Milton's Imagery and the Visual Arts

ROLAND MUSHAT FRYE

MILTON'S IMAGERY AND THE VISUAL ARTS

Iconographic Tradition in the Epic Poems

Princeton University Press *Princeton, New Jersey*

Copyright © 1978 by Princeton University Press

Published by Princeton University Press, Princeton, New Jersey
In the United Kingdom: Princeton University Press, Guildford, Surrey

All Rights Reserved

Publication of this book has been aided by a grant from the
John Simon Guggenheim Memorial Foundation

This book has been composed in Linotype Janson

Printed in the United States of America
by Princeton University Press, Princeton, New Jersey

Illustrations printed by the Meriden Gravure Company,
Meriden, Connecticut

LIBRARY OF CONGRESS CATALOGING IN PUBLICATION DATA

Frye, Roland Mushat.
    Milton's imagery and the visual arts.

    Bibliography: p.
    Includes index.
    1. Milton, John, 1608-1674—Knowledge—Art.
2. Milton, John, 1608-1674. Paradise lost.
3. Milton, John, 1608-1674. Paradise regained.
4. Ut pictura poesis (Aesthetics)   5. Art—Themes,
motives.   I. Title.
PR3592.A66F78   821′.4   77-24541
ISBN 0-691-06349-4

For My Ever Bonnie Jean

"Heaven's last best gift, my ever new delight"

Contents

List of Illustrations   xi
List of Abbreviations   xxi
Preface and Acknowledgments   xxiii

Part One
INTRODUCTION
  I. *Purposes, Presuppositions and Methods*   3
 II. *Milton's Visual Imagination and the Critics*   9
III. *Milton's Awareness of the Visual Arts*   20
       The Puritans and the Arts   20
       Milton's Exposure to the Visual Arts   23
       Milton's References to the Visual Arts   31

Part Two
THE DEMONIC WORLD
 IV. *The War in Heaven and the Expulsion of the Rebel Angels*   43
       Panoply and Ordnance   43
       Individual Combat and Mass Conflict   50
       The Fall of the Rebel Angels   56
  V. *Visual Images of the Demonic*   65
       The Theological and Artistic Problem   65
       From Blue Angel to Hideous Fiend   66
       Milton and the Hideous Fiends   71
       Beautiful and Humanoid Devils   77
       Milton and the Humanoid Devils   81
 VI. *Demonic Associations: Comparisons and Disguises*   92
       Visual Comparisons   92
       Disguises   98
       Serpents   101
VII. *Sin and Death*   111
       The Infernal Trinity   111
       Death   113
       Sin   118
VIII. *Hell*   125
       The One Exclusion: Physical Torture   125
       The Seeming Inconsistencies of Hell   127
       Pandaemonium, The High Capitol/Capital   133
       Entrances and Exits   138

Part Three
THE HEAVENLY WORLD

IX. *Images for the Divine* — 149
God the Father and God the Holy Spirit — 149
God the Son — 154

X. *The Vision of Angels* — 169
Angelic Wings — 169
Angelic Movement — 171
Individual Appearance — 176
Activities and Moods — 180

XI. *Heaven* — 189
The Problems — 189
Access to Heaven: The Golden Stairs — 190
Heaven as Community, City, and Garden — 192
Light and Color Images — 198

Part Four
THE CREATED WORLD

XII. *Infinite Space and the Paradise of Fools* — 209

XIII. *Landscape Art and Milton's Garden of Eden* — 218
Landscape as Mood and Mimesis in Renaissance Aesthetics — 218
Italian Gardens — 221
Landscape and View Paintings — 227

XIV. *The Garden of Eden in Milton and in Pictorial Art* — 235
Larger Features of the Landscape — 235
Fauna and Flora — 239
Vegetable Gold — 251

Part Five
THE HUMAN WORLD

XV. *Adam and Eve* — 259
The Creation of Adam and Eve — 259
Nude Beauty — 262
Adam — 266
Eve — 272
The Love of Adam and Eve — 280

XVI. *The Fall and its Effects* — 286
The Fall — 286
The Effects of the Fall — 291
The Education of Adam: Books XI–XII — 297
The Expulsion — 308

Part Six
THE WORLD REDEEMED

XVII. *Paradise Regained* — 319
The Wilderness Temptations in Pictorial Art and the
Problems of *Paradise Regained* — 319

Incidental Images and Panoramic Views 321
"Paysage Moralisé": The Wilderness and the Grove 329
Extra-Biblical Temptations 334
The Biblical Narrative Envisioned 341

Conclusion 347

Bibliography 351

Index 381
General 381
To Milton's Poetry 404

Illustrations 409

List of Illustrations

NOTE TO THE READER

The arrangement of illustrations for this study poses certain problems which could not be resolved at reasonable expense. Most plates serve a multiple purpose and are referred to several times within the text; different iconographic features of a single picture may be cited in widely separate chapters, so that it is impossible to arrange the plates in a sequence which is equally accessible from all parts of the book. The only way to avoid the distraction to the reader of having to jump back and forth between plates would have been to supply individual reproductions to go with each reference within the text, but that would require the publication of several thousand additional illustrations, at prohibitive expense.

In the sequence adopted here, the illustrations follow the general order of the principal analyses in the text. Considering the alternatives available (arrangement by order of first references in my text, or by the historical chronology of the art works, or by medium or school, etc.), this system minimizes but cannot eliminate the difficulties. For example, pictorial representations most directly relevant to Milton's Sin are numbered 91-98, grouped according to the treatment of Sin in Chapter VII, but some of these plates are also referred to elsewhere. Furthermore, that chapter which analyzes Sin perforce also refers to representations of the hybrid serpent-woman as the tempter of Adam and Eve in paintings of the Fall, whereas those pictures are placed in other groupings according to the sections of text to which they primarily apply. Art works which form part of a coherent series (such as the Signorelli frescoes on the Last Judgment at Orvieto, the Medici tapestries on Adam and Eve, and the *Genesis B* illuminations of the Hexapla) are kept together in the plates, and details follow the works from which they are selected. I regret that no more convenient arrangement was possible.

Numbers in the margins throughout indicate the figure or plate numbers of the illustrations to which the text refers.

Unless otherwise indicated, all photographs are by courtesy of museum or library to which the work belongs. Grateful acknowledgment is here made to each of those named below for permission to publish, and for the photographic reproductions, as indicated for each illustration.

In Color

I. *Christ Separating the Sheep from the Goats*, sixth-century mosaic, S. Apollinare Nuovo, Ravenna (Scala-Art Reference Bureau).

II. Simone Martini (1284-1344), *Annunciation* (detail), Gallerie degli Uffizi, Florence (Scala-Art Reference Bureau).

III. *The Heavenly City*, sixth-century mosaic, S. Apollinare in Class, Ravenna (Scala-Art Reference Bureau).

IV. Medici Tapestries, Flemish, ca. 1550, *The Fall* (detail), Accademia, Florence (Scala-Art Reference Bureau).

V. Medici Tapestries, Flemish, ca. 1550, *God Clothing Adam and Eve* (detail), Accademia, Florence (Scala-Art Reference Bureau).

VI. Abraham van Linge, *The Fall*, 1641, University College Chapel, Oxford (Thomas Photos).

VII. Peter Paul Rubens (1577-1640), *Adam and Eve in Paradise*, Mauritshuis, The Hague.

VIII. Luca Giordano (1632-1705), *St. Michael Archangel*, Kunsthistorisches Museum, Vienna.

In Black and White

1. Ortelius, "China," from *Theater of the Whole World*, 1606, University of Pennsylvania Library.

2. Jocodus Hondius, *Christian Knight Map*, 1597, British Library, London.

3. *Christus Victor*, early sixth-century mosaic, Oratory of St. Andrew, Ravenna (Alinari—Art Reference Bureau).

4. Spinello Aretino (active 1373-d. 1410/11), *Expulsion of the Rebel Angels*, S. Francesco, Arezzo (Alinari—Art Reference Bureau).

5. Peter Bruegel (ca. 1525/30-69), *Fall of the Rebel Angels*, Musées Royaux des Beaux-Arts, Brussels (photo A.C.L., Brussels).

6. Lucas Cranach (1472-1553), *War in Heaven*, Luther's 1522 Wittenberg New Testament, Princeton University Library: Scheide Collection (Willard Starks photo).

7. Anonymous, *War in Heaven*, Tyndale's 1534 Bible, Princeton University Library: Scheide Collection (Willard Starks photo).

8. Jacopo Tintoretto (1518-94), *Michael and the Dragon*, S. Giuseppe di Castello, Venice (Anderson—Art Reference Bureau).

9. Detail of Figure 8. (Anderson—Art Reference Bureau).

10. G. Glover (?), *The Fall of the Rebel Angels*, in Thomas Heywood, *The Hierarchie of the Blessed Angells*, 1635, sig. Ee 3v., University of Pennsylvania Library.

11. Luca Giordano (1632-1705), *Michael and Lucifer*, Palacio Real, Madrid (photo MAS).

12. *Satan Leading His Troops Out of Hell*, thirteenth-century English Apocalypse, Bodleian Library MS Tanner 184, p. 56, Oxford.

13. Jacques Callot (1592/3-1635), *The Temptation of Saint Anthony*, National Gallery: Rudolf L. Baumfeld Collection, Washington.

14. *The Devil and the Invention of Gunpowder*, frontispiece in Johannes Brantzius, *Les Artifices de feu*, 1604, Folger Shakespeare Library, Washington.

15. Dragon, from Flavius Renatus Vegetius, *De re militari*, Augsburg, 1472, University of Pennsylvania Library.

16. *Michael and the Expulsion of the Rebel Angels*, in the Sforza Book of Hours, ca. 1490, British Library add. MS 34298, fol. 186v., London.

17. Peter Paul Rubens (1577-1640), *Michael and the Expulsion of the Rebel Angels*, Alte Pinakothek, Munich.

18. Piero della Francesca (1410/20-92), *Michael and the Dragon*, National Gallery, London.

19. Antonio Pollaiuolo (ca. 1432-98), *Michael and the Dragon*, Museo Bardini, Florence (Alinari—Art Reference Bureau).

20. Juan Jimenez, *Michael and the Dragon*, ca. 1500, Philadelphia Museum of Art: John G. Johnson Collection.

21. Detail of Figure 20.

22. Jacobello del Fiore (d. 1439), *Michael and the Dragon*, Accademia, Venice (Alinari—Art Reference Bureau).

23. Giovanni Lanfranco (1582-1647), *Michael Chaining Satan*, Museo Capodimonte, Naples (Alinari—Art Reference Bureau).

24. Paolo Farinati (1524-1606), *Michael and Lucifer*, S. Maria in Organo, Verona (Alinari—Art Reference Bureau).

25. Dionisio Calvaert (ca. 1545-1619), *The Virgin with Child and Michael*, S. Giacomo Maggiore, Bologna (Alinari—Art Reference Bureau).

26. Detail of Figure 25 (Alinari—Art Reference Bureau).

27. Lorenzo Lotto (ca. 1480-1556), *The Fall of Lucifer*, Palazzo Arcivescovo, Loreto (Alinari—Art Reference Bureau).

28. Guido Reni (1575-1642), *Michael and Satan*, S. Maria della Concezione, Rome (Alinari—Art Reference Bureau).

29. Domenico Beccafumi (1484/6-1551), *Michael and the Fallen Angels*, Pinacoteca, Siena (Alinari—Art Reference Bureau).

30. Detail of Figure 29 (Alinari—Art Reference Bureau).

31. Thomas de Leu (1562-ca. 1620) after Antoine Caron, *A Giant Destroyed by Jupiter*, The Art Museum, Princeton University.

32. Hendrik Goltzius (1558-1617), after Cornelius van Haarlem, *The Disgracers: The Fall of Icarus*, The Art Museum, Princeton University.

33. *Lucifer's Presumption and Expulsion*, early eleventh-century Anglo-Saxon illumination, *Genesis B*, Bodleian Library MS Junius 11, p. 3, Oxford.

34. *The Fall of the Rebel Angels into Hell*, *Genesis B*, p. 16.

35. *Creation of Man and the Ladder to Heaven*, *Genesis B*, p. 9.

36. *Temptation of Eve*, *Genesis B*, p. 24.

37. *The Fall* and *Postlapsarian Prayers*, *Genesis B*, p. 31.

38. *The Remorse of Adam and Eve*, *Genesis B*, p. 34.

39. *The Tempter-Demon Returns to Hell*, *Genesis B*, p. 36.

40. *Recrimination and Alienation of Adam and Eve*, *Genesis B*, p. 39.

41. *Judgment of Adam, Eve, and the Serpent*, *Genesis B*, p. 41.

42. *Fall of Rebel Angels*, eleventh-century Anglo-Saxon illumination, Aelfric Manuscript, British Library MS Cotton Claudius B IV, p. 2, London.

43. *Fall of the Rebel Angels*, late fourteenth-century Italian illumination in, *Treatise on the Seven Vices*, British Library add. MS 27695, fol. 1v., London.

44. *Expulsion of the Rebel Angels*, early sixteenth-century oak bas-relief, King's College Chapel, Cambridge (Royal Commission on Historical Monuments).

45. Limbourg Brothers, *Expulsion of the Rebel Angels*, early fifteenth-century *Très Riches Heures du Duc de Berry*, fol. 64v., Musée Condé, Chantilly.

46. Limbourg Brothers, *Satan and Hell*, early fifteenth-century *Très Riches Heures du Duc de Berry*, fol. 108, Musée Condé, Chantilly.

47. Luca Giordano (1632-1705), *St. Michael Archangel*, Kunsthistorisches Museum, Vienna.

48. Guyart Desmoulins, Illumination for Bible Historiale, 1390, Bibliothèque Royale Albert Ier MS 9001, fol. 19, Brussels.

49. John Droeshout, *Michael and the Demons*, in Thomas Heywood, *The Hierarchie of the Blessed Angells*, 1635, sig. Tt 1v. University of Pennsylvania Library.

50. L. Cecill, *The Ladder of Angels and the Fall of the Devils*, frontispiece in Heywood, *The Hierarchie of the Blessed Angells*.

51. Marco d'Oggiono (ca. 1475-ca. 1530), *The Angelic Triumph over Satan*, Brera, Milan (Alinari—Art Reference Bureau).

52. Master LD, *Pride*, mid-sixteenth-century French engraving, University of Pennsylvania Library.

53. *Lucifer Enthroned, Christ Creating* and the *Jaws of Hell*, fourteenth-century English illumination, Holkham Bible, fol. 2, British Library add. MS 47682, London.

54. Sarcophagus of Junius Bassus, fourth century, Vatican Museum (Alinari—Art Reference Bureau).

55. *Satan in Hell*, thirteenth-century mosaics, Baptistry Cupola, Florence (Alinari—Art Reference Bureau).

56. *Christ Creating* and the *Fall of the Rebel Angels*, fourteenth-century English illumination, Queen Mary's Psalter, British Library Roy. MS2 BVII, fol. 1v. London.

57. *Devils, Hell-Hounds and Hell*, later fifteenth-century illumination, Missal of Poitiers, Bibliothèque Nationale MS lat. 873, fol. 164, Paris.

58. *Christ the Judge and Devils*, in *Treatise on Antichrist*, fifteenth-century French illumination, Bodleian Library MS Douce 134, fol. 98, Oxford.

59. Andrea da Firenze, *Christ in Limbo* (detail of demons), ca. 1365, Spanish Chapel, S. Maria Novella, Florence (Alinari—Art Reference Bureau).

60. Michelangelo Buonarroti (1475-1564), *Last Judgment*, Sistine Chapel, Vatican (Alinari—Art Reference Bureau).

61. Detail of Figure 60, *Charon Delivers the Damned* (Alinari—Art Reference Bureau).

62. Detail of Figure 60, *Charon* (Alinari—Art Reference Bureau).

63. Detail of Figure 60, *Hades* or *Screaming Demon* (Alinari—Art Reference Bureau).

64. Detail of Figure 60, *Papal Chancellor as Devil* (Alinari—Art Reference Bureau).

65. Detail of Figure 60, *Head of Devil* (Alinari—Art Reference Bureau).

66. Detail of Figure 60, *One of the Damned* (Alinari—Art Reference Bureau).

67. Detail of Figure 60, *Christ in Judgment* (Alinari—Art Reference Bureau).

68. Hieronymus Bosch (1450-1516), *Hell* from *Garden of Earthly Delights*, Prado, Madrid (Anderson—Art Reference Bureau).

69. Raphael (1483-1520), *Michael and the Dragon*, Louvre, Paris (Musées Nationaux).

70. Raphael (1483-1520), *Michael Vanquishing the Devil*, Louvre, Paris (Musées Nationaux).

71. David Teniers II (1610-90), *Dives in Hell*, National Gallery, London.

72. *The Blessed* and *The Damned*, seventeenth-century wax models, Victoria and Albert Museum, London.

73. Nardo di Cione and Andrea Orcagna (?), *The Inferno*, ca. 1350, Camposanto, Pisa (Alinari—Art Reference Bureau).

74. Luca Signorelli (ca. 1441/50-1523), *The Last Judgment: The Damned in Hell*, Cathedral, Orvieto (Alinari—Art Reference Bureau).

75. Luca Signorelli, *The Last Judgment: The Damned in Hell* (detail) (Alinari—Art Reference Bureau).

76. Luca Signorelli, *The Last Judgment: The Reception of the Damned into Hell* (detail) (Alinari—Art Reference Bureau).

77. Luca Signorelli, *The Last Judgment: Angels Conducting the Elect* (Alinari—Art Reference Bureau).

78. Luca Signorelli, *The Last Judgment: The Calling of the Elect* (Alinari—Art Reference Bureau).

79. Nicolò di Liberatore (Alunno) (1425/30-1502), *The Virgin Delivers a Child from Satan*, Galleria Colonna, Rome (Alinari—Art Reference Bureau).

80. Giovanni Lanfranco (1582-1647), *The Virgin Delivers a Child from Satan* or *The Salvation of a Soul*, Museo Capodimonte, Naples (Alinari—Art Reference Bureau).

81. Jean Tavernier, *The Devil Asks for a More Flattering Portrait*, in *Miracles de Nostre Dame*, ca. 1456, Bodleian Library MS Douce 374, fol. 93, Oxford.

82. Domenichino (1581-1641), *The Guardian Angel*, Museo Capodimonte, Naples (Alinari—Art Reference Bureau).

83. Carlo Bononi (1569-1632), *The Guardian Angel*, Pinacoteca Civica, Ferrara (Alinari—Art Reference Bureau).

84. Pietro Tacca (1577-1640), *Devil Running a Foot Race*, Museo Capodimonte, Naples (Soprintendenza alle Gallerie).

85. *Leviathan and the Seamen*, late twelfth-century illumination, Bestiary, Bodleian Library MS Ashmole 1511, fol. 86v., Oxford.

86. Peter Bruegel the Younger (1564-1638), *Orpheus in Hades*, Palazzo Pitti, Florence (Brogi—Art Reference Bureau).

87. Anonymous, *The Fall*, mid-sixteenth-century Italian oil, author's collection.

88. Lucas Cranach (?), *The Garden in Eden*, illustration for Genesis in Luther's 1534 Bible, Princeton University Library: Scheide Collection (Willard Starks photo).

89. Crispin van de Passe I (1565-1637), *Christ Triumphing over Sin, Death and Hell*, from Thomas Scott, *Vox Dei*, London, 1623, Folger Shakespeare Library, Washington.

90. Gaetano Zumbo (ca. 1656-1701), *The Corruption of Corpses*, Bargello, Florence (Alinari—Art Reference Bureau).

91. *The Soul Fights Temptation*, engraving, frontispiece to Edward Benlowes, *Theophila*, 1652, Folger Shakespeare Library, Washington.

92. Engraving, Scylla in frontispiece to Book XIV of Sandys' translation of Ovid's *Metamorphoses*, London, 1632, sig. Hhh4v, University of Pennsylvania Library.

93. Giovanni Bologna (1529-1608), Siren in Neptune Fountain, Bologna (Alinari—Art Reference Bureau).

94. *Truth the Daughter of Time*, Italian earthenware dish, ca. 1540-50, Victoria and Albert Museum, London.

95. Agnolo Bronzino (1503-72), *Allegory*, National Gallery, London.

96. Detail of Figure 95, Deceit.

97. *Frau Welt*, early fifteenth-century illumination, Codex Latinus monacensis, Bayerische Staatsbibliothek MS 8201, fol. 95, Munich.

98. *Frau Welt*, fifteenth-century woodcut, British Library, London.

99. Nardo di Cione (d. 1366), *The Inferno*, S. Maria Novella, Florence (Alinari—Art Reference Bureau).

100. Fra Angelico (ca. 1400-1455), *Last Judgment*, Museo di S. Marco, Florence (Alinari—Art Reference Bureau).

101. Herri met de Bles (Civetta) (d. 1550), *The Inferno*, Doge's Palace, Venice (Anderson—Art Reference Bureau).

102. El Greco (1541-1614), *Allegory of the Holy League*, also called *The Dream of Philip II* and *Adoration of the Holy Name of Jesus*, Prado, Madrid (Anderson—Art Reference Bureau).

103. Duccio di Buoninsegna (ca. 1255/60-1315/18), *Christ in Limbo*, Cathedral Museum, Siena (Alinari—Art Reference Bureau).

104. Maerten van Heemskerck (1498-1574), *Death and Judgment*, Hampton Court Palace.

105. Giambattista Fontana (1525-87), *Last Judgment*, Institute of Fine Arts, New York.

106. Michelangelo (1475-1564), *God the Father Separating Land and Water*, Sistine Chapel, Vatican (Alinari—Art Reference Bureau).

107. Raphael (1483-1520), *The Vision of Ezekiel*, ca. 1516, Palazzo Pitti, Florence (Alinari—Art Reference Bureau).

108. *Omnipotent Hand of God*, twelfth-century mosaic, Apse of S. Clemente, Rome (Alinari—Art Reference Bureau).

109. *Adam and Eve*, frontispiece to Genesis, Geneva Bible, 1583, University of Pennsylvania Library.

110. Jacopo Tintoretto (1518-94), *St. George and the Dragon*, National Gallery, London.

111. *Christ-Logos as Creator*, thirteenth-century mosaic, Atrium of S. Marco, Venice (Alinari—Art Reference Bureau).

112. *Christ in Judgment*, thirteenth-century mosaic, Baptistry, Florence (Alinari—Art Reference Bureau).

113. Raphael (1483-1520) and his school, *God Creating the Animals*, Vatican Loggia (Alinari—Art Reference Bureau).

114. Peter Paul Rubens (1577-1640), *The Fall of the Damned into Hell*, Alte Pinakothek, Munich.

115. Nardo di Cione and Andrea Orcagna (?), *Last Judgment*, ca. 1350, Camposanto, Pisa (Alinari—Art Reference Bureau).

116. *Abraham Entertains the Angels*, sixth-century mosaic, S. Vitale, Ravenna (Alinari—Art Reference Bureau).

117. *Censing Angel*, thirteenth-century sculpture, South Transept, Westminster Abbey, London.

118. *Angelic Musician*, fifteenth-century carving, Holy Sepulchre Church, Cambridge.

119. *Angel in Feathered Mail*, early Tudor sculpture, King's College Chapel, Cambridge (Royal Commission on Historical Monuments).

120. Fra Filippo Lippi (1406-69), *Annunciation*, Palazzo Barberini, Rome (Alinari—Art Reference Bureau).

121. Paolo Veronese (1528-88), *Consecration of St. Nicholas* (detail), National Gallery, London.

122. Jacopo Tintoretto (1518-94), *The Resurrection* (detail), Scuolo di San Rocco, Venice (Alinari—Art Reference Bureau).

123. Andreas Giltlinger (fl. 1563-80), *Nativity with Annunciation to Shepherds*, Rosengarten Museum, Constance.

124. Carlo Crivelli (d. 1495/1500), *Annunciation*, National Gallery, London.

125. *Christ Child on Sunbeam*, early thirteenth-century illumination, from *Enfancie de Nostre Seigneur*, Bodleian Library MS Selden supra 38, fol. 24, Oxford.

126. Studio della Robbia, *Michael*, ca. 1475, Metropolitan Museum: Harris Brisbane Dick Fund, New York.

127. Perugino (ca. 1445/50-1523), *Virgin in Glory with Saints and Angels*, Pinacoteca Nazionale, Bologna (Alinari—Art Reference Bureau).

128. Gianlorenzo Bernini (1598-1680), *Ecstasy of St. Theresa* (detail), S. Maria della Vittoria, Rome (Alinari—Art Reference Bureau).

129. School of Verrocchio (1435-88), *Raphael and Tobias*, National Gallery, London.

130. *Raphael and Tobias*, anonymous engraving after Maerten van Heemskerck (1498-1574), Rijksbureau voor Kunsthistorische Documentatie, The Hague.

131. Carlo Crivelli (d. 1495/1500), *Pietà*, Philadelphia Museum of Art: John G. Johnson Collection.

132. Jacopo Tintoretto (1518-94), *Paradise* (detail), Doge's Palace, Venice (Alinari—Art Reference Bureau).

133. Anonymous late fourteenth-century painter, *Wilton Diptych*, National Gallery, London.

134. Donatello (1386-1466), *David*, Bargello, Florence (Alinari—Art Reference Bureau).

135. Ludovico Carracci (1555-1619), *The Praise of Angels*, S. Paolo, Bologna (Alinari—Art Reference Bureau).

136. Antonio Bettini, *Ladder of Salvation*, from *Monte Santo di Dio*, Florence, 1491, Library of Congress: Rosenwald Collection.

137. Fra Angelico (ca. 1400-55), Paradise detail of *Last Judgment*, Museo di S. Marco, Florence (Alinari—Art Reference Bureau).

138. Giovanni di Paolo (1403-82/3), *Paradise*, Pinacoteca, Siena (Alinari—Art Reference Bureau).

139. *Last Judgment*, late fifteenth-century illumination, Utrecht Book of Hours, Bodleian Library MS Douce 93, fol. 46v., Oxford.

140. Augustine's *City of God*, early fifteenth-century illumination, Philadelphia Museum of Art: Philip S. Collins Collection (given by Mrs. Philip S. Collins in memory of her husband).

141. Alonso Cano (1601-67), *The Vision of St. John* (detail), 1635-37, Wallace Collection, London.

142. *Last Judgment*, early fourteenth-century illumination, Holkham Bible, fol. 42v., British Library, London.

143. Giorgio Vasari (1511-74) and others, *Triumph of Cosimo I*, Palazzo Vecchio, Florence (Alinari—Art Reference Bureau).

144. Pietro da Cortona (1596-1669), *The Triumph of Glory*, Palazzo Barberini, Rome (Alinari—Art Reference Bureau).

145. Peter Paul Rubens (1577-1640), *Apotheosis of Buckingham*, National Gallery, London.

146. Peter Paul Rubens (1577-1640), *Apotheosis of James I*, Whitehall Banqueting House, London (Royal Commission on Historical Monuments).

147. Sandro Botticelli (ca. 1445-1510), *Primavera*, Gallerie degli Uffizi, Florence (Alinari—Art Reference Bureau).

148. Medici Tapestries, Flemish, ca. 1550, *Creation of Adam*, Accademia, Florence (Alinari—Art Reference Bureau).

149. Medici Tapestries, *Adam Taken into the Garden* (Alinari—Art Reference Bureau).

150. Medici Tapestries, *Adam Names the Animals* (Alinari—Art Reference Bureau).

151. Medici Tapestries, *Eve Presented to Adam* (Alinari—Art Reference Bureau).

152. Medici Tapestries, *The Fall* (Alinari—Art Reference Bureau).

153. Medici Tapestries, *The Judgment of Adam and Eve* (Alinari—Art Reference Bureau).

154. Medici Tapestries, *Expulsion of Adam and Eve* (Alinari—Art Reference Bureau).

155. Cecchino Salviati (Francesco de' Rossi) (1510-63), *The Fall*, Galleria Colonna, Rome (Vasari, Rome).

156. *Story of Adam and Eve*, early fifteenth-century illumination, Bedford Book of Hours, British Library add. MS 18850, fol. 14, London.

157. Mabuse (Jan Gossaert) (d. ca. 1533), *The Fall* from the Malvagna Triptych, Museo, Palermo (Alinari—Art Reference Bureau).

158. Jan Bruegel the Elder (1568-1625), *Garden of Eden*, Victoria and Albert Museum, London.

159. Jan Bruegel the Elder (1568-1625), *Garden of Eden*, Galleria Doria, Rome (Alinari—Art Reference Bureau).

160. Limbourg Brothers, *Story of Adam and Eve*, early fifteenth-century, *Les Très Riches Heures du Duc de Berry*, fol. 25v., Musée Condé, Chantilly.

161. *The Fall*, late thirteenth-century illumination, Bible and Prayer Book, British Library add. MS 11639, fol. 520v., London.

162. *The Fall*, manuscript illumination ca. 1500, from the Grimani Breviary, Biblioteca di S. Marco, Venice (Alinari—Art Reference Bureau).

163. Lucas Cranach (1472-1553), *Paradise*, Kunsthistorisches Museum, Vienna.

164. Albrecht Dürer (1471-1528), *The Fall*, National Gallery of Art: Rosenwald Collection, Washington.

165. Frans Floris (ca. 1517-70), *The Fall*, Palazzo Pitti, Florence (Alinari—Art Reference Bureau).

166. Mabuse (Jan Gossaert) (d. ca. 1533), *Adam and Eve*, Rhode Island School of Design (Walter H. Kimball Fund), Providence.

167. Cornelius van Haarlem (1562-1638), *Adam and Eve in Paradise*, Rijksmuseum, Amsterdam.

168. *Terrestrial Paradise*, engraved title page to John Parkinson, *Paradisi in Sole*, 1629, Princeton University Library.

169. Michelangelo Buonarroti (1475-1564), *The Fall and Expulsion*, Sistine Chapel, Vatican (Alinari—Art Reference Bureau).

170. *The Paradise of the Senses in Eden*, unsigned engraving, ca. 1600, Huntington Library (Kitto Bible) San Marino, California.

171. Peter Paul Rubens (1577-1640), *The Fall*, Prado, Madrid (Anderson—Art Reference Bureau).

172. Pietro di Puccio, *The Story of Adam and Eve*, ca. 1390, Camposanto, Pisa (Alinari—Art Reference Bureau).

173. Jacopo Tintoretto (1518-94), *The Fall*, Accademia, Venice (Alinari—Art Reference Bureau).

174. Lucas Cranach (1472-1553), *The Fall*, Courtauld Institute: Lee Collection, London.

175. Andrea Pisano (ca. 1290-ca. 1349), *The Creation of Adam*, Campanile, Florence (Alinari—Art Reference Bureau).

176. Andrea Pisano (ca. 1290-ca. 1349), *The Creation of Eve*, Campanile, Florence (Alinari—Art Reference Bureau).

177. *The Judgment of Adam and Eve*, thirteenth-century mosaic, Atrium of S. Marco, Venice (Alinari—Art Reference Bureau).

178. Lucas Cranach (1472-1553), *Eve*, Gallerie degli Uffizi, Florence (Alinari—Art Reference Bureau).

179. Secondo Maestro, *Story of Adam and Eve*, mid-twelfth century, S. Zeno, Verona (Alinari—Art Reference Bureau).

180. Joannes Sadeler I (1550-1600) after Marten de Vos, *Adam and Eve*, Huntington Library (Kitto Bible), San Marino, California.
181. Michelangelo Buonarroti (1475-1564), *Creation of Adam*, Sistine Chapel, Vatican (Alinari—Art Reference Bureau).
182. Lucas van Leyden (1494?-1533), *Creation of Eve*, University of Pennsylvania Library.
183. Albrecht Dürer (1471-1528), *Adam*, Gallerie degli Uffizi, Florence (Alinari—Art Reference Bureau).
184. Albrecht Dürer (1471-1528), *Eve*, Gallerie degli Uffizi, Florence (Alinari—Art Reference Bureau).
185. Masolino (ca. 1383/4-1447?), *The Fall*, S. Maria del Carmine, Florence (Alinari—Art Reference Bureau).
186. Pseudo Met de Bles, *The Fall*, Pinacoteca, Bologna (Alinari—Art Reference Bureau).
187. Antonio Rizzo (fl. 1465-85), *Adam*, Doge's Palace, Venice (Alinari—Art Reference Bureau).
188. Antonio Rizzo (fl. 1465-85), *Eve*, Doge's Palace, Venice (Alinari—Art Reference Bureau).
189. Masaccio (1401-28), *The Expulsion*, S. Maria del Carmine, Florence (Alinari—Art Reference Bureau).
190. Hans Holbein (1497/8-1543) (attributed to), *The Fall*, Luther Bible, Lyons, 1544, Princeton University Library: Scheide Collection (Willard Starks photo).
191. Hans Baldung Grien (1484/5-1545), *Adam and Eve*, 1511, National Gallery of Art: Rosenwald Collection, Washington.
192. Hans Baldung Grien (1484/5-1545), *Adam and Eve*, 1519, National Gallery of Art: Rosenwald Collection, Washington.
193. Michelangelo Naccherino (1550-1622), *Adam, Eve and Satan*, Boboli Gardens, Florence (Alinari—Art Reference Bureau).
194. Detail of Figure 193 (Alinari—Art Reference Bureau).
195. Marcantonio Raimondi (ca. 1480-1534), *Apollo and Hyacinth*, Institute of Fine Arts, New York.
196. Benvenuto Cellini (1500-71), *Apollo and Hyacinth*, Bargello, Florence (Alinari—Art Reference Bureau).
197. Paolo Uccello (1396/7-1475), *The Expulsion*, Chiostro Verde, S. Maria Novella, Florence (Alinari—Art Reference Bureau).
198. Raphael (1483-1520), *The Fall*, Vatican Apartments (Alinari—Art Reference Bureau).
199. Cristoforo Solario (fl. 1489-1520), *Adam*, Cathedral, Milan (Alinari—Art Reference Bureau).
200. Cristoforo Solario (fl. 1489-1520), *Eve*, Cathedral, Milan (Alinari—Art Reference Bureau).
201. Michelangelo Buonarroti (1475-1564), *The Risen Christ*, S. Maria sopra Minerva, Rome (Alinari—Art Reference Bureau).
202. Peter Lely (1618-80), *Oliver Cromwell*, 1653, Palazzo Pitti, Florence (Alinari—Art Reference Bureau).
203. William Faithorne (1616-91), *John Milton*, Princeton University Library.
204. Paolo Farinati (1524-1606), *The Judgment of Adam and Eve*, SS. Nazaro e Celso, Verona (Alinari—Art Reference Bureau).
205. Andrea del Minga (ca. 1540-96), *The Expulsion of Adam and Eve*, Palazzo Pitti, Florence (Brogi—Art Reference Bureau).
206. Albrecht Altdorfer (1480-1538), *Fall of Man*, National Gallery of Art, Washington.
207. Joannes Saenredam, *Vertumnus and Pomona*, 1605, and *Adam and Eve*, 1597, Princeton University Library (Willard Starks photo).
208. Lucas Cranach (1472-1553), *Venus and Cupid*, National Gallery, London.
209. Jean Cousin (1490-1560), *Eva Prima Pandora*, Louvre, Paris.
210. *Adam and Eve*, anonymous engraving in Joseph Fletcher, *Perfect-Cursed-Blessed Man*, 1628, sig. E2v, Huntington Library, San Marino, California.
211. Jean Duvet (ca. 1485-1561), *The Marriage of Adam and Eve*, National Gallery of Art: Rosenwald Collection, Washington.
212. *Adam and Eve*, anonymous engraving, frontispiece to Genesis in the Matthew Bible, London, 1537, University of Pennsylvania Library.
213. Joannes Saenredam after A. Bloemart, *Adam and Eve*, ca. 1600, Huntington Library (Kitto Bible), San Marino, California.
214. Hans Brosamer (1500-54), *Adam and Eve*, Frontispiece to Genesis in Luther Bible, 1565, Huntington Library (Kitto Bible), San Marino, California.
215. Lucas van Leyden (1494?-1533), *Adam and Eve*, National Gallery of Art: Rosenwald Collection, Washington.
216. Hans Burgkmair (1473-1531), *The Fall*, National Gallery of Art: Rosenwald Collection, tion, Washington.
217. Rembrandt van Ryn (1606-69), *The Fall*, National Gallery of Art: Rosenwald Collection, Washington.

218. Albrecht Dürer (1471-1528), *The Fall*, National Gallery of Art: Rosenwald Collection, Washington.
219. Rembrandt van Ryn (1606-69), *Postlapsarian Adam and Eve*, Pierpont Morgan Library, New York.
220. *Stories from Genesis*, eleventh/twelfth-century Byzantine ivory (detail), Cleveland Museum of Art: gift of J. H. Wade, John L. Severance, W. G. Mather, and F. F. Prentiss.
221. Nardo di Cione and Andrea Orcagna (?), *The Triumph of Death*, ca. 1350, Camposanto, Pisa (Alinari—Art Reference Bureau).
222. Detail of Figure 221 (Alinari—Art Reference Bureau).
223. Andrea Orcagna (1308-68), fragment of *The Triumph of Death*, Museo S. Croce, Florence.
224. Joannes Sadeler I (1550-1600) after Marten de Vos, *Jabal*, Huntington Library (Kitto Bible), San Marino, California.
225. Joannes Sadeler I after Marten de Vos, *Jubal* (Kitto Bible).
226. Joannes Sadeler I after Marten de Vos, *Tubalcain* (Kitto Bible).
227. Joannes Sadeler I after Marten de Vos, *Lamech's Lament* (Kitto Bible).
228. Joannes Sadeler I after Marten de Vos, *The Sons of God and the Daughters of Men* (Kitto Bible).
229. Joannes Sadeler I after Marten de Vos, *Enoch's Ascent* (Kitto Bible).
230. Dono Gazzola (?) and Bernardo Strozzi (1581-1644), *The Expulsion*, Castelvecchio, Verona.
231. *Debate between Christ and Satan*, fourteenth-century English illumination, Holkham Bible, fol. 11v., British Library, London.
232. *Christ and Satan*, thirteenth-century stained glass, ca. 1225, Victoria and Albert Museum, London.
233. Lorenzo Ghiberti (1378-1455), *Christ and Satan*, Baptistry, Florence (Alinari—Art Reference Bureau).
234. Dirk Vellert (fl. 1511-44), *Christ and Satan*, National Gallery of Art: Rosenwald Collection, Washington.
235. Abraham Bloemaert (1564-1651), *Christ and Satan*, Huntington Library (Kitto Bible), San Marino, California.
236. Henric Hondius I (1573-ca. 1649) after I. van Lier, *Christ and Satan*, Huntington Library (Kitto Bible), San Marino, California.
237. *Ancient Rome*, illumination in Giovanni Marcanova, *Antiquitates*, 1465, Princeton University Library (Willard Starks photo).
238. Giovanni Francesco Venturini (1650-1710+), engraving of Ligorio's *Rometta* in the Tivoli Gardens, Princeton University Library.
239. Grünewald (ca. 1470/80-1528), *St. Anthony and St. Paul the Hermit*, ca. 1510-15, Isenheim Altarpiece, Unterlinden, Colmar.
240. Antonio Tempesta (1555-1630), *Christ and Satan*, from first Arabic Gospels, 1590-91, Huntington Library (Kitto Bible), San Marino, California.
241. *Christ and Satan*, engraving in Greek New Testament, 1563, Huntington Library (Kitto Bible), San Marino, California.
242. Hans Schaufelein (ca. 1483-1539/40), *Christ and Satan*, Institute of Fine Arts, New York.
243. D. P., *Christ and Satan*, 1642, Huntington Library (Kitto Bible), San Marino, California.
244. Hieronymus Cock (1510-70), *Christ and Satan*, National Gallery of Art: Rosenwald Collection, Washington.
245. Detail of Figure 244, National Gallery of Art: Rosenwald Collection, Washington.
246. Sandro Botticelli (ca. 1445-1510), *Christ and Satan*, Sistine Chapel, Vatican (Alinari—Art Reference Bureau).
247. Detail of Figure 246 (Alinari—Art Reference Bureau).
248. Cornelius Galle after Marten de Vos, *Christ and Satan*, Huntington Library (Kitto Bible), San Marino, California.
249. *Christ and Satan*, eleventh-century illumination, Matilda of Tuscany's Gospel Book, Pierpont Morgan Library MS 492, fol. 43, New York.
250. *Diabolical Feast*, seventeenth-century woodcut in Guazzo's *Compendium Maleficarum*, 1608, Folger Shakespeare Library, Washington.
251. Jacopo Tintoretto (1518-94), *Christ and Satan*, Scuola di San Rocco, Venice (Alinari—Art Reference Bureau).
252. Detail of Figure 251 (Alinari—Art Reference Bureau).
253. Pieter Pieterse (?), *Banquet Larder*, ca. 1600, Van Abbe Museum, Eindhoven, Holland.
254. Michelangelo Aliprandi (fl. 1560-82), *Temptation of St. Anthony*, SS. Nazaro e Celso, Verona (Alinari—Art Reference Bureau).
255. Martin Schongauer (d. 1491), *Temptation of St. Anthony*, ca. 1470, National Gallery of Art: Rosenwald Collection, Washington.

256. Grünewald (ca. 1470/80-1528), *Temptation of St. Anthony*, Isenheim Altarpiece, Unterlinden, Colmar.

257. Peter Bruegel the Elder (1525/30-69), *Temptation of St. Anthony*, Ashmolean Museum, Oxford.

258. Annibale Carracci (1560-1609), *Temptation of St. Anthony* (detail), National Gallery, London.

259. C. Jegher (1596-1652/3) after Rubens, *Christ and Satan*, Huntington Library (Kitto Bible), San Marino, California.

260. *Christ and Satan*, thirteenth-century mosaic, S. Marco, Venice (Alinari—Art Reference Bureau).

261. Mattia Preti (1613-99), *Christ and Satan*, Museo Capodimonte, Naples (Alinari—Art Reference Bureau).

List of Abbreviations

AnM	*Annuale Mediaevale*
CL	*Comparative Literature*
CLS	*Comparative Literature Studies*
EA	*Etudes Anglaises*
ELH	*ELH: A Journal of English Literary History*
ELN	*English Language Notes*
ELR	*English Literary Renaissance*
EM	*English Miscellany*
E&S	*Essays and Studies by Members of the English Association*
ES	*English Studies*
Expl	*Explicator*
HLQ	*Huntington Library Quarterly*
HTR	*Harvard Theological Review*
JAAC	*Journal of Aesthetics and Art Criticism*
JEGP	*Journal of English and Germanic Philology*
JHI	*Journal of the History of Ideas*
JWCI	*Journal of the Warburg and Courtauld Institute*
MLN	*Modern Language Notes*
MLQ	*Modern Language Quarterly*
MLR	*Modern Language Review*
MP	*Modern Philology*
MQ	*Milton Quarterly*
MS	*Milton Studies*
N&Q	*Notes and Queries*
PMLA	*Publications of the Modern Language Association of America*
PQ	*Philological Quarterly*
QR	*Quarterly Review*
REL	*Review of English Literature*
RenQuar	*Renaissance Quarterly* (formerly Renaissance News)
RES	*Review of English Studies*
SCN	*Seventeenth-Century News*
SEL	*Studies in English Literature, 1500-1900*
SN	*Studia Neophilologica*
SP	*Studies in Philology*
TLS	*Times Literary Supplement*
TSE	*Tulane Studies in English*
TSLL	*Texas Studies in Literature and Language*
UTQ	*University of Toronto Quarterly*
UTSE	*University of Texas Studies in English*

Preface and Acknowledgments

THE relation between Milton's epic imagery and the visual arts has been much on my mind for some twenty-five years, whether in travel or at home, in museums or in libraries, and the last decade has been almost entirely devoted to research on this subject. In the course of this delightful preoccupation, I have been assisted in ways financial and scholarly and personal, which I am now happy to acknowledge.

Financially, my work in the United States and in Europe was generously supported not only by my own university, but by a number of foundations and learned academies. The *in situ* Italian research was largely carried out in 1971 during a sabbatical from the University of Pennsylvania, with further support from the American Council of Learned Societies and the American Philosophical Society, and with gracious hospitality extended by the American Academy in Rome. Research grants from the National Endowment for the Humanities for the summer of 1973 and 1974 made possible extensive work in libraries and museums in the United States, in England, and in Spain, and the purchase then and later of many valuable photographic reproductions. The award of a Guggenheim Fellowship and of membership in the Institute for Advanced Study made possible the basic writing of the book during the academic year 1973-74, spent in the immensely stimulating and pleasant atmosphere of the Institute in Princeton. Gordon Ray, the President of the Guggenheim Foundation, has, with this project as with many others, expressed an interest and encouragement which go beyond the duties of the office which he so eminently fills. The Guggenheim Foundation has, in addition, provided a substantial subvention for the publication of this book.

Many scholars have been generous in sharing their learning with me. The late James Holly Hanford, that great dean of Miltonists in his day, was among the first to offer encouragement for this research, and the present "Dean," C. A. Patrides, has followed my progress with generous assistance, unfailing friendship, and helpful suggestions from the very beginning. Rensselaer W. Lee, Marquand Professor Emeritus at Princeton, who holds doctorates both in literary and in art history and who has contributed seminal work in relating the two fields, has been strong in his support throughout.

Art historians prove to be a particularly helpful group, even to literary historians who have strayed out of their preserve, and I am especially grateful for suggestions from John R. Martin and David R. Coffin of Princeton University. Similarly, Malcolm Campbell and Paul F. Watson at the University of Pennsylvania, Ulrich Middeldorf of Florence, Harold E. Wethey of the University of Michigan, William S. Heckscher, Emeritus Professor from Duke University, and the late Millard Meiss of the Institute for Advanced Study have all been helpful in various ways.

Student research assistants who have worked with me for a full year each on this project include Georgianna Ziegler, Jacquelyn Mitchell, Debra Doyle, and John Shea, while another student, Theresa Ormsby-Lennon, has assisted with materials in the Vatican Library.

Ministro Antonio Carloni of Florence, who knows his city so intimately, has been helpful in numerous ways, both official and unofficial, through correspondence and in person.

Mrs. Kenneth Setton, preeminent wife of the eminent historian at the Institute for Advanced Study, was alone responsible, through her diplomacy, resourcefulness and charm, for obtaining certain photographs which are vital to my argument, and which would surely have been unobtainable if she had not so kindly intervened on my behalf in Italy.

United States Foreign Service Officer Samuel R. Gammon and Dr. William K. Braun, former U. S. Cultural Attaché in Rome, were also helpful in ways both diplomatic and cultural.

Thomas G. Waldman, Lyman W. Riley, Neda M. Westlake and others in the University of Pennsylvania Libraries have been consistently helpful, as have Thomas Lange and Mina R. Bryan for the Rare Book Collection and Scheide Library at Princeton University. During his own leave of absence, Charles C. Price of the Chemistry Department at the University of Pennsylvania kindly took a number of photographs for me in Germany.

Lessing J. Rosenwald has been typically gracious in allowing access to his unrivalled collections of graphic art, and Ruth Fine has not only advised me about the Rosenwald, of which she is the knowledgeable curator, but about other collections as well.

Mrs. Arthur Vershbow assisted me by examining prints illustrating classical texts in the fine collections which she and her husband have assembled, as well as in the Harvard libraries.

For assistance given while I was working at the Henry E. Huntington Library and Art Gallery, Mary Isabel Fry, Carey Bliss and R. R. Wark are especially to be thanked, as are Horace Groves and Kirsten Mishkin at the Folger Shakespeare Library, and Rosalie B. Green at the Index of Christian Art in Princeton.

During my research into manuscript illuminations in Britain, W. O. Hassall and his staff at the Bodley Library in Oxford (especially Maureen Pemberton and Martha Lively), as well as the staff at the British Library in London, were unfailingly helpful. Malcolm Cormack of the Fitzwilliam Museum in Cambridge (now at Yale with the Mellon Collection), and M. A. Cecil of the Wallace Collection in London, were particularly kind. Father Thomas Glover of the Oratory of St. Philip Neri at the Chiesa Nuova in Rome conducted me through the superstructure of that church to allow a close view of some paintings there, and other clergymen elsewhere have been similarly thoughtful.

The Vatican Library, the Bibliothèque Nationale in Paris, the British Library in London, and innumerable cathedral, college and other libraries on the continent and in Britain have shared their resources with me, as acknowledged in the proper places, while the National Gallery and the Victoria and Albert Museum were generous in opening their libraries to use while I was working in London. Conservateur François Avril of the Bibliothèque Nationale in Paris intervened to solve a particularly thorny problem for me there.

Dr. Giovanni Battista Perotti, Administrator of the Galleria Colonna in Rome, generously contributed splendid photographs of Salviati's *Adam and Eve* from the collections of that gallery.

In the Photographic Archives Department of Fratelli Alinari in Florence, Signorina Alessandra Corti was most helpful, while Janet Snow at the Art Reference Bureau in Ancram, New York, has assisted with unfailing efficiency in acquiring many photographs and permissions for publication in this volume.

Separate acknowledgments for permission to reproduce works of art, and for photographs, are made for each entry in my List of Illustrations.

My superb secretary, Eileen Cooper, has prepared more versions of the notes for this book, of correspondence connected with it, and of the text, footnotes, and plate lists which eventuated in the printed version, than either of us cares to remember. Throughout, she worked with an interest, good cheer and accuracy which are rare indeed, and for which I am deeply grateful.

I also wish to acknowledge once again, as with past publications, the pleasure and satisfaction which I have found in dealing with the Princeton University Press. The process of publishing this heavily illustrated volume has involved complications hitherto unimagined by a literary historian, and as a result of such complications some four years will have elapsed between the initial completion of my manuscript and the actual publication. In the meanwhile, I have received splendid support from many people at the Press, ranging from editor to designer to compositor to director. My first work there for this particular volume was with Mary E. D. Laing, who was helpful with many suggestions and in other ways. I wish to express my especial gratitude to my editor, Margot Cutter, for her learning, her fine eye for style, and her common sense.

My son was present during many phases of this research, both in museums in America and abroad, and by his keen observations contributed at many points. I am happy to say that my wife was present at every point and in every place, enriching all with her wit, intelligence, perception, and grace, as she has in my life for over thirty years. To her the whole is, appropriately, dedicated.

In addition to these, I have been fortunate in having expressions of interest from many friends, who often generously inquired far beyond the range of their usual concerns, and who are too numerous to mention by name, though I hope that, in reading this, they will name themselves.

To express my thanks to all these supporters, friends, and colleagues at home and abroad, I must revert from my role as Miltonist to my role as Shakespearean, and adapt *Macbeth* to say, "More is their due than more than all can pay."

ROLAND MUSHAT FRYE

University of Pennsylvania
Philadelphia, Pennsylvania
June 15, 1977

Part One

Introduction

Purposes, Presuppositions and Methods

IN his epic poetry, Milton has for the most part described the indescribable and the inaccessible. He could not look up into the sky and examine directly the wings of angels or the chariot of the Almighty, nor could he survey the landscape of the Heaven of heavens. Satan, his demonic legions, and his infernal kingdom were equally inaccessible. Even the Garden in Eden, the most this-worldly of all his settings in *Paradise Lost*, was admittedly no longer existent, and he had no direct access to its flora and fauna or to its ruling monarchs, Adam and Eve. These were the principal subjects of his epic, and for none of these could he rely on direct inspection in shaping his visual descriptions. Consequently, any analysis of the visual qualities of *Paradise Lost* which appraises Milton's verse as a mirror held up to nature applies a largely inappropriate standard for judgment and comparison. I say largely, but not always, inappropriate, for, as we shall see, there are descriptions which directly and effectively evoke nature in its own terms.

But though Milton was describing the indescribable, he was not describing the undescribed.[1] We may find many objective visual counterparts to Milton's epic descriptions if we look primarily to art rather than to nature, for his subjects had been central to Western art for centuries, and treatments of them were to be found throughout England and the continent. If we are to understand and appreciate Milton's visual descriptions, therefore, we must look not only to the natural world but especially to the great panorama of paintings, mosaics, and sculptures which represent the same subjects and personalities which form the center of his epic concern.

The observations made thus far concern primarily *Paradise Lost*, but also apply to a somewhat lesser degree to *Paradise Regained*. The Temptation in the Wilderness was not accessible to direct observation by Milton or anyone else, and although Palestine could be visited, Milton did not visit it, and the Rome he knew was radically different from the Rome presented to the Son by Satan on the mountain. The events recounted in *Paradise Regained* are not so far removed from

---

[1] Samuel Johnson objected to the "inconvenience" of Milton's epic design that "it requires the description of what cannot be described, the agency of spirits," and notes that even Adam and Eve "are in a state which no other man or woman can ever know" (see John T. Shawcross, ed., *Milton 1732-1801. The Critical Heritage*, London, 1972, pp. 304, 305). Mark Van Doren, *The Noble Voice: A Study of Ten Great Poems*, New York, 1946, p. 127, judges that Milton "had to create certain of his symbols out of nothing; to pretend; to go the long way around, which is not the way of poetry at its best." When the pictorial tradition is taken into account, however, it becomes apparent that Milton was by no means creating *ex nihilo*.

ordinary human experience as are those in *Paradise Lost*, but they were not subject to direct observation by Milton and his initial audience. Again, the story of Christ in the Wilderness had been presented in objective visual forms for centuries before Milton's time by European artists, and the works of those artists provided a reservoir of images in terms of which men and women had been accustomed to imagining the physical components of the authoritative accounts in the Gospels.

My purpose here is to study the ways in which artists represented the scenes, events, and characters that Milton treats poetically in his epic works. Over the centuries prior to Milton's time, the arts had developed an extensive vocabulary of visual imagery relating to sacred subjects. Unfortunately, that vocabulary has been very largely lost to modern readers.

In addition, a similar loss of familiarity with the Biblical and classical traditions handicaps the modern reader in ways with which we are all relatively familiar, and which are frequently lamented. Douglas Bush, for example, notes that "Milton and his early readers knew the Bible and the common classics far better than we do and were far more likely to use and to catch overtones from both sources." Thus we are not only in danger of missing important meanings introduced by way of allusion, but perhaps even more in danger of overlooking those simple overtones and undertones of irony and ambiguity which contribute density and depth to the poetry. That readers in earlier generations were widely aware of the rich heritage of classical and Biblical literature gave the poet an immense advantage, which Davis P. Harding succinctly described when he pointed out how, by allusions to that heritage, "the traditional poet is able to achieve clarity in plan and economy in execution. His art, therefore, is principally an evocative art; that is, he extends and enriches his meanings by a strategy of deliberate allusiveness to the poetry of the past."[2] The "evocative" and "allusive" operate in much the same way in relation to the visual traditions as in relation to the literary traditions. An awareness of the visual heritage of art will enrich our responses to *Paradise Lost* and *Paradise Regained* in very much the same fashion as an awareness of the Hebrew, Greek, and Roman past.

Our task here, then, is to recover the vocabulary of visual images which Milton and his readers may reasonably be expected to have known. The major elements of that vocabulary can be recovered and made available to us. Beyond that, differences in visual dialect will be cited only as they may cast light upon Milton's own usage. Throughout, the purpose is to marshal visual resources which will enable us to read the epic poems with greater awareness and sensitivity.

I have no interest in arguing that I have discovered particular and individual "sources" for the descriptive passages in Milton. I shall engage in considerable analysis of individual works of art, and of particular details, but such analyses are undertaken to show the traditional ways of seeing things that the arts can reveal to us, and not to identify a particular painting or sculpture as the source for this or that line in Milton. Here an analogy to Milton's knowledge of words may be

[2] Douglas Bush, "Ironic and Ambiguous Allusion in *Paradise Lost*," *JEGP* 60 (1961), 634; Davis P. Harding, *The Club of Hercules*, Urbana, 1962, p. 1.

helpful: just as we are rarely concerned with when and how Milton added a particular word to his vocabulary, so we need not be especially concerned about when he first encountered some visual motif. Such identifications may be interesting but are not likely to be very significant, and it is in any case unlikely that they could be demonstrated with any high degree of probability. For both words and images, it should be enough to establish the common patterns of usage, and then to see how Milton adopted, adapted and expanded these, and also what he ignored or changed.

Similarity can rarely be taken as a proof of direct dependence in these matters. Literary works were continually feeding the imagination of visual artists, who in their turn offered pertinent stimulus to writers. Where visual motifs have been long established and widely employed, as is true for most of Milton's epic subject matter, the precise direction and line of influence is often impossible to determine. If a particular description is found to be unique to Milton as a poet, and the same visualization appears in only one work of art, the probability that one depends upon the other may seem to be high. Even so, we should consider that the two artistic imaginations may have been operating quite creatively and quite independently of each other, or that they may have relied upon a common source or a common tradition, and we must be careful not to mistake analogues for sources.[3]

In discussing the literary traditions upon which Milton drew, Robert M. Adams has said that Milton "approached few authors in the spirit of a man seeking permission to hold an opinion or borrow an expression, but sat over most of his library as a judge, if not as a conqueror."[4] The same patterns will be found in Milton's evocations of artistic traditions. Genius does not manifest itself in a mechanical reproduction of what has gone before, and for Milton it surely did not do so: his departures from the established visions of art may be just as important as his reliance upon them.

As we are not interested in tracing the direct sources of Milton's descriptions, neither are we concerned with the direct influences exerted by Milton on later art. That subject has already been broached in Marcia Pointon's book on Milton's illustrators, as well as in shorter pieces by other scholars.[5] Horace Walpole long since took Milton to be the poetic inspirer of the development of eighteenth-

[3] For a valuable analysis of such problems, see John M. Steadman, "Tradition and Innovation in Milton's 'Sin': The Problem of Literary Indebtedness," *PQ* 39 (1960), 93.

[4] Robert M. Adams, *Ikon: Milton and the Modern Critics*, Ithaca, N.Y., 1955, p. 176.

[5] Marcia R. Pointon, *Milton and English Art*, Toronto, 1970. See also C. H. Collins Baker, "Some Illustrators of Milton's *Paradise Lost* (1688-1850)," *The Library* 5th ser. vol. 3 (1948), 1-21, 101-19; Suzanne Boorsch, "The 1688 *PL* and Dr. Aldrich," *Metropolitan Museum Bulletin* 6 (1972), 133-50; Helen Gardner, "Milton's First Illustrator," in *A Reading of "Paradise Lost,"* Oxford, 1965, pp. 121-31; Merritt Y. Hughes, "Some Illustrators of Milton: The Expulsion from Paradise," *JEGP* 60 (1961), 670-79; John Dixon Hunt, "Milton's Illustrators," in *John Milton: Introductions* (ed. John Broadbent), Cambridge, 1973, pp. 208-25; Edward Morris, "John Gibson's Satan," *JWCI* 34 (1971), 397-99; John T. Shawcross, "The First Illustrators of *PL*," *MQ* 9 (1975), 43-46; Kester Svendsen, "John Martin and the Expulsion Scene of *Paradise Lost*," *SEL* 1 (1961), 63-73; and Joseph A. Wittreich, Jr., " 'Divine Countenance': Blake's Portrait and Portrayals of Milton," *HLQ* 38 (1975), 125-60, and also his impressive *Angel of Apocalypse: Blake's Idea of Milton*, Madison, Wisc., 1975.

century English landscape gardens, and Helen Gardner agrees that it was Milton's conception which spread over Europe as *le jardin anglais.*[6] Certainly Milton's Garden of Eden lacks the formal regularity of most seventeenth-century gardens, whether in Italy or in England, for which Milton substituted a natural expansiveness and variety. That subject, again, is not within our interests, but I hope that some other scholar may take it up, for it could be a fascinating and rewarding study.

A final disclaimer must be made: this study does not focus upon putative relations between Milton's poetry and Baroque or Mannerist art. A number of studies have been made of that subject; many critics have referred to such relationships, with varying degrees of effectiveness, and I shall treat examples of these when I deal with the critical literature. A case can surely be made for restricting a comparison of art and literature to a single period in history,[7] but my purpose is not to disclose the cultural spirit of Milton's century; it is rather to consider the relations between his poetic descriptions and the visual traditions accessible to him and to his early readers. The cultural roots which nourished John Milton go very deep, and penetrate beyond the baroque expressions of the seventeenth and the mannerist expressions of the sixteenth centuries. Milton's genius was so eclectic, drawing upon such a wide range of historical and cultural influences, that a restriction of our investigation to one or two centuries would unduly narrow and perhaps even cripple our attempt to understand the visual components and references of his work. Jean Hagstrum has eloquently warned that a central focusing on the "time-spirit" can lead us to neglect the uniqueness of the individual artist in favor of a preoccupation with the uniqueness of his epoch. In such a preoccupation, "the terms of critical analysis pass undiscriminatingly from one work to another, even from one art to another," as genuine understanding is displaced by idols of the marketplace.[8]

The vast extent of Milton's cultural awareness has never ceased to amaze commentators, and quite rightly so. Surely, no great poet has ever been so learned, and the very weight and mass of his knowledge would have burdened and suffocated a lesser mind. Far more impressive than his learning, however, is the genius he displayed in distilling, transmuting, and applying that learning with the most perfect tact in his own artistic creations. The learning was not only mastered by the poet, but was made subservient to the poetry. When Helen Gardner calls him the "grand assimilator," and when D. C. Allen refers to his "combining imagination," they provide phrases which convey his particular genius.[9] He could appar-

[6] See Edward Malins, *English Landscaping and Literature 1660-1840*, London, 1966, pp. 1-2; Gardner, *A Reading of "Paradise Lost,"* p. 79; and John R. Knott, Jr., *Milton's Pastoral Vision: An Approach to "Paradise Lost,"* Chicago, 1971, p. 46, for a comment on Gardner.

[7] See for example, Helmut A. Hatzfeld, *Literature through Art: A New Approach to French Literature*, New York, 1952, p. 211.

[8] Jean H. Hagstrum, *The Sister Arts: The Tradition of Literary Pictorialism and English Poetry from Dryden to Gray*, Chicago, 1958, p. xiv.

[9] Gardner, *A Reading of "Paradise Lost,"* p. 81, and D. C. Allen, "Milton's Amarant," *MLN* 72 (1957), 257. For Milton's synthetic and integrating genius, see also Charles G. Osgood, *The Classical Mythology of Milton's English Poems*, New York, 1964, pp. xliii and lxviii; Harry F. Robins, *If This Be Heresy*, Urbana, 1963, p. 180; Walter Clyde Curry,

ently carry knowledge as if in solution until the moment of need, when he precipitated it into new fusions of perfect aesthetic propriety.[10] Even his frequent citation of the classics seems to have been largely from memory, yet his references are usually correct.[11]

If Milton generally relied upon an accurate memory for his references to literature, he may be presumed to have done much the same thing for his allusions to the visual tradition. What Elizabeth Pope has to say about Milton's reliance upon the traditions out of which he fashioned *Paradise Regained*, we may apply also to Milton's use of the visual traditions: "Milton often does not trouble to define his terms or to explain himself at length: he takes it very much for granted that everyone of any intelligence will understand the key phrases, the casual allusions, and the implied connections between events that were so obvious and so significant in his own day."[12]

Without a knowledge of the visual lexicon available to Milton and his contemporaries, it is all too easy to find in him a blindness that is really our own. Bernard Berenson's words on the approach to unfamiliar forms of art are equally pertinent here: ". . . let anyone give us shapes and colors which we cannot instantly match in our paltry stock of hackneyed forms and tints, and we shake our heads at his failure to reproduce things as we know they certainly are, or we accuse him of insincerity."[13] No one has a perfect dictionary to assist in understanding a great poet or a great painter, but it is incumbent upon us continually to improve and expand the dictionaries we do have.[14]

Though Milton's descriptions drawn directly from nature are often extraordinarily effective, the principal analogues to the subject matter he treats in the epics are to be found in the visual arts rather than in nature. It is the arts which have enabled the mind of man to "see" the supernatural, and the arts which have stocked the mind with images for envisioning the principal incidents of *Paradise Lost* and in somewhat different ways of *Paradise Regained*. In using art to illuminate literature, we are paralleling one of the major efforts of art historians in our time, but reversing the primary direction of most such efforts, for their principal endeavor has been to use literature for the interpretation of the visual arts. So eminent an authority as Millard Meiss has shown, however, that the interchange actually

---

Milton's Ontology, Cosmogony and Physics, Lexington, Ky., 1957, p. 11; Christopher Ricks, *Milton's Grand Style*, Oxford, 1963, p. 76; J. M. Evans, *"Paradise Lost" and the Genesis Tradition*, Oxford, 1968, p. 219; Northrop Frye, *The Return of Eden*, Toronto, 1965, p. 5; Mason Hammond, "Concilia Deorum from Homer through Milton," *SP* 30 (1933), 16.

[10] See James H. Sims, *The Bible in Milton's Epics*, Gainesville, Fla., 1962, p. 252.

[11] Charles G. Osgood maintains that "it seems impossible that he ever adapted them directly from the printed text, or that his relation to them was sustained in any degree by the open book" (*The Classical Mythology of Milton's English Poems*, p. xlv).

[12] Elizabeth Pope, *"Paradise Regained": The Tradition and the Poem*, Baltimore, 1947, p. 122.

[13] Bernard Berenson, *Italian Painters of the Renaissance*, New York, 1964, p. 173.

[14] See Stanley Stewart, *The Enclosed Garden: The Tradition and the Image in Seventeenth-Century Poetry*, Madison, Wisc., 1966, p. 182.

operates in both directions, and has called for further study of the ways in which art influences the human imagination in general.[15]

The relating of the visual arts to Milton's epic poetry will be carried out in as explicit a manner as possible, so as to elucidate the details of Milton's treatment as well as the more general outlines. At times Milton provides a remarkably complete description of some scene, while on other occasions only a few details suffice for his purposes.[16] Generations of Christian art had sensitized readers to a wide range of pictorial images which could be brought to mind by a few deft phrases, and that visual range is what we shall here attempt to recover. Milton was too sophisticated a poet not to be aware of the traditional association evoked by his visual allusions, any more than he would have been unaware of the associations aroused by his classical imagery. We may, and I think must, assume that his use of visual allusions was consciously directed to reinforce and undergird both his poetic and his religious purposes. But although this assumption is, as I believe, valid, it has not commanded universal assent, either in the past or today, as a survey of Milton criticism will show.

[15] Millard Meiss, *Painting in Florence and Siena after the Black Death: The Arts, Religion, and Society in the Mid-Fourteenth Century*, New York, 1964, pp. 106 and 131, and *passim*.

[16] Even as late as the eighteenth century, the poet Thomson impressed readers with his exquisite pictorial qualities, and was able "to create a vivid tableau of a few details that may strike us as meager or vague," as Jeffry B. Spencer has shown in *Heroic Nature: Ideal Landscape in English Poetry from Marvell to Thompson*, Evanston, 1973, p. 292.

II

Milton's Visual Imagination and the Critics

MILTON's visual imagery was often praised by early critics of his verse; when faults were found, they usually had to do with too much specificity, rather than vagueness, in his descriptions. The principal charges of visual inadequacy came later, a century and more after Milton's time.

In the eighteenth century, painters who commented on the subject were united in regarding Milton's descriptions as remarkably and memorably pictorial.[1] William Hogarth's interest in Milton is well known, and he was not only inspired to paint scenes which Milton described (as in his famous *Satan, Sin, and Death*), but took passages from Milton as defining that "serpentine line" which he postulated as the basic element in pictorial beauty.[2] The painter and editor Jonathan Richardson wrote that "Milton's pictures are more sublimely great, divine and lovely than Homer's, or Virgil's, or those of any other poet, or of all poets, ancient or modern," and he favorably compared Milton's verbal landscapes, portraits, and history paintings to the works of the greatest Renaissance and baroque artists.[3] Henry Fuseli was so moved by Milton's visual imagination that he spent much of the last decade of the eighteenth century painting scenes illustrating Milton's verse, while William Blake produced major works inspired by Milton's visual descriptions, and J.M.W. Turner repeatedly cited Milton in explanatory notes to his own paintings.

Critics for the most part concurred in the judgment of the painters. In Newton's 1749 edition of Milton we find a number of specific comparisons between Milton's descriptions and famous works of art, as also in Todd's edition of 1801.[4] In his essay for *Spectator* number 321, Joseph Addison included among the "beauties of the fourth book" of *Paradise Lost* those "pictures of Still-Life, which we meet with in the description of Eden, Paradise, Adam's Bower, etc."[5] Writing on art and literature in a treatise published in 1745, the French critic Abbé le Blanc

---

[1] Spencer, *Heroic Nature*, p. 12.

[2] William Hogarth, *The Analysis of Beauty, with the Rejected Passages from the Manuscript Drafts and Autobiographical Notes* (ed. Joseph Burke), Oxford, 1955, p. 160.

[3] Jonathan Richardson, *Explanatory Notes and Remarks on Milton's "Paradise Lost,"* in *The Early Lives of Milton* (ed. Helen Darbishire), London, 1932, p. 328, and Spencer, *Heroic Nature*, p. xvi; for similar comments by Thomas Newton, see Shawcross, *Milton: 1732-1801*, pp. 154-55.

[4] Arthur E. Barker, ". . . And on his crest sat Horror," *UTQ* 11 (1942), 434, and Shawcross, *Milton 1732-1801*, p. 406.

[5] John T. Shawcross, ed., *Milton: The Critical Heritage*, London, 1970, p. 183. Addison's objections to Milton's decorum will be taken up at later points.

commented that one could not read Milton's *Paradise Lost* "without perceiving that he had a hundred times in his life taken pleasure in seeing the sun, sometimes gild the horizon, and reanimate all nature; and at others, withdraw its rays, and leave her buried in the horrors of darkness." Like others of his time, Abbé le Blanc was impressed not only by Milton's description of the physical presence of nature, but also by his skill in introducing the reader to a feeling for the nature he describes: "Milton does not only describe the coolness of the morning, and the beautiful enamel of a meadow, or the verdure of a hill; he expresses even the sentiments of joy and pleasure these objects excite in our soul: and gives us the satisfaction of thinking, that as we feel the same sensations he does, we have the happiness to see nature with the same eyes."[6] In the course of our study, we shall repeatedly recur to this theme, and to the skill with which Milton induces us not only to share but to appropriate his awareness.

In the century after his death, the visual elements of Milton's poetry were more often praised than condemned, but quite as significant are the kinds of condemnation that developed during this period. Adverse criticism maintained that Milton was far too concrete and explicit in his description of spiritual subjects. Most early critics did not read Milton in this unfavorable way, and showed little or no embarrassment over his physical presentation of spiritual realities, because Christendom had long employed a doctrine of accommodation by which objects and actions could be interpreted according to their spiritual significance rather than their literal meaning. That understanding of accommodation (found alike in the Fathers of the Church and in the Protestant reformers) continued to be influential, but it was subject to gradual and steady erosion during the eighteenth century and thereafter. Along with erosion, we see more and more signs of embarrassment, both among some of the faithful and among others, over the physicality of many of Milton's descriptions. An increasingly literal understanding of the Scriptures in some circles thus combined with a heady suspicion of mythology in the Age of Reason to condemn Milton for a too detailed visualization of his supernatural scenes. Without trying to distinguish which of these two trends, which were often mixed and always complex, is at the point of the complaint, it is possible to trace briefly the course of such objections, and doing so will throw important light upon the history of Milton's reputation.

In *The Political History of the Devil* of 1726, Daniel Defoe castigated Milton for describing Hell as a local place, and found Hell's "Gates of burning Adamant" (II, 436) an absurdity.[7] Twelve years later, an anonymous author in the *Gentleman's Magazine* similarly criticized Heaven's "blazing portals" because Milton's description does "very much resemble the Heaven which Nurses portray to their Children, when, in the Simplicity of their Hearts, they would nurture them in what they think Piety."[8] The very preciseness of such descriptions in Milton's epics was considered dangerous, as "making room for the grossest and most absurd Kind of

---

[6] Shawcross, *Milton 1732-1801*, pp. 133-34.

[7] B. Eugene McCarthy, "Defoe, Milton, and Heresy," *Milton Newsletter* 3 (1969), 71.

[8] Shawcross, *Milton 1732-1801*, p. 95 and *PL* VII, 574ff.

Enthusiasm"—that grand bugaboo of the eighteenth century. Milton was seen as "sensualizing our Ideas of Heaven to a Degree that may have ill Effects," and indeed his poetic conceptions were said to be "every whit as sensual as the Mahometan's."[9] A little supernaturalism went a long way in the *Aufklärung*, and the supernatural descriptions in *Paradise Lost* went considerably beyond anything of the kind in Holy Writ. Voltaire would obviously be more annoyed by bad taste than by bad theology, and he characterized that elaborate demonic structure Pandemonium as "a contrivance" which he found "very preposterous."[10] Here, the objection by the chief apostle of Reason provides a counterpart to the objection raised by the dissenter Defoe. It may all be summarized in David Hume's description in 1757 of *Paradise Lost* as "a work not wholly purged from the cant of former times."[11]

The objection to overly concrete descriptions in *Paradise Lost* was most often lodged against the War in Heaven. In 1698, the Reverend Charles Leslie, apparently attempting to protect Christianity from the ridicule of the deists, attacked Milton on the grounds that his narrative descriptions imposed a considerable mythological stain upon the Christian faith.[12] Very much the same kind of attitude was displayed in 1721-22 when John Dennis declared that he did not believe even one syllable that Milton had written about the angelic wars—as though a literal belief were being called for.[13] A decade later, John Clarke objected strenuously to angels fighting and suffering in armor, when they could prevent or deliver themselves from pain merely by removing the armor, and he traced Milton's usage to "this absurdity by Homer, who set his gods a fighting in the *Iliad*; a thing not only ridiculous but profane in him...."[14] A similar profaneness was attributed to Milton by an anonymous writer for the *Gentleman's Magazine* in 1738 who found the poet "so free with the Scriptures of God's Word, as to introduce so many circumstances purely invented [which showed him] to have but little Respect for those Holy Books."[15] These and other adverse judgments preceded Samuel Johnson's attacks upon Milton for mixing the spiritual and the material, though Johnson of course operated on a higher critical plane.

The earliest of these attacks upon the War in Heaven pointed out the source of the problem. Writing in 1695, Sir Samuel Morland objected that *Paradise Lost* was a "jest with God's Word" much fitter for poets and "Painters who, when they have got to the top of their Parnassus, frame to themselves Ideas of what chimeras or goblins they please."[16] Aside from his pejorative judgment, Morland did identify here a major shaping influence upon Milton's imaginative account of the Battle of the Angels: the painters and other artists who had spread throughout Europe just

[9] *Ibid.*, pp. 101-2.

[10] Shawcross, *Milton: The Critical Heritage*, p. 253.

[11] Shawcross, *Milton 1732-1801*, p. 238.

[12] Shawcross, *Milton: The Critical Heritage*, p. 117.

[13] *Ibid.*, p. 236.

[14] *Ibid.*, p. 263.

[15] Shawcross, *Milton 1732-1801*, p. 94.

[16] Sir Samuel Morland, *The Urim of Conscience*, London, 1695, pp. 13 and 14, as quoted in Robert H. West, *Milton and the Angels*, Athens, Ga., 1955, pp. 119 and 118.

those visual images which Milton evoked. In Morland's mind, the ancient traditions of visualizing the conflict between the powers of light and the powers of darkness had already become discredited, and they would be almost entirely ignored in eighteenth-century criticism of Milton.

Without recourse to the visual tradition, many later critics treated Milton's vivid descriptions of angels and devils at war as though they were his own pernicious and even ridiculous interpolations. Even the precedent of Homer was insufficient to justify Milton's tangible descriptions of spiritual beings and spiritual conflicts. In such matters, our perceptions are governed not only by our native abilities but also by the traditions in which we have been trained to understand and imagine. A later chapter of this book will be devoted to reconstructing the ways in which the War in Heaven was imagined in European art up to Milton's time, and to demonstrating the close associations between Milton's descriptions and the pertinent art works—associations which Morland had recognized at least in general terms only twenty-one years after Milton's death.

Thus far, the evidence indicates that for the first century or so after his death Milton was widely regarded by critics, poets, and painters as strikingly effective in his visual descriptions. It is significant that the principal objections to *Paradise Lost* concerned what were regarded as overly physical and specific visualizations, and that these objections were based on intellectual and religious premises rather than on aesthetic ones. The controversy expanded, however, from these bases.

Dr. Samuel Johnson's objections to the War in Heaven are well known and were taken by Robert West in his *Milton and the Angels* as epitomizing and spawning a whole critical tradition.[17] To these we shall turn later. Perhaps even more important than Johnson's analyses of those passages in *Paradise Lost* has been his majesterial and memorable dictum that Milton saw nature through the spectacle of books.[18] It is sad, but apt, to recall that poor Johnson was himself so very nearly blind throughout his life that he scarcely ever saw nature directly at all, and so might be taken as an extraordinarily bad witness on this subject. His stature as a critic, however, is indisputable, and his bad judgments have sometimes been as influential as his good. Walter Savage Landor replied that "if ever there was a poet who knew [nature] well, and described her in all her loveliness, it was Milton," and fired back a bon mot of his own that Johnson "saw Nature from between the houses of Fleet Street," but it was of no avail against the Grand Cham of the English enlightenment.[19]

Coleridge was the next major critic to belittle Milton's visual imagination. He did recognize one artistic counterpart to a famous description in *Paradise Lost* —that of the creation of the animals—but he regarded this as the extent of the artistic influence upon Milton, and he commented that "Milton is not a picturesque,

---

[17] See West, *op. cit.*, pp. 108-12, for a perceptive analysis.

[18] Samuel Johnson, *Lives of the English Poets* (ed. George Birkbeck Hill), New York, 1967, I, p. 178.

[19] Joseph Anthony Wittreich, Jr., *The Romantics on Milton: Formal Essays and Critical Asides*, Cleveland, 1970, p. 319.

but a musical poet."[20] Hazlitt demurred, and made much of the "vividness with which [Milton] describes visible objects," referring especially to "the grandeur of the naked figure" in Adam and Eve, who "convey to us the ideas of sculpture."[21] Coleridge's emphasis on Milton's verbal music cannot be faulted, for Milton is almost above rivalry in the depth and variety of his aural beauties. But the strength of one faculty does not necessitate the atrophy of another. Hazlitt (without directly attacking Coleridge) disputed that "common perversion of criticism" that Milton's

> ideas were musical rather than picturesque, as if because they were in the highest degree musical, they must be (to keep the sage critical balance even, and to allow no one man to possess two qualities at the same time) proportionally deficient to other respects. But Milton's poetry is not cast in any such narrow, commonplace mold; it is not so barren of resources. His worship of the Muse is not so simple or confined. A sound arises like a 'steam of rich distilled perfumes' [*Comus*, 556]; we hear the pealing organ, but the incense on the altars is also there, and the statues of the gods are arranged around![22]

In our own century, the debate was reopened, or at the very least reinvigorated, by T. S. Eliot, when he declared that "Milton may be said never to have seen anything." Eliot held that we should not attempt to see very clearly any scene Milton depicts, and declared that "I am happiest where there is least to visualize." Going far beyond Coleridge, he postulated for Milton a psychological law under which "a dislocation takes place, through the hypertrophy of the auditory imagination at the expense of the visual and tactile."[23] Few critical remarks have been more provocative—of both agreement and disagreement. As much the Grand Cham of twentieth-century letters as Samuel Johnson had been in the eighteenth, and perhaps accorded even more authority than Coleridge in the nineteenth, Eliot exerted a massive influence. Samuel Johnson once commented upon a remark of King George III that if the King had said it, it was so, and it was just in this sense that many twentieth-century readers honored the critical opinions of T. S. Eliot.[24]

Like a stone thrown into a pond, Eliot's comments sent eddies circling out toward every point of the compass. Some critics have gone beyond him, as did F. R. Leavis in his reference to Milton's "sensuous poverty."[25] While not entirely unsympathetic with Eliot's view, Mario Praz nonetheless associated Milton with the visual artists, and yet could still refer to "the aural exclusiveness of his mature

---

[20] *Ibid.*, p. 245.

[21] *Ibid.*, pp. 370 and 382.

[22] *Ibid.*, p. 382.

[23] T. S. Eliot, *On Poetry and Poets*, New York, 1957, p. 162, first published as "A Note on the Verse of John Milton," *Essays and Studies* XXI (1936), 32-40.

[24] The influence of Eliot's charge against Milton is traced by Patrick Murray, *Milton: The Modern Phase*, London, 1967, pp. 31-49, and *passim*.

[25] F. R. Leavis, *Revaluations: Tradition and Development in English Poetry*, London, 1936, p. 47.

inspiration."[26] Even Jean Hagstrum found little that is sharply visualized in Milton, while suggesting that the poet is "more intent on having us feel in a kind of kinaesthetic sensation the full opulence of nature itself, than in having us see its particulars."[27]

Eliot had a tremendous impact, and his views have continued to be influential, but it is fair to say that his extreme position has failed to convince most readers. Numerous critics have launched counterarguments against him.[28] The poet and art connoisseur, Laurence Binyon maintained that Milton "shows a painter's eye,"[29] and Louis L. Martz concluded a close analysis of some of Milton's typical descriptions with the comment that "one wonders how there could ever have been any questions of Milton's visual imagination."[30] Like Jeffry B. Spencer, most Milton critics would probably refer to certain "technical limitations on his pictorialism," but also like Spencer they would go on to affirm that he "possesses a strong visual sense."[31] Don Cameron Allen has asserted the strength of Milton's visual powers in poetry,[32] and Wayne Shumaker has affirmed the full sensory, including visual, effectiveness of Milton's verse.[33]

Even among those critics who have rejected T. S. Eliot's strictures, there has been little tendency to conduct a full and systematic study of Milton's visual descriptions. There can be no doubt that the cumulative judgments of those three great critics, Johnson, Coleridge, and Eliot, have had an inhibiting effect. Also inhibiting has been the awareness of Milton's blindness, even though it affected him at most for only the last thirty of the sixty-six years of his life. In this connection, critics have frequently assumed a kind of automatic decline in visual memory and descriptive effectiveness due to the loss of sight, accompanied by a gain in the vitality of the other senses. Theodore Banks, for example, writes of Milton that "his visual sense . . . weakened, but his other senses—smell, hearing, and touch—

[26] Mario Praz, "Milton and Poussin," in *Seventeenth-Century Studies Presented to Sir Herbert Grierson*, Oxford, 1938, p. 193.

[27] Hagstrum, *The Sister Arts*, p. 126.

[28] See, for example: Christine Brooke-Rose, "Metaphor in *Paradise Lost*: A Grammatical Analysis," in *Language and Style in Milton* (ed. Emma and Shawcross), New York, 1967, p. 296; Phyllis MacKenzie, "Milton's Visual Imagination: An Answer to T. S. Eliot," *University of Toronto Quarterly* 16 (1946), 17-29; Christopher Grose, "Some Uses of Sensuous Immediacy in *Paradise Lost*," *HLQ* 31 (1968), 215; and Theodore H. Banks, *Milton's Imagery*, New York, 1969, p. 124. Banks also points out the considerable scope and significance of Milton's "images drawn from the various arts," p. 36.

[29] Laurence Binyon, "A Note on Milton's Imagery and Rhythm," *Seventeenth-Century Studies Presented to Sir Herbert Grierson*, p. 187.

[30] Louis L. Martz, *The Paradise Within: Studies in Vaughn, Traherne, and Milton*, New Haven, 1964, p. 129. The passages to which Martz directly refers are *PL* VII, 309-28 and 463-73. On pp. 147-48, Martz discusses the similarity to Milton of the 1641 windows by Abraham van Linge in University College, Oxford, to which we shall later turn.

[31] Spencer, *Heroic Nature*, p. 102, and see also pp. 108-9.

[32] Don Cameron Allen, *The Harmonious Vision, Studies in Milton's Poetry*, Baltimore, 1970, pp. 95ff.

[33] Wayne Shumaker, *Unpremeditated Verse: Feeling and Perception in "Paradise Lost,"* Princeton, 1967, pp. 211-13.

became more quick and sharp. In so doing, they showed a development character-istic of a man who goes blind."[34] Similarly, John Peter refers to Milton's descrip-tions as "bold and broad impressions, where the density given by detail is not needed," and associates this characteristic with his blindness.[35] We have already noted Eliot's hypothesis that the auditory imagination sharpened at the expense of the visual. But such hypotheses, though often announced, have never to my knowl-edge been supported by a thorough study of the evidence, and I doubt that such a study would support them.

Milton himself prepared for the French oculist Thévenot a careful report of his affliction, and he must be assumed to have given a full and accurate account on the basis of which he hoped that this distinguished physician could effect a cure. According to his own statement, the first signs of eye trouble began when he was a mature man of about thirty-six, some five years after his return from Italy, and he gives no hint of serious trouble before about 1644. Over the next several years his sight progressively deteriorated until at the age of forty-two or forty-three he was totally blind.[36] The fact that he was blind during his later years, and particu-larly during the composition of his two epic poems, does not mean that he was shut off from visual imagination, and should not blind us as readers to the visual possibilities of his verse. In the authoritative study *Milton's Blindness*, based on medical evidence and her own experience of blindness, Eleanor G. Brown has settled that question: persons who do not lose their sight until after the seventh year apparently are able to retain a clear visual memory of people and things they saw before blindness, what she calls "the retention . . . of mental pictures."[37]

Recognizing the importance of this visual memory, Marjorie Nicolson has argued persuasively that the telescope "has much to do with the vast canvas of *Paradise Lost*,"[38] and that Milton's visit to the volcanic Phlegraean Fields near Naples contributed much to his later descriptions of Hell. With her customary

[34] Banks, *Milton's Imagery*, p. 137. For a brief discussion of the critical linking of Milton's blindness with characteristics of his imagery, see Leland Ryken, *The Apocalyptic Vision in "Paradise Lost,"* Ithaca, N.Y., 1970, p. 220.

[35] John Peter, *A Critique of "Paradise Lost,"* New York, 1960, p. 85.

[36] William Riley Parker traces the chronology of Milton's affliction in *Milton: A Biog-raphy*, London, 1968, pp. 286, 324, 389, 393, and 408. Milton's account, prepared for Dr. Thévenot, is given in John Diekhoff, *Milton on Himself: Milton's Utterances Upon Himself and His Works*, New York, 1939, pp. 94-97. It is sometimes said that Milton's postscript and signature on a petition to the commissioners for sequestration of royalist estates, of 25 Feb-ruary 1651, is labored and indicates the writer's increasing blindness, but an eminent literary historian who has for years worked extensively with seventeenth-century handwriting in the Public Records Office and elsewhere recently wrote me that all the Chancery manuscripts he examined were worse than this postscript.

[37] Eleanor G. Brown, *Milton's Blindness*, New York, 1934, pp. 57, 107, and 133. Earlier V. P. Squires had compared the early and late poems without finding any appreciable difference in references to nature ("Milton's Treatment of Nature," *MLN* 9 [1894], 462). In a comparable situation with a musician, few musicologists would argue that the deaf Beethoven did not retain an effective musical memory or that he could not hear the music stored in his mind.

[38] Marjorie Nicolson, "The Telescope and Imagination," *MP* 32 (1935), 235 and 259.

forthrightness, she denied that "Milton's sources are to be found primarily in books," and asserted that he "often drew from actual experience"[39]—a principle we shall see validated again and again.

If we seek principally for literary and erudite readings of Milton, we may find them, but in the process we can sometimes lose the primary meaning of simple and straightforward descriptions. As a case in point, we may take Milton's references to flowing water as an "amber stream" (*PL* III, 358-59 and *PR* III, 288-89). G. Stanley Koehler attributes these to the influence of Greek science, mythology, or legend.[40] For a far simpler explanation one has only to cross the Apennines between Florence and Venice, as Milton did, and look down the gorges to the streams below, which have a decidedly amber color.[41] There need be no emblematic significance in such descriptions, nor need we seek for distant literary sources, where a merely literal rendition of what the eye perceives is explanation enough. Or there may be a conjunction of visual experience with literary reference. The Villa Poggio at Caiano, for example, was early known as Ambra, from the stream that runs through its grounds and figures in the poetry of Poliziano and of Lorenzo the Magnificent. For another Miltonic reference to running water, we may recall the "milky" stream from which both Adam and Samson are said to drink, (*PL* V, 306 and *SA* 547-51) and which Samson describes as "a fresh current [which] flow'd . . . translucent, pure. . . ." Maud Bodkin finds the epithet "milky" incongruous "if related to any visual image of clear water, . . . clear water is not 'milky.' The aptness of the word must spring, not from any appeal to the eye, but from some overtone of organic emotional response."[42] Here Bodkin is being precious, for the reference is not to still water, but to fast moving water, and any experienced trout fisherman would have been able to tell her that "milky" or "white" are adjectives accurately applied to such fast-moving, churning, and therefore foaming, clear water. Milton is not introducing us to archetypes here, but rather to nature itself. Once again, if we are to read Milton aright, we must look at *things* as well as at words and ideas.

That important point is not lost on Arnold Stein, who finds in Milton an "unromantic love [for the beauty of nature], with no nervous quiver in the sensuousness; the beauty celebrated is firmly founded on order." Of Milton's vivid "liquid lapse of murmuring streams" (*PL* VIII, 263), he reminds us that we should not be so engulfed in the music that we ignore other powers in the description: "one ought not to miss the fact that Adam is *seeing* the water and that the sound of the water owes something to the very exact meaning of lapse—the falling, running downward movement, discontinuous within the continuous, that causes the liquid murmuring."[43]

[39] Marjorie Nicolson, "Milton's Hell and the Phlegraean Fields," *UTQ* 7 (1938), 500-13, with the quotation from p. 513.

[40] G. Stanley Koehler, "Milton's Use of Color and Light," *Milton Studies* 3 (1971), 66.

[41] The same may be observed elsewhere in the Apennines, as indeed in other countries.

[42] Maud Bodkin, *Archetypal Patterns in Poetry*, New York, 1958, p. 106.

[43] Arnold Stein, *Answerable Style: Essays on "Paradise Lost,"* Seattle, 1967, pp. 85 and 144-45.

In his readings of Milton, Stein refers us not only to nature but also to art. In a suggestive article, he notes that "the traditional *descriptio rei* of Renaissance rhetoric was associated with painting," and points out how Milton in his descriptions "arranges depths and chiaroscuro" so that "the final effects may approximate those of painting."[44] In a similar vein, Helen Gardner writes that "we read *Paradise Lost* best if we read it in the spirit in which we look at great Renaissance paintings of Christian subjects."[45] Brief expressions of such views may be encountered with increasing frequency in criticism since the Second World War. The late Holly Hanford suggested that there was a direct connection between Milton's poetry and the art he saw in Italy, but unfortunately he was unable to work out those connections in detail.[46] C. A. Patrides has treated the subject broadly in a number of interesting lectures and in a persuasive article.[47] There was also one doctoral dissertation completed in 1955, which remains unpublished,[48] but as yet there has been no detailed and full-length study of Milton and the visual arts.[49]

There have, to be sure, been a number of treatments of Milton and the Baroque, ranging in length from short comparisons to articles and books. These comparisons can be helpful, if the terms are defined with sufficient precision. Thus, when Helen Gardner compares Milton's poetry to Baroque art, she is exemplary in the specification of what she means: "his vast glooms and burst of brilliant light, . . . the energy with which he assaults our feelings . . . , single moments of intense feeling, the attempt to do more than one thing at once: to make sculpture move and architecture dance, to combine weight and lightness, mass and fluidity, to express the inexpressible, to play tricks with light and darkness—all this we have come to find imaginatively satisfying in the Baroque style, the child of the classical, but venturing far beyond its limits. Milton is an adventurer of this kind."[50]

[44] Arnold Stein, "Milton and Metaphysical Art: An Exploration," *ELH* 16 (1949), 120 and 123. See also his *Answerable Style*, p. 151.

[45] Gardner, *A Reading of "Paradise Lost,"* p. 28; see also pp. 34, 50-51, and 71-2. For brief references by E.M.W. Tillyard, see *The Miltonic Setting, Past and Present*, Cambridge, 1938, pp. 70 and 120.

[46] James Holly Hanford, *John Milton, Englishman*, New York, 1949, p. 97. In private conversations Professor Hanford expressed even more hope than in his published works. See also his "Milton in Italy," *Annuale Mediaevale* 5 (1964), 49-63.

[47] C. A. Patrides, "John Milton: The Poet Who Gave us Paradise," *The Observer* (Color Supplement), August 13, 1969, pp. 3-9.

[48] Amy Lee Turner, *The Visual Arts in Milton's Poetry*, a Rice University Ph.D. dissertation of 1955. As Rice did not begin to publish its dissertations in microfilm until well after 1955, Turner's thesis came to my attention only after all my basic research had been completed. Her work includes some useful observations and pertinent allusions, but it is spotty, as when Hieronimus Bosch is repeatedly alluded to as a Protestant, though he died in 1516, before the break with Rome. One is also surprised to read that the Florentine Baptistry was in pagan times "a round temple dedicated to Mars" (p. 278), as this false legend is repudiated even in popular guidebooks. The work is interesting, and reads like a travel diary by an intelligent reader of Milton, or a guide to travel for such a reader.

[49] A much earlier work by Ida Langdon (*Milton's Theory of Poetry and Fine Art: An Essay with a Collection of Illustrative Passages from His Works*, New Haven, 1924) is a survey, sweeping through the whole field of what are called the "fine arts." An essay, as the title indicates, it is primarily useful for its copious quotations from Milton's works.

[50] Gardner, *A Reading of "Paradise Lost,"* p. 44.

Such references, and they may be found in other critics, are helpful and enlightening, but many discussions of the Baroque in connection with Milton tend to befuddle the issues, too often relying on high levels of abstraction and suggesting premature conclusions.[51]

The terms "Mannerist" and "Baroque" arose out of art criticism, where they can have considerable meaning, but they may also be used loosely even there, as art historians have pointed out. René Huyghe, for example, comments that after years of neoclassical preoccupation, the Baroque was discovered, and "everything was now seen in relation to the Baroque; the only effect of this attempt to reduce every problem to a single principle has been confusion."[52] Walter Friedlaender also warned against the unproductive attempt "to include completely different trends under a common denominator like 'The Art of the Baroque,'" and recommended that such terms only be "used when they mean something very definite and circumscribed."[53] If such warnings are necessary for art history, then even greater wariness would seem to be needed when these terms are imported into literary analysis. Within certain contexts and for certain purposes, they may be useful, but until more fundamental work has been done to establish their critical precision and appositeness for literature, I must agree with Wellek, Tuve, and others that we should do our major interpretive work with other tools.[54]

Some basic studies have already been carried out, from which we can profit here. From Mario Praz we learn of Milton's apparently limited interest in the emblem literature: "Traces of an acquaintance with emblems can be detected in Milton (when in the *Doctrine and Discipline of Divorce* he speaks of 'two carcases chained unnaturally together or, as it may happen, a living soul bound to a dead corpse,' he seems to allude to Whitney's emblem for *Impar coniugium* suggested by Mezentius' cruelty)."[55] Elsewhere Praz saw possibilities for a fuller correlation, and in a sophisticated article suggested major similarities between Milton and Poussin.[56] H.V.S. Ogden has written an instructive and stimulating article entitled "The Principles of Variety and Contrast in Seventeenth-Century Aesthetics, and in Milton,"[57] and in joint authorship with his wife has produced an authoritative

[51] Northrop Frye, *The Return of Eden*, p. 18, provides another brief but helpfully specific comparison.

[52] René Huyghe, "Baroque Art" in *Larousse Encyclopedia of Baroque and Renaissance Art*, New York, 1967, p. 329.

[53] Walter Friedlaender, *Mannerism and Anti-Mannerism in Italian Painting*, New York, 1970, p. 81.

[54] See René Wellek, "The Parallelism between Literature and the Arts," *English Institute Annual (1941)*, New York, 1942, p. 59; and Rosamond Tuve, "Baroque and Mannerist Milton?" in *Essays by Rosamond Tuve* (ed. Thomas P. Roche, Jr.), Princeton, 1970, pp. 262-80.

[55] Mario Praz, *Studies in Seventeenth-Century Imagery*, Rome, 1964, p. 228. In the later light of this study, Erwin Panofsky was apparently wrong to assume that the emblem books were an important influence upon Milton's imagery; see his *Meaning in the Visual Arts*, New York, 1955, p. 163. More recently, Ludomir Konecny has suggested emblem influences in Milton's early "Poem at a Vacation Exercise," in his note "Young Milton and the Telescope," *JWCI* 37 (1974), 368-73.

[56] Mario Praz, "Milton and Poussin," p. 209, and *On Neoclassicism* (trans. Angus Davidson), Evanston, Ill., 1969, p. 38.

[57] *JHI* 10 (1949), 159-82.

study of seventeenth-century English taste in landscape art, which is often appo-site to Milton.[58] In Jeffry Spencer's recent book on ideal landscape and English poetry we find a number of useful observations about Milton. As early as 1947, Elizabeth Pope reproduced in her book on *Paradise Regained* several visual repre-sentations of the Temptation in the Wilderness, which was a pioneering thing to do at that time even though she did not fully explore the possibilities of artistic relevance.

Other studies will be cited in later chapters, but even the fullest available treatments of Milton and the visual arts are either limited in subject or incidental to some different interest. It has been assumed at best that the subject could be adequately treated by occasional allusions, while at worst it has been ignored—mostly the latter. Even a scholar so sophisticated both in the visual arts and in literature (though primarily post-Miltonic) as Jean Hagstrum can repeat Leigh Hunt's assumption that Milton learned nothing from art.[59] Hagstrum's judgment represents what is probably the majority view: "Milton had been to Italy and had seen Renaissance art, and the diligent investigator will doubtless find more than one reflection. But they will remain few, and the search for correspondences promises little to students of Milton's imagery." Similarly, John Arthos in his study of *Milton and the Italian Cities* passed over entirely the wealth of Italian paintings simply because he felt that they were not sufficiently relevant to Milton.[60]

A close and systematic examination of the visual evidence will, I believe, lead us to a substantially different understanding.

[58] Henry V. S. and Margaret S. Ogden, *English Taste in Landscape in the Seventeenth Century*, Ann Arbor, 1955. These similarities were further analyzed by Marjorie B. Garber in a study published after the writing of my book—"Fallen Landscape: The Art of Milton and Poussin," *ELR* 5 (1975), 96-124.

[59] See Wittreich, *The Romantics on Milton*, pp. 454-55.

[60] Hagstrum, *The Sister Arts*, p. 125, and John Arthos, *Milton and the Italian Cities*, London, 1968, p. 118, both of whom have subsequently indicated to me, in private corre-spondence, that they have modified these opinions.

III

Milton's Awareness of the Visual Arts

THE PURITANS AND THE ARTS

PURITANISM was a vast, explosive, and protean movement, embracing not only the fanatical and bigoted but also the most cultivated of tastes. It is understandable that we should wish to reduce such a diverse phenomenon into some simple phrase or some simple characterization, but it is impossible to do so without falsifying the issues. The reputation of seventeenth-century Puritans has suffered severely because, having lost their revolutionary struggle, the Puritans could then scarcely defend themselves against the ridicule of the victors. A stereotype has thus emerged of the Puritan as, among other things, essentially antiaesthetic, and William Dowsing, the notorious "image breaker" who rejoiced in the destruction of "superstitious pictures," is sometimes taken as the typical figure of his group. If typical at all, Dowsing was so only of one special sub-group of the Puritans, and although I am unaware of his having given even a single sign of any kind of good taste, it is only fair to him to note that his opposition was not to art as such, but to what he regarded as the idolatrous potential of certain images. Though often overestimated, mob action by Puritans also resulted in the destruction of, or damage to, some works of art, as when mobs threw stones at the Laudian statue of the Virgin and Child over the door of St. Mary's Church in Oxford. That incident is worth noting, but it is as important to note that when the Puritan leaders came into authority, they did not destroy this controversial image but removed it from its place and stored it away. What was at issue was religion, not aesthetics, and when responsible Puritans removed specific examples of what they felt would be offensive to God, they were not attacking the visual arts as such.[1]

In popular folklore, nonetheless, the Puritans are given principal credit for the artistic poverty of England. The respected curator of one of the leading British museums recently remarked that Oliver Cromwell and his men had mutilated all

[1] Erwin Panofsky pointed out that it was only "comparatively rare forms of Protestantism which objected to the representational arts in principle." On the protean character of Protestantism in relation to art, Panofsky commented: "Let me repeat that Protestant art is as variable as Protestant doctrine and that its historical fate was codetermined by an infinite number of additional factors." ("Comments on Art and Reformation," in *Symbols in Transformation: Iconographic Themes at the Time of the Reformation; An Exhibition of Prints in Memory of Erwin Panofsky* [ed. Craig Harbison], Princeton, 1969, pp. 9 and 12.) For a correction of the oversimplification of the Protestant attitudes, Louis Réau, *Iconographie de l'art chrétien*, 3 vols. in 6, Paris, 1955-59, I, p. 452, points out that Jacob Jordaens, the most sensual, the most carnal of all the Flemish painters, was a Calvinist convert.

the figures in the Lady Chapel and in the Chantry Chapel of Ely Cathedral, whereas the destruction in the former took place during the Reformation of the early and mid-sixteenth century, one hundred years before the Puritan interregnum, and there was never any destruction in the latter, for there the rough-hewn figures erected by Bishop West about 1534 were simply never completed. In the late eighteenth century, "true taste" replaced "true religion" as the supreme arbiter, and the grand old Norman screen or *pulpitum* was removed from the east end of the nave at Ely with as few qualms as the early Protestant zealots under King Edward VI had removed saints' images. We badly need a thorough scholarly history of changes and destruction in England's artistic patrimony over the centuries, and when such a history is written, I suspect it will show that as much art was lost due to changes of taste as to changes of faith. The "restorers" of churches may be the worst culprits of all: as Gothic was sacrificed to neoclassicism in the eighteenth century, so the latter in its turn fell prey to the Gothic revival of the nineteenth.

Through all these changes, Oliver Cromwell and the Puritans are the legendary villains. Close historians know better, of course, and the words of Christopher Hill are particularly instructive:

> Historians are beginning to appreciate how much the interregnum in general and Cromwell in particular did for British education and British cultural life. But the legend of the philistine Puritan, hostile to art and culture, dies hard in popular imagination. Dr. Nuttall has, I hope, established the fact that most cathedrals whose desecration is conventionally ascribed to Oliver Cromwell were in fact desecrated by sixteenth-century bishops or (more rarely) by the troops of either side in the civil war in the course of military operations or out of control of their officers. The only reliable evidence we have on the subject invariably shows Cromwell trying to protect the monuments of antiquity.[2]

Again, Hill notes that "Dr. Scholes has taught us to see [Cromwell's] court as an important patron of music: so it was of painting, sculpture and literature."[3] In his authoritative history of classical sculpture collected in England, Michaelis observes that "Cromwell exerted himself more than anyone, though not always with success, to restrain a barbarous squandering of art treasures," and in an informative

---

[2] Christopher Hill, *God's Englishman: Oliver Cromwell and the English Revolution*, Harmondsworth, 1970, p. 189. In a more recent study, John Phillips (*The Reformation of Images: Destruction of Art in England, 1535-1665*, Berkeley, 1975) has taken a somewhat more unfavorable view of the Puritan destruction, though he recognizes that "there was a tremendous exaggeration of destruction for purposes of propaganda," and that "how many of these accounts are true, of course, will probably never be known," because the destruction in earlier times "combined with the lack of good descriptive inventories, have blocked the possibility of fully assessing the destruction" (pp. 193, 195). Though Phillips fails to account for the full complexity and range of viewpoints among the Puritans of the interregnum, he does recognize that when Cromwell assumed the direction of affairs, he not only halted the dispersion of works of art, but even began to some extent to increase the national collections (pp. 199-200).

[3] Hill, *Cromwell*, pp. 190-91.

article entitled "Two Cultures? Court and Country under Charles I," P. W. Thomas demonstrates that in their attitudes toward culture, the Puritan and Parliamentary Party was not very different from the Royalist Party.[4] In their study of English taste in the seventeenth century, the Ogdens summarize:

> The significant thing about the Commonwealth period is that, in spite of the political and social unrest, the polite pursuits of Englishmen continued without much apparent slackening. . . . The Restoration initiated a period of relative stability, in which the fine arts could flourish with increasing vigor, but it is a mistake to think of the Commonwealth period as one of narrow Puritanism breaking the continuity of English culture. The evidence here presented shows clearly that the growth of interest in the fine arts in general, and in landscape in particular, continued without pause during the whole of the Revolution and Commonwealth period.[5]

The dispersal of the art treasures assembled by King Charles I is assuredly one of the great tragedies of this period, for the English royal collection was one of the finest in Europe. The sale of these art works was prompted, not by antipathy to beauty, but by economic necessity in order "to settle the very considerable sums of money which the King owed by way of arrears of wages and salaries to his servants and debts outstanding for provisions supplied to the Royal Household." The Puritans' execution of the King had disposed of him, but not of his extensive personal debts, which became the responsibility of the new regime. Attempting to establish itself in the popular favor, and fearing the effects of further unpopular taxes, "Parliament hit upon the expedient of paying off the King's debts by the sale of his personal belongings. In July 1649, some six months after the King's death, Parliament, therefore, passed an Act, forfeiting the goods and chattels of the late King and the Queen and the Prince on account of 'their several delinquencies'."[6] In his history of Whitehall Banqueting House, Per Palme recounts that "in 1653 the traditional villain of this iconoclastic chapter [i.e., Oliver Cromwell] energetically put an end to the wholesale dispersal of Stuart splendor," and began to recover the royal furniture and to reserve the hangings at Hampton Court, and in other ways to preserve the national heritage.[7] Among other works, Raphael's "cartoons" were preserved for the nation, but much had been lost, irretrievably lost, of a priceless heritage, often sold at a fraction of its true worth.

What Milton thought of these transactions, we do not know. We do know

[4] Adolf Michaelis, *Ancient Marbles in Great Britain*, Cambridge, 1882, p. 30, and P. W. Thomas, "Two Cultures? Court and Country under Charles I," in the *Origins of the English Civil War*, ed. Conrad Russell, London, 1973, pp. 168-93. I am indebted to Christopher Hill for calling the latter to my attention.

[5] Henry Ogden and Margaret Ogden, *English Taste in Landscape in the Seventeenth Century*, p. 73b.

[6] W.L.F. Nuttall, "King Charles I's Pictures and the Commonwealth Sale," *Apollo* 82 (October, 1965), 302.

[7] Per Palme, *Triumph of Peace: A Study of the Whitehall Banqueting House*, Stockholm, 1956, p. 83.

that his own official quarters were hung with art works, for when Mylius went to meet "the great Milton" at Whitehall on October 20, 1651, he reported that he passed through anterooms hung with splendid wallpaper and tapestries. The comment is so brief as to be tantalizing, but at least we do know that the hangings were there, though we have no way of knowing what they represented.[8] For the cultivated Puritan, the objection to images revered in ways which seemed idolatrous in no way implied an objection to images elsewhere.[9]

MILTON'S EXPOSURE TO THE VISUAL ARTS

Whether or not he was particularly fond of art, no intelligent man living in the seventeenth century (even one who went blind in his forties) could have avoided the many impressions of art surrounding him. Woodcuts, engravings, and etchings transmitted copies of great masterpieces throughout Europe, and popularized works of many lesser men who also carried on the visual tradition. In England the flowering of native art in the Middle Ages was almost stifled by the dynastic wars of the fifteenth century, the disinterest of the Tudors, and the changing ecclesiology of the Reformation, but the great visual heritage was still to be encountered in stained glass, wood carving, and stone sculpture in most parish churches, colleges, cathedrals, and even in public buildings. For those cultivated Englishmen who took a continental tour (as increasing numbers did), there was also the great treasury of European art, seen at first hand. All of this was available to that "fit audience though few" for which Milton wrote, and provided a vast reservoir of images upon which readers could draw in reading his epic poems.

There is no doubt that the fifteen months Milton spent abroad, including a year in Italy, in 1638-39 were immensely formative in his intellectual and poetic development. It was a common practice for English travelers in Milton's time to keep a journal or diary of such a tour, recording what had been seen, enjoyed, and learned.[10] In view of the importance Milton always assigned to his own reactions and opinions, it seems to me highly likely that he kept such a personal record and that it was subsequently lost. But little is to be gained by constructing arguments without evidence, and to speculate upon what Milton's travel diary might have revealed about his observation of art on the continent would only be a waste of energy.

In *The Reason of Church Government*, Milton described his program of preparation as a poet, placing first "devout prayer to that Eternal Spirit who can enrich with all utterance and knowledge." "To this," he goes on to say, "must be

[8] Parker, *Milton: A Biography*, pp. 400-401, and J. Milton French, *The Life Records of John Milton*, 5 vols., New Brunswick, 1949-58, III, pp. 82-83.

[9] See William G. Madsen, *From Shadowy Types to Truth: Studies in Milton's Symbolism*, New Haven, 1968, pp. 2 and 166-80, for a brilliant demonstration of the Protestant attitudes on such issues, and a refutation of one of the most persistent idols of the marketplace.

[10] John W. Stoye, *English Travellers Abroad 1604-67: Their Influence in English Society and Politics*, London, 1952, p. 197, refers to the "current belief that it was right and proper, pertaining to the educational purposes of a tour, to keep such a record" as a travel journal or diary.

added industrious and select reading, steady observation, insight into all seemly and generous arts and affairs," pursuits which he said he had been encouraged to undertake by the confidence of many, including his Italian friends.[11] The three critical phrases here—"select reading, steady observation, insight into all seemly and generous arts and affairs"—may be interpreted as appositive, but it makes more sense to see them as serial and incremental. Observation and insight are not merely refinements or variations upon "industrious and select reading," but additional and supplementary avenues to knowledge. The word observation appears again when Milton, in his tractate *Of Education*, recommended travel to "make wise observation."[12]

Milton himself, in his various references to his Italian journey, made clear that he saw the sights, and his good Italian friend Carlo Dati noted that Milton had "viewed with care full many a place," to apprehend "everywhere all that each has to offer."[13] Dati then cited other aspects of the impression Milton made upon his friends in Italy, referring to his linguistic abilities, literary learning, and social heartiness, so as to cover the whole range of gentlemanly accomplishments, and I take works of art to be included in the phrase "viewed with care."[14] "Viewing" and "seeing the sights" in Milton's time, usually referred to the observation of antiquities, great architecture, and other works of art, as may be illustrated by John Evelyn's comment in his diary that "travelers do nothing else but run up and down to see sights, that come into Italy"—Evelyn's account of his own Italian journey, only a few years after Milton's, serves to define the terms in just the sense which I have given them.[15]

Milton's friends would certainly have encouraged him to take an interest in art, for such an interest was considered essential to the complete gentleman of the time. In Florence, his friends Gaddi, Dati, and Frescobaldi were all members of distinguished patrician families, and the Frescobaldi may well have been second in Florence only to the Medici in prestige. The Gaddi family had not only contributed to the creation of great art in Florence by the ancestral painters Taddeo and Agnolo, but had a famous and rich collection of art in their palazzo when Milton was there.[16] Besides a notable library, the Palazzo Gaddi contained much fine modern and ancient sculpture, antiquities from Egypt, and paintings by Leonardo, Del Sarto, and other great masters.[17] It would be interesting to know the full

[11] John Milton, *The Works of John Milton*, 18 vols. in 21 (ed. Frank Allan Patterson, *et al.*), New York, 1931-38, III, p. 241, hereafter referred to as the Columbia Edition and abbreviated *CE*.

[12] *CE* IV, pp. 290-91.

[13] Letter, *CE* I, pp. 164-65, and James Holly Hanford, *John Milton, Englishman*, New York, 1949, pp. 81 and 96-97, for Milton's sightseeing.

[14] Antonio Francini of Florence referred to Milton's quest "of the sciences and the arts," and here the treatment is so general as not to specify (though presumably to contain) a reference to the visual arts as such (*CE* I, pp. 160-61).

[15] John Evelyn, *Diary*, 6 vols. (ed. E. S. De Beer), Oxford, 1955, II, p. 431, and *passim*.

[16] Demetrio Guccarelli, *Stradario storico biografico della città di Firenze*, Rome, 1969, p. 299. See also Enrico Barfucci, *Giornale fiorentino*, Florence, 1961, p. 52.

[17] John Arthos, *Milton and the Italian Cities*, p. 20.

extent of this collection, but for this kind of information there are usually only scattered and scanty references, so that it is generally not known which paintings represented the artists mentioned. Such difficulties are encountered again and again in trying to establish the holdings of seventeenth-century European collections. Occasionally, it is possible to identify a piece which had been in the Gaddi collection—for example, the bozzetto in gilt wax and wood of the *Descent from the Cross* by Jacopo Sansovino, which is now in the Victoria and Albert.[18]

Milton's friend Carlo Dati, the youngest member of the circle of his intimates in Florence, became a scholar of considerable prominence, writing on art history and contributing a collection of biographical studies of leading artists which was published at about the same time as Milton's *Paradise Lost*. Two of the Dati palaces survive, one marked "Canto de' Dati" on the exterior, and the other now known as the Baldovinetti Palace, from the family that acquired it after the extinction of the Dati line in 1767. Both palaces are on the south side of the Arno. The Frescobaldi palaces are also on the south bank, directly adjoining the Ponte S. Trinita, the ancient one standing behind the one along the river. The newer palace, "a magnificent example of Florentine Baroque" designed by Bernardo Radi with niches containing busts of the Medici Grand Dukes Ferdinando I, Cosimo II, and Ferdinando II, was erected about 1640.[19] Unfortunately, I have been unable to ascertain the precise date the palace was completed, and so cannot say whether it was still under construction or recently finished when Milton was in Florence. Milton's friend was Bishop Piero Frescobaldi, who at the time of Milton's Florentine stay was parish priest of the church at Artimeno, where the Medici were seasonal parishioners, and who shortly thereafter became Mitred Prior of the Church of San Lorenzo in Florence, the ancient parish church of the Medici which houses their tombs. In the seventeenth century, such ecclesiastical appointments not only showed that young Piero was singled out as a rising prince of the Church but also indicated close personal and family ties with the reigning Medici grand dukes.[20] The seventeenth century being what it was, it is unthinkable that men such as Gaddi, Dati, and Frescobaldi (to mention only the Florentines of whom we know most) would not have seen to it that Milton was introduced to the fine arts. The same is true of his friend Giovanni Battista Manso, the Marquis of Villa in Naples, and Lucas Holstenius, the curator of the Vatican collection, in Rome.[21] With friends such as these, Milton could have gained entrance virtually everywhere, and must be presumed to have seen a great deal.

[18] See Sir John Pope-Hennessey *Catalogue of the Italian Sculpture in the Victoria and Albert Museum*, London, 1964, vol. III, pl. 439 and 440, and vol. II, p. 418, for the history of ownership.

[19] Georg Kauffmann, *Florence: Art Treasures and Buildings*, London, 1971, 349-50. Piero Bargellini, *Florence*, Florence, 1969, p. 278, dates the older Frescobaldi palace in the thirteenth century.

[20] For an account of Piero, and for the present location of the palaces of Milton's friends in Florence, see Roland Mushat Frye, "Milton's Florentine Friend, Bishop Frescobaldi: A Biographical Note and Portrait," *Milton Quarterly* VII (1973), 74-75.

[21] There is an interesting bronze plaque, allegorizing the life of Holstenius, erected in his memory in 1663 for his tomb in Sta. Maria dell'Anima in Rome, by Antonio Giorgetti, which

Milton was in Venice, as in Naples, for only one month, compared to a total of four months in Rome and another four months in Florence. It is only in Venice that he makes no mention of Italian friends, an understandable omission given the traditional clannishness of the Venetians: officially, at least, the association of Venetian patricians with foreigners was frowned upon, and other English travelers, too, mention fewer Italians in Venice than anywhere else. Richard Lassels' *An Italian Voyage* of 1670 notes that it was harder for foreign visitors to make friends and contacts in Venice than elsewhere in Italy. Lassels nonetheless did see the Treasury of St. Mark's and went through the Doges Palace very thoroughly, noting its art works.[22]

Though affording fewer social contacts, Venice had much else to offer, and cultivated Englishmen of Milton's age made the most of its artistic treasures. Sir Henry Wotton, who had sponsored Milton elsewhere, had been a long-time English ambassador in Venice, where he acquired a large collection of art for himself and for others.[23] Indeed, English emissaries in Venice in the early seventeenth century were generally deputed to find art works for English collectors like the Earl of Arundel and the Duke of Buckingham.[24] While Milton was in Venice in 1639, Basil Fielding was still resident there. Like Wotton and Carleton before him in that post, Lord Fielding collected paintings for himself and others, and was also known in Venice for his musical interests. He shared many of Milton's loyalties and associations—his sympathies were with Parliament, and he would soon return home to command troops under the banner of Parliament in the Civil War—but despite this, we have no record of any contact between the two. Sir Henry Wotton, however, must certainly have opened some avenues for Milton in Venice. We know how carefully Wotton studied the pictures in churches and elsewhere in Venice, and how he conveyed to England not only examples of Venetian art, but also an understanding of that art. Surely, Wotton's advice to the young Milton on his travels would have included an insistence on the value of art, knowingly appreciated.

Much could be seen in Italy by the English traveler even without Milton's

---

is represented by an early copy in the Victoria and Albert Museum in London. The portrait bust, and an engraving of the whole tomb, are reproduced as figs. 6 and 9 in Jennifer Montagu, "Antonio and Gioseppe Giorgetti," *The Art Bulletin* 52 (1971), 278-98. As for Manso, the earliest biographer of Milton says that this nobleman showed Milton "the rarities" of Naples, which in the seventeenth century would presumably include works of art (French, *Life Records*, I, p. 399).

[22] Richard Lassels, *An Italian Voyage, or a Complete Journey through Italy*, Paris, 1670, pp. 378-80.

[23] Frances A. Yates, "Paolo Sarpi's 'History of the Council of Trent,'" *JWCI* 7 (1944), 135-38. Wotton exercised his first artistic embassy by assembling pictures for Sir Robert Cecil, and he later arranged for Daniel Nys, an artist, to go through Italy in search of interesting works. It may well be that Wotton was one of the early influences in forming the acquisitive tastes of Charles I, even while he was Prince of Wales. See A. Lytton Sells, *The Paradise of Travelers: The Italian Influence on Englishmen in the Seventeenth Century*, London, 1964, p. 74.

[24] For the English ambassadors to Venice, see Stoye, *English Travellers Abroad*, p. 212, and Arthos, *Milton and the Italian Cities*, p. 115.

influential friends. The catacombs in Rome had been rediscovered in the early years of the century by Antonio Bosio, and his authoritative study of them in 1632, *Roma Sotterranea*, had generated enthusiasm and excitement even beyond the circles of scholarship. Roman Catholic apologists used the artistic evidence on the walls of the catacombs to support the claims of the Roman Church in debates with Protestants, and as Milton arrived in Rome only six years after the publication of this magnificent volume, he must certainly have been aware of the current arguments. At issue were such matters as the honor given to saints, and the celebration of the Lord's Supper, as well as other doctrinal differences. John Evelyn went down into the catacombs to inspect them in 1645, as did many other visitors, and Milton may have too, given his interest in both the controversial issues and Christian history.[25]

Public museums as we know them today are an innovation of the nineteenth century, but there was one early exception: the collection of antiquities given by Pope Sixtus IV to the conservatori, or municipal officials of Rome, in the fifteenth century. It was displayed, for the benefit of all visitors and for the aggrandizement of Rome, in the Palace of the Conservatori on the Capitoline Hill. Succeeding popes, including Innocent VIII and Leo X, added to the original collection, and by Milton's time it included many of the primary works which are to be seen on the same site today.[26] Michelangelo's patron, Pope Julius II, was also an avid admirer of classical marbles, and he provided a new building at the Vatican in which to display them. Though not technically a museum, the Belvedere served many of the same purposes. The *Laocoon* was installed there in 1506, shortly after its discovery, to be followed in relatively short order by the *Venus Felix*, the *Commodus*, the *Apollo Belvedere*, *Cleopatra* (now identified as Ariadne), the Belvedere "torso," and the statues of the river gods Tiber and Nile. Thus, many of the most famous examples of classical art to be seen by the twentieth-century traveler in Rome were also available to Milton and his contemporaries.

Though the Vatican picture galleries as we know them are a later addition, the greatest art works in the Vatican complex, then as now, were the wall paintings by such painters as Botticelli, Michelangelo, and Raphael, and there appears to have been no difficulty in gaining access to these. The guidebooks all list them as available for viewing, and the accounts of contemporary travelers indicate that such opportunities were taken. In the 1630s English travelers were welcomed everywhere and apparently desired to see everything, and unlike Moryson and Leithgow fifty years before, were no longer content with seeing merely ancient Rome.[27] Even so staunch an Anglican as John Evelyn, and that staunch Protestant Francis Mortoft, were impelled to go into the great Roman Catholic churches

---

[25] See Ernest S. Bates, *Touring in 1600*, New York, 1911, p. 109. The Catacombs of Calixtus and of Cyriaca (subsequently destroyed) were open in the time of Milton's visit; see Turner, *The Visual Arts in Milton's Poetry*, pp. 302-3.

[26] Roberto Weiss, *The Renaissance Discovery of Classical Antiquity*, Oxford, 1969, p. 191.

[27] Stoye, *English Travellers*, p. 189, and Clare Howard, *English Travellers of the Renaissance*, New York, 1914, p. 168.

and study their artistic and architectural treasures.[28] Like Milton, these and others of his English contemporaries traveled with more leisure than the twentieth-century tourist, and saw far more.

It is little short of amazing how much they could and did see.[29] Even before the establishment of modern museums and galleries, the great collections in palaces and villas of the nobility were opened to them. No doubt the gentle susceptibility to tipping on the part of Italian servants was as apparent then as it is now; at all events, the palaces were somehow opened to travelers, and were thoroughly inspected and reported on. Francis Mortoft reports a careful tour of the Borghese with its sculptures and paintings, as well as a similarly close acquaintanceship with the Vatican, the Palazzo Farnese, the Villa Medici, and the Villa Montalto with its modern and ancient treasures. He even penetrated as far as the bed chamber in the Villa Ludovisi, and he was able also to "crash" a musical party given by Queen Christina at the Palazzo Pallavicini, during which he was much impressed by the mosaic landscapes and the tables made of precious stones.[30]

Milton's contacts made it unnecessary for him to slip into parties uninvited. We know that he was personally welcomed and escorted into the Palazzo Barberini by Cardinal Francesco Barberini and followed this introduction with a leisurely visit the next day. Not only Urban VIII, but the whole Barberini family were great collectors and patrons of the arts, and their palace presented an "assembly of the best the world had to offer." Much of this was collected under the direc-

[28] See Evelyn, *Diary*, II, *passim*, and *Francis Mortoft His Book. Being His Travels Through France and Italy 1658-59* (ed. Malcolm Letts), London, 1925, *passim*.

[29] The numerous and readily available guidebooks provide invaluable background information for us. Among the principal works were J. H. von Pflaumen's *Mercurius Italicus* and François Schott's three-volume *Itinerarii Italiae rerumque Romanorum*. Turner, *The Visual Arts in Milton's Poetry*, p. 288, indicates that Inigo Jones in 1613-14 relied upon Palladio's *L'antichità di Rome* and *Le descritione delle chiese*, while Peacham found *Icones statuarium quae hodie visuntur Romae* useful, and John Raymond, who visited Rome in 1646, chose *Itinerario d'Italia*, *Roma antica*, and *Roma moderna* (the last two presumably by P. Totti). Other useful works included *B. Marliani urbis Romae topographica*, 1588; Bartolommeo Rossi's *Ornamenti di fabriche antiche e moderni dell'alma citta di Roma*, 1600; Totti's *Ritratto di Roma*, 1638; Filippo de' Rossi's *Ritratto di Roma moderna*, 1645; and Giovanni Baglione's *Le vite de' pittori . . .* , 1642. *L'antichità di Roma*, 1688, by Andrea Fulvio was highly regarded. The guide material assembled by Fioravante Martinelli was republished in 1969 with superb maps and other illustrations in Cesare D'Onofrio's *Roma nel seicento*. The 1679 *Painter's Voyage of Italy*, which is a translation of Giacomo Barri by W. L. [William Lodge] is primarily a brief and bare list of paintings and their locations in Italy, which provides no iconographical evidence and shows not even the slightest signs of critical discernment, beyond the bare fact of inclusion and exclusion.

"Views" and maps are reproduced in Amato Pietro Frutaz, *Piante e vedute di Roma e del Vaticano dal 1300 al 1676*, Vatican City, 1956, and in J. M. Wiesel and B. Cichy, *Rom, Veduten des 14-19 Jahrhunderts*, Stuttgart, 1959.

Among the useful books on the cities Milton knew in Italy are: Giuseppe Martinelli (ed.), *The World of Renaissance Florence* (trans. Walter Darwell), New York, 1968; Paolo Portoghesi, *Rome of the Renaissance* (trans. Pearl Sanders), London, 1972; Paolo Portoghesi, *Roma Barocca; The History of an Architectonic Culture*, (trans. Barbara Luigia La Penta), Cambridge, Mass., 1970.

[30] Mortoft, *His Book*, pp. 97, 110ff., 119ff., 124ff., 128ff., 146ff., and 151ff.

tion of Cardinal Francesco, for whom Milton expressed an almost unbounded admiration.[31]

The opening of the Italian treasures to heretical Englishmen testifies not only to the inherent generosity of the Italian temperament, but probably also to the ingenuity of that fraternity of guides who then as now were a fixture of the Italian scene. We know relatively little about how these men operated but we do get occasional glimpses. John Evelyn, for example, found early in his stay a "Sights-man" who provided him entrance into, and a conducted tour of, the Farnese Palace.[32] It is known, too, that "the English Jesuits in Rome—Oxford scholars, many of them—engaged the attentions of such of their university friends or their countrymen who came to see Italy, offering to show them the antiquities, to be guides and interpreters."[33] It may well be that Milton's introduction at the Jesuit English College in Rome, and his presence at dinner there, according to the register, on October 30, 1638, may have come about as a result of his taking on just such a guide. The Vatican curator Holstenius (or even Cardinal Barberini, though the latter is less likely) could well have been expected under the conditions and courtesies of the time to have arranged for Milton to have an expert guide, who would provide entrée into private as well as public buildings.

In Florence, Milton's eminent and noble friends would have made things still easier for him. He would not necessarily have had to rely on them as there seems to have been fairly ready access for an Englishman of the time to the full range of Florentine art. The Stone brothers, sons of the English sculptor Nicholas Stone, made extensive studies in the Medici collections, and the diaries of young Nicholas show that on a number of occasions when he was copying in the Duke's collection, the Duke himself came by and commended his work; this was during the summer of 1638 when Milton was also in Florence.[34] In the 1640s, Evelyn also made a detailed report on the Medici art collection, and there seems to have been little difficulty in obtaining access not only to the Palazzo Vecchio and the Uffizi but also to the grounds and gardens of the ducal residence at the Pitti. In the 1650s Francis Mortoft reports that he went through all three floors of the Pitti Palace, and saw "all these chambers" with their works of art.[35]

[31] Letter to Holstenius, in French, *Life Records*, I, pp. 391-92 and 410-11. Hanford (*John Milton, Englishman*, p. 94) assumes that Milton's memory played him false, and that he was greeted by Antonio Barberini, but Parker and Arthos accept Milton's account as correct. Surely Milton would not have made so obvious a mistake, especially about a man with whom he had later had a long private visit. Francesco's kindnesses to other visiting Englishmen are treated in Arthos, *Milton and the Italian Cities*, pp. 68-69, and his oversight of the Barberini Collection on p. 76. For the Barberini's influence on art, see Francis Haskell, *Patrons and Painters: A Study in the Relations Between Italian Art and Society in the Age of the Baroque*, New York, 1963, pp. 24-62. For the palace itself, see Anthony Blunt, "The Palazzo Barberini," *JWCI* 21 (1958), 256-87.

[32] Evelyn, *Diary*, II, p. 214.

[33] Howard, *English Travelers*, p. 86.

[34] Stoye, *English Travellers*, p. 205, and Turner, *The Visual Arts in Milton's Poetry*, p. 277.

[35] Mortoft, *His Book*, p. 57, and for Evelyn, *Diary*, II, pp. 186-93.

Among the highly reputed arts of the time was garden landscaping, and the English traveler was as much impressed by the Italian gardens as by the churches, the art collections, and the antiquities. Many gardens are mentioned which are no longer familiar to us, but the Boboli Gardens in Florence, the Gardens of the Villa d'Este at Tivoli, and the Borghese Gardens were as much a source of delight then as now, and were as frequently commented on.[36]

Many works of art readily accessible to travelers in Milton's time no longer exist today. The Rosary Chapel of SS. Giovanni e Paolo in Venice, containing paintings by Tintoretto, Palma the Younger, Corona, G. F. Bassano, Titian, and Giovanni Bellini, was destroyed by fire in 1867. The Paleo-Christian mosaics of the fifth century in San Antonio Abbati in Rome were destroyed in 1686, while reconstruction of the Vatican itself has led to the destruction of frescoes which were clearly visible in Milton's time. In addition to such losses, gradual weathering has taken its toll of paintings on the exterior walls of buildings. Late in the fifteenth century in Rome it became popular to paint exteriors in fresco or sgraffito, a practice so prevalent in the sixteenth century that the whole city was characterized by gaiety of color and line.[37] Some of these paintings still exist, in Rome and elsewhere, though in a much decayed form. An example is the facade of the Palazzo Ricci on the same street as the English College in Rome where Milton dined in 1638. In Florence similarly faded designs may be seen on the Palazzo Capponi and a number of other buildings.[38] In Venice, some of the greatest artists were commissioned to paint such murals, among them Giorgione and Titian for the Fondaco dei Tedeschi, and Tintoretto for the Palazzo Zen and the Palazzo Brandolino, but these frescoes have not survived. Such works of art, now so sadly lost to us, displayed in the most public of walls to delight the passers-by on every street in the principal cities of Italy, should at least remind us that art was inescapable in the Italy Milton knew and loved.

It would be possible to go on indefinitely cataloguing what travelers saw, and what they thought worthy of being seen, in Italy in the seventeenth century, but enough has been said to establish the point. Travelers in Milton's time, blessed with more leisure and encouraged by the social and cultural ideals of the well-educated gentleman, saw many more works of art than most modern tourists, even intelligent ones. It had been established that the cultural and educational ideal included extensive exposure to the arts by the time Milton made his Italian journey, and, as I understand him, Milton was a man likely to live up to such an ideal. When Milton's earliest biographer says that in Italy he saw "the rarities of the place" and

[36] Sells, *The Paradise of Travelers*, pp. 191-92, 212, and 221; Lassels, *An Italian Voyage*, p. 190; Mortoft, *His Book*, pp. 57ff. and 151ff.; and John Raymond, *Il Mercurio Italico*, 1648, pp. 31-39. Italian gardens of Milton's time are treated by E. March Phillipps, *The Gardens of Italy* (ed. Arthur T. Bolton), London, 1919, which still has some value though superseded by such works as David R. Coffin's authoritative *The Villa d'Este at Tivoli*, Princeton, 1960, and *The Italian Garden* (ed. David R. Coffin), Washington, 1972.

[37] Portoghese, *Rome of the Renaissance*, comment on figs. 327 and 328.

[38] Bargellini, p. 278. The interior Davanzati frescoes are illustrated in Giuseppe Martinelli, *The World of Renaissance Florence*, pp. 60 and 62.

when his nephew John Phillips writes that "he met with many charming objects," I think the evidence permits us to assume with some confidence that among those "rarities" and "charming objects" he included the masterpieces of art with which the cultivated Englishman was expected to be familiar.[39]

MILTON'S REFERENCES TO THE VISUAL ARTS

From a study of Milton's own words, and of words written about him by those who knew him, one gets some sense of his awareness of the arts—moreso, indeed, than is sometimes supposed. The evidence remains fragmentary, and I will not base my case for the relevance of the visual arts to the reading of Milton's poetry upon it, but as evidence it should be examined.

Among the works generally ascribed to Milton, the most extensive treatment of art is found in the first essay of the Columbia Manuscript, under the title "Of Statues & Antiquities." The editors of the Columbia Edition judged it proper to include this essay "among works probably Milton's."[40] It has received practically no attention from scholars. Archeologists to whom I have shown it have expressed astonishment at the sophistication, thoroughness, and practical insight it contains. None had been aware of its existence, and all expressed surprise that anything of this kind had been written so early in the development of archeology as the seventeenth century, when the field was practically restricted to amateurism and commercial exploitation. The document, then, is one of considerable importance in the history of archeology and of art appreciation.

The manuscript was among the private papers of Milton which came into the hands of the great collector Sir Thomas Phillipps of Middle Hill, Broadway, in Worcestershire, in the earlier nineteenth century. I am less confident than the Columbia editors, however, that it is probably Milton's own composition, though of course it may be. The principal features of Milton's prose style do not appear here, but this may be due to the nature of the document, which is simply a memorandum, and as such would offer neither the incentive nor the opportunity for the rhetoric typical of Milton's major prose. The document is undated, as are most of those included in the Columbia Manuscript; only Milton's "letter to a friend" is given a particular date—October 20, 1659. At that time—or even later, or indeed during the preceding decade—it seems highly unlikely that Milton

---

[39] Joseph Milton French, *Life Records*, I, p. 372, and Helen Darbishire, ed., *The Early Lives of Milton*, pp. 20 and 56. The Oxford English Dictionary defines "object" as "something being seen" and "something placed before the eyes or presented to the sight or other senses." These are the principal and primary seventeenth-century meanings which can be assigned to the word in this particular sentence, though other early meanings use "objects" to refer to statements, obstructions, and for teleological, metaphysical, and grammatical senses, none of which can apply here. See also n. 21, above.

[40] Printed for the first time, and since ignored, in *CE* XVIII, pp. 258-61. The notes to this edition, pp. 519-20, conclude that "Milton's interest in Greece as evidenced alike in his plan to visit it in his youth and his desire to have Christendom unite to free it later in life, make one suspect that this plan to recover Greek antiquities was not only approved but perhaps composed by himself."

would have been interested in an elaborate plan for the recovery of ancient Greek art. The most plausible hypothesis is that the essay was prepared in connection with Milton's planned visit to Greece, whether in England before his departure, or in Italy before he had changed his itinerary and decided to return to England without visiting Greece. Had it been prepared in Italy, it might still have been written in English, but it would more likely have been written in either Latin or Italian. Thus it appears most probable (although it is impossible to establish with certainty) that the document was prepared prior to Milton's departure from England in the spring of 1638. On this basis, I suggest that the document was associated with Sir Henry Wotton or some member of his circle, and that it was either presented to Milton as it now stands or that Milton wrote it down as a digest of the advice given him. In any case, the document clearly indicates an interest on Milton's part in the actual, physical recovery of ancient art, even to the techniques and methods of excavation.

The memorandum opens with a classification of things to be sought, and a sub-classification within the general headings. Statues are referred to as especially desirable, and "the naked ones are of greatest value." Sculpture is classified as free-standing, fully rounded figures, and as reliefs, and the latter are further divided into the standard classifications used in Milton's time. There are references also to brass sculpture, as well as lamps, vases, and metals, and care is taken to point to the need to provide, for the marble statues, blocks of the same kind of Grecian marble to be used in mending and repairing broken pieces.

The places at which digs may most profitably be carried out are also indicated, with three given preeminence, and it is noted that "the ruines will direct one where to dig." Provisions should be made for "carts and draggs" for moving the statues, and brief directions are given for their crating and shipment. The memorandum is specific even on small points, such as the need to prepare "cases of boards" for the best pieces, while the others can be placed in the ballast of the shipping vessels, although here care must be taken not to load anything in ships where "butts of oyle lye on top of them, for many things have bin spoyled by that meanes." For statues too large to be carried away whole, there are careful instructions on the kinds of saws to be used for dissecting them, and the archeologist "must be very carefull to gather together all the smallest bits and fragments that are to be found or digged up neare to any Statue, and put them up in boxes."

Venetian territories in the Greek world should be avoided, for they have been largely explored already, and attention should be turned to Turkish Hellas. In order to search there, the archeologist must get "a passe or safe conduct from the Great Turk procured by the ambassador at Constantinople," and be provided with bills of exchange, letters of credit, and the like. At the end, in shipping back the treasures found, "he must send home bills of lading, expressing everything that he sendeth, with the name of the Master, and of the ship," etc. The archeologist is advised that he "must alwayes weare poor apparell," and that he should never allow the Turks to think that he is seeking anything of any great value; furthermore, "he must never be without great store of Tobacco, and English Knives, to present the Turks withall," and it is also noted that "the men that he employes to dig, he must pay by the day." All told, the document is a fascinating one, and makes us wish even more (as Milton surely did) that he had been able to complete his tour by a long visit to the ancient Greek world. The fact that Milton kept this memorandum in his personal papers, however he acquired the information and whoever wrote it down, is strong evidence of his interest in classical art.

Other and briefer references to art are found scattered throughout Milton's works. Few poets or critics have equaled, and none have excelled, Milton's exalted view of the office of the poet, and it is noteworthy that he associated painters with poets on the same high level of human endeavor. The power of kings, as such and when exercised apart from righteousness, he tells us, is comparable to that of highway robbers, and below that of painters and poets.[41] He was too sophisticated an observer, however, to suppose that artistic success was in itself a mark of virtue, and although true beauty can be achieved only by those who are truly good, a false impression of beauty which will nonetheless overwhelm observers can be produced by a display of mere technical powers. Pandemonium falls within this class of art, Milton tells us, when he associates it with the artful monuments of totalitarian power in Babel and Egypt:

> And here let those
> Who boast in mortal things, and wondering tell
> Of Babel, and the work of Memphian kings,
> Learn how thir greatest monuments of fame,
> And strength and art are easily outdone
> By spirits reprobate, and in an hour
> What in an age they with incessant toil
> And hands innumerable scarce perform.
>
> (I, 692-99)

Though referred explicitly to Babylon and Egypt, the comparison might also be applied to those "greatest monuments of fame" which Milton had seen in Italy— e.g., the Colosseum, the Pantheon, St. Peter's, and the Capitol in Rome, and in Florence the Hall of the Five Hundred in the Palazzo Vecchio, and the Chapel of Princes in San Lorenzo, each of which might have contributed something to his imaginative picture of Pandemonium.

Though Milton regards power (and even artistic power) as delusory apart from goodness, he never depreciates the technical aspects of art; in his own practice, he had perfected a technical mastery so great that, in comparison with him, most other poets seem only gifted amateurs.[42] By assigning a similar eminence to painting as to poetry, he would seem to judge technical mastery on the part of a visual artist as equally important, and he implies that a critic of the visual arts must also acquire some technical mastery: "None," he writes in *The Apology*

---

[41] *The First Defense*, CE VII, p. 263.

[42] See Donald R. Pearce, "The Style of Milton's Epic," in *Milton: Modern Essays*, (Arthur E. Barker, ed.), New York, 1965, p. 380.

Against a Pamphlet, "can judge of a painter or statuary but he who is an artist, that is, either in the practick or the theory, which is often separated from the practick."[43] In that expression, he places the role of the critic considerably above what most artists would grant it, but he will not allow the critic the right to determine the significance of an art work. A painting must be sufficiently convincing as an imitation of reality to convey its own subject and significance without need for an appended motto, even a motto by the artist himself. This point is made in the attack upon King Charles, who has cast himself as a martyr, and the aesthetic parallel is drawn as though it were self-evident: "He who writes himself martyr by his own inscription is like an ill painter, who by writing on the shapeless picture which he hath drawn is fain to tell passengers what shape it is, which else no man could imagine."[44] In *Logic*, Milton notes that "there are in a picture two things—the subject or archetype and the art of painting," but the earlier allusion to the "ill painter" clearly indicates that this invaluable distinction does not allow the subject to be praised for itself, apart from the artistry with which it is rendered.[45]

Milton refers to "landscape" more often than to any other form of the arts. The word entered English as a technical term to describe the well-known products of Dutch art; within a few decades of its first appearance Milton in "L'Allegro" refers to "the lantskip round," while *Paradise Lost* is marked by several references, to "the darkened lantskip," "so lovely seem'd/ That lantskip," and to "Discovering in wide lantskip all the East/ Of Paradise and Eden's happy plains," and there are many poetic landscape views in which the technical term itself does not appear.[46] In addition to direct uses of the word, and poetic adaptations of the subject, there is also the metaphoric application when Milton promises in his tractate *Of Education* to "straight conduct ye to a hillside, where I will point ye out the right path of a virtuous and noble education."[47]

The representation of landscape has at least a cousinly relationship to maps, or to put it another way the distance between the two may be bridged by those topographical views which were so popular in Milton's time. For a long while before Milton, maps had been regarded as highly decorative, and frequently appeared on the walls of palaces as well as humbler dwellings.[48] The walls of the Vatican display a famous series of such paintings, and the Palazzo Vecchio in Florence has another series, while less opulent places might display popular geographical prints which range from simple lines and masses to the incorporation of pictures of buildings, human activities, and rural or naval scenes. The popularity

[43] *CE* III, p. 346.

[44] *Eikonoclastes, CE* v, p. 283.

[45] *CE* XI, p. 11. The distinction Milton makes ("*exemplum cive archetypus, et ars pigendi*") is perhaps more familiar in our age under the terms material and formal principles, as developed in Heinrich Wölfflin, *Classic Art: An Introduction to the Italian Renaissance* (trans. Peter and Linda Murray), New York, 1968, pp. 82-83.

[46] "L'Allegro," 70 and *PL* II, 491, IV, 153, and V, 142.

[47] *Of Education*, in *CE* IV, p. 280.

[48] See Joan Evans, *Pattern: A Study of Ornament in Western Europe from 1180 to 1900*, 2 vols., Oxford, 1931, I, pp. 176-78.

of such works is attested by the young Milton's advice to his fellow students at Cambridge to visit the world by studying maps, an interest shared by Robert Burton, among others.[49] It has led a number of scholars to postulate sources, or at least analogues, for passages in *Paradise Lost* that treat scenes also illustrated in popular maps of the time. Thus Frank L. Huntley, following Allan H. Gilbert, identifies in Ortelius a fine picture of the scene described by Milton as the plain where "*Chineses* drive/ With sails and wind thir cany waggons light."[50] Amy Lee Turner has been especially successful in finding analogues to Milton in the maps available to him: she postulates the engraved figures of Hondius' "Christian Knight Map" as influential in the development of Milton's Satan, Sin, and Death, and she follows up a suggestion made as early as 1939 by George W. Whiting that the beautiful compass rose in Jansson's *Sea Atlas* may have been influential in shaping conception of the winds in *Paradise Lost* x, 695-707.[51]

For Englishmen of Milton's time, tapestries were among the most popular and best known expressions of art, and we have already noted that handsome tapestries adorned the walls of the offices in Whitehall where Milton served as Latin Secretary of State, though we do not know their subject. Milton referred to some such works in *Eikonoclastes* when he described a person who was "struck as mute and motionless as a Parliament of tapestry."[52]

Sculpture furnishes Milton with an illustration, which suggests some actual familiarity with the processes of carving: "in things artificial seldom any elegance is wrought without a superfluous waste and refuse in the transaction. No marble statue can be politely carved, no fair edifice built, without almost as much rubbish and sweeping."[53] In *Pro Se Defenso*, Milton declared that no Englishman was more given than he to prizing and applauding the Dutch for their arts, and though the word here may have a more general significance than the fine arts, it would at least seem to include them and perhaps even to point particularly to them, for it occurs seriatim along with references to Dutch industry and ingenuity, which would cover other forms of art in the general sense.[54]

References in *Paradise Lost* are frequent to mosaic work and other forms of

---

[49] *Prolusion* III, *CE* XII, pp. 169-70, and Ogden and Ogden, *English Taste in Landscape*, pp. 57 and 61.

[50] *PL* III, 438-39, and Frank L. Huntley, "Milton, Mendoza, and the Chinese Land-ship," *MLN* 69 (1954), 404-7. Allan H. Gilbert, in the entry in his *A Geographical Dictionary of Milton*, New Haven, 1919, p. 263, adds to Masson's sources the *History of China* by Mendoza, published in Spanish in 1585 and in English in 1588, and mentions maps by Mercator and Ortelius which illustrate the scene, though he does not reproduce them.

[51] Amy Lee Turner, "Milton and Jodocus Hondius the Elder," *Milton Newsletter* 3 (1969), 26-30, and "Milton and Jansson's Sea Atlas," *Milton Quarterly* 4 (1970), 36-39. Evert M. Clark, "Milton's Abyssinian Paradise," *UTSE* 29 (1950), 129-50 suggests certain passages in *Paradise Lost* which may have been influenced by Milton's study of maps.

[52] *CE* v, p. 288; in the *First Defense*, he refers to tapestries at one remove, through Virgil's line "purpurea intexti tollunt aulaea Britanni," which he treats as an emblem of "no true Britains, but painted ones, or rather needle-wrought men" (*CE* VII, p. 485). There was a difference, which Milton cites here, between painted and woven hangings.

[53] *Church Government*, in *CE* III, pp. 223-34.

[54] *CE* IX, p. 105.

inlaid stone, which appear to have been favorites with Milton. We are told that Mammon characteristically walked with his head "always downward bent," so as to admire "the riches of heaven's pavement, trodden gold" (*PL* I, 679-84). Though I know of no gold in mosaic floors, there was inlaid brass in many, and beautifully impressive mosaic patterns may be found in such Roman churches as St. John Lateran, San Marco, Santa Maria in Aracoeli, Santa Maria in Cosmedin, and Santa Maria in Trastevere. The cathedral at Siena was especially famous for its inlaid floors, illustrating stories which might directly or indirectly contribute to the final illumination of the faithful soul by a process of accommodation. Mammon's fault was that he concentrated on the beautiful symbol itself, rather than allowing it to inspire him to raise his eyes to the divine reality it was intended to suggest.

Early Christian art used mosaic tesserae to stunning effect in the representation of flowers and shrubs, as may be seen in the Baptistry of St. John Lateran in Rome, among other places. The references to the "wrought mosaic" and "rich inlay" of flowers in the Garden of Eden has offended some readers, who are confused by the use of minerals to establish the color of flowers (*PL* IV, 699-701). Milton not only refers to flowers here in their own terms and by their own names, but he proceeds to describe how they "Broidered the ground, more coloured than stone/ Of costliest emblem" (*PL* IV, 701-3). For those who are familiar with the great examples of the Paleo-Christian mosaics to be seen in Rome and elsewhere, that allusion not only makes the colors and shapes more sparkling in their beauty, but elevates the description above the mere commonplaces of an ordinary garden. Milton's words, moreover, may elicit not only the masterpieces of mosaic art but also of that *pietre dure* work which was one of the great prides of Florence under the Medici dukes. In this work, stones of brightest and richest hues were cut with infinite care, and placed together to create pictures of flowers, animals, mythological and human figures, emblems, and even landscape scenes. It is to such effects of incredible opulence and staggering beauty that Milton is referring in his association of the Garden with mosaic and inlay. Works of this kind, which have since lost their great popularity, attracted the attention and enthusiastic comment of English travelers in Italy during the seventeenth century.

In a similar vein Milton refers to enameled work, and presents the flora of Eden "with gay enamelled colours mixt" (*PL* IV, 148-49). In interpreting such passages, Broadbent has quite rightly referred us to the brilliant colors used in miniatures and jewelry, and I believe he was the first to do so.[55] From the late Middle Ages down into Milton's own time, enameled pictures produced in the town or school of Limoges had been intensely popular; they were often imitated in other forms, and the word "enamel" was used even to designate the imitations.

[55] John B. Broadbent, "Milton's Paradise," *MP* 51 (1954), 165. Broadbent notes (175) the application of enameled images to nature by Spenser, Drayton, Waller, and Marvell, while John R. Knott, "Symbolic Landscape in *Paradise Lost*," *Milton Studies* 2 (1970), 40, indicates that the literary usage was conventional. For full analysis of the artistic aspects of Milton's enameled imagery in Heaven and in Eden, see the chapters on those subjects below, especially pp. 200-5 and 249-55.

"Gay enamelled colours" are thus far from implying any metallic deadness, but refer instead to one of the most vibrant and entrancing mediums of art.[56]

The delight which Milton would lead us to take in precious stones and metals is also associated with stained glass windows. The familiar lines of "Il Penseroso" show appreciation of the whole ambience of Gothic art:

> But let my due feet never fail
> To walk the studious cloister's pale,
> And love the high embowed roof,
> With antique pillars massy proof,
> And storied windows richly dight,
> Casting a dim religious light.
>
> (155-60)

The love of Gothic architecture is explicitly stipulated and we are led to share the experience of it, to feel ourselves surrounded by its beauty and power; that much is unmistakable. But the brief lines on the stained glass reveal an even more subtle appreciation. Even so perceptive a critic as Jean Hagstrum misses the point here. Citing these lines to indicate that it is Milton's practice "to approach the pictorialist conventions and then to withdraw into other forms of expression," he argues that "the 'storied windows richly dight' of 'Il Penseroso' are almost at once blurred and shadowed by the 'dim religious light'."[57] To argue thus is to ignore the special properties of stained glass windows, which Milton treats so acutely as to show himself to be something of a connoisseur. Such windows can be properly revealed only by the "dim" light which they themselves transmit; any other light, far from revealing their beauty, will in fact deface it. In his authoritative study of stained glass, Lewis Day writes that "it is not generally understood how completely the effect of glass depends upon the absence of light other than that which comes through it. Every ray of light which penetrates into a building excepting through the stained glass does injury to the colored window."[58] Milton has not approached a pictorial presentation and then withdrawn: he has in fact displayed the most alert awareness, in all of English verse, of the visual power of stained glass art.

Milton's visual descriptions, whether the result of direct visual observation or a reliance upon artistic traditions, must be recognized as reflections of only one part of his acute awareness and perception through all the senses. Immediately after the visual descriptions just discussed, he supplements and completes our aesthetic experience by joining aural to visual effects:

> There let the pealing organ blow
> To the full-voiced choir below,
> In service high, and anthems clear,

[56] See also Ernest W. Tristram, *English Medieval Wall Painting: The Thirteenth Century*, 2 vols., Oxford, 1950, I, pp. 405-7; and the treatment of Palissy enamels in John Shearman, *Mannerism*, Harmondsworth, 1969, pp. 128-30.

[57] Hagstrum, *The Sister Arts*, p. 127.

[58] Lewis Day, *Windows: A Book about Stained and Painted Glass*, London, 1897, p. 383.

> As may with sweetness, through mine ear,
> Dissolve me into ecstasies,
> And bring all heaven before mine eyes.
>
> (161-66)

To that symphony of eye and ear he then adds effects on the other senses: the feeling of "hairy gown and mossy cell," the odor of "every herb" and even the taste of the dew. No poet, writing in English at least, excels Milton in the power to elicit our total sensuous response to his verse. Milton's Paradise, as Helen Gardner has reminded us, "is a paradise of all the senses," while G. Wilson Knight declares that "his use of smell and taste is probably more abundant than that of any English poet but Keats."[59] Milton's description of the meal shared by Raphael with Adam and Eve evokes the delights of the most refined gourmet:

> What choice to choose for delicacy best,
> What order, so contrived as not to mix
> Tastes, not well joined, inelegant, but bring
> Taste after taste upheld with kindliest change . . . .
>
> (v, 333-36)

Few indeed have so fully appreciated the implications of the Biblical declarations that God's creation is good, and few have so commended its innocent pleasures for the faithful man, who wisely enjoys "these delicacies/ I mean of taste, sight, smell, herbs, fruits, and flowers" (*PL* viii, 526-27). In Italy Milton had been exposed to those Renaissance gardens in which Eugenio Battisti tells us that "the aroma of spices and flowers [were] all arranged by skillful artists," the effect being to provide just the kind of sensuous enjoyment that Milton described in his Eden, and we should remember that in England he commended the joy to be found "in those vernal seasons of the year, when the air is calm and pleasant," from walks in the country where "it were an injury and sullenness against nature not to go out and see her riches, and partake in her rejoicing with heaven and earth."[60]

It is not merely the music of sounds which he leads us to appreciate, but even the beauty of silence, as in his description of Eden's fig tree, which formed

> a pillared shade
> High overarched, and echoing walks between.
>
> (ix, 1106-7)

Donald R. Pearce aptly describes the effect of these lines: "It is the pictured stillness in the lines, not any verbal resonance, that strikes us. The image is that of pastoral arcades gulfed in some large, dreamlike silence, punctuated by intermittent

[59] Gardner, *A Reading of "Paradise Lost,"* p. 80, and G. Wilson Knight, *The Burning Oracle: Studies in the Poetry of Action,* London, 1939, p. 85.

[60] Eugenio Battisti, "*Natura Artificiosa* to *Natura Artificialis,*" in *The Italian Garden* (ed. David R. Coffin), p. 8, and *Of Education* in *CE* iv, p. 290. While preparing this manuscript for the press, I have read Charlotte F. Otten's excellent " 'My Native Element': Milton's Paradise and English Gardens," *MS* 5 (1973), pp. 249-67, and I find that we have independently made a number of similar observations.

footsteps. It is a piece of soundless phantasy."[61] Elsewhere Milton elicits in us an almost muscular response, as when he describes the headlong and precipate fall of Lucifer so vividly that we virtually participate in it:

> Him the Almighty Power
> Hurled headlong flaming from th' ethereal sky
> With hideous ruin and combustion down
> To bottomless perdition, there to dwell
> In adamantine chains and penal fire,
> Who durst defy th' Omnipotent to arms.
>
> (I, 44-49)

Examples such as those I have cited provide only a brief glimpse of the full range of Milton's sensuous effects, but close readers will be able to fill in the spectrum of our responses. Just as Milton achieves his musical effects by converting us at the same time into musical instruments and into musicians, so too with all of his sensuous powers: we are led to respond to the utmost extent of our own alertness. Bernard Berenson commended Italian Renaissance art above all for what he called its "tactile values," its ability to evoke in us sense responses comparable to those of the picture before our eyes, and I suggest that Milton was just as successful in his epic embodiment of similar tactile values.[62]

[61] Donald R. Pearce, "The Style of Milton's Epic," p. 379.
[62] Bernard Berenson, *The Italian Painters of the Renaissance*, pp. 63, 72, 85, 153, and 157. I have found particularly helpful on Mulciber's fall Christopher Ricks, *Milton's Grand Style*, p. 41.

Part Two
The Demonic World

IV

The War in Heaven and the Expulsion
of the Rebel Angels

PANOPLY AND ORDNANCE

THE War in Heaven initiated all the subsequent action in *Paradise Lost*, and has initiated much of the critical controversy since. It has always had strong defenders, of course, and most readers recognize the power and beauty of its execution, but powerful objections have been leveled against it, as we have already seen. "The confusion of spirit and matter which pervades the whole," as Dr. Johnson put it,[1] is close to the heart of all these objections: angels are spiritual in their essence, and should not be made to appear in full armor, charging with lances, and hacking away with swords, as they do in Milton's account. Mark Van Doren finds the result "outlandish," while John Peter calls it "a fiasco," full of "monstrous curiosities" and "Disney-like panoramas," and William Empson stigmatizes it all as "unusually stupid science fiction."[2]

Milton appears to have no suspicion that such objections could arise. Having reminded his audience of the well-known theory of accommodation, according to which matter and physical action could be taken as symbolic of spiritual reality, he rushes ahead without the slightest sign of misgiving. His angelic armies march in mid-air in "perfect ranks," move in "cubic phalanx," as "squadroned angels" (VI, 71-75, 399-400, and XII, 367-68). Moloch, "furious king," threatens to drag Gabriel at his chariot wheels, and Gabriel later threatens Satan with the same ignominy (VI, 355-62, and IV, 965-66). On both sides, the angels are dressed in helmets (VI, 543, 840), and in "bright arms," or "armed in adamant and gold," as each his "adamantine coat" girded well, and grasped "his orbed shield" (II, 812, VI, 110, 541-43). The battle itself is fought in the finest tournament style, with "arms on armour clashing" (VI, 209), and under a blow from Michael, Satan finds "all his armour stained, ere while so bright" and other demons are "Mangled with ghastly wounds through plate and mail" (VI, 334, 368). After the battle, all the heavenly ground was "with shivered armour strown," and even with the bodies of "foaming steeds" (VI, 388-91).

It is not denied that these are fine epic actions, magnificently narrated; what is at issue is their propriety to a battle between faithful and rebellious angels. Waldock states the unfavorable case with greater consistency and logic than any other twentieth-century critic. Of the armored angels, he writes that "Milton *had* to give them armour, of course, once having conceived the battles in Homeric

[1] Samuel Johnson, *Lives of the English Poets*, I, 184-85.
[2] Mark Van Doren, *The Noble Voice*, pp. 133-34; John Peter, *A Critique of "Paradise Lost,"* pp. 76-78; and William Empson, *Milton's God*, London, 1965, p. 54.

terms," but he feels that the Homeric precedent provides insufficient justification, and that Milton was wrong in choosing to cast his "spiritual" themes in traditional Greek pagan terms. It was incumbent on Milton in his epic "to demonstrate that his ideas, when worked out in detail, could make at least some show of coherence and common sense,"[3] and in this Waldock judges that Milton failed.

Even so sympathetic a critic as Wayne Shumaker writes that Milton's account "generates grotesqueries which the poet himself is unwilling or unable to resolve," so that the warfare is "the wrong metaphor for Milton's purpose."[4] If Milton had chosen to introduce this metaphor, as a fresh version of his own, and had sought to induce his "fit audience" to accept it only by virtue of his poetic magic, then the critique of Shumaker, like that of Waldock, might perhaps be just. But at this point he was simply invoking firmly established visual associations—so firmly established, indeed, that he can scarcely be expected to have chosen any other metaphor for his theme.

What Waldock and Shumaker ignore is the variation, from one historical epoch to another, in what is regarded as acceptable in works of the imagination. Milton's ideas are "worked out in detail" so as to accord with a centuries-old tradition in which the angelic struggles had been painted and carved throughout Europe, and Milton could rely upon his first readers to accept in his narrative descriptions what they accepted elsewhere. For a poet, as for a painter, "coherence and common sense" are in large part a function of what the imaginative background of his audience allows him to assume. Armored angels battling demons with the weapons of chivalry were a commonplace of the imaginative world inherited by Milton and his contemporaries.[5]

One of the earliest Christian representations of armor in the triumph of light over darkness is a mosaic in the Oratory of St. Andrew in Ravenna, executed shortly after 500 A.D., which shows Christ the Warrior, clad in Roman armor, with a crossed spear in his hand, standing in triumph upon a lion and a serpent, which represent the devil and sin. Other early treatments were equally allegorical.[6]

3

[3] A.J.A. Waldock, *"Paradise Lost" and Its Critics*, Cambridge, 1964, pp. 108-10.

[4] Shumaker, *Unpremeditated Verse*, p. 126.

[5] Samuel Johnson declared that "no precedents can justify absurdity" (*ibid.*, 185), but *per contra* what is or is not regarded as absurd is often governed by precedent.

[6] In Eph. 6:11-18, Paul advises the Christian to put on "the whole armor of God," which he allegorizes in an immensely influential passage and which in some measure surely influenced the treatment by Milton. This conception is touched on by Robert H. West, "Elizabethan Belief in Spirits and Witchcraft," *Studies in Shakespeare*, Miami, 1952, p. 71. It is important to recognize, too, that physical warfare had been used as a visual metaphor for the struggle of rival values long before the Christian era, whether that struggle was understood as representing culture against barbarism, order against anarchy, or reason against the passions. The frieze of the Siphnian Treasury at Delphi (530-25 B.C.) shows the warfare of the gods against the giants; the west pediment of the Temple of Zeus at Olympia (465-57 B.C.) shows the battle of the Lapiths and Centaurs; the altar of Zeus and Athena at Pergamum (197-59 B.C.) presents the gods against the giants; while sculptures for the Parthenon in Athens (447-32 B.C.) show all these symbolic struggles, and add the warfare of the Greeks against the Amazons; these and other instances are treated by John Barron, *Greek*

Beginning in the fifth or sixth century, and continuing through the Middle Ages, artists expressed the struggle within and for the human soul, the conflict between virtues and vices, in dynamic battle scenes between armed antagonists.[7] This metaphor was as popular in England as on the Continent. Thirteenth-century wall paintings of the symbolic action in the Painted Chamber of Westminster Palace, destroyed by the fire of 1834, would have been clearly visible in Milton's time, along with many other treatments of the psychomachia.[8]

Though the battle between the Vices and the Virtues was represented as taking place in armor from very early times, it was not always so with the War of the Angels. Until well into the thirteenth century, Michael, whether with or without his angelic armies, is represented most typically in a long robe with straight folds.[9] Even so, he was often armed with sword and shield.[10] As the archangel delegated to conduct the dead, Michael is also represented as holding the scales of judgment in one hand, and as such he continues to be shown in long robes in many representations until well after the Renaissance. As the chieftain of heavenly armies, however, and as the heavenly champion, he more and more often appears in full armor in medieval ecclesiastical painting and sculpture,[11] as also in manuscript illuminations.[12] In fifteenth-century English church decoration, the fully armored and armed angel becomes predominant,[13] and remains standard until, and indeed after, Milton's time.[14]

The treatment of the demonic forces was less consistent. When the devil was represented as a great dragon, it would obviously have been inappropriate to clothe him in armor. Similarly, the degenerately bestial devils of the kind represented by

---

Sculpture, New York, 1970, pp. 49, 74, 89, and 155. The altar from Pergamum shows the rebellious giants as partly animalized, in preview of what Christian artists would do with the rebellious angels.

[7] Adolph Katzenellenbogen, *Allegories of the Virtues and Vices in Mediaeval Art from Early Christian Times to the Thirteenth Century*, New York, 1964, vii.

[8] Ernest W. Tristram, *English Medieval Wall Painting: The Twelfth Century*, Oxford, 1944, pls. 72-73 and 76-77; and by the same author, *English Medieval Wall Painting: The Thirteenth Century*, 2 vols., Oxford, 1950, II, pls. 19-21, and I, p. 105 for the discussion.

[9] Emile Mâle, *Religious Art from the Twelfth to the Eighteenth Century*, New York, 1949, p. 89; hereafter abbreviated as *Religious Art*.

[10] Arthur Gardner, *A Handbook of English Medieval Sculpture*, Cambridge, 1935, figs. 29 and 49.

[11] Mary P. Perry, "On the Psychostasis in Christian Art," *Burlington Magazine* 22 (1912-13), 102-3.

[12] Walter Birch and Henry Jenner, *Early Drawings and Illuminations, an Introduction to the Study of Illustrated Manuscripts, with a Dictionary of Subjects in the British Museum*, London, 1879, pp. 225-26.

[13] Tancred Borenius and E. W. Tristram, *English Medieval Painting*, Florence and Paris, 1927, pls. 77 and 79, and Fred H. Crossley, *English Church Monuments*, London, [c. 1921], p. 141.

[14] Armored cherubs in the sky are found in a very unusual print by Erhard Altdorfer, in the Lubeck Bible of 1533, reprinted in Max Geisberg, *Die Deutsche Buchillustration in der ersten Halfte des XVI Jahrhunderts*, 9 vols., Munich, 1930, VII, pl. 307, where the "baby" angels appear startlingly inappropriate in their armor, like little Renaissance princes, with the added advantage of wings.

4, 5 Spinello Aretino would look ridiculous in armor, and the whole purpose of the distorted forms of the devils in the visual traditions of Bosch and Bruegel would be lost if their forms were covered with armor. Basically, armor on the devils had to await that change in artistic tradition which came about the year 1500 and which invested the demonic with a large measure of human beauty.[15]

The early printed Bibles issued by the Protestants, while continuing the tradition of armored angels, also gave considerable impetus to the conception of the demonic armies in armor. This mode was firmly established in the first edition of Luther's German translation, the 1522 Wittenberg Bible, where Cranach illus-trated the rebel angels as knights clad in full plate armor, mostly with their bea-
6 vers up, and led by a crowned King Satan. Cranach's elegantly attired devilish warriors strike us as great courtiers engaged in one of the courtly tournaments of the time. Twelve years later, in 1534, Tyndale's New Testament appeared as the first English Protestant version. The War in Heaven woodcut in Tyndale's Bible is based directly upon the Cranach print, both in its composition and in its
7 general conception, but there are significant differences. Here the faithful angels are unmistakably clothed in European fashions, whereas the satanic forces are shown in Turkish dress and armor, thereby reminding us of Milton's emphatic association of Satan with the "great Sultan" and of his followers with the barbaric and pagan hordes of Asia (I, 348, 764). Variations upon these treatments, estab-lished so early, occur in later editions of the Bible and in related prints, as in Jean Duvet's Apocalypse series which shows the battle of the angels carried on with a full range of weapons—daggers, swords, spears, maces, and even bow and arrow, while banners and flags are also apparent. The *Michael and Lucifer* by Tintoretto in the Church of S. Giuseppe di Castello in Venice pictures Satan in fine Renais-
8, 9 sance armor and cloak, a figure retaining charm, dignity and power even in defeat. In 1635, Thomas Heywood's *The Hierarchie of the Blessed Angels* presented a verbal description of the conflict as conducted with spiritual weapons only, after the fashion some critics would have preferred for Milton.[16] Even so the artist responsible for the illustrations to Heywood's text showed one falling angel
10 dressed in Roman trunk armor, so strong had the tradition become (Fig. 10, left center). Beautiful examples of Satan in armor are found in paintings now at the
11 Ascensione a Chiaia in Naples and at the Palacio Real in Madrid, executed by Luca Giordano at about the same time as the composition of *Paradise Lost*, and though these could not possibly have exerted any direct influence upon Milton, they do serve our purpose of establishing the continuity of this important element of the visual tradition.[17]

[15] Bodleian Library MS Auct. D. 4.17 fol. 20v. shows demonic forces in armor as early as the thirteenth century, but this treatment was not common.

[16] Thomas Heywood, *The Hierarchie of the Blessed Angels*, London, 1635. See the comment of C. A. Patrides on Heywood's spiritual conflict in William B. Hunter, C. A. Patrides, and J. H. Adamson, *Bright Essence: Studies in Milton's Theology*, Salt Lake City, 1971, p. 159. A reading of Heywood's account should remove all doubt about whether or not Milton had chosen the most effective way for telling his story, but then very few of us read Heywood.

[17] *PL* I, 547, describes a "forest huge of spears," which leads Jean Hagstrum (*The Sister*

The descriptive recklessness of which some critics accuse Milton may seem to reach an intolerable climax in the way he refers to the mounts upon which the angelic chivalry rides. Milton repeatedly insists that the demonic military maneuvers are carried out on "fiery steeds," that the faithful angels in "thick embattled squadrons bright" are mounted in chariots and on "fiery steeds," and he concludes that the field after the battle is strewn not only with the panoply of war but with the bodies of "fiery foaming steeds" (II, 531, VI, 16-17, and 389-91). In so careful a poet as Milton, this iteration and reiteration can only mean that we are expected to envision mounted troops, cavalry in the sky, but it is important to observe that Milton does not specify what kinds of mounts were used by this cavalry. The generic term "steeds" can refer to horses, as most readers probably assume almost instinctively, but Milton does not restrict himself in this way and his consistent ambiguity here allows his readers to choose as they will between two traditional modes for envisioning the demonic cavalry.[18]

In a thirteenth-century English Apocalypse a crowned Satan, mounted on a centaur which is protected by the kind of chain mail used for chargers, leads forth his mounted troops, also represented as centaurs.[19] In Dürer's Apocalypse series, as in Hans Burkmair's, a similar scene represents troops of horses with lions' heads and tails like serpents, all in the sky, while a *Last Judgment* by the sixteenth-century Cretan painter Klotzas shows devils riding griffinlike steeds.[20]

The tradition of angels on horses as such was apparently not widespread in the Middle Ages, and though Réau finds some instances of the Archangel Michael

12

Arts, pp. 124-25) to comment that "I see a reflection of the spears and banners of Piero della Francesca's 'Battle of Constantine' in Arezzo, Italy, or of Paolo Uccello's 'Rout of San Romano' in the National Gallery, London." Other examples may be found in the wall paintings of the Hall of the Five Hundred in the Palazzo Vecchio in Florence and in the anonymous paintings at Hampton Court of the *Battle of Pavia* and the *Meeting of Henry VIII and Maximilian I*. In each of these instances, what is represented is the "hedgehog" formation which would have been familiar both to Milton and to the artists from military drills and maneuvers in their own times; see Maurice Ashley, *The English Civil War*, London, 1974, p. 73.

[18] Shumaker, *Unpremeditated Verse*, pp. 124-25, reads "steeds" as meaning horses and balks at this representation, but his reference to it as an "indolent acceptance of an inappropriate tradition" leaves open the possibility that he may be aware of the numerous artistic treatments of mounted cavalry in heaven.

[19] Bodleian Library MS Tanner 184, p. 56.

[20] See Heinrich Wölfflin, *The Art of Albrecht Dürer*, London, 1971, pp. 65-66, and for the Burgkmair print, Max Geisberg, *Die Deutsche Buchillustration*, III, pl. 121. And at the Hellenic Institute in Venice there is another painting, by Klotzas or an artist of the same school, in which a black and distorted Satan rides in a flaming chariot, with a long spear in his hand. Callot did a drawing entitled "Design for Hell Chariot" which is now at the Louvre and is reproduced as figure 35 in Howard Daniel, *Devils, Monsters and Nightmares: An Introduction to the Grotesque and Fantastic in Art*, New York, 1964. Satan's chariot is described by Vondel in *Lucifer* (Watson Kirkconnell, *The Celestial Cycle: The Theme of 'Paradise Lost' in World Literature, with Translations of the Major Analogues*, Toronto, 1952, pp. 410 and 413) and illustrated in a print, presumably by Salomon Savry, reproduced in Joost von den Vondel, *Werken*, Amsterdam, 1927-40, V, p. 603. In my observation, Satanic chariots are rarely found in art.

mounted on horseback, these are rare.[21] In the sixteenth century, armored angels mounted on horses in the sky became a commonplace, especially of course in illustrations of the Apocalypse.[22] We have already noted examples in the first Luther Bible and in Tyndale's English New Testament. In the Bishops' Bible of 1568, there is an additional feature of God the Father on horseback pursuing his enemies at a full gallop.[23]

Jacques Callot's fascinating 1635 engraving, *The Temptation of St. Anthony*, combines tradition and innovation in a fabulous vision of great power where demons armed with spears charge through the air on mounts which may be described either as dragonlike horses or as horselike dragons. The contrasts with Milton are as significant as the similarities: in the first place, Callot is not depicting the War in Heaven, but a later episode in the continuing struggle. Even more significant is the difference in tone and attitude: Milton's War is described with pervasive irony, by which Satan's handsome and heroic warriors are consistently and subtly undercut, whereas Callot uses a blunt but powerful satire. Levron comments that Callot has reduced heroic warfare to a parody, "où les soldats et les officiers aux brillant costumes sont remplacés par des diables sordides."[24] There is much of the influence of Hieronymus Bosch in Callot's print, but it is a Bosch thoroughly Gallicized, with the mature sophistication of seventeenth-century France.

Of special pertinence to our interests is the presence of the demonic cannon in Callot. Firing from a position left of center in the lower part of the picture, this artillery piece is a monstrous contrivance of diablerie: mounted on wheels, it has the rear legs and haunches of a dragonish beast, while the mouth of the cannon is literally a devil's mouth, extending out from the barrel to hideous effect and firing projectiles. In a preliminary drawing, now in the Hermitage collection in Leningrad, Callot provided a more mechanical cannon; in both instances the significance for us is the association of artillery with the demonic forces.[25]

Milton has been severely criticized for allowing Satan to invent artillery for use during the War in Heaven (VI, 482-627).[26] The anonymous writer for the

---

[21] Réau, *Iconographie*, II, i, pp. 47 and 49. A lesser authority on iconography might be suspected of misidentifying the warrior saint in the Choir of St. George in Bamberg Cathedral as Michael, but I presume that Réau is to be trusted.

[22] Max Geisberg, *Die Deutsche Buchillustration*, VII, pl. 309.

[23] Such illustrations are generally to be found in connection with the Book of Revelation, though there are of course also independent prints of the same kind. In addition, there are other instances of horses in heaven in Biblical illustrations. The Bible Historiale furnished examples from the late thirteenth century, and in another manuscript of the same work from the mid-fourteenth century, in the British Library: Harley MS 4381 fol. 158, and Royal Coll. MS 19 D. II fol. 174v. One might also note the tradition of God's chariot, represented in the Utrecht Psalter for Psalm 67 (Psalm 68 in the Authorized Version) in which God brandishes a spear while trampling his enemies in a chariot drawn by four horses in heaven. More will be said of the divine chariot at another point.

[24] Jacques Levron, *Le Diable dans l'art*, Paris, 1935, p. 87.

[25] L. Ugloff, "Drawings by Jacques Callot for the Temptation of Saint Anthony," *Burlington Magazine* 67 (1935), 220-24, with illustrations.

[26] Milton has also been praised for the correspondence between Satan's deployment of artillery and certain standard military maneuvers of the sixteenth and seventeenth centuries;

Gentleman's Magazine of 1738 called it a ridiculous circumstance, and Voltaire found the incident "very low and ridiculous in Heaven."[27] Yet the association of the devil with gunpowder and cannon was originated neither by Milton nor by Callot, but is part of a much longer tradition in literature, in art, and on the stage. Spenser had referred to a cannon as a "divelish yron Engin wrought/ In deepest Hell, and framd by Furies skill," and Watson Kirkconnell traces the demonic use of artillery through *L'Angeleida* by Valvasone, to the earliest known literary introduction in Ariosto's *Orlando Furioso* of 1516.[28] An illustration of the devil instructing the inventor of gunpowder (Milton also says that the inventor was inspired by "devilish machination"—VI, 504) occurs in the 1604 edition of *Les Artifices de feu* by Johannes Brantzius. As early as 1472 there was a representation of a cannon as a demonic dragon which appeared in *De re militari*, issued at Augsburg by Flavius Renatus Vegetius, and in Verona by Robertus Valturius, and in all subsequent editions I have seen of this work. Here the association is purely visual: the great dragon of the Apocalypse *becomes* a cannon.

14

15

French mystery plays repeatedly included the cannon in the demonic arsenal. In one mystery, probably by Eustace Mercade who died in 1440, there are two scenes which serve as a prologue to the Harrowing of Hell. In these, Lucifer and Satan prepare for Christ's assault by barricading the defenses of Hell, and "culverins and cannons are included in the defenses."[29] This was not an isolated instance: Gustave Cohen tells us that cannons and culverins were actually fired by devils on the stage, and that the demonic artillery on occasion actually harmed actors and spectators. A drawing based on the Passion Play at Valenciennes in 1547 illustrates three such cannons firing missiles from a battlement of Hell.[30] Perhaps such examples on the continental stage served to introduce the image into the graphic arts. At all events, visual representations would have prepared Milton's contemporaries to appreciate the aptness of the epic association of the demonic with artillery.[31]

---

see Harold H. Scudder, "Satan's Artillery," *N&Q* 195 (1950), 334-37, with references to earlier treatments by Keightly and Hanford.

[27] Shawcross, *Milton: The Critical Heritage*, p. 256, and *Milton 1732-1801*, pp. 94-95.

[28] Literary parallels may be found in Spenser's *Faerie Queene* I, vii, 13; Shakespeare's *Henry V*, III Prol. 33; Valvasone's *L'Angeleida* II, 20, and Ariosto's *Orlando Furioso* IX, 89-91; see Watson Kirkconnell, *The Celestial Cycle*, pp. 81 and 577-78. Of related interest are Edgar Wind, *Pagan Mysteries in the Renaissance*, New York, 1968, p. 108, and Gardner, *A Reading of "Paradise Lost,"* pp. 68-69.

[29] D.D.R. Owen, *The Vision of Hell: Infernal Journeys in Medieval French Literature*, Edinburgh, 1970, p. 237.

[30] See Bibliothèque Nationale MS fr. 12536, illustrated opposite p. 70 in Gustave Cohen, *Histoire de la mise en scène dans le théâtre religieux français du moyen âge*, Paris, 1906, while further discussions are found on pp. 93, and 160-61. I am indebted to Professor D.D.R. Owen for calling my attention to this evidence.

[31] From Milton, the motif apparently feeds back into the visual arts in England in at least one instance: a church monument erected to the elder Dr. Plot at Borden, Kent, which dates only four years after the first publication of *Paradise Lost*, shows the Archangel Michael trampling on the defeated Satan, with the heavenly artillery in the background, above. See Katharine A. Esdaile, *English Church Monuments: 1510-1840*, New York, n.d. (1946?), fig. 109, and p. 115, and also Esdaile in *The Times*, 10 August, 1938.

INDIVIDUAL COMBAT AND MASS CONFLICT

No artist could possibly include within a single canvas the imaginative sweep and epic scope of Milton's War in Heaven. Few, indeed, made the attempt to represent the war as a whole, though there were notable examples which achieved great *16* stature. The Sforza Book of Hours,[32] completed at Milan about 1490, presents a carefully selected and highly dramatic picture in a small space, while other artists painted large versions teeming with action and power, such as we find in the *4, 5, 17, 11* renditions by Spinello Aretino, Peter Bruegel the Elder, Rubens, Luca Giordano *16, 47, VIII* and others to which we shall turn in various connections. But the vast majority of visual representations epitomized the conflict in the two figures of Michael and Satan,[33] as in the paintings by Piero della Francesco and Pollaiuolo, and it is with *18, 19* such treatments that we shall begin. By definition, Michael was at once the hero, the favorite, and the victor, clad in the full armor of God.[34]

Satan, on the other hand, was usually presented in some thoroughly unattractive guise, and although there were exceptions to this rule, as we shall see in the next chapter, the rule did obtain until about 1500. Then there came a change which may be observed in the painting by Juan Jiminez in the Philadelphia Museum *20, 21* of Art. Here the Satan is conglomerate, with a serpent's tail, the hairy flanks of a satyr, and a pair of handsome horns on his forehead. What is striking about this painting is the face of the fallen angel: it is the face of a distressed and tragic prince. The sad eyes and the furrowed brow suggest a suffering which has not often been pictured in Satan before—a suffering caused by inner loss, anguish, and distortion of the psyche. There are wounds here far deeper than those which Michael's spear serves merely to betoken. Deep scars of thunder have entrenched this face, and it is the face not of some petty scarecrow demon or scullery fiend, but of a great archangel ruined, an early visual premonition of Milton's Lucifer.

Somewhat later in the sixteenth century, Andrea del Sarto painted a *Dossal with Four Saints* for the Chiesa del Paradiso in Vallombrosa (whose fallen leaves Milton immortalized as an image for the fallen angels on the Lake of Hell). Here we have a fine and princely devil, with a neat Van Dyke beard and elegant horns, nude and quite human, kneeling before an imperious Michael, and trying in vain to wrest away his sword.[35] In the first decade of the seventeenth century, Hans Reichle produced a Michael statue which is now at the Zeughaus in Augsburg. In it the devil is a fine humanoid figure except for talons growing on his fingers and toes, and is given the tragic and agonized face of an older man, looking indeed a bit like Michelangelo.[36] In the mid-seventeenth century, Alessandro Algardi

[32] British Library add. MS 34294, fol. 186v.

[33] See Alfons Rosenberg, *Michael und der Drache*, Freiburg im Breisgau, 1956; the popularity of the subject is indicated by the six pages needed to list examples in A. Pigler, *Barockthemen*, 2 vols., Budapest and Berlin, 1956, I, pp. 397-402.

[34] He was not always so clad: the Tintoretto painting in Dresden, and the print for Heywood's *Hierarchie*, Sig. Tt v. show him in robes.

[35] This painting is now in the Uffizi in Florence; unfortunately, I have been unable to obtain a photograph or even to find a printed reproduction.

[36] See Herbert Keutner, *Sculpture: Renaissance to Rococo*, Greenwich, Conn., 1969, fig. 130.

produced a *Michael and Satan* for San Michele in Bosco, Bologna (now in the Museo Civico), which was reproduced in a bronze example to be seen at the Victoria and Albert Museum. Here Satan's toes and fingers are barely clawed, and he has hairy thighs and buttocks with a scaly tail, but there are no horns, and the face is taut, with an open mouth, crying out or even screaming, though more in defiance than in despair. The representation of Satan as a fallen prince was carried on well after Milton's time, as in the work by Francesco Solimena in the Vatican Picture Gallery.

The visual renditions of Michael and Satan approached Milton's conception in supplying Michael with armor and Satan with some physical beauty and a tragic or heroic face. Beyond those points of significant resemblance, there were equally significant differences. Most Renaissance and later artists did not allow the two great antagonists to face each other foot to foot, arm to arm, and eye to eye. Where the great War in Heaven is reduced to these two figures, Satan is usually prostrate beneath the standing, victorious figure of Michael, a scene Milton never describes but which artists never tired of painting. Closer to Milton is Tintoretto's representation of an impressive Satan battered down till he stoops "on bended knee" (VI, 194), but in the epic that discomfiture is only temporary and soon he is fighting again. Even when Michael's descending sword has shattered Satan's weapon, and sheared Satan's side, so that "Satan first knew pain,/ And writhed him to and fro convolved," Satan in *Paradise Lost* is saved the ignominy of lying prone and groveling at Michael's feet. His loyal followers close in about him, and bear him away on their shields (VI, 327-40). The debasement of Satan occurs later in *Paradise Lost*, of course, for as a storyteller Milton could hold it in preparation and suspense as a painter or sculptor could not do.

16, 20 69, 70 8, 9

If we may adopt an expression from photography, the artist has only a one-shot opportunity to capture his subject, a single exposure in which to express its form and suggest its meaning. To show Michael and Lucifer in dubious battle, hand to hand as apparently equal antagonists, might appear to suggest something which the central Judeo-Christian tradition has persistently denied, that is, the essential equality of the forces of good and evil. The artist must epitomize in a single moment and a single stance the final significance of the *mythos*, and this he usually did by showing Michael as the champion of good in undisputed victory. Artists, theologians, and plain Christian folk all knew that many skirmishes and even many campaigns in the Holy War were won by Satan, but nonetheless evil was an aberration and distortion of life, destined to suffer complete and ultimate defeat. Even when the great mythic struggle was not epitomized in two figures, and when the artist was given sufficient scope to present the whole conflict of the War in Heaven, his canvas had not only to catch the struggle at some particular moment, but also to convey the ultimate victory of God's faithful. By using space, whether the cubic space of sculpture or the flat space of painting, the artist had to suggest or to represent an ultimate victory in time.

The poet, on the other hand, worked in a primarily temporal mode, and though he could never achieve the full graphic reality of the visual artist, he could suggest subtleties and ironies, and convey developments, which were not possible for the painter or the sculptor. In *Paradise Lost* one picture follows another, each qualifying or altering what went before, so as to form final impressions of great complexity. On the first day of the War in Heaven, Michael and Lucifer approach their personal encounter on apparently equal terms,

> to such heighth
> Of Godlike power: for likest Gods they seemed
> Stood they or moved, in stature, motion, arms
> Fit to decide the empire of great Heaven.
> Now waved thir fiery swords, and in the air
> Made horrid circles; two broad suns their shields
> Blazed opposite, while expectation stood
> In horror. . . .

(VI, 300-7)

The only artist to my knowledge who dared to depict the contest in such a way as to suggest the equal terms Milton described was Luca Giordano in the latter years of the seventeenth century. In his painting at Madrid the antagonists seem almost equally formidable, but even so the position of Satan's raised left arm and averted face suggests a lack of confidence alien to Milton's Lucifer. Other artists were even less venturesome, but some did manage to convey the sense of a real contest. As a dragon, the devil may wrap his tail about Michael's waist or about his legs, or as a distorted fiend he may grapple for Michael's spear with one hand, and brandish a mace in the other, or claw up at Michael from below, techniques which are also adopted by humanoid devils.[37] Though a humanoid Satan is rarely allowed to face Michael in a combat such as that depicted by Luca Giordano, the fifteenth-century painter Antonio Pollaiuolo (c. 1432-98) does face Michael with a frighteningly formidable, erect, and vicious dragon.

Although Milton does not directly describe the familiar picture of the heavenly champion standing in triumph over the defeated body of his adversary, his medium allows him considerable leeway,[38] and he repeatedly alludes to such a scene. Belial refers to the fallen angels in Hell as having been not only "thus expelled" but also "thus trampled" (II, 195), while Satan himself is fearful lest

---

[37] For tail-wrapping, see the *Coronation of the Virgin with Saints* by Jacopino da Bologna (fl. 1350-80) at the Pinacoteca in Bologna, and the French statue of 1475 in the medieval section of the Metropolitan Museum in New York. Fiendish counterattacks appear in the anonymous French painting of the fifteenth century in the Musée Calvet at Avignon, and in Crivelli's Demidoff Altarpiece in the National Gallery, London. Humanoid counterattack may be seen in the *Michael and the Devil* by Bonifacio di Pitati (1487-1553) in the Zanipolo Church in Venice, and the *Virgin Enthroned with Saints* by Juan de Juanes (1523-79) in the Philadelphia Museum of Art.

[38] The triumph and stance of the victor on the body of the vanquished has been traced back to the East in antiquity; it was adapted to Christ's victory over Sin and Death, and to the victory of the Virtues in their conflict with the Vices in the psychomachia in the early developments of Christian art, and was notably revived in the latter part of the fourteenth century; see Katzenellenbogen, pp. vii, 14-17; Ormonde M. Dalton, *Byzantine Art and Archaeology*, New York, 1961, p. 672; and Millard Meiss, *Painting in Florence and Siena after the Black Death*, pp. 49-51.

God's angels "descending tread us down/ Thus drooping" (I, 327-28). Later, the epic voice reminds us that the Messiah "shall tread [Satan] at last under our feet" (X, 190). Not only was Michael represented in art as treading or trampling on demons of various types, but so also was Christ, in general symbolic terms in early Byzantine representations, and in very specific terms throughout Western Europe in representations of the Harrowing of Hell. In addition to Milton's modified acceptance of the "trampled" Satan, there are other major convergencies with art. "Gnashing for anguish and despite and shame" aptly describes many a satanic face in the humanoid representations, while the "writhed him to and fro convolved" (VI, 328, 340) perfectly describes the long tradition of serpentine adversaries, twisting under Michael's blow, a reaction which was also carried over into the humanoid representations insofar as the human anatomy would allow.

3

21-26

If the defeated Satan is rarely apathetic in art, the victorious Michael usually is. One of the most consistent features of the visual tradition is the patent denial of anger or anxiety to the archangel, even at the height of the struggle, or of deep satisfaction even in the moment of triumph. An early example from the cathedral in Cortona, a sculptured work presumably of the seventh century, may be taken as setting the tone. Here Satan is presented as a dragon, and Clement provides us a vivid impression of the effect: "the beast curls his tail in air and lifts his head as high as possible, holding his mouth wide open, into which Saint Michael presses his lance without a struggle. The whole effect is that of some calm and common-place occurrence, and is in striking contrast with the spirit of the conflict which is represented, . . ."[39] A remarkable congruence joins this early example with the main stream of the later tradition. Even as he prepares to deliver the coup de grace, the archangel seems serenely aloof and spiritually at peace.

Of Raphael's Michael, Oskar Fischel notes that "his sword triumphs without a struggle," and even where the fight is full of action, as it is in Tintoretto's painting in Dresden, the victory seems easy and assured.[40] Lorenzo Lotto's Michael floats effortlessly in the sky over a falling Lucifer, while Paolo Farinati's Michael is so abstracted in holy thoughts that his face is slightly averted from the grisly King of Hell whom he is about to dispatch with his spear. In Dionisio Calvaert's painting, Michael presents a blessed soul to the outstretched arms of the infant Jesus, upon whom he gazes in rapt fealty, meanwhile controlling his fallen antagonist by a light pressure from the toes of his right foot in Satan's eye socket, while Satan gestures furiously and gnashes his teeth. The eyes of Guido Reni's Michael are fixed upon the prone figure of a ruffianly devil, but his thoughts are apparently elsewhere. The bronze Michael by Michael Frey at St. Michael's Church, Munich, is totally intent upon his enemy, in a concentration of mind as well as of eye, but his face remains peaceful and aloof, unclouded by anger or any trace of passionate involvement.

69

27

24
25

26

28

[39] Clara Erskine Clement, *Angels in Art*, Boston, 1896, p. 58. Clement contrasts this dispassionate scene "with the superhuman combat depicted by later artists," and the contrast is valid for such works as those by Bruegel and Rubens, but many later examples conform remarkably to the spirit of this early sculpture.

[40] Oskar Fischel, *Raphael*, 2 vols., London, 1948, I, p. 32.

The mood of these works is likely to puzzle viewers today: the serenity of Michael's face seems to contradict his involvement in the action, or his achievement of victory. We will be more understanding of the approach of these artists if we recall that anger and pride are sinful passions, and as such are not within the emotional range of faithful angels. Michael in his integrity must fight and overcome Satan, but he must do so without debasing passions. This fact created difficulties for the visual artists, for they had to portray at the same time the strenuously involved arm and the serenely detached face of Michael, and in larger compositions, of the other angels too. Milton's problem was simpler, for he could essentially ignore the faces of Michael and his cohorts while describing to us their intense dedication and strenuous action. The faithful angels in *Paradise Lost* regard Satan and his adherents with absolute contempt, but without degrading emotion. Milton provides a graphic description of how ire, envy, and despair dim, change, and mar Satan's visage (IV, 114-17), but there is never any such marring of the angelic faces. When Michael encounters Satan on the field of battle, the most he shows is a "hostile frown/ And visage all inflamed" (VI, 260-61)—and this is as much as we ever find in the visual arts: recall the intense and alert face, with furrowed brow, of Pollaiuolo's Michael, and Rubens' Michael with his face flushed from the superhuman effort of his struggle.

I have seen no painting of the conflict in which Michael (or any other faithful angel) is shown as bleeding, and neither does Milton allow them to bleed, though he does say that they feel pain. With the devils, the situation is again different, and examples exist in which all major types of devil are shown bleeding. Thus, the neck of the dragon is bleeding in the polyptych by Cenni di Francesco at the Getty Museum and in the painting by Piero della Francesca, while Spinello Aretino shows blood exuding from the sword wound in the shoulder of the satyrlike fiend in the upper left portion of his fresco, and there is blood on the point of Michael's spear where it enters the jaws of the humanoid devil in the painting by Juan Jiminez, just as bloodstains appear on the neck and on the side of the demonic figure who stretches half-prone across the foreground of Beccafumi's *Fall of the Angels*; finally, the central figure of the falling demon in Rubens' great Michael painting in Munich appears to have a bloody coxcomb. Though most devils in art do not bleed, there were enough examples to provide ample visual precedent for the way Milton describes the wound Michael inflicted upon Satan:

> from the gash
> A stream of nectarous humour issuing flowed
> Sanguine, such as celestial spirits may bleed. . . .
>
> (VI, 331-33)

The "jaculation dire" (VI, 665) of mountains which the faithful angels hurl upon the followers of Satan is partly derived from classical precedents,[41] and partly from Revelation 6:16, where mountains and rocks fall upon the Satanic forces to hide them from the face of God. Milton's use of the hills as weapons is unmistakably based in literary traditions, and artistic renderings were sufficiently rare

[41] Hesiod, *Theogony*, 713-20, and Ovid, *Metamorphoses*, I, 154-56.

as to influence poet and reader less than is true elsewhere, but they should at least be mentioned briefly if only because comparisons of the visual and verbal treatments are aesthetically instructive and may help us to avoid critical misjudgments.

One famous representation of Jupiter heaping mountains upon the fallen giants was executed by Julio Romano in the Sala dei Giganti in the Palazzo del Té at Mantua, a painting that impressed Fynes Moryson and many other travelers.[42] Other artists who rendered the same subject include Antoine Caron and Thomas de Leu, Guido Reni, and Salvatore Rosa. Even the cannon founders entered the act with a high-relief scene on the barrel of a cannon, signed I. O. Mazzaroli in 1688.[43] The pictures are similar in showing a chaotic scattering of fallen giants, all thrown down in confusion, and some with large rocks heaped upon them. If one insists upon actual mountains in such a scene, one must be prepared for the virtual obliteration of the giants from our sight beneath a mass of tumbled hills, which would destroy the narrative point of the painting. The painters, therefore, are forced to employ boulders rather than hills, and to rely upon us not to be too literalistic in our demands. The poet has problems of his own with the scene, though the problems are naturally different: Milton must thus rely upon us to grant him poetic license in his description, and not to inquire too eagerly, as I think Shumaker does, about the torrents of "Rocks, Waters, Woods" that would stream down from the hills upon the angels who are throwing them (VI, 644-45).[44] Milton leaves visual realism far behind, and achieves a brief masterpiece of poetic description, compounded almost equally of suggestiveness and precise detail. The story is fraught with rational inconsistencies which neither poet nor painter can fully resolve, though each can achieve a workable solution somewhat different from that of the other.

While we are considering parallels to Milton's story in classical myth and before we turn to artistic representations of the Fall of Rebel Angels, we should also note the visual rendering of mythological figures falling through space. Greek and Roman literature furnishes several possible parallels to the Biblical story of Lucifer's fall. One of these, the fall of Saturn or the setting planet, was taken over by astronomy and was so illustrated in art,[45] but in other instances, as with Phaeton, a fall through the sky was often allegorically equated with the Fall of Lucifer.[46] Capitalizing upon the sixteenth century's fascination with what Harry Levin has called "overreachers," and following the earlier paintings of Cornelius

[42] Sells, *The Paradise of Travelers*, p. 155, and see also Frederick Hartt, *History of Italian Renaissance Art*, New York, [c. 1969], p. 527.

[43] The Reni painting is illustrated as figure 182 in Gian Carlo Cavalli and Cesare Gnudi, *Guido Reni*, Florence, 1955; the Mazzaroli relief is in the Wallace Collection in London; the Rosa painting is reproduced in *Salvator Rosa: His Etchings and Engravings after His Work*, published by the Ringling Museum of Art, Sarasota, Fla., 1971, entry 24 and fig. 25B8. Other art works on the subject are listed in Pigler, II, 88-91.

[44] Shumaker, *Unpremeditated Verse*, pp. 128-29.

[45] An illustration from the fourteenth-century manuscript of Albumasar, *Introductio in astrologiam* is reproduced in Fritz Saxl, *A Heritage of Images: A Selection of Lectures* (eds. Hugh Honour and John Fleming), Harmondsworth, 1970, fig. 40.

[46] Jean Seznec, *The Survival of the Pagan Gods; The Mythological Tradition and its Place in Renaissance Humanism and Art*, New York, 1953, p. 93.

van Haarlem, Goltzius completed in 1588 a series of four prints called "The Disgracers," which shows Tantalus, Icarus, Phaeton, and Ixion, all falling and tossing through space with such visual conviction that the viewer almost feels himself to be falling as precipitately as they.[47] To find the common ground in technique, rather than merely in subject matter, between these visual treatments and Milton's poetic descriptions of figures plummeting downward would carry us far toward understanding the relations between two major forms of art. Even more effectively than his greater contemporaries Rubens and Bruegel in their paintings of the Fall of Icarus, Goltzius seems to me to have conveyed through his masterly foreshortening the tactile impression of falling bodies, hurtling through space.[48]

THE FALL OF THE REBEL ANGELS

Milton frequently develops the reader's response to events and places in *Paradise Lost* by incremental repetition, returning several times to the same subject so as to provide various perspectives upon it and modifications of it. For the Fall of the Rebel Angels, he provides at least nine viewpoints: first there is a brief description by the epic voice, then successively by Satan, Moloch, Belial, Beelzebub, Sin, Chaos, followed by the angelic song, and climaxed by Raphael's full account (I, 44-48, 169-77, and 325-30; II, 77-81, 165-68, 374, 767-77, 993-98; III, 390-99; and VI, 824-77). For these accounts, Milton could turn to the Bible for rather scanty references, totalling only about thirty verses in all, and to the rich and elaborate versions of the hexameral tradition.[49] There was, moreover, no dearth of visual representations of the subject, which had been illustrated for at least seven centuries prior to Milton's time.

As for the process of the fall into Hell, Milton provides two somewhat different accounts.[50] According to one of these, the rebels are merely driven over the battlements of Heaven and allowed thereafter to fall of their own weight, as it were. The epic voice mentions no pursuit beyond the walls of Heaven, while in the angelic song of praise and in Raphael's long description, we are shown only an unimpeded fall through space (I, 44-48; III, 390-99; and VI, 824-77). The fallen angels, on the other hand, frequently mention a pursuit: Satan refers to "Ministers of vengeance and pursuit," to "His swift pursuers from Heaven Gates," and says that "the fierce foe hung on our broken rear/ Insulting, and pursued us through the deep. . ." (I, 169, 326; II, 78-79). Belial declares that "we fled amain, pursued," while Sin says that they were "driven" headlong, and only Beelzebub is noncom-

[47] F.W.H. Hollstein, *Dutch and Flemish Etchings, Engravings, and Woodcuts c. 1450-1700*, 19 vols., Amsterdam, 1949-1969, VIII, p. 103.

[48] George Galavaris, *The Illustrations of the Liturgical Homilies of Gregory Nazianzenus*, Princeton, 1969, pp. 131-32, discusses the relations between the illustrations of the stories of Phaeton and Icarus with the manuscript illuminations of the Fall of Lucifer.

[49] See primarily Isa. 14:12-23, Luke 10:18, and Rev. 8:10-11, 12.7-17, and 20.1-3, along with the other references catalogued by James H. Sims, *The Bible in Milton's Epics*.

[50] Allan H. Gilbert argues that these two versions represent separate stages in Milton's composition (*On the Composition of "Paradise Lost," A Study of the Ordering and Insertion of Material*, Chapel Hill, 1947, pp. 121-22).

mittal when he refers merely to having been "hurled headlong" (II, 165, 772, and 374). Chaos, too, mentions Heaven's "victorious bands pursuing" (II, 997-98).

The artistic tradition also provides two versions, identical with those of *Paradise Lost*. In the earlier Middle Ages, the demons are characteristically represented as free-falling figures, and are not pursued by troops of angels. The reason is that in these pictures the Deity is directly and solely responsible for the expulsion, while the faithful angels do no more than observe. In the Anglo-Saxon illustrations for *Genesis B*, in the Aelfric Manuscript, and in the fourteenth-century Italian *33, 42* manuscript *Treatise on the Seven Vices*, it is the Christ-Logos who effects the *43* expulsion over the wall of Heaven, but he does not pursue beyond that line.[51] Each of the three manuscripts conform to Milton's conception in these details. *Genesis B* *33* also shows the Son casting spears of thunder, as in Milton, whereas the other two show him enthroned as in Milton but accomplishing the expulsion merely by command and presence. In various manuscripts of the Bible Historiale,[52] the expulsion is effected as if by mere fiat of the whole Trinity seated together, while in the *45* *Très Riches Heures du Duc de Berry* and in the wood carving at King's College Chapel, Cambridge, it is by the raised arm of the Eternal Father alone. In none of *44* these instances is there a pursuit by the faithful angels. On the other hand, when Michael and his angelic troops are charged with expelling the demons, there frequently is a hot pursuit, as for example in Spinello Aretino, Luca Giordano, *4, 47, VIII* Bruegel, and Rubens. In his concerted effort to provide visual conviction to an *5, 17* action which no man can possibly have seen, Milton employs both artistic traditions.

When Milton describes the "deformed rout" of the falling angels, and writes that they were "scorcht and blasted," he implies that their appearance is already changed from what it was in Heaven, but he does not make that change explicit or detailed (VI, 372, 387). Having conveyed the confusion of the angelic fall as graphically as words alone could allow, he merely hints at the deformity of the demons and leaves that subject shrouded in vagueness, at the same time tantalizing and thwarting our curiosity when he writes "O how fallen! how changed . . .!" (I, 84). When we turn to the visual arts, we find two traditional ways of representing the falling and fallen angels. According to one popular medieval version, the rebel angels are immediately transformed into reptiles and/or hideous fiends as soon as they precipitate over the brink of Heaven. The other view, which is closer to Milton's, allowed for a gradual deterioration during the fall.

Let us first note examples in which the devils are instantly transformed to ugliness. The Bible Historiale of Guyart Desmoulins, an illuminated manuscript dating from about 1390, provides a fine before-and-after view of the rebel angels. *48* In Heaven, they are still winged and dressed in white robes, though their postures

[51] The careful survey of medieval legend and literature by P. E. Dustdoor ("Legends of Lucifer in Early English and in Milton," *Anglia* 54 (1930), p. 248) failed to find any instance of "the Messiah's intervention in the conflict," but there are many instances in the pictorial tradition.

[52] For the development of this visual tradition, see Adelheid Heimann, "Trinitas Creator Mundi," *JWCI* 2 (1938-39), 47.

seem to indicate that they have already undergone a spiritual fall, for two are seated on thrones, holding their heads, a third has already dropped his head to his knees, and a fourth is in the process of plunging over the sill of Heaven. Below that sill, the same number of angels are shown as black demons, plunging headlong into a flaming cauldron within the open jaws of a monster whale. In the stained glass window of the early sixteenth century at King's College Chapel in Cambridge, the falling devils are monsters rather like those of Grünewald and Bosch, while Bruegel's are distorted in similarly imaginative ways. In English engravings, Droeshout in 1635 and Vaughan in 1652 represented the falling angels as hideous and bestial.[53]

Now it should be apparent that Milton systematically preserves both the appearance and the dignity of his devils in his direct descriptions of them, but at one crucial point he compares the expelled demons to a herd of goats. Having told us that the Son chose "not to destroy, but root them out of Heaven," Milton describes the action through a memorable simile: "The overthrown he raised, and as a herd/ Of goats or timorous flock together thronged/ Drove them before him . . ." (VI, 855-58). Alastair Fowler in his edition comments on this image that "Milton might at least have agreed that it lowers the rebels drastically."[54] The "lowering" is surely there, for Milton's simile does evoke, *sotto voce* as it were, one major element of the visual tradition which otherwise he ignores. Christ's apocalyptic parable of separating the sheep from the goats (Matthew 8:28-32) had for centuries justified artists in picturing the devils as goat-men, and Spinello Aretino's representative *Expulsion of the Rebel Angels* shows them being driven out of Heaven as a herd of satyr-demons, more goatish even than the ancient satyrs themselves.[55] A comparison rather than an identification, Milton's simile evokes analogies from both the artistic and the Biblical traditions, and contributes depth and complexity to its context. Within the consistency of Milton's larger visualizations of the falling angels, it is no more than a slightly divergent hint, but it does remind us that the description of heroic and godlike forms applies only to the outward appearance of Satan and his followers. That measure of visual dignity and beauty which Milton so carefully preserves for them is an important element of their capacity to tempt, but it masks an inner reality comparable to the goatish devils of the old tradition, which Milton would not have us entirely forget.

The other artistic tradition represented a gradual degeneration of the rebel angels which allowed them to maintain some part of their beauty even as they fall. A case in point is the illustration for the thirteenth-century Breviary of St. Louis, which Didron describes as follows:

[53] An illustration to Elias Ashmole's *Theatrum Chemicum Britannicum*, reproduced in Arthur M. Hind, Marjorie Corbett, and Michael Norton, *Engraving in England in the Sixteenth and Seventeenth Centuries*, 3 vols., Cambridge, 1952-64, III, pl. 32.

[54] John Carey and Alastair Fowler, *The Poems of John Milton*, New York, 1972, *PL* VI, 856-57 n., hereafter referred to as Fowler n. (for *PL*) and Carey n. (for *PR*).

[55] In "The Conclusion of Book VI of *Paradise Lost*," *SEL* 3 (1963), 109-17, Mother Mary Christopher Pecheux also suggests an enriching analogy with the devils turned into a herd of swine which rushes over the Gadarene precipice (Mark 5:1-13).

The forms of Lucifer's army, just falling out of Heaven where the Lord is seated amidst his adoring hosts, are angelic still. They have the nimbus, wings and robes of prismatic colors, red, blue, green, etc., on a golden ground. But the features are already undergoing a transformation, the mouth changing to an open throat, the nose to a beak. When they enter the gulf [hell's open jaws] they have neither a nimbus nor robes; a tail projects behind, feet and hands are changed to paws, nails become as claws, and all the skin resembles that of a monkey; the face is no longer human, but bestial and monstrous.[56]

The so-called Byzantine Painters' Manual summarizes this iconography:

Lucifer and all his army fall from Heaven. The angels above are full of beauty; those below are angels of darkness; lower still they are darker and blacker; still lower, they are half angels, half demons; finally they are altogether black and hideous demons. At the bottom and in the midst of the abyss Lucifer, most fearful and blackest of all, lies forward on the ground, looking upward.[57]

The incorporation of this scheme into many paintings attest its general appeal, and it is unlikely that many viewers missed its striking allegorical significance.[58] Operating on these visual premises, artists could represent the devils not only as beautiful angels and as hideous fiends within a single picture, but could also exploit the dramatic possibilities of change from the one state to the other.[59] It is not surprising that such visual and dramatic possibilities would exert particular appeal upon Milton.

This more relevant tradition of the expulsion of Lucifer begins in England with the illustrations for the Anglo-Saxon poem known as *Genesis B*, which were drawn during the second quarter of the eleventh century, but may represent copies of a manuscript from the tenth century.[60] The Anglo-Saxon illumination of the Fall of the Rebel Angels is divided into four zones. In the upper zone, Lucifer is shown about to mount the throne in an ornate palace, holding the scepter in his left hand (this sinister gesture has obvious significance), while angels

33

[56] Adolphe N. Didron and Margaret Stokes, *Christian Iconography* (trans. E. J. Millington), New York, 1968, II, pp. 110-12, with illustration. The reference is to the Breviary of St. Louis, MS 1186 in the Bibliothèque de l'Arsenal, Paris.

[57] Didron, *op. cit.*, II, p. 266. Erwin Panofsky, *Meaning in the Visual Arts*, p. 75n. discusses the significance and dating of this Manual.

[58] Anna Brownwell Jameson, *Sacred and Legendary Art*, 2 vols., New York, 1970, I, pp. 65-66.

[59] In his attempt to establish the stages of Milton's composition, Allan Gilbert, *On the Composition of "Paradise Lost,"* p. 96, writes as follows: "Satan's inconsistencies about his failing luster and his unfailing might are apparently a result of stratified composition." In light of the pictorial tradition, there is no inconsistency between Satan's fading luster and his continuing might, and thus no evidence of stratified composition.

[60] See J. B. Trapp, "The Iconography of the Fall of Man," in *Approaches to "Paradise Lost": The York Tercentenary Lectures* (ed. C. A. Patrides), London, 1968, pp. 240ff. and notes.

honor him, and four in particular bring him crowns to represent his presumption upon deity. In the next lower panel, Lucifer is presenting peacock feathers to his angelic followers, as symbols of pride, while just below we see the Christ-Logos, with spears in hand, expelling the rebel angels. In the bottom zone, Satan has already fallen into the open jaws of Hell, represented as the mouth of a whale to whose teeth he is bound, while his angelic followers tumble down after him. Their bodies are tossing about in the air, and some are falling feet first towards Hell; the "headlong" fall which Milton three times insists upon, and which we find in most later pictures, had not yet become firmly established. For our present interests, what is most significant about this illustration is the continuing beauty of the falling angels—though Lucifer himself is sweltering in the flames, and shows the development of talons on his hands and feet, he is by no means a hideous fiend. His followers maintain a generally angelic appearance, though the twisting movements of the fall deprive them of the dignity they had shown above. The uppermost figure is still clothed in angelic robes, while the lower bodies have been stripped of their robes and left only with primitive loin cloths. All have lost their angelic coronets, so that their hair flows wildly, but all maintain angelic wings.

This extraordinarily interesting manuscript accords with Milton's descriptions at a number of points, as we shall see. It had been acquired by Archbishop James Ussher, who passed it on to Francis Junius at some unknown date before Junius left England in 1651 to return to Holland. When and how Ussher acquired the manuscript we do not know, and though he was seeking such things as early as 1603, he may not have found this until he returned to England from Ireland after 1640. Before Junius published the manuscript in Amsterdam in 1655, Somner had seen it and made a transcript of it. At least one foreign visitor is known to have been intimate both with Milton and with Junius, and it is by no means unlikely that Milton knew Junius.[61] Even if we assume, as some scholars have, that Milton knew *Genesis B*, we cannot be certain that he saw it early enough before his total blindness in 1652 to have been able fully to appreciate the illuminations.[62] For my purposes, those illuminations are important as establishing early instances of the development of a particular visual tradition which leads into *Paradise Lost*, and not as definitive sources in themselves for Milton's conception.

[61] David Masson, *The Life of John Milton*, 6 vols., New York, 1946, IV, p. 351, and VI, p. 557n.

[62] The manuscript has been three times edited in this century, first by Sir Israel Gollancz for the British Academy in 1927, next by George P. Krapp for Columbia in 1931, and finally by B. J. Tinner for Oxford in 1948. The illuminations have been finely treated by Barbara Raw in *The Story of the Fall of Man and of the Angels in Junius XI and the Relationship of the Manuscript Illustrations to the Text*, a 1953 University of London dissertation. A brief and effective summary and comparison of Milton's narrative with that of the Anglo-Saxon poet is found in Charles W. Kennedy, *Early English Christian Poetry*, London, 1952, pp. 28-31, while S. Humphreys Gurteen provides a longer analysis in his *The Epic of the Fall of Man: A Comparative Study of Caedmon, Dante, and Milton*, New York, 1896, and P. E. Dustdoor has provided a helpful article in his "Legends of Lucifer in Early English and in Milton." J. W. Lever argues for the influence of the *Genesis B* manuscript in "*Paradise Lost* and Anglo-Saxon Tradition," *RES* 23 (1947), 97-106, to which argument a strong piece of evidence is added by J. M. Evans in his "*Paradise Lost*" *and the Genesis Tradition*, p. 255, while Kirkconnell in *The Celestial Cycle*, p. 512, is unconvinced of any direct influence.

Another eleventh-century Anglo-Saxon illustration of the expulsion of the   *42*
rebel angels is found in the Aelfric Manuscript in the British Museum. Though
the draughtsmanship is less finished, the general conception is quite similar to that
of *Genesis B.* The angels fall over the precipice of Heaven, indicated here as in
the *Genesis B* illumination by a straight line or sill; none have wings, and all are
stripped of their angelic robes, some falling nude and others with primitive loin
cloths. None have horns or misshapen feet, and none have tails except for Satan
himself, who is pinioned at an upsidedown angle within a mandorla gripped by the
jaws of Leviathan. In body and face, there is relatively little to distinguish between
the faithful and the falling angels, except that in the latter the hair is no longer
neatly dressed, and in Satan has become scraggly, a feature we shall see further
developed in the succeeding centuries. The demons do lack the serenity and dignity
that mark the adoring angels above, but they have not yet become hideously distorted. They do, however, without exception fall headlong in this illustration.
In early manuscripts illuminated on the Continent, the fallen angels are also precipitated towards Hell head first—still in robes, and adorned with angelic wings
and halos.[63] Such a treatment is found in an Italian *Treatise on the Seven Vices*
of the later fourteenth century. Here the demons fall headlong through a starry   *43*
space, past an irregular line, after which there is darkness, the open jaws of hell,
and flames.[64] In the early fifteenth-century *Très Riches Heures du Duc de Berry,*[65]   *45*
the Limbourg brothers show a handsome, crowned and gracefully winged Satan
plunging headfirst toward the Lake of Hell, accompanied by smaller but still
beautiful rebel angels in blue robes with golden wings.

A little more than a century later, an oak choir screen was installed in King's
College Chapel, Cambridge, which contains a beautiful lunette in bas relief of the   *44*
fall of the rebel angels. Again, the demons are humanoid rather than fiendish in
appearance. One of the fallen figures is bearded (a frequent feature of the devils,
whether handsome or hideous) and is distinguished in appearance. Some figures
tumble wildly through space, but one dives rather gracefully. Milton's taste for
music must surely have brought him to this chapel, which provided the finest
music in his university then as now, and if, as he sat and listened, he examined the
carvings of the chapel, he may have become familiar with this one. Its mixture of
physical confusion with physical beauty, and of despair with aspiration, has much
in common with the descriptions in *Paradise Lost.*

Similarly flattering views of the devils may be found in Heywood's *Hierarchie*
of 1635 in an engraving of beautiful angels tumbling through the air and into the   *10*
jaws of hell. They are still dressed in angelic robes, and one wears a military
cuirass. Their faces are intended to represent loveliness, though their gestures and
expressions are distraught. Heywood's title page presents another view of the   *50*
same incident. Here, the angels are older (the other print is of childlike cherubs),

[63] See the illustration from an Old Spanish Apocalypse reproduced in Wilhelm Neuss,
*Die Apokalypse des Hl. Johannes in der Altspanischen und Altchristlichen Bibel-Illustration
(Das Problem der Beatus-Handscriften)*, Munster in Westfalen, 1931, II, pl. CLXVII.

[64] British Library, add. MS 27695 fol. 1v.

[65] For a superb facsimile of this work, see the volume edited by Jean Longnon and
others, New York, 1969.

and are nude rather than robed. Their bodies are perfectly human, and even handsome, though their gestures indicate distress and guilt. Only the bottom-most figure, Satan, shows slight horns and asses ears as he precipitates into the open jaws.[66]

20, 21   Returning to the Continent, let us recall the tragic-heroic face on the Satan under the feet of the triumphant Michael painted by Juan Jiminez about 1500, and the demons painted at about the same time by Signorelli for the Cathedral at

74-76   Orvieto. From this time forward, humanoid devils became increasingly popular in pictures of the War and the Expulsion. In a stickily sweet vulgarization of Leonardo da Vinci's style, Marco da Oggione painted Michael in the sky with raised sword, flanked somewhat below by figures of Gabriel and Raphael, supervising

51   the headlong fall of Satan into a pit in the earth. Satan's body is purely humanoid, and was apparently intended by Marco to pass for beautiful, with the exception of his feet, which have turned into harpy talons. He has the face of an obvious melodramatic villain, with hooked nose, scowling brows, and a turned-down open mouth, as though he were saying "Curses! Foiled again!" There are small dark horns on his head, but his deformity remains strictly limited. When we come to

27   the painting by Lorenzo Lotto, executed somewhat later in the sixteenth century for the Archbishop's Palace at Loreto, there is no deformity whatsoever. With no horns and no claws, adorned with angels wings, Lotto's Satan is as comely in face and figure as is the Michael who drives him down through the clouds.[67] Indeed, he is if anything more beautiful than his victorious antagonist, and even his fall is graceful. At about mid-century, Pellegrino Tibaldi represented the same action in a fresco for the Poggi Chapel in the Church of San Giacomo Maggiore at Bologna. There, the principal figures of angels and demons differ only in that the demons have claws on their hands and feet, but there is a smaller figure, just to the right of center, which represents the old hideous figure and face of the horned devil, com-

52   plete with bat wings. In France, the engravings of the *Fall of Pride* by Master LD shows a handsome humanoid Satan marred only by small horns and by harpy feet, and surrounded by other beautiful figures, both male and female. The *Fall of the Rebel Angels* painted by Charles Lebrun shows the falling figures moving through various stages of distortion, the greatest distortions being in the lowest part of the picture.[68]

    The greatest seventeenth-century paintings of the falling angels were executed by Rubens and by Luca Giordano, and these are interesting both for their similari-

[66] Heywood, *Hierarchie*, sig. Ee 3v., and title page.

[67] John Steadman refers to this painting in *Milton's Epic Characters; Image and Idol*, Chapel Hill, 1968, pp. 294f., and quotes from Bernard Berenson, *Lorenzo Lotto*, London, 1956, p. 133: "Contrary to the Renaissance tradition of representing Lucifer as a monster, Lotto shows him as an angel of great beauty." Strictly speaking, since Berenson regarded the Renaissance as ending in 1500 or 1520, he is correct; but it is necessary to recognize that in a larger sense Lotto's picture is not a rare exception.

[68] Henri Zerner, *The School of Fontainebleau*, London, 1969, pl. LD 86. In the fall of Envy, on the other hand, this "finest Fontainebleau artist" shows hideous and deformed demons at the flaming gate of Hell (*ibid.*, pl. LD 88 and p. 21). Lebrun's painting was engraved by Loir and may be found in the Kitto Bible, 11031-32.

ties to, and differences from, Milton's descriptions. In the center of Rubens' composition there is a hideous, many-headed dragon, but our attention is primarily attracted to the humanoid forms of the other falling demons. Though twisted and contorting, their bodies maintain considerable beauty, while their fingers and toes have already grown into menacing talons. It is in their heads that we see the most frightening effects of their crime, as Rubens reintroduces facial features of the most monstrous distortion. Though Milton differs from Rubens in this matter, the two represent strikingly similar visions of the nature of the fall itself. Rubens paints what Milton's Satan described when "the fierce foe hung on our broken rear/ Insulting, and pursued us through the deep" (II, 78-79). Rubens' demons are "hurled headlong" or "driven headlong" through space (I, 45, and II, 374 and 772). Like Moloch who "fled bellowing" (VI, 362), each demon's mouth is open, as in a united scream which perhaps signifies astonishment and pain as much as defiance and despair. The clashing lines of humanoid torsos and limbs, embroiled with serpentine heads, claws, and tails, produces in oil upon canvas just those impressions which Milton described as "hideous ruin and combustion," "deformed rout . . . and foul disorder," an overwhelming sense of "ruin upon ruin, rout on rout, confusion worse confounded" (I, 46; VI, 387-88; and II, 995-96). Milton's favorite descriptive word for this scene is "rout" (I, 747; II, 770, 995-96; IV, 3; VI, 387-88, 598, 873; and X, 534). The aspect of rout appealed to Rubens as much as it did to Milton, and he treated it not only in his *Fall of the Angels*, but also in his *Mary Immaculate as Woman of the Apocalypse*, and in his *Fall of the Damned into Hell*, all in terms which are relevant to Milton's description. Action, conflict, and violent movement, in which the seventeenth century took so much delight, could find no fuller expression than in the War in Heaven, and it was in this century that the greatest painting of the subject was created by Rubens, and the greatest poem by Milton.

    After Rubens, the next major artist to be fascinated by the subject was Luca Giordano, who painted it first in 1657 and four times thereafter.[69] These paintings continue those features of confusion and rout that we have seen visualized by Rubens and described by Milton, but Luca refuses to give his falling devils the deformed faces that Rubens did. In his painting at Naples, they maintain a striking beauty both of face and of figure, though they are obviously distraught in spirit, and Satan himself is still beautiful, still clad in handsome Roman body armor, and carries his sword with him to Hell, just as Milton provides weapons for his demons on the Lake of Fire. In his painting at Vienna, the subsidiary devils do show signs of the spouting of satyr's ears and horns, and the body of one is turning into a serpentine tail, but Luca implies that their degeneration is more spiritual than physical.

    Luca provides another arresting detail, in that Satan's throne is cast down from Heaven with him: in the Vienna painting, he falls seated on his throne (which is difficult to see in our Fig. 47), whereas in the Naples version the throne falls

(margin references: 17; 17, 114; 47; VIII)

[69] See Oreste Ferrari and Giuseppe Scavizzi, *Luca Giordano*, 3 vols. [Naples?], 1966, III, pl. 56, 110, 348, 349, and 350.

separately, and carries on it the Latin inscription "Similis Ero Altissimo"—literally spelling out the attempt to usurp upon the Godhead. That representation, with or without explanatory motto, allows the artist to give visual expression to the cause of Lucifer's fall even as he is shown falling from Heaven. Though Luca's interpretation is quite orthodox, he is unusual in representing Satan as precipitated toward Hell while enthroned, or accompanied by his throne.[70] In the eleventh century Anglo-Saxon *Genesis B* manuscript, Lucifer is shown in Heaven approaching a throne under a magnificent canopy, while attendant angels prepare to present him

33, 53   with crowns; three centuries later the artist of the Holkham Bible shows the rebel angels offering a crown to an enthroned Satan, while other angels turn away in sadness and dismay. Luca's visualization—which Milton, because of his blindness, could not have seen even in an engraved copy—provides an interesting use of the throne, roughly contemporary with *Paradise Lost* but different from it. Though Milton draws our attention to Lucifer's heavenly throne when God the Father foresees his intent "to erect his throne/ Equal to ours, throughout the spacious North," and also when Satan enters the battle seated upon "his gorgeous throne" (v, 725-26 and VI, 103), there is a different throne in Pandemonium, which is described with even more gorgeous elaboration, for reasons we shall discuss in the chapter on Hell. First, however, we must relate Milton's visual conceptions of the devils to the broader traditions of treating the demonic in art.

[70] For the removal from Heaven of the throne of Satan, see the apocryphal Book of John the Evangelist in Montague R. James, *The Apocryphal New Testament*, Oxford, 1924, p. 189. The removal itself is illustrated in a Florentine rendering of the cycle of Michael, dating from about 1260, reproduced as figure 832 in George Kaftal, *Iconography of the Saints in Tuscan Painting*, Florence, 1952. The painting of the Expulsion by Bruegel at Eindhoven shows, above the rout of falling angels, an empty golden throne, which symbolizes Lucifer's lost glory, left behind in Heaven—reproduced clearly as plate 22 in Max Dvorak, *Die Gemälde Peter Bruegels das Alteren*, Vienna, 1941.

V

Visual Images of the Demonic

THE THEOLOGICAL AND ARTISTIC PROBLEM

REPRESENTING the demonic in any visual form, whether in painting, sculpture, or mosaic, invites insoluble problems. It is not only difficult, but indeed impossible, to contain the full Christian understanding of evil within a single image. Theologically, sin is not a created entity, but a perversion of created good. Milton and Genesis both insist that everything created was declared by the Creator to be good, so that evil remains an essentially mysterious distortion and perversion. Satan, by seeking to exalt himself in power to equality with God, debased himself and destroyed any possibility of fulfillment within his created potential. As St. Augustine put it, "he became less than he had been, because, in wishing to enjoy his own power rather than God's, he wished to enjoy what was less."[1]

Men have always been tempted to exalt their own will above the will of God, and to love themselves (or some other good created by God) more than they love God himself. As this perennial temptation is both presented by Satan, and symbolically represented in his person, he must be viewed as singularly attractive to man. On the other hand, both in what he presents and in what he represents, Satan is essentially a perversion and distortion of created good, and therefore should be understood as a distortion of created beauty. In the Christian understanding of this tension, the demonic is essentially hideous and destructive, but perennially appeals to a man under appearances which are both attractive and tempting. Consequently the devil is not only the father of lies, but himself is the ultimate lie: falsification is the heart of his being. Satan and his followers represent at once the source, the apotheosis, and the definition of sin. This conception contributes to the understanding and management of human life, and to the analysis of actual as well as theoretical choices. The conception is fraught with ambiguity and irony, and since ambiguity and irony are particularly accessible to a writer, it is also singularly well adapted for presentation in literature.

But what of art? How can an artist in a single vision represent a being who is at one and the same time hideously deformed and marvelously attractive? Faced with that problem, the visual artist can obviously achieve only a limited success: to the extent that his art work emphasizes the attractiveness of the demonic, it will proportionally minimize or even ignore the destructive and distorting elements; conversely, the more effectively the image presents the inner ugliness and distortion of evil, the less effectively will it suggest the power to tempt. It is inevitable

---

[1] Augustine, *Earlier Writings*, trans. and ed. John H. S. Burleigh, Philadelphia, 1953, p. 237.

that visual representations of the demonic tend either to emphasize depravity at the expense of attractiveness, or attractiveness at the expense of depravity.

The dilemma, as it concerns our interests here, may be posed in the words of two critics. Maximilian Rudwin wrote that "rationally conceived, the Devil should be by right the most fascinating object in creation. One of his essential functions, namely temptation, is destroyed by his hideousness. To be effective in the work of temptation, a devil might be expected to approach his intended victim in the most fascinating form he could command." Just as Rudwin regards portrayals of the devil to be falsified by hideousness, so Ruskin regards them as falsified by beauty: "I am aware of no effort to represent the Satanic mind in the angelic form which has succeeded in painting," he writes, and also declares that "the elevation of the form necessary to give it spirituality destroys the appearance of evil."[2]

FROM BLUE ANGEL TO HIDEOUS FIEND

When the Fall of Man was carved on the sarcophagus of Junius Bassus in the fourth century, the devil was represented in fidelity to Genesis as a serpent coiled about the Tree of Knowledge. Otherwise, he appeared in paleo-Christian art simply as a blue angel, as he does in the famous sixth-century mosaic at Ravenna, which shows a beardless young Christ separating the sheep from the goats, the sheep on his right hand accompanied by a faithful angel colored red, and the goats on his left hand accompanied by a reprobate angel colored blue. Aside from the differentiating signal of color, the two angels are virtually indistinguishable and the devil is at least as attractive in appearance as the faithful angel.[3]

In the visual arts of the first Christian millennium, the attractive features of the demonic were emphasized and the outward depravity minimized. An ivory carving of the fifth century shows Christ expelling a demon, the demon represented by a little figure extruding from the head of the victim, with raised arms and free to the waist—but not much different in appearance from the victim himself. A sixth-century illuminated manuscript, treating a similar incident, shows what appears to be a winged figure rising above the head, entirely free, and unlike what we are accustomed to regarding as a demon.[4] In the church at Baouit, Egypt, a sixth-century fresco shows a devil with an angelic head.[5] The ninth-century Bible of St. Gregory still shows a well-formed Satan, though with clawed nails and a black halo.[6] The black halo was not universal, but demonic figures in this period

---

[2] Maximilian Rudwin, *The Devil in Legend and Literature*, Chicago, 1931, pp. 37-38. But oddly, though Rudwin sees this, he is unable to avoid the facile opinion that Satan is Milton's hero in *Paradise Lost* (see p. 10). John Ruskin, *Works*, ed. E. T. Cook and Alexander Wedderburn, London, 1903-4, XI, p. 174, and IV, p. 318, from *The Stones of Venice* and *Modern Painters* respectively.

[3] For a general overview, see E. Kirschbaum, "L'angelo rosso e l'angelo turchino," *Rivista di archeologia cristiana* 17 (1940), 209-48.

[4] By the thirteenth century, the pictorial traditions had radically altered, and expelled demons show all those features that we customarily associate with the hideously demonic (see J.-M. Charcot and P. Richer, *Les Démoniaques dans l'art*, Paris, 1887, pp. 5 and 10).

[5] Reproduced in Levron, *Le Diable dans l'art*, fig. 2.

[6] *Ibid.*, fig. 3, and pp. 16-17.

were given a dusky shading to suggest their repudiation of the light of God. The ninth-century Utrecht Psalter shows a personification of Hades chewing on sinners, an unattractive figure to be sure, but not so distorted in appearance as he was later to become. In the same manuscript, the devil trampled upon by Christ in Limbo is still humanoid, while some devils are shown with snaky hair, or with horns.[7] In eleventh-century Anglo-Saxon manuscripts, the fallen angels tend to be either nude or clothed only in loin cloths; their hair is shaggy, while some may develop tails, claws in the place of nails, and take on a dark or even black color. Still, most of the devils are humanoid in appearance, and not unattractive: the denigration of the appearance of Satan had barely begun.

33, 34, 37
39, 42

Parallel developments may be seen in the illustrations to Psychomachia manuscripts, delineating the struggle of Vices and Virtues for the human soul. The earliest illustrators gave the Vices all the charms with which Prudentius (348-405) had endowed them in his great Christian poem, but the influence of the Rheims School of Carolingian miniaturists brought about a change. Thereafter, "most of the Vices are caricatured as weird powers of darkness. Their hair, in tufts and unkempt, and their garments, often consisting merely of a tattered loin-cloth, give an immediate impression of violence and wildness."[8] That description could apply to some of the demons in Anglo-Saxon manuscripts, but by about 1130 the progression has gone so far that the Vices are shown accompanied by a writhing dragon and represented as "naked demons with flaming hair, who struggle in their last convulsions" at Aulnay, while at Argenton-Château they "appear as naked demons with claws on hands and feet. The faces are often so distorted that they resemble the masks of enraged beasts."[9] In her study of representations of the deadly sins in medieval manuscripts, Rosamond Tuve reports that the familiar sins typically show an outrageous ugliness, and observes that "as far as I have seen, verbal and pictorial ugliness is reserved for the morally ugly."[10]

Concomitantly, the devil developed from the blue angel of early Christian art into the frightful monster of the Middle Ages, but we would be mistaken to assume that this change in representation implied an essential change in theology. The early Christians regarded the devil as no less degenerate morally than did their medieval descendents, while medieval men were just as aware of demonic attractiveness as were the early Christians. Since a visual representation that would adequately include both aspects of the Christian conception of the demonic was impossible, there were inevitably variations along the spectrum between the visual poles, some being closer to one pole, some to the other. The emphasis in pictorial representations thus changes, under influences which we shall trace, until we find almost universally that devils are shown with such deformities as huge heads, gross eyes,

[7] Ernest T. De Wald, *The Illustrations of the Utrecht Psalter*, Princeton, n.d., fols. 78r., 79r., 8r., and 1v.

[8] Katzenellenbogen, *Allegories of the Virtues and Vices*, p. 7 and pl. II.5.

[9] *Ibid.*, pp. 17 and 18.

[10] Rosamond Tuve, *Allegorical Imagery: Some Medieval Books and Their Posterity*, Princeton, 1966, pp. 191-92. Owen, *The Vision of Hell*, p. 60, indicates that one of the forms of torment for the damned was "the horrible sight of demons and dragons."

distorted nostrils, emaciated limbs, talons, tails, horns, bat wings, and instruments
of torture. On all sides we see what Levron has called "les diables grimaçants,"
"cette image affreuse," "un masque hideux," "aux gestes fous."[11] As the inspirer
of all moral depravity and deformity, Satan is presented with an "abundance of
ugliness," his body distorted in every conceivable way and often compounded of
many different animal forms, and his countenance "filled with scorn, lust, and
envy."[12]

A number of influences effected this marked change, and something should be
said of several of the most important of these. In the first place perhaps is the
ancient Jewish and Christian association of the demons with goatlike creatures, for
satyrs had an evil connotation even in the Old Testament.[13] Anderson summarizes
the influence of this conception: "What we might call 'the basic devil' was probably derived from the faun of classical mythology, for this creature, half goat,
half human, was associated by the early Christians with the devils, elves, and fallen
angels who all inhabited the wild woods."[14] The influence of the satyr upon
medieval and later pictures of the devil could be widely illustrated.[15] A typical
example may be seen in the fresco painted in 1365 by Andrea da Firenze for the
Spanish Chapel at S. Maria Novella in Florence.

British legends also contributed importantly to hideous representations of the
devils. One famous story tells how St. Guthlac "was carried up into the air and
down to Hell by horribly deformed beings which the author describes in great
detail." These demonic conceptions were graphically represented in twelfth-
century illuminations which were widely imitated, first in the Lower Rhine, and
then elsewhere on the Continent.[16] Further British influences may be traced to
accounts of a vision which the Irish knight Tundalus was said to have experienced
in 1149, in which he saw at the entrance of Hell "the enormous jaws of an animal,
with huge teeth between which flames shot forth and seized the condemned. This
notion of Hell, which prevailed especially in England, is fixed in numerous pictures
of the eleventh and twelfth centuries, and was transferred from England to the

---

[11] Levron, *Le Diable dans l'art*, pp. 14, 20, and 42.

[12] Birch and Jenner, *Early Drawings and Illuminations*, p. 97.

[13] See Isa. 13:21, and the sometimes associated references to devil-worship in Lev. 17:7 and
2 Chron. 11:15. Also, see above, p. 58.

[14] M. D. Anderson, *The Imagery of British Churches*, London, 1955, p. 138. Morton
Bloomfield, *The Seven Deadly Sins*, East Lansing, Mich., 1952, pp. 28 and 62, recognizes
the contribution of the classical satyr to Christian conceptions of the devil, but feels that the
influence has been overemphasized.

[15] When Medina drew Satan as a satyr in his illustration for Book III of *Paradise Lost*,
he was drawing upon a well-established convention. Gardner, *A Reading of Paradise Lost*,
p. 130, seems to imply that there was some originality in Medina's choice, but there was
very little.

[16] Adolph Goldschmidt, "English Influence on Medieval Art on the Continent," in
Medieval Studies in Memory of A. Kingsley Porter, II, Cambridge, Mass., 1939, pp. 721-22
and fig. 16. The influence of these treatments upon later Temptations of desert saints, as in
Schöngauer's *Legend of St. Anthony*, is obvious.

Continent."[17] British paintings and carvings of the devils and their kingdom reached a terrifying ferocity, but changing tastes after the Renaissance and Reformation made these works seem repulsive, and according to Ernest W. Tristram such paintings "have perhaps been intentionally defaced more often and more thoroughly than anything in our wall-painting."[18] It is interesting to recall that William Shakespeare's father, while an official of the corporation of Stratford-upon-Avon, was given the responsibility for obliterating such murals in the Guild Chapel, which he apparently first attempted to deface by scratching and later plastered over entirely. Enough examples have fortunately been preserved, however, to make unmistakably clear the extent of the British influence on the Continent.

In addition to the classical and British influences, Islamic art also contributed to the development of fantastic and monstrous forms. These were imported into Western Europe, where they became motifs of Romanesque style in the grylli that adorned the margins of medieval manuscripts, and also in the stone carving of churches, where Saint Bernard at least felt that they generally conveyed no direct theological meaning.[19] While the precise significance and influence of these distorted forms is notoriously difficult to establish, they surely reinforced distorted images already characteristic of the demonic.[20]

Such pictures are often loosely referred to as grotesque, but properly speaking the word "grotesque" and the grotesque in art are traceable to the discovery about the year fifteen hundred of Nero's Grottoes of the Domus Aurea in Rome. The wall pictures found there introduced Renaissance artists to a classical style hitherto unknown, a style marked by the breaking up of natural forms into constituent parts, and the redistribution of those parts into new and fantastic shapes, which reinforced certain tendencies developed in the medieval representation of the demonic. Also in the sixteenth century, printed manuals on ancient religions drew especially from the late classical periods when deities were imported into Rome from the Orient. As Jean Seznec writes, "it is not the Olympians alone, but a complete barbaric pantheon which is summoned before our eyes by the illustrations

[17] *Ibid.*, p. 721. The Museo Galdiano in Madrid has a gruesome *Vision of Tundal* attributed to Bosch.

[18] Ernest W. Tristram, *English Wall Painting of the Fourteenth Century*, London, 1955, p. 4.

[19] Sir E. Maunde-Thompson, "The Grotesque and the Humorous in Illuminations of the Middle Ages," *Bibliographica* 2 (1896), 309-32, *passim*, and Emile Mâle, *Religious Art*, p. 49.

[20] Jurgis Baltrušaitis, *Le Moyen Age fantastique: antiquités et exotismes dans l'art gothique*, Paris, 1955, is especially helpful in tracing the antecedents and analogues to deformed demons. A general study of the place of monsters in European art and culture is Rudolf Wittkower, "Marvels of the East: A Study in the History of Monsters," *JWCI* 5 (1942), 159-97. Readers may also be interested in René de Solier, *L'Art fantastique*, Paris, 1961, and also (although they are less immediately useful) in Marcel Brion, *Art fantastique*, Paris, 1961, and Luther B. Bridaham, *Gargoyles, Chimeres, and the Grotesque in French Gothic Sculpture*, New York, 1969. A collection of authoritative studies and revealing reproductions may be found in a publication by the Centro Internazionale di Studi Umanistice (Enrico Castelli), entitled *L'Umanesimo e il demoniaco nell'arte*, Rome, 1952.

in Cartari: the horrible three-headed Hecate; Aphroditos, the bearded Venus, with comb in hand; the Apollo of Elephantinopolis, with blue skin and ram's snout; the unspeakable Typhon, whose scaly body bows his soft, snakelike legs— in a word, creatures of the strangest and most misshapen sort, a nightmare mythology, the vision of Saint Anthony in the desert."[21]

These influences were just that—influences—for they did not create the conception of the demonic as hideously deformed. In the patristic period, Saint John Chrysostom called the devil mania, frenzy, impossible to reduce to rationality, while at the Reformation John Calvin referred to him as "the sphere of atrocity and horror under the name of a person."[22] In his twentieth-century survey of Christian teachings on the devil, Denis de Rougemont says that Satan is the "absolute antimodel."[23] Just as the first millennium had emphasized visually the attractiveness of the demonic (without losing awareness of its inherent distortions), so the Middle Ages emphasized those distortions (without losing awareness of the attractiveness).

The distorted devils created in the Middle Ages showed a remarkable tenacity in the art of succeeding centuries. Typical of the fifteenth century in the north, Van Eyck's great diptych at the Metropolitan Museum in New York portrays, in Erwin Panofsky's words, "hideous demons who merge with their victims in a seething mass of tortured confusion."[24] Later in the fifteenth century, Hieronymus Bosch created his startlingly depraved imps, giving new vitality to the old techniques by joining together hideously incommensurate forms and initiating a new

68, 5, 13   sub-tradition which continued into Milton's own century. In the sixteenth century, Michelangelo personified the forces of hell in a horrifying black face with scream-

63   ing mouth and bared teeth, and Raphael contrasted to the grace of his Michael the

69   violent ugliness of the demon. In mid-sixteenth century, Bronzino painted the devil still with a batlike face, blood-tipped horns, and webbed hands ending in talons, while several decades later Alessandro Allori presented female-breasted demons with Medusa heads.[25] Bosch-like distortions continue to appear in paintings into the seventeenth century, as in the canvas by Frans Francken in the Victoria and Albert Museum and the picture by Teniers the Younger in the National Gallery

71   in London.

The wax effigy of a Damned Soul executed toward the end of the seventeenth

---

[21] Seznec, *The Survival of the Pagan Gods*, p. 252. I suspect that Milton's association of his demonic princes with pagan deities and idols (1, 364-521) is more than once related to the "barbaric pantheon" whose entry into post-Renaissance Europe is recounted by Seznec. See also Seznec's "Temptation of Saint Anthony in Art," *Magazine of Art* 40 (1947), 87-93.

[22] Quoted by Bernard Leeming, "The Adversary," in *Satan*, New York, 1952, p. 39, and Heinrich Quistorp, *Calvin's Doctrine of the Last Things*, Richmond, Va., 1955, p. 119.

[23] Denis de Rougemont, *The Devil's Share*, New York, 1952, p. 14.

[24] Erwin Panofsky, *Early Netherlandish Painting, Its Origins and Character*, 2 vols., Cambridge, Mass., 1966, 1, pp. 238-39.

[25] The Bronzino is in the Eleanora Chapel in the Palazzo Vecchio, and the Allesandro Allori painting in the Galeria Colonna in Rome. For Ruskin's critique of the stereotype by Bronzino, see his *Modern Painters* in *Works* IV, p. 319.

century in the style of Zumbo, contains horned devils of the satyr type (but interestingly modified to suggest the features of pre-Columbian Indian gods), with conspicuous fanglike teeth and red tongues stuck out at the damned in mockery. Even the once dignified devils of the Byzantine tradition had disappeared by the seventeenth century, and such Greek artists as Kavertzàs, Klotzas, Zanfurmaris, and Apakas had turned to the distorted image, as may be seen in the Hellenic Institute in Venice.

72

Sixteenth- and seventeenth-century woodcuts and engravings often followed the same patterns, as in the illustrations for the Apocalypse by Dürer and by Jean Duvet, while in the seventeenth century Jacques Callot presents us with diableries which have become almost ends in themselves, riots of Gallic fantasy which extend, even while thoroughly modifying, the monsters of Bosch and Breugel. The distorted image was perpetuated even in relatively commonplace household utensils: thus a sixteenth-century Casteldurante vase shows Satan with conspicuous horns and the homely face of an old man, while a painted porcelain of 1566 provides him with a satyr's head and harpy feet, and an ink stand by Ferdinando Tacca of the mid-seventeenth century shows the martyrdom of St. Lawrence supported by devils who are horned, clawed, bat-winged, and harpy-footed.[26]

13

Similar treatments of the demonic are found in England during the sixteenth and seventeenth centuries. In the superb early Tudor windows of King's College Chapel in Cambridge, the devils of window number 10 conform to the types envisioned by Bosch and Grünewald, and though the fine 1635 window in Queen's College Chapel, Oxford, may lack the imaginative flair of those at Cambridge, the demons are no less hideous. Even so late as 1664, the *Last Judgment* painting by Isaac Fuller for Magdalen in Oxford continued the same types. Throughout the Tudor and Stuart periods, most English book illustrations showed demons as almost entirely distorted and ugly.[27]

MILTON AND THE HIDEOUS FIENDS

For several reasons, Milton simply could not adopt the conventional ugliness of the devil for his own epic purposes. In the first place, he could not have been unaware of the oversimplification which the visual medium necessarily imposed. His poetic medium, on the other hand, allowed him to achieve a synthesis inaccessible to an artist, while both his poetic and his religious sophistication required that he do so. Though Satan is in no sense the hero of *Paradise Lost*, whether heroism is defined in moral or in epic terms, Milton chose to give his demonic prince a tremendously

[26] To be found respectively at the Capodimonte and the Villa Floridiana in Naples, and at the Victoria and Albert in London.

[27] Examples may be found in Hind, Corbett, and Norton, *Engraving in England in the Sixteenth and Seventeenth Centuries*, vol. ii, pls. 18, 118, 182; vol. iii, pls. 24, 32, 41b, 51, 92, 163, and 178. Volume iii, plate 129c, presents the only exception in this collection, George Glover's illustration of the falling angels for Thomas Heywood's *Hierarchie* of 1638; see my Figs. 10 and 50.

attractive aura; otherwise, his epic would not have accorded with his own realistic understanding of human experience. The devils of *Paradise Lost* could not be visualized in such a way as to appear simply repulsive.

Nor could they be so presented as to appear simply ridiculous. In the later Middle Ages, the distorted fiend had become a kind of burlesque, and demonic ugliness had reached a point of absurdity.[28] Such demons frequently were more humorous than monitory: as Maunde-Thompson put it, artists frequently made their devils "so absurdly ugly that we can only laugh at them."[29] Crossley reminds us that the devil became "the clown of the medieval stage," and by the fifteenth century "his brood became the subject of satire, descending to pot-house revels . . . . the butt of many a crude joke."[30] Such conceptions made the valid theological point that the demonic is ultimately ridiculous before the goodness of God and the faithfulness of his saints, but the sustained atmosphere of burlesque and *reductio ad absurdam* which was so effective on the stage and in many medieval art works would simply have destroyed the texture of an epic.

For these and other reasons, Milton dissociates his Satan from the distorted image, and he insists more upon internal than external deformity in his devils. Ruskin commented that whereas artists who gave Satan an angelic form were misguided, "Milton succeeds only because he separately describes the movements of the mind and therefore leaves himself at liberty to make the form heroic."[31] The greatness of Milton's achievement in the demons consists largely in the "combination of splendor and desolation" which he accords them, to use the fine phrase of Isabel MacCaffrey.[32] The desolation is inward, while the splendor is outward and is not entirely lost until the final degradation of the demons in Book x, with their transformation into loathsome serpents.[33]

The young Milton's descriptions of the devil had accorded almost entirely with the hideous image. *In Quintum Novembris* presents a purely conventional demon with pitch-black wings, sighing fire, and with flashing eyes and grinding teeth.[34] The "Hymn on the Morning of Christ's Nativity" describes how "th' old Dragon under ground . . . . Swinges the scaly horror of his folded tail," and in those two lines provides a perfect verbal epitome of the visual tradition of the Satanic dragon.[35] In *Paradise Lost* the emphasis was dramatically shifted, and we are shown a demonic form which

> had not yet lost
> All her original brightness, nor appeared

[28] Réau, *Iconographie* II, i, p. 60.

[29] Maunde-Thompson, "The Grotesque and the Humorous," 314.

[30] Fred H. Crossley, *English Church Craftsmanship*, London, 1941, p. 80.

[31] Ruskin, *The Stones of Venice*, in *Works* XI, p. 174.

[32] Isabel G. MacCaffrey, *"Paradise Lost" as "Myth,"* Cambridge, Mass., 1959, p. 127.

[33] It is also well to recall here the comment by Christopher Grose, "Some Uses of Sensuous Immediacy in *Paradise Lost*," HLQ 31 (1968), 222: "Milton can express the full terror of the devils only by declaring overtly the failure of figurative language."

[34] *In Quintum Novembris*, 36-47.

[35] "Hymn on the Morning of Christ's Nativity," 168 and 172.

Less than archangel ruined, and th' excess
Of glory obscured.

(I, 591-94)

Until the tenth book of *Paradise Lost*, Satan and his followers are persistently (though not invariably) invested with dignity, but the exceptions to this rule require careful consideration.

The first reference to a major disfiguration of Satan comes when he has reached the earth and alighted upon Niphates. Like so much else about Satan, this transfiguration on the mount underscores his reversal of the role of the true Messiah, and particularly of the Messiah's own transformation on a later mount. For Satan, the change is described as sudden and violent. Looking down from his post in the sun, Uriel "soon discerned his looks/ Alien from Heaven, with passions foul obscured" (IV, 570-71). Like Uriel, the epic voice also calls our attention to a Satan who has become "disfigured more than could befall/ Spirit of happy sort" (IV, 127-28). Those lines briefly summarize and explain the entire rationale for visual deformity in the demons, but Milton carefully refrains from giving us a detailed description: the gorgeous plumage of angelic wings is not explicitly replaced with the membrane of a bat,[36] and we are told nothing of horns and hooves and a tail. If the disparate parts of zoological nature have been dismembered and reassembled in some bizarre and heterogeneous form, we do not know it. Though an outward deformity is unmistakably acknowledged, Milton purposely keeps it vague, and focuses our attention instead upon the more generalized outward sign of an inner and spiritual disgrace: "his gestures fierce . . . and mad demeanor" (IV, 128-29). In a later book, God the Father refers in rather similar terms to his "scornful enemies" who "laugh as if transported with some fit/ Of passion" (X, 625-27). We do not have here that madly prancing devil of the visual tradition, which we may see exemplified in Queen Mary's Psalter, or to speak more exactly we only have so much or so little of that figure as each of us may find helpful to imagine as we read those lines. *Paradise Lost* provides no such "épouvantail burlesque" as Réau finds in art: Milton gives us strong hints of "le diable grimiçant," of "cette image affreuse," complete with "gestes fous," and yet his emphasis remains primarily moral.[37]

Other references convey the same generalized effect, evoking the impressions created by the distorted image but refusing to allow the specific visual details of that distortion to obliterate the continuing attraction of the demonic. Satan is "the grisly King," and his visage is "marred" by evil passions (IV, 821 and 116). The devils display a "shuddering horror," their eyes are "baleful," "aghast," and "scornful," and their faces are repeatedly characterized as "frowning" (II, 616;

56

---

[36] Satan is never described as a bat in *Paradise Lost*, but so fixed even today is the visual association which art long ago established between flying demons and flying bats, that D. C. Allen sees him in just this way: "restless, a great bat he speeds around the earth" (*The Harmonious Vision: Studies in Milton's Poetry*, Baltimore, 1970, p. 107).

[37] It would be interesting to see exactly how the devils appeared and behaved in the "ougly Hell" which Ben Jonson introduced into his *Masque of Queenes* (1609) as "a spectacle of strangeness, producing multiplicitie of gesture"; see Shearman, *Mannerism*, p. 157.

1, 56; VI, 149; II, 106, 713, 719; and IV 924). And when Satan first observes the love between Adam and Eve, it is with "jealous leer malign" (IV, 503). Those words and phrases could be applied with great accuracy to many a devil in art: those horrible eyes of the demons in *Paradise Lost* are strikingly reminiscent of the fiendish stares of Michelangelo's Charon and Hades. But in general Milton's emphasis is on kinesic significance rather than on physical morphology. Where Hieronymus Bosch joins contrary and conflicting forms together into the hateful images of his demons, Milton internalizes those conflicts within an outwardly appealing Satan, and has Satan himself refer to feeling "Torment within me, as from the hateful siege/ Of contraries" (IX, 121-22). Where Nardo di Cione and Andrea Orcagna illustrate the self-destructiveness of evil by showing fiends torturing sinners in Hell, Milton again internalizes by having Satan declare that "only in destroying I find ease," but "thereby worse to me redounds" (IX, 128-29).

Such recognition by the damned of their lostness is not often encountered in visual art, but it does occasionally appear. In the left panel of Bosch's *Inferno* in the Doge's Palace, Venice, we see one of the damned seated, his chin in his hand and his head bowed in deep dejection, and a similar self-recognition may be found in the Last Judgment window of 1635 in Queen's College, Oxford. As we might expect, it is Michelangelo who provides the most moving examples, but for the most part psychological disturbances are represented in the visual arts by various forms of physical distortion.

Gastrocephalic demons are a persistent motif in medieval art, with faces represented in their stomachs or even pudenda: this iconography implies the loss of control by right reason, and the usurpation of the passions, and it would be difficult to imagine a more effective means of conveying that meaning in purely visual terms.[38] As a poet, Milton can make the same point without minimizing the appeal of the demons, by describing them as fallen angels "who reason for their law refuse,/ Right reason for their law, and for their king/ Messiah" (VI, 41-43). Whereas Raphael paints his devil a swarthy red, as if he carried the fires of Hell always with him, Milton has his Satan declare that "which way I fly is Hell, myself am Hell." Similarly, whereas many devils are shown breathing fire, as in Leandro Bassano's *Last Judgment*, in Birmingham, Alabama, Milton can simply say of Satan that "the hot Hell . . . always in him burns,/ Though in mid Heaven" (IV, 75, and IX, 467-68). The conception which the Anglo-Saxon artist conveys in *Genesis B* by having Satan chained to the teeth of Leviathan, is communicated in purely psychological terms in *Paradise Lost* when Abdiel accuses Satan of being "to thyself enthralled" (VI, 181). Each of these instances illustrates the poetic internalizing of conceptions which an artist could only present in objective visual form.

But though Milton does put the traditional distortions at some distance from his devils,[39] he cannot ignore those distortions entirely, so firmly were they fixed

[38] Réau, *Iconographie* II, i, p. 61, and Emile Mâle, *The Gothic Image; Religious Art in France of the Thirteenth Century* (trans. Dora Hussey), New York, 1958, p. 378.

[39] Ruskin, *Works* XI, p. 174.

in the imagination of Western man. Milton's most detailed evocation comes in five verses describing hell:

> Where all life dies, death lives, and nature breeds,
> Perverse, all monstrous, all prodigious things,
> Abominable, unutterable, and worse
> Than fables yet have feigned, or fear conceived,
> Gorgons and hydras, and chimeras dire.
>
> (II, 624-28)

Focusing on the last verse in this passage, Addison remarked that "the monstrous animals produced in that infernal world are represented by a single line, which gives us a more horrid idea of them, than a much longer description would have done."[40] The point is eminently well taken.

Even where Milton refers to some very particular physical detail of the distorted image, he keeps it at some remove from the devils themselves. Up to Milton's time, devils were more often represented with the taloned feet of harpies than with the cloven hooves which have in succeeding centuries become more popular. *46, 51, 52* Milton provides this conventional visual detail in Hell, but ascribes it to his "harpy-footed furies" rather than to the devils themselves (II, 596). As with the feet, so with the head: Milton refers to the shaggy and bristling "horrid" hair which characterized the painted devils, but again he puts this at some remove. *33, 34, 42* In his flight from Hell to earth, Satan is likened to *56, 59*

> a comet burned
> That fires the length of Ophiucus huge
> In th' Arctic sky, and from his horrid hair
> Shakes pestilence and war.
>
> (II, 708-11)

Strictly speaking, Milton applies that description not to his Satan, but only to a body, a comet, with which he compares Satan. Here we see almost epitomized what Burke praised as Milton's ability to set "terrible things . . . in their strongest light by the force of a judicious obscurity."[41]

The predatory activities of the devils are represented in art not only by showing Satan chewing on a sinner but also by pictures of devils manhandling and

---

[40] Addison, *Spectator* 309, in Shawcross, *Milton: The Critical Heritage*, p. 176.

[41] Edmund Burke, *The Sublime*, 1757, p. 44 (II, iii), and see the discussion by Arthur E. Barker, ". . . And on his Crest Sat Horror: Eighteenth-Century Interpretations of Milton's Sublimity and His Satan," *UTQ* 11 (1942), 421-36, especially p. 430. For a discussion of actual comets of which Milton may have known, and of the association of "hair" with the tail of comets, see William B. Hunter, Jr., "Satan as Comet: *Paradise Lost*, II, 708-11," *ELN* 5 (1967), 17-21; Donald C. Baker, "On Satan's Hair," *N&Q* n.s. 4 (1957), 69-70, proposes that the "horrid" snaky locks of Medusa may be suggested by the conjunction with Ophiucus, "the serpent-bearer." Tristram, *English Wall Painting of the Fourteenth Century*, p. 91, points out that not only demons, but men possessed by demons, show the characteristic of horrid hair in medieval painting.

73, 55, 79
74-76, 61
dragging people about. Medieval artists were especially given to producing such scenes, but we even find them in Signorelli and Michelangelo, as physical *raptus* is used to symbolize all demonic exploitations of humanity. Milton never shows the fallen angels overtly engaged in such acts of predation, but he does several times compare Satan to a predatory bird or animal, as when he "walked up and down alone bent on his prey" (III, 441). The poetic strategy here has been effectively analyzed by Knott:

> By showing Satan as a fiend "bent on his prey" Milton invested him with some of the terror that informs medieval conceptions of a bestial devil. Without demonizing the fallen angels in the manner of Andreini, whose Satan has talons and cloven feet and is served by pride in the form of a savage dog, Milton nevertheless preserved enough of Satan's demonic aspect to suggest the immense capacity for destruction of the powers with which man must reckon. Seen as a predator, Satan has at least a distant kinship with those black, hairy devils with claws and beaks who carry off sinners to their damnation.[42]

The hideous and distorted fiends developed in the Middle Ages and continued into the seventeenth century did not fit Milton's needs, but though rejected, that tradition was not irrelevant to him, and it was too strong to be ignored. Indeed it provided an imaginative consciousness from which it was difficult to escape, and much of Milton's poetic energy was devoted to freeing his readers from imagining the devils only, or even primarily, within the distorted image. Writing under those conditions, Milton would probably have been unable to conceive of any reader who could interpret Satan as the moral and social hero of his epic. What Kenneth Muir has written in another context is also applicable here:

> It was not necessary for a seventeenth-century reader to put in a "good morning's hate of Satan" as a protection against too much sympathy: he believed in Satan and both by conviction and training he would hate him heartily. This means that he would be less likely than a modern reader to be swept away by the sheer grandeur of the poetry, and though he would be prepared to admit that Satan possessed certain good qualities, he would tend to think that heroism when exerted in the worst of causes ceased to be a virtue. Gangsters are often brave, but it is only the immature who think that they should therefore be admired.[43]

Milton recognized that the traditionally deformed fiend would exert a downward pull upon the imagination of his readers, and he consequently attempted to compensate for that drag by his own poetic exaltation of Satan. It was coincident with the loss of the older visual and conceptual understanding of Satan that some readers began to feel that Milton had made the devil the hero of his poem. Fortu-

---

[42] Knott, *Milton's Pastoral Vision*, p. 130. Valvasone, Andreini, and Vondel maintained many elements of the distorted model, as may be evidenced by Kirkconnel, *The Celestial Cycle*, pp. 81, 402, 414-15, 598-99, and *passim*.

[43] Kenneth Muir, *John Milton*, London, 1960, p. 145.

nately those who so misread *Paradise Lost* have remained a small minority, but the fact that such a minority exists at all is due at least in part to Milton's efforts to correct and compensate for a popular image which he found too one-sided and over simple for his own uses.[44]

Sophisticated readers need to be aware not only of what Milton incorporated in his epic but also of what he excluded from it. The range of the visualization of devils in art was surprisingly broad, and it not only provided Milton with much to reject, but also with much on which he could build. We shall now turn to those elements of the visual tradition which were more congenial to Milton's own conception and more directly supportive of his descriptions.[45]

BEAUTIFUL AND HUMANOID DEVILS

The visual conception of Satan as beautiful in face and figure never died out completely, and though it was only a minority tradition in the Middle Ages, that tradition was continuous down to the time of the Renaissance. Thus we find in the twelfth century at Salzburg in the illuminated manuscript of the "Riesenbibel von Saint Peter" that the devil over whom Michael triumphs is still angelic and still handsome.[46] The door of Benevento Cathedral shows a striking bronze relief, executed in the twelfth century, in which Judas is shown hanging by his neck from the branch of a tree, with his bowels bursting out, and a demon appears like a handsome angel to take away his soul.[47] The *Last Judgment* of the Cathedral at Torcello represents Satan in the form of a handsome Antichrist, strikingly reminiscent of the beauty of Christ himself.[48] The finely illustrated *Life of St. Anthony Abbot*, executed in 1426 for the monastery of Saint Antoine de Viennois, provides almost a full range of demonic types. One illumination shows a dual temptation of the saint, one by a devil appearing in the form of a rather homely monk, and the other by a devil in the guise of Christ—and it is a particularly beautiful version of

[44] The error of some readers, rather than of the poet, in elevating Satan to the heroic center of *Paradise Lost* is analyzed by James G. Nelson, in the *Sublime Puritan; Milton and the Victorians*, Madison, Wisc., 1963, p. 67, and he notes perceptively that "the seventeenth-and-eighteenth-century reader reacted to Milton's Satan with horror and revulsion. But by the close of the eighteenth century, that strangely modern feeling of aspiration, that insatiable desire to know all things and do all things and scorn all restraint, was beginning to permeate the culture of the Western World." The development of a visual romantic iconography of Satan as hero may be traced through the illustrations in Pointon, *Milton and English Art*, and the other works cited in note 5 to chapter 1, above.

[45] It has too often been assumed by critics that the visual arts presented Milton only with demonic visions which he had to reject outright, as may be noted in the comments of Thomas Newton (Shawcross, *Milton 1732-1801*, pp. 154-55), Jonathon Richardson (Barker, ". . . And on his Crest Sat Horror," 434), William Hazlitt (*Lectures on the English Poets*, in *Works* [ed. E. P. Howe], 21 vols. London, 1930-34, v, p. 65), and Don M. Wolfe (*Milton and His England*, Princeton, 1971, entry 111).

[46] Reproduced in Ernst Frisch, *Mittelalterliche Buchmalerei Kleinodien aus Salzburg*, Vienna, 1949, p. 25.

[47] Gertrude Schiller, *Ikonographie der christlichen Kunst*, Gütersloh, 1966-71, II, fig. 278.

[48] Reproduced in Roland Villeneuve, *Le Diable dans l'art*, Paris, 1957, opposite p. 96.

Christ, complete with crossed halo, the only identifying features of the demonic being two very small horns. These two temptations take place in a loggia, above and outside which there is a horde of the usual scruffy little devils.[49] A similarly broad range of demonic images appears in the *Très Riches Heures* by the Limbourg brothers, also from the first part of the fifteenth century.[50]

45, 46

Sometimes medieval artists, while denying devils the beauty of the examples just cited, nonetheless gave them a perfectly acceptable human appearance. We find one example in the *Christ in Limbo* mosaic in the nave of Saint Mark's in Venice, in which the Risen Lord is represented as standing on a startled-looking old fellow clad only in a loin cloth, with a rather brownish but not black skin and with graying hair. One fifteenth-century Book of Hours in the Bibliothèque Nationale shows a plain and peasantlike Satan approaching Job under the guise of a shepherd, while another in Philadelphia shows stricken Job visited by a Satan with a neatly trimmed beard and richly dressed like a great lord.[51] When the devil is made to seem (or to be disguised as) quite presentable, telltale attributes may be added which seem primarily designed to identify him for the viewer, rather than to degrade his presence. An example may be seen in the first doors cast by Ghiberti for the Baptistry in Florence, in the panel of the Temptation of Christ, in which the devil displays the dignified bearing and authoritative presence of an Old Testament patriarch in his face and gestures; even the ram's horn on his temple is small and neatly curled along his skull, but the batlike wings and taloned feet make his identity as a demon unmistakable. A striking contrast between a handsome and a typically distorted devil may be found in an illuminated French manuscript of about 1456, which shows a fashionably dressed devil approaching a painter who has just drawn a hideous fiend, and asking him for a more flattering portrait.

233

81

In the High Renaissance we find what Réau called the rehabilitation of Satan, the recovery of a sense of him as "un ange déchu," and his restitution to "la dignité fière d'un ange rebelle que la défaite n'a pas dégradé."[52] The new conception was given monumental expression by Luca Signorelli in the awesome frescos of the *Last Judgment* which he painted for the cathedral in Orvieto between 1499 and 1502. Signorelli's dramatic line and superb modeling endowed his demons with a terrible energy rarely seen before. No longer monsters, they are displayed as human nudes in violent and destructive action, in every variety of pose, going about their business of attacking men and women with a dedication which is all the more horrible for being so obviously joyless. The human form itself, which

74-76

---

[49] Reproduced as plate IV.2, in Rose Graham, "A Picture-Book of the Life of St. Anthony the Abbot," *Archaeologia* 83 (1933), opposite p. 13.

[50] Jean Longnon, *et al.*, The *"Très Riches Heures"* of Jean, Duke of Berry, provide helpful comments opposite pls. 65 and 91.

[51] Reproduced as plate XII in V. Lerouquais, *Supplément aux livres d'heures manuscrits de la Bibliothèque Nationale*, Macon, 1943, and as plate XVI opposite p. 102 in Edwin Wolf, II, *A Descriptive Catalogue of the John Frederick Lewis Collection of European Manuscripts in the Free Library of Philadelphia*, Philadelphia, 1937.

[52] Réau, *Iconographie*, II, i, p. 62.

had long since been effectively adapted to conveying the sense of angelic serenity and beauty, here gives fit expression to the terrible sublimity of damnation, in these "lean naked men, in whose hollow eyes glow the fires of hate and despair."[53] Yet for all their heartless ferocity, Signorelli's demons maintain a dignity, a sense of tragic loss, an aura of depraved nobility. With all that they have lost, they still have authority, but it is an authority "only supreme/ In misery" (IV, 91-92). To these fallen princes, all good has become bane and "never can true reconcilement grow/ Where wounds of deadly hate have pierced so deep" (IX, 122f., and IV, 98f.). Nowhere in art up until this time are comparisons with Milton so easy and instructive. Signorelli's demonic kingdom as a whole conveys the sense of Satan's plans for "Earth and Hell/ To mingle and involve," to make of Hell and earth "one realm, one continent/ Of easy thoroughfare" (II, 383-84, and X, 392-93). And the deeply etched lines of those tortuous demonic faces express as well as paint ever could Satan's self-taught message to himself:

> So farewell Hope, and with Hope farewell Fear,
> Farewell Remorse: all good to me is lost;
> Evil be thou my good; by thee at least
> Divided empire with Heaven's King I hold
> By thee, and more than half perhaps will reign;
> As man ere long, and this new world shall know;
>
> (IV, 108-13)

or again,

> Nor hope to be myself less miserable
> By what I seek, but others to make such
> As I, though thereby worse to me redound:
> For only in destroying I find ease
> To my relentless thoughts.
>
> (IX, 126-30)

Among Signorelli's demons, face after face suggests lines with which Milton describes his "Spirits of purest light" now "gross by sinning grown," "looks/ Alien from Heaven, with passions foul obscured," their "lustre visibly impaired" and "faded splendor wan," countenances in whose "look defiance lowers" with "shuddering horror pale and eyes aghast" (VI, 660-61; IV, 570-71, 850, 870, and 873; and II, 616).

In the Orvieto frescos, almost all that remains of the hideous image of the   74-76
Middle Ages are horns and scraggly hair. And even these are so varied in their application by Signorelli that they take on an individual significance for each face which makes them original. Signorelli's conceptions influenced Michelangelo's *Last Judgment* in the Sistine Chapel, and when that painting was unveiled in 1541 it showed devils of the same Olympian stamp. Relying on little more than   *61, 64, 65*
horns and asses' ears to identify his devilish princes, Michelangelo conveyed an

---

[53] J. A. Symonds, *Sketches in Italy*, Leipzig, 1883, p. 105.

understanding of the demonic powers in which hateful and attractive qualities are carefully intermingled. When he took the Papal Chancellor as the model for one of his demonic chieftains, he still maintained for him the grave bearing of a powerful statesman. Prior to Signorelli and Michelangelo, nothing like this had been seen, but now we find ourselves very close to Milton's own vision. In his Chancellor of Hell, Michelangelo had achieved with color and line very much the same effects as Milton had imagined for his own Beelzebub:

64

> with grave
> Aspect he rose, and in his rising seemed
> A pillar of state; deep on his front engraven
> Deliberation sat and public care;
> And princely counsel in his face yet shone,
> Majestic though in ruin: sage he stood
> With Atlantean shoulders fit to bear
> The weight of mightiest monarchies.
>
> (II, 300-7)

Signorelli and Michelangelo did not merely repudiate the total hideousness of the typical medieval devils, but they provided a new beginning for artistic conceptions. They may be said to have stopped the degeneration of the devils at some midpoint between Heaven and Hell, and to have maintained for them even in Hell an only partially defaced image. Furthermore, they endowed their fallen angels with that nude beauty of physique which Renaissance artists admired in classical antiquity. Michelangelo was the greater artist of the two, but Signorelli was the greater innovator, and their influence upon later art was profound. Even when signs of demonic deterioration were included in these devils, it was clear that their artistic creators were seeking, as Milton was, "visages and stature as of gods," and that they wished to suggest what Milton described as "Godlike shapes and forms/ Excelling human, princely dignities" (I, 570, and 358-59). Some artists even went considerably beyond Signorelli and Michelangelo and presented demons of an unblemished physical beauty. We may see examples of such in Beccafumi's *Victory of Michael*, and in Tintoretto's *Michael and Lucifer*, as well as in other works to which we shall turn in due course. I can well imagine some traditionalist, unweaned from the older ways, looking at these new images of the demonic and saying very much what Abdiel said to Satan in *Paradise Lost*:

29, 30
8, 9

> Oh Heaven! that such resemblance of the Highest
> Should yet remain, where faith and fealty
> Remain not!
>
> (VI, 114-16)

Artists who refused to allow the devils to maintain the fulness of heavenly beauty to which Abdiel referred, nonetheless maintained it in large measure, though of course in varying ways. Some artists gave their devils handsome human bodies, but also fiendishly distorted faces, as did Rubens in his *Expulsion of the*

Rebel Angels. Rubens, however, did not always carry his partial distortions so far,   *17*
and in his *Allegory in Honor of the Franciscan Legend*, in Philadelphia, we find
a devil whose handsome body is set apart only by bat wings and tail, and whose
face though painfully distorted is not in any conventional sense monstrous. The
painting of *Michael and the Angelic War* which Federico Zuccari executed for the
Chapel of Angels in the Gésu Church in Rome shows a full range of demonic
conceptions: the falling angels retain their human bodies, with or without wings,
but their faces become distorted, horns begin to appear, and hands and feet
produce claws, as they tumble in confusion toward the Lake of Fire. One demonic
head in the lower left emerges from the lake as a Signorelli-type demon, though
melodramatic, while the one to the right is that of a hideous ape-man with fangs,
gnawing upon his own wrist—so much is included, in fact, that one wonders
whether Zuccari might have been attempting to cover the whole gamut of the
visual tradition. Guido Reni's *St. Michael* in S. Maria della Concezione in Rome
shows Satan with a well-formed and athletic human torso, though the body has
been turned into a serpentine tail below the waist. A seventeenth-century French   *28*
version of *Michael and the Devil* by Pierre Biardeau casts the devil with traits only
slightly distorted, and more nearly those of a rather vulgar wrestler.[54] The tradition
in Europe as a whole never returned to the medieval extremes of bestiality and
monstrosity. At most, the faces attain the kind of hideousness shown in Rubens'
Expulsion, but more generally demonic attributes are restricted to horns, bat
wings, or harpy feet. Even so, the bodies themselves usually represent physical
grace and athletic beauty, and graceful human figures compensate for much in the
way of incidental distortions. Sixteenth- and seventeenth-century artists produced
numerous devils that are quite fairly and constructively comparable with those of
Paradise Lost, and to such comparisons we will now turn.

MILTON AND THE HUMANOID DEVILS

Once the artists began to arrest the deterioration of the rebel angels, the range of
devil types appearing in the visual arts inevitably widened. With a new freedom to
represent Satan at almost any stage between the purely angelic and the totally
deformed, each artist responded in his own way to the possibilities. As a result,
a broad new spectrum of demonic types came into being. As we explore the
demonic images within that spectrum, we can find many counterparts to Milton's
descriptions.

Few critics have questioned the skill with which Milton manages the degeneration of his rebel angels,[55] through a succession of time frames for the description

[54] Reproduced in Levron, *Le Diable dans l'art*, fig. 44, and discussed pp. 92-93.

[55] Waldock not only doubts the skill but even denies the degeneration: "It is not merely
that the Satan of the first two books reenters altered: the Satan of the first two books to all
intents and purposes *disappears*: I do not think that in any true sense we ever see him again."
Again, he declares that "I do not think, in other words, that the term 'degeneration,' applied
to the downward course of Satan, has any validity. . . . The changes do not generate themselves from within: they are imposed from without. Satan, in short, does not degenerate:

of Satan's decline.[56] The major stages of the process are summarized by John M. Steadman: "Instead of completing Lucifer's metamorphosis at the time of his expulsion, Milton depicted his gradual degeneration in several stages: a grossness of texture as early as the Angelic War; the partial obscuration of his brightness with the fall; and, finally, his transformation into a serpent at the conclusion of his enterprise against man."[57]

The first vision Milton gives us of Satan and the reprobate angels shows them rolling on the fiery Lake of Hell:

> he with his horrid crew
> Lay vanquisht, rolling in the fiery gulf
> Confounded though immortal.
>
> (I, 51-53)

When Satan speaks to Beelzebub, it is

> With head up-lift above the wave, and eyes
> That sparkling blazed, his other parts besides
> Prone on the flood, extended long and large
> Lay floating many a rood, . . .
>
> (I, 193-96)

Thereafter,

---

he is degraded" ("*Paradise Lost*" *and its Critics*, pp. 81-82, and 83). Waldock's contentions have been effectively refuted by Steadman in "Archangel to Devil: The Background of Satan's Metamorphosis," *Milton's Epic Characters*, pp. 281-97, and in "Milton's Rhetoric: Satan and the 'Unjust Discourse,'" *Milton Studies* 1 (1969), pp. 67-91. Thomas Kranidas also provides an effective analysis of Waldock's charge in *The Fierce Equation: A Study of Milton's Decorum*, The Hague, 1965, pp. 119ff., in which discussion I particularly like the following observation (p. 129): "Milton's Satan is a consistently developed figure of decreasing energy. He helps us to know God through a series of marvelously engineered inversions. But Satan is defined, too, by the very immutability and pure rational assertiveness of God."

[56] Arnold Stein has observed that "for the poet a picture, however rich in details, need not be confined to one frame. The picture may move imperceptibly into a second picture and then into a third, the foreground of one becoming the background of the next, and so on. And yet the effect (except perhaps for the technique of the close-up) may remain closer to the effect of painting than of cinema" ("Milton and Metaphysical Art: An Exploration," *ELH* 16 [1949], 123.)

[57] Steadman, *Milton's Epic Characters*, p. 297. Steadman correctly emphasizes the importance of Milton's postponement of the final deterioration of the devils until after the Fall of Man, and he charts the gradual degeneration with definitive care, but the postponement itself was less innovative than he suggests (p. 282): "Through this innovation he was able to present his devils initially in a heroic light. Satan himself, through shorn of 'th' excess of Glory,' was no 'Less than Archangel ruined,' still endowed with much of his 'Original brightness.' His companions were likewise 'Godlike shapes and forms Excelling human.' This introductory portrait of the fallen angels as defeated heroes rather than as distorted fiends constituted a far greater variation on tradition than Milton's subsequent account of their transformation into serpents." See also Evans, "*Paradise Lost*" *and the Genesis Tradition*, p. 231.

Forthwith upright he rears from off the pool
His mighty stature; on each hand the flames
Driven backward slope their pointing spires, and rolled
In billows, leave i' th' midst a horrid vale.

(I, 221-24)

The impressions created by these descriptions are surprisingly close to the details in the foreground of Beccafumi's view of Hell at Siena. The Lake of Fire stretches back from the lower edge of the painting, and on it we see a number of prostrate and "rolling" forms. Parallel to that lower edge there is a figure, slowly rearing himself from the waist, but with his lower parts "extended long and large." Just to the left of this figure is another, who has already risen; where his feet strike the lake, "the flames/ Driven backward slope their pointing spires." These agreements in detail between the poem and the painting are quite explicit. Somewhat similar, though less extensive, agreements may be found with the handsome oak carving in the choir screen at King's College Chapel in Cambridge, where we see some forms still tumbling down toward the Lake of Fire, and others already attempting to arise from it, though none has yet done so. In one figure in particular, the lower half of the body is still "extended long and large" while the head is being lifted up above the wave.

29, 30

44

A comparison of Milton's lines with these two sixteenth-century art works treating the same subject allows us to see that Milton's specification of detail is such as to permit more than a mere generalization, and to define a closer kinship with Beccafumi than with the Cambridge bas relief. The similarity to the former work is so pronounced that Frederick Hartt has suspected that Beccafumi's painting may have influenced Milton.[58] Given Hartt's broad experience in distinguishing between visual sources and visual analogues, his suspicion here may be correct. Widely held opinions about the "generality" of Milton's visual imagery surely need to be modified in the face of evidence that within a few lines he gives us sufficient visual detail to allow one distinguished art historian to identify a particular art work as the possible source of a descriptive passage in *Paradise Lost*.[59]

Having made these observations, however, it is important also to observe that no one could take a pencil and create Beccafumi's image simply by following the details Milton gives us: great epic poetry is rarely that specific, and I am prepared

[58] Frederick Hartt, *History of Italian Renaissance Art*, p. 511.

[59] In purely physiological terms, a comparison might be made between Satan raising his head above the lake and those statues of river gods which post-Renaissance Europeans found so attractive. Examples are the effigies of the Nile and the Tigris, taken from the Baths of Constantine in the sixteenth century and placed below the left and right stairways to the Palazzo Senatorio, and the statue of the Tiber placed in the Vatican Belvedere immediately after its discovery in 1512. Such figures exerted considerable influence on artists, as may be exemplified in the copy adapted by Vasari in the mid-sixteenth century for a tomb in San Pietro in Montorio. The subject matter, however, is entirely different from Milton's, and I merely mention such works because of the similarity of pose.

to argue that this restriction applies generally, and not merely to John Milton.[60] Helen Gardner is surely correct when she comments that "I cannot feel that Milton would have done better to give us a sharply visualized picture of Satan instead of thus stimulating in us a play of feeling before this huge prone figure."[61] My suggestion is that Milton has gone as far as an epic poet may be expected to go without losing himself, and his reader, in a plethora of extraneous visual detail.

The reverse of this limitation upon the poet may be seen to restrict the communicative powers of the painter and the sculptor. Let us look again at the bas relief in Cambridge, where we see two of the fallen figures stretching their arms outward and upward in gestures which are at once powerfully moving and inherently ambiguous: what does it mean? We may recall the interest in Lucifer's reactions after his fall which are displayed in medieval commentaries and homilies, and which receive poignant poetic expression in the Anglo-Saxon *Christ and Satan*, where Satan laments that he "may not reach with my hands to the Heavens above, nor thither lift up mine eyes."[62] As the early English poet explicitly included that longing in his characterization of the fallen Lucifer, so Milton with equal explicitness excludes it, as when he has his Satan declare, "Farewell happy fields/ Where joy forever dwells: Hail horrors, hail/ Infernal world, and thou profoundest Hell/ Receive thy new possessor" (I, 249-52). Neither the Anglo-Saxon poet nor Milton leave us in doubt as to whether or not Satan longs for Heaven, but those yearning gestures in the Cambridge woodcarvings remain permanently evocative and mysterious.

29   Now let us return to Beccafumi's painting, and to that prominent figure in the left foreground who with open mouth and extended arm so attracts our attention. Is his open mouth uttering a cry of despair? Or is he addressing the "profoundest Hell" with something like "Hail horrors, hail . . ."? Or is he reaching the peroration of a spirited address to "the fellows of his crime" (the artist could scarcely make Milton's subtle poetic distinction which describes them as "the followers rather"), urging them to "Awake, arise, or be forever fallen" (I, 606, and 330)? The painting remains shrouded in a powerfully moving ambiguity, and the painter should not be criticized for telling us no more than his art can profitably tell.

It is important also to note the extent to which Beccafumi has ennobled his demons. To be sure, he has provided in the center, just below the victorious figure of Michael, a conventional dragon with many heads, swinging "the scaly horror

---

[60] E. H. Gombrich (*Symbolic Images: Studies in the Art of the Renaissance*, London, 1972, p. 3) makes the same point about the relations between picture and literary text: "The crucial difference between the two of course lies in the fact that no verbal description can ever be as particularized as a picture must be. Hence any text will give plenty of scope to the artist's imagination. The same text can be illustrated in countless ways. Thus it is never possible from a given work of art alone to reconstruct the text it may illustrate." Insightful comments on the generalized, rather than particularized, imagery of poetry are made by P. N. Furbank, *Reflections on the Word "Image,"* London, 1970, pp. 6-8, and *passim*.

[61] Gardner, *A Reading of "Paradise Lost,"* p. 50.

[62] *Christ and Satan*, 168-73, and Charles W. Kennedy, *Early English Christian Poetry*, p. 33.

of his folded tail," as he falls into a volcanic pit; and just below that serpentine form, we can barely make out a more-or-less humanoid figure plodding over the burning soil in a half crouch which may suggest to twentieth-century man the familiar pose of Neanderthal, and would in the sixteenth century have suggested debasement and defeat. But the fallen angels in the foreground, to whom Beccafumi primarily directs our attention by his use of highlights and composition, are of extraordinary physical beauty and grace. Beccafumi is here unmistakably attempting to paint "godlike shapes and forms/ Excelling human, princely dignities" (I, 358-59), and he does so by displaying the "mighty stature" which also characterized the classical divinities in post-Renaissance art (I, 222). The once glorious haloes are gone, as in Milton's Lucifer "shorn of his beams" (I, 596), and the hair has that scraggly and unkempt look which Milton described in his astronomical simile as "horrid" (II, 710).[63] Within their differing media, Beccafumi and Milton are quite clearly attempting to convey very similar, though not necessarily identical, conceptions of the fallen host upon the Lake of Hell. The manner in which each succeeds, and fails, reveals basic distinctions between the arts. Beccafumi creates beautiful human forms, but to what extent can an explicitly painted human body reveal something which excels the human body? How far can an artist go beyond his own skillfully defined lines and volumes to announce "Godlike shapes and forms/ Excelling human, princely dignities"? The very precision of the painter in some measure limits his power to suggest more than he can visually define, and it would be uncouth of us to demand more. Conversely, the poet is limited in the details he can convey through merely verbal descriptions, but he is unlimited in his ability to suggest.

Let us now turn to another question, and consider the extent to which the fallen angels have deteriorated. Signorelli's devils are marred in ways which deny them the physical beauty of Beccafumi's, though I find that they thereby have acquired a measure of tragic grandeur which Beccafumi did not attain. Milton's descriptions might seem to place his demonic hosts somewhere between the conception of Beccafumi and that of Signorelli, but precisely where I do not judge it either possible or desirable to determine. It is instructive, nonetheless, to see why this is so. Signorelli's devils fall considerably behind Beccafumi's in attaining godlike shapes and forms which excel the human, and so may seem at a further remove from Milton, who can so much more effectively suggest the supernal and superhuman. But there is another sense in which Signorelli comes closer to Milton's vision than does Beccafumi, and this is in the representation not only of "regal port," but also of "faded splendour wan," to use Milton's words (IV, 869-70). Beccafumi's devils have not yet so "gross by sinning grown" as have Signorelli's, nor is their "lustre visibly impaired" to the same extent (VI, 661, and IV, 850). In neither case has the angelic form yet lost "All her original brightness, nor

74-76

29, 30

---

[63] J. B. Broadbent, "Milton's Hell," *ELH* 21 (1954), 167, says the phrase "'shorn of his beams' suggests a woodcut sun after a haircut," which indeed it does, but, what is more important, it reminds us of the loss of the nimbus. I can recall no representation in art of devils with angelic haloes in Hell, though haloes are occasionally assumed as disguise elsewhere.

appeared/ Less than archangel ruined, and th' excess/ Of glory obscured" (I, 591-94), but surely we can with more feeling say of Signorelli's devils as Satan says of Beelzebub, "How fallen, how changed!" (I, 84). As Beccafumi succeeds admirably in capturing the lingering sense of angelic perfection, so Signorelli succeeds in communicating that tragic loss of grandeur, and the resemblance to the devils' "sin and place of doom obscure and foul" (IV, 840). The point of the comparison should now be clear: Milton's descriptive lines cannot be equated with any single visual model, such as are exemplified in Beccafumi and Signorelli, for Milton deploys his verbal explicitness with sufficient conceptual vagueness (or if one prefers, he deploys his verbal vagueness with such specificity) that he succeeds in incorporating the effects of both these artists (and others as well) within a single poetic vision.

In one sense, then, Milton's descriptions achieve more than can be incorporated by an artist into any single work, but there is another way in which Milton's devils may be quite constructively associated with the devils in particular paintings. The framing of the demonic image upon human models, which Signorelli so significantly achieved, opened possibilities for demonic characterization in painting which were inaccessible to artists operating within the limits of the medieval tradition. So long as artists restricted themselves to total ugliness in the representation of devils, the fiends might differ in the iconographic significance conveyed by their particular combination of distortions, but these differences were essentially allegorical. One demon might, for example, be primarily associated with lust, and another with greed or envy, but beyond those terms distinctions were quickly blurred. Examples of such allegorical associations may be found in the Hell painting by Fra Angelico in Florence, in the frescoes in Pisa and Florence attributed to Nardo di Cione and Andrea Orcagna, in Taddeo di Bartoli's *Hell* in San Gemignano and so on down through the works of Bosch. With the sixteenth century, however, the possibility of individuation entered, and we can find devils differentiated from each other by features which correspond to the differences Milton posited between Beelzebub, Moloch, and Belial.

73

68

Here, as in any such interdisciplinary analysis, qualification is necessary. It is certainly difficult, and I think in the final analysis impossible, to establish simple equations between a particular characterization in verbal art and another characterization in visual art. For several years, I have tried the following experiment with bright undergraduate English majors. After they have completed a close study of the Shakespearean presentations of Hamlet and of Lear, I have shown a number of Renaissance and later portraits of intelligent young princes and authoritative old kings, and have asked each student to identify the artistic version which comes closest to the literary characterizations. The identifications have been so varied that no pattern emerges. This is admittedly a rather simple-minded experiment, but it does serve to illustrate the extraordinary complexity of our responses to the human face and figure. Shakespeare's Duncan may have overstated the case when he said that "there's no art to find the mind's construction in face," but if there are ways to read the human physiognomy, they remain very much within the realm of indefinite art rather than of precise science.

Somewhat the same difficulties emerge if we attempt to move in the other direction, from a visual characterization to a verbal explanation. Alberti long since commented on the difficulty of distinguishing between a laughing and a crying face, but the difficulties only begin there. Thus, studies of the figures in Raphael's *School of Athens* in the Vatican have led to radically different identifications, as Anton Springer showed in 1883. More recently, E. H. Gombrich has listed fifteen different meanings which have resulted from as many different readings of the face of Venus in Botticelli's *Primavera*.[64]

Even though precise equivalence is impossible to establish, general comparisons may be fruitful. Consideration of several paintings of two different subjects will clarify the possibilities. In representing Michael's conflict with Satan, in the later fifteenth century, Antonio Pollaiuolo chose to present Satan as a formidable dragon; previously the miniaturist of the Sforza Book of Hours portrayed him as a hideously ugly fiend. These pictures, and others like them, raise a number of questions in the mind of a thoughtful viewer, who is led to reflect on the nature of the Adversary, but in abstract terms: thus the physical threat from the dragon may be converted into a moral threat, and the physical ugliness of the hideous fiend into a moral ugliness. With such images, we rarely raise questions of personality and personal motivation in human terms, but once the humanoid devil is put into the picture, such questions inevitably arise, as they do for example with the painting by Guido Reni. As we reflect upon that figure, we tend to do so in terms of such human issues as personality, motivation, and characterization.

19, 16

28

The same distinctions arise from considerations of paintings which treat the psychomachia, or struggle for a human soul, in which the soul is frequently represented as a child. In the painting by Niccolò Alunno, the Virgin in a mandorla in the sky oversees a literal tug-of-war for a baby, between a human mother (does she perhaps represent the Church?) and a fiendish demon. In the seventeenth century, Lanfranco paints essentially the same subject, though here the Virgin herself is raising the child by hand into the clouds; the devil in this instance is almost completely humanoid, with a graceful body and sad though comely face, marked as exceptional only by his faun's ears. Other seventeenth-century paintings of the psychomachia theme often replace the Virgin with a guardian angel, as we see in Domenichino, and also in Carlo Bononi. In both these instances, the demons are much more nearly comparable to Lanfranco's than to Niccolò's, but the sneering frustration of Domenichino's demon suggests a personality quite distinct from that of Bononi's dark seducer, as both are distinguished from the elegant wistfulness of Lanfranco's. Metaphysical concepts lie behind all of these paintings, but the shift to humanoid forms for the demonic introduces other considerations as well, considerations which are essentially those of character delineation and differentiation. In the paintings which I have cited as treating the contest for a human soul, the demons seem to share perversity and gentleness, even perhaps traces of decadence and effeteness, whereas Guido Reni's devil has no gentleness, no touch of the effete: he is a powerfully virile old ruffian. Similar ruffianly qualities may be found in the demons portrayed in the Michael paintings by Paolo

79

80

82, 83

28

24-26

---

[64] Gombrich, *Symbolic Images*, pp. 39; 86 and 221n. 7, and fig. 74; 38, and 204n. 23.

Farinati and Dionisio Calvaert. In the latter, we see the face of a furiously enraged
barbarian, glaring at his conqueror with shrewd and malevolent eye. The humanoid
demons just discussed fall into two sets, each sharing certain personal characteristics, whether of thuggery or effeteness. None of these painters, and no perceptive
viewer of their time, would have thought that these characteristics exhausted the
meaning of the demonic, broadly considered, but each set suggested certain characteristics to be found within the diabolical spectrum.

Such paintings as these contributed to preparing the European imagination
for the kinds of characterization and character differentiation which Milton provides in the second book of *Paradise Lost*. Indeed, Milton's characterization of
Moloch and Belial correspond with the two different visualizations of devils we
24-26, 28 have just identified in art. To the malignant ruffians of Farinati, Calvaert, and Reni,
we may compare Moloch, "the strongest and fiercest spirit/ That fought in
Heaven; now fiercer by despair," as Milton describes him before he begins to
speak, who "ended frowning, and his look denounced/ Desperate revenge, and
battle dangerous/ To less than gods" (II, 44-45, 106-8). On the other hand, the
80, 83 gently effete and graceful demons painted by Lanfranco and Bononi represent
essentially the type of Belial, "in act more graceful and humane" than Moloch,
and whom Milton described in terms strikingly applicable to the would-be seducers
in those paintings:

> A fairer person lost not Heaven; he seemed
> For dignity composed and high exploit:
> But all was false and hollow; though his tongue
> Dropt manna, and could make the worse appear
> The better reason, to perplex and dash
> Maturest counsels: for his thoughts were low;
> To vice industrious, but to nobler deeds
> Timorous and slothful.
>
> (II, 110-17)

Of the other leaders who address the demonic council in Pandaemonium,
Mammon is given no physical description whatsoever, but is merely introduced
to speak, and allowed to characterize himself by his own words. Milton gives
Beelzebub a verbal portrait which is just as careful and explicit as those he constructed for Moloch and Belial, and Beelzebub is as radically individuated from
them by his physical appearance as by his ideas. We have already compared him
64 with Michelangelo's Chancellor of Hell, and if that comparison is recalled, visual
analogues to Milton's portrait gallery of Satan's deputies will be as complete as his
physical descriptions allow. As for the alignment of Milton's demonic chieftains
with the devils of art, I am interested neither in establishing one-for-one sources
nor one-for-one equations, but I would suggest that Milton provides sufficiently
explicit detail in his descriptions of Moloch, Belial, and Beelzebub to enable us to
align each of them with a distinctive physical type in the artistic tradition of
his time.

Of the relations between Milton's Satan and art, so much has already been said in outlining the major traditions, and so much will be said in connection with his activities in Eden, that it seems appropriate at this point only to single out a few characteristic features. Milton repeatedly insists upon the "diminisht" brightness of his Satan, but even so enough lustre remains to establish a qualified and comparative brilliance: "Darkened so, yet shone/ Above them all th' archangel" (I, 599-600; IV, 835-40, 846, 850, 869-70).[65] The visual tradition of a darkened Satan was sufficiently strong that it could not be denied, but Milton so carefully qualified it as to separate his ruined archangel by many light years from any debased and vulgar conception.

As Satan shines above the demonic host, so, too, "he above the rest/ In shape and gesture proudly eminent/ Stood like a tower" (I, 589-91). Satan is compared to Leviathan, his shield to the moon, his spear to the mast of some great ship, but his followers are compared to locusts and swarms of insects. Upon entering Pandaemonium, the "incorporeal spirits to smallest form/ Reduced their shapes immense" while the great demonic lords sat "in thir own dimensions like themselves," Satan still exalted above the rest (I, 789-93). When all are turned to serpents,

> still greatest he the midst,
> Now dragon grown, larger than whom the sun
> Ingendered in the Pythian vale on slime,
> Huge Python, and his power no less he seemed
> Above the rest still to retain.
>
> (x, 528-32)

At no point can we make a precise measurement of Satan, but the impression he makes upon us is overwhelming in its power.[66] The relative size of the various demons, clearly established by analogy and comparison, corresponds to the relative size in medieval art, where Satan appears gigantic in comparison with his followers. *73, 55* That comparison tends to be lost after the Renaissance (but see Droeshout's *Michael and the Demons* in Heywood's *Hierarchie*).[67] Where humanoid devils are *49*

[65] Milton achieves a comparable balance in treating the reasons for Lucifer's revolt in Heaven, as Evans points out in his *"Paradise Lost" and the Genesis Tradition*, p. 223: "The chief difficulty lay in finding a motive for his rebellion which was neither too good nor too bad. If it was too good, God would seem unjust; if it was too bad, the Devil would seem silly. To a poet of Milton's sensibilities the literary implications of the second conclusion must have seemed no less abhorrent than the theological implications of the first, for he took great pains to avoid either."

[66] An early comparison of Dante's almost exactly measured Satan with the vast but implied bulk of Milton's may be found in Thomas Macaulay, "Milton," in *Works*, New York, 1900, v, pp. 14-15. Stanley E. Fish, *Surprised by Sin: the Reader in "Paradise Lost,"* New York, 1967, p. 27, comments interestingly on the Satanic similes of size, and another stimulating analysis may be found in Furbank, *Reflections on the word "Image,"* p. 10. The relation of Milton's conception to giants in literature has been treated in D. T. Starnes, "Tityos and Satan," *N&Q* 197 (1952), 379-80, and John M. Steadman, "Milton's Giant Angels: An Additional Parallel," *MLN* 75 (1960), 551-53.

[67] Mâle, *Religious Art*, p. 56. John Trapp is correct as to precedents for Satan's size and

portrayed in sixteenth- and seventeenth-century art, Satan is usually not distinguished by his huge size, though a dragon may occasionally be introduced which
is more massive than any other demonic form. Though it had been superseded for
a century and a half before Milton undertook the writing of *Paradise Lost*, the
medieval perspective was still widely in evidence, and Milton chose to incorporate
it into his descriptions, rather than to follow the more general practices of contemporary artists.

As for the plebian demons, several minor points should be added to what has
already been said, and these apply primarily to their activities. Here, the most
important thing to note is a difference between Milton and the artists: Milton's
epic story denied the demons the opportunity for directly engaging in those sadistic
tortures which kept them fiendishly busy through several centuries of art. Milton
keeps them busy, nonetheless, perhaps assuming that idle hands are not the devil's
workshop, contrary to the conventional proverb (II, 521-628). Most of these
activities have no artistic counterparts of which I am aware, though they do fit well
within the epic traditions of literature. Of demonic tournaments, I can find a
parallel only in Jacques Callot's *Temptation of Saint Anthony* where mounted
devils charge through the air with lance and spear, and one instance surely does
not establish a significant tradition for our purposes. If demons were ever painted
in the process of holding theological seminars and debates, I am unaware of the
fact, though it seems an eminently appropriate concern in view of the nature of
much theologizing. Neither can I cite instances of demons exploring Hell, like
Elizabethan voyagers. As for athletic devils who "in swift race contend,/ As at th'
Olympian games or Pythian fields," I have found only one example in art, but it
is amusing enough to mention (II, 529-30). At the Museo Capodimonte in Naples,
there is a small bronze figure executed in the earlier seventeenth century by Pietro
Tacca which is identified by the outsized title of "Devil Running a Foot Race with
Serpent about his Waist." The little devil is quite humanoid, with a face less distinguished than well-formed, a bald head with small horns and something like a
Chinese topknot at the back of his skull (not visible in my plate). He is enjoying
himself, and he moves gracefully. Although he indeed appears to be running a race,
it is only with himself, and I have found no other instances of this motif.

Milton also allows his devils to divert themselves by creating music both vocal
and instrumental, and in this detail he does correspond with one persistent element
of the *diablerie* tradition in art. In the panel of his *Garden of Earthly Delights*
depicting Hell, Hieronymus Bosch provides a veritable orchestra of damnation,
playing upon over-sized musical instruments to accompany a vocal chorus of the
damned, while the same artist's *Last Judgment* in Vienna shows an "infernal con-

---

for the demonic council, but not as to his incomparable majesty in ruins, when he writes that
"no rendering of Satan's majesty in ruins—or indeed of the demonic council—is to be found
anywhere (except in Milton illustration) before the Satan-hero, Romantic school of criticism,
though Satan is often of giant size" ("Iconography," in *John Milton: Introductions* [ed. John
Broadbent], Cambridge, 1973, p. 178).

cert . . . conducted by a black-faced monster whose belly glows like a furnace."[68]
Jacques Callot represents a hideous vocal and instrumental orchestra of devils to
the left foreground, on a balcony, in his *Temptation of Saint Anthony*. Finally,   *13*
Milton's younger contemporary, Teniers the Younger, painted a scene entitled
Dives Admitted to Hell in which a very reluctant Dives is welcomed at the entrance
to Hell by an orchestra of monsters playing upon musical instruments. The iconog-   *71*
raphy of infernal music was there for Milton to draw upon, but he radically
changed the effect so that "the harmony . . ./ Suspended Hell, and took with
ravishment/ The thronging audience" (II, 552-55). We need not question that the
music would have seemed beautiful in Hell, for here as elsewhere Milton has
given the devil his due, but the irony would not have escaped those who knew the
tradition lying behind this motif.

Milton describes other devils who "with vast Typhoean rage more fell/ Rend
up both rocks and hills, and ride the air/ In whirlwind; Hell scarce holds the wild
uproar" (II, 539-41). Parallel to this wild uproar, art works devoted to Hell provide
pictures of general hell-raising and whirlwind rides through the air, as well as the   *74*
cavorting of witches' sabbaths, but I know no instances of devils tossing about
hills and rocks. By ignoring entirely those tortures with which the artists had
perennially occupied their devils, and by introducing his own occupations for them,
Milton set himself at his furthest remove from the established iconographic tradition
of the demonic. Elsewhere both he and his readers could have found strong visual
reinforcement for his demonic descriptions somewhere within the artistic traditions which had come down to them. This was true not only of Milton's direct
descriptions of the devils, but also in Satan's disguises, in his offspring Sin and
Death, and in those comparisons and allusions with which Milton enriched his
diabolical conceptions. To those we shall now turn.

[68] Walter S. Gibson, *Hieronymus Bosch*, London, 1973, p. 56. Signorelli provides no
demonic orchestra or vocal chorus, but his frescoes do contrast the cacophony of demonic
noisemakers with the harmony of angelic musicians.

VI

Demonic Associations: Comparisons and Disguises

VISUAL COMPARISONS

MILTON provides visual impressions of his devils not only in *propriae personae*, but also through *personae de mimo*, if we may borrow and expand a term from Roman drama. The *personae de mimo* extend and channel our sense of the demonic both by epic similes and by demonic disguises. Both means are visual: though neither represents a univocal description, whether through simile or disguise, we may be led to see something that is not itself devilish in ways which assist our understanding of the devils themselves.

Perhaps the most memorable of the visual images associated with Satan through epic similes occurs early in the first book, where he lies floating on the Lake of Hell,

> Prone on the flood, extended long and large
> Lay floating many a rood, in bulk as huge
> As whom the fables name of monstrous size,
> Titanian, or Earth-born, that warred on Jove,
> Briareos or Typhon, whom the den
> By ancient Tarsus held, or that sea-beast
> Leviathan, which God of all his works
> Created hugest that swim th' ocean stream:
> Him haply slumbering on the Norway foam
> The pilot of some small night-foundered skiff,
> Deeming some island, oft, as seamen tell,
> With fixed anchor in his scaly rind
> Moors by his side under the lee, while night
> Invests the sea, and wished morn delays:
> So stretcht out huge in length the Archfiend lay
> Chained on the burning Lake, . . .
>
> (I, 195-210)

T. S. Eliot praised Milton here, in one of the most notable backhanded compliments in recent literary criticism, for his "happy introduction of so much extraneous matter" and his "skill in extending a period by introducing imagery which tends to distract us from the real subject."[1] Eliot's characterization of this passage as distracting and extraneous was surely one of his less happy ventures into Milton

---

[1] T. S. Eliot, "Milton," *Proceedings of the British Academy* 33 (1947), 74-75.

criticism, for the Leviathan symbol had been closely associated with Satan for several hundred years in European literature. The tradition was widespread in the bestiaries and elsewhere, and the literary antecedents of the simile have been so fully explored that we may be sure, as D. M. Hill has said, that "the devil was a whale, and everyone knew it."[2] An Elizabethan wall painting executed between 1603 and 1625 at Hardwick House portrays the same scene, and it is easy to extend the list of such pictures, which often have great charm.[3] The one which I have chosen is from a twelfth-century Bestiary in the Bodleian Library which indicates the historical depth of this visual tradition, though Milton's readers would for the most part know it from more recent examples. Just as Leviathan lured seamen to anchor on the seeming security of his great bulk, only then to plunge to the bottom of the sea and destroy them, so Satan had already lured his angelic followers to Hell and would so lure many deceived men and women in future ages.[4]

85

Milton's next important visual description occurs in the extended simile for the fallen hosts of Satan, thick-scattered on the Lake of Hell:

> His legions, angel forms, who lay intranst
> Thick as autumnal leaves that strow the brooks
> In Vallombrosa, where th' Etrurian shades
> High overarcht imbower; or scattered sedge
> Afloat, when with fierce winds Orion armed
> Hath vext the Red Sea coast, whose waves o'erthrew
> Busiris and his Memphian chivalry,
> While with perfidious hatred they pursued
> The sojourners of Goshen, who beheld
> From the safe shore their floating carcasses

[2] D. M. Hill, "Satan on the Burning Lake," *N&Q* 201 (1956), 158. Fuller analyses are: James Whaler, "Animal Simile in *Paradise Lost*," *PMLA* 47 (1932), 536, and "The Miltonic Simile," *PMLA* 46 (1931), 1050; Kester Svendsen, *Milton and Science*, Cambridge, Mass., 1956, pp. 33-35; C. S. Lewis, *The Discarded Image: An Introduction to Medieval and Renaissance Literature*, Cambridge, 1964, p. 150; John M. Steadman, "Leviathan and Renaissance Etymology," *JHI* 28 (1967), 575-76. More recently, Jason Rosenblatt has suggested that the floating of the fallen legions "is an indication of their spirit-like buoyancy as well as of their wickedness," and associates the imagery with Rashi's *Commentary*, in "Structural Unity and Temporal Concordance: The War in Heaven in *Paradise Lost*," *PMLA* 87 (1972), 36.

[3] Rosemary Freeman, *English Emblem Books*, London, 1970, p. 92; see also the three examples reprinted as figure 218 in Francis Klingender, *Animals in Art and Thought to the End of the Middle Ages* (ed. Evelyn Antal and John Harthan), Cambridge, Mass., 1971, and the comments on pp. 386-87; Amy Lee Turner provides a woodcut from Gesner's *History of Animals* as plate 18 in her dissertation; M. D. Anderson cites a roof boss illustrating the scene at Queen Camel, Somersetshire, in *History and Imagery in British Churches*, London, 1971, p. 248.

[4] For the Christianized interpretation of the sea monster in the Andromeda myth, see Tuve, *Allegorical Imagery*, pp. 35-36, with three illustrations; see also figure 11 (p. 131) of Lucie Schaefer, "Die Illustrationen zu den Handschriften der Christine de Pizan," *Marburger Jahrbuch für Kunstwissenschaft* x, 119-208.

> And broken chariot wheels; so thick bestrown
> Abject and lost lay these, covering the Flood,
> Under amazement of thir hideous change.
>
> (1, 301-313)[5]

Few passages in *Paradise Lost* have attracted more devotees than the lines on Vallombrosa. Like numerous others, Mario Praz assumes that these verses recall a personal experience: "Doubtless Milton had enjoyed walking through the woods of Vallombrosa, but when the image came back to his mind it was in the mould of a classical simile, it was the 'heroic' image recreated by his detachment from reality."[6] Perhaps the experience was personal, but there is a problem here: the trees in Vallombrosa in Milton's time were not deciduous. As evidence, we have Della Bella's engraving of Vallombrosa,[7] dated 1637, in which we can identify nothing but evergreen trees, so that, at least in modern usage, it would have been needles that "strow the brooks in Vallombrosa." On the other hand, the Oxford English Dictionary tells us that the use of needle for "one of the sharp slender leaves of the fir and pine trees" does not date before 1798, so perhaps Milton's "leaves" was not inaccurate after all. What matters here is surely not his fidelity to the regional botany of Vallombrosa, but rather his evocation in a lovely musical phrase of an effective visual image redolently appropriate to his epic sense.

The highly apposite comparison to autumnal leaves and scattered sedge captures the sense of numbers, and also of fall and of waste, in natural imagery which is powerfully evocative, but the primary artistic parallels come in the reference to the overwhelming of the Egyptian cavalry in the Red Sea. The inclusion in Milton's epic simile of this episode serves several purposes: while the association of the fallen angels with Pharaoh's army does afford them a certain epic elevation, the association is double-edged, and at the same time identifies them with a desperate and despised tyranny. Furthermore, the incident had served through centuries of Jewish and Christian analysis to symbolize God's deliverance of his people from oppression, and Milton's placing of it at just this point serves to remind his readers of the ultimate victory of God over his enemies.[8]

---

[5] In *A Critique of "Paradise Lost,"* p. 12, John Peter notes in this succession of similes "how beautifully the images have been turned back upon themselves and resolved, leading us back where we started, with the picture of myriads of soldierlike forms stretched in defeat on the sea of fire."

[6] Praz, *On Neoclassicism*, p. 30. Cecil N. Bowra, *From Virgil to Milton*, London, 1945, pp. 240-41, points out that "the comparison of spirits in the underworld to fallen leaves is of great antiquity."

[7] The engraving is reproduced as illustration 37 in Don M. Wolfe's *Milton and his England*, Princeton, 1971. Banks, though unaware of this print, did note that as early as 1789 "the streams at Vallombrosa could not be thickly covered with leaves because the high over-arching trees consist almost entirely of evergreens" (*Milton's Imagery*, p. 100).

[8] Kurt Weitzmann, *Aus den Bibliotheken des Athos*, Hamburg, 1963, pp. 41-43, discusses the motif in Byzantine art, and Alexandre de Laborde, *La Bible Moralisée illustrée*, 5 vols., Paris, 1911-27, v, p. 164, notes that "Pharon molestant les Israélites, c'est le diable qui détruit le peuple par l'orgueil, la luxure et l'avarice." John M. Steadman's "The Devil and Pharoah's Chivalry," *MLN* 75 (1960), 197-201, is a useful article, showing that Milton's "comparisons are rooted in Christian exegetical tradition. Commentators on Exodus 14 and 15 had likened

Important as these suggestions undoubtedly are, they are ancillary to the visual function of the image here, which is to stimulate the reader to imagine uncounted and uncountable numbers of forms, strewn upon the waves, masses of bodies as overcrowded and overlapping as the leaves in Vallombrosa. Appropriate as it is on other accounts, the story of the drowning of the Egyptian army as we find it in Exodus 14:23-31 does not necessarily suggest such overwhelming numbers, but the treatment of the story in art had developed to the point where it could be taken as a visual symbol for an incalculable swarming and thronging of the dead and dying. Heinrich Wölfflin cites the typical paintings of this scene as examples of ineffective composition, so overcrowded as to diminish their aesthetic appeal, as if the intent were to show in a single small canvas the entire population of Egypt drowning.[9] The massing of drowned figures becomes conspicuous in illuminated manuscript as early as the eighth or ninth century: in one example the front rank of Pharaoh's soldiers is indicated by only four faces, but behind them stretches a line of helmets which is apparently intended to suggest an almost endless succession, and later representations add spears in a series of striking perpendiculars, obviously intended to give the same effect.[10] Early Bible illustrations provide just the visual sense Milton wished to convey, as we may see in the Cologne Bibles, and in Burgkmair's later illustration.[11] *The Crossing of the Red Sea* in the Galleria Spada in Rome by Andrea Donducci (Il Mastelletta) shows so many Egyptians that one wonders why the waves are not drowned, while the version by Santi di Tito in the Studiolo of Francesco I in the Palazzo Vecchio has the Egyptians crowded together into an almost indistinguishable and faceless mass, and this tradition continues at least until the painting by Luca Giordano executed in 1681 for Santa Maria Maggiore in Bergamo. In the traditions of Biblical art, Milton could probably have found no other image which had been so persistently characterized by "thick bestrown" figures.[12] The "broken chariot wheels" to which Milton

---

the destruction of the Egyptian army to the punishment of the rebel angels, the Red Sea to the fiery lake of Hell, and Pharoah himself to Lucifer. Similarly Isa. 34:4 ('And all the host of heaven shall be dissolved . . . and all their host shall fall down, as the leaf falleth off from the vine, and as a falling fig from the fig tree') had been interpreted as an allusion to the Last Judgment and the final expulsion of the evil spirits from their aerial seats into Hell" (p. 198). See also John T. Shawcross, "*Paradise Lost* and the Theme of Exodus," *Milton Studies* 2 (1970), 3-26, and J. B. Broadbent, "Milton's Hell," pp. 181-84.

[9] Heinrich Wölfflin, *Classic Art*, pp. 54-55, and 217; Wölfflin also complained that despite all the violence of action, the painters did not represent "a single Jew as excited about it."

[10] Bibliothèque Nationale, Paris, Psalter, MS gr. 139, fol. 419v., and the Homilies of Gregory of Nazianzus, MS gr. 510, fol. 264v. The Index of Christian Art at Princeton contains two dozen or so instances of similar illustrations prior to 1400. It should be noted, however, that the few representations surviving from the fourth and fifth centuries do not show such overcrowding.

[11] James Strachan, *Pictures from a Mediaeval Bible*, Boston, 1961, pl. 31 on p. 45, and F.W.H. Hollstein, *German Engravings, Etchings, and Woodcuts c. 1400-1700*, Amsterdam, 1954ff., v, p. 91.

[12] At least one thirteenth-century manuscript illustrated the drowning hosts of Pharaoh in direct association with the fallen legions of Satan; see the reproduction in Laborde, *Bible Moralisée*, 1911, i, pl. 48.

refers are almost always conspicuous in this scene whenever it appears in art: examples are to be found in the mosaics of the atrium of Saint Mark's in Venice, in the intarsia work of Fra Damiano in the choir of San Domenico in Bologna, as well as the work by Lorenzo Lotto in Santa Maria Maggiore in Bergamo, in the oil painting on alabaster executed by Antonio Tempesti now in the Galleria Doria, and in the painted screen at Essex Cathedral, to cite only a few instances.[13]

The single simile for the demons upon which Milton most frequently insists is that comparing them to swarms of insects. When Satan calls upon his followers to arise, they appear like "a pitchy cloud/ Of locusts, warping on the eastern wind,/ That o'er the realm of impious Pharaoh hung/ Like night, and darkened all the Land of Nile" (1, 340-43). Later, when the demons enter Pandaemonium, it is as a hissing and "thick swarmed" flight of bees (1, 767-76). In *Paradise Regained*, Satan's repeated assaults upon Christ, and rejections by him, are again given an insect comparison:

> as a swarm of flies in vintage time,
> About the wine-press where sweet must is poured,
> Beat off, returns as oft with humming sound.
>
> (*PR*, IV, 15-17)

Literary antecedents are not hard to find: the plague of locusts which was visited upon Egypt, as described in Exodus 10:12-15, is picked up again and integrated into an apocalyptic vision in Revelation 9:1-11. The bee simile has attracted considerable scholarly attention, and has been aligned with previous literary uses, but James Whaler concludes that Milton's application "is absolutely new."[14] Claes Schaar has demonstrated that the motif of a bee simile was firmly established in Neo-Latin poetry treating the "Council in Hell" well before Milton's time, and Kingsley Widmer has summarized the uses in Homer, Virgil, and Tasso, though his subsequent comment that "the glorification of work in the Protestant ethos may well have influenced the tone of the insect similes" seems somewhat less than perceptive.[15]

In her impressive study of the sources of Milton's Pandaemonium, Rebecca W. Smith associates Milton's bee simile with the coat of arms of the Barberini family, and points out that "when Milton was in Rome in 1638 the Barberini symbol, a bee, was everywhere prominent, and the followers of the Barberini Pope, Urban VIII, were often referred to as bees."[16] The Barberini insignia, with its bees, appeared frequently in the artistic monuments which the family patronized, most

---

[13] The Biblical account indicates that the Egyptians had trouble with their chariot wheels, and seems to suggest that these came off, though the Authorized Version provides no very clear translation of Exod. 14:25.

[14] Whaler, "Animal Simile," 551; see also John M. Steadman, "The Bee-Simile in Homer and Milton," *N&Q*, 201 (1956), 101-2; Davis P. Harding, "Milton's Bee-Simile," *JEGP* 60 (1961), 664-69.

[15] Claes Schaar, "Vida, Ramsay, and Milton's Bees," *ES* 46 (1965), 417-18, and Kingsley Widmer, "The Iconography of Renunciation: The Miltonic Similes," *ELH* 25 (1958), 261.

[16] Rebecca W. Smith, "The Sources of Milton's Pandaemonium," *MP* 29 (1931), 197.

famously on the great baldachino by Bernini in St. Peter's, where "the Barberini bees crawl up the columns and hang down on the bronze leaves from the cornice," and also in the great apotheosis ceiling glorifying the family, which Pietro da Cortona had painted for the Palazzo Barberini shortly before Milton visited there.[17] *144*
Smith cites the literary association of the Roman Church with a beehive, and notes Milton's own reference to "the bees of Trent," but she does not seem aware that the bee image was also applied to the Protestant clergy, and that it was used in reference to young men training for the ministry at the eminently Protestant Sidney Sussex College in the Elizabethan statutes for that Cambridge college,[18] evidence which tends to undercut her arguments associating the bees only with the Roman priesthood.

Even with all this attention to sources and analogues, I have found no recognition of the long-standing tradition which visually associated insects with the devils. Based in part upon the Biblical symbol of swarming locusts, this tradition developed in such a way as to include a broad range of stinging insects, sometimes seen as hornets, wasps, or bees, and sometimes as conglomerates of various insect forms. In the illustrations of Revelation 9 in the *Trèves-Cambrai* manuscripts of the eighth and ninth centuries the insects are real locusts and not monstrous forms, but as the illustrations continue through the Middle Ages various features are added, especially stinging tails.[19] In early Protestant Bibles, the scorpion-tailed locusts of Revelation 9 are shown with insect faces, as in the 1534 Tyndale New Testament, *97*
in the 1537 Matthew Bible, and in the Bishops' Bible of 1568, to cite representative examples. Insectlike devils appear in the *Fall of the Rebel Angels* by Dirk Bouts in the Louvre, and in the painting of the same subject by the elder Bruegel in *5*
Brussels, as well as in the *Last Judgment* fragment by Bosch at Munich, while they hover in flight over Hell in Civetta's *Inferno* at the Doge's Palace in Venice, and *101*
also in the *Orpheus in Hades* by Peter Bruegel the Younger in the Palazzo Pitti. *86*
Similar demonic representations or symbols appear in paintings of the Temptation of St. Anthony by Bosch at the Prado and by the elder Bruegel in Washington. The same conception may be found in seventeenth-century England in the *Last Judgment* window of 1632 at Magdalen College, Oxford, where insect devils are shown hovering in dark clouds over Hell, and in the engraving of Michael's victory which appears in Heywood's *Hierarchie* of 1635. *49*

Milton's intended audience could scarcely have ignored this widespread tradition of treating the devils as insects, and Milton's similes are sufficiently explicit to have elicited quite precise visual images. In view of this apposite visual association, certain critical analyses must be reappraised. Although John F. Huntley may be correct in one sense in writing that the bee simile "removes the reader from deep involvement with Satan's activity and restores him with a note of pastoral tran-

[17] Haskell, *Patrons and Painters*, pp. 35, 51-52.

[18] Smith, "Sources of Milton's Pandaemonium," 195-96, and C. W. Scott-Giles, *Sidney Sussex College. A Short History*, Cambridge, 1951, p. 25.

[19] M. R. James, *The Apocalypse in Art*, London, 1931, p. 36; and the English illuminations for Rev. 9:1-10 in the thirteenth-century Douce Apocalypse (MS Douce 180) and the fourteenth-century MS Univ. Coll. 100, both in the Bodleian Library.

quility," the reader also needs to be aware that Satan's activity is presented here within the framework of a widely recognizable symbolism, and that any note of pastoral tranquility is heavily qualified by irony.[20] Theodore Banks' analysis of the insect imagery is equally limited: though it is true enough to say as he does that the description of bees "gives a detailed and accurate picture of the activities of a bee colony," and that flies inspire "annoyance and disgust,"[21] in ignoring the visual arts he is precluded from appreciating the full resonance and power of Milton's visual description.[22]

DISGUISES

Milton's descriptions of Satan's disguises are, for the most part, more directly related to nature than to art—though the serpentine disguise is an exception which will be treated in a separate section. Before Satan chooses to mask his deception of Eve within the form of a serpent, he has already moved through a series of other forms. Having first deceived Uriel in the guise of a "stripling cherub," he becomes in succession a wolf, cormorant, lion, and tiger as he explores the Garden; he then crouches as a toad at Eve's ear and appears to her in a dream as an angel; finally, in Book IX he enters the Garden as a mist. In each instance, as Raymond B. Waddington has written, "Milton exploits a consistent level of irony through the idea that Satan thinks he is effectively disguising himself, while the disguises only reveal his nature more effectively to the judicious spectator."[23] Wolves and predatory cats were used as symbols for evil even in the Bible and not infrequently appear in purely symbolic form in art, whereas the cormorant was associated with gluttony during the Middle Ages, and evil black birds represented the devils in numerous Christian treatments,[24] but so far as I can determine there is no artistic precedent for Satan's use of them to disguise himself in Eden. Milton's narrative here is probably too complex to allow comparable visual treatment, unless the picture were to be accompanied by an explanatory text. Animals could of course be given visual attributes which would unmistakably associate them with the devil, as we see in the horned lion introduced by Carracci into his *Temptation of St. Anthony* in London. Pictures of Eden are abundant with animals, but no such signal identifies them as demonic, with the single possible exception of Bosch's Eden panel in

258

[20] John F. Huntley, "The Ecology and Anatomy of Criticism: Milton's Sonnet 19 and the Bee Simile in *Paradise Lost*, I. 768-76," *JAAC* 24 (1966), 388.

[21] Banks, *Milton's Imagery*, pp. 165 and 153. For perceptive literary analyses of the locust image, see Broadbent, "Milton's Hell," 182-83, and Ricks, *Milton's Grand Style*, p. 129.

[22] There is also a hornet simile in *Samson Agonistes*, 19-22, and an interesting commentary in Ricks, *Milton's Grand Style*, p. 52.

[23] Raymond B. Waddington, "Appearance and Reality in Satan's Disguises," *TSLL* 4 (1962), 398; a similar point is made in Steadman's "Ethos and Dianoia: Character and Rhetoric in *Paradise Lost*," *Language and Style in Milton* (ed. Emma and Shawcross), p. 223.

[24] Pss. 7:2, and 1 Pet. 5:8; see also the appropriate entries in Réau, *Iconographie*, as well as Klingender, *Animals in Art and Thought*, p. 375, and Owen, *The Vision of Hell*, pp. 38, 46, 191, and 198.

the *Garden of Earthly Delights* where a number of very anomalous animals do appear.

Even when Satan's disguises have no direct parallels in art, Milton's descriptions evidence acute visual perceptions of nature. Satan takes the form of

> a tiger, who by chance hath spied
> In some purlieu two gentle fawns at play,
> Straight couches close, then rising changes oft
> His couchant watch, as one who chose his ground
> Whence rushing he might surest seize them both
> Gript in each paw.
>
> (IV, 403-8)

Though Milton could never have seen a tiger hunting in the wild, these lines do attest to his close observation of the physical movements of smaller hunting cats, and finely convey a visual experience. Where the description breaks down as accurate observation—cats rarely if ever seize two victims at once, gripped in each paw—it is because he has quite properly altered the facts to accord with his narrative. A strong visual impression of mist moving along the ground is provided when Milton describes Satan "like a black mist low creeping," and has Satan declare that he will "thus wrapt in mist/ Of midnight vapor glide obscure, and pry/ In every bush and brake" (IX, 180, 158-60).

Milton also describes Satan as "squat like a toad, close at the ear of Eve" (IV, 800). This conception appears nowhere in artistic treatments of the Fall,[25] though the association of the toad with the devils was widespread and has frequently been noted by scholars.[26] In medieval art, the devil was sometimes shown entering a man in the physical form of a toad,[27] and in scenes of Hell, devils often appear as toads who devour the sinners,[28] as in the mosaic of the Florentine Baptistry. When attached to the sexual organs of a woman, toads in hell inevitably signified punishment for lust, but otherwise they did not necessarily do so.[29]

55

[25] Howard Schultz, "Satan's Serenade," *PQ* 27 (1948), 17-26, considers the originality of Milton's account; for Eve's dream itself, as related to the contemporary lore of dreams and demons, see William B. Hunter, Jr., "Eve's Demonic Dream," *ELH* 13 (1946), 255-65. Trapp, "Iconography," p. 178, observes that Satan does not appear as a toad in the temptation of Eve except in Milton illustrations, but cites a curious half-toad in Lucas van Leyden.

[26] Michael Fixler has associated Satan's disguise here with the froglike forms assumed by evil spirits in Rev. 16:13-14, in "The Apocalypse within *Paradise Lost*," in *New Essays on "Paradise Lost"* (ed. Thomas Kranidas), Berkeley, 1969, p. 164; Waddington, "Appearance and Reality," p. 392, cites the proverbial, popular, alchemical, and necromantic "connotations which certainly put the toad in Satan's camp"; while Steadman, "Eve's Dream and the Conventions of Witchcraft," *JHI* 26 (1965), 567-74, shows that Eve's dream of flight contains certain resemblances to the flights attributed to witches and notes that "Satan's disguise as a toad recalls one of the most conventional forms which familiar devils assumed in their association with the sorceress" (567-68).

[27] Bridaham, *Gargoyles, Chimeres, and the Grotesque*, x.

[28] Mâle, *The Gothic Image*, p. 381.

[29] Klingender, *Animals in Art and Thought*, p. 302, and Katzenellenbogen, *Allegories of the Virtues and Vices*, p. 58.

Milton's placing of the toad at Eve's ear is of course appropriate because Satan is speaking to her fancy, but it also sets the representation apart from those lascivious toads in art, for Eve's fall was not occasioned by sexual lust.

Toads also figured prominently, from the late Middle Ages through the seventeenth century, in tomb sculpture and various forms of *memento mori*. The bodies of the deceased were often represented by stone carvings intended to show just how decayed and decomposed they would look after death, and in these *transis* we encounter not only slithering worms who crawl in and out of the body, but as frequently see toads engaged in eating away at the heads of these figures.[30] A colored wax relief in the Victoria and Albert Museum called *Time and Death*, executed by Zumbo in the second half of the seventeenth century, epitomizes this tradition by showing an enormous toad squatting directly behind a human skull.[31]

A third and more significant comparison to art has been suggested by A. B. Chambers, who relates the speaking of the toad to Eve's ear with the speaking of the dove to Mary's ear at the Annunciation.[32] It was a commonplace of Christian theology that the incarnate Word entered into the Virgin not by her uterus but by her ear, which explains the iconography of those visual representations showing the dove of the Holy Spirit descending from Heaven on a ray of light directly into her ear. As God sends the Word of salvation to the Virgin's ear, so does Satan convey the word of damnation to Eve's. Milton's staging of Satan's first approach to Eve acquires unexpected richness when it is allowed to suggest visual allusions to such scenes in art.

124

While Satan is squatting like a toad at Eve's ear, Eve is dreaming of him as a beautiful angel visitant. We know several examples of mystery plays in which Satan appears to tempt Eve in Eden under the guise of a beautiful angel, and these examples would seem to suggest the appearance of similar representations in art, but I know of none from the later Middle Ages or the Renaissance.[33] Satan does appear as a beautiful angel to tempt Eve in several illuminations of the *Genesis B* manuscript, in accordance with the text of that Anglo-Saxon poem, but even if Milton saw those illuminations, very few others did, and we must conclude that Milton's presentation of the demonic tempter in Eve's dream is without direct counterpart in works of art readily accessible to him and to his readers. Satan's

36, 37

[30] Erwin Panofsky, *Tomb Sculpture: Four Lectures on its Changing Aspects from Ancient Egypt to Bernini* (ed. H. W. Janson), New York, 1964, p. 64, and fig. 258; and Eugene Bach, "Le Tombeau de François Ier de La Sarra-Montferrand à La Sarraz," *Congrès Archéologique de France* 110 (1952), 369-74.

[31] R. W. Lightbown, "Time and Death: A New Relief by Zumbo," *Victoria and Albert Museum Bulletin* 3 (1967), 43.

[32] A. B. Chambers, "Three Notes on Eve's Dream in *Paradise Lost*," PQ 46 (1967), 191-93.

[33] John K. Bonnell, "The Serpent with a Human Head in Art and in Mystery Play," *American Journal of Archaeology* 2nd ser., 21 (1917), pp. 279 and 283, cites the Anglo-Norman *Jeu d'Adam* of the mid-twelfth century as presenting Satan to Eve at first in *propria persona*, and also a fourteenth-century Cornish play which describes Satan appearing as an angel. See also Evans, *"Paradise Lost" and the Genesis Tradition*, pp. 195-96 and 202. Trapp, "Iconography," p. 169, finds in *Genesis B* the first artistic representation of the Tempter in the Garden as other than a speaking serpent.

appearance as an angel of light was not infrequent in art, but did not occur broadly in connection with Eve, and Milton's descriptions of him in this guise will be treated in the chapter on angels.[34]

SERPENTS

Milton provides lengthy descriptions of serpents at three points in *Paradise Lost*: in Book VII, we encounter the newly created order *serpentes*, as yet unsullied by any demonic associations; in Book IX, the descriptions are more detailed and elaborate, as this "fittest imp of fraud" represents the incarnate disguise for Satan's successful temptation of Eve; finally, in Book X we have the transformation of Satan and his followers into serpents, representing now the fullest available symbols of the sinister and debased.[35] The connotations inherent in Milton's descriptions at these three points of course differ in obvious and even predictable ways, but between Book VII and Book IX there are at least two rather curious denotative differences. The "hairy mane terrific" has disappeared entirely by Book IX when Satan enters into a serpent with "burnisht neck of verdant gold," and the absence of the earlier mane is indicated for a second time by the description of the serpent's "sleek enamelled neck" (VII, 497, and IX, 501 and 525).[36] The earlier account also describes the serpents as having wings (VII, 484),[37] a feature which does not appear at all in the more detailed descriptions of Book IX.

[34] Thomas Kranidas, "Satan's First Disguise," *ELN* 2 (1964), 14, makes the interesting suggestion that the disparity between Satan's appearance as a cherub and his reality is intentionally humorous, "a little joke on the matter of 'decency'" in Anglican usage. Trapp, "The Iconography of the Fall," p. 261, notes that "all early examples of differentiation between devil and serpent are English and range from the early eleventh to the fourteenth century" (see also pp. 240-41). Steadman, "Eve's Dream and the Conventions of Witchcraft," 570, points out that dream lore held that devils tempted women under the guise of angels of light.

[35] *PL* IV, 3-4 contains a passing but significant reference to the Dragon of the Apocalypse.

[36] It is interesting that Virgil described those sea serpents who devoured Laocoön as having manes (*Aeneid* II, 203-7), and it may well be that Milton simply borrowed Virgil's conception, and then forgot that he had done so. I have the impression that I may have seen other maned serpents at the Tree of Knowledge, but I can recall only one, that beautifully marked creature who is twined about the Tree in the mosaic at S. Apollinare in Classe, Ravenna.

[37] D. C. Allen, "Milton's Winged Serpents," *MLN* 59 (1944), 537-38, traces the conception of winged serpents back through science and legend to Isaiah 30. In art, winged serpents appeared at the Tree in a print of the Fall engraved by Theodor de Bry in the 1590 Frankfurt-am-Main edition of *Admiranda Narratio fida tamen, de commodis et incolarum ritibus Virginiae*, as also in paintings by Giorgio Vasari and Philippe Thomassin (pls. 171-72 in Ernst Guldan, *Eva und Maria*, Graz-Cologne, 1966). In each of these instances, the winged serpent coiled about the Tree has an adult human face, though wings are comparatively rare in such a configuration. Putto-headed serpents at the Tree are more often shown to be winged, as in the Holkham Picture Bible, the fifteenth-century French Book of Hours at the Bodleian Library, and in the sixteenth-century title-page print for Witart's *Traité des Misadventures de Personages Signalez*, Paris, 1578. Wings are even more common on those strange sphinx-like and camellike "serpents" which are sometimes placed at the Tree in medieval illuminations (see those reproduced in the John Rylands Library, *The Beginnings of Printed Book Illustration*, Manchester, 1933, pls. 10 and 11; in Laborde, *Bible Moralisée*, IV, pl. 788; in

The mane and wings give the creature a mythological aura distinguishing it from anything to be observed in nature. As a balance to these unnatural features, Milton treats the movements of the snakes in two lines which are models of acute observation and accurate description: "These as a line their long dimension drew,/ Streaking the ground with sinuous trace" (VII, 480-81). It is hard to see how that serpentine movement could be verbalized with greater visual precision, or given greater visual conviction. Even the alternating slow and fast movements which are characteristic of a crawling snake are conveyed through the contrasting speeds of the two lines—slowly drawing up the tail, and quickly thrusting forward the head and foreparts—as the aural effect is made to reinforce the physical image. Such passages convey direct and credible impressions of nature itself.

The most interesting serpent in *Paradise Lost* is, of course, the serpent-tempter of Book IX. The visual tradition provided Milton with several possible prototypes here, some quite well known and others not. At one point or another, he refers to each of the more popular types. On the other hand, he ignores all those esoteric forms which may be lumped together within an omnium-gatherum made up of medieval representations of the Tempter as a sphinx, a camel, or a salamander. J. B. Trapp observes that "in the Byzantine Octateuchs, and in them only, the Tempter is a composite, long-necked quadruped, with a camel's body and the head of a snake, the body of the snake forming the neck of the camel."[38] Just as curious, but usually more attractive, are those paintings which show the Tempter as a salamander, with a human face, a motif which enjoyed some limited popularity in the fifteenth century.[39] We find no hint of these creatures in *Paradise Lost*.

By Milton's time, the visual arts almost always represented the Tempter in the Garden either as a hybrid serpent with a human head or torso, or as a snake pure and simple. Of these, the zoomorphic serpent is the more ancient and persistent motif. The earliest known representations of the Fall show the serpent as a simple snake, coiled about the Tree, as we see him in the carved relief on the fourth-century sarcophagus of Junius Bassus at the Vatican.[40] Pictorial representations of serpents coiled about trees were well known in pre-Christian antiquity, and these ancient images doubtless supplied visual models for the development of Early Christian iconography. We should not, however, be deceived by the visual continuity here into postulating a continuity of meaning, as is sometimes done, but

---

Bonnell, "The Serpent with a Human Head," fig. 2; in Charles Wall, *Devils*, London, 1904, p. 63; and in *The Saint Albans Psalter* (ed. Otto Pächt), London, 1960, pl. 14). Dragons are frequently shown with wings: Biblical references connecting Satan with a dragon or serpent are provided in Edward Langton, *Satan: A Portrait*, London, n.d., pp. 38-40 and *passim*; Biblical passages relevant to Milton's verse are catalogued in Sims, *The Bible in Milton's Epics*.

[38] Trapp, "The Iconography of the Fall," p. 261 and pl. 7.

[39] This motif has been carefully traced by Robert A. Koch in "The Salamander in Van der Goes' *Garden of Eden*," *JWCI* 28 (1965), 323-26 and plates.

[40] Trapp, "The Iconography of the Fall," p. 261, notes that the earliest Christian monuments all show the serpent proffering the fruit in its mouth, but on p. 228 he qualifies this by saying that this motif does not appear in the catacomb and other early wall-paintings but only on sarcophagi.

should keep in mind that in the Summerian and Greek myths the serpent guards the tree, whereas in the Biblical interpretation the serpent has usurped the tree.[41]

In the late twelfth century, we encounter for the first time what was to become an immensely popular and persistent representation—the combination of a serpent's body with a woman's head or torso. This motif appears on an altar at Klosterneuburg, executed in 1181 by Nicolas of Verdun. The first extant literary reference to it occurred in Peter Comestor's commentary on Genesis, where the Venerable Bede is credited with explaining the appearance of the serpent with a woman's face as a reflection of the appeal of like to like in the Temptation of Eve.[42] In an influential article, John K. Bonnell marshaled evidence to show that this innovation was due to stage practice in the mystery plays, and though his argument is not accepted today in quite the sense in which he first advanced it, it is clear that religious drama at the least supplied strong reinforcement to the iconographic detail.[43] Whatever the origins, the developments are clear, as summarized by M. D. Anderson: "As the dialogue between Eve and the serpent developed in the later mystery plays, the popularity of the human-headed serpent increased, and there is a tendency for the tree to become a thick bush in which the body of an actor could have been hidden while his tail was prominently displayed below."[44]

There were a number of variations upon this basic representation. One of these showed the serpent with the head of a child or putto, as in the 1494 Lübeck Bible, and in Titian's painting of about 1570, later copied by Rubens, in addition to *171* medieval instances.[45] In the sixteenth and seventeenth centuries, we find a number of paintings in which the human portion of the hybrid is male, as with the beautiful figures painted by Vasari and Salviati.[46] An anonymous painting, from mid-six- *155, VI*

---

[41] Examples of the motif in pre-Christian art are reproduced in plates 1 and 4 in John Armstrong, *The Paradise Myth*, London, 1969, but when Armstrong discusses the snake at the Tree in *Paradise Lost*, he overlooks the critical distinction cited above.

[42] Trapp, "The Iconography of the Fall," p. 262; Rudwin, *The Devil in Legend and Literature*, p. 44; and Evans, *"Paradise Lost" and the Genesis Tradition*, pp. 170 and 181-82. No known work by Bede contains the reference ascribed to him, and the matter remains a bit of a mystery. Wall, *Devils*, p. 68, suggests that the first instance of a serpent with a human head appears in the Catacomb of St. Agnes, but recognizes that the painting may well not be contemporary with the formation of the catacomb.

[43] Bonnell, "The Serpent with the Human Head," 290-91; see also Trapp, "The Iconography of the Fall," p. 262, and Réau, *Iconographie* II, i, p. 84.

[44] Anderson, *Imagery of British Churches*, pp. 88-89.

[45] Theodor Ehrenstein, *Das Alte Testament in der Graphik*, Vienna, 1936 II, pl. 5, and Trapp, "The Iconography of the Fall," p. 254.

[46] Salviati painted a similar version of his *Fall* for the Church of S. Maria del Popolo in Rome, which is less interesting than the one reproduced here by courtesy of the Galleria Colonna; Trapp, "The Iconography of the Fall," p. 263, notes that he is aware of no certain instance before the Renaissance, and cites one painting attributed to Bronzino; identical engravings of the serpent with a male torso appear in the *Typus Praedestinationis*, Antwerp, 1630, and in Biverus, *Sacrum Oratorium* published by Plantin in 1634. Occasionally, the serpent may be shown with two heads, the female one addressing the man and the male head addressing the woman. See Didron *Christian Iconography*, II, p. 140 and Wall, *Devils*, p. 67; examples of two-headed serpents are reproduced in Laborde, *Bible Moralisée*, IV, pls. 759 and 768.

teenth-century Italy and strongly under the influence of Michelangelo, shows an enormously muscular male serpent-devil observing Eve's persuasion of Adam in what must surely be the only amusing representation of the Fall in art. In the latter part of the century, Andrea del Minga presents the serpent with a male torso and face, showing huge self-satisfaction at his triumph.

The serpent with a "lady visage" was vastly popular, so much so that it may be said to have dominated artistic conceptions of the Fall for three hundred years. In the sixteenth century, however, the zoological serpent again came into prominence, and the Tempter was quite often represented simply as a snake for the remainder of the period of our interest.[47] The visual influences shaping the seventeenth-century imagination were so divided that one might equally well expect a seventeenth-century poet to describe the Tempter as a serpent with a human torso, after Michelangelo and Raphael, as to follow Dürer and Cranach in thinking of a zoomorphic snake.

The choice would by no means have been automatic, and the fact that Milton chose as he did is significant. As for the human-serpent hybrid, Milton had two possibilities. He could have chosen a serpent with the torso and head of a man, which would have provided further possibilities for the beautification of his Satan. Had he done so, however, he would have opened the way for a sexual interpretation of the Fall (the handsome male serpent seducing Eve) which he obviously wished to avoid. A description of the serpent as "woman to the waist, and fair" would have led to different, but equally undesirable, possibilities. Milton indisputably believed in the subjection of wives to husbands, but he was not an antifeminist and could scarcely have put a "lady visage" on his Tempter without seeming to some readers to invite an identification of the devil with woman. Misinterpretation could also arise if the serpent-demon were given not just a feminine face but the actual face of Eve, as artists sometimes did. Even so astute a critic as Broadbent falls into the trap which Milton carefully avoided, when he reads *Paradise Lost* through the palimpsest of Raphael's Adam and Eve fresco, with its Eve-faced serpent, and suggests that Eve "has fallen in love with herself."[48] Had Milton wished to convey Broadbent's interpretation, he could scarcely have done better than to describe the scene Raphael painted, but he chose not to do so, and critics should not read into his poem an alien description. That Milton was strongly influenced by traditional images of the hybrid female-serpent, there can be no doubt, but he associated that image with the person of Sin, not with the episode of the Fall of Man.[49]

There is still another iconographically important example of the hybrid serpent-woman which we should consider because of its striking similarity to that passage in *Paradise Lost* (IV, 388-89) where the sight of Adam and Eve makes Satan "melt" into tears. This is the second such reference in Milton, the first being to those "tears such as angels weep" which Satan shed at the sight of his fallen

---

[47] Steadman, " 'Sin' and the Serpent of Genesis III," *MP* 54 (1957), 219.
[48] Broadbent, *Some Graver Subject*, London, 1960, p. 246.
[49] See Steadman's already cited " 'Sin' and the Serpent of Genesis III."

legions (I, 619-21). While Fowler is correct in noting the existence of "a strong iconographical tradition of angels mourning," and though one could cite many examples of angels actually shedding tears, as at the Crucifixion, none of these examples applies to the fallen angels.[50] Even in representations of Christ's *Harrowing of Hell*, where the demons are most distraught and come closest to mourning, I have never seen any shed even a single tear.[51]

The only representation I have been able to find of a tearful devil occurs in a marble statuary group of Adam, Eve, and Satan, carved in 1616 by Michelangelo Naccherino, in which the Tempter is shown with the lady visage and torso, and weeping over the first parents. It is an undistinguished, though competent, piece of journeyman sculpture by a pupil of Giambologna, but it is dramatically effective, in a saccharine kind of way, and apparently appealed strongly to the Medici, for they gave it what is perhaps the most conspicuous location in the Boboli Gardens, placing as a frontispiece to their garden this reminder of the lost paradise in Eden. In the seventeenth century, the principal entrance to the Boboli was through the Annalena entrance off the Via Romana. From that handsome gateway, a broad and graveled path leads into the grounds only to deadend after about fifty yards in a conspicuous grotto containing Naccherino's statuary group, at which point the path turns right to move on through the landscaped grounds. Today, visitors most commonly enter the Boboli Gardens alongside the Pitti Palace, and if they follow the full compass of those gardens, they may exit by the Annalena Gate, but in this way they come out with the grotto behind them, and rarely see it or the Naccherino figures inside. If we assume that Milton entered by the customary seventeenth-century route, he could not possibly escape seeing Naccherino's sculptured group. It represents a tearful Adam and Eve standing, with Eve leaning on Adam as though for support. At their feet is a seated demonic serpent-woman, her tail coiled behind Adam's feet. The Tempter looks up at them in pity and is reduced to tears. Art historian Eve Borsook describes the effect as "mawkish," and her judgment is impeccable.[52] Both in Naccherino and in Milton, Satan "melts" at the sight of Adam and Eve, and in both the demonic tears represent a sticky sentimentality.[53] I suggest that Milton was impressed by this unusual representation when he was in Florence, and that he either kept the image in mind or that it surfaced from his unconscious memory when he came to write that superbly ironic description of Satan weeping over his victims.

Even after he had decided to present his Tempter within the zoological form of a serpent, Milton still had other choices to make. Compositionally, the serpent

193, 194

[50] Fowler, *PL* I, 620n.

[51] There may be instances in the Hexameral literature, and something similar to Milton's account is found in Theodore Beza's *Abraham's Sacrifice*, lines 805-7.

[52] Borsook, *Florence*, p. 291; Borsook provides a map of the Boboli Gardens with number keys on p. 286, where Naccherino's marble group is numbered 41.

[53] Naccherino may merely have blundered into his effect, whereas Milton knew exactly what he was doing, despite Waldock's naive misreading of Satan here as "really sad, really regretful" (*"Paradise Lost" and its Critics*, p. 89). Evans (*"Paradise Lost" and the Genesis Tradition*, p. 229) catches the true spirit of Milton's treatment when he says that Satan is here acting "like a typical Elizabethan revenger."

was sometimes represented in a more or less erect posture, standing and/or moving alongside Eve; more often the serpent was represented as coiled around the trunk of the Tree. Milton chooses the first type for his primary narrative, in which there is a good deal of physical movement, but he does not ignore the latter type. That latter representation was so popular and so firmly fixed in the European imagination that seventeenth-century readers would have expected to find it somewhere in *Paradise Lost*, as indeed they could, though Milton had removed it from the Fall itself and placed it in Satan's report to Eve of how he acquired knowledge of the fruit: "About the mossy trunk I wound me soon,/ For high from ground the branches would require/ Thy utmost reach or Adam's" (IX, 589-91). That description of the scene accords well with most of the pictorial versions of the sixteenth and seventeenth centuries, which show the serpent wrapped about a trunk where the fruit is at a height requiring Eve to reach high. In his brief vignette, Satan also describes "all other beasts" as gathered about the Tree, as they frequently appear in paintings of the Fall and especially in Cranach, but as they do not appear at the Fall itself in *Paradise Lost*, when Milton wishes to concentrate all our attention upon Tempter, the tempted, and the fatal fruit. Milton has thus introduced virtually every visual detail which his audience had been conditioned to expect in accounts of the Fall, but has deployed them so that each contributes at a different point according to the demands of his own epic.

152, 171,
174
174

As for the actual tempter-serpent at the Fall, Milton chose to give him the dignity of standing like "some orator renowned/ In Athens or free Rome, where eloquence/ Flourished" (IX, 670-72). This standing serpent is an interesting phenomenon, and we may well be curious as to where Milton came upon the conception. Edward C. Baldwin in 1929 challenged the formerly held notion that the erect serpent was Milton's own imaginative invention, and sought instead to identify it with descriptions found in extracanonical Jewish writings.[54] Though stories of the erect serpent are surely to be found in rabbinical lore, Baldwin unfortunately ignored one critical difference: rabbinical descriptions always accord the serpent both hands and feet, which the serpent in *Paradise Lost* unmistakably lacks.[55] The rabbinical stories say of the serpent that "like man he stood upright upon two feet, and in height he was equal to the camel" before the Fall, and that after the Fall his hands and feet were hacked off. Angels descended to do the hacking, and the serpent's anguished cries "could be heard from one end of the world to the other."[56] A Miltonist who reads these stories will be impressed at once that they are not the kind of thing which was likely to have appealed to John Milton. Such a serpent as Baldwin suggests is probably related to the camellike tempter of the Byzantine manuscripts, but the conception certainly does not conform to Milton's.

[54] Edward C. Baldwin, "Some Extra-Biblical Semitic Influences upon Milton's Story of the Fall of Man," *JEGP* 28 (1929), 366-401.

[55] Baldwin was apparently not unaware that the rabbinical serpent was a biped (see his pp. 371 and 387), but was unwilling to allow this inconvenient fact to stand between him and his conclusion.

[56] The stories are to be found in Louis Ginzberg, *The Legends of the Jews*, Philadelphia, 1909-38, vol. I; for the quotations, see pp. 71 and 78, and the notes thereon in vol. V.

J. B. Trapp has identified several erect serpents in art, which correspond directly with Milton's descriptions. Of the first, he is somewhat uncertain—that found in Gallery K of the catacomb of St. Priscilla in the Via Salaria in Rome—but three are quite pertinent. These are in the Grandval Bible of about 840, in an eleventh-century Exultet Roll from southern Italy, and in the 1538 Bible published by Trechsel at Lyon.[57] Trapp has clearly established the existence in art prior to Milton of what we might call Miltonic serpents, but the artistic tradition was considerably broader than his four examples might suggest. In the Judgment scene which takes place immediately after the Fall, the artist of *Genesis B* shows the serpent standing erect while being judged. On the bronze doors of Augsburg   *41* Cathedral, dating from the first quarter of the eleventh century, serpents are represented standing on their tails, as also in the twelfth-century fresco of St.-Savin in Poitou,[58] while numerous examples may be found from the fourteenth and fifteenth centuries.[59] The motif enters the sixteenth century with a tapestry of 1518 at La Chaise-Dieu, Haute-Loire, which shows very much the same type of undulating erect serpent as was found in the Middle Ages.[60] By this time, the visual motif of the standing serpent had acquired a long history and wide distribution throughout Europe, but its most significant days lay just ahead, for both quantity of exposure and quality of production. In 1534, Luther's German Bible appeared for the first time with a frontispiece prepared by Lucas Cranach for Genesis which continued to be used in later issues. Cranach's print shows the uni-   *88* verse as a circle, with the Garden of Eden in the center medallion: and there, on a meadow in the midst of the Garden, Adam stands talking with Eve, while an erect serpent stands a bit forward and to the left, in alert concentration upon their every word and gesture. The motif of the Miltonic serpent reaches what is almost its finest artistic expression here, but Cranach was to be outdone by a Flemish tapestry of the mid-century, to which we shall turn shortly. In the meanwhile, there appeared in the Bibles published at Lyons a print attributed to Holbein but which I cannot conceive of his having executed, which represents the artistic nadir of this particular type: here we see the erect serpent standing like a carrot, topped not by the usual serpentine head, but by the bloated and unpleasantly dyseptic visage of an elderly dowager. Several decades later, Hieronymus Wierix did a   *190* pleasant but undistinguished version of the erect serpent moving by the coiling of its tail,[61] and in the seventeenth century the same type is shown in a *Judgment of Adam and Eve* in the triptych of the *Last Judgment* attributed to G. Klotzas, in the Hellenic Institute at Venice.

Of these representations, the vast majority would impress most viewers as convincing members of the order *serpentes*, when considered for shape and general

---

[57] Trapp, "Iconography of the Fall," pp. 227, 237, 239, and 256.

[58] Réau, *Iconographie*, II, i, p. 86.

[59] Guldan, *Eva und Maria*, figs. 48-50; M. Funck, *Le Livre belge à gravures*, Paris and Brussels, 1925, p. 19; Wilhelm Worringer, *Die Altdeutsche Buchillustration*, Munich, 1912, fig. 6 on p. 37.

[60] Guldan, *Eva und Maria*, fig. 68.

[61] Reproduced in Ehrenstein, *Das Alte Testament in der Graphik*, fig. 48.

appearance.[62] What does contradict our direct observation of serpents in nature, of course, is the erect stance and curious movements of these snakes. Both in the paintings and in *Paradise Lost*, the means of locomotion are zoologically impossible, but imaginatively conceivable. In an interesting article on Milton's serpent, the poet John Ciardi assumes that Milton had "to invent a rather fanciful rear-wheel drive, details of which he well-advisedly keeps a bit vague." Ciardi finds Milton's descriptions here to be "ridiculous," but goes on to make the conventional apology that Milton's visual inadequacy is more than redeemed by his music, calling the whole passage "an example of poetry elevated to sublimity by the rich and powerful development of its diction into music-like themes."[63] The musical effects are beyond question successful, but there is surely need to challenge Ciardi's judgment that the description itself is ridiculous. What Ciardi wittily describes as the "rear-wheel-snake" would not have seemed odd to an audience whose visual imagination had been shaped by a centuries-old artistic tradition of just such snakes.[64]

Milton was providing a precise and accurate verbal transcription of this whole visual tradition. His tempter-serpent did not move "with indented wave," crawling along,

> Prone on the ground, as since, but on his rear,
> Circular base of rising folds, that towered
> Fold above fold a surging maze, his head
> Crested aloft, and carbuncle his eyes.
>
> (ix, 496-500)

In this traditional view, the serpent moves by touching parts of his rear coils to the ground, while most of his fluctuations are above the ground: "So varied he, and of his tortuous train/ Curled many a wanton wreath in sight of Eve" (ix, 516-17). In so doing, the tempter-serpent makes the devious appear straightforward, and Milton carefully keeps this moral significance before us, but he does not thereby sacrifice any acuteness of the visual sense: "He leading swiftly rolled/ In tangles, and made intricate seem straight,/ To mischief swift" (ix, 631-33).

The particular iconographic tradition upon which Milton was drawing in these verses reached what I regard as its finest artistic expression in a series of tapestries executed in Flanders and delivered to the Medici in Florence during the *148-54* 1550's. This series treats the Eden saga from the Creation of Man through the *IV, V* Expulsion from the Garden. Again and again the visual details of these tapestries accord most strikingly with those of *Paradise Lost* in ways which have not pre-

[62] Even apart from the minority which are shown with human heads, professional herpetologists might find instances of inaccurate details, but these are not directly pertinent to our concerns either in art or in poetry.

[63] John Ciardi, "A Poem Talks to Itself," *Saturday Review* (January 24, 1959), 12.

[64] The illustrations of *Paradise Lost* indicate how the tradition was lost. Medina's engraving for Tonson's 1688 edition (and even more, his original drawing in the Victoria and Albert Museum) shows a still reasonably traditional version of the standing serpent, though not so credibly executed as the earlier examples we have cited. With E. F. Burney's engraving for the 1799 edition and the copies of Flaxman for the 1808 *Poems*, the artists are so far removed from the tradition that all credibility and even balance is lost, and what we see is pure fantasy.

viously, to my knowledge, been called to the attention of Miltonists. Milton was in a position to have seen these tapestries while he was in Florence in 1638-39, but there is no way to demonstrate beyond doubt whether or not he did.

The serpent in the Fall tapestry provides an almost perfect visual counterpart *152, IV* to Milton's verbal description: green and gold thread was used to achieve what Milton described as the "burnisht neck of verdant gold, erect . . . ," and Milton's designation of his eyes as "carbuncle" precisely captures the stonelike hardness, shape, and deep-red color of those eyes (IX, 500-501). Milton's words also vividly convey the posture of this serpent as he "fluctuates disturbed, yet comely, and in act/ Raised, as of some great matter to begin" (IX, 668-69). Milton's medium allows him as a poet to go beyond the artist, and to introduce a direct comparison to "some orator renowned/ In Athens or free Rome," and by that simile he adds depth and dignity to the figure of the Tempter, but at the same time he keeps the visual impression before us of one who "stood in himself collected," and we are told that "so standing, moving, or to heighth upgrown/ The Tempter all impassioned thus began" (IX, 670-78).

In Book X we have Milton's final descriptive identification of Satan with serpents, and here there is no disguise, only revelation. When the triumphant Satan returns from earth to mount his "throne of royal state," his triumph speedily becomes horror, and the applause turns into a dismal hissing, as he and all his followers feel themselves transformed into loathsome serpents. What had once concealed his identity has now become an expression of his essence, and his pretense to Godhead has reached full fruition in a bestial incarnation. Milton had accorded him great beauty, and had preserved that beauty so long as it could possibly contribute to his epic and his religious purposes, and then at the moment of greatest dramatic intensity he transformed all the demonic princes into a pit of swarming vipers.[65] We have by now seen many artistic versions of the Fall of the Rebel Angels which showed the transformation of Satan from splendid Lucifer to repulsive fiend, sometimes portraying the change through increasingly distorted images, inch by inch from top to bottom of a canvas. Pictures and carvings of demons with humanoid torsos and serpentine lower quarters exist in numbers too great to count, but all such representations are only arrested images; the artists cannot carry us visually throughout the process of transformation itself. Take for example the humanoid devil whom Guido Reni has shown under the feet of Michael, where all below the waist is coiling serpent. Reni can make us see that stasis as Satan's situa- *28* tion, even as expressing something of his essence, but he cannot show us an on-going process, in which the serpentine scales steadily invade the whole body, until it becomes one writhing mass. Only a poet could do that, and Milton did with incomparable sensuous immediacy:

[65] Literary sources and analogues have been suggested in considerable numbers: see particularly Merritt Y. Hughes, "Satan Now Dragon Grown (*PL* X, 525)," *EA* 20 (1967), 356-69, and especially 366-67, and also Katharine Garvin, "Snakes in the Grass," *REL* 2 (April, 1961), 11-27. A similar incident may be found in Phineas Fletcher, *The Purple Island* (1633), Canto VII, 11, reprinted in Kirkconnell, *The Celestial Cycle*, p. 282.

His visage drawn he felt to sharp and spare,
His arms clung to his ribs, his legs entwining
Each other, till supplanted down he fell
A monstrous serpent on his belly prone,
Reluctant, . . .

(X, 511-15)

Here and throughout his description of that serpentine transformation, Milton has given us not a single picture, but rather a series of pictures in motion. Elements of the traditional iconography are surely present here, but Milton has made of them a new synthesis which only a poet could conceive and which only he among poets has created to such visual and tactile effect.

VII

Sin and Death

THE INFERNAL TRINITY

In the allegorical figures of Sin and Death, Milton achieved a virtually perfect adaptation of religious ideas to character and story.[1] Sin is "conceived" in the mind of Satan when he decides to supplant the Supreme Deity, and springs forth from his head in the beautiful form of his "perfect image" (II, 764). She does not represent sins, though she is their mother, but only Sin itself, the usurpation upon Deity. She is not even a part of creation in any proper sense, and suggests the creature's repudiation of his created being in order to "be God," with a consequent warring upon the whole created order. Satan's love for her, and intercourse with her, is but the sealing of his union with his own self-deified self. This incestuous union of Satan (as creation repudiated) with Sin (as pseudo-creation) brings forth Death, the enemy of all creation and of all life. The relation between these two extensions of Satan's perverted being is one of repulsion-attraction, culminating in Death's rape of Sin. From this second incestuous union are born the Hell Hounds. This yelping horde of monsters, products of a union marked equally with lust and hate, symbolizes those myriad sins which Satan has spawned upon the universe.

The incident is rife with all the "loathsomeness" which Voltaire found in it, and to which he objected that it "cannot but shock a reader of delicate taste."[2] Had Milton been in a position to reply to Voltaire's objection, I am confident that he would have said, quite simply, "yes, that is just the response I wished to evoke." Through this Infernal Trinity of Satan, Sin, and Death, Milton was able to associate the demonic with distortions and horrors equal to those which characterized the hideous fiends of tradition, while still preserving the attractiveness of Satan. In this way, he incorporated into his epic vision both the seductive appeal of evil, and the revolting depravities which result from that appeal. As Knott has pointedly observed, "Milton scarcely could have suggested the hideousness of evil without resorting to allegory, since he was unwilling to compromise Satan's dignity by endowing him with the attributes of a medieval demon. By giving Sin and Death an independent existence, Milton was able to establish them as forces outside of nature driven by a demonic compulsion to destroy it."[3]

[1] A contrary judgment is expressed by William Empson, *Milton's God*, p. 59: "The episode of Sin is bad allegory, because it makes the biology of the angels too hard to get clear." Though Empson is often wrong, he is almost always intelligent, which makes this comment particularly puzzling; surely he puts the cart before the horse, as though Milton's purpose in this allegory was to illustrate the biology of the angels. But perhaps he is being whimsical.

[2] Shawcross, *Milton: The Critical Heritage*, p. 254. Voltaire strangely fails to understand certain aspects of the allegory, for instance the meaning of the incest.

[3] Knott, *Milton's Pastoral Vision*, p. 131.

Milton did not create the Infernal Trinity *ex nihilo*, but his conception differs in interesting ways from earlier forms. First among these was the demonic triprosope, or three-faced Satan, whose most famous example comes in the final canto of Dante's *Inferno*. Each of the three faces is endowed with a mouth, and each mouth of the metaphysical author of all treason is chewing upon one of the three greatest human traitors, Judas, Cassius, and Brutus. Dante's description conveys the ultimate futility of Satan's attempt to usurp the place of God, an attempt which can only redound upon himself as his own countenance becomes a grotesque parody of the Holy Trinity. This profound insight into the nature of the demonic pretension was not even originated by Dante. At least as early as 1225, a stained glass window from Troyes Cathedral represented the devil with three faces: the central one combines the features of a monkey with those of a parrot (both creatures known for their attempts to imitate higher forms of being), while two serpent heads emerge from his temples. In 1303, Giotto painted Satan in the Scrovegni Chapel as an elephantine king of Hell, enthroned with two serpents coming out of his ears, while the Florentine Baptistry mosaic of about 1290 shows a much slimmer Satan with a bull-like head out of whose ears serpents extend, while each mouth devours a human sinner. The *Inferno* in the Camposanto at Pisa, perhaps painted by Orcagna, shows Satan as king of Hell without the serpents, but with three demonic faces in his head, and the same arrangement was followed at San Gimignano by Taddeo di Bartoli about 1393. In the later fifteenth century, Botticelli did at least two sketches of the three-headed Satan, while Grünewald about 1523-24 represented the demonic trinity by three heads monstrously joined within a common halo. The last version with which I am familiar appears in the dome fresco of the Last Judgment painted in 1578 for the Cathedral of Florence by Vasari and Federigo Zuccari.

In addition to the three-faced Satans in the Dante pattern, we find also a tradition of separating and at least symbolically individuating the three persons of the Infernal Trinity in ways which at least approach the Miltonic pattern. The analogues and potential sources of Milton's conception of Sin and Death have been carefully and fruitfully explored in the literary background,[4] but here as elsewhere too little attention has been devoted to comparable treatments in the visual arts. Amy Lee Turner has suggested a possible source for Milton's demonic trinity in "The Christian Knight Map of the World" engraved by Hondius, where we see

---

[4] See the notes in the edition by Hughes, and that by Fowler, as well as the following articles: Arlene A. Swidler, "Milton's *Paradise Lost* ii, 866-70," *Expl.* 17 (1959), item 41; Dustdoor, "Legends of Lucifer in Early English and in Milton"; Robert C. Fox, "The Allegory of Sin and Death in *Paradise Lost*," *MLQ* 24 (1963), 354-64; Steadman, "Grosseteste on the Genealogy of Sin and Death," *N&Q* 204 (1959), 367-68, and "Milton and Saint Basil: The Genesis of Sin and Death," *MLN* 73 (1958), 83-84; Dick Taylor, Jr., "Milton's Treatment of the Judgment and the Expulsion in *Paradise Lost*," *TSE* 10 (1960), 61. For the classical background for such personifications, see T.B.L. Webster, "Personification as a Mode of Greek Thought," *JWCI* 17 (1954), 10-21, and E. H. Gombrich, "Personification" in *Classical Influences on European Culture A.D. 500-1500* (ed. R. R. Bolgar), Cambridge, 1971, pp. 247-57.

the Christian surrounded by figures labeled Diabolus, Peccatum, and Mors.[5] Of these, Diabolus is too distorted to conform to Milton's Satan, while Mors is too osseous, but Peccatum comes very close to Sin in being a woman to the waist, but thereafter a serpent, who rolls on the coils of a snaky tail ending in a sting. The differences cited render the map dubious as a source, but as an analogue it is both valuable and suggestive.

A similar analogue may be found in the engraving by Crispin van de Passe I for Thomas Scot's *Vox Dei* of 1623, where Christ stands triumphant on the three figures of a skeleton representing Death, a toothy whale's maw representing Satan or Hell, and a serpentine form with a lovely female head representing Sin. Though the trinitarian plan is analogous to what we find in *Paradise Lost*, the details here differ at least as much as in the Hondius engraving, and I doubt that we shall ever find a precise equivalent in art to Milton's descriptions. As always, Milton was eclectic, and for a satisfactory comparison between his allegorical figures and pictorial traditions we must cast our nets far more widely. When we do so, we shall find that Milton's Sin incorporates more elements from pictorial tradition than does Death, and since Death presents less complex problems, we shall begin with him.

89

DEATH

For hundreds of years before Milton's time, tombs had been adorned with the recumbent figures of the deceased, reclining undisturbed as if in sleep,[6] but following the ravaging of Europe by the Black Plague in the fourteenth century those peaceful and reassuring figures gave way to new and horrendous images of death.[7] From the first appearance in Tuscany of "a decayed corpse, consumed by snakes and toads" in the fourteenth century, through the first visualization of the Dance of Death in the fifteenth century, the tradition of macabre representations became increasingly widespread while the number of gruesome details multiplied. In place of the peacefully sleeping *gisant* or the kneeling *orantes* which adorned monuments

[5] Amy Lee Turner, "Milton and Jodocus Hondius the Elder."

[6] From the eleventh century on, Life and Death were often placed near the Cross at the Crucifixion, but these personifications represent a different tradition; see Gertrud Schiller, *Iconography of Christian Art* (trans. Janet Seligman), Greenwich, Conn., 1971, II, pp. 114-15.

[7] See Meiss, *Painting in Florence and Siena after the Black Death*, especially pp. 74-75; Emile Mâle, *Religious Art*, pp. 140-47; Henriette s' Jacob, *Idealism and Realism: A Study of Sepulchral Symbolism*, Leiden, 1954, especially pp. 46-47; and Erwin Panofsky, *Tomb Sculpture, passim*; Raimond van Marle, *Iconographie de l'art profane au moyen-âge et à la renaissance*, The Hague, 1931-32, II, pp. 361-414; T.S.R. Boase, *Death in the Middle Ages: Mortality, Judgment and Remembrance*, London, 1972, especially pp. 102, 106, and 109. For brief but helpful résumés of the theme as developed into modern times, see G. Duthuit, "Représentations de la Mort," *Cahiers d'art* 14 (1939), 25-39; E. Carleton Williams, "The Dance of Death in Painting and Sculpture in the Middle Ages," *Journal of the British Archaeological Association*, 3rd ser., I (1937), 229-57, and "Mural Paintings of the Three Living and the Three Dead in England," *Journal of the British Archaeological Association*, 3rd ser., VII (1942), 31-40.

in earlier centuries, we now have the decaying, ghastly, and worm-infested cadavers known as the *transis*. Sometimes two images appear together, as in the tomb of the Duchess of Suffolk at Ewelme in Oxfordshire, where one effigy represents the Duchess in idealized beauty, and another shows her corpse as if in the actual process of physical decay.[8] Frequently, inscriptions in Latin or in the vernacular were appended to remind the viewer that his own body would be subject to the same desiccation and corruption, and to admonish him to think of the state of his soul.

Three stages of death were represented in these admonitory *transi* carvings, and those stages are enumerated in the epitaph for Henry Chichele in Canterbury Cathedral. The first stage was the *caro vilis*, meaning the vile flesh, in which the corpse was presented as lifeless, and sometimes shown with the incisions made by the embalmers. The second stage was the *vermis*, in which worms were shown crawling in and out of the body, as the flesh rotted away in the process of decomposition. The final stage was the *pulvis*, in which either a simple skeleton, or a shriveled-up corpse or mummified body might be represented.[9] Skeletons were represented with some flesh hanging like rags from the bones until the sixteenth century, when the completely fleshless skeleton became increasingly popular.

During the Italian Renaissance, there had been a period of respite from the atrocious realism of such presentations of death, but with the sixteenth century and the Counter Reformation a new ghoulishness became apparent, culminating in the seventeenth century. As Mâle summarizes the process, "the tombs of the fifteenth century were consoling; those of the seventeenth are appalling."[10] The devotional exercises introduced by the Jesuits were strongly influential here, urging men to think more of the immortal state of the soul than of the temporal state of the body. Death was presented as ghastly, and viewers were shocked into recognition and preparation. Mâle has indicated both intent and effect:

> The image of Death seems to be even more forbidding in the seventeenth century than in the fifteenth. The Dance of Death preserved a generalized character: it expressed the theological idea that Death, after Adam's transgression, became one with human nature and represented the price of sin. In the seventeenth century the menace of Death is more direct: it is aimed not at man in general, but at each Christian in particular. The vacant-eyed skulls sculpted on tombs look into the eyes of the passerby, command him to stop and put to him that fearful question which is basic to *The Spiritual Exercises*: "You want to wait until tomorrow to be just, temperate, charitable, but are you sure of tomorrow?"[11]

Although the Dance of Death seems to me no less horrible because of its generalized character, Mâle is surely correct in his emphasis upon the highly individuated

[8] Anderson, *History and Imagery in British Churches*, p. 148.
[9] Jacob, *Idealism and Realism*, p. 48.
[10] Mâle, *Religious Art*, p. 182.
[11] Emile Mâle, *L'Art religieux de la fin du XVIe siècle du XVIIe siècle et du XVIIIe siècle*, Paris, 1951, p. 227.

and particularized threat of Death in seventeenth-century art. In Protestant as in Roman Catholic tombs, the viewer was repeatedly reminded that he, too, would soon be food for worms, with the strong suggestion that now was the time for repentance and the beginning of a Christian life. In November of 1639, the Jesuits celebrated a mass in the Gesù in Rome for the repose of the souls of their benefactors, and staged a pageant of Death as a part of the service. Menacing skeletons were prominently featured in the action, and one seized hold of Adam and Eve after they have "eaten" their death, but the frightening prospects were put into proper theological perspective by a mournful figure of Death, stricken with grief because it has been conquered, as an inscription indicates: "as in Adam we die, so in Christ we live."[12] In art works throughout the seventeenth century, the fragility of human life was again and again emphasized, as we have seen in the sculpture by Zumbo in which wax figures represent the various stages of decomposition before our very eyes, while toads, worms, and rats gnaw the rotting flesh.

90

Whereas Voltaire correctly recognized the shocking quality of Milton's allegory, he might have been less offended by what he regarded as Milton's excesses had he recalled the visual alternatives available in the sixteenth and seventeenth centuries. When considered against the background just sketched, Milton's conception of Death will appear both restrained and tactful. This restraint becomes more marked the more closely we compare the details of Milton's description of Death with the visual counterparts in art. Milton concentrates upon psychological terror, and minimizes the physical, even eliminating the most basic of its elements. Here Broadbent reads carelessly when he associates Milton's Death with Holbein's woodcuts of the Dance of Death, and with the emblems where "Death is the skeleton, pitiably clad in rags or ragged flesh, that Milton and his literary sources describe." Milton describes nothing of the sort: his Death is not a skeleton, and there is not even a hint of rags and flesh. But as Broadbent sees it, Death was treated "as in a cartoon." He thinks Milton "had inklings that more could be done with it" but that he "failed largely because the cartoon treatment was more congenial to him," and he refers to what he calls "repellent organic imagery."[13] But there is no organic imagery associated directly with Death in *Paradise Lost*, and the analogy to a cartoon breaks down entirely when we reflect that cartoons are based upon lines, and note that Milton emphatically denies the relevance of line or contour to his Death. Death is

> the other shape
> If shape it might be called that shape had none
> Distinguishable in member, joint, or limb,
> Or substance might be called that shadow seemed. . . .
>
> (II, 666-69)

There is not even a single bone here. What we have is an example of poetic legerde-

---

[12] James Lees-Milne, *Saint Peter's*, Boston, 1967, p. 261, and *Relazione del Solenne Funerale e Catafalco fatto dalli Padri della Compagnia di Giesu*, Rome, 1639, for an account of the pageant, which was enacted after Milton had left Rome.

[13] Broadbent, *Some Graver Subject*, p. 131.

main achieved through the masterly use of oxymoron: there must be some "shape" if there is to be any image at all, but that shape is itself shapeless, as Milton immediately indicates. We have the shuddering effects of the *caro vilis*, the *vermis*, and the *pulvis*, but are denied every single detail which went into those grisly visions. Coleridge's comment on these lines is as nearly definitive as criticism can be:

> The grandest efforts of poetry are where the imagination is called forth, not to produce a distinct form, but a strong working of the mind, still offering what is still repelled, and again creating what is again rejected; the result being what the poet wishes to impress, namely, the substitution of a sublime feeling of the unimaginable for a mere image. I have sometimes thought that the passage just read might be quoted as exhibiting the narrow limit of painting, as compared with the boundless power of poetry: painting cannot go beyond a certain point; poetry rejects all control, all confinement. Yet we know that sundry painters have attempted pictures of the meeting between Satan and Death at the gates of Hell; and how was Death represented? Not as Milton has described him, but by the most defined thing that can be imagined—a skeleton, the dryest and hardest image that it is possible to discover; which, instead of keeping the mind in a state of activity, reduces it to the merest passivity,—an image, compared with which a square, a triangle, or any other mathematic figure, is a luxuriant fancy.[14]

Having denied his Death any distinguishable members, or joints, or limbs, Milton does allow him the attributes traditionally associated with Death. His color is black —"black it stood as night," and in another instance "her black attendant Death" (II, 670, and VII, 547)—a characteristic which attends many artistic versions of Death, from the medieval illuminated manuscripts in which he is shown "black as soot" down through the great figures of Death painted black for the 1639 pageant in the Gesù Church.[15]

The artists sometimes armed Death with a spear or dart, sometimes with a scythe: Milton gives the scythe to Time—"whatever thing/ The scythe of Time mows down" (x, 605-6)—and instead arms Death with "a dreadful dart," elsewhere referred to as his "deadly arrow" (II, 672, 811, and XI, 491). In Bosch's *Death and the Miser*, at the National Gallery in Washington, Death is armed with a dart or long arrow, while Peter Bruegel the Elder in his *Triumph of Death* supplies scythes to the skeletal marauders in the foreground and darts to those in the background. Milton's English contemporary Thomas Cross uses both in his *Memento Mori* engraved at about the time Milton was beginning to concentrate upon *Paradise Lost*.[16] Both of these attributes were associated with Death, and yet

[14] S. T. Coleridge, *Coleridge's Shakespearean Criticism* (ed. John Middleton Raysor), London, n.d. [1962?], II, pp. 103-4, and see also Ruskin, *Works*, IV, p. 291.

[15] Didron, *Christian Iconography*, II, p. 156.

[16] Jacob, *Idealism and Realism*, pp. 62 and 235, traces the origin of the spear as an attribute of Death to about 1470, while Erwin Panofsky, *Studies in Iconology*, New York, 1939, pp. 69-90, traces the use of the scythe. Osgood cites similarities and differences between

the choice between them was not arbitrary: the scythe seems more appropriate for mass destruction, whereas the spear or dart was the weapon most appropriate for individual targets, particular persons.

Milton's contemporaries were so accustomed to artistic views of Death attacking individual human beings with a spear that Milton's version would have come as something of a shock, albeit a shock full of recognition and significance: the first threat of Death's spear is not against man, his accustomed victim in art, but against Satan, and his ultimate threat at the end of time is also against Satan (XII, 432). The image of Death shaking his dreadful dart against a frightened human soul is here transposed to represent the return of evil upon itself, to imply the self-destructive, self-defeating qualities of Sin and of Satan's kingdom. Milton not only introduces an encounter of epic proportions, in accord with his literary form, but by at once invoking and revising the visual tradition he introduces a strong note of Christian hope in the very presence of the demonic trinity.

Another traditional attribute which Milton provides Death is "the likeness of a kingly crown" (II, 673). The image was a common one, and yet Milton's treatment of it has uncommon iconographic overtones. It is particularly striking because the only crown in Hell is the crown of Death. Milton provides Satan with the most stunningly ornate throne in literature, but he never gives fallen Satan the dignity of a crown. In this Milton is at odds with a popular element of visual tradition, in which Satan is frequently shown with a crown.[17] Milton's choice is always significant both for what he includes and what he excludes: here he is purposely using familiar visual details to suggest an important understanding: Satan is not supreme even in Hell, despite his fustian that it is "better to reign in Hell than serve in Heaven" (I, 263), for he has brought forth out of his own pretension an offspring who is now crowned as his superior and who will eventually destroy even him. Death makes his claim in unequivocal words when he declares to Satan that in Hell "I reign king, and to enrage thee more,/ Thy king and lord" (II, 698-99). In the dramatic encounter between Death and Satan, we see a prefiguration of the end of Satan.

Ultimately Christ's heel will crush both Sin and Death, and "fix far deeper in [Satan's] head their stings" (XII, 432), but in the meanwhile they have important dramatic and symbolic roles to play as surrogates for the repulsiveness and horror which in the visual tradition had accumulated about the devils themselves. Within the divine plan, they serve for refuse disposal, "to lick up the draff and filth/

Thanatos in Euripides and Milton's Death, and notes that Thanatos carries a sword not a dart (*The Classical Mythology of Milton's English Poems*, pp. 26-27). See also the *Memento Mori* by Thomas Cross, reproduced as plate 169b in Hind's *Engraving in England in the Sixteenth and Seventeenth Centuries*, vol. III.

[17] English pictures of Death as King of Terrors are treated in Frederick Burgess, *English Churchyard Memorials*, London, 1963, p. 220, and Frank Kendon, *Mural Paintings in English Churches During the Middle Ages*, London, 1923, p. 195; see also Erwin Panofsky, *Albrecht Dürer*, Princeton, 1971, p. 153 and pl. 207, and F. Douce, Holbein's *Dance of Death*, London, 1858, pls. 13, and 15. For a fine literary analysis of Milton's Death, see Joseph H. Summers, *The Muse's Method: An Introduction to "Paradise Lost,"* New York, 1968, pp. 47-55.

Which man's polluting sin with taint hath shed/ On what was pure, till crammed and gorged, nigh burst/ With suckt and glutted offal, . . ." (x, 630-33). In his perverse and unwitting accord with providence, Satan promises Sin and Death that they will "be fed and filled/ Immeasurably, all things shall be your prey," and this is the only promise which he ever keeps (II, 843-44). Death is the ultimate and infinite scavenger, and his appetite is ravenous. Metaphorically, he is like some great vulture, drawn by "a scent . . . Of carnage, prey innumerable," and can "taste/ The savor of death from all things there that live" (x, 267-69). Pining with an eternal famine, he declares that all life "too little seems/ To stuff this maw, this vast unhidebound corpse" (x, 597-607).

This devouring of human bodies, the insatiable appetite "to stuff this maw" with carnage, corresponds primarily with representations of Satan in art, rather than with pictorial renditions of Death itself. Visually, Satan was characterized as gluttonously engorging himself with human sinners, stuffing his jaws with them as he sits upon his throne in hell, in art works extending from the thirteenth century into the seventeenth. This widespread visualization of Satan as the great devourer engorging humanity is theologically apposite, but Milton could scarcely afford to incorporate this imagery into his epic Satan, and so he reverses the visual roles conventionally associated with Satan and Death. As he has done elsewhere, so here he preserves the attractiveness of Satan, and associates the revolting image with Death who replaces his father as the devourer of human flesh.[18]

SIN

Aside from the physical attributes of blackness, crown, and dart, and the future activity of devouring, Milton purposely describes Death in such a way that he can be visualized only numinously and minimally. Sin, on the other hand, is visualized with the most vivid and graphic details. Let us note the earliest description which Milton provides of Sin sitting at the Gate of Hell:

> The one seemed woman to the waist, and fair,
> But ended foul in many a scaly fold

[18] For Satan devouring sinners, see also Nicolò Pisano's pulpit carving in Siena, and the Last Judgment paintings by Giotto at Padua, by Taddeo di Bartoli at San Gimignano, and by Vasari and Zuccari in Florence. I have not cited the open maw of Leviathan swallowing sinners into Hell, though it is metaphorically apposite; see figs. 33, 42, 43, 48, 102, 104. It is far more difficult to find pictorial images of Death devouring mankind, though one occasionally encounters hints to this effect, as in Baldung Grien's *Death and the Woman* where Death is apparently chewing on a woman even as he kisses her (reproduced in van Marle, *Iconographie*, II, p. 398). A somewhat related visual concept appears in the *Last Judgment* by Van Eyck at the Metropolitan in New York, where the specter of Death is shown under the feet of a victorious Michael, as Death defecates the bodies of the damned into Hell, a conception which was taken over in a later painting by Petrus Christus; see Panofsky, *Early Netherlandish Painting*, I, pp. 238-39. Michael Lieb, *The Dialectics of Creation: Patterns of Birth and Regeneration in "Paradise Lost,"* Amherst, Mass., 1970, p. 29, discusses the association with Satan in *Paradise Lost* of intestinal and digestive imagery.

Voluminous and vast, a serpent armed
With mortal sting: about her middle round
A cry of Hell Hounds never ceasing barked
With wide Cerberean mouths full loud, and rung
A hideous peal: yet, when they list, would creep,
If aught disturbed thir noise, into her womb,
And kennel there, yet there still barked and howled
Within unseen. Far less abhorred than these
Vexed Scylla bathing in the sea that parts
Calabria from the hoarse Trinacrian shore.

(ii, 650-61)

Three visual elements are combined here: the fair shape of a woman above the waist, the scaly folds of a serpent below, and around the middle the yelping Hell Hounds. To each of these some attention must now be given.

The literary ancestry of Sin has been thoroughly explored,[19] and within recent years there has been increasing interest in the visual analogues. As early as 1917, John H. Bonnell suspected that there might have been some connection between Milton's Sin and the visual tradition, but his suggestion was made with great reticence: "Milton may have a shadowy recollection of some of the numerous examples of Christian art in which the serpent tempter is given a form half woman and half serpent."[20] In 1948, C. H. Collins Baker suggested other loose visual parallels when he wrote that "Ripa's image of Deceit is somewhat alike: a woman; from the middle down, two serpent's tails," and then went on to propose a quite precise one: "Francis Barlow's representation of 'The World' in his frontispiece to Canto iv of Benlowes' *Theophila* (1652) might almost have been in Milton's eye when he described Sin."[21] In 1956, John M. Steadman made the first unequivocal association of Milton's Sin with pictorial representations of the serpent-woman in

91

[19] For the literary background, Ann Gossman has suggested the influence of Prudentius in her "Milton, Prudentius, and the Brood of Sin," *N&Q*, 202 (1957), 439-40; somewhat exotically, John Illo postulates the South American opossum as Milton's inspiration in his "Animal Sources for Milton's Sin and Death," *N&Q* 205 (1960), 425-26; major contributions have been made by Steadman in "Tradition and Innovation in Milton's 'Sin': The Problem of Literary Indebtedness," already cited, and in his "Sin, Echidna and the Viper's Brood," *MLR* 56 (1961), 62-66, and Steadman's lists have been extended by Robert C. Fox, "Milton's Sin: Addenda," *PQ* 42 (1963), 120-21; a more recent study is by Timothy J. O'Keeffe, "An Analogue to Milton's 'Sin' and More on the Tradition," *Milton Quarterly* 5 (1971), 74-77. With questionable results, Lynette R. Muir sought to derive the hell hounds in Sin's womb from Malory's Questing Beast, in "A Detail in Milton's Description of Sin" *N&Q* 201 (1956), 100-101. Kirkconnell reprints some of the less accessible literary parallels in the *Celestial Cycle*, pp. 273, 282-83, and 604. John M. Patrick is surely correct when he places primary emphasis on the suggestions of attraction-revulsion in the double nature of Sin in his "Milton, Phineas Fletcher, Spenser, and Ovid—Sin at Hell's Gates," *N&Q* 201 (1956), 384-86.

[20] Bonnell, "The Serpent with the Human Head," p. 275n.

[21] C. H. Collins Baker, "Some Illustrators of Milton's *Paradise Lost* (1688-1850)," p. 6. Baker has apparently misread the legend appended to the Benlowes' illustration: it is the Flesh (holding glass), not the World, who resembles Milton's Sin.

the Garden of Eden, and in the same year Ann Gossman acknowledged the same possibility.[22]

As the place of this image in the iconography of the Fall has already been outlined, there is no need to repeat that history here. The motif was carried into the High Renaissance by Michelangelo and Raphael, among others, and into the seventeenth century by Naccherino. By observing the essential characteristics of the demonic serpent-woman, but shifting her from the Tree of Knowledge to the Gate of Hell, Milton was able to endow his monstrous figure of Sin with more credibility than might have accrued from a literary convention alone. With his description of Sin, furthermore, he had included at one or another point in *Paradise Lost* allusions to almost every major visual form used for depicting the Adversary in the Garden:[23] serpent-woman, serpent coiled about the Tree, erect serpent, and even the early and rare Anglo-Saxon angelic tempter.[24]

Milton's direct association of Sin with the nymph Scylla—"Vexed Scylla bathing in the sea" (II, 660)—connects with another visual tradition. J. F. Gilliam pointed out the connection between Milton's description and Christian iconography when he cited Saint John Chrysostom's conception of Sin: "And if a painter drew her, he would not seem to me to err depicting her thus, as a woman, bestial in form, barbarous, breathing fire, hideous, and black, such as the pagan poets describe their Scyllas."[25] Milton's linking of Scylla with Sin accords with Chrysostom, but a thoroughly horrendous conception was not the only possible interpretation of Scylla, as we may see in Ovid's *Metamorphoses* XIV, 40-74, and the engraved illustration for this passage in Sandys' 1632 edition. In this illustration, the nymph's lower parts have already been transformed at the command of jealous Circe into the snarling dogs' heads which Ovid compared to Cerberus, but Scylla shows neither displeasure nor discomfort at this development, and the stance of her body might otherwise be described as coy or even demure. Ugly conceptions of the siren, as exemplified by Chrysostom, were in time ameliorated until she became a beautifully tempting creature. The fish-siren appeared in art only in the eighth century, and the image became virtually indistinguishable from that of the mermaid.[26] This shapely creature with her two scaly tails amply embodied the enticements of the flesh, and appeared in carvings and paintings throughout England and

(Margin numbers: 169, 198, 193, 194, 92)

---

[22] Steadman, "Sin and the Serpent of Genesis III," and Ann Gossman, "Milton, Prudentius and the Brood of Sin," 440.

[23] We have noted above (p. 102) that Milton ignored the omnium-gatherum of sphinx, camel, and salamander.

[24] Beautiful demonic females often appear, though without serpentine elements, in paintings of the temptation of wilderness saints in circumstances more relevant to *PR*. See, for example, Rose Graham, "A Picture-Book of the Life of St. Anthony the Abbot," *Archaeologia* 83 (1933), pp. 1-26; Benno Geiger, *Magnasco*, Bergamo, 1949, pl. 320; and see A. Aspland, *A. Tempesta*, Holbein Society, 1873, pp. 19-21, for the thirty plates by Tempesta published in 1597 under the title *Vita S. Antonii Abbatis*. Other examples are reproduced in Wall, *Devils*, p. 77; Kaftal, *Iconography of the Saints in Tuscan Painting*, fig. 41; Bartolomeo Nogara, *Art Treasures of the Vatican*, New York, 1950, pp. 143 and 154.

[25] J. F. Gilliam, "Scylla and Sin," *PQ* 29 (1950), 346-47.

[26] Réau, *Iconographie*, I, p. 122.

the Continent.[27] Some of the finest examples adorn the *Neptune Fountain* executed by Giovanni Bologna for the public square in Bologna, which Montaigne praised *93* so highly. The seductiveness is inescapable. The association of the mermaid, as the female among the fallen angels, with the "devil's dam" is particularly significant for Milton's introduction of Sin as the devil's mistress.[28]

To return to the serpent-woman in the Garden, a close scrutiny of the frescoes of the Sistine Ceiling will show that Michelangelo had endowed her with two serpentine tails, which appear to be joined to the hip like legs. Bonnell sees this as *169* the creation of a new type, possibly under the influence of the bifurcated mermaidens of art and the Scylla of classical poetry.[29] There is also a double tail on the serpent in Titian's 1570 painting at the Prado. Any substitution of a serpentine coil or coils for legs inevitably suggested some form of evil in Renaissance and later art. The snaky tails could be fitted to a male torso as well as a female, as we may see in a painting by Federico Zuccari and in prints by Iacomo Franco and Henry Peacham, as well as in the emblems of Cesare Ripa, and in many wood carvings.[30] Whether male or female, such figures usually symbolized deceit, fraud, or slander.[31] A painted earthenware dish, executed at Urbino about 1540 to 1550, pictures the *94* "Rescue of Truth by Time from Falsehood," where Falsehood is represented with an attractive female body and face (though there are serpents in her hair), while her legs turn first into the hairy thighs of a satyress and then into the scaly coils of a sea monster.

Bronzino's famous *Allegory* at the National Gallery in London includes a *95* related conception, though in it the serpentine coil is singular rather than bifur- *96* cated. The painting was once found puzzling until Panofsky sorted out the meanings. As Panofsky puts it, the serpent-woman

> really looks at first like a charming little 'girl in a green dress.' But the dress cannot fully conceal a scaled, fish-like body, lion's or panther's claws, and the tail of a dragon or serpent. She offers a honeycomb with one hand while she hides a poisonous little animal in the other, and moreover the hand attached to her right arm, that is the hand with the honeycomb, is in reality a left hand, while the hand attached to her left arm is in reality a right one, so that the figure offers sweetness with what seems to be her 'good' hand but is really her 'evil' one, and hides poison in what seems to be her 'evil' hand but is really her 'good' one. We are presented here with the most sophisticated symbol of perverted duplicity ever de-

[27] Bridaham, *Gargoyles, Chimeres, and the Grotesque*, figs. 36 and 396, and F. H. Crossley, *English Church Craftsmanship*, p. 83.

[28] For a witty and learned article which traces some of these significances, but does not note the Miltonic use of them, see A. A. Barb, "Antaura: The Mermaid and the Devil's Grandmother," *JWCI* 29 (1966), 1-23.

[29] Bonnell, "The Serpent with a Human Head," p. 275.

[30] See A. Petrucci, *Panorama della incisione italiana*, Rome, n.d., pl. 72; and Fritz Saxl and Rudolf Wittkower, *British Art and the Mediterranean*, London, 1948, p. 41.

[31] Didron, *Christian Iconography*, II, pp. 148-52.

vised by an artist, yet curiously enough it is a symbol not rapidly seized upon by the modern observer.[32]

With all his acuteness, in this fascinating analysis Panofsky made one of his rare errors, due probably to the uncleaned state of the painting: what Deceit holds in her right hand is not "a poisonous little animal" but rather the scorpionlike sting at the tip of her own serpentine tail, a close visual association with her counterpart in *Paradise Lost* whom Milton described as ending "foul in many a scaly fold/ Voluminous and vast, a serpent armed/ With mortal sting" (II, 651-53).

The instances we have just considered each symbolize some aspect of Deceit or Falsehood, but the image may have wider implications, as in an allegorical engraving by Flötner, in which the serpent-woman represents Bad Company. Gertrud Schiller identifies the image as symbolizing the sovereignty of Sin in general rather than in any particular sense, as indeed it does.[33] In the stained glass "Window of Chariots" executed in Rouen about 1525, there is a series of three parts, each of which represents a triumphal procession: in the first, Adam and Eve are shown before their fall in a golden chariot attended by the Virtues; in the second, we see the consequences of the original sin, in that an allegorical Sin now rides triumphant in the chariot, in the form of a serpent with a woman's bust; in the third, we have the Virgin Mary seated in the chariot as the second Eve, accompanied by angels, prophets, and patriarchs.[34]

In the "Christian Knight Map" executed by Hondius in the late 1590's, we have already observed that the figure of Sin accords closely with Milton's description, though she does differ in having the serpentine hair of Medusa. Hondius' engraving of Peccatum is at least collaterally related to a popular figure in fifteenth-century illustrations known variously as Sin, the World, or Frau Welt, of which we shall consider two examples. The earlier of these is from a manuscript dated 1414, and the later is a fifteenth-century German woodcut. The overall significance of the two images is the same, though there are variations in details of illustration and of meaning. In each instance a female body is balanced on a crane's leg, indicating instability. In the woodcut, there is only one leg, which is bitten by a cadaverous figure of Mors, to indicate the end of Sin in Death. In the manuscript illumination, Frau Welt has two lower limbs, one of them a serpent, also labeled Mors, which bites the crane's leg, labeled Vita, to show the end of all creaturely pretensions. In the woodcut, the right hand holds a cup signifying unchastity, while in the manuscript the cup betokens greed. The left hand of the woodcut figure holds a pronged fork which signifies avarice, while the limp left arm in the other illustration represents sloth. In both instances the headdress contains peacock feathers, as symbols of pride. The manuscript version gives the woman a belt about the waist which is labeled avarice, and from which coins are leaking. Here we have the summation of all or most of the mortal sins into a single figure repre-

[32] Erwin Panofsky, *Studies in Iconology*, pp. 89-90.

[33] Reproduced in van Marle, *Iconographie*, II, p. 105, with brief comment on 101; Schiller, *Iconography*, II, p. 160.

[34] Mâle, *Religious Art*, pp. 138-39, and reproduction in Elisabeth Von Witzleben, *Stained Glass in French Cathedrals*, New York, 1968, fig. 90 and pp. 79-80.

senting Sin itself, seen as a comely woman above the waist, and represented in animal forms below.[35]

The woodcut figure shows the cadaverous Death with a serpent crawling out of his bowels, recalling the *vermis* motif with which we have already dealt. In the manuscript illumination, there is a somewhat similar detail, and one of considerable relevance to Milton's description of Sin: two hounds extend their necks and heads from the waist of Frau Welt with labels identifying them as Wrath and Envy. Whether they are coming out of her body, or only out of her waistband, cannot be determined. However that may be, we have here an association of "hell hounds" with the belly of a woman representing Sin. The iconographical significance for Milton is obvious.

In the Missal of Poitiers we find different and yet related representations. *57* Here there are two demonic figures, the one chained to the snout of Leviathan, and the other figure below him and to the left. Both represent the distorted image, bringing together incommensurate parts of many animal forms into frightening new images of tremendous vitality. Each of these demons is gastrocephalic, and in each stomach the mouth gapes wide to reveal figures within. From the open stomach of the lower demon, there protrudes a doglike head, while serpents extend from the midriff of the superior fiend, and behind these are seen a number of animalistic faces. The relevance to Milton of the small animalistic demons moving in or out of the torsos of these larger devils becomes even clearer when we recall that Milton's term "hell hound" had for centuries stood as a synonym for demon.[36]

In Milton, the Hell Hounds were engendered by Death's rape of his mother Sin. Produced by the interaction between mortality and the creaturely presumption to deity, they represent the myriad sins produced by the Original Sin. Sin herself describes her offspring as

> These yelling monsters that with ceaseless cry
> Surround me, as thou sawest, hourly conceived
> And hourly born, with sorrow infinite
> To me, for when they list into the womb
> That bred them they return, and howl and gnaw
> My bowels, their repast; then bursting forth
> Afresh with conscious terrors vex me round,
> That rest or intermission none I find.

(II, 795-802)

[35] For the iconography of these representations, see E. H. Gombrich, *Symbolic Images*, p. 137; Fritz Saxl, "A Spiritual Encyclopedia of the Later Middle Ages," *JWCI* 5 (1942), p. 128; and Campbell Dodgson, *Catalogue of Early German and Flemish Woodcuts . . . in the British Museum*, London, 1903, I, pp. 115-16. The Peccatum figure in Hondius' map was first associated with Sin by Amy Lee Turner, "Milton and Jocodus Hondius the Elder."

[36] M. Rudwin, *The Devil in Legend and Literature*, p. 39. In Ripa, Sin ("Peccato") is represented as a masculine figure, with Medusa-like hair, bound round with serpents at the waist, and with one serpent entering the chest to bite the heart. I am indebted to Amy Lee Turner's dissertation for this parallel, which she reproduces as her plate 24. See Cesare Ripa's *Iconologia*, Padua, 1618, p. 401. Ripa's emblem apparently derives from a different tradition from the one just traced.

The artists, though restricted to a single view and time frame, do give visual expression to the distortion and terror which Milton communicates. The hounds emerging at the waist of Frau Welt are shown with open mouths, as though giving voice to "a hideous peal" and "ceaseless cry" (II, 656 and 795).

If Milton's Death represents for the most part an invisible horror, modified by traditional attributes from the visual tradition, his Sin is a conglomerate of visual horrors. To preserve his demons as epic figures and credible tempters, he dissociates them from direct identification with the horrible forms so often seen in art. It is in conjunction with Sin and Death that he most directly summons distorted images to our minds with such expressions as "hell hounds," "night-hag," "grim" and "execrable shape," "goblin," "grisly terror," "snaky sorceress," "hellish pest," "phantasm," "yelling monsters," all "with terrors and with clamors compassed round" (II, 654, 662, 681-82, 688, 704, 724, 735, 743, 795, and 862). It is in Sin and Death that Milton has concentrated most of his direct references to the visual monstrosities of the traditional demons, and principally, of course, in Sin. Satan's first response to these two is to say that he never saw "till now/ Sight more detestible," but after he learns their parentage he refers to them as "dear daughter . . . and my fair son" (II, 744-45, and 817-18). Satan had already taken evil as his good, and here he accepts ugliness as beauty, even though in himself he still preserves a large measure of outward luster. Milton's visual strategy is superb: relying upon the easy familiarity of the visual traditions with which his details accord, he conveys in poetry an understanding of the demonic which for complexity and balance is beyond the possibilities of any single work of visual art. Whatever he may have owed to the influence of any particular painting or piece of sculpture remains of secondary importance, even if demonstrable. His dependence on the visual arts was at once general and eclectic, and he expected his readers to respond on the basis of a broad cultural awareness of the images he evoked.

THE ONE EXCLUSION: PHYSICAL TORTURE

MILTON's understanding of Hell was expressed through accommodation, and took the infernal symbols as primarily applicable to a permanent cast of mind, rather than to physical geography, though geography contributed to those symbols. Whereas Heaven represents personal existence everlastingly centered in the love of God, and radiating from there through the love of God's creatures, Hell is existence centered in the love of self and of Satan, with consequently distorted relations to creation. Whenever a lesser good or a positive evil is exalted in place of the wholeness of God, there the Satanic ideal is followed, and the lesser good becomes a positive evil insofar as it asserts its own supremacy. When Satan declares that "The mind is its own place, and in itself/ Can make a Heaven of Hell, a Hell of Heaven," he is telling only half of the truth, so as to encourage both himself and Beelzebub (I, 254-55). Alone, he admits that "which way I fly is Hell; myself am Hell," for he carries his torments within him (IV, 75, and IX, 120-21). Milton editorializes that "from Hell/ One step no more than from himself" can Satan fly "by change of place," for Hell "always in him burns/ Though in mid Heaven" (IV, 21-22, and IX, 467-68). Satan's repudiation of good and pursuit of evil ("Evil by thou my good," IV, 110) is in effect a choosing of Hell, and he himself admits that "in Heaven much worse would be my state" (IX, 123).

Of this development in Satan, Arnold Stein aptly comments that "the circle has now closed; he has adjusted so entirely to the 'unchanged' part of his mind, the Hell within, that he *needs* Hell."[1] What Stein calls to our attention here would be impossible to paint, at least in its full implications. Some distraught demons raging in the presence of virtue may suggest an inner need for Hell—but only if we bring the preformed insight to the painting: it can proceed from us to the painting, and come back from the painting enriched, but we cannot derive it *de novo* from the art work alone. Extending his analysis of Satan to include all the fallen angels, Stein comments that "their bringing good out of evil really means thriving under evil by adjusting entirely to place: 'our torments also may in length of time/ Become our elements.' "[2] When Milton describes Hell as a place, he is objectifying the psychological realities to which the demons have adjusted, the only forms of existence to which their psychic pretensions can adjust.

As we read *Paradise Lost*, we find direct descriptions of almost every feature

[1] Arnold Stein, *Answerable Style*, p. 11.
[2] *Ibid.*, p. 44.

of Hell as it had been presented in art[3]—almost, but not quite, for there is one very important exception: the traditional tortures and torture chambers, which fascinated so many artists and so many viewers, are virtually eliminated. No one could sensibly maintain that Milton's Hell is a comfortable place, but neither do we find there any scholastic delight in developing and categorizing particular afflictions and torments. In numerous medieval and some Renaissance paintings, Hell is divided into little cubicles, often based upon Dante's *Inferno*, in each of which exquisite pains are allocated to logically appropriate vices. In some representations, devils are even shown afflicting each other. Milton's Hell is neither so specified nor so specialized: "a universe of death," its details combine to impress us with a place or a state "where all life dies, death lives, and nature breeds,/ Perverse, all monstrous, all prodigious things,/ Abominable, inutterable, and worse/ Than fables yet have feigned, or fear conceived . . ." (II, 622-27). The physical features of Milton's Hell are outward and visible signs of inward and spiritual disgrace. Broadbent has stated the case exactly in writing that Milton's Hell "is not a torture-chamber where specialized punishments are meted out to helpless convicts, but the material abode of the irredeemably damned."[4] It may be objected that there were no human sinners in Hell at the time Milton wrote of it, and so he could not show those "specialized punishments," but in *Paradise Lost* Milton again and again wrote predictively of the future—human history in its heights and depths, the Divine Incarnation, and the Last Judgment are all presented. In the Paradise of Fools, Milton introduced the punishment of human folly, and he could as well have described proleptically the punishment of more vicious sinners in Hell. That he did not do so is surely significant.

Though we need not dwell for long upon the individualized tortures of art, something must be said about them, because it is important to recognize what Milton rejected as well as what he accepted. As early as the eleventh century, specialized punishments in Hell were being envisioned in the series on the south porch of Toulouse Cathedral, and in the next century at Conques we see Avarice hanged like Judas, with a purse about his neck, "while Lust is symbolized by a couple chained together for all eternity."[5] Many such symbols preceded Dante, but were given wide circulation and authority in the *Divine Comedy*, which along

[3] For a general study of Hell and the devils in art, see Centro Internazionale di Studi Umanistice (Enrico Castelli), *L'Umanesimo e il demoniaco nell' arte*, Rome, 1952. Changes in the religious attitudes toward the doctrine of Hell are traced in Daniel P. Walker, *The Decline of Hell: Seventeenth-Century Discussions of Eternal Torment*, London, 1964. For treatments of Hell in Byzantine art, see Klaus Wessel, ed., *Reallexikon zur Byzantinischen Kunst*, Stuttgart, 1966-, and Selma Jónsdóttir, *An 11th Century Byzantine Last Judgment in Iceland*, Reykjavík, 1959. Studies already cited in the preceding chapters on demonology will also contain much of value on pictorial representations of Hell.

[4] Broadbent, "Milton's Hell," 165. Ernest Schanzer, "Milton's Hell Revisited," *UTQ* 24 (1955), 136-45, treats Hell as a geographical adjustment to the spiritual state of the fallen angels, and Northrop Frye, *The Return of Eden*, p. 82, finds "no relish of damnation" in *Paradise Lost*. We are not, for these reasons, to assume as Woldock does (*"Paradise Lost" and Its Critics*, p. 93) "that Milton's Hell is very much a nominal one."

[5] Katzenellenbogen, *Allegories of the Virtues and Vices*, p. 58, and Mâle, *Religious Art*, p. 56.

with *The Vision of St. Paul* influenced artists in the later Middle Ages to specify in detail all the sins and their appropriate punishments.[6] There were exceptions, of course, and of these Giotto comes closest to Milton with a Hell which is described by Millard Meiss as "a place more of disorder than of excruciating pain," but a more typical representation will be found in "Orcagna's fresco in Santa Croce, where the faces of the damned are torn by the claws and teeth of wildly sadistic devils."[7] We find much the same Dantean specificity in the infernos at S. Maria Novella in Florence and in the Camposanto at Pisa and even in the *Last Judgment* of the gentle Fra Angelico.

99, 73
100

The differences between the images used in such pictures and in *Paradise Lost* are extraordinarily important, and those distinctions must be preserved. Even so sophisticated a mind as Erwin Panofsky can ignore them, as he did when he described the *Hell* by Van Eyck as "a spectacle as horrifying as any canto in Dante or Milton."[8] The proper balance is struck by Helen Gardner: "As Milton is so constantly compared with Dante to Dante's advantage, it is worth saying here that it is surely to Milton's credit that he showed so little inventiveness in imagining tortures or degrading the enemies of God and man by showing them grotesquely deformed and contorted."[9]

THE SEEMING INCONSISTENCIES OF HELL

Apart only from the tortures he ignores, Milton's visual imagery evokes the mood of the Hell which artists had for so many centuries painted. In Hell, the light becomes darkness, for without God the demons' only permanent dwelling will be in gloom. Their landscape is sterile, a fiery gulf with volcanic peaks and icy wastes —inimical to the created life they have rejected and upon which they have declared war. Their home is in one sense a deluge, in another a dungeon, and their headquarters is the burnt gold Pandaemonium with its pompous throne. Climate, landscape, and architecture, as Milton describes them, all conform to visions of Hell which art had forged for the Western imagination. What Whiting said of the literary tradition can also be said of the artistic tradition: "The essential ideas, the crude materials are present, waiting, as it were, for the shaping power of the imagination. Milton breathed into these traditional and familiar ideas the breath of life."[10]

Many features were brought together into that vision of Hell. Some of those features may appear incongruous if abstracted, and their visual conjunction unnatural; but the very incongruity and unnaturalness are appropriate to Hell. As the

[6] Réau, *Iconographie*, II, ii, p. 752, and Anderson, *History and Imagery in British Churches*, pp. 126-27.

[7] Meiss, *Painting in Florence and Siena after the Black Death*, pp. 84 and 83.

[8] Erwin Panofsky, *Early Netherlandish Painting*, I, pp. 238-39, in reference to the diptych in the Metropolitan in New York.

[9] Gardner, *A Reading of "Paradise Lost,"* pp. 45-46. It may be objected that there are no human sinners available for torture in Milton's Hell, but Milton did not hesitate to introduce prophetic scenes of other kinds, and he produces none which foresee the traditional tortures of Hell.

[10] George W. Whiting, "Tormenting Tophet," *N&Q* 192 (1947), 230.

physical objectification of the denial of Creation and of createdness, Hell must be disjointed and grotesque. F. R. Leavis referred categorically to "Milton's failure to give us a consistently realized Hell at all,"[11] but Kenneth Muir replied that "to some readers the very inconsistency gives a nightmare quality which could not have been achieved in any other way."[12] Surely Muir's view here is the correct one, from an exclusively literary point of view, and when Milton's literary descriptions are allowed to evoke the visions of the visual arts, they take on a credibility which makes any seeming inconsistency quite irrelevant.

Allan H. Gilbert has gone somewhat beyond Leavis, though to be sure on another line of analysis. Seeking to discover the stages of the writing of *Paradise Lost*, Gilbert points to Milton's description of Hell as both deluge and dungeon, and of Pandaemonium as both palace and metropolis, and postulates these features as strata lines in his development of the original drama into an epic poem.[13] Gilbert's arguments often seem strained as literary analysis, and when the visual tradition is considered they lose virtually all their force: in art, Hell was a deluge and a dungeon, a metropolis and a palace, all at the same time, on the same canvas, or in the same mural. A consideration of representative art works will show how such "contradictory" elements were in fact conjoined in the visual imagination. In the illuminations for *Genesis B*, Hell is a huge and toothy maw of Leviathan, and it is also in the same representation a walled city with towers; in the mosaic of the Florentine Baptistry, it is a lake of fire, with burning land, and huge mountain peaks colored both a lurid dark red and a whitish red as well (symbolizing the Hell of fire and the Hell of ice?); in the Spanish Chapel, it is two caves in a desolate rocky landscape, but protected by a wall and door; in Nardo di Cione's painting for Santa Maria Novella in Florence, it has a towered palazzo, surrounded by a crenelated wall, but also consists of underground lakes, swamps, deserts, and caves; the Hell panel of Bosch's *Garden of Earthly Delights* shows not only a grisly metropolis but both a burning lake and a frozen lake upon which the damned skate toward a hole in the ice; Joachim Patinir, in *Charon Crossing the Styx* at the Prado, shows Hell as partly a lake of fire, and partly buildings. Civetta's immensely complicated *Inferno* in Venice shows lakes of fire, volcanic mountains, sterile rocky peaks, bridges, towers, furnaces, walls, portcullis gates, and other structures; Michelangelo shows both a lake and a dismal shore. The oak carving at King's College Chapel in Cambridge shows Leviathan's jaws, barren land, mountains, and

34

55

99

68

101

61

44

---

[11] F. R. Leavis, *The Common Pursuit*, New York, 1952, p. 20, in support of earlier criticisms by Eliot and Waldock.

[12] Muir, *John Milton*, p. 147.

[13] Gilbert, *On the Composition of "Paradise Lost,"* pp. 99-100, 105-6. Useful distinctions between various senses of Hell in Milton are both possible and desirable, as we may find in Joseph E. Duncan, "Milton's Four-in-One Hell," *HLQ* 20 (1957), 127-36, and in C. A. Patrides, "Renaissance and Modern Views on Hell," *HTR* 57 (1964), 217-36. Marjorie Nicolson, *John Milton: A Reader's Guide to His Poetry*, New York, 1966, pp. 193-200, accurately distinguishes between three aspects of Milton's Hell: the burning landscape, Pandaemonium, and the hellish world explored in Satan's absence, but she does not find these mutually contradictory.

a city; Beccafumi provides burning lakes, mountains both volcanic and cold, and burning sand; El Greco portrays a bridge, buildings, a lake of fire, and Leviathan's jaws. The conjunction of all these features within single panoramas provided universally recognized visions which would have been invoked in the imaginations of Milton's readers by his descriptions. Both Leavis' denial of a consistently recognizable Hell in *Paradise Lost* and Gilbert's hypothesis that the different physical features identify separate strata of the epic's composition raise problems which simply disappear in the light of the traditional vision of Hell.

29, 30
102

The darkness with which Milton shrouds his Hell is, for many readers, the most striking element of his description. It is not just that the forms in Hell are dark, but that we must look through a veil of darkness to see them, indeed to see anything. Dark, or words derived directly from dark, appear some three dozen times in the first two books of *Paradise Lost*, which also abound with such variant phrases as "the gloomy deep," "the dusky air," and "this mournful gloom" (I, 152, 226, 244). Such light as is found in Hell is not the divinely creative light of Heaven, but the ominous light of fire, so that nothing is seen except by the light of destruction: it is the appropriate setting for Satan who finds ease "only in destroying" (IX, 129). As we respond to Milton's descriptions, we feel ourselves enveloped in lurid darkness:

> Seest thou yon dreary plain, forlorn and wild,
> The seat of desolation, void of light,
> Save what the glimmering of these livid flames
> Casts pale and dreadful?
>
> (I, 180-83)

Milton's repeated emphasis on this factor permeates Hell with monotony, but Milton's creation of that impression is far from monotonous. By the skillful variation of sight and sound within his lines, Milton pictures the infernal monotony and desolation without once allowing our interest to flag.

Problems have arisen, of course, and one of the major cruces of modern criticism arises from the following description of what Satan first sees:

> At once as far as angels'ken he views
> The dismal situation waste and wild,
> A dungeon horrible, on all sides round
> As one great furnace flamed, yet from those flames
> No light, but rather darkness visible
> Served only to discover sights of woe,
> Regions of sorrow, doleful shades, where peace
> And rest can never dwell, hope never comes
> That comes to all. . . .
>
> (I, 59-67)

Here we are introduced to flames without light, a conception which is later expressed as the "black fire" of Hell (II, 67). But the phrase which has created most difficulty for critics is "darkness visible."[14] T. S. Eliot posed a central problem when he wrote that Milton's description was "difficult to imagine."[15] Literary source studies have identified many possible sources and certain analogues to Milton's phrase in writings extending back from the seventeenth century to the time of the book of Job, but although these establish Milton's conception as a literary commonplace, they cannot make that commonplace easily conceivable, and so do not answer Eliot's basic objection.[16] After surveying much of this literary tradition, John E. Hankins still quite properly admits that "we may well be puzzled as to the exact visual image which the 'fire without light' is intended to convey."[17]

The problem is readily resolvable only when we turn to the evidence of the visual arts. There we find Hell consistently shrouded in the "black fire," and "darkness visible" to which Milton refers. Even the colors which would be mixed to depict a normal fire are mingled with darks and blacks in representations of Hell. In an illuminated picture of the Fall of the Rebel Angels executed by W. de Brailes about 1240, now at the Fitzwilliam in Cambridge, the background color for Heaven is gold, while the background for Hell is black, against which only enough light is allowed to the figures to delineate them. A fourteenth-century *Last Judgment* in the Chancel of Sant' Anastasia in Verona shows the apostles, angels, saints, all clearly delineated even after the passage of six centuries, but when we come to the Hell portion of the fresco at the lower right, the devils and the damned are too dark to see, and Hell is obliterated in a gloom too deep to penetrate. This extreme is rare; artists usually provide just enough light in Hell for the scene to be visible as well as dramatic. In the *Très Riches Heures du Duc de Berry*, the blue and glittering gold which predominated during and before the Fall of the Rebel Angels, gives way in Hell to combinations of gray, black, and red, to create a

---

[14] Vincent B. Leitch, "The Landscape of Hell in *Paradise Lost*, Book I," *Xavier University Studies* 9 (Fall, 1970), 27-28.

[15] T. S. Eliot, "Milton," p. 75.

[16] See Job 10:22; Robert West, *Milton and the Angels*, p. 205n. 18; Kirkconnell, *The Celestial Cycle*, p. 601 and *passim*; Whiting, "Tormenting Tophet," 228; Ann Gossman, "Two Milton Notes," *N&Q* 206 (1961), 182-83; three articles by John Steadman: "John Collop and the Flames without Light," *N&Q* 200 (1955), 382-83, "Milton and Patristic Tradition: The Quality of Hell-Fire," *Anglia* 76 (1958), 116-28, and "Grosseteste on the Genealogy of Sin and Death," 367-68; Edgar F. Daniels, "Thomas Adams and Darkness Visible," *N&Q* 204 (1959), 369-70; while Owen, *The Vision of Hell*, pp. 88, 150-51, and 166, cites black fire references in medieval French literature. There have been other attempts to explain the phrase. Allen puts it in the historical context of the theology of light and darkness (*The Harmonious Vision*, p. 103). In a brilliant recognition, Jackson Cope points to Milton's strategy of setting the "darkness visible" of Hell opposite the "brightness . . . invisible" of Heaven (V, 598-99) (*The Metaphoric Structure of "Paradise Lost,"* Baltimore, 1962, p. 94). John Peter provides a valid rhetorical justification when he notes that "a sort of vibrancy is set up within the phrase, not unlike that of the armature in an electric buzzer, a restlessness and vigor of language unobtainable in any other way" (*A Critique of "Paradise Lost,"* p. 39). Valuable as these considerations are, they still do not answer Eliot's objection.

[17] John E. Hankins, "The Pains of the Afterworld: Fire, Wind, and Ice in Milton and Shakespeare," *PMLA* 71 (1956), 486.

suitably dark and yet flaming atmosphere for the infernal forge.[18] The *Last Judg-*   *45, 46*
ment in the Grimani Breviary at Venice shows the blessed in fresh shades of blue
and pink, in contrast to the dark brownish and black scenes of the damned.[19] There
were some variations, of course, and some innovations in the coloring, but artists
consistently used some form of dark light for Hell. In the infernos painted by
Hieronymus Bosch, we are not only looking at psychologically and morally dark
deeds, but we are looking at them through a light which is darker than anything we
see elsewhere. Even artists so radically different as Bosch and Raphael agreed on   *68*
this, and the infernal landscape which Raphael painted as background for his
Michael and the Dragon provides striking pictorial echoes of the lurid Hell storms   *69*
of Bosch, as even the supreme painter of light mixed his palette with darkness in order to represent Hell.[20] Similar "darkness visible" pervades the Hell scenes in Patinir's *Crossing the Stygian Lake* and Coecke van Aelst's *St. John the Evangelist* in
the Prado. In the *Inferno* by Civetta, the light again is dark and dreary, and there is   *101*
only enough of it to allow us to make out those who, in Milton's words, "sit in
darkness here/ Hatching vain empires" (ii, 377-78). Beccafumi may create a
somewhat more phosphorescent surface glow, yet the effect as our eyes penetrate
into the background depths of his canvas is precisely that of a darkness visible in
which we can barely make out the movement and shape of the "doleful shades."   *29, 30*
In Guido Reni's seventeenth-century painting, the gloom has descended even more
pervasively, and it is only as our eyes become accustomed to the darkness of his
infernal landscape that we can begin to pick out some details of Lucifer's new
realm. What we find in the paintings is also present in stained glass windows,   *28*
where the phenomenon of darkness visible is equally striking. In the seventeenth-
century stained glass Judgment scenes executed by the Van Linge family in Oxford, and in the early Tudor version at Saint Mary's Church in Fairford, one must
look long and hard before shapes begin to emerge and pervasive darkness yields to
vision. Once we acknowledge the relevance to *Paradise Lost* of the artists' representations of the infernal world, even those hitherto puzzling phrases "black fire"
and "darkness visible" are recognized as accurate visual renditions.[21]

"Like Satan's our eyesight seems to be working its way through the gloom,"
as Ants Oras has observed in a brilliant article. "It is with the slightest of verbal
touches that much of the canvas is filled, but every touch tells. The procedure
here is 'realistic,' if one wants to use the word: this is the way one begins to see at
night; yet it also preserves the terror of the unknown, which Milton clearly wishes
to evoke."[22] Oras perceptively compares Milton's chiaroscuro effects to those of

[18] For color reproductions, see Limbourg Brothers, *The Très Riches Heures*, pls. 65
and 91.

[19] Folio 469, in the Biblioteca Marciana.

[20] Oskar Fischel, *Raphael*, I, pp. 31-32.

[21] Readers may wish to consult the popularity of night and twilight scenes in the art of
the Low Countries, as traced in Wolfgang Stechow, *Dutch Landscape Painting of the Seventeenth Century*, London, 1966, pp. 173-82 and pls. 345-69.

[22] Ants Oras, "Darkness Visible—Notes on Milton's Descriptive Procedures in *Paradise
Lost*," in *All These to Teach* (ed. Robert C. Bryan), Gainesville, Fla., 1965, pp. 137 and 133.

Rembrandt, and his use of perspective to that found in Rembrandt, Poussin, and Claude Lorrain, but he makes no direct comparison between Milton's inferno and the infernos of art. What Oras says of our ordinary and natural night vision applies almost equally to the vision of Hell in art. The dark light was always there, at least from the Middle Ages onward, but in the sixteenth century with Beccafumi, and into the seventeenth with Guido Reni, we have that additional element of indistinctness. In paintings by Bosch, Civetta, and other earlier artists, we see everything through a cloud of darkness, but the forms retain a linearity which is distinct and unmistakable. In the works of later artists and in stained glass, the pall of darkness is so heavy that at first we do not make out the forms in the background, and even when we do they preserve a certain haziness. What Northrop Frye has written about Milton's descriptions in the first book of *Paradise Lost* could apply with equal validity to these works of art: "A number of huge clouded forms begin to come out of a kind of sea and gather on a kind of shore."[23] It is true that the poet can present indistinctness more fully than the painter can, but a comparison between the paintings of Bosch and Civetta, on the one hand, with those of Beccafumi and Guido Reni, on the other, will indicate how much closer the two later artists were to the mysterious shrouding of vision which Milton provides in Hell.

What we see through the darkness is a "fiery gulf," with "floods and whirlpools of tempestuous fire," a "boiling ocean" (I, 53, 77, and II, 183). From this burning lake we turn to a "land that ever burned/ With solid, as the lake with liquid fire," with a "singed bottom all involved/ With stench and smoke," while in the background "there stood a hill not far whose grisly top/ Belched fire and rolling smoke" (I, 228-29, 236-37, and 670-71). Later, we hear of Hell spouting "her cataracts of fire," as Milton's descriptions of the fiery landscape itself are completed (II, 176). Poetry could scarcely go further in providing a credible picture, and it is curious that anyone who has read these passages could ever have doubted the power of Milton's visual descriptions. What we see here could have been derived directly from volcanic landscapes in nature, and Marjorie Nicolson has posited that Milton was here drawing upon his recollections of his visit to the Phlegraean Fields in southern Italy: "the topographical details are as clearly indicated as if Milton were drawing a map of the district."[24] More recently, Irwin R. Blacker has suggested also that the geysers of the Larderello area near Florence may have suggested Milton's infernal topography, and the two areas may well have been synthesized in Milton's imagination to influence the Hell of *Paradise Lost*.[25] Nicolson argued rightly that Milton often drew upon his own experiences, and suggested that we should not always insist upon finding his sources in books, which have occupied the primary attention of source hunters.[26] These studies by

---

[23] Northrop Frye, *Return of Eden*, p. 17.

[24] Nicolson, "Milton's Hell and the Phlegraean Fields," 501.

[25] Irwin R. Blacker, "Did Milton Visit Hell?" *SCN* 9 (1951), 54.

[26] Nicolson, "Milton's Hell," 513; for useful analyses of possible literary sources, see the following: Whiting, "Tormenting Tophet"; D. T. Starnes, "Gehenna and Tophet," *N&Q* 192 (1947), 369-70; Alfred L. Kellogg, "Some Patristic Sources for Milton's Gehenna," *N&Q* 195 (1950), 10-13; Hankins, "The Pains of the Afterworld," 482-95; Leitch, "The

Nicolson and Blacker demonstrate the acuteness both of Milton's observation and of his poetic descriptions by showing how effectively Milton does indeed evoke natural scenery.

For most of Milton's early readers, of course, those same descriptive phrases would have been more likely to evoke the nearly universal visions of the representational arts than the landscape of two provincial regions in Italy. It is difficult to conceive of a cultivated European audience of Milton's time whose imaginations had not been prepared by the visual arts to associate graphic and visual details with Milton's cumulative references to dreary plains, the glimmering of livid flames from burning lakes and burning lands, and thundering Aetnas belching smoke and mineral fury. A single line from *Paradise Lost* epitomizes the infernal landscapes of art: "rocks, caves, lakes, fens, bogs, dens, and shades of Death" (II, 621). What John Peter aptly calls the "lunar sterility," and "the dismal geography of Hell . . . . made up of desolate and meaningless accretions," would have evoked the most vivid and powerful images in the minds of Milton's contemporaries.[27]

PANDAEMONIUM, THE HIGH CAPITOL/CAPITAL

One of the first actions of the fallen legions is the erection of Pandaemonium, under the skilled supervision of Mulciber,[28] who had built in Heaven, but to far different effect from what we see emerging in Hell:

> Anon out of the earth a fabric huge
> Rose like an exhalation, with the sound
> Of dulcet symphonies and voices sweet,
> Built like a temple, where pilasters round
> Were set, and doric pillars overlaid
> With golden architrave; nor did there want
> Cornice or frieze, with bossy sculptures graven;
> The roof was fretted gold. Not Babylon,
> Nor great Alcairo such magnificence
> Equalled in all their glories, to enshrine
> Belus or Serapis their Gods, or seat

Landscape of Hell in *Paradise Lost*, Book I." For the Lake of Hell in Anglo-Saxon art and literature, see M. B. McNamee, "*Beowulf*—An Allegory of Salvation?" in *An Anthology of Beowulf Criticism* (ed. Lewis E. Nicholson), Notre Dame, Ind., 1963, pp. 343-46. Neither Nicolson nor I would wish to do without such valuable studies, but they do need to be supplemented in other directions.

[27] Peter, *A Critique of "Paradise Lost,"* p. 46.

[28] Panofsky, *Studies in Iconology*, pp. 33-49, discusses paintings of the Mulciber-Vulcan myth by Piero di Cosimo (1461-1521) and others, and connects them with the mythographic tradition of the early building of houses and cities. A contrast between the buildings Milton ascribes to his Vulcan and the crude log structure of the mythographic tradition as painted by Piero will show how Milton has exalted Vulcan's skill while debasing his character. See Piero's *Vulcan and Aeolus as Teachers of Mankind* (Ottawa) reproduced as plate IX in Panofsky, *op. cit.*

> Their Kings, when Egypt with Assyria strove
> In wealth and luxury. Th' ascending pile
> Stood fixt her stately highth. . . .

(I, 710-23)

In an influential article published in 1931, Rebecca W. Smith made a meticulous survey of St. Peter's Church as Milton would have seen it while in Rome, and then suggested that Milton drew his description of Pandaemonium "largely from his recollections of the church and its surroundings."[29] This thesis has been widely accepted, and Marjorie Nicolson even declares that "all the details mentioned in the description of Pandaemonium were there" at St. Peter's when Milton saw it.[30] The identification deserves close analysis, under which it will lose much of its plausibility.

One frequently cited difference between the two structures concerns the orders of the architecture: Pandaemonium is Doric, St. Peter's is Corinthian. This may seem a minor difference to us, but it would not have been so in Milton's time, when the differentiation between the orders was assigned prime importance. The Classical and Renaissance heritage was so crucial to Milton and his contemporaries that they would no more have confused a building in the Doric order with one in the Corinthian order than T. S. Eliot and his contemporaries would have confused a Neoclassical church by Wren with a neo-Gothic church by Pugin. Furthermore, the architrave and the roof of Pandaemonium were of gold, whereas in St. Peter's these elements were not even bronzed. It does not help here to cite John Evelyn's comment that in St. Peter's "the *volto*, or roof" is all "overlaid with gold," as Smith does, for Evelyn is explicitly describing the interior and its ceiling (*volto*), not the exterior roof in our sense, and *Paradise Lost* contains no hint that the ceiling of Pandaemonium is overlaid with gold. An equally striking difference between the ceilings of the two buildings involves shape: the ceiling in St. Peter's is a coffered barrel vault, after the fashion of Renaissance and Baroque architecture, whereas Milton explicitly refers to "the arched roof" of Pandaemonium (I, 726).[31] As for the "porches wide" which Milton ascribes to Pandaemonium, the plural is critical; by contrast, there is only one conceivable porch on the St. Peter's which Milton could have known, for it was only many years after he had returned to England that the Bernini Colonnade was added (I, 762). Finally, the most striking visual feature of St. Peter's is its universally admired dome, usually referred to as a cupola in Milton's time, and there is not the slightest suggestion of a dome or a cupola on Pandaemonium.

In view of this accumulation of radical architectural differences, any identification of St. Peter's with Pandaemonium becomes untenable. Such similarities as do

---

[29] Rebecca Smith, "The Source of Milton's Pandaemonium," 187-98, quoted from 187.

[30] Nicolson, *A Reader's Guide*, pp. 196-98; see also Irene Samuel, *Dante and Milton: The Commedia and Paradise Lost*, Ithaca, N.Y., 1966, p. 110.

[31] Citing Henry Wotton as authority ("Elements of Architecture," *Reliquiae Wottonianae*, London, 1672, p. 29), Amy Lee Turner, *The Visual Arts in Milton's Poetry*, p. 370, identifies the roof of Pandaemonium's hall as "a vaulted roof in the Gothic manner."

exist—the hanging lamps, and the inner rooms—were shared with innumerable other structures throughout Europe, nor would it be difficult to find other buildings with such capacious rooms that people walking into them appeared to be dwarfed, as for example in the Hall of the Five Hundred in the Palazzo Vecchio in Florence. Although Hagstrum has commented that "actually we do not see very much" through Milton's description of Pandaemonium,[32] I suggest that we see as much as a poet can show us without being diverted into extraneous detail, and we certainly see enough to recognize that Pandaemonium is not an infernal version of St. Peter's.

This conclusion is important for at least two reasons. In the first place, it is ideationally significant that Milton did not introduce into his universal Christian epic any degrading identification of Pandaemonium with the chief church of Roman Catholicism. Milton's days of sectarian controversy and bickering were over, and it is incumbent upon us not to read into *Paradise Lost* sectarian biases not demonstrably present. In the second place, we should recognize that what Milton has given us in Pandaemonium is actually a promiscuous architectural monstrosity, a bastard compound of Doric order and classical architrave and frieze with a Gothic arched roof,[33] and surrounded by wide porches after the fashion of the loggias of the Uffizi courtyard in Florence or the covered walkways of the Ducal Palace in Venice. The joining of architectural elements in Pandaemonium is so promiscuous that the building cannot even be convincingly described as Baroque, though that effort has of course been made.[34] It is not only by his comparison of Pandaemonium with the barbaric works of Babel and of Memphian kings that Milton ridicules his demons, but by the very structure of their art. Left to their diabolical imaginations, they frame what Broadbent has brilliantly described as "a primitive, overdecorated, vulgar palace, the home of cruel and heathen despotism." The result architecturally is indeed "very preposterous," as Voltaire observed, but Voltaire judged wrongly that this "contrivance" did not fit "the serious spirit of Milton," for as Broadbent has observed, "even 'the serious spirit of Milton' could be ironical, and show us what the devils were like by playing on our own devilish bad taste."[35] The visual language of Pandaemonium amounts to what the French call *goût de la surcharge*, and what could be more appropriate?[36]

[32] Hagstrum, *The Sister Arts*, pp. 125-26.

[33] It is relevant that in Neoclassical stage design, bastard architecture such as we find in Pandaemonium was restricted to comedy. According to Panofsky, *Meaning in the Visual Arts*, p. 197n., "It should be noted that in Serlio's stage designs the 'tragic scene,' destined for plays which, up to the advent of the 'bourgeois tragedy' in the eighteenth century, involved only royalty and princes, exclusively consists of Renaissance buildings, whereas the 'comic scene,' destined for plays about ordinary folk, shows a mélange of Renaissance and Gothic structures."

[34] See Wylie Sypher's *Four Stages of Renaissance Style*, Grove City, N.Y., 1955, pp. 210-11.

[35] Broadbent, "Milton's Hell," 178 and 180, and Shawcross, *Milton: The Critical Heritage*, p. 253. In *Some Graver Subject*, p. 108n., Broadbent refers to the "architectural promiscuity" of Pandaemonium.

[36] Many elements surely entered into Milton's descriptions of Pandaemonium, or lay relevantly behind those descriptions. Of the rising of Pandaemonium (1, 710-12), Marjorie

When Milton allowed his industrious crew of devils to construct buildings in Hell, he was supported by a visual tradition which goes back at least as far as the Utrecht Psalter of the ninth century, where the infernal palace is shown with flames issuing from it.[37] The early eleventh-century artist of *Genesis B* repeatedly *34* showed Hell with crenelated walls and towers; in an illuminated English Apocalypse of the fourteenth century, Hell is shown as a Norman castle;[38] Lochner's *Last Judgment* at Cologne shows a soot-darkened fortress, with one flame-colored tower flanking the gate; Juan de Flandres in a painting at the Metropolitan in New York shows Michael triumphing over a dragon, and holding a shield in which is reflected the dark and dreary cityscape of Hell.

The Hells of Bosch contain many buildings, as in *The Garden of Earthly* *68* *Delights*, while the Hell panel of Bosch's *Haywain* shows demons in the actual process of erecting a tower in Hell: one carves a beam with an axe, another climbs a ladder holding a tray of mortar, while others operate a windlass to lift supplies to the top of the construction, and still others place bricks with trowels and mortar. Walter H. Gibson comments on the rarity of "circumstantial detail" in Bosch's infernal construction crew: "Towers abound in medieval descriptions of Hell, but the devils are usually too busy ministering to their victims to engage in such architectural enterprises."[39] Like Bosch, Milton is unusual in depicting the building process itself, but conforms to the visual convention in placing buildings in Hell.

In Raphael's vision, Michael triumphs over Satan in a dreary infernal waste, *69* with a gloomy Kremlin-like structure in the left background; the choir screen

---

Nicolson writes that "here the ears of some modern critics catch echoes of a masque presented at court on Sunday after Twelfth Night in 1637 (three years after the production of *Comus*), in which the 'spectacle' was of the opening of the earth and the rising of a 'richly adorned palace, seeming all of goldsmith's work' " (*A Reader's Guide*, p. 196). See also Merritt Y. Hughes' note on this passage in his *Complete Poems and Major Prose*, New York, 1957, and John G. Demaray, "The Thrones of Satan and God: Backgrounds to Divine Opposition in *Paradise Lost*," HLQ 31 (1967), 21-33. Enid Welsford persuasively suggests masque influence for the Pandaemonium episode (*The Court Masque*, Cambridge, 1927, pp. 312-13), as also does Hughes (*Complete Poems*, I, 710-17n.). William G. Riggs points out that architecture and music were closely associated in the Renaissance understanding of aesthetics (*The Christian Poet in "Paradise Lost*," Berkeley, 1972, p. 171).

[37] DeWald, *The Illustrations of the Utrecht Psalter*, fol. 5.

[38] Bodleian Library, MS. Univ. Coll. 100, fol. 82.

[39] Gibson, *Hieronymus Bosch*, p. 76. Bosch's conception of Hell is filled with distorted monster-demons, but if we could clear these out of the picture, we should see similarities between his Hell and Milton's, as Broadbent has observed: "The only Hell comparable with it [Milton's]—and then lacking its dramatic personalities—is the top of Bosch's Volet of Hell. There, in red and black, are the desperate activity, the dark Satanic mills, the building and destruction, the hurrying to-and-fro, the flames reflected in a carcassed lake of blood. The paint is laid on with gusto, your attention distracted by environing curiosities, but as you look it steadies, like Milton's vision, into a pattern that offers just enough scope for the recognition of your own devilry, and yet remains integral to the composition" (*Some Graver Subject*, pp. 108-9). Once we have excluded the "environing curiosities" with which Bosch has populated his Hell, the comparison works quite well, but Broadbent's words could be applied to many other examples in art besides those by Bosch.

carving for King's College Chapel in Cambridge shows purposeless buildings whose arches seem to lead nowhere save from waste to waste, while in the same chapel the Limbo window allows the buildings of Hell to show certain attractive features of Florentine quattrocento architecture; a propaganda engraving of 1527 representing the *Descent of the Pope into Hell* shows the Pope riding into the infernal city between two flaming buildings which could also be fifteenth-century Florentine.[40] A follower of Huys presents a largely architectural Hell in his *Last Judgment* at Philadelphia, as does Bonifacio da Pitati in his *Dives and Lazarus* at the Academy in Venice, and in Civetta's *Inferno* we have a virtual metropolis, while the same tradition is carried into the seventeenth century by the French artist Callot, by the Dutch Jacob van Swanenburgh, and by such Greek expatriates in Italy as Klotzas and Apakas.[41]

    To summarize, between the ninth and fifteenth centuries Hell was frequently represented by a single building of varying complexity, though it had been shown as early as the eleventh century to be a large walled city. From the fifteenth century onward, artists added building to building, until they were portraying Hell as a vast metropolis. It is such a visual tradition which Milton is invoking in his references to the "city and proud seat/ Of Lucifer," and to the demonic "metropolis" (x, 424-25, and 439). Here we find a visual explanation for what has seemed to be Milton's confusion as to whether Pandaemonium is a single building or an entire city. The manuscript of *Paradise Lost* (I, 756) identifies it as Satan's "capitoll," which was later corrected by the hand of a different amanuensis to read "capitall," a reading which is followed by the "capital" of the first two printed editions. Helen Darbishire prefers the first word as more precise, and attributes the change to an "officious corrector," but Milton apparently vacillated between the two readings, either of which can be defended.[42] Though Milton describes only the erection of a single building, he elsewhere explicitly designates a city and a metropolis, which is what the visual tradition would have prepared his readers to expect and to imagine. In his poetic depiction, Milton does not copy any single visual source, but goes beyond all available analogues to provide Satan with a capitol/capital of unrivaled panache and pretentiousness.

    As for the palace so for the throne: there were scores upon scores of enthroned Satans in art, but there was no throne exactly like that described in *Paradise Lost*:

[40] Hollstein, *German Engravings*, III, p. 232.

[41] The Callot etching is reprinted as figure 57 on p. 104 of Allardyce Nicoll's *Stuart Masques and the Renaissance Stage*, London, 1937; Swanenburgh is reproduced in the Centro Internazionale *Demonaico*, pl. XL; and the seventeenth- and eighteenth-century Byzantine paintings may be found in the Hellenic Institute in Venice. Interacting with the tradition of the pictorial arts was the tradition of the stage, where architecture was characteristic of Hell from the Middle Ages on, as may be seen in Owen, *The Vision of Hell*, pp. 16, 83-84, and 265, and in Cohen, *Histoire de la mise en scène*, pp. 92-99. The hexameral uses may be traced through Kirkconnell's *Celestial Cycle*. Inigo Jones did a sketch of Hell for the masque *Brittania Triumphans* of 1638 which included a cave's mouth, a lake, and a burning city with towers, battlements, and buildings (see Nicoll, *Stuart Masques*, fig. 72 on p. 115).

[42] Helen Darbishire, *The Manuscript of Milton's "Paradise Lost," Book I*, Oxford, 1931, p. 68.

> High on a throne of royal state, which far
> Outshone the wealth of Ormus and of Ind,
> Or where the gorgeous East with richest hand
> Showers on her kings barbaric pearl and gold,
> Satan exalted sat, by merit raised
> To that bad eminence; and from despair
> Thus high uplifted beyond hope, aspires
> Beyond thus high, insatiate to pursue
> Vain war with Heaven, and by success untaught
> His proud imaginations thus displayed.
>
> (II, 1-10)

If that throne outshines everything on earth, it outshines far more all that can be found in the traditional infernos of art. In the thirteenth and early fourteenth centuries, it was customary to represent Satan as seated on a chair made of dragons and serpents, as in the mosaic at Torcello, in the pulpits at Siena and Pisa, in the Arena Chapel in Padua, and in the Florentine Baptistry. Somewhat later, as at the Camposanto in Pisa, we see Satan represented as though he were seated on a close stool, from which he defecates the sinners whom he has engorged, dropping them like so many feces into the lowest parts of Hell; this conception reached its height, or perhaps more appropriately its depth, in the revolting throne upon which Satan sits to defecate in the Hell panel of Bosch's *Garden of Earthly Delights*. It is occasionally possible to find Satan's throne pictured in a fairly straightforward way as a royal chair of state, but even so the heavily distorted Satan seated upon it precludes the possibility of achieving Milton's effects.[43] As a general rule, the artists used a visually debased throne as yet another means for ridiculing Satan, whereas Milton employed a gorgeous throne so as to expose Satan by exalting him. Milton heightens, enhances, and dignifies both his demons and their Hell, allowing them to glorify themselves according to their own image; but at the same time, by a beautifully sustained irony, he manages to unmask them through the uninhibited pretentiousness of their attempts at self-elevation.

ENTRANCES AND EXITS

Any narrative treatment of Hell, whether literary or pictorial, must provide the infernal kingdom with entrances and exits. Through these, devils come and go on various missions, or sinners are admitted for their final punishment, or Christ enters on his mission of harrowing Hell and freeing the Old Testament saints from Limbo. The Biblical references to Hell treat the subject in a persistently metaphorical way and were never designed to give any accurate or even detailed topography. The artistic visualizations were elaborated from details picked up here and there in the Biblical accounts and imaginatively expanded through succeeding centuries. There are three principal types. Revelation 20:1 refers to the bottomless pit in which the

[43] Two examples of more straightforward thrones are reproduced from sixteenth-century prints in Jurgis Baltrušaitis, *Réveils et prodiges: Le gothique fantastique*, Paris, 1960, p. 329.

Dragon was imprisoned, and from this verse eventually stem hundreds of pictures in which the entrance to Hell is shown as an open pit or an open cave. A second conception showed the entrance to Hell as the open jaws of a giant sea monster, based ultimately upon the treatment of Leviathan in the forty-first chapter of Job, which had been associated with Hell as early as Saint Gregory the Great, and increasingly thereafter.[44] Finally, there was the gate of Hell, as referred to in Matthew 16:18 and elsewhere. These three basic types were sometimes pictured singly, but perhaps more often in various combinations and permutations. The usage was primarily metaphorical, and only a basic misunderstanding of the conception could lead us to seek or to expect consistency. It is impossible to find an authoritative map of Hell, whether in Scripture, in theology, in the hexameral writings, or in art. In each instance, the writer or artist served the purposes of his own design and the same is true for Milton: to expect in *Paradise Lost* a consistency of imagery here is to look for something which Milton felt himself under no obligation to supply. Milton and his contemporaries would surely have been amused, and probably exasperated, by the twentieth-century debate between Robins and Curry as to whether the infernal gate is in the wall or in the roof of Hell.[45]

Let us begin with the type which shows the opening to Hell as either a pit or a cave. Access to the "pit" might be through a cave opening in the side of a hill, as in the Spanish Chapel fresco, or as a simple hole in the level ground, as in the painting by Marco da Oggione. In Byzantine representations of Christ in Limbo, "the mouth of Hell, where shown at all, is indicated by a cavernous entrance" toward which "Christ advances over the broken valves of a door," combining both the gate and the pit-opening motifs.[46] Pit or cave openings may be seen at Pisa in the Camposanto frescoes of the *Triumph of Death*, and in the *Christ in Limbo* by Duccio di Buoninsegna at Siena, while we see similar treatments in the fifteenth-century illuminated French manuscript *Treatise on Antichrist* at the Bodleian Library, in Fra Angelico's *Last Judgment* at San Marco in Florence, and in the painting of Christ in Limbo by the school of Pacher at Princeton, as well as in the Utrecht Psalter. Representations in the sixteenth century include the Limoges Crucifixion Triptych at the Ashmolean, a *Christ in Limbo* by Civetta and the seventeenth-century *Dives in Hell* by Teniers the Younger, while in the Stuart masques "Hell scenes were usually of a cavernous kind."[47] In accordance with this visual convention, Milton frequently refers to the "pit" of Hell, and once to the many ways, "all dismal," which lead to Death's "grim cave" (I, 91-92, 381, 657; II, 850; IV, 965; VI, 866; X, 464; and XI, 468-70).

At least equally popular were representations of the entrance to Hell as the open jaws of Leviathan. As early as the *Genesis B* manuscript, Satan was represented as chained to the teeth of a giant whale, while his followers are shown falling pell mell into the whale's jaws. Meyer Shapiro identifies this hell mouth

59

51

221

103

100

71

33

---

[44] Emile Mâle, *Gothic Art*, pp. 379ff.

[45] H. F. Robins, "Satan's Journey: Directions in *Paradise Lost*," *JEGP* 60 (1961), p. 705, and Curry, *Milton's Ontology*, pp. 149-51 and 153.

[46] Dalton, *Byzantine Art and Archaeology*, p. 662.

[47] Nicoll, *Stuart Masques*, p. 68.

as "a typical English motive," and notes that most examples of it before the twelfth century are English.[48] Emile Mâle finds the conception entering French art in the twelfth century at Conques, where "the entrance is the maw of a monster which swallows up the condemned," though behind this we see the related motif of the door of Hell.[49] The maw of Leviathan had become almost universal in the thirteenth century, and continued thereafter, both on the continent and in England.[50] The bizarre nature of this motif subjected it to the possibilities of parody, as we see in the monstrous mouth enclosing the fireplace at Palazzo Thiene at Vicenza, in the entrance to the dining room in the Sacred Grove at Bomarzo, and in the doors and windows designed by Federico Zuccaro for his palace in Rome, all executed in the sixteenth century.[51] Despite the parodies, Leviathan's jaws continue to be treated seriously as the opening to Hell in El Greco's *Dream of Philip II* in both the version at London and the one in the Escorial, in the *Inferno* by Jacob van Swanenburgh at Danzig, in Rubens' *Franciscan Legend* at Philadelphia, and in Marten van Heemskerk's *Death and Judgment* at Hampton Court Palace. When Milton refers to the "mouth of Hell" and to its "ravenous jaws," or when he writes of the falling angels that "Hell at last/ Yawning received them whole, and on them closed," he was using a very ancient symbolism, but one which had by no means yet lost its visual force and vitality. In these words, brief though they are, Milton sketched a picture which would have been instantly recognized by his contemporaries (VI, 875; X, 288, 636-37; XII, 42).[52]

In each of these instances, Milton was able to evoke a visual image of considerable specificity by the use of very few words, but his treatment of the gates of Hell is far more elaborate. When he refers to "the huge portcullis," or to "the bars of Hell," and "the dismal gates," he is apparently evoking the standard range of visual conceptions. We may see instances of the grated or barred portcullis in *Genesis B*, in the *Last Judgment* after the manner of Huys, and in Civetta's *Inferno*. But Milton wishes to do more than merely evoke the standard versions of Hell's gates: he seeks something which multiplies and compounds everything of the kind in art:

> And thrice threefold the gates; three folds were brass,
> Three iron, three of adamantine rock,

[48] Meyer Shapiro, "Cain's Jawbone that did the First Murder," *Art Bulletin* 24 (1942), p. 211.

[49] Mâle, *Religious Art*, p. 56.

[50] Emile Mâle, *Gothic Image*, pp. 379-80, and M. D. Anderson, *History and Imagery in British Churches*, pp. 123-27.

[51] Shearman, *Mannerism*, p. 121.

[52] Michael Lieb analyzes the digestive and scatological imagery which Milton associated with the demonic world in the *Dialectics of Creation*, pp. 20, and 28. John R. Knott, Jr., associates this imagery of hellish mouth and jaws with the pictures of the devil in Hell: "Satan himself was often represented with the legs of unfortunate sinners protruding from his mouth. God's promise to seal the 'ravenous jaws' of Hell takes on more force if we have such images in mind, as many of Milton's contemporaries would have had" (*Milton's Pastoral Vision*, p. 146). In chapter VII, I discuss the same motif in connection with Death.

> Inpenetrable, impaled with circling fire,
> Yet unconsumed.

(II, 645-48)

Though the fire is customary enough, everything else about those gates is unique.

In art, the gates of Hell appear most frequently in representations of Christ in Limbo, where they tend to be very simple devices indeed. What Christ breaks down in order to rescue the patriarchs is rarely more than a rather sturdy door made of a single material. Schiller presents many versions, and though it is not always possible to determine certainly the materials of the door, it generally appears to be made of metal or of heavy wood. Iron hinges, bolts, and locks are often conspicuous as well.[53] The fresco in the Spanish Chapel also postulates the breaking of a masonry wall, a representation which may be found elsewhere. But I have seen no gate of Hell in art which would even remotely correspond to Milton's conception. For his epic purposes, Milton requires gates far more formidable and massive than any which he could simply evoke from the trained imaginations of his contemporaries, so he specifically excludes the traditional oak, and substitutes brass, iron, and adamantine rock, each in three folds, as he magnifies and multiplies the conventional image.

In Milton's visualization, those uniquely "dismal gates" did not open upon some part of earth, as in Dante, nor indeed upon any part of the created universe. In *Paradise Lost*, Hell is outside everything else, apart from everything else. This visualization is not merely poetic carpentry, but conveys a critical aspect of Milton's understanding. As Winifred Hunt has commented, "Paradise in a world already lodging Hell [as in Dante] would not glisten from a setting pure enough for Milton's purpose. Paradise on a wholly uncorrupted earth, with Hell beyond Chaos, does."[54] But more is involved than protecting the purity of Eden, for Milton's theological conception of Hell as "beyond the pale" is here expressed in perfectly appropriate visual imagery. Whether Milton conceived of this idea on his own, or found it in theology, I do not know; I seriously doubt that he took it directly from art, but it was there as a visual tradition he could evoke, and evoke it he did. In painting, the created universe was represented as a circle or a globe, just as Milton described it in *Paradise Lost*. In the Psalter illuminated by de Brailes in the mid-thirteenth century, we see this full circle represented with Christ enthroned at the center, and the rebel angels falling out of that golden globe into a lower region where the background is painted black, as they tumble into the ravenous jaws of Hell's mouth. In the following century, the Holkham Picture Bible shows Christ setting the bounds of the global universe with a compass, below and outside of

103

59

---

[53] Schiller, *Ikonographie*, III, figs. 99-171. In polar opposition to Milton's "thrice threefold" strengthening of the gates are the flimsy gates executed in woodcarvings for the high altar of the Nicholas Church in Kalkar, Niederrhein, executed by Master Loedewich about the year 1500. This door is made of rustic slats, such as might be found on an outhouse or privy, and the implications for Hell are unmistakable (*ibid.*, fig. 163).

[54] Winifred Hunt, "On Even Ground: A Note on the Extramundane Location of Hell in *Paradise Lost*," *MLQ* 23 (1962), 17-18.

53
56 which we see the jaws of Leviathan, while Queen Mary's Psalter allows only the slightest intersection between the circles representing the created universe and Hell. In the sixteenth century, Bruegel's *Fall of the Rebel Angels* pictures Michael and his hosts pursuing the already grossly deformed rebel angels down toward Hell,
5 far below the luminous globe of the created universe above them. In Civetta, Hell is a grim metropolis on a barren and fiery plain, above which we see represented
101 the globe of a Ptolemaic universe with planets orbiting within it—as close a visual equivalent as one could possibly hope to find to Milton's poetically described "firm opacous globe/ Of this round World" (III, 418-19).

The Chaos which separates Hell from the Universe in *Paradise Lost* is essentially unpaintable:

> Before their eyes in sudden view appear
> The secrets of the hoary deep, a dark
> Illimitable ocean without bound,
> Without dimension, where length, breadth, and highth,
> And time and place are lost.

(II, 890-94)

That description is exclusively literary, and its defining terms prohibit even the possibility of finding an equivalent in art. Painting, sculpture, and mosaic work are alike in presenting a scene through dimension, through length, breadth, height, and place—but Milton explicitly cancels every dimension, every limit, every measure.[55] In Whitney's *Emblems*, Chaos is represented by a confusion of lines and shapes crossing each other, in the center of which are the Greek letters which spell out the word,[56] but here art is abandoned in favor of a labeled cartoon. In the *Last Judgment* diptych by Van Eyck, the skeletal specter of Death has its bat wings labeled *Chaos Magnum* and also *Umbra Mortis*, for even Van Eyck could present Chaos only by personification. Lorenzo Lotto executed a curious allegory entitled *Magnum Chaos* in intarsia for Santa Maria Maggiore in Bergamo, but again we are involved only in allegory.[57] But Milton's description of Chaos remains unique; nowhere is his exploitation of the literary mode more complete than here, and nowhere are we further removed from any direct relevance to the art tradition. Yet, although he virtually abandons the visual, he continues to employ a powerfully sensuous imagery as he describes how

> eagerly the fiend
> O'er bog or steep, through straight, rough, dense, or rare,

[55] For the absence of apposite sources for Milton's Chaos in Greek mythology, see Osgood, *Classical Mythology*, p. 22; for a comparison with Neoplatonic doctrines, see Walter C. Curry, "Milton's Chaos and Old Night," *JEGP* 46 (1947), 38-52; for the history of Demogorgon (whose divinity is ultimately traceable to a grammatical error), see Jean Seznec, *The Survival of the Pagan Gods*, p. 222.

[56] Geoffrey Whitney, *Emblems*, Leyden, 1586, p. 122 (facsimile ed. Henry Green, 1866).

[57] See Berenson, *Lorenzo Lotto*, p. 64 and pl. 177. Other instances of personified Chaos may be found by consulting the Index of Christian Art at Princeton.

With head, hands, or feet pursues his way,
And swims or sinks, or wades, or creeps, or flies.

(II, 947-50)

We *feel* in our bones every struggling inch of Satan's progress through an invisible void, and nowhere did Milton more fully achieve those tactile responses which Berenson regarded as essential to great art.[58]

Satan has scarcely emerged from Chaos when Milton tells us of the great bridge which Sin and Death will make through Chaos to link Hell with Earth. A precedent may be found in the warning of Matthew 7:13 that "wide is the gate, and broad is the way, which leadeth to destruction," but Rajan is surely correct when he describes the bridge as "a causeway which Milton's imagination built, even though its diabolical span encompasses scriptural and Virgilian texts."[59] Milton's imagination is as always the shaping factor, yet he was not asking his readers to envision a total novelty, for Hell had been pictured with bridges for at least a century and a half before *Paradise Lost*. These bridges are conspicuous, broad, and capacious, and as such begin to appear in the late Renaissance.

There was an earlier bridge, appearing both in literature and art, but it differed in crucial ways from what we find in post-Renaissance art and in Milton. This earlier bridge was known as the "Bridge of Dread," and is described by M. D. Anderson as "narrow, slippery, sharp-edged or set with spikes, over which the spirits of the dead must cross," and she cites an example in a twelfth-century Doom painting at Chaldon, Surrey.[60] Both the virtuous and the vicious must cross it, or fall from it, as a test of moral fitness. This bridge is always represented as narrow in the extreme: it may vary from the width of a hair or thread, to that of a sword's edge, to that of a single plank, but the righteous cross it with ease.[61]

The bridges of Hell which we find in sixteenth- and seventeenth-century art are conceived and visualized in radically different ways. In the first place, they provide no access to Heaven, but are a purely infernal phenomenon: every symbolic and visual indication defines those on these bridges as already damned, precluding the possibility of testing the virtuous. In the second place, these bridges are no longer perilously narrow, but broadly capacious and capable of heavy traffic. Whether the post-Renaissance artists were aware of the significance earlier attached to the Bridge of Dread seems to me highly dubious, though some attempts have been made to suggest that they were.[62] Whatever may be made of this

[58] Berenson, *Italian Painters of the Renaissance*, pp. 63, 85, and 153.

[59] B. Rajan, *The Lofty Rhyme*, Coral Gables, Fla., 1970, p. 58. See also E.M.W. Tillyard, "Causeway from Hell to the World," *SP* 38 (1941), 266-70.

[60] M. D. Anderson, *History and Imagery in British Churches*, p. 127.

[61] Howard R. Patch, *The Other World*, Cambridge, Mass., 1950, pp. 95-97, 112, 125, and 203; Owen, *The Vision of Hell*, pp. 4, 12, 20, 28-29, 34, 43-44, and 152; and L. D. Ettlinger, "Virtituum et Viciorum Adumbracio," *JWCI* 19 (1956), 155-56.

[62] Anthony Blunt, "El Greco's 'Dream of Philip II': An Allegory of the Holy League," *JWCI* 3 (1939-40), 58-69, attempts to show that El Greco was aware of the ancient meanings, but his argument remains dubious as we may see by consulting Neil Maclaren and Allan

historical background, bridges became a standard feature of the infernal landscape from Bosch on. The Hell panel of Bosch's *Garden of Earthly Delights* shows a conspicuous bridge in the upper center, while Coecke van Aelst's *St. John the Evangelist* shows a bridge leading into Hell and others within Hell, and Civetta's *Christ in Limbo* has at least one bridge, in the lower left, of Hell. In Civetta's *Inferno*, the bridge is conspicuously placed in the upper left of the landscape, just below the horizon, where it moves off in the direction of the globe of the Universe in the center, and may connect with it, though the painting is sufficiently dirty that description must remain uncertain. In the very center of this painting there is another bridge, across which demons and the damned move. In El Greco's *Dream of Philip II* (also sometimes referred to as *Adoration of the Holy Name of Jesus* and as *Allegory of the Holy League*), there is also a bridge within Hell and another which apparently leads out of Hell, though its destination is not made clear, and we find much the same thing in Fontana's engraved *Last Judgment*. The *Inferno* painted by Jacob van Swanenburgh features a conspicuous bridge, from which some sinners are falling into the burning lake below, and which exits from Hell on the sinister side of the painting, though once more the destination is not explicit.

In the *Death and Judgment* painting by Marten van Heemskerk, at Hampton Court Palace, the visual scheme is made unmistakably clear: the bridge leads from Earth to the huge open maw of Leviathan in Hell. In the Heemskerk painting we have a precise visual equivalent of Milton's bridge between Hell and Earth as "a passage broad,/ Smooth, easy, inoffensive down to Hell," but in the others as well we have close visual analogues (x, 304-5). In each instance we see "a broad and beaten way/ Over the dark abyss, whose boiling gulf/ Tamely endured a bridge . . . ," "the work by wondrous art/ Pontifical, a ridge of pendant rock/ Over the vexed abyss" (II, 1026-28, and x, 312-14).

Dr. Johnson strenuously objected to Milton's bridge, and wrote that "this unskillful allegory appears to me one of the greatest faults of the poem; and to this there was no temptation, but the author's opinion of its beauty."[63] At this point a century of radical change separated Johnson the critic from Milton the poet, and Johnson's history is obviously in error, for the "temptation" of the Bridge was already there for Milton, quite apart from "the author's opinion of its beauty." It is not a question of whether Milton could have created his Bridge without the preparation of art; to deny that he could have done so is to ignore the creativity of genius. Had Dr. Johnson's exposure to art more nearly equaled his knowledge of literature, he would not have been shocked by the physicality of the bridge constructed by Sin and Death. With his imagination so prepared, he would have been able to appreciate the brilliance with which Milton at once adopted and transformed an ancient visual conception.

As with the bridge, so elsewhere in Milton's Hell: the poet was not creating

---

Braham, *The National Gallery Catalogue: The Spanish School*, London, 1970, p. 30. Also interesting is Allan Braham, "Two Notes on El Greco and Michelangelo," *Burlington Magazine* 108 (1966), 307-8.

[63] Samuel Johnson, *Lives of the English Poets*, I, 186.

de novo, but was skillfully evoking in the imaginations of his readers physical elements which had been indelibly impressed upon the European mind over many centuries by visual artists. Milton resolutely excluded the graphic torments and torture chambers of the traditional Hell, but he employed every other major motif of that tradition. In doing so, he relied upon his words and phrases to elicit visual counterparts with which his readers would be familiar, but he transforms even that which he elicits. His demons achieve in Hell a dignity and a style they never attained in art, yet even when he elevates to their greatest magnificence the established motifs, he keeps the old degrading inferno in our minds as the background of reality against which the fallen angels construct their illusion.[64]

[64] Arnold Stein, in *Answerable Style*, p. 44, puts it that "outside the area where some material superiority seems to have been gained over place by mind lies the classic Hell with all its static horrors."

Part Three
The Heavenly World

IX

Images for the Divine

GOD THE FATHER AND GOD THE HOLY SPIRIT

MILTON's presentation of God the Father is generally regarded as the greatest weakness of *Paradise Lost*. It is also the least visual aspect of the poem. Anthropomorphic representations of the Eternal Father had dominated art from at least the twelfth century, but the Father is presented by Milton in sternly abstract terms, not only as to his "appearance" but even as to his vocabulary when he speaks.[1] Nothing in Milton is further removed from the visual than his God the Father, whom the angelic choir describes as "unspeakable, who sit'st above these Heavens/ To us invisible, or dimly seen/ In these thy lowest works" (v, 156-58).

In his insistence upon the invisibility of the Father, Milton is closer to the first millennium of Christian art than to the centuries which immediately preceded him. Images of God the Father are exceedingly rare in the early art of Christendom, and are almost always connected with the creation of man, though even that scene is far more often shown with the Christ-Logos as creator.[2] Anthropomorphic representations of God the Father increase after the first millennium, and fall into three general types: the Ancient of Days, the Papal or Imperial Majesty, and the Christian Jupiter of the Renaissance.[3] The Ancient of Days may have originated during the iconoclast controversies, and by the eleventh century was firmly established in Byzantine art. In purely facial terms it might be difficult to distinguish this Father from one of the patriarchs such as Abraham, though the divine halo and other attributes made the identification clear.[4] This representation had the disadvantage of making the Eternal Father into a kindly old gentleman much burdened with years, and in the fourteenth century efforts were made to provide him with attributes of exaltation and glory which would be immediately impressive to the viewers of the art works. Thus we begin to see God the Father dressed in papal or imperial robes, and this God-pope or God-emperor was increasingly popular until the Renaissance.[5] In the Renaissance, there was a perhaps inevitable tendency

[1] Arnold Stein, *Answerable Style*, p. 128, writes that "language and cadence are as unsensuous as if Milton were writing a model for the Royal Society and attempting to speak purely to the understanding." Isabel G. MacCaffrey, in "The Theme of *Paradise Lost*, Book III," in *New Essays on Paradise Lost* (ed. Thomas Kranidas), pp. 71-72, notes that "the rhetoric can be described as a kind of skeletal or paradigmatic idiom, its language stripped of sensuous implication."

[2] Walter Lowrie, *Monuments of the Early Church*, London, 1901, p. 259.

[3] Réau, *Iconographie*, II, i, pp. 7-9.

[4] Dalton, *Byzantine Art and Archaeology*, p. 670.

[5] Panofsky, *Early Netherlandish Painting*, I, p. 213, and Mâle, *Religious Art*, p. 108. For British developments, see M. D. Anderson, *Imagery of British Churches*, pp. 81-82.

to represent God the Father as a Jupiter figure, far removed from the Hebrew imagery and reflecting a new Hellenism. Epitomizing this tendency are the figures of God in Michelangelo's Sistine Ceiling and in Raphael's *Vision of Ezekiel*. Of the latter Berenson has written: "Is it thus that Jehovah revealed himself to his prophets? Is it not rather Zeus appearing to a Sophocles?"[6] Milton might well have asked the same question.

Of the three visual types of God the Father as represented in art, none appears in *Paradise Lost*. Milton's religious scruples were certainly a factor here: most English Protestants probably objected in greater or lesser degree to visual delineations of God the Father, and most Puritans surely did. As for the Godhead itself, Milton followed the precedents of his coreligionists and of the early Church in making the Son the only visual and operative principal of deity. Relying upon those precedents again, however, he did provide a kind of visual aura for the first person of the Trinity by the use of synecdoche and attributes. "Although *Paradise Lost* contains no single descriptive passage depicting God as a total physical being, there are many ascriptions of individual human parts to the Deity," as Leland Ryken puts it. "Milton's anthropomorphism takes the form of the rhetorical figure of synecdoche, in which a whole person is designated by one of its parts or aspect."[7]

Of the synecdochic symbols the hand was by far the most ancient, deriving eventually from the familiar language of the Psalmist referring to "the hand of God," and "the arm of the Lord." In early Christian art, as Lowrie writes, "it was usually by a mere hand or arm stretched from a cloud that the presence of God was represented, and the artist was relieved of the necessity of depicting the deity in human form."[8] This feature continued into the Middle Ages and beyond, representing the benediction, command, or judgment of God the Father: "C'est une *main parlante* qui traduit la pensée et la volonté de l'Eternel."[9] This "speaking hand" could be widely illustrated from Paleo-Christian times through the Protestant period of Milton himself, but the variations were relatively minor and the artistic potential limited, so I give here only one illustration, a twelfth-century mosaic from the Church of San Clemente in Rome. Milton repeatedly refers to the hand

---

[6] Berenson, *The Italian Painters of the Renaissance*, pp. 213-14. Perhaps Berenson's opinion needs to be balanced by that of Ruskin, who took such treatments "as mere symbols, the noblest that could be employed, but as much symbols still as a triangle, or the Alpha and Omega, nor do I think that the most scrupulous amongst Christians ought to desire to exchange the power obtained by the use of this symbol in Michelangelo's creation of Adam and Eve, for the effect which would be produced by the substitution of any other sign in place of it" (*Modern Painters*, in *Works*, IV, p. 318). Aside from Michelangelo, however, there were few artists who could invest the symbol with its intended meaning.

[7] Leland Ryken, *The Apocalyptic Vision in "Paradise Lost,"* pp. 128-29.

[8] Lowrie, *Monuments of the Early Church*, pp. 263-64, and see also Jacob, *Idealism and Realism*, p. 232, for the use of this feature on early Christian tombs.

[9] Réau, *Iconographie*, II, i, p. 7. The Rabbinic and Biblical contexts for the hand of God are treated by Jason P. Rosenblatt, "Structural Unity and Temporal Concordance: The War in Heaven in *Paradise Lost*," 35-36. In another context (without direct reference to art) E. W. Taylor observes that the "guiding hand" of the opening line of *Samson Agonistes* is "the commonest shorthand for God and His Providence" ("Milton's *Samson*: The Form of Christian Tragedy," *ELR* 3 [1973], 311).

as a symbol of the power, command, blessing, or control of the Almighty, and in so doing he is supported by the visual tradition, but his treatment of the motif can scarcely be thought of as primarily visual.[10]

God's ear, nostrils, and feet also figure symbolically in *Paradise Lost*, but here there is very little visual tradition to support the associations, which are primarily derivative from, and refer back to, Old Testament accounts. The eye of God, like his hand, was at once a Biblical and an artistic symbol of deity. Milton's use of such symbols does provide some visual references for his God the Father, but the visualization remains minimal and the synecdoche becomes very nearly an abstraction.[11] Only once does Milton go beyond a bare synecdoche of the throne and eye of God, and give us a little sketch:

> Now had the Almighty Father from above,
> From the pure Empyrean where he sits
> High throned above all highth, bent down his eye,
> His own works and their works at once to view.
>
> (III, 56-59)

That description provides a brief vignette which could be traced through innumerable paintings back to medieval drama in which God was seated in a gallery, looking down upon the action of the main stage.[12] Given Milton's consistently nonvisual treatment of God the Father, this description is somewhat surprising.

While Milton's synecdoches are visually limited, the attributes with which he surrounds his Eternal Father receive somewhat more visual development. The "skirts" of God are a case in point:

> thou shadest
> The full blaze of thy beams, and through a cloud
> Drawn round about thee like a radiant shrine,
> Dark with excessive bright thy skirts appear. . . .
>
> (III, 377-80)

In the Sistine Ceiling, Michelangelo has God the Father "drawn round" with an operative radiant shrine or "skirts" in the creation scenes, but he pictures God as a vital and dynamic human figure within that shrine. Here Milton's Protestantism appears most decisively: he accepts the attribute of the radiant cloud or whirling skirts as a kind of frame, but removes the image of God. What he gives us as a frame of attributes is entirely conventional, and may be found in such fifteenth-

106

---

[10] References to the hand appear in *Paradise Lost* as follows: II, 174; III, 279; V, 606; VI, 139, 747, 762, 807, 835, 892; VII, 500; IX, 344; X, 64, 772, 1058; XI, 372; XII, 457; and *PR* III, 187. In accordance with both literary and artistic tradition, most of these references are to the right hand. Satan and his hosts, parodying the Divine in this as in all else, also make frequent references to their hands or to the Satanic "right hand": I, 732; II, 727; V, 864; and VI, 154.

[11] See Leland Ryken, pp. 130-31. Edgar Wind, *Pagan Mysteries*, pp. 231ff., traces other backgrounds for the eye as a symbol.

[12] W. L. Hildburgh, "English Alabaster Carvings as Records of the Medieval Religious Drama," *Archaeologia* 93 (1949), 68.

century painters as Benozzo Gozzoli and Francesco di Giorgio, and in sixteenth-century masters such as Jan Mostaert and Tintoretto.[13]

109

The use of a cloud surrounding God, but without an anthropomorphic representation of the Deity, was a frequent Protestant device, as may be seen in the frontispiece of the Geneva Bible of 1583. The use of the Hebrew letters for God in the center of a cloud, or the use of an eye there, provided little that could be developed visually, even if a hand were also shown reaching down below the clouds.[14] Milton tries to invigorate the scene by scent when he refers to "incense clouds," and he provides some tint of color in the "golden cloud" from which the voice of God emerges, but he has in the final analysis very little to show (VII, 599, and VI, 28).

The clouds surrounding God were traditionally associated with light, in a paradox which presented at once God's hiding of himself and revelation of himself. This conception is probably more accessible to poetic expression than to expression in art. Milton can describe his "eternal King" as "fountain of light, thyself invisible/ Amidst the glorious brightness where thou sitest/ Throned inaccessible," and we are able to follow his meaning, or he can enthrone the Deity in Heaven upon "a flaming mount, whose top/ Brightness had made invisible," and again we understand (III, 375-77; V, 598-99), for a poet can write of the invisible as a painter cannot possibly paint it. In treating this ancient Christian conception, a painter can rely only upon hints and suggestions as Tintoretto does in his *Saint George Slaying the Dragon*, where God the Father appears amidst circles of light in which his own distinctive brightness almost disappears, though not quite.[15]

110

The scales are another attribute of God the Father which Milton introduces into *Paradise Lost* when Gabriel and Satan are on the verge of conflict, and "Th' Eternal to prevent such horrid fray/ Hung forth in Heaven his golden scales" (IV, 996-97). Primarily traceable to Biblical usage, but also paralleled in Classical epics,[16] the divine scales appeared with great frequency in art. In the early centuries of Christian iconography, the scales were held by the hand of God from Heaven, and it is only later that the instrument was largely transferred to an association with the Archangel Michael.[17] With or without reference to art, Milton reverts to the earlier usage and ascribes the scales to the hand of God, visible alike to Satan and Gabriel, as it would be highly inappropriate at this point to have Michael intervene.[18]

Milton's descriptions of God the Father represent a visual *via negativa*, and at

[13] Gozzoli's fresco for the Camposanto in Pisa is reproduced in van Marle, *Iconographie*, I, p. 166; the painting by Francesco di Giorgio of *The Coronation of the Virgin* is in the cathedral at Siena; Tintoretto's *Jacob's Dream* is reproduced in Francis P. B. Osmaston, *The Art and Genius of Tintoret*, I, pl. CIV.

[14] See Bateman, *The Doom Warning All Men to Judgemente*, London, 1581, sig. A1.

[15] For the problems and opportunities which painters found in light, see Millard Meiss, "Light as Form and Symbol in some Fifteenth-Century Paintings," in *Renaissance Art* (ed. Creighton Gilbert), New York, 1970, pp. 43-68.

[16] Isa. 40:12, and Dan. 5:27; *Iliad*, VIII, 69-72, and XXII, 209, and *Aen.* XII, 725-27.

[17] Perry, "On the Psychostasis in Christian Art," p. 103, and Réau, *Iconographie*, II, i, pp. 49-50.

[18] Panofsky, *Early Netherlandish Painting*, I, 270-71 traces the use of scales both in the

most the visual arts merely support his use of attributes and symbols which were equally accessible in literature. Nowhere else does he so completely diverge from the major artistic traditions of the five or six centuries before his own time; that he does so is clearly the result of widely held Protestant convictions.

There is one other divergence from tradition to which particular attention should be called for it reveals Milton introducing a descriptive feature which is all his own: Milton's Eternal Father is a smiling and even a laughing God. The Son predicts, of his own work of redemption, that his Father will "look down and smile," out of Heaven, while elsewhere the Father "smiling" speaks to his Son (III, 257, and V, 718). In *Paradise Regained* (I, 129), the Father "smiling spake" to Gabriel about the beginning of Christ's mission of redemption. Elsewhere, God laughs in derision at his demonic adversaries, and Raphael suggests that he may be moved by scientists to "laughter at their quaint opinions wide" (V, 737, and VIII, 78). Sin declares that the Father "sits above and laughs" at the near fatal confrontation between Death and Satan (II, 731). Finally, "great laughter was in Heaven" at Nimrod's assault upon Heaven itself in building the great Tower of Babel (XII, 59). Some heavenly laughter appears to be scornful of God's puny enemies, but the divine smiles are more beneficent, as in response to the providential redemption of man.[19] So far as I have been able to determine, there is no counterpart anywhere in art to Milton's smiling and laughing Deity, a fact which makes his description all the more significant.[20]

The Holy Spirit figures in both of Milton's epics under the familiar form of the dove. In *Paradise Regained*, Milton invokes the "Spirit . . ./ With prosperous wing full summed to tell of deeds/ Above heroic," where the "summed" is a reference to the full perfection of a bird's wings (*PR* I, 8, 14-15). When Milton invokes his "Heavenly Muse" at the beginning of *Paradise Lost*, he makes his meaning clear by a vivid description of the Spirit of God at Creation:

> Thou from the first
> Wast present, and with mighty wings outspread
> Dove-like satst brooding on the vast Abyss

Last Judgment and in classical combat, and Katzenellenbogen (*Allegories of the Virtues and Vices*, p. 55) notes that the figure was applied to Justice from very early times. Adelheid Heimann, "Three Illustrations from the Bury St. Edmunds Psalter and their Prototypes: Notes on the Iconography of Some Anglo-Saxon Drawings," *JWCI* 29 (1966), 51-52, provides information on the history of the figure in early English times.

[19] On the divine laughter, see Leland Ryken, *The Apocalyptic Vision*, p. 137.

[20] Shumaker (*Unpremeditated Verse*, p. 20) emphasizes the importance of noting both "what is admitted into the work as image and idea and what is kept out." The variation from an established iconographic scheme is at least as important as adherence to it. An interesting example of this important principle may be found in Paul Atkins Underwood, "The Fountain of Life in Manuscripts of the Gospels," *Dumbarton Oaks Papers* no. 5 (1950), p. 43: "When a pagan architectural type with fixed significations, such as the mausoleum of Roman Imperial times, was taken as model for a Christian Baptistry, an analogy was drawn between the traditional signification of the type and the new function to which it was put. The 'allegories' thus established were usually rather apt, and the parallelism of meaning between a mausoleum and a Baptistry was peculiarly so, for among the connotations of the rights of Baptism is that which associates it with death, burial, and resurrection."

> And madest it pregnant: What in me is dark
> Illumine, what is low raise and support.

(I, 6, 19-24)

The last two lines provide the traditional theological understanding of the operation of the Holy Spirit within man, providing both understanding and strength, while the first four lines present a picture of the original creative activity of the Spirit, based in the first chapter of Genesis. Of that scene, Milton later gives another account:

> Darkness profound
> Covered th' Abyss: but on the watery calm
> His brooding wings the Spirit of God outspread,
> And vital virtue infused, and vital warmth
> Throughout the fluid mass, . . .

(VII, 233-37)

In these passages, Milton sought to evoke in the reader's mind the familiar image of the dove of the Holy Spirit, but at the same time it was necessary for him to go beyond that simple image to convey a massiveness and pervasiveness of power which could not be suggested by any simple picture of a dove. At most, then, his description must be "dove-like" without actually representing a dove. In conveying that conception, Milton could rely on greater support from the magnificent poetry of Genesis than from anything in the visual tradition, though artists had frequently used the dove to represent the Spirit of God moving upon the water.

GOD THE SON

Milton's resolute insistence upon the invisibility of the Father is balanced by a like insistence that the Son shows "the radiant image of his glory" (III, 63). It is the Son "In whose conspicuous countenance, without cloud/ Made visible, th' Almighty Father shines,/ Whom else no creature can behold," and "he full/ Resplendent all his Father manifest/ Expressed" (III, 385-87, and X, 65-67). That seems clear enough, and conveys the universal Christian doctrine that God the Father may be fully seen only through his image reflected in the Son. But what Milton appears to give with his right hand, he decidedly takes away with his left. When the Father addresses the Messiah as "effulgence of my glory, Son beloved,/ Son in whose face invisible is beheld/ Visibly, what by deity I am,/ And in whose hand what by decree I do," the paradox is neatly concealed by Milton's poetic sleight-of-hand: "in whose face invisible is beheld/ Visibly" (VI, 680-84). Here indeed the music almost carries us away, and we may very well be persuaded that we have seen something "visibly" even though we are told that it appears in a "face invisible."[21] A bit later we read of the Son that "he all his Father full expressed/

---

[21] Another interpretation is possible here: "invisible" may be intended as a noun so as to read "in whose face [the] invisible is beheld/ Visibly." But Milton usually capitalized nouns, and "invisible" is not capitalized. I agree with Fowler (VI, 684n.), and take the expression to be

Ineffably into his face received," which is in effect to say that the Son's face fully expressed inexpressibly his Father (VI, 720-21). Milton is apparently fearful that if he were to specify physical features even in the Son, he might unduly narrow our impression and response, perhaps especially since the Son has not yet become incarnate. What Milton wishes us to see revealed is psychological, moral, intellectual:

> Beyond compare the Son of God was seen
> Most glorious, in him all his Father shown
> Substantially expressed, and in his face
> Divine compassion visibly appeared,
> Love without end, and without measure grace.
>
> (III, 138-42)

Throughout, Milton shows great poetic tact in concealing what he is not revealing, because many centuries of art had persuaded Christians to assume, however unconsciously, that they knew the appearance of the Son. Actually there were two standard representations, and the bearded figure with which we are most familiar is the more recent of the two. Universally until the fourth century, and often for several centuries thereafter, Christ was represented as a beardless young man, usually conceived as the Good Shepherd but sometimes as the young Prince or Emperor.[22] Even after its early popularity waned, this representation continued for many centuries, and came to indicate the celestial being, the second person of the Trinity. As such, we see the Son appear in the Creation cupola in the atrium of San Marco in Venice. The widespread usage of this figure to represent the preexistent Christ-Logos might lead us to visualize the Son in this way throughout *Paradise Lost*, but we have no explicit warrant in Milton for doing so.

I, 3

III

The other representation, which became dominant after the fourth century, showed the Son as a bearded man of about thirty years of age. This type is sometimes referred to as the Nazarene, and reflects Near Eastern influences as well as the once prevalent fashion for philosophers and teachers to wear beards. This conception was increasingly used in representations of Jesus during his earthly ministry, and also after his ascension to Heaven. It might be tempting to assume this appearance for the Son in *Paradise Regained*, but again Milton provides no explicit warrant for doing so. In a somewhat comparable case, Shakespeare gives conflicting hints as to whether or not his King Lear is bald (the Fool refers to his "bald crown" and Lear to his "white head" [1.4.170, and 3.2.6]), but Milton gives no indication whatsoever as to whether or not his Son is bearded. As for facial and physical characteristics, the Son in Milton's epics is described in no more visual terms than the Father.

---

an oxymoron. Certainly Milton leaves the matter ambiguous, and scrupulously avoids providing physical features for the Son's face.

[22] Pierre du Bourguet, *Early Christian Painting*, New York, 1965, pp. 15-17; Dalton, 670-72; Lowrie, *Monuments of the Early Church*, 218-19; and Antonio Bosio, *Roma Sotterranea*, Rome, 1632, pp. 237-52, *passim*.

But there are major differences. Whereas the Father is never shown in action, but only in judgment and contemplation, the Son is repeatedly and dramatically active. Presumably this is what God the Father means when he declares that the Son expresses visibly "what by decree I do" (VI, 683). It is by his action that the Son is described in *Paradise Lost*, whether as victor in the War in Heaven, as Creator of the universe and of man, or as friend and judge of Adam and Eve in Eden. On this casting of the Son in each of these roles, scholars have said that Milton was in one way or another introducing a new element into the tradition of the hexamera. Whether this contention is true of the literary and theological traditions I do not know, though I am inclined to doubt it, but Milton was certainly supported in each instance by a strong visual tradition, as we shall now see.

Milton's insistence upon magnifying the role of the Son—which is obvious throughout *Paradise Lost*—is nowhere clearer than when he casts him as victor and "hero" in the War in Heaven. Dustdoor declares that "in none of the versions of the legend in Middle English literature, so far as my knowledge of it goes, is there any indication of . . . the Messiah's intervention in the conflict."[23] Perhaps so, but the visual arts, as we have seen, provide ample evidence of that triumphant intervention. The point is important enough to justify a brief recapitulation. In the illumination of the ninth-century Utrecht Psalter, there are numerous examples of Christus Victor with shield, spear, bow, and arrows.[24] In the eleventh-century Aelfric Manuscript, we see Christ enthroned in a mandorla, raising his hand in a gesture of command to expel black-haired humanoid devils. *Genesis B* comes even closer in some ways to Milton's description, with the "thunders" and "arrows" of the Almighty in the raised right hand of the Son who drives the rebel angels over "the bounds" and "the verge of Heaven" (*PL*, VI, 713, 836, 845, 854, 859, and 865).

The fourteenth-century Italian *Treatise on the Seven Vices* does not show the weapons which Milton and the Anglo-Saxon artist provide, but does represent the chariot in which Milton places the Son at the climax of the action (VI, 749-66, 835-55). Here the good angels only stand and watch, as they do in *Paradise Lost*, while Christ in his chariot raises his right hand and by that mere gesture expels the rebel angels, who are seen plunging into Hell. If we return to the Utrecht Psalter of the ninth century, we find the Son trampling over his enemies as he rushes forward brandishing a spear (presumably a thunderbolt) in a chariot drawn by four horses. An anonymous mid-sixteenth-century woodcut shows Christ riding victoriously in the chariot, and by the simple raising of his hand condemning his opponents to Hell. The Modena Triptych, an allegory of the Christian warrior attributed to El Greco, shows Christ in the chariot of Ezekiel with Hell's mouth below.[25] Finally, there is also a 1590 print of the same subject by Andrea Andreani.[26]

---

[23] Dustdoor, "Legends of Lucifer," 248.

[24] DeWald, *The Illustrations of the Utrecht Psalter*, fols. 34v., 73v., 85, 85v., and *passim*.

[25] Both reproduced in Lydie Hadermann-Misguich, "Deux nouvelles sources d'inspiration du polyptyque de Modène," *Gazette des Beaux-Arts* 63 (1964), pp. 356-57. Schiller, *Ikonographie*, III, figs. 662-63, shows that the visual motif of Christ in a chariot is also an Eastern variant on the Majestas Domini.

[26] Harold Wethey, *El Greco and His School*, 2 vols., Princeton, 1962, II, 198. For Raphael's very different treatment of the subject, see Fischel, *Raphael*, I, pp. 273-74.

The artistic tradition exemplified by these pictures would have provided strong visual support for Milton's description of the chariot.

Welsford has suggested parallels in the "idealized versions of masqued triumphs," particularly that in which the chariot of the Fairy Prince exits from the great gate of Oberon's Palace to the sound of music, but though I have no desire to challenge the relevance of that analogue, it alone is not sufficient to meet the objections raised to Milton's provision of a chariot in the War in Heaven. When Van Doren, for example, objects that no recorded reader has failed to find Milton's introduction of a chariot on the plains of eternity "outlandish, either for its intrusion, or for its excess," he can scarcely be answered by references to masques set in fairyland, however interesting these analogies may be, but his objection may be countered by citing the widespread occurrence in the visual arts of Christ mounted in a chariot in Heaven as he overcomes his enemies.[27] Not only was Christ so mounted in the arts, but so also were Enoch, Elijah (with Biblical precedent), and a host of pagan gods, all traveling chariot-borne above the clouds.[28] What Milton was asking his audience to imagine was well within their accustomed visual frames of reference, for artists had established direct associations between the Merkabah chariot of Ezekiel 1:4-28 and the War in Heaven long before Milton wrote *Paradise Lost*.[29]

Milton has Christ not only mount the divine chariot, but mount a throne in that chariot.[30] This enthronement and this throne come at the numerical center of *Paradise Lost*, as Qvarnström has demonstrated, so that the physical structure of

[27] Welsford, *The Court Masque*, pp. 311-12, and Van Doren, *The Noble Voice*, pp. 133-34.

[28] See Bosio, *Roma Sotterranea*, p. 161, for the heavenly chariot; for Early Christian adaptations of the sun chariot to Christ, see Bourguet, *Early Christian Painting*, p. 17, and fig. 130, and John Beckwith, "Byzantium: Gold and Light," in *Light in Art* (ed. Thomas B. Hess and John Ashbery), New York, 1971, pp. 69-70; for pagan chariots of divinity, see the British Library's *Illustration of Early Italian Engravings*, London, 1909, pls. AI 1-15, and Guy de Tervarent, *Attributs et symboles dans l'art profane 1450-1600*, Geneva, 1958, 75-77. In his note to VI, 749-59, Fowler cites representations of triumphal chariots and observes that "the triumph of a god or allegorical abstraction was one of the principal motifs of Renaissance and Baroque art."

[29] I presume that what Røstvig has said about Milton would apply in the arts, namely that the divine chariot was understood as a "figure of consonant harmony, which is in all the works of God's Providence" (Maren-Sofie Røstvig, "Images of Perfection," in *Seventeenth-Century Imagery* [ed. Earl Miner], pp. 21-22). See also Jason Rosenblatt, "Structural Unity and Temporal Concordance: The War in Heaven in *Paradise Lost*," pp. 31-32 and 39; Kester Svendsen, "Milton's Chariot of Paternal Deity," *N&Q* 193 (1948), 339; and J. H. Adamson, "The War in Heaven: Milton's Version of the *Merkabah*," *JEGP* 57 (1958), 690-703.

[30] For a suggestive essay, see John G. Demaray, "The Thrones of Satan and God: Backgrounds to Divine Opposition in *Paradise Lost*," *HLQ* 31 (1967), 21-33. Earl Baldwin Smith, *Architectural Symbolism of Imperial Rome and the Middle Ages*, Princeton, 1956, p. 83, connects the divine throne with the Roman imperial throne, and cites Eusebius' eulogy of Constantine. The rainbow throne of the Western tradition in art may be interestingly compared and contrasted with Byzantine representations of the empty throne prepared for the coming of Christ as Judge, for which see Dalton, *Byzantine Art and Archaeology*, p. 666; Walter Lowrie, *Art in the Early Church*, New York, 1969, pp. 85-86; and Réau, *Iconographie*, I, p. 54.

the epic is precisely Christocentric.[31] The throne Milton thus centrally introduces is not merely the symbol of majesty in general, but has very specific iconographic significance: it is the rainbow throne, with "colors of the showery arch" (VI, 759). This throne has developed from Biblical roots, but as is also often the case, the artistic development has so altered the original that it is possible to see that Milton's description relies primarily upon art rather than upon Scripture. Revelation 4:3 describes the throne of God and adds that "there was a rainbow round about the throne." In art, that rainbow was removed from its position encircling the throne, and was converted into the throne itself. Showing Christ on the rainbow throne was a semantic semaphore to identify his function either as the Pantokrator or All-Ruler (especially in the first millennium), or as the Supreme Judge in the Last Judgment. When these visual signals are recognized, Milton's description takes on greater richness and depth, for as the Son mounts his rainbow throne to expel the rebel angels, he assumes a familiar iconographic pose which emphasizes his supremacy not only in this one combat with the powers of darkness, but also alludes graphically to him as the All-Ruler throughout history and as the ultimate consummation at the end of time.

Pictures of Christ seated upon a rainbow go back at least as far as a seventh- or eighth-century Palestinian icon from Sinai, and the motif enters Italy as early as the ninth century,[32] where it may most conveniently be seen in a mosaic of about 820 in the Church of S. Maria in Domnica in Rome. In medieval illuminated manuscripts, this representation was the "almost invariable type" used for Last Judgment scenes.[33] It may be seen in the *Last Judgment* of the Florentine Baptistry, in that of Notre Dame in Paris, and frequently thereafter on the continent as in the sixteenth-century *Last Judgment* at Münster by Hermann Tom Ring.[34] In England the motif had, if anything, an even greater popularity than on the continent, and may be found in examples dating from the eleventh into the seventeenth centuries.[35] This traditional imagery did not want in popularity during the Tudor period, when it may be found in King's College Chapel in Cambridge, in the early sixteenth-century window of St. Mary's Church at Fairford in Gloucestershire, and in many printed books.[36] It appears also in the fine stained glass windows introduced into Magdalen Chapel and Queen's College Chapel in Oxford during the 1630s and 1640s. By his introduction of the rainbow throne Milton was not only able to evoke

112

[31] Gunnar Qvarnström, *The Enchanted Palace. Some Structural Aspects of Paradise Lost*, Stockholm, 1967, p. 64.

[32] Schiller, *Ikonographie*, III, fig. 674, and Walter W. S. Cook, "The Earliest Painted Panels of Catalonia," *Art Bulletin* 6 (1923), 44f.

[33] Birch and Jenner, *Early Drawings aand Illuminations*, p. 257.

[34] Centro Internazionale, *Demonaico*, pl. LIII.

[35] Eric G. Millar, *English Illuminated Manuscripts from the Xth to the XIIIth Century*, Paris and Brussels, 1926, pls. 17, 39, 69, and 75; Ernest W. Tristram, *English Medieval Wall Painting: The Twelfth Century*, pls. 3, 54, and 75, and *English Medieval Wall Painting: The Thirteenth Century*, I, 469; Tancred Borenius and E. W. Tristram, *English Medieval Painting*, pl. 85; and M. D. Anderson, *The Imagery of British Churches*, p. 135 and pl. 1.

[36] Royal Commission on Historical Monuments, *An Inventory of Historical Monuments in the City of Cambridge*, London, 1959, pl. 147; Coverdale's 1540 Bible for Rev. 4:3; and Stephen Bateman, *A Christall Glasse of Christian Reformation*, London, 1569, sig. Oii v.

a familiar visual image but even more important he was able through that image to move readers to recall the meanings universally associated with it.

The Creation provided another opportunity which Milton seized upon in his systematic epic aggrandizement of the Son. In postulating the Son as the divine Creator, or perhaps more precisely as the creative agent of the Godhead, Milton was not heretical, but he was certainly out of step with the majority opinion among theologians and Biblical commentators. Rajan writes that "in interpreting the first chapter of Genesis the general opinion is that all three persons of the Trinity participated in the process of creation; the decisive role that Milton assigns the Son is so unusual that the awkward reservation of VII, 587 becomes necessary to preserve appearances."[37] Visualization of the Trinity posed problems for the artists which were gigantic and introduced possibilities which were grotesque. Though there are artistic representations of the Trinity as three divine figures, the Church disapproved of these because they almost inescapably suggested tritheism.[38] In the sixteenth and seventeenth centuries it was almost universal practice to represent God the Father as the divine agent at Creation. The most famous and influential instances occur in Michelangelo's Sistine Ceiling and in Raphael's paintings in the Vatican. Later Italian artists including Veronese and Tintoretto generally followed those precedents, and so, too, did those northern artists who contributed to illustrating the Lutheran Bibles.[39]

In choosing to have the Creation executed by the Son, Milton not only broke with prevailing theological opinion but also with a visual convention which had been dominant for two hundred years in art. Milton's reasons for doing so were of course literary and theological, but his decision accorded with very early and widespread visual treatments of the subject. For the first twelve centuries and more of Christian art, the Creator was usually shown with the typical physiognomy and figure of the young Christ-Logos, and only rarely as the Father. It was only in the fourteenth century that the Creator was figured by an old man with a crown.[40]

Considered abstractly, one might think it immaterial whether the Father or the Son were represented as the Creator, but there are considerable differences in visual impact. These differences become apparent when we consider and compare the Creation mosaics of S. Marco in Venice with the frescoes by Michelangelo in the Sistine. By focusing upon the figure of the creating Father, Michelangelo conveys power, authority, *majestas* to an almost unparalleled degree, but lesser artists use the same iconographic theme to much the same purpose. As Creator, the Eternal

106, 181

---

[37] B. Rajan, *The Lofty Rhyme*, pp. 60-61.

[38] Gerhart B. Ladner, *Ad imaginem Dei; The Image of Man in Medieval Art*, Latrobe, Pa., 1965, p. 9; Heimann, "Trinitas Creator Mundi," p. 42; Anderson, *History and Imagery in British Churches*, p. 95; and Meiss, *French Painting in the Time of Jean de Berry*, London, 1967-68, II, figs. 600-3. For a general study, see Wolfgang Braunfels, *Die Heilige Dreifaltigkeit*, Dusseldorf, 1954.

[39] Ph. Schmidt, *Die Illustration der Lutherbiebel 1522-1700*, Basel, 1962.

[40] Réau, *Iconographie*, II, i, pp. 66-68; Mary Laura Gibbs, "The Creation of Eve," in *Five Themes from Genesis* (ed. Robert A. Koch and Nina R. Bryan), Princeton, 1972, p. 4; and Jan van der Meulen, "A Logos Creator at Chartres and its Copy," *JWCI* 29 (1966), 82-100.

Father almost always conveys an aura of command and control, if not also of sternness. Visually, a very different aura is conveyed by the Son as Creator, and the artist can thus emphasize gentleness and graciousness, as in the S. Marco mosaics. The Christ-Logos not only brings the universe into being, but seems to be sharing creation with his creatures, to be communing with Adam and Eve to a degree we can scarcely expect from a patriarchal figure of the Eternal Father. By showing the Son in the role of Creator, Milton achieves several effects also to be found in comparable art works: without derogating from the divine power, he places his emphasis upon divine grace and compassion, with the consequence that there is a subtle enhancing of our sense of human freedom within a divine-human community of love and acceptance.

The same effects accrue when Milton shows the Son as the judge of Adam and Eve after their fall, but before we turn to that subject we must complete our consideration of the Son's role as Creator. On the first day,

> He took the golden compasses, prepared
> In God's eternal store, to circumscribe
> This Universe, and all created things:
> One foot he centered, and the other turned
> Round through the vast profundity obscure,
> And said, thus far extend, thus far thy bounds,
> This be thy just circumference, O World.
> Thus God the Heaven created, thus the Earth. . . .
>
> (VII, 225-33)

Both Sims and Fletcher trace this usage to Proverbs 8:27: ". . . he set a compass upon the face of the deep," as the Authorized Version puts it, but as Fletcher notes, Milton's Hebrew would surely have allowed him to recognize that the reference in the original is to a circle placed on the face of the deep, or an enclosed space, rather than to the geometrician's compasses.[41] Fletcher acknowledges that Dante also introduced the compasses into his epic, but insists that Milton's use is traceable to the Rabbinic commentaries.[42] The precise sorting out of sources and influences in such a matter can be extraordinarily complex, and is usually inconclusive. What we do know is that the compasses were an almost invariable attribute of the Creator in the European imagination, both in art and in literature. As early as 1935, Merritt Y. Hughes noted that "the divine hand, drawing the circle in Chaos, was a familiar printer's ornament and must have been etched on Milton's memory," and a few years later George W. Whiting and Grant McColley both pointed to the widespread use of the compasses in church art and in religious books.[43] Illuminated

[41] James H. Sims, *The Bible in Milton's Epics*, p. 266, and Harris F. Fletcher, *Milton's Rabbinical Readings*, Urbana, Ill., 1930, pp. 100-9. The compasses are also sometimes read into Isa. 40:12 (though Sims does not do so), but Milton would have known better; see Anderson, *The Imagery of British Churches*, pp. 87-88.

[42] Fletcher, *Milton's Rabbinical Readings*, p. 102.

[43] Hughes, *Paradise Lost*, 1935, note to VII, 225; George W. Whiting, "The Golden Compasses in *Paradise Lost*," *N&Q* 172 (1937), 294-95; Grant McColley, "Milton's Golden

manuscripts from as early as the Anglo-Saxon period employed the compasses as symbolic of the Creation, and though compasses do not appear in English churches before the fifteenth century, they became immensely popular in church decoration thereafter.[44] Out of this richness of visual analogues, I have chosen to illustrate the motif by the fourteenth-century Holkham Bible, where we see the Son as Creator centering one foot on the compass and turning the other "round through the vast profundity obscure," to set the "just circumference" of the universe.

    53

    The single art work which comes closest to Milton's descriptions of the creation is the famous *Creation of the Animals* in the so-called Raphael Bible in the ceiling of the Vatican Loggia. Whereas most artistic representations show the animals fully formed and standing upon the earth, flying through the air, or swimming in the sea, this painting by Raphael and his school is extremely unusual and may have been unique at the time: we see the animals forcing their way out of the earth itself, as if by parturition. Because of its novelty and its majesty, the painting attracted considerable attention. Among English travelers of Milton's time, Richard Lassels and John Evelyn specifically mention it, and it was frequently copied in prints and other art forms.[45] Coleridge was the first to notice the similarities between this painting and Milton's description, and he asserted that Milton "certainly copied" the painting in what he takes to be the only direct influence of art upon the poet. Though Coleridge's own knowledge of art was so limited that he confused Raphael's Loggia ceiling with the Michelangelo ceiling in the Sistine Chapel, his suggestion here has much to commend it.[46] Don M. Wolfe in his illustrated life of Milton is quite properly more cautious than Coleridge, yet he assumes that Milton may very well have called up his memories of this picture when he described a similar scene in *Paradise Lost*.[47] Milton's description is indeed strongly reminiscent of Raphael:

    113

Compasses," *N&Q* 176 (1939), 97-98. Whiting's *Milton and this Pendant World*, Austin, 1958, pp. 104-28, traces the interesting development of this traditional symbolism, and illustrates it as I do here by reprinting the illumination from the Holkham Bible. The relevance of the pictorial tradition has been underscored by Gardner, *A Reading of "Paradise Lost,"* p. 72. Had the anonymous critic of 1738 been cognizant of this virtually universal visual attribute, he might not have been so ready to conclude that "the fancy would be apt to make one laugh" (Shawcross, *Milton 1732-1801*, p. 95).

    [44] Heimann, "Three Illustrations from The Bury St. Edmunds Psalter," pp. 51-52; W. O. Hassal, ed., *The Holkham Bible Picture Book*, London, 1954, p. 59; and M. D. Anderson, *The Imagery of British Churches*, pp. 87-88.

    [45] Amy Lee Turner, *The Visual Arts in Milton's Poetry*, p. 293. Lanfranco and Nadobocchi engraved a set of thirty-four sheets of Raphael's ceilings entitled *Vetus Testamento*, which was published in 1607 and which Richard Symonds purchased in 1650 or 1651 (Stoye, *English Travellers Abroad*, pp. 210-11) to take home to Essex. Another version appeared in 1649 under the hand of Nicholas Chapron, while Bartsch lists examples also executed by Borgiani (B XVII.316.4). Other prints may be found in Kitto Bible I, 50, 91, and 93. Raphael's scene was copied in a Majolica dish, made in Pesaro, marked and dated 1540, which is now in the Ashmolean Museum in Oxford, while the Galleria Colonna in Rome has an ebony desk with an ivory bas-relief of the scene executed by the brothers Francis and Dominic Steinhard, late in the seventeenth or early in the eighteenth century.

    [46] S. T. Coleridge, *Specimens of the Tabletalk*, London, 1885, II, 83-84.

    [47] Wolfe, *Milton and his England*, p. 112.

> The Earth obeyed, and straight
> Opening her fertile womb teemed at a birth
> Innumerous living creatures, perfect forms,
> Limbed and full grown: out of the ground up rose
> As from his lair the wild beast . . .
>
> . . . .
>
> The grassy clods now calved, now half appeared
> The tawny lion, pawing to get free
> His hinder parts, then springs as broke from bonds,
> And rampant shakes his brinded mane; the ounce,
> The libbard, and the tiger, as the mole
> Rising, the crumbled earth above them threw
> In hillocks; the swift stag from under ground
> Bore up his branching head . . . .
>
> (VII, 453-70)

The closest thing we find to this description in literature before *Paradise Lost* is Lucretius's account of how mother Nature brought forth the animals from the earth, but that treatment is a far cry from Milton's, whereas Raphael's conception is very close indeed.[48] Though Raphael's "tawny lion" has a "brinded mane," as indeed a lion should have on any count, he does not shake it nor is he in the process of breaking free from the bondage of the earth, but stands erect and self possessed. Elsewhere in the painting, however, the grassy clods are indeed calving, and the leopard and the tiger do paw their way to freedom out of the earth, as also does a bear, and instead of Milton's stag who "bore up his branching head" there is an antelope who emerges from the earth between a unicorn and an elephant, and in the lower foreground a handsome white horse rears up his head above the earth.

Obviously, Raphael and Milton were each representing a single conception of the creation of the animals, and the conception was quite rare. The extent to which Milton's description corresponds to Raphael's painting of this unusual interpretation is as complete as such things are ever likely to be, granted that Milton could not have seen the painting for some twenty-five years and that his blindness at the time of the composition of *Paradise Lost* would have prevented him from consulting an engraved reproduction. Like Coleridge and Wolfe, I incline to the opinion that Milton's poetic description was influenced by his recollection of the Raphael painting. His close correspondence with Raphael in his visualization of the creation of the animals makes even more conspicuous his divergence from Raphael in his presentation of the Creator: for Raphael, the Creator is unmistakably God the Father.

As Milton insists upon casting the Creator of Genesis 1-2 in the *persona* of the Son, so, too, with the divine judge of Adam and Eve after their Fall. Genesis is content with calling this person merely "the Lord God." Comparing the episode in *Paradise Lost* with the previous literary and exegetical tradition, Dick Taylor

---

[48] J. M. Evans, *"Paradise Lost" and the Genesis Tradition*, pp. 127-28, discusses the possible influence of Lucretius.

concluded that "Milton is unique, so far as I have been able to find, in having the Son deliver the Judgment."[49] Taylor may be correct in asserting the uniqueness of Milton's conception here, and so far as I know he has not been disproved by reference to hexameral literature and commentary. On the other hand, Milton's staging of the scene had long been made familiar by the visual arts, and the presence of so many instances of the Son as Judge in art suggests that there may well have been a similar tradition in literature, hitherto overlooked. In an illumination of this scene executed about the year 1000 in the Noailles Bible in the Bibliothèque Royale in Paris, it is the Son who sits in judgment, as also on Saint Bernward's bronze doors set up in 1015 in Saint Michael's Church, Hildesheim.[50] In the middle of the twelfth century, the bronze doors executed by Secondo Maestro for the Church of San Zeno in Verona show the Son in the same action, and a medieval Bible Moralisée[51] represents Christ carrying the cross as he walks out of the Garden between Adam and Eve at their expulsion, thus expressing a visual equivalent of the words of the Son in *Paradise Lost* that "the worst on me must light" (x, 73). Nicolò Pisano's fine thirteenth-century carving for the cathedral at Orvieto shows the familiar figure of the Son, though here he is passing judgment from a cloud rather than on the earth.[52] These and many other artists recognized, as did Milton, that the judgment of Adam and Eve would appear most fully merciful if it were delivered by one who would himself endure the sentence *in extremis*. The early thirteenth-century mosaic in the atrium of S. Marco in Venice may be taken as epitomizing the tradition Milton evokes. In it we see the Son passing judgment with a cruciform halo about his head and a cross in his hand, again emphasizing the association of the judgment with the sacrificial redemption. The divine hand is extended in a gesture which is at once solemn and gentle, and the same combination may be read in the divine face. Here as in *Paradise Lost* we see "with what mild/ And gracious temper he both heard and judged/ Without wrath or reviling," indeed "pitying while he judged," as one "in whose look serene,/ When angry most he seemed and most severe,/ What else but favor, grace, and mercy shown?" (x, 1046-48, 1059, 1094-96).

177

The means Milton took for the epic enhancement of the Son's role in *Paradise Lost*—sole victor over the rebel angels, creator of the universe, friend and judge of Adam and Eve—have been widely noted among critics, and students of the hexameral and exegetical traditions have classified Milton's treatments on these counts either as unique or extremely rare. When judged against the background of art, however, Milton is seen within a continuum which embraced many representations parallel to his own. On that the evidence cited here is unmistakable. But Milton would not have adopted these conceptions of the role of the Son simply because of their ancient and once widespread employment in art any more than he accepted theological doctrine simply because it was orthodox. Highly individual

[49] Taylor, "Milton's Treatment of Judgment and the Expulsion in *Paradise Lost*," 71.

[50] Anna Brownwell Jameson and Lady Eastlake, *The History of our Lord as Exemplified in Works of Art*, London, 1864, I, 109-10.

[51] Laborde, *La Bible Moralisée*, III, pl. 496.

[52] Jameson and Eastlake, *op. cit.*, I, 109.

as he always was, Milton chose what accorded with his own religious analysis and the requirements of his epic. In his poetic descriptions, furthermore, he chose just those visual elements which had been demonstrated in the experience of art as conveying most effectively the understanding of Christian heroism which is fundamental throughout *Paradise Lost*.

Whereas in those matters alternatives were available to Milton, it was universally understood of the Last Judgment that the Son would preside as supreme judge. Beyond that central feature, details of the visualization could and did vary, and Milton's choices of details to include, exclude, and add are both interesting and significant. Milton provides four fairly detailed descriptions of the Last Judgment, and each is of course prophetic. The first two are spoken by God the Father, initially in Book III after the Son has volunteered to redeem man even before the Fall, and again in Book x after the Fall and the arrival of Sin and Death on earth. Later, two descriptions are given by Michael to Adam in the final book of the epic. We shall take these up thematically, beginning with the prediction by God the Father to the Son, of the time:

> When thou attended gloriously from Heaven
> Shalt in the sky appear, and from thee send
> The summoning archangels to proclaim
> Thy dread tribunal: forthwith from all winds
> The living, and forthwith the cited dead
> Of all past ages to the general doom
> Shall hasten, such a peal shall rouse their sleep.
> Then all thy saints assembled, thou shalt judge
> Bad men and angels, they arraigned shall sink
> Beneath thy sentence; Hell, her numbers full,
> Thenceforth shall be for ever shut.
>
> (III, 323-33)

The summoning angels are almost invariably shown in the Last Judgment in art, where again almost invariably they are represented as sounding trumpets to awaken the dead, as "such a peal shall rouse their sleep"—these are all givens of Christ's prophecy in Matthew 24:29-31. Milton does not need to be more explicit, and is not, whereas the artists invariably had to decide upon some specific visual scheme: the resurrected dead pushing aside their tombstones, or perhaps merely rising directly from open graves, or even appearing by parturition out of the earth itself like Milton's animals at the Creation.[53]

Remaining noncommittal on those details, Milton then proceeds, in the last three verses quoted, to the sentencing of "bad men and angels," who "shall sink" beneath the sentence of Christ. They are not hurled down by the judgment of God, nor pursued by angels, nor dragged by demons; they merely sink down toward Hell. Milton's conception here is quite uncommon. Rubens' painting in Munich shows them jettisoned toward Hell under the vigorous and harrying pursuit of

[53] See Mâle, *Religious Art*, pp. 161-63.

Michael, while demons fly about to push and drag them downward. In none of the four descriptions of the Last Judgment in *Paradise Lost* do angels pursue or even commit the damned humanity to Hell, as in some Western and many Byzantine versions; and there are no demons to seize, maul, and manhandle the damned, or to drag them screaming into torments. In avoiding such melodramatic scenes, Milton was not only bypassing the standard medieval vision of the Last Judgment, but also the one still current in the major art of the sixteenth and seventeenth centuries. In Michelangelo, Charon violently swings his oar as a club to beat the passengers out of his boat and onto the shore of Hell. In the Last Judgment dome executed for the Florentine Duomo by Vasari and Zuccari, the damned are tossed about and torn by devils, while the painting in the Doge's Palace by Palma the Younger shows angels with drawn swords driving the damned down toward Hell, while horned and fire-breathing demons snatch at them. In the painting by Leandro Bassano in Birmingham, Alabama, fire-breathing devils pitchfork the damned toward various torments on the fiery lake, and almost equal violence and horror characterize the Hell in the Last Judgment window executed for Queen's College Chapel in Oxford by Abraham van Linge in the early seventeenth century. Against this background, it is surely significant that in Milton's first description of the Last Judgment, bad men and angels merely sink beneath the sentence of Christ, as though inexorably weighted down by their sins.

61, 62

In three of Milton's four descriptions of the Last Judgment, primary emphasis falls upon the joys of the blessed, but he also develops a view devoted entirely to the final judgment and disposition of evil. The words are spoken by the Father to the Son:

> at one sling
> Of thy victorious arm, well-pleasing Son,
> Both Sin, and Death, and yawning grave at last
> Through Chaos hurled, obstruct the mouth of Hell
> Forever, and seal up his ravenous jaws.
>
> (x, 633-37)

In this prophetic vision, that slinging action strikingly corresponds to a motif introduced into the visual consciousness of Western Europe about the middle of the fourteenth century, when the devastations of the bubonic plague had altered life in a spiritual as well as a physical sense. In the Doom paintings of that time, the serene Christ of previous centuries was replaced by an angry, denouncing figure, radically different from what had been seen before.

The innovation probably appeared first in the Camposanto frescoes at Pisa, and the influence spread from there. Millard Meiss describes this new representation of Christ as Judge: "For the first time in the representation of the Last Judgment he addresses the damned alone, turning on them with an angry mien, his arm upraised in a powerful gesture of denunciation."[54] In the previous century or two, Tuscan artists had usually turned Christ's eyes, and often even his head and body, toward

115

---

[54] Meiss, *Painting in Florence and Siena after the Black Death*, pp. 76-77.

the redeemed as a mark of his special concern for them, and his raised hand was shown as a sign of blessing. In the earliest Christian art, Christ was depicted on sarcophagi and in apsidal mosaics with his hand raised high in what has usually been taken as blessing.[55] There is no possibility of confusing that gesture with Milton's description in *Paradise Lost* or with what Meiss finds in Tuscan paintings after the terrible ravages of the Black Death. Meiss traces the continuous development of this new conception in which Christ is pictured as though "moved to denunciation alone," through the fifteenth and sixteenth centuries, until we find both its crescendo and its most famous exemplar in Michelangelo's *Last Judgment* in the Sistine Chapel.

67

There the emphasis is upon the overwhelming violence of the judgment; there the raised right arm of the Son is terrifying, poised as if for a split second before dashing sinners into Hell and inexorable doom.[56] Milton's pervasive emphasis in his descriptions of the Last Judgment is radically different from that of Michelangelo, but at this particular point in his epic immediately after the triumph of Satan and the ominous arrival of Sin and Death on earth, Milton needs to evoke the most powerful and definitive image of divine wrath and retribution. He does so in the passage under discussion, but it is interesting that the divine vengeance here is vented upon the personifications of evil (Sin, Death, and grave) rather than upon God's erring fallen creatures. Even so, that "one sling" of the Son's "victorious arm" produces what is probably the most Michelangelesque vision in *Paradise Lost*.

But in their overall presentations of the Last Judgment, as in so much else, Michelangelo and Milton could scarcely be further apart. In general terms as well as in specifics, Milton's descriptions of the Last Judgment principally concentrate upon redemption and restoration. Immediately after the first description, in which the evil sink and Hell is shut, we have this:

> Meanwhile
> The world shall burn, and from her ashes spring
> New Heaven and Earth, wherein the just shall dwell
> And after all their tribulations long
> See golden days, fruitful of golden deeds,
> With Joy and Love triumphing, and fair Truth.
> Then thou thy regal sceptre shalt lay by,
> For regal sceptre then no more shall need,
> God shall be all in all.
>
> (III, 333-41)

[55] Walter Lowrie contends, however, that it was merely "the gesture commonly used by orators . . . a common gesture of address, alloquy" (*Art in the Early Church*, New York, 1969, p. 84).

[56] This impression is so strong that it has led Réau, *Iconographie*, II, ii, pp. 753-54, to conclude that Michelangelo is no longer thinking of the Christ of the Gospel, and to interpret the entire fresco as the triumph of the paganization of Christian art, but this interpretation is surely excessive.

In Michael's descriptions as well as in those by God the Father, the emphasis is the same: the Son

> thence shall come,
> When this world's dissolution shall be ripe,
> With glory and power to judge both quick and dead,
> To judge th' unfaithful dead, but to reward
> His faithful, and receive them into bliss,
> Whether in Heaven or Earth, for then the Earth
> Shall all be Paradise, far happier place
> Than this of Eden, and far happier days.
>
> (XII, 458-65)

Pivoting upon only half a line devoted to the unfaithful dead, Michael brings the full weight of emphasis down upon the new paradise here, and he does much the same in his final depiction of how Christ will appear:

> Last in the clouds from Heaven to be revealed
> In glory of the Father, to dissolve
> Satan with his perverted world, then raise
> From the conflagrant mass, purged and refined,
> New Heavens, new Earth, ages of endless date
> Founded in righteousness and peace and love,
> To bring forth fruits Joy and eternal Bliss.
>
> (XII, 545-51)

The grace, hope, and joy of Milton's descriptions go far beyond what is usually found in the Last Judgments of the visual arts. Here, as in other ways, Signorelli is perhaps closest to Milton, at least in certain of his scenes. Milton suffuses his Last Judgment scenes with serenity and joy. He does not give us any verbal portraits of individuals showing those responses within the framework of his Doom pictures, and to have done so in his verse would have been to distract attention from the universal triumph of goodness, perhaps even to dilute it.[57] Signorelli, on the other hand, can convey a sense of universal joy and blessedness only by multiplying expressions of individual reactions among the joyfully resurrected saints and their welcoming angels. In the different ways appropriate to their aesthetic media, Milton   77, 78
and Signorelli achieve much the same effect.

   Where Milton goes beyond all the treatments of the Last Judgment with which I am familiar in literature and in art is in his insistence upon the final closing down and even annihilation of Hell. First there is the prophesy by God the Father that Hell "shall be for ever shut," which is followed by his later promise "to seal up [Hell's] ravenous jaws" (III, 333; X, 637). The "mouth of Hell" and its jaws to which Milton refers were immensely familiar, as we have already seen in the

---

[57] Adam, of course, increasingly expresses a sense of joy and triumph, but he is not within the framework of the Doom descriptions.

chapter on Hell. Thousands of art works show those jaws gaping wide, and I know of no instance in any visual representation of the Last Judgment in which they are shown to be sealed up and forever shut. Cultivated readers among Milton's contemporaries could scarcely have overlooked both what he omitted in the way of physical horrors and what he added here in the way of reassurance—that vivid and surprising detail of the shutting down of Hell. Milton returns to this promise in his last description of the Doom, when Michael informs Adam that the Son will "dissolve/ Satan with his perverted world" (xii, 546-47).[58] Here, as elsewhere, Milton places the fullest weight of his emphasis upon the restoration of golden days, ages of eternal bliss, "with Joy and Love triumphing, and fair Truth." With the Son at its center and providentially overseeing every crucial development within the epic, *Paradise Lost* is permeated with the most profound cosmic optimism. And to a remarkable degree, Milton conveys that optimism by means of his visual descriptions.

[58] Fowler is surely correct when he annotates "dissolve" at xii, 546, as meaning "annihilate, destroy."

X

The Vision of Angels

ANGELIC WINGS

ANGELS without wings would be inconceivable to most people. It is hard to imagine the Annunciation without Gabriel descending on broad and colorful wings, or kneeling before the Virgin with his brilliant plumage spread to view. That choir of heavenly hosts who sang to the shepherds at the Nativity of peace on earth and good will toward men are again imagined as borne aloft by their wings even as they sing. And so, too, for the Old Testament angels who visit Abraham or the parents of Samson, and so on: we almost invariably think of these angelic visitors as winged. So nearly universal is this traditional vision, that many people are shocked when they learn that those familiar wings have no Biblical warrant, but are a graceful addition to the Biblical accounts supplied by art.[1] With his profound knowledge of the Bible both in Hebrew and in Greek, Milton would certainly have known that he was following an artistic rather than a Scriptural conception in his description of the winged angels.

For the first four centuries of the Christian era, angels were presented without wings. Then, early in the fifth century, the new image of the angel appears. We may see the two images almost side by side in the fifth-century mosaics of the Church of Santa Maria Maggiore in Rome, where the angel visiting Joshua appears, just as the Biblical text requires, as an unwinged warrior-messenger, whereas on the triumphal arch of the same church the Virgin and Child are represented as surrounded by winged angels. Not long thereafter, the new image became fixed in the Christian imagination, and continued with only minor changes for centuries. Fritz Saxl summarizes the development: readers of "the Bible visualized the scenes quite differently from the way in which the authors of the text intended it to be understood. The impact of the pagan image on the Christian mind was so strong that it made people imagine something that was not in the written text or was even contrary to it."[2]

To refer to the winged angel as a "pagan image" is historically valid. The visual conception of the winged angel was directly based upon the classical representation of the winged Victory. Indeed, the common Roman motif of two winged Victories or Nikes holding between them a wreath of triumph was taken over

---

[1] The seraphim of Isa. 6:2 and the "four living creatures" of Ezek. 1:6 and 11 have six wings and four wings respectively, but these creatures are not angels in the Biblical sense.

[2] See Saxl, *A Heritage of Images*, p. 24, and pp. 21-26 for a brief history of angels in art. See also Dalton, *Byzantine Art*, p. 675, and for a specialized study, Gunnar Berefelt, *A Study on the Winged Angel: The Origin of a Motif*. Stockholm, 1966.

intact into Christian art, though a cross was inserted within the wreath. An example
is the pair of figures above the Abraham mosaic of the sixth century at San Vitale
in Ravenna. The early Christian adaptation of the familiar Roman Victory composition was a brilliant stroke:[3] triumph was understood in paganism and Christianity
in radically different ways, and the insertion of the cross (an emblem of shame in
classical culture) within the wreath of Victory served both to announce the new
conception and to suggest the shallowness of the old. So it was that the Nike was
gradually merged with the angel, but with the understanding that angels were
messengers of God, not projections of human pride, and that true victory was the
gift of God, not the self-assured achievement of man.

Beneath the Christianized Nikes in Ravenna, we see that the three angelic visitors to Abraham and Sarah are fitted with haloes but conspicuously lack wings.
Within a few centuries such wingless angels were almost entirely supplanted, and
by Milton's time they were rarely found in art of any kind. Between the fifteenth
and seventeenth centuries, they may be seen in Piero della Francesco's paintings of
the Death of Adam, in Michelangelo's *Last Judgment*, and occasionally in Rembrandt, but these are exceptional cases. So far as Panofsky could determine, the
only wingless angels to be found in Northern art of the fifteenth century appear
in Van Eyck's *Ghent Altarpiece*.[4]

Milton's acceptance of the artistic rather than the Biblical angel was far from
perfunctory. He lavished great care upon his depictions of angels' wings, and endowed them with extraordinary plastic beauty. "In describing angels' wings,"
Thomas Greene observes, "Milton describes more than wings; he endows his
creature with a grace and energy and poise and beauty beyond the concern of the
prophet—qualities reminiscent of antique and High Renaissance sculpture."[5] In this
regard, medieval representations could be found in England on at least as high a
plane as those available on the continent. M. D. Anderson informs us that "in no
other country have the plastic possibilities of angels' wings been so richly exploited
as in England." She cites in particular the great tradition of English angel roofs
"where winged figures are carved upon every projection of the hammer-beam
roofs, tier above tier of wings soaring up into the darkness of the rafters," like
Milton's angels who "numberless were poured" and ranked "in full frequence"
(VII, 197, and *PR* I, 128-29, II, 130).[6] English woodcarvers and stone carvers alike
were notably adept at providing beautifully plumed wings and downy feathers,
as may be seen in medieval examples chosen from Westminster Abbey and from
Holy Sepulchre Church in Cambridge, and in the Renaissance work for King's

[3] For the influence of Nike, see Réau, *Iconographie*, I, p. 53, and Bourguet, *Early Christian Paintings*, p. 24. Illustrations of early Jewish art showing winged angels may be found in
H. Leclercq, *Manuel d'archéologie chrétienne*, Paris, 1907, I, pp. 516-22.

[4] Panofsky, *Early Netherlandish Painting*, I, p. 214.

[5] Thomas Greene, *The Descent from Heaven: A Study in Epic Continuity*, New Haven,
1963, pp. 379-80.

[6] Anderson, *Imagery of British Churches*, p. 138. For the winged angels in Anglo-Saxon
illuminations, see O. Elfrida Saunders, *A History of English Art in the Middle Ages*, Oxford,
1932, figs. 10-12.

College Chapel.[7] In England, this tradition was primarily sculptural (though the carvings were polychromed), while the fullest painted exploitation of the wings of angels came on the continent.

117-19

Milton's treatment of angelic wings emphasizes shape and movement, but color is also introduced in a somewhat secondary way. For the stripling cherub, Milton describes "many a colored plume sprinkled with gold" but allows his readers to imagine what other hues they will. He also puts gold into the wings of Michael, and in addition he specifies purple and blue (v, 280-85), but beyond this he does not go. Gold was especially popular for angel wings in mosaics, and probably appeared more frequently than any other color in paintings, whether "sprinkled" over the other colors of the plumes as for Milton's stripling cherub and angel of the Annunciation, or covering large areas as on the wings of Michael in *Paradise Lost* and in Titian's *Annunciation* in the Scuola di San Rocco and in Martini's. But at least from the Quattrocento on, there were no standard colors prescribed and applied in angels' robes and wings. Artists could adopt such bright or muted hues as best fitted the overall design of their work, and usage varied widely. "Radiant," "dazzling," and "bright" are the words Milton repeats in describing the appearance of his angels: Gabriel's ranks are seen as "radiant files/ Dazzling the moon" (IV, 797-98); Raphael "seems another morn/ Risen on midmoon" (v, 310); Adam notes after the Fall that "those heavenly shapes/ Will dazzle now this earthly, with their blaze/ Insufferably bright" (IX, 1082-84); Michael descends with his "cohort bright" which appears to Adam to draw "o'er the blue firmament a radiant white" (XI, 127 and 206). G. Stanley Koehler is surely correct when he observes that in general "Milton's interest in light outweighs his interest in color."[8] This emphasis certainly reflects the ancient symbolic contrasts between light and darkness, but it may also represent to some degree an influence upon Milton of the visual heritage of England, which was principally plastic and sculptural rather than coloristic and painterly.

120

II

ANGELIC MOVEMENT

The wings of Milton's angels are intensely beautiful, but they are also so functional that without them much of the action of his epic would be inconceivable. Aerial movement is perhaps the most striking and pervasive visual quality conveyed by Milton's descriptions of the angels. His angels plummet through space, wheel about, ascend again, dive once more, or move forward with a steady and irre-

[7] For further examples, see F. E. Howard and F. H. Crossley, *English Church Woodwork*, London, n.d., pp. 115-30 *passim*, 179, and 187; Crossley, *English Church Craftsmanship*, pp. 82-83 and figs. 66-67; and Gardner, *English Medieval Sculpture*, p. 297 and figs. 366-68.

[8] Koehler, "Milton's Use of Color and Light," 73. Of many useful comments made by critics on this subject, the following should be particularly noted: Allen, *Harmonious Vision*, pp. 98-103; Albert R. Cirillo, "Tasso's *Il Mondo Creato*: Providence and the Created Universe," *Milton Studies* 3 (1971), 83-102; Merritt Y. Hughes, "Milton and the Symbol of Light," *SEL* 4 (1964), 1-33; Josephine Miles, "From 'Good' to 'Bright': A Note on Poetic History," *PMLA* 60 (1945), 766-74; and Ryken, *Apocalyptic Vision*, pp. 38-41, and 78-79.

sistible power. Here comparisons between *Paradise Lost* and Baroque paintings become almost inevitable, as when Jeffry Spencer notes in both forms of art how "soaring or plunging angels test the boundaries of a limitless universe."[9] In *Paradise Regained* as well, Spencer finds "the familiar Baroque preoccupation with forms plunging downward or floating in mid air." Commenting on the climactic incident when "Satan smitten with amazement fell" and Christ was rescued from the pinnacle of the Temple by "a fiery globe/ Of angels on full sail of wing .../ Who on their plumy vans received him soft/ From his uneasy station, and upbore/ As on a floating couch through the blithe air," (*PR* IV 562, 581-85), he observes that we have here something quite similar to a Baroque painting:

> Like a figure from a Last Judgment fresco, Satan plummets down to Hell while Christ, cloud-borne by angels, comes to rest in an earthly paradise landscape where he is refreshed by heavenly food and drink. As a final touch, angelic choirs celebrate his triumph; in a conventionally composed painting of the scene they would fill the sky or upper air above the figure of Christ in his landscape setting. For an epic containing little more action than a series of dramatized debates between Christ and Satan, the Baroque theatricality of the landscape contributes a good deal to the pictorialization of themes that would be otherwise almost totally abstract, ethical, and intellectual.[10]

Dynamic and rapid movements, which delighted the Baroque artists and Milton alike, were also to be seen in the art of the sixteenth century when techniques were developed which continued in popularity throughout the seventeenth. Moving angels had been seen before, of course, but in earlier centuries they typically seemed to swim deliberately through the air or pace along in slow and stately fashion.[11] Wölfflin attributes the new development primarily to Signorelli, followed by Raphael, and notes that later "foreshortening and increased movement were added, as well as flight into, or out of, the depth of the picture."[12] Of Raphael's *St. Michael*, Fischel comments that "the heavenly combatant comes down like a thunderbolt on his arch enemy," and that "the saint has almost alighted from the course of a swooping downward flight which the next moment he is to resume; his body is still in its gliding rush through the air."[13]

70

As the painters' experimental understanding of foreshortening and perspective improved, it became possible to give the illusion of actual flight, and physical movements ranged from the most sedate through the most dynamic and bravura gestures. We see an angel hurtling out of the sky to make a dramatic pivot and

121

present the mitre and crozier in Veronese's *Consecration of St. Nicholas*, while in

[9] Spencer, *Heroic Nature*, p. 106.
[10] Spencer, *Heroic Nature*, p. 136.
[11] Wölfflin, *Classic Art*, pp. 221-23; Jameson, *Sacred and Legendary Art*, I, p. 77; Dalton, *Byzantine Art*, p. 653; Tristram, *English Medieval Wall Paintings: The Fourteenth Century*, p. 25.
[12] Wölfflin, *Classic Art*, 223n.
[13] Fischel, *Raphael*, I, p. 32.

the next century Rembrandt's *Sacrifice of Isaac* at Munich has the hurtling angel come to rest in mid-air just at the most graceful point to grasp Abraham's wrist and prevent the execution. Osmaston maintains that Tintoretto was perhaps the greatest master of such effects:

> Most obvious of all perhaps is Tintoret's quite exceptional, and in certain cases unsurpassed power to depict the angelic flight. His work illustrates almost every type of such movement we can imagine, from the exquisite poise in mid-air of the suspended angel in the *Resurrection and Three Senators*, . . to the headlong flight in extreme perspective of the angel in the *Descent into Hades* of the S. Cassiano Church, or the more serene return of the two archangels in the *Paradise* to their King of kings.[14]

Tintoretto's effects were indeed varied, as may be illustrated in his *Resurrection*   *122* where one angel is standing gracefully on the ground, another is on the very point of springing into flight, and two others are shown in wheeling aerial maneuvers— each executed with great credibility.

Milton's descriptions are at least as varied, and his range as wide. Uriel moves swiftly along on a sunbeam, as straight and direct as space will allow, while Raphael speeds "with steady wing/ Now on the polar winds, then with quick fan/ Winnows the buxom air," to remind us of the "soar/ Of towering eagles" (IV, 555-56, and V, 266-71). When Raphael alights, "like Maia's son he stood,/ And shook his plumes, that heavenly fragrance filled/ The circuit wide" (V, 285-87). When Gabriel's angelic guards fly, they are said to "coast," and when they part ranks, it is by a "wheeling" maneuver (IV, 782-85). In these motions of the faithful angels, one is impressed by harmonious continuity as well as power: they move with the grace and beauty of supernal athletes.

Satan's flight is more sudden, more jerky, and even when he "winds with ease/ Through the pure marble air" his flight is "precipitant" and his way "oblique" (III, 563-64). When he takes to his wings, his physical actions are sudden and agitated: he "uplifted spurns the ground," and "springs upward like a pyramid of fire/ Into the wild expanse" (II, 929, and 1013-14). As he makes his way through Chaos, we are impressed that his heroism is overwhelming but the very unnatural-ness of his adventure denies him the grace of movement which he can on occasion show elsewhere and which the blessed angels always show:

> nigh foundered on he fares,
> Treading the crude consistence, half on foot,
> Half flying; . . .
> O'er bog or steep, through straight, rough, dense, or rare,
> With head, hands, wings, or feet pursues his way,
> And swims or sinks, or wades, or creeps, or flies.
>   (II, 940-42, and 948-50)

We are overwhelmed by the sheer energy and determination Milton has led us to

[14] Osmaston, *Art and Genius of Tintoret*, I, 117.

see in these lines, but which even more pervasively he has led us to feel in every bone and muscle until we virtually ache in tactile response. But magnificent though Satan's energy is, his movements here are awkward, ungainly, and even uncouth. Milton expresses the demonic repudiation of spiritual grace by visualizing a powerful but physically ungraceful action.[15]

The spiritual beauty of the faithful angels is given its counterpart in the physical beauty of their movements, ranging from the stately serenity of musicians like those of Signorelli to the dynamic majesty of a Baroque angel in full flight, but the physical violence of the moving Satan suggests something vaguely and remotely approaching the obscenity of the typical medieval devils. The mobility of Milton's angels, both fallen and unfallen, fills in the full visual range of imaginable possibilities. How much of that range Milton could have imagined without the suggestive assistance of pictorial art must remain ultimately undemonstrable, but a comparison of his descriptions with art does help us as readers to appreciate the diversity of the visual effects he achieved.

That diversity has been properly admired,[16] but one episode has impressed major critics as excessive and even contrived: this is the movement of Uriel from the sun to earth, "gliding through the even/ On a sun beam, swift as a shooting star," and his return on the same "bright beam" (IV 555-56 and 590). Addison dismissed this description as "a prettiness that might have been admired in a little fanciful poet, but seems below the genius of Milton," while Dr. Johnson treated it along with other examples of "the confusion of spirit and matter" which he regarded as major flaws of the epic. For Johnson, it was simply inadmissible to describe the animated body of Uriel as supported by an immaterial ray of light.[17]

In the Age of Reason such representations would be rare, but from the Middle Ages through the sixteenth century they appear in one form or another in numerous art works. In the *Nativity with Annunciation to Shepherds* painted in 1522 by Andreas Giltlinger, cherubs slide happily down a broad beam of light extending from the head of God the Father to the feet of the Virgin, like small children shooting down slides in a playground. In other instances, angels walk, stand, or kneel upon light: in the *Martyrdom of St. Christopher*, which Tintoretto painted about 1560 for the Church of the Madonna dell' Orto in Venice, an angel appears to be walking down rays of brilliant light to present a crown and palm frond of victory to the saint, while in the *Scenes from the Life of John the Baptist* of 1510 by Granacci an angel is poised above the ground, kneeling on horizontal rays of light as though on a platform.[18] Angels are not infrequently shown hovering about

123

[15] See Broadbent, *Some Graver Subject*, p. 87 for a similar judgment of demonic motion in Book I.

[16] Allen, *The Harmonious Vision*, p. 99.

[17] Addison, *Spectator* 321 in Shawcross, *Milton: The Critical Heritage*, pp. 185-86; Johnson, *Lives of the English Poets*, I, p. 185.

[18] The Granacci painting is in the Metropolitan Museum in New York; the Tintoretto is reproduced as plate 96 in Hans Tietze, *Tintoretto: The Paintings and Drawings*, London, 1948, where also see figure 167 for Tintoretto's *Annunciation* of about 1575-84, in which the angel appears to be walking down clouds as though they were stepping stones, in order to greet the Virgin.

a beam of light, without quite riding on it, as in Veronese's *Adoration of the Magi* in the National Gallery in London, and angels appear to be moving up the light beams to Heaven in the *Martyrdom of St. Ursula and the Eleven Thousand Virgins* painted by the Master of the St. Ursula Legend in the last decade of the fifteenth century, and now on display at the Victoria and Albert Museum.

The dove of the Holy Spirit is a more frequent traveler on light beams, moving along without the slightest effort and with no sign of any need to beat his wings for self-propulsion. In paintings of the Annunciation, this motif is almost standard during the Renaissance and after, the dove appearing to glide directly down the beam of light. Representative examples may be found in Annunciation paintings by Fra Filippo Lippi in the National Gallery in Washington, by Domenico Michelino in Philadelphia, by Crivelli in the National Gallery of London, by *124* Titian in the Scuola di San Rocco in Venice, by Veronese at the Uffizi in Florence, and by Artemisia Gentileschi at the Capodimonte in Naples.

A similar conception represents the Christ Child at the Incarnation as floating or gliding down rays of light out of Heaven.[19] This scene is painted as early as the first half of the fourteenth century, remaining popular throughout the fifteenth century, and represented even as late as the sixteenth century, most accessibly in the frontispiece of one of the earliest English Protestant Bibles, the 1537 Matthew Bible.[20] Eventually, theologians feared that such a representation would mislead the ignorant to believe that the Christ Child came from Heaven in this infantile form, and thus did not draw human nature from Mary, so that the scene was officially disapproved and gradually disappeared. A somewhat similar instance, unrelated to the Christ Child, occurs in a fifteenth-century manuscript illumination of the creation of a human soul. Adelheid Heimann describes the scene: "A man and wife lie in a bed . . . . The upper left hand corner of the room opens, the Holy Trinity becomes visible, and sends a child down to the couple on a ray of light." The infant is actually toddling down through the air toward its parents, with outstretched arms, its feet supported only by the light rays emanating from the Deity.[21]

Another version of riding the sunbeam introduces elements of vivacity and charm that are perhaps even closer to Milton's conception. Though not heretical, this tradition was undeniably apocryphal. The fictional narratives recounting the infancy of Jesus, which became great favorites in the Middle Ages, told of the games the divine Child played. Among these was the enticing pastime of sliding down a sunbeam, as some other child might slide down a banister rail. Medieval illuminations convey the unmistakable *joie d'esprit* of this conception. Perhaps *125* Milton was displaying a similar *joie d'esprit* when he described Uriel "gliding

[19] David N. Robb, "The Iconography of the Annunciation in the Fourteenth and Fifteenth Centuries," *Art Bulletin* 18 (1936), 480-526, especially 525-26; see also Meyer Shapiro, " 'Muscipula Diaboli,' the Symbolism of the Mérode Altarpiece," in *Renaissance Art* (ed. Creighton Gilbert), New York, 1970, p. 26.

[20] For other English instances, see Anderson, *History and Imagery in British Churches*, p. 94. Dozens of continental examples are reproduced in Giacomo Prampolini, *L'Annunciazione nei pittori primitivi italiani*, Milan, n.d., and in Gertrud Schiller, *Iconography*, 1, figs. 99-104, 129, and pp. 45-46.

[21] Heimann, "Trinitas Creator Mundi," 52 and pl. 8d.

through the even/ On a sunbeam (IV, 555-56). Whether he should have introduced this episode amidst the high seriousness of his epic must remain a matter of personal taste, but I for one find it delightful.

INDIVIDUAL APPEARANCE

Milton's first full and detailed description of an individual angel is of Satan's disguise as he approaches Uriel on his way to earth. Uriel, "the sharpest sighted spirit of all in Heaven," is completely taken in and addresses the imposter as "fair angel" (III, 691 and 694), so perfect is the counterfeit:

> And now a stripling cherub he appears,
> Not of the prime, yet such as in his face
> Youth smiled celestial, and to every limb
> Suitable grace diffused, so well he feigned;
> Under a coronet his flowing hair
> In curls on either cheek played, wings he wore
> Of many a colored plume sprinkled with gold,
> His habit fit for speed succinct, and held
> Before his decent steps a silver wand.
>
> (III, 636-44)

It would be difficult to find another literary description which so graphically evokes the visual tradition, as we shall now see.

In the first line of this description, the reference to the "stripling cherub" shows a reliance upon art rather than theology, for it postulates age differences among the angels which were accepted in art but rejected in theology. Jameson summarizes the orthodox understanding that "there is no such thing as an old angel, and therefore there ought to be no such thing as an infant angel," and West applies this principle directly to Milton: "If Milton had any kind of warrant for this, it is certainly from art, not from angelology, whose authorities often complain of the artists' liberty in showing ageless angels as children or young men. Theologians virtually all agree that angels are not one younger than another and that they do not age."[22] Milton compounds this "mistake" later in the epic when he describes Michael as "prime/ In manhood where youth ended," but there was ample and indeed wholesale warrant in art for this conception of varying ages among the angels (XI, 245-46). Michael's appearance in the "prime" of manhood accords with Giordano's painting of the "giovane arcangelo," and I presume that Milton's "stripling cherub" is somewhat younger as he is not yet in the prime.[23]

In the earliest Christian art, and apparently throughout Byzantine art, infant

[22] Jameson, *Sacred and Legendary Art*, I, p. 51, and Robert H. West, *Milton and the Angels*, p. 104.

[23] Ferrari and Scavizzi, *Giordano*, I, p. 47, and III, p. 56. The descriptive phrase "not of the prime" applied to Satan's disguise may refer to rank in the celestial hierarchy rather than to age. At all events, Milton's "stripling cherub" does unmistakably show differences in the age of his angels.

angels were unknown, but they entered French art at the end of the twelfth century and became a virtual obsession in fifteenth-century Italian art. Ages were represented from earliest childhood, where the little angels were often almost literal adaptations of Classical putti and amorini, into boyhood, adolescence, young manhood, and full maturity.[24] On different occasions the same artist accords different ages to his angels, and we find a chubby child angel in the *Stemma* of the Ginori family executed by Della Robbia, along with a graceful adolescent *Michael* executed by the same studio, and in Perugino's *Madonna in Glory with Saints* at Bologna we have three different ages represented in the same picture, ranging from early infancy through adolescence and into manhood. Satan's angelic disguise which "so well he feigned," with a face where "youth smiled celestial" and where suitable grace was diffused in every limb, could be duplicated indefinitely in examples from pictorial art.[25]

126

127

Crowns, coronets, and fillets were frequent in the hair of angels from the earliest times. Early Christian and Byzantine art usually allowed a simple fillet to suffice, and Mâle reports that sometime after 1380 the hair was encircled with bands of gold.[26] Pietro Lorenzetti provides slight coronets, and so does Giotto. Hugo ver der Goes in his Portinari triptych paints lovely crowns composed of precious metals and gems, and Ortolano in his *Annunciation* at the Capitoline in Rome provides Gabriel with a jeweled crown of fine goldsmith's work. Like wings, crowns do not appear on angels in the Bible but in one form or another they were immensely popular in art into the early sixteenth century, after which they rarely appear.[27] Though the motif was uncommon by his own time, it obviously appealed to Milton, for he gave the assembled angels golden crowns, Uriel a golden tiara, and a coronet to the stripling cherub (III, 352, 625, 640). The cherubic coronet is presumably less distinguished than the archangelic tiara.[28] Beneath the coronet, Milton describes the cherub's "flowing hair" which "in curls on either cheek played." This coiffure is frequently encountered in art, as in the angels of Crivelli and Bernini.

124, 128

Thus far Milton's depiction of this stripling cherub scarcely serves to individualize him, except perhaps for his youth: his appearance is so commonplace that he could be illustrated by thousands of other angels. In the last two lines of the description, however, Milton introduces two more specialized attributes: the silver staff, and the robe girded up for speed succinct. Both are familiar features, but they do serve to indicate something very interesting about Satan's choice of

---

[24] Mâle, *Religious Art*, pp. 106-7; Evans, *Pattern*, I, p. 112; and Wölfflin, *Classic Art*, pp. 221-23.

[25] Rex Clements, "The Angels in *Paradise Lost*," *QR* 264 (1935), 285, suggests comparisons with the creations of Cimabue, while Margaret Bottrall, "The Baroque Element in Milton," 38, sees this as "just such an angel as poised the dart above the swooning Saint Teresa in Bernini's altarpiece" (Fig. 128).

[26] Jameson, *Sacred and Legendary Art*, 74-76, and Mâle, *Religious Art*, p. 106.

[27] The only comparable Biblical incident is in Rev. 4:10, where the twenty-four elders cast their golden crowns before the throne of God, but elders are certainly not angels.

[28] Differences in rank between angels were often denoted by the richness of their costume and appearance, from sixth-century Ravenna on.

disguise. The "silver wand" goes back to the earliest days of Christian art, as in the Church of Saint Agata in Ravenna where the angels carry the wandlike silver sceptres of Greek royalty. The tradition continues to appear throughout the Middle Ages, as in Duccio's *Angel* in the Johnson Collection at the Philadelphia Museum, and into the Renaissance and beyond, though it is often varied with a staff of some other material, as in the golden staff of Jacob Jordaens' *Flight into Egypt* at the Walters Gallery in Baltimore.[29] That the wand would not and should not be a universal attribute of all angels is apparent: it is appropriate only for a standing or walking angel, rather than for a flying angel, and it is only in these circumstances that it is represented in art. For several centuries prior to Milton's time, it probably appeared most frequently when carried by Raphael in one hand as he leads the boy Tobias with the other, or carried by a guardian angel who is similarly leading his human charge on the pilgrimage of life.

Here the attribute of the staff merges with the "habit fit for speed succinct." The phrase describes angelic robes which are girded up by a belt or sash or tucked up in some other way, so as to allow free movement of the legs, as we see in Titian's *Tobias and the Angel* at the Accademia in Venice. In a similar painting by a follower of Verrocchio, the angel has not only belted his under garment but is holding up his outer robe with his hand. In these and other instances with Tobias, the angel is known to be Raphael, and the scene was taken as epitomizing the relationship between the guardian angel and the human soul.[30] Guardian angels also appeared in art without Tobias, but with some unidentified child who symbolized the human soul. Here again the angelic robes were shown girded up, as in the paintings by Domenechino and Carlo Bononi.

In Netherlandish art, Raphael and the unarmed guardian angels are typically represented with both these attributes.[31] The Digital Index for the Art of the Low Countries (DIAL) shows both staff and tucked-up robes in treatments of the subject by the Master of the Prodigal Son at Castle Grünewald near Berlin, by D. van Alsloot at the Antwerp Museum, by B. Fabritius at Nimes, by E. van der Neer at the Rijksmuseum in Amsterdam, as well as in privately owned paintings by Abraham van Dijk, Jasper van der Lanen, and P. H. Lankrink. Abraham Bloemaert made no less than three versions (in the Minneapolis Institute of Art, in the Hermitage at Leningrad, and in a private collection), while there are graphic works by Hans Bol and Marten van Heemskerck, and a drawing by Rembrandt in the Marignane Collection in Paris.[32] An engraving after Marten van Heemskerck illustrates this standard conception: whether Raphael or any other guardian angel was intended, the expected appearance was with staff and girded robes.

129

82, 83

130

[29] See Jameson, *Sacred and Legendary Art*, p. 74.

[30] Clement, *Angels in Art*, pp. 106-7; Mâle, *Religious Art*, pp. 187-89; E. H. Gombrich, *Symbolic Images*, p. 28. Pigler, *Barockthemen*, I, pp. 520-26, provides a long list of guardian angel representations.

[31] West, *Milton and the Angels*, p. 50, shows that many Protestants believed in guardian angels.

[32] These works are illustrated under DIAL numbers 72C53, 55, 56.1, 57, 58, 58.1, 61.1, and 47 I 22.31.

Normally angels in art are not so dressed, for neither walking clothes nor a staff are necessary to their usual operations. Milton thus provides, for those who are able to catch it, a hint fraught with powerfully ironic significance: Satan enters the created world not only disguised as an angel, but even disguised in a form which artistically sophisticated readers could readily identify as the usual form of the guardian angel. It has long been recognized that Milton's choice of Raphael as instructor for Adam and Eve was based upon his traditional role as guardian angel *par excellence*, and also that the explicit comparison of Asmodeus to Satan upon the latter's entering of Eden (IV, 166-71) was to place him in precise antithesis to Raphael, since it was from the demon Asmodeus that Raphael protected Tobias. One scarcely needs a knowledge of art to appreciate those allusions, but the nexus of associations takes on a new depth of meaning when we recognize that in his first disguise Satan assumes the appearance most frequently associated with the guardian angel, the protector and guide of human souls.

In contrast to the stripling cherub, Milton's description of the faithful angels in Eden shows them, either implicitly or explicitly, as dressed in one or another form of armor, except for the first appearance of the angelic guards captained by Gabriel. These "unarmed youth of Heaven" have hung their "celestial armory" nearby while they "exercised heroic games" (IV, 550-54).[33] Even so, Gabriel is described as "the winged warrior" and his angelic command is soon assembled "in warlike parade" (IV, 576 and 780).

A more explicit description is given of Michael when he comes to instruct Adam in the eleventh book—"his starry helm unbuckled," he carries a spear in his hand and "by his side/ As in a glistering zodiac hung the sword,/ Satan's dire dread," while "over his lucid arms/ A military vest of purple flowed/ Livelier than Meliboean" (XI, 240-49). As we have already discussed at considerable length the development of armored images of Michael in the pictorial arts, we now need only to touch upon some of the incidental details of Milton's description. The application of the adjective "lucid" to describe the armor provides a certain range of color and light, without prescribing a particular hue. Milton's purpose is to suggest the dazzling light and splendor thrown off by the armor, and lucid in this sense could suggest gold or silver or white armor. The color of Michael's armor was not uniform in painting—it could even be a gun-metal color as in the painting by Bonifacio de Pitati in the Zanipolo Church in Venice, or dark blue as in the *Virgin with Angels* by Ghirlandaio in the Uffizi, or deep green as in the painting by Juan Jiminez. Such dark armor was exceptional, however, and even when it occurs the dark oils used for the metal can display a surprising luminosity, as they do in Juan Jiminez and Rubens. Michael is more often shown in gold or silver or white armor, and whatever the color, the armor is usually shining and reflecting the light, so that Milton's "lucid arms" evokes the typical picture of Michael.

Cloth of various kinds is often represented in these paintings, whether in military vests, as in Milton's description, or in cloaks, sleeves, kilts, and stockings. Here

20

17

*5, 22,
25, 28, 29*

---

[33] It is interesting to contrast these peaceful and Olympian sports with the destructive games in which the devils delight in *PL* II, 532-8.

again there was no uniform color scheme: the mosaic in San Marco shows Michael with a blue kilt and a red cloak, while the stained glass in King's College Chapel represents his robe as gray green, but Milton's description conforms with the majority of the visual representations I have seen, in which Michael's clothing is painted within the purple, violet, or lavender range of the spectrum.[34] The spear and the sword were common attributes of Michael throughout Europe.[35] Milton's description of Michael as he comes to meet Adam after the Fall accords with the most usual artistic practice after the Middle Ages, and was sufficient to elicit familiar visual imagery appropriate to what Milton calls the "majesty . . . solemn and sublime" of this angelic "Prince above princes" (XI, 232-36 and 298).

Raphael differs from the other angels in that he is not dressed in plate armor but in mail—indeed, in "feathered mail" (V, 284). It is appropriate that Raphael as the sociable spirit should not wear the formidable plate armor of Michael; by clothing him as he does Milton is able to accord this angelic visitor an air of heavenly mystery, without making him awesome. This angelic costume had long been popular in England.[36] It was a logical adaptation of that ancient scale armor which consisted of small overlapping plates of metal, leather, or horn.[37] Replacing the hard scales with soft feathers was a simple matter, and made possible the easy costuming of actors who portrayed angels in the mystery plays so that they could assume on the medieval stage a distinctive and recognizable form. From the stage, the armor spread rapidly throughout English ecclesiastical art in a standard form precisely described as "feathered mail."

119

ACTIVITIES AND MOODS

As Milton ran counter to traditional theology and pneumatology when he ascribed different ages to his angels, so, too, when he referred to sad and weeping angels.

[34] Koehler, "Milton's Use of Color and Light," 56-57, treats the iconographic propriety of purple for Michael, with its implications of military and political power. Allen, *Harmonious Vision*, p. 98, says that purple was probably red in Milton's eye but does not substantiate the claim, and I remain unconvinced by it. Broadbent, *Some Graver Subject*, p. 270, says that Milton's Michael "appears like Raphael's."

[35] Scales were another popular attribute of Michael, and were frequently found on the continent but rarely in England, according to Peter Brieger, *English Art 1216-1307*, Oxford, 1957, p. 181. R.L.P. Milburn, *Saints and Their Emblems in English Churches*, London, 1949, p. 184, says that a total of 690 English churches were dedicated to Michael during the Middle Ages.

[36] E. S. Prior and A. Gardner, *Medieval Figure Sculpture in England*, Cambridge, 1912, p. 516; W. L. Hildburgh, "An English Alabaster Carving of Saint Michael Weighing a Soul," *Burlington Magazine* 89 (1947), 129-31, and "English Alabaster Carvings as Records of the Medieval Religious Drama," *Archaeologia* 93 (1949), 51-101; Anderson, *Imagery of British Churches*, p. 137; Perry, "On the Psychostasis in Christian Art," 102-3; and E. S. Prior, "The Sculpture of Alabaster Tables," *Illustrated Catalogue of the Exhibition of English Medieval Alabaster Work*, London, 1913, for more general background.

[37] See Sir Guy Francis Laking, *A Record of European Armour and Arms Through Seven Centuries*, London, 5 vols., 1920-22, I, pp. 40-42 with illustrations, and George Cameron Stone, *A Glossary of the Construction, Decoration and Use of Arms and Armor*, Portland, Me., 1934, p. 544.

When he explains that angels can eat and digest earthly food and that they enjoy a sex life comparable to human sexual intercourse, he again "enters into questions debated among angelologists and almost unanimously decided against his view."[38] In the visual arts we find consistent support for his sad or tearful angels, while there was one popular example of angels who can eat, frequently repeated. As for sex, art by the seventeenth century contained many unmistakably male and female angels, but never showed them making love.

"Tears such as angels weep" were not unusual, though Milton was highly innovative, as we have seen, (above, pp. 104-5) in ascribing them to Satan. For the faithful angels to be shown as sad or as weeping would have been quite expected, so often had they appeared so in renderings of the Passion. What artists had traditionally shown as angelic concern for the Second Adam was transferred in *Paradise Lost* to the First Adam. When the unwelcome news of the Fall of Man reached the angels in Heaven, "displeased/ All were who heard; dim sadness did not spare/ That time celestial visages, yet, mixt/ With pity, violated not their bliss" (x, 22-25). An eleventh-century ivory carving of the Crucifixion in the Victoria and Albert Museum pictures weeping angels, who wipe tears from their eyes with their robes, while Giotto and Cavallini show angels tearing at their breasts in anguish over the Crucifixion.[39] The *Pietà* by Carlo Crivelli in the Philadelphia Museum shows child angels whose weeping distorts their faces almost to ugliness.[40] Though Milton explicitly declares that the angels' displeasure did not spare their celestial visages, he avoids the excesses of such paintings by adding that this dim sadness "violated not their bliss." The extent to which pity and sorrow changed the appearance of these angels in *Paradise Lost* we do not know, and we do not need to know, for Milton only wishes to summon before our eyes a fleeting sign of the compassion the faithful angels feel for humanity.

131

Most angelologists denied that angels could concoct and digest food as Raphael does in the al fresco meal in Book v.[41] Without any close parallels in epic and hexameral writings, this episode has raised many critical eyebrows, and a few critical gorges.[42] According to Kranidas, the history of this subject is "almost a history of the understanding of Milton's decorum," and unfortunately a study of pictorial art enables us to add little if any fresh insight to that history.[43] There is

---

[38] West, *Milton and the Angels*, pp. 104 and 106.

[39] Clement, *Angels in Art*, p. 210.

[40] In Milton's own century, the same conception was visually portrayed by Poussin in his *Lamentation for Christ*, now at the Alte Pinacotek in Munich, and by Francesco Albani's *Ecce Homo*, now in the Galleria Colonna in Rome. Ryken, *The Apocalyptic Vision in "Paradise Lost*," p. 21, discusses "the accommodated nature" of Milton's details, and the same could be said of the artistic analogues.

[41] West, *Milton and the Angels*, p. 106; John R. Knott, Jr., "The Visit of Raphael: *Paradise Lost*, Book v," *PQ* 47 (1968), 36-42; Curry, *Milton's Ontology*, pp. 160 and 221-22; and Virginia R. Mollenkott, "A Note on Milton's Materialistic Angelology," *SCN* 22 no. 1 (1964), item 9.

[42] P. L. Carver, "The Angels in *Paradise Lost*," *RES* 16 (1940), 415-31, provides theological background.

[43] Kranidas, *The Fierce Equation*, p. 150.

surely nothing new in suggesting an association between the meal shared by Raphael with Adam and Eve and the meal shared in Genesis by the three angels visitant with Abraham and Sarah,[44] but that Biblical incident had long been popular in art, and representations in virtually every medium showed the angelic visitors seated at table and being served human food. From the earliest church art through the Middle Ages and into Milton's time, this episode was taken as a representation of the Holy Trinity, and the suggested intimacy between God and man made it strongly appealing in almost every age.[45] As late as 1641, the stained glass window executed by Abraham van Linge for University College, Oxford, represented the familiar scene in the familiar way, with the angels being served by Abraham, while Sarah like a timid Eve peeps out of the door in the background.

The sex life of the angels was introduced by Milton in a discussion, not as a description, and its purpose was to underscore his conviction that sexual love was intrinsically sure (VIII, 612-630).[46] Though one can occasionally find examples in art of affectionate gestures between angels, there are no paintings of actual angelic love-making, and indeed Milton's allusion to a joining "easier than air with air" scarcely could be painted (VIII, 626).

Milton also wrote that "spirits when they please/ Can either sex assume" (I, 423-24), which accords both with the standard pneumatology and with pictorial tradition. Réau points out that the Christian development of the winged Victory into an angel involved the abandonment of Nike's femininity,[47] and he finds no unmistakably female angels until the fifteenth century;[48] thereafter he notes their great popularity among Baroque artists, while Wölfflin refers to "those agile girlish figures" of Renaissance art, and to "the girl-angels" of Botticelli and Filippino Lippi.[49] Berefelt finds beautiful female angels firmly established after the fifteenth century.[50]

Although there was no sexual differentiation between angels in the catacombs, Bosio's magnificently illustrated *Roma Sotterranea* of 1632 is full of Baroque engravings of angels as decorative supports and in margins, and in these we frequently see unmistakably feminine angels with breasts, along with nude cherubs and even adult angels with male sex organs.[51] In England, we also find seventeenth-century differentiation of the angels, as in the anonymous paintings of about 1600 at Muchelney Abbey, where the nave vault is "peopled with angels of both sexes,

---

[44] Sims, *The Bible in Milton's Epics*, pp. 202-205, and Jason P. Rosenblatt, "Celestial Entertainment in Eden: Book V of *Paradise Lost*," *Harvard Theological Review* 62 (1969), 411-27.

[45] Braunfels, *Dreifaltigkeit*, figs. 1-10, and Pigler, *Barockthemen*, I, pp. 36-38.

[46] See Dennis Burden, *The Logical Epic: A Study of the Argument of "Paradise Lost,"* Cambridge, Mass., 1967, pp. 158-59.

[47] Réau, *Iconographie*, II, i, pp. 34-35.

[48] Trapp, "Iconography," p. 177 avers to the contrary that until the later Middle Ages, angels were as frequently feminine as masculine. See also Gardner, *English Medieval Sculpture*, p. 142, and Anderson, *Imagery of British Churches*, p. 137.

[49] Wölfflin, *Classic Art*, pp. 223 and 235.

[50] Berefelt, *A Study on the Winged Angel*, pp. 96-111, treats the historical developments.

[51] Bosio, *Roma Sotterranea*, pp. 51, 53, 61, 81, 97, and 287; 101, 157, 229, 287, 337, 391, and 577.

dressed in Elizabethan costume."[52] The spandrel of the east gate of Canterbury Quad of Saint John's College in Oxford is decorated with carvings, erected by Archbishop Laud between 1631 and 1636, which show bare-breasted female angels.[53] This visual tradition allowed Milton considerable flexibility of treatment, so that Adam could refer to the angels as "spirits masculine . . . without feminine," and yet without contradiction Eve could be thought of as an angelic figure when the epic voice refers to "her heavenly form/ Angelic" (x, 890-93 and IX, 457-58). What Wölfflin had called the "girl-angels" of the Quattrocento may suggest the figure which Milton basically wished to evoke here, but he avoids any possibility of confusion with the androgynous angels by adding that Eve was "more soft and feminine."[54]

Among the most notable features of the traditional angelology was the systematic division of angels into strata of ranks and degrees known as the celestial hierarchy. Milton does not precisely conform to this elaborate system, though he does of course identify angels within a hierarchy of service to God, one having more authority and responsibility than another. In this regard he agrees with most Protestant writers who "avoided strict classification of angels, preferring to speak vaguely of the 'unconfused orders Angellick'."[55] As in *Paradise Lost*, the traditional angelic orders were not ignored in pictorial art, but they were not so frequently represented as I had expected. We find the full range of orders displayed about the central lantern in the Florentine Baptistry, and also in the work by Giovanni di Balduccio and others for the Portinari Chapel in Sant' Eustorgio, while the *Last Judgment* painted in the fifteenth century by John Brentwood for Richard Beauchamp's tomb chapel in Saint Mary's Church, Warwick, shows a consistent differentiation according to "skilled theological knowledge."[56] Otherwise, systematic representations of the whole celestial hierarchy are rare in comparison with the total number of angels available to us in art.

What is not rare is the movement of angelic ranks in concentric circles about the divine center.[57] This representation minimizes or even ignores the separate orders so as to emphasize order itself, and the result is a powerful visual assertion of

[52] Edward Croft-Murray, *Decorative Painting in England, 1537-1837*, London, 1962, I, pl. 46 and pp. 30 and 188.

[53] It is possible that these figures represent winged Victories, as in Poussin's *Coronation of David* (reproduced in Friedlander, *Nicholas Poussin: A New Approach*, New York, n.d. fig. 25) but the crucial point is that Milton's contemporaries could have interpreted them as angels on the basis of the developing iconography. See Berefelt, *A Study on the Winged Angel*, p. 105.

[54] Ricks, *Milton's Grand Style*, p. 57, treats objections raised to this comparison by Bentley and others; such objections appear to be even less apposite in view of the visual tradition.

[55] C. A. Patrides, "Renaissance Views on the Unconfused Orders Angellick," *JHI* 23 (1962), 267. See also C. A. Patrides, "Renaissance Thought on the Celestial Hierarchy: The Decline of a Tradition," *JHI* 20 (1959), 155-66; Dustdoor, "Legends of Lucifer," 220-23; Rex Clements, "The Angels in *Paradise Lost*," *passim*; and West, *Milton and the Angels*, pp. 133-36.

[56] *La Cappella Portinari in Sant' Eustorgio a Milano* (ed. R. Cipriani *et al.*), Milan, 1963, figs. 30-37 and pp. 46-47, and Boase, *Death in the Middle Ages*, p. 67.

[57] Clement, *Angels in Art*, 25-26.

harmony. Milton makes much of this angelic formation in his descriptions, repeatedly referring to the orbs or circles or globes of the angelic hosts, usually centered on the Father or on the Son (*PL* III, 60-62; v, 594-96 and 631; *PR* I, 171, and IV, 581-83). This circling movement about the divine throne or thrones enhances our understanding of the proper ordering of life as centered upon and directed toward the Godhead "fixed forever firm and sure" within a sea of created change and flux (VII, 586).[58] That meaning is of course primary, but it is enhanced by the visual suggestiveness of the descriptions. From at least the thirteenth century, artists working in churches and cathedrals had ranked the whole populace of Heaven in concentric circles about the Deity or the Virgin,[59] and the same may be found in illuminated manuscripts.[60] This visual imagery was still very much alive through Milton's time, and may be illustrated in the globe of angels surrounding Christ in Raphael's *Disputa* at the Vatican, in the orb of angels surrounding the Holy Spirit in Tintoretto's *Adoration of the Holy Spirit* at the Galleria Colonna, in the ceiling for the Chapel of Angels by Federico Zuccari at the Gesù in Rome, in Guido Reni's *Christ in Glory with Angels* in the cupola of the Chapel of the Sacraments in the cathedral at Ravenna, and in Andrea Camassei's painting of the angels in "full and frequent" ranks circling about God in the ceiling of Room VI of the Palazzo Barberini in Rome. This visual tradition is epitomized in Tintoretto's *Paradise* which covers a large wall in the Doge's Palace with so many adoring angels that no reproduction in book size is possible of that magnificent evocation of "orbs of circuit inexpressible" about the divine presence (v, 594-95). A detail can indicate how Tintoretto places the Virgin along with the Son within his divine circle of light, while about the divinity "all the sanctities of Heaven/ Stood thick as stars, and from his sight received/ Beatitude past utterance" (III, 60-62). Aside from the Virgin, the similarity is precise, down to the visual image of "thick as stars." Satan's presumptuous imitation of deity may be seen here as elsewhere, and Milton twice shows Satan surrounded by "a globe of fiery seraphim" (II, 511-13, and I, 616-18).

132

Another typical angelic formation in art which appears also in Milton is the flying maneuver by which angels support and carry the Deity. It is to this that Satan alludes in his contemptuous dismissal of Gabriel even "though Heaven's King/ Ride on thy wings" (IV, 973-74). The same image is developed in *Paradise Regained* when the Son is rescued from the pinnacle of the Temple by "a fiery globe/ Of angels on full sail of wing," and carried "As on a floating couch through the blithe air" (*PR* IV, 581-85). The Son is upborne on just such a soft sail of "pluming vans" in the *Paradise* of Tintoretto, as is the Father in the choir-screen

132

[58] Ryken, *The Apocalyptic Vision*, p. 106, provides an insightful analysis of this theme.

[59] Mâle, *Religious Art*, p. 82.

[60] Walter Oakeshott, *The Sequence of English Medieval Art, Illustrated Chiefly from Illuminated Manuscripts, 650-1450*, London, 1950, pl. 18, reproduces an illumination of John's Gospel dating from about 1020; see also Millar, *English Illuminated Manuscripts of the XIVth and XVth Centuries*, pl. 83, and Ludwig Volkmann, *Iconographia Dantesca*, Leipzig, 1897, pl. 4. Visual presentations clearly antedate the use by Dante.

carving at King's College Chapel, and the Virgin in the painting by Niccolò di 44
Liberatore.[61] 79

In a third representation of the angelic hosts massed in the presence of God, Milton shows them seated: ". . . the sons of light/ Hasted, resorting to the summons high,/ And took their seats; till from his throne supreme/ Th' Almighty thus pronounced his sovran will" (XI, 80-84).[62] The seating of angels in the presence of God was especially popular in the art of the fourteenth and fifteenth centuries, as we can see in the Last Judgments by Giotto at Padua and by Cavallini in the Church of Saint Cecilia in Trastevere in Rome, in the Quattrocento paintings of the *Assumption of the Virgin* by Botticini at the National Gallery in London, and in the *Coronation of the Virgin* by Jacobello del Fiore at the Accademia in Venice. The motif is represented here in a miniature painting from the *Très riches heures* by the Limbourg brothers. Neither in Milton nor in pictorial art am I aware of any 45 instance of the faithful angels having to prostrate themselves before the Deity, but Satan institutes this reverence for himself among his followers: "Towards him they bend/ With awful reverence prone, and as a God/ Extol him equal to the highest in Heaven" (II, 477-79). By introducing that demonic prostration of the rebellious angels in Hell, Milton achieved a fine visual contrast with the dignity of the faithful angels seated upon their thrones in Heaven.

Haloes had for so long been supplied by the artists to their angels as to be virtual commonplaces, and though in Milton's time the halo was often omitted in paintings, Milton alludes to it twice in *Paradise Lost*, as "beaming sunny rays" and simply as "beams" in the angelic hair (III, 625, 362). Less ordinary was Milton's provision of flower and leaf garlands for his angels—a fashion which evidences a somewhat old-fashioned taste on the part of the poet. He first tells us of the use of amarant by angels to "bind their resplendent locks" (III, 352, and 361); elsewhere, he is less specific as to the plants used, and merely describes the angels "with fresh flowerets crowned" (V, 636). In each case, we see in *Paradise Lost* what is known in pictorial art as "l'angelo inghirlandato." The garland itself was variously composed: of olive leaves, of roses, of other flowers, or of amarant. This decorative feature was immensely popular in the fourteenth and fifteenth centuries, when it appeared that no respectable angel would be seen without flowers in his (or her) hair. The motif is represented in the works of Simone Martini, Ambrogio Lorenzetti, Fra Angelico, Matteo di Giovanni, Piero della Francesca, Domenico Ghirlandaio, Filippo and Filippino Lippi, Piero Pollaiuolo,

[61] The Son is similarly borne up in an oval of angels in the Last Judgment paintings by Giotto at Padua and by Giovanni di Paolo in Siena, while the latter artist so presents the Father in his *Baptism of Christ* (Robert Hughes, *Heaven and Hell in Western Art*, New York, 1968, p. 121) as does Marco Benefial in his *Judgment of Adam and Eve* at the Galleria Corsini in Rome, and the Virgin is shown with the same support in Masolino da Panicale's *Assumption* at the Capodimonte in Naples. *PL* III, 520-21, refers to a human soul being carried to Heaven in the same fashion.

[62] Rev. 4:4 provides seats for the "four and twenty elders" but apparently none for the angels; the tradition of seated angels seems to have been an artistic extrapolation from this verse.

133

Botticelli, and Pintorricchio, while in England during the same centuries it is found in the Holkham Bible, in the Wilton Diptych, and in many of the stone angels in King's College Chapel.[63] The fashion declined in the sixteenth century, though seventeenth-century examples may be found in angels by Domenico Feti, Orazio Gentileschi, and Baciccia in the Galleria Corsini in Rome, and elsewhere as well.[64] These flowered chaplets go well beyond mere decoration in art, for they actually modify our impression of the wearers. By adding an olive wreath, Simone Martini is able to qualify the austerity of his angels without diminishing their dignity, while the circlet of flowers in the golden hair of Fra Filippo Lippi's angels

II, 120

increases our sense of their beauty, innocence, and grace. The same attractive effects are achieved by Milton when he weaves flowers about the hair of his angels.

Something more needs to be said about Milton's references to amarant as a plant. As has long been recognized, the word "amarant" here refers to the unfading or *amaranton* inheritance or crown promised to the faithful Christian in 1 Peter 1:4, and literary uses of the symbol have been traced down to the time of Milton.[65] D. C. Allen, who wrote a useful article identifying similarities between Milton's use of amarant and treatments of it by Clement of Alexandria, has shown that Clement denied any physical, earthly basis for the flower.[66] According to Allen, Milton's amarant "is not a real flower at all but an ideality inexpressible in terms of earthly flora. . . . As a consequence, this flower, beyond the things of earth, has neither color nor form: it is an emblem of immaculateness enhancing the visual interpretation of the accompanying panels and lifting them above a mundane commentary."[67] In a fundamentally metaphorical sense, Allen is of course correct, and Milton tells us that this plant was "for man's offense/ To Heaven removed" (III, 355-56). But the denial of any botanical and visual reality to the plant is incorrect.

Far from being a purely metaphysical construct, the amarant in fact existed as a real flower known as *genus amaranthus* which was famous, among gardeners as well as theologians, for its remarkably long life.[68] Milton might have seen this flower in the Borghese Gardens, and probably elsewhere in Italy as well.[69] According to Guy de Tervarent, this plant was known to the Greeks, who were so much impressed by the persistence of its blossoms that they gave it the name amarant.[70]

[63] Examples from most of these Italian artists, and others as well, may be seen in the illustrations to Giacomo Prampolini, *L'annunciazione nei pittori primitivi italiani*, *passim*, which I cite for the convenience of readers and not because the flowered wreaths were restricted to the angel of the Annunciation.

[64] In the same gallery is an eighteenth-century example by Pompeo Batoni, while a seventeenth-century example by Alessandro Tiarini is found in the Church of San Michele in Bosco, Bologna, and a sixteenth-century example by Morone in the National Gallery in London.

[65] C. Ruutz-Rees, "Flower Garlands of the Poets, Milton, Shakespeare, Spenser, Marot, Sannazaro," in *Mélanges offerts à M. Abel Lefranc*, Paris, 1936, pp. 85 and 88.

[66] Allen, "Milton's Amarant," 257.

[67] Allen, *Harmonious Vision*, p. 99.

[68] Arnold Whittick, *Symbols, Signs and Their Meaning*, Newton, Mass., 1960, p. 131.

[69] Georgina Masson, "Italian Flower Collectors' Gardens in Seventeenth Century Italy," in David R. Coffin, *The Italian Garden*, p. 67.

[70] G. de Tervarent, *Attributs et symboles dans l'art profane*, p. 15.

It would thus appear that the flower originally inspired the literary myth, rather than the contrary, though whether Milton actually saw the flower, we have unfortunately no way of knowing.

In addition to its well-attested literary popularity and its horticultural reputation, the flower was given considerable visual exposure in art. An Italian Renaissance medal made for Marius Equicola featured a crown of amarant with the words "immortalitas amaranthi,"[71] and one of Alciati's emblems pictures Thetis covering the grave of Achilles with the ever-fresh amaranthus.[72] But amarant was not only associated with the heroes of classical antiquity and the would-be immortals of the Renaissance. It was introduced for great heroes of the faith early in the fifteenth century when Donatello carved a beautiful marble wreath of amarant about the head of his *David*, where the appearance of the plant may be most clearly seen. *134* H. W. Janson suggests that this iconography may have been suggested to Donatello by a Florentine humanist such as Niccolò Niccoli.[73] The earliest work in which the amarantine chaplet was applied to angels seems to be the *Angel with the Crown of Amarant* carved by Nanni di Banco for the Porta della Mandorla in the cathedral at Florence. Here again we see an instance of what Janson has called "the general pattern of 'cross-breeding' between theology and philosophy, between literature and the fine arts, that molded the intellectual and artistic climate of the new age."[74] At all events, the allegorical purpose is at work not only in Milton but in pictorial art, and in both the addition of flowered chaplets to the hair of angels introduces yet one more visual suggestion of grace and joy.

Similar effects were achieved, both in the visual arts and in *Paradise Lost*, by the introduction of angelic music and dance. There is some Scriptural basis for this conception, as we find in Revelation 5:8 where the twenty-four elders make music (but elders are not angels), in Job 38:7 where the morning stars sing, and in Psalm 148:2-3 where angels are said to join in praise of God, and these Scriptural warrants were widely developed into a vast conception of celestial harmony. As Knott reminds us, "the dominant mood of Heaven is festive, in keeping with Milton's view of dynamic communal praise as the highest expression of the love of God," a view which found enthusiastic expression in the visual arts as well.[75] This vision of angelic music is often represented in English churches, where we find many a triforium or roodloft carved with angelic musicians, such as those in Holy Sepulchre Church and King's College Chapel, Cambridge.[76] On the continent, *118* too, Heaven was envisioned as a cheerful place in which angels were engaged in making a joyful noise with musical instruments and with song.[77] Representative examples in Italy may be found in the cantorias of Donatello and Della Robbia,

[71] *Ibid.*

[72] Andrea Alciati, *Omnia Emblemata*, Paris, 1618, cxxxv on p. 636.

[73] H. W. Janson, *The Sculpture of Donatello*, 2 vols., Princeton, 1957, ii, 6-7.

[74] Janson, *loc. cit.*, and 221.

[75] Knott, *Milton's Pastoral Vision*, p. 86.

[76] M. D. Anderson, *History and Imagery in British Churches*, p. 159; Fred H. Crossley, *English Church Monuments*, London, 1921, p. 145 and *English Church Craftsmanship*, pp. 81-83.

[77] Panofsky, *Early Netherlandish Painting*, i, 270.

which would still have been seen in the Florentine cathedral in 1639, in Raphael's sixteenth-century *Ecstasy of Saint Cecilia* now at Bologna, and in the angelic musical celebration which Guido Reni painted in 1615 for his *Glorification of Saint Dominic* in the Church of Saint Dominic at Bologna. Choirs of singing angels and orchestras playing upon harps, pipes, organs, and stringed instruments were a nearly universal part of the visual imagination of Europe, judging by the art works.

All of these would have supplied visual reinforcement for Milton's numerous descriptions of angelic music-making (III, 365-71, and 416-17; IV, 677-88; V, 178, 546-48, 619-27; VI, 93-96, 167-68; VII, 256-60, 275, 557-64, 594-634; X, 641-43; and *PR* I, 168-72). It would be an exaggeration to suggest that Milton's descriptions are visually detailed and precise in these passages: they clearly are not and they would have lost something of their effect had they been made too specific. Milton is not only making his own music with his verse, but is relying upon generalized imagery to bring before the mental eyes of his readers traditional visions of harmony and joy. It is to our advantage as readers if we recognize not only the harmony of sound but the harmony of line and movement in these passages. It is such a perception which lies behind John Addington Symonds' acute observation of Signorelli's frescoes at Orvieto that "a Miltonic harmony pervades the movement of his angelic choirs. Their beauty is the product of their strength and virtue."[78] In the *Praise of Angels* painted by Ludovico Carracci for S. Paolo in Bologna, we find another artistic effect comparable to Milton's. Here spontaneity and diversity are apparent throughout, implying an inner-directed order even in apparent disorder, a freedom inherent in the disciplines of love and service, which is very much what Milton implies in his description of the angelic song and dance which moves through "mazes intricate,/ Eccentric, intervolved, yet regular/ Then most, when most irregular they seem" (V, 622-24).

[78] John Addington Symonds, *Sketches in Italy*, p. 106.

XI

Heaven

THE PROBLEMS

THE imaginative topography of Heaven should express the nature of God and of the faithful angels just as effectively as Hell expresses the nature of Satan and his fallen legions. Judged on those grounds, Milton's Heaven must be regarded as a success; indeed, once we have accepted the propriety of accommodating spiritual truth through physical images, it would be difficult to fault it as an expression of divine will and angelic beatitude. Serenity, peace, love, joy, and harmonious communion are not only spiritually present within the inhabitants of Heaven, but are amply suggested by its physical environment.

And yet Harry Levin is surely correct in saying that "most of Milton's readers are more at ease with the diabolic, we must admit, than with what Allen Tate has called 'the angelic imagination.'"[1] The problem may be endemic to the subject itself. When Bernini set out to carve two marble heads representing a blessed and a damned soul, he inevitably found the subject of damnation to be more dramatic than that of beatitude, and in medieval paintings of the Last Judgment it is usually Hell which first attracts and longest holds the attention of the viewer.[2] Even if we desire beatitude, we can scarcely claim to find it so exciting as damnation. We may admire humility but we are fascinated by ambition, and tranquility attracts our attention less than do agitation and disturbance. The turbulent is inherently more dramatic than the serene. Perhaps it is inevitable for the concord of Milton's Heaven "to be contrasted with the energetic discord elsewhere, in Hell or even Chaos, and to seem merely lethargic in comparison," as John Peter has expressed it.[3]

If Milton could be asked about all this, I suspect that he would maintain his Heaven to be every bit as successful as his Hell in purely literary terms, and that he would claim our confusion of serenity with lethargy to be more a theological than a critical problem. He would admit, I believe, that he, too, instinctively found hatred more dramatic than love, and war more interesting than peace, and would claim that the reasons for this decadent human preference had been clearly explained in *Paradise Lost*. He might then go on to claim that his description of Heaven gave as effective an expression of perfection as could be reasonably expected of an imperfect creature.

[1] Harry Levin, *The Myth of the Golden Age in the Renaissance*, Bloomington, Ind., 1969, p. 180.
[2] "Hell is always made more explicit than Heaven" according to Frank Kendon, *Mural Paintings in English Churches during the Middle Ages*, p. 125.
[3] John Peter, *A Critique of "Paradise Lost*," p. 86.

Our primary concern here is not with the dramaturgy but with the scenography of Heaven, and Milton has made use of every major element of the artistic tradition to make that scenography vital and convincing. Whether or not he was able to "bring all Heaven before mine eyes," as he had written in "Il Penseroso," it is demonstrable that the celestial imagery in *Paradise Lost* is remarkably inclusive in its appeal to memories of the Heavens envisioned and foreshadowed in pictorial art. The artists would doubtless have agreed with Milton that Heaven was literally "inimitable on earth/ By model, or by shading pencil drawn," but certain conventions had been established, and these were exploited again and again in paintings and in mosaics as the most effective and appealing visual accommodations of the invisible, and it is upon those same visual conceptions that Milton primarily relies in describing Heaven in *Paradise Lost* (III, 508-9).

ACCESS TO HEAVEN: THE GOLDEN STAIRS

Getting into Heaven is a matter of no small importance and of some reputed difficulty. For God the Son and for the faithful angels, there is no problem, but merely a matter of returning home: the Son is conveyed in the chariot of paternal deity, and the angels on their own wings.[4] Milton also introduces an elaborate golden stair to connect the created world with the great gate of Heaven (III, 501-25). In representational art, such stairs were often used by angels, but Milton obviously prefers to have his angels fly from one point of the universe to another, and so the stairs are apparently not needed by the angels and we never see them used by man within the current action of the epic.[5] But we should not assume them to be a purposeless addition. For over a thousand years, Christians had been accustomed by the visual arts to imagine a ladder especially designed for the faithful souls to climb on their pilgrimage to Heaven. As we examine this *scala coeli* in art, and Milton's evocation of it in *Paradise Lost*, we shall see the pertinence of his descriptions.

Milton bases his account explicitly in Genesis 28:12: "the stairs were such as whereon Jacob saw/ Angels ascending and descending, bands/ Of guardians bright" (III, 510-12). The earliest illustration of this subject with which I am familiar dates from the mid-fourth century in the New Catacomb of Via Latina, where figures are shown ascending and descending the ladder while Jacob dreams.[6] The strong attraction which the ladder subsequently exerted on the Christian imagination was in good measure due to its allegorization by a sixth-century Greek clergyman named John Climacus into an elaborate guide for Christian life and

35, 50

---

[4] The expulsion of the rebel angels over the "precipice," "pitch," or "brow" of Heaven (I, 173; II, 772; VI, 51-2) has already been treated in Chapter IV, but for comparable views of the edge of heaven, see figs. 33, 42, 43 here, and in Anderson, *History and Imagery*, pl. 41.

[5] The ladder has been identified with the golden chain linking the created world with Heaven in *Paradise Lost* (II, 1005-6 and 1051-53) by Don Cameron Allen, "Two Notes on *Paradise Lost*," *MLN* 68 (1953), 360-61, and this identification has been denied by Harry F. Robins, "Milton's Golden Chain," *MLN* 69 (1954), 76. If Milton intended such an identification, he has not made himself clear.

[6] Bourguet, *Early Christian Painting*, pl. 128. Réau, *Iconographie*, II, i, p. 147, cites an artistic representation of the ladder in the Synagogue at Dura-Europas.

salvation. The ladder as a symbol came to have not only personal significance for each individual, but a larger meaning for the whole community of believers. Patrides' erudite study of Christian historiography concludes that for Christians "history is like Jacob's Ladder, 'ascending by degrees magnificent' toward the Celestial City, the Christ's presence not only suffused everywhere in the ladder but, according to Renaissance commentators, the ladder itself."[7]

The Heavenly Ladder in art came to show a number of more or less standard features.[8] The Byzantine Painters Manual prescribed that Christ should be at the head of the ladder, and stretch out his hands to assist the struggles of the faithful, or to crown them with flowers as they finish their ascent.[9] In the Renaissance, the ladder was sometimes elaborated into a handsome stairway, as in the paintings by Raphael in the Vatican and Tintoretto in the Scuola di San Rocco. In some examples, God the Father is shown at the head of the stairway, while in others it is God the Son and in Vecchietta's painting in the Pilgrims' Hall of the Ospedale di S. Maria della Scala in Siena it is the Virgin, but in any case the Divinity evidences concern with eyes fixed upon the faithful souls who are struggling to ascend to Heaven.

To those familiar with this traditional visualization, there is a fine irony in Milton's picturing of Satan at the foot of this stair:

> Satan from hence now on the lower stair
> That scaled by steps of gold to Heaven gate
> Looks down with wonder at the sudden view
> Of all this World at once.

(III, 540-43)

In that posture, Satan unwittingly parodies God, for as the Deity traditionally stood at the head of the ladder looking down in blessing, Satan here stands at its foot looking down with malevolence. There were, furthermore, many medieval representations of Satan standing at the foot of the ladder to divert or dislodge climbers from their ascent.[10] That picture appears in England as early as the year 1200 on the west wall of the church at Chaldon in Surrey, and thereafter achieved some popularity in other British churches as well as on the continent.[11]

[7] C. A. Patrides, *Milton and the Christian Tradition*, Oxford, 1966, p. 227, and by the same writer *The Grand Design of God*, London, 1972. See also Whiting, *Milton and This Pendant World*, pp. 61-63, 83, and 87. Madsen, *From Shadowy Types to Truth*, p. 87, identifies this as "the ladder of love," while Professor Røstvig discusses the Neoplatonic significance of the ladder in "Images of Perfection," p. 6. Bloomfield, *The Seven Deadly Sins*, p. 120, comments on the related ladder of Virtues, and the meanings of the various steps.

[8] For a study of this visual tradition, see John Rupert Martin, *The Illustration of the Heavenly Ladder of John Climacus*, Princeton, 1954.

[9] Didron, *Christian Iconography*, II, 380.

[10] Martin, *op. cit.*, pp. 11-12, 15, 19, and *passim*, and Katzenellenbogen, *Allegories of the Virtues and Vices*, pp. 22 and 24.

[11] Reproduced in Boase, *Death in the Middle Ages*, fig. 36. See also Tristram, *English Medieval Wall Paintings: the Twelfth Century*, pp. 37 and 86 and pl. 48, where the ladders are classified into various types, and Anderson, *History and Imagery in British Churches*, pp. 126-27 and pl. 41. For French fifteenth-century usage, see Mâle, *Religious Art*, pp. 162-63.

The continued popularity of the ladder in Milton's time is attested by a list running to about two pages in Pigler's *Barockthemen*, but the widest diffusion of course came through prints and engravings, of which England produced its fair share. Anne of Denmark was memorialized after her death by an anonymous allegorical engraving entitled "The Scala Coeli of the Gratious Queene Anne" in which Anne is shown recumbent on her tomb, with a ladder ascending to Heaven from her head. The title page of Matthew Griffith's *Bethel, or a Forme for Families* of 1634 shows the ladder of Heaven with human and angelic spirits upon it, as it extends into the Empyrean.[12] The title page of Heywood's *Hierarchie of the Blessed Angells* contrasts the headlong falling figures of the demons on the right with the dignity of the angels ascending and descending the Ladder of Heaven on the left.

Milton states that "each stair mysteriously was meant" (III, 516), but he does not go on to specify those meanings. Pictorial representations sometimes labeled each step of the ladder with a different virtue, as we find in a woodcut in Bettini's *Monte Santo di Dio*, of 1477 and 1491, where the ladder is shown resting on the ground of Humility, and proceeding through rungs labeled Prudence, Temperance, Fortitude, Justice, and so on, until finally Wisdom is reached, at which point the ladder disappears into the curved arc of the universe, where Christ stands in Heaven. The ladder with labeled rungs was often, though not always, identified with the development of monastic and priestly virtues. So useful a scheme may have been taken over and employed visually in Protestant engravings, but if such Protestant prints exist, I have been unable to find them, and none of the English examples which I have cited carry identifications of each stair. Milton may have had in mind the scale of virtues which Michael later recommends to Adam as summarizing his education on the Mount of Vision: beginning with knowledge, moving through deeds, faith, virtue, patience, temperance, and charity, "the soul/ Of all the rest," but so far as I know that particular set does not exist outside of *Paradise Lost* (XII, 581-84).[13] At all events, Michael's monitory list includes the kind of virtues traditionally attached as labels to the stairs "mysteriously meant."

HEAVEN AS COMMUNITY, CITY, AND GARDEN

By the time of the Renaissance, Christians had been instructed by pictorial art to think of Heaven in terms of three familiar scenes: the community of the faithful, whether including angels only or angels and human saints; the garden of Paradise beautified with flowers, fruits, and trees; and the City of God, sometimes abbreviated to appear as a single building.[14] The three scenes are combined by Fra An-

[12] Reproduced in Hind, *Engraving in England*, II, pl. 31, and III, pl. 144a.

[13] Elsewhere, Adam refers to "the scale of Nature . . . whereon/ In contemplation of created things/ By steps we may ascend to God," whereas Raphael refers to love founded in reason as "the scale/ By which to heavenly love thou mayest ascend" (V, 509-12 and VIII, 589-92).

[14] Panofsky, *Early Netherlandish Painting*, I, p. 270, and Lotte Brand Philip, *The Ghent Altarpiece and the Art of Jan van Eyck*, Princeton, 1971, pp. 57-58.

gelico in his *Last Judgment* in the Museo di S. Marco in Florence. There we see *100*
Christ in Judgment in the center, surrounded by orbs of angels, and flanked on *137*
either side by human saints representing the community. When the blessed souls,
just emerged from open graves, join hands with angels for a beautifully serene
dance, we again have symbols of community. The dance takes place in a flowery
landscape about a fountain (the garden), beyond which we see the pink walls of
Heaven, with brilliant yellow light flowing from the gate (the City). Like Fra
Angelico, Milton employs all three conceptions in his visualization of Heaven.

The early medieval symbol for the community was far simpler, consisting of
Abraham seated with faithful souls in his lap to suggest the human saints in Heaven,
while angels were ranged about the regnant figure of the Son.[15] Thereafter, there
was a gradual disappearance of Abraham, and a progressive crowding of the scene
with angels or saints or both.[16] Sometimes the Father was represented along with
the Son and the dove of the Holy Spirit as in the *Paradise* by Palma Giovanni at
the Corsini in Rome, or the Son shares his glory with the Virgin as in *The Last
Judgment* at Pisa. Typically, in both of these scenes the Deity is surrounded by *115*
faithful angels and saints. Milton's religious convictions disinclined him from a
visual representation of the Godhead, as we have seen, and precluded him entirely
from glorifying the Virgin, but apart from those exceptions, his descriptions of
the heavenly community correspond well with the established visual images. As
Heaven in *Paradise Lost* is populated with angels, the treatment of angelic appearance and activities in the preceding chapter covers the community aspects of
Heaven, and so needs no further development here.

Heaven was also represented as a delectable garden or landscape, filled as in
Paradise Lost with "the sons of light" enjoying "their blissful bowers/ Of amarantin
shade, fountain or spring,/ By the waters of life . . ./ In fellowships of joy"
(XI, 77-80). The Biblical roots of this conception may be found in the waters of
life referred to in the Apocalypse and the Psalms, and in the love garden of the
Song of Songs, allegorically interpreted as prefiguring the blessings of Paradise.[17]
From those beginnings, exegetical and creative literature alike developed the conception of the enclosed garden, and artists gave it a visual reality which became
firmly fixed in the European imagination.

This heavenly landscape becomes almost indistinguishable from the landscape
of the Garden in Eden, for, as Réau has summarized the tradition, "L'art ne distingue pas le Paradis céleste du Paradis terrestre."[18] As accommodation, Heaven
represents the perfection of the human capacity for dreams as well as for achievements, and attempts to suggest that which surpasses both. Heaven, then, is the
master image of which Hell is a parody and the Garden of Eden an earthly infer-
ence. Or, put somewhat differently, the Celestial Paradise is an extrapolation of
perfection conceivable on earth, Hell is a complete reversal of that perfection, and

---

[15] Mâle, *Gothic Image*, 383.

[16] Boase, *Death in the Middle Ages*, pp. 51-53.

[17] There was also influence from classical descriptions of Elysium, as has been noted,
inter alia, in Knott, *Milton's Pastoral Vision*, p. 78.

[18] Réau, *Iconographie*, II, ii, p. 750.

the terrestrial paradise of Eden a deduction from the heavenly image. Knott accurately perceives this interrelation: ". . . the true image of perfection in *Paradise Lost* is Heaven. Although the landscape of Eden is much more fully and convincingly realized, it can only be regarded as a 'shadow' of the hills and valleys of Heaven, which stand for a bliss beyond the threat of change."[19]

When Milton describes the landscape of Heaven, he is in no wise innovative, and an awareness of the artistic representations of the Celestial Paradise is important to a full appreciation of his achievement. It is not that he provides precise and detailed descriptions of scenes represented in any particular art works; on the contrary, his pastoral descriptions are general and evocative, rather than meticulously drawn. But if our minds have been stocked with the traditional images of the visual arts, we will find his descriptive phrases to be extraordinarily rich and visually allusive. The paintings by Fra Angelico and Giovanni di Paolo exemplify the kind of impression which Milton sought to convey: here we see his blessed spirits who "on flowers repose" and who are "with fresh flowerets crowned" amidst the "happy fields" where "hill and valley smiled" (v, 635-36; I, 249; VI, 784).

137, 138

Architecture was also employed to provide visual symbols for Heaven. Based in the Apocalyptic imagery of the New Jerusalem, this conception was expressed in many and varied forms, from the most simple architectural feature of a canopy[20] through to the representation of an entire cityscape comparable to what Ryken has called the "urban skyline" of Milton's Heaven.[21] "In the thirteenth century a simple arcade was supposed to be the door of Heaven—a pure symbol, almost a hieroglyphic," and sometimes the heavenly city was represented merely by a Gothic tabernacle.[22] By the mid-fifteenth century, that simple church door and tabernacle had developed into an elaborate cathedral facade, as may be observed in Stephen Lochner's *Last Judgment* at Cologne. This ecclesiastical symbolism for Heaven, highly popular as it was in the Middle Ages, is adopted only twice by Milton, when he describes the return of the Son into the "temple of his mighty Father" and also when angels frequent "this high temple" (VI, 890, and VII, 148). More usually, Milton's descriptions give the impression of a fortified city. English artists had represented the towers of Heaven as early as the twelfth century, and views of Heaven as a fortified city were popular in the fourteenth- and fifteenth-century Doom paintings.[23] Similar representations are to be found in great numbers on the continent. From sixth-century mosaics, through medieval illuminations and into the Neoclassical paintings of the seventeenth century, artists filled Heaven with visual counterparts of Milton's high walls, battlements, and watchtowers (II, 343, 1047-52).

III

139-41

[19] Knott, *Milton's Pastoral Vision*, p. 53.

[20] The history of canopies representing Heaven is traced by Karl Lehmann, "The Dome of Heaven," *Art Bulletin* 27 (1945), 1-27. It is interesting that Milton never associates "dome" with Heaven, but the world in our sense did not appear in English until 1656, according to the OED.

[21] Ryken, *Apocalyptic Vision*, pp. 120-21.

[22] Mâle, *Religious Art*, pp. 162-63.

[23] Tristram, *English Medieval Wall Paintings: the Twelfth Century*, pp. 16, 43, 51, and 85; and Anderson, *History and Imagery in British Churches*, p. 125.

On those conventional features Milton is clear enough, but he leaves the shape of the Celestial City unspecified and even ambiguous: at one point Heaven is referred to as a "whole circumference," and at another as a "quadrature," while the epic voice describes it as "extended wide/ In circuit, undetermined square or round" (II, 353, and 1047-48; x, 381). Faced with this ambiguity, scholars may be tempted to find a resolution on the basis of Biblical accounts, where the shape of the Holy City is unmistakably represented as square or even cubical.[24] Such evidence cannot, however, be taken as dispositive, for Milton did not tie himself literally to Scripture. Whereas most scholars have opted for the square Heaven, W. C. Curry not only maintains that Heaven is circular, but provides a diagram so illustrating it.[25] Under the circumstances of Milton's description, a decision to eliminate either the circular or the rectilinear Heaven can only be Procrustean.

It is interesting that within the pictorial tradition there was a similar vacillation between square and round. Kirschbaum's *Lexikon der Christlichen Ikonographie*, and Schiller's *Iconography* alike illustrate both shapes.[26] The round conception is exemplified here from an illuminated manuscript of Augustine's *City of God* dating *140* from about 1410, and the squarish conception from the *Vision of St. John* painted *141* between 1635 and 1637 by the Spanish artist Cano.

This discrepancy in pictorial art, and Milton's introduction of it into his descriptions, may I think be understood in terms of conflicting symbolisms. During the Middle Ages and for a long while thereafter, topographical views even of earthly cities lacked surveying accuracy, and were often conceived symbolically rather than geographically: thus in medieval drawings the classical city of Rome was sometimes shown in the shape of a lion simply because the lion was the king of animals. Even in the sixteenth century, the presumably scholarly maps reconstructing ancient Rome which were issued by Marco Fabio Calvo show little regard for the historical topography, and represent a square Rome for Romulus and a circular city for Augustus.[27] Symbolic habits of mind continued to be important, even after more accurate topographical representations of cities had been introduced. Symbolically, the square and the circle were regarded as the primary and perfect geometrical forms, and so it was appropriate to apply both to Rome as the master city of the known world and to the New Jerusalem as the master city of the universe.

The squaring of the circle had long been regarded as a tantalizing problem, symbolizing in some sense the possibility of resolving the interactions between time

[24] Rev. 21:16, Ezek. 45:2 and 48:16.

[25] Curry, *Milton's Ontology*, p. 156, and for the opposing view, Robins, "Satan's Journey: Direction in *Paradise Lost*"; see also Hughes, "Satan Now Dragon Grown," 359, and Knott, *Milton's Pastoral Vision*, p. 54.

[26] Engelbert Kirschbaum, *Lexikon der Christlichen Ikonographie*, 7 vols., Freiburg im Breisgau, 1968-74, II, pp. 394-99, and figs. 1-3 and 5; Schiller, *Iconography*, II, figs. 527 and 531. Réau, *Iconographie*, II, ii, pp. 721-23, concentrates on the square city. Helen Rosenau, *The Ideal City in its Architectural Evolution*, London, 1959, provides a further illustration of a circular version of Heaven in her plate vb. The frontispiece to Isaiah in the 1537 Matthew Bible shows Heaven as circular.

[27] Weiss, *The Renaissance Discovery of Classical Antiquity*, pp. 90 and 96-97.

and eternity. The solution to the problem might not be achieved in any mathematically satisfying way, but a solution could be suggested which was satisfying to even more basic human needs. The Renaissance delighted in drawing of the figure of a man whose outstretched arms and legs touch the corners of a square, at just the points where the circumference of a circle overlies the square. Symbolically, these intersections were taken to indicate how the straight lines of finitude and the unending lines of eternity were reconciled by the figure of man, as *imago dei*. This conception formed the basis or model for the new domed churches erected by Renaissance architects, which visually represented the creation of God, bringing the finitude of the square or cubical shape at the crossing of transept and nave into contact with the infinity of the dome. The most famous architectural expressions of this essentially theological idea may be found in Michelangelo's St. Peter's in Rome and Wren's St. Paul's in London, in which the crossing of the church merges almost unperceptibly into the crowning dome.

Furthermore, the circle had appeared to be the form of completeness and perfection as understood by the classical tradition, just as the square represented the same conceptions in the Scriptural tradition.[28] Had Milton chosen between these two shapes, he would on either count have excluded meanings and implications which he was apparently unwilling to lose. Milton chose to have it both ways: his Heaven has a circumference, and is a quadrature; in a bold gesture of visual oxymoron, the circle and the square merge together in the Empyreal Heaven of *Paradise Lost*. What was expressed as visual tour de force in Michelangelo's St. Peter's becomes visual paradox in Milton's Heaven, and both suggest the humanly impossible union of all perfections in the mind of God.

The perfect and harmonious blending of circle and square in Heaven differs radically from the tasteless jumble of conflicting styles in Pandaemonium. In the contrasting descriptions of Heaven and Hell in *Paradise Lost* we find yet another instance of what Isabel MacCaffrey has called "Milton's habitual method of playing his images and archetypes against each other," and what have often been noted by critics as poetic foils may be paralleled almost exactly in the visual foils between Heaven and Hell in pictorial art.[29] Visual antitheses between symbolic cities may be found in art of the Judeo-Christian tradition as early as the murals of the synagogue at Dura-Europos, "where the Tabernacle and the Temple of the sun-god are placed as counterparts and express religious and moral opposites."[30] In the Apocalypse, the contrast between "Jerusalem" and "Babylon" was elevated to a metaphysical plane, and artists made the most of the dramatic contrast. Summarizing the developments of that contrast in medieval and later Christian art, Réau declares that "l'enfer est conçu comme le contraire du Paradis."[31]

---

[28] Rosenau, *The Ideal City*, pp. 25-26. A more problematical influence may be postulated for the early Protestant preference for circular church buildings in France. This preference was systematically advocated for Protestant churches by Henrik de Keyser, *Architectura Moderna*, published by Salomon de Bray in 1631.

[29] MacCaffrey, *"Paradise Lost" as Myth*, p. 174.

[30] Rosenau, *The Ideal City*, pp. 19-20.

[31] Réau, *Iconographie*, II, ii, p. 751.

The contrast could be traced through many pictorial works, but for our purposes it may be exemplified in Fra Angelico's *Last Judgment*. On Christ's right hand are the blessed and Heaven, and on his left are the damned and Hell. Perhaps the first thing we notice is that the light of Paradise stands in direct visual contradiction of the darkness of Hell, but that is only one contrast in an elaborate scheme of foils. Between Heaven and Hell we see epitomized the differences between a loving community and an antagonistic conglomerate: in the one, hands reach out and join as signs of mutual love and acceptance, whereas in the other, hands are instruments of oppression and sadism. In the one, we see the circle of a harmonious dance, while in the other, there are many circles packed with miserable figures imprisoned together but isolated in themselves. Again, the garden produces green vegetation enlivened with colored fruit and flowers, while on the opposite side we see only a dreary universe of successive caves devoted to endless destruction. Finally, there is the contrast between the rose-colored city and the black dungeon. Such antitheses may be found in many art works, and the alert reader can cite comparable antitheses in *Paradise Lost*.

100

The gates of Heaven and Hell were particularly subject to presentation as foils. In *Paradise Lost*, such contrasts are carefully developed and consistently emphasized: the gates of Heaven throw light out into the universe whereas Hell casts forth smoke and flame (VII, 575, and II, 888-89); the gates of Heaven are rich with enameled imagery, while those of Hell are dark and obscenely forbidding (III, 505-8, and II, 644-48); the opening of the infernal portals is accompanied by the grating noise of harsh thunder, whereas those of Heaven open to harmonious sound (II, 880-83, and VII, 205-7). The contrasting of the two gates in art does not, and indeed could not, follow each of the points of the poetic contrast, but we can see a comparable device at work both in the Holkham Picture Bible and in the Utrecht Book of Hours. In the Holkham, the contrast is largely one of lines, the designs of masses over the gate of Heaven corresponding geometrically to the similar lines of the gate of Hell. The heavenly gate is overhung by a canopy upon which musical angels welcome the newly arrived human souls. Corresponding to that canopy in Heaven, Hell has a chimney draft, and the lines of the angelic organ are paralleled by the flue lines in this chimney. The heavenly gate is an open door, an entrance to something beyond, whereas the hellish counterpart is an absolute dead end, a fire place backed by a chimney wall. The geometrical contrasts are the setting for the psychological: in Heaven the human souls are warmly welcomed by serene angels, whereas in Hell human souls are dragged and wheeled into torment by raging fiends. In the Utrecht manuscript we see a similar foiling, though with somewhat different details: the architectural lines of the two gates almost parallel each other, but here the hellish gate is open, leading to the terrifying, toothed and flaming jaws of Leviathan, where devils cart and haul souls to perdition. The gate of Heaven is shut, but Saint Peter is unlocking it with his keys, and the wondering human souls will be admitted to the joyful reception of the angels crowding the celestial battlements.

142
139

Milton's careful contrasting of Heaven and Hell was composed some centuries after the similar pictorial treatments cited, but I do not propose that he was directly influenced by them: indeed, though he might well have seen Fra Angelico's *Last Judgment*, it is highly unlikely that he could have seen the two illuminated manuscripts. Furthermore, the details chosen do not precisely overlap as between the epic and the pictures, and the artists themselves were not uniform in the specifics of their contrasts. What is important is the convention of picturing Hell as a perverse visual counterpart to Heaven, and of elaborating that antithesis through a series of carefully emphasized and paralleled details. Here the poet was imagining and visualizing according to patterns which had long before been popularized by the visual arts.

LIGHT AND COLOR IMAGES

Light and color are constituent elements of all painting and mosaic work, regardless of subject, but they have distinctive roles to play in artistic representations of Heaven. In one traditional symbolism, Heaven was predominantly suggested by gemlike and precious metallic colors, while in another it was represented through pure, radiating light. Milton uses both, but light is the visual element of his Heaven which critics have most often emphasized.

In Heaven, we are overpowered by what D. C. Allen has called "an unlimited cascade of light," and Ryken comments that "Heaven's dazzling brightness is, along with its height, its most consistently mentioned characteristic."[32] Not only is God directly associated with and expressed by light, but the angels are repeatedly characterized by the brightness of their appearance, as "spirits of purest light" (VI, 660). Allen's observation is worth quoting:

> Throughout the whole poem blessedness is associated with the complete comprehension of the increate light, the essence of immaculateness. Its "sacred influence" pours over the walls of Heaven (II, 1034-40), and the battlements of Paradise are approached by a drawbridge of light (III, 510-18). The creatures who people the capital of God are "progeny of light" (V, 600) or "sons of light" (XI, 80). This is Biblical phrasing but it is in keeping with the nature of God, *Pater luminum*, and of Christ, *Lux mundi*.[33]

Milton's use of, and contrast between, light and darkness was so effective as to change the direction of English imagery: Josephine Miles has shown that after him "*bright* and *dark*, as representative descriptive adjectives superseded *true* and

---

[32] Allen, *Harmonious Vision*, p. 98, and Ryken, *Apocalyptic Imagery*, p. 79. Ryken provides further references in critical literature on pp. 78-79, and on pp. 38-41 an interesting philosophical and theological analysis of Milton's use of light. Hughes, "Milton and the Symbol of Light," surveys received opinion and studies the role of light in *Paradise Lost*, while Albert R. Cirillo, "Tasso's *Il Mondo Creato*: Providence and the Created Universe," has much of value to say about the divine and human significance of light in *Paradise Lost*, with reference to Tasso's similar uses.

[33] Allen, *Harmonious Vision*, p. 102.

false as representative judgmental adjectives, and heaven and earth began to shine forth pictorially in their depth and height, air and mass, light and shadow."[34]

From the Bible on, light was one of the principal metaphors for the Kingdom of Heaven. Central as it was to writings which preserved the faith and explained it, light was equally important in the art works which illustrated it. Up until the fifteenth century, divine light was very largely represented through colors, but in the early Renaissance this conception began to shift in ways which are traced by Patrik Reutersward in a brilliant article on the color of divine light.[35] Whereas medieval churches had been flooded with the "dim religious light" reflected through stained glass windows, the fifteenth century saw the development of new attitudes, in which church interiors were "flooded by a warm light with hardly any spots of color," of the kind we may see in Jan van Eyck's Berlin *Madonna*. In the following decades, "this warm light was to become cooler and cooler," until about the year 1500 we find that the light inside a church was thought of as virtually white.[36] After van Eyck, divine light came more and more to be thought of "in terms of intensity rather than hue."[37] The overall change may be exemplified in the rendering by the Master of Saint Giles of the interior of Saint-Denis, where everything is "depicted with painstaking accuracy" except for the polychromy of the interior sculptures and of the windows, all of which are treated as colorless, and "no allusion is made to the stained glass windows of which Abbot Suger had been so proud. The Master of Saint Giles deliberately rendered the daylight of the church as if there were no colored panes in the windows at all."[38]

We can perhaps most clearly understand this development by following the visual history of the halo. In the earliest centuries of Christian art, as in the mosaics at Ravenna, the halo was represented as a round plate of metal or precious stone, usually of gold; this treatment continued throughout the Middle Ages, and even may be seen in the representations by Fra Angelico of Paradise. As the fifteenth century progressed, that plate gave way more and more, to be replaced by transparent circles of light, and finally by simple glories of brightness. The new treatment may be epitomized in Tintoretto, of whom Berenson wrote that he rendered light "as if he had it in his own hands to brighten or darken the heavens at will and subdue them to his own moods," a comment equally applicable to Milton.[39] In Tintoretto's great *Paradise* mural in Venice, light emanates from the head of Christ, and in a blazing glory streams out in separate rays upon the blessed.

Baciccia's painting of the ceiling of the Gesù in Rome, begun the year after the publication of *Paradise Lost*, represents Heaven as a cloud of dazzling light with many rays emanating from the sacred monogram IHS in the center of the sky. Milton's description of Heaven as a dazzling brightness of light was in direct accord

3

137

132

---

[34] Miles, "From 'Good' to 'Bright': A Note on Poetic History," 770.
[35] Reutersward, "What Color is Divine Light?" in *Light* (eds. Hess and Ashbery), pp. 101-24.
[36] *Ibid.*, pp. 106-8.
[37] *Ibid.*, p. 110.
[38] *Ibid.*, pp. 106-7.
[39] Berenson, *Italian Painters of the Renaissance*, p. 39.

with these artistic representations. As was so often the case in the Renaissance and later centuries, classical and Christian influences converged to a single effect, and Joan Evans writes that "color, one of the chief glories of ornament, was deliberately relinquished in certain schemes; the men of the Renaissance who saw antique sculpture denuded by time of its former color accepted a marble fairness as a standard of beauty."[40] Thus Bernini followed the practice of the Renaissance in denying polychrome to his statuary, but his *Ecstasy of Saint Theresa* is typical in its massive and Baroque use of light, which pours down as in benediction upon the ravished saint through a specially designed window in the ceiling.

128

But Bernini did not concentrate upon pure white light alone for his effects: he also recovered and restated the earlier emphasis on hard metallic substances. Thus golden rays and brazen shafts of light from his great Gloria envelop the Cathedra Petri at the focal point in the apse of St. Peter's in Rome, and illustrate the reinvigoration of the old metallic symbols for heavenly glory. Like Bernini, Milton also uses both of the traditional means for envisioning beatitude and the heavenly state —brilliant light, and brilliant metals and stones.

The description of Heaven in terms of precious metals and stones, which was bequeathed by the Bible and developed in the hexameral literature, had its artistic as well as literary expressions, and Milton's usage suggests a conscious attempt to draw upon all these traditions in order to enrich our perception of Heaven. Gold is everywhere encountered in his Heaven, and precious stones abound. The firmament is of crystal, the throne of sapphire inlaid with pure amber, the walls are of sapphire, and the pavement is "like a sea of jasper," and elsewhere we have reference to the "bright sea of jasper or of liquid pearl," or the "clear hyaline" and "glassy sea" (I, 682; II, 1049-50; III, 363-64, 541 and 518-19; VI, 757-59, and 772; VII, 619). The gates of Heaven are made of diamond and gold, "thick with sparkling Orient gems" (III, 505-7), an appropriate frontispiece to the whole structure which Milton assembled with such great relish.[41]

In literary criticism, Leland Ryken has provided the most perceptive analysis of Milton's metallic and mineral descriptions, calling such passages as I have cited "enameled imagery," and it will be helpful to survey his observations before turning to the pictorial tradition. Ryken finds that Milton's choice of imagery evokes both brilliance of color and hardness of materials, two elements which he sees as "reinforcing each other and often indistinguishable from each other."[42] By "combining visual and textural hardness of surface," such enameled imagery depicts "a transcendental realm whose permanence forms a contrast with the transient world of earthly experience."[43] The enameled imagery is also often couched in terms of what Ryken calls "mystic oxymorons," as in "living sapphire" or "flowing jasper," or "liquid pearl" (II, 1049-50, III, 363, and 518-19): "The result is a picture of contradictions, since in earthly experience something cannot be

---

[40] Evans, *Pattern*, II, pp. 8-9.
[41] Koehler, "Milton's Use of Color and Light," 74.
[42] Ryken, *The Apocalyptic Vision*, p. 86.
[43] *Ibid.*, p. 87.

simultaneously fluid and static in its essential nature. The solution to the contradiction is to recognize that these contradictory motifs share the same principle which underlies individual mystic oxymorons, the principle of combining two empirical phenomena to suggest a transcendental realm in which the sum is greater than the parts."[44] The literary effect is there brilliantly summarized, but more than a conceptual tradition is involved, for Milton's enameled imagery evokes strongly visual responses as well, responses which had long been imaginatively identified with Heaven in pictorial art.[45]

From the earliest Christian art through Milton's time, precious metals and precious stones had been used to suggest Paradise by their visual and tactile properties. Such materials were not thought of as lacking in color, as some critics have assumed Milton's use of them intended, but were conceived as possessing certain uniquely attractive and significant color properties, symbolizing the highest levels of human and superhuman life. In the imperial portraits and divine icons at Ravenna, gold was "conceived as light materialized," so that "gold and light provided the firmament beneath which the divine and imperial liturgies could be enacted like a sacred drama," as John Beckwith puts it.[46] The Byzantine use of gold as a ground and background dominated art for centuries, and even after Western art no longer used gold as a symbol of surrounding eternity, "a foil of golden tones" was sometimes used to overlay a painting, as in the sacred subjects of Tintoretto.[47] *132* It is in these terms that we should understand Milton's frequent references to gold in the scales of judgment, gates of heaven, compasses, crowns, rivers, censers, sceptres, chains, clouds, cups, hinges, harps, and ladders of *Paradise Lost*, for as Koehler has put it with impressive understatement, "Milton gilded rather heavily his images of perfection and power."[48] As the most precious metal known to man, gold was employed visually to remind us of the most precious life available to man, that of Heaven. That Milton could also show gold put to sinful uses by demons and fallen men should not lead, as it sometimes has, to oversimplified readings: as with sex, Milton would have our reactions to gold in *Paradise Lost* depend upon the principle of contextual definition.[49]

Milton's repeated association of enameled imagery with Heaven is related not only to the use of gold foil but also to the visual effects of mosaic tesserae. The mosaics used to decorate Early Christian churches differed from pagan mosaics in the use of color more than in any other single feature: whereas the classical mosaics were often executed in black and white, or otherwise consisted of rather muted colors, the Paleo-Christian mosaics almost always were ablaze with color, as the brilliant patterns of tesserae cast a glittering polychrome light throughout the

[44] *Ibid.*, p. 91.

[45] For the use of enameled imagery in descriptions of the Garden in Eden, see below, Chapter XIV, pp. 249-55.

[46] John Beckwith, "Byzantium: Gold and Light," pp. 75 and 72.

[47] Otto Demus, *Byzantine Art and the West*, New York, 1970, pp. 232-38.

[48] Koehler, "Milton's Use of Color and Light," 59.

[49] Especially pertinent here is the analysis in Ryken, *The Apocalyptic Vision*, pp. 86-87, where further references are provided. We shall return to these issues in Chapter XIV.

church.⁵⁰ As James Rosser Johnson describes it, "the irregular setting of the tesserae causes the reflected light to be broken up into twinkling and glittering effects which change with the movement of the spectator, enhancing and animating the scene before him and dematerializing the wall."⁵¹ Milton could have observed the gemlike colors of such mosaics in many churches when he was in Rome—in S. Costanza, S. Pudenziana, S. Passede, or S. Agnese. Sometimes marble chips and semiprecious stones were introduced into the designs, but most often the tesserae were made of a vividly chromatic vitreous paste. The effect is a dazzling brilliance of color: light reflects from the tesserae as though from the facets of precious stones. In this regard, later revivals of mosaic work never quite equaled the Paleo-Christian achievement, but a workshop for mosaics was established by the Vatican late in the sixteenth century, and among the Barberini both Cardinal Francesco and Pope Urban VIII sponsored its work, which is amply evidenced in St. Peter's.⁵² For hundreds of years rich, jewellike color dominated the church interiors of Christendom. In illustrating the purpose and effect of this tradition, Hagstrum cites Paulus Silentiarius' contemplation of the Church of St. Sophia as a response not only "to space, form, and size but chiefly to color and light; the gleam of gold and marble, of mosaics and silver candlesticks. Gold is precious in and of itself and therefore possesses symbolic value. But its chief glory is that it reflects light throughout the immense spaces of the church. The gold and gem of altar and column are even more splendid at night, when they reflect light in such a way that one imagines a kind of nocturnal sun: smiling, roseate, resplendent."⁵³ Such historic uses of precious metals and gems to lift the Christian's imagination from earth to Heaven provide the key to many of Milton's color images.⁵⁴ The ecclesiastical art we have just discussed and Milton's enameled imagery of Heaven may be explained in the words of Miguel de Molinos: ". . . the Church is the image of Heaven on earth. How should it not be adorned with all that is most precious?"⁵⁵

When the Christian passed from the light of every day through the doors of a Gothic cathedral and into the nave, he was introduced into a radically different atmosphere, as the outside light "passed through the sacred figurations in the stained

⁵⁰ Ferdinando Rossi, *Mosaics: A Survey of their History and Techniques*, New York, 1970, p. 79. If we recall the widespread popularity of aquatic scenes dramatizing the motif of the fish and the fisherman in the Early Christian mosaics (Rossi, pl. 14 and pp. 38-42), and also the glassy substance of the tesserae, we may find reinforcement for "the clear hyaline, the glassy sea" in Milton's Heaven (VII, 619), but I think it unlikely that Milton's primary reference in these phrases is so technical: it is far more probable that he was intent upon portraying a calm, unruffled surface in the heavenly sea, as we might describe a lake as being crystal clear or as reflecting like a mirror.

⁵¹ James R. Johnson, *The Radiance of Chartres: Studies in the Early Stained Glass of the Cathedral*, New York, 1965, p. 9.

⁵² Rossi, *Mosaics*, pp. 82-84.

⁵³ Hagstrum, *The Sister Arts*, p. 51.

⁵⁴ Patrick Trevor-Roper, *The World Through Blunted Sight: An Inquiry into the Influence of defective Vision on Art and Character*, London, 1970, p. 67, notes the frequent association of color with minerals in Milton. The author, an ophthalmologist, is apparently unaware of traditional symbology in these areas.

⁵⁵ Quoted in *Larousse Encyclopedia of Renaissance and Baroque Art* (ed. René Huyghe), p. 332.

glass and showered color down to the pillars and the pavement."[56] The same sapphire which Milton so delighted to associate with the structures of Heaven had long been associated with stained glass windows and their effects: "Suger, the famous twelfth-century abbot of Saint-Denis near Paris, claims to have ground up sapphires in order to obtain the blues of his panes. This obviously expensive procedure may have been wishful thinking rather than reality. It is, however, interesting and significant for the often made comparison of stained glass with precious stones; jewels were many times described as sources of light."[57] Not only did Abbot Suger claim to have mixed precious gems in the formation of stained glass, but he explicitly cited intimations of Heaven in the gems themselves:

> Thus when—out of my delight in the beauty of the House of God—the loveliness of the many-colored gems has called me away from external cares and worthy meditation has induced me to reflect, transferring that which is material to that which is immaterial, on the diversity of sacred virtue; then it seems to me that I see myself dwelling, as it were, in some strange region of the universe which neither exists entirely in the slime of the earth nor entirely in the purity of Heaven; and that, by the grace of God, I can be transported from this inferior to that higher world in an anagogical manner.[58]

D. C. Allen and others have surely been correct in emphasizing Milton's use of brilliant natural lighting as a symbol for divine light, but Milton's use of precious stones and jewels is equally natural and visual in reference, and equally powerful in suggestion. Johnson writes appositely in his *The Radiance of Chartres*: "As a cabochon jewel does not transmit directed rays of light—seeming rather to glow from within—so do ancient windows diffuse and transform the light of day into the 'new light' of the Celestial Jerusalem. . . . The windows, with their richness and depth of color, invite the contemplation and intoxication of the viewer as he is lured to explore inner mysteries of light in precious stones."[59] The environing light of the sun, and the enclosed light of jewels, supplement each other, and between them we have the range of Milton's color symbolism for Heaven.

Whether or not we believe that Abbot Suger actually ground precious stones in the manufacture of glass, there can be no doubt that the manufacture of imitation gems and of stained glass were closely associated. Johnson concludes from his study of both processes that "it is apparent that methods as well as nomenclatures and uses are frequently interchangeable," and that they suggest "an absorbing interest in a wide range of light-bearing objects which glow and radiate with an uncommon power."[60] In each instance, we are dealing with traditional visual symbols for *nobilitas* by which was meant "that quality of divine light which precious

[56] Reutersward, "What Color is Divine Light," p. 103.
[57] Florens Deuchler, "Gothic Glass," in *Light* (eds. Hess and Ashbery), p. 59.
[58] Quoted by Patrick Nuttgens, *The Landscape of Ideas*, London, 1972, pp. 42-43.
[59] Johnson, *The Radiance of Chartres*, p. 63.
[60] James R. Johnson, "Stained Glass and Imitation Gems," *Art Bulletin* 39 (1957), pp. 222 and 223.

stones and metals as well as stained glass were said to contain to a far greater degree than ordinary materials."[61] So designed, the interior decorations of Ste. Chapelle first impressed the early fourteenth-century philosopher Jean de Jandun of Senlis as though he were "carried off to Heaven and let in to one of Paradise's most beautiful chambers."[62]

Jeweled and metallic colors were still visible in hundreds of churches and cathedrals in Milton's time. We know of their early appeal to him from the lines in "Il Penseroso" where he described "storied windows richly dight,/ Casting a dim religious light"[63] which combined with "the pealing organ" and "the full voiced choir" to bring "all Heaven before mine eyes" ("Il Penseroso," 159-66). The jeweled light which shone in Christian churches for fifteen hundred years is recaptured by Milton in order to bring Heaven before the eyes of his seventeenth-century readers, but his enameled imagery may find other visual counterparts from the sixteenth and seventeenth centuries as well.

In the late sixteenth century, the Medici established at Florence the Opificio delle Pietre Dure for perfecting a new variety of stone mosaic work, which by the time of Milton's visit was famous throughout Europe. This form of mosaic was known as *commesso* work.[64] It employed not only hard stones (*pietre dure*) but brightly and variously colored stones such as porphyry, lapis lazuli, agate, and others, which were closely set together in such a way as to provide brilliantly polychromatic effects. Smaller works were designed as panels for cabinets and as table tops, and reproduced flora, fauna, and landscapes with surprising fidelity. On a far larger scale, *commesso* work was used to adorn the Medici Chapel of the Princes in S. Lorenzo with a magnificence scarcely to be rivaled in Europe. John Evelyn, who visited Florence only a few years later than Milton, was enthralled by the splendor of colored and semiprecious stones in this chapel, which he called "the third Heaven if any be on earth."[65] As the enameled imagery of Gothic windows had elevated the thoughts of others into Paradise, a similar effect was achieved by the polished and polychromatic *pietre dure* of this chapel. Like other contemporaries, Evelyn was also much taken with smaller inlaid work of flowers, animals, and "landscapes like the natural."[66] A Florentine decree of 1602 sought to restrict the use of *pietre dure* to "the ornament of churches and chapels to the honor of God," and though secular work was done, this medium was principally intended to contribute *ad majoram gloriam dei*.[67]

Art works such as those I have been describing bring into Milton's own time effective visual exemplars of enameled imagery, used to the same effects that

[61] Reutersward, "What Color is Divine Light," pp. 103-4.

[62] *Ibid*., pp. 105-6.

[63] Tasso, like Milton, was also deeply moved by "the splendors of Gothic stained glass," as E. K. Waterhouse shows in "Tasso and the Visual Arts," *Italian Studies* 3 (1946-48), pp. 149-50.

[64] Rossi, *Mosaics*, pp. 105-79, provides the finest analysis of *commesso*.

[65] Evelyn, *Diary*, II, pp. 198f.

[66] Evelyn, *Diary*, II, pp. 191, 198, 253, etc. He was equally delighted with the mosaics showing natural scenery in San Marco in Venice (II, p. 437).

[67] Rossi, *Mosaics*, pp. 130, 133-35, 141.

Milton sought to elicit. When Joseph Warton objected to Milton's use of such imagery as "having no relative beauty as pictures of nature," he was missing Milton's entire point: in *Paradise Lost* as in pictorial art, enameled imagery was employed to lead us through nature and beyond it to a supernatural vision.[68] Milton was evoking effects which were firmly established in the visual arts, and can be traced back through the *pietre dure* work of the Mannerist and Baroque periods, the stained glass windows of the Gothic artists, and the tesserae of the earliest Christian workers in mosaics. Which particular works within that long development impressed him most, we cannot now determine, but the influence of the whole tradition upon his epic descriptions can scarcely be denied. Heaven was visualized as radiant with gemlike beauty, as we may see illustrated in the mosaic   *III* from S. Apollinare in Classe near Ravenna. There we find but one of many similar visions of that Heavenly City Milton described:

> The work as of a kingly palace gate
> With frontispiece of diamond and gold
> Embellished, thick with sparkling Orient gems
> The portal shone, . . .
>
> (III, 505-8)

[68] Warton in Shawcross, *Milton 1732-1801*, p. 227. Warton's objection was primarily directed against the use of enameled imagery in Eden.

Part Four
The Created World

XII

Infinite Space and the Paradise of Fools

INFINITE spaces, extending far beyond any power of human vision but within the imaginative grasp of the mind, must surely have struck every thoughtful reader as being among the great creations of *Paradise Lost*. Milton has given us a poetic universe limitless in its expanse, and has persuaded us that we can see it all, that we can comprehend with the mind's eye what the physical eye simply cannot encompass. The achievement is metaphysical, of a vastness and penetration beyond the range of even the most powerful telescope.

Although the finite range of a telescope cannot show us that infinity of space which Milton enables us to imagine, Milton's vision would probably have been impossible had it not been for the invention of the telescope. Marjorie Nicolson has argued that case persuasively, and has also recreated for us the immense excitement with which Milton and his contemporaries first became acquainted with "the glass of Galileo" and so "viewed the vast immeasurable abyss,/ Outrageous as a sea, dark, wasteful, wild" (v, 261-62 and vii, 211-12). "Nowhere in poetry," Miss Nicolson writes, "do we find more majestic conceptions of the vastness of space than in the work of this blind poet, in those scenes of cosmic perspective in which we, like Satan on the one hand, God on the other, look up and down to discover a universe majestic in its vastness."[1]

Also relevant to Milton's descriptions of space was the development in the sixteenth and seventeenth centuries of illusionist ceiling paintings. Germain Bazin summarizes the seventeenth-century achievements:

> All through this century there was a steady development in that type of ceiling painting which gives the spectator a feeling of being overhung by a whole world of flying figures, that hover and soar in an imaginary palace, or through the open sky. This painting of figures in space was especially Baroque in spirit; its full flights take place mainly in the churches, since their size lent itself better to effects of perspective than did the inadequate dimensions of the rooms in palaces. Domenichino, Lanfranco, Pietro da Cortona, and Giovanni Battista Gaulli exemplify the principal stages of this art, before it reached its apogee with Padre Andrea Pozzo (1642-1709). This Jesuit priest, who also wrote several

[1] Marjorie Nicolson, "The Discovery of Space," *Medieval and Renaissance Studies: Proceedings of the Southeastern Institute of Medieval and Renaissance Studies, Summer, 1965,* (ed. O. B. Hardison, Jr.), Chapel Hill, N.C., 1966, p. 57, and *passim.* See also by the same author "The Telescope and Imagination."

treatises on perspective, painted the *Glory of St. Ignatius* (1691-1694) on the ceiling of the Church of St. Ignatius in Rome, creating the masterpiece of this illusionist style.[2]

Margaret Bottrall has long since pointed out how "Milton's fondness for figures hurtling through space" and for scenes of aerial perspective "recall the gorgeous animation of the painted ceilings,"[3] and has particularly cited Satan's descent to earth:

> then from pole to pole
> He views in breadth, and without longer pause
> Down right into the world's first region throws
> His flight precipitant, and winds with ease
> Through the pure marble air his oblique way
> Amongst innumerable stars, that shone
> Stars distant, but nigh hand seemed other worlds,
> Or other worlds they seemed, or happy isles. . . .
>
> (III, 560-67)

In what I regard as the most persuasive analysis in his *Milton, Mannerism and Baroque*, Roy Daniells aligns Milton's aerial descriptions with the Baroque presentation of "depth, recession, and diagonal penetration of space" which suggests "by its sweep a completion beyond its mechanical limits." As in painting, so too in architecture, Baroque artists create the "illusion of limitlessness within walls which were in fact the boundaries of an assigned space."[4] Such comparisons between Milton's verse and Baroque art are sufficiently explicit to allow us to know exactly what we are being asked to accept, and also to appraise the evidence,[5] and I for one find the Baroque relevance here to be at once persuasive and enlightening.[6]

Even before the seventeenth century, artists had provided something of the same illusion of infinite space, and often to much the same effect.[7] Lotte Brand Philip has thus written of our response to the Ghent Altarpiece that "with his eyes drawn into the freedom of an unlimited distance, the beholder experiences a visual foretaste of eternal bliss."[8] Bernard Berenson has argued that religious emotion and response in a viewer is most persuasively produced by effective space composition, and his comments are as pertinent to *Paradise Lost* as to the paintings of Perugino and Raphael:

[2] Germain Bazin, *Baroque and Rococo*, London, 1964, p. 39.

[3] Bottrall, "The Baroque Element in Milton," 40.

[4] Daniells, *Milton, Mannerism and Baroque*, pp. 53, 87.

[5] See also Spencer, *Heroic Nature*, pp. 105-6 and 136, for his reference to illusionist ceilings.

[6] Stimulating analyses of Milton's spatial imagery may also be found in MacCaffrey, *"Paradise Lost" as Myth*, pp. 44-73, in Cope, *The Metaphoric Structure of "Paradise Lost,"* pp. 72-148, and in Ryken, *The Apocalyptic Vision*, pp. 175-78.

[7] For a useful history of the pictorial rendering of space, see Miriam S. Bunim, *Space in Medieval Painting and the Forerunners of Perspective*, New York, 1940.

[8] Philip, *The Ghent Altarpiece and the Art of Jan van Eyck*, p. 107.

The religious emotion—for some of us entirely, for others at least in part —is produced by a feeling of identification with the universe; this feeling, in its turn, can be created by space-composition; it follows then that this art can directly communicate religious emotion—or at least all the religious emotion that many of us really have, good church members though we may be. And indeed I scarcely see by what other means the religious emotion can be directly communicated by painting—mark you, I do not say represented. If, then, space-composition is the only art intrinsically religious, since the Perugian school is the great mistress of this art, we see why the paintings of Perugino and Raphael produce, as no others, the religious emotion.[9]

It is in a sixteenth-century artist that Berenson finds the closest approximation to Milton's handling of space, citing Lorenzo Lotto's *Coronation of the Virgin*: "The Madonna prostrates herself in space, separated by what seems an endless stretch of ether from Christ and God the Father, who are crowning her. The space between the human and the Divine has never been indicated with more spiritual suggestiveness. Lotto attains here a sublimity which is rare elsewhere in painting, and which I can compare to Milton only."[10]

Whereas we cannot claim to account for Milton's spatial consciousness in *Paradise Lost* merely by reference to similar conceptions in paintings before and during his own time, such developments presumably helped him to describe, and his readers to imagine, the limitless panoramas of *Paradise Lost*.[11] Such spatial similarities between Milton and art as have been outlined thus far in this chapter have been widely accepted by critics, and scarcely need further development here. But it is possible to go further and to suggest ways in which particular art works, and a particular use of illusionistic ceilings, may throw light upon one of the most puzzling passages in *Paradise Lost*.

The Paradise of Fools or Limbo of Vanity has been a persistent center of controversy in *Paradise Lost* (III, 440-97) ever since 1712 when Addison judged it more appropriate for a poem by Spenser or Ariosto than by Homer, Virgil, or Milton, and concluded that it did not have "probability enough for an epic."[12] Lacking Addison's convictions about Classicism, modern readers may not be so disturbed concerning the epic propriety of the episode, but there have been grave doubts concerning its pertinence to the thematic and intellectual structure of *Paradise Lost*. These may be summarized in Norma Phillips' reference to "that

[9] Berenson, *Italian Painters of the Renaissance*, pp. 202-3.

[10] Berenson, *Lorenzo Lotto*, p. 91.

[11] It would be dangerous, however, always to expect a synchronous development in painting and in literature, and Millard Meiss has reminded us that in some respects "the historical evolution of the arts of painting and literature did not exhibit a close chronological conformity. Because of motives, conditions, and accidents peculiar to each, related impulses appeared at somewhat different times, as they not infrequently do" (*Painting in Florence and Siena after the Black Death*, p. 158).

[12] Addison, *Spectator* 297, in Shawcross, *Milton: The Critical Heritage*, p. 166.

perennial question of the *raison d'être* of the Limbo, its sudden intrusion into the action of the poem, its baffling isolation, even its inconclusiveness."[13] Within the context of Milton's time, however, it is possible to read Milton's acute visual creation of the Limbo as neither intrusive, nor isolated, nor inconclusive, but as a superbly integrated and apposite parody of human pretension in one of its most notable artistic forms.

Milton's Paradise of Fools is a fitting memorial for those vain souls "who in vain things/ Built their fond hopes of glory or lasting fame,/ Or happiness in this or th' other life, . . . / Nought seeking but the praise of men" (III, 448-53). There are more than enough such in any age, but in Milton's age there was one form of artistic monument which precisely accords not only with the purpose but also with the appearance of the Paradise of Fools—this was the apotheosis ceiling. Influenced by classical conceptions of the apotheosis of heroes and emperors, these illusionist paintings were designed to confer immortality upon princes of Church or State by dramatically staging their divinization upon a ceiling which seemed to open into eternity. Such works were not only monuments to fame, but were in themselves renowned for the virtuosity of their *trompe l'oeil* effects. Those effects are masterful and even awesome—if one accepts the proffered illusion; if not, the illusionist space collapses in upon itself to appear "th' unaccomplished works of nature's hand,/ Abortive, monstrous, or unkindly mixed" and all the exalted figures tumble together as though "a violent cross wind from either coast/ Blows them transverse ten thousand leagues awry/ Into the devious air" (III, 455-56, 487-89). Milton's Limbo of Vanity is the *reductio ad absurdum* of the apotheosis ceiling, both as to its visual and its intellectual content.

Such ceilings began to appear in the sixteenth century, as we may see in the *Glorification of the Medici Pope Leo X* (the excommunicator of Martin Luther) in the Palazzo Vecchio. Even more apposite is the *Triumph of Cosimo I* in the Room of the Five Hundred of the same palace, executed by Vasari and his assistants. This latter painting shows the coronation of the Grand Duke, who is enthroned in the clouds and surrounded by a circling orb of cherubs, just as Milton and so many others imagined the angels in Heaven to circle about the throne of God himself. The message is clear and unmistakable: the prince is either a god or an angel demigod, and is flaunting that assumption of godhead which devastated mankind in Eden and has plagued it throughout history. Such a conception contradicted Milton's most profound convictions, both republican and religious.

At least as offensive to Milton would have been the ceiling fresco in the Grand Saloon of the Palazzo Barberini, which was nearing completion by Pietro da Cortona about the time Milton was personally received there by Cardinal Francesco Barberini in 1639. Variously known as the *Allegory of Divine Province*, or *Triumph of Divine Wisdom*, or *Triumph of Glory*, this massive ceiling painting was a blatant glorification of the Barberini family and of the Barberini pope, Urban

143

[13] Norma Phillips, "Milton's Limbo of Vanity and Dante's Vestibule," *ELN* 3 (1966), 182. Esmond L. Marilla, "Milton's Paradise of Fools," *ES* 42 (1961), 159-64, provides helpful analysis.

VIII, whose arms are being elevated into the Empyrean. Bodies, robes, insignia, and   *144*
implements, both ecclesiastical and civil, toss about in the atmosphere. Here we
have an ultimate illusionism of effect, as our eyes are carried through the painting
itself and into infinite space. Pietro's technique was masterly, and his effect almost
overwhelming.

   Similar paintings, seeking similar effects, were to be found in Milton's England.
The Duke of Buckingham, the favorite successively of King James I and of King
Charles I, commissioned Rubens to paint *The Apotheosis of Buckingham*, which
the Duke modestly set into the ceiling of his closet in York House.[14] Executed
between 1625 and 1627, the painting was still on view at the time of the inventory
of 1635,[15] and was something of a cause célèbre both among Buckingham's political
supporters and among his opponents. Whether Milton saw it we do not know, but
others of his persuasion did, and commented upon it. The anonymous controversial
pamphlet *Felton Commended* described it as follows: "Antwerpian Rubens' best
skill made him [Buckingham] soare, Ravish't by heavenly powers into the skie,
Opening and ready him to deifie In a bright blisfull pallace, fayrie ile."[16] Rubens'
original conception is now preserved only in a small sketch in the National Gallery
in London, but it is possible on this and other bases to know that this apotheosis   *145*
painting, like so many others, was crowded with figures floating and tossing about
in space: Minerva, Mercury, the three Graces, Medusa, Virtue, Abundance with a
cornucopia, and so forth. However successful artistically, and that success cannot
be disputed, *The Apotheosis of Buckingham* would have struck Milton as blasphemous. Describing the effect of Rubens' apotheosis paintings, Walter Friedlaender declares that "the divine is not made human, but rather the two extremes
approach in another way; Man becomes God, and the apotheosis takes on all its
ancient meaning. . . . The Kingly Man, and God, are one."[17]

   What Rubens did for Buckingham he did on an even more grandiose scale
for King James I, and for the divine right of monarchy of the Stuarts, on the
ceiling of the Banqueting House at Whitehall. Conspicuously placed, and made
famous alike because of Rubens' own massive reputation and the royal propaganda
of Charles I, these paintings were widely known by Englishmen, and famous
throughout Europe. It is inconceivable that Milton did not know them well, because his office was located in the same building when he served as Secretary of
State for Latin Affairs, with responsibility for discrediting just that divine right
theory which the canvasses glorified. There are three major compositions, cele-
brating at either end of the Hall respectively the *Benefits of the Government of*

[14] Similar ceilings executed in England by Rubens and his followers are illustrated in
Croft-Murray, *Decorative Painting in England*, pls. 63-69, and 84-85.

[15] Randall Davies, "An Inventory of the Duke of Buckingham's Pictures, etc., at York
House in 1635," *Burlington Magazine* 10 (1906-7), 376-82.

[16] Quoted by Oliver Millar, *The Age of Charles I: Painting in England 1620-1649*, London, 1972, p. 19. Germaine Bazin maintains that "the few square feet of a picture were enough
to enable Rubens to suggest far greater depth of limitless space than Padre Pozzo had created
with all his artifices of perspective" (*Baroque and Rococo*, p. 67).

[17] Friedlaender, *Mannerism and Anti-Mannerism in Italian Painting*, p. 83.

146 *James I*, and the *Union of England and Scotland*, while in the large oval of the center there is the *Apotheosis of James I*.[18] The program was perhaps designed by Archbishop Laud.[19]

These illusionist paintings expressed in unmistakable visual form those pretensions to deity which Milton regarded as the original sin. In *Paradise Lost* it was by "affecting Godhead and so losing all" that Adam and Eve fell, as they succumbed to the Satanic temptation to "be as gods," "to put on gods," to take on "higher degree of life" and be "gods, or angels demigods" (III, 206; IX, 708-14, 934, and 937). Every evil in *Paradise Lost* is traceable to this particular sin—the sin of self-sought apotheosis: by it, Satan falls from Heaven, Adam and Eve fall from Paradise, and from this same originating sin proceed all the manifold wickednesses and human distortions, personal and social, recounted in the final two books of the epic. For the most part, Milton treats such pretensions to aposwtheosis soberly, though from time to time he will introduce sardonic and ironic humor. In the Limbo of Vanity passage, he subjects the whole range of such pretension to uproarious parody. His theme here is the same as his theme throughout *Paradise Lost*: here we see Empedocles who sought "to be deemed a god," and the builders of the Tower of Babel who sought to rival Heaven, and those who would still build new Babels, "had they wherewithal" (III, 466-71).

The physical atmosphere of Milton's Limbo is marked by turbulence, tossing movements, unexpected postures, and twistings about. Fitting as it is to reward secular pretensions, the Limbo also provides an apt habitation for religious superstition and presumption:

> Here pilgrims roam, that strayed so far to seek
> In Golgotha him dead, who lives in Heaven;
> And they who to be sure of Paradise
> Dying put on the weeds of Dominic,
> Or in Franciscan think to pass disguised.
>
> (III, 476-80)

They lift their feet at the base of the stairs to Heaven just as Satan will be shown to do a few lines further along—and we should not miss this visual correspondence (III, 540-43)—when they are once again caught up and tossed about through purposeless gyrations:

> A violent cross wind from either coast
> Blows them transverse ten thousand leagues awry
> Into the devious air; then might ye see
> Cowls, hoods and habits with their wearers tossed
> And fluttered into rags, then relics, beads,

[18] See John Charlton, *The Banqueting House, Whitehall*, London, 1964; Per Palme, *Triumph of Peace, a Study of the Whitehall Banqueting House*; and Julius S. Held, "Rubens' Glynde Sketch and the Installation of the Whitehall Ceiling," *Burlington Magazine* 112 (1970), 274-81.

[19] Croft-Murray, *Decorative Painting in England*, p. 35.

Indulgences, dispenses, pardons, bulls,
The sport of winds: All these upwhirled aloft
Fly o'er the backside of the world far off....

(III, 487-94)

The introduction of religious paraphernalia extends the significance of Milton's Limbo beyond the symbols of political and social power which are represented in the apotheosis paintings of Cosimo I and of James I, and may accord more closely with details of the Barberini *Triumph*.[20] This and other allegorical treatments in Italian art which Milton may have seen, such as the *Assumption of the Virgin* that Lanfranco painted between 1625 and 1627 for the Church of San Andrea della Valle, would naturally contain somewhat similar religious objects to those Milton describes, but the tossing about of robes, regalia, and insignia in the Whitehall ceiling is equally apposite in visual form.

Italian paintings executed after Milton had returned to England, and English paintings after he had become totally blind, carried the convention of the apotheosis and illusionist ceilings to even greater extremes. Filippo Gherardi covered the whole ceiling of the Church of San Pantaleo in Rome with the *Triumph of the Name of Mary*; in 1672 Baciccia began the celebrated *Adoration of the Name of Jesus* for the ceiling of the nave in the Gesù; and Cozza decorated the ceiling of the Library of the Collegeo Innocenziano to much the same effect. The ultimate expression of illusionism was created for the nave of San Ignazio when the Jesuit Pozzo painted there the *Triumph of Saint Ignatius* in the 1690s.[21] Any of these works could be taken as actualizations of the visual schema of Milton's Limbo of Vanity, though direct influence is of course out of the question. Displaying remarkable technical competence, such ceiling paintings were greatly admired, and were propagandistically effective as adaptations of the Baroque into what was often called "the Jesuit style."

To take these works seriously, and as art they surely deserve at least that, the viewer must be prepared to ignore a certain implausibility in the whole procedure. Of Rubens' ceilings glorifying James I and the Stuart monarchy, Julius Held points out that "it is essential to remind ourselves that terms like 'rightside up' and

[20] Objections have also been raised to the "shocking anti-Catholicism" of the Limbo of Vanity: Ann D. Ferry declares unequivocally that "the chief target of this parody is Catholicism," while Rex Clements maintains that "medievalism in all its forms" is the target (Ann D. Ferry, *Milton's Epic Voice*, Cambridge, 1963, p. 139, and Rex Clements, "Angels in *Paradise Lost*," 284). The passage is an attack upon many forms of religious hypocrisy and pretension, but it is such an attack as devout Catholics have often made (see *inter alia* Dante's *Inferno* XXVII, 82-93, and Ariosto's *Orlando Furioso* XXXIV, 73ff.), and it must surely be relevant that few Catholics have found the passage objectionable. Milton was writing a universal Christian epic, and his achievement went far beyond the individual biases of personal and sectarian opinion which we find in his prose writings. Fine critical analyses of the passage may be found in: F. L. Huntley, "A Justification of Milton's 'Paradise of Fools'," *ELH* 21 (1954), 107-13, and Merritt Y. Hughes, "Milton's Limbo of Vanity," in *Th' Upright Heart and Pure* (ed. Amadeus P. Fiore), Pittsburgh, 1967, pp. 7-24.

[21] Reproductions of the Gherardi, Baciccia, Cozza, and Pozzo paintings may be found in Ellis Waterhouse, *Italian Baroque Painting*, London, 1962, pp. 68-74.

'upside down' have no meaning and indeed are misleading when applied to paintings on a ceiling."[22] By refusing to admit or accept that limitation, one sees in these ceilings a visual counterpart to Milton's Limbo, "something like decorative nonsense," as Waterhouse described the work of Cozza. As for Pozzo's *Apotheosis of Saint Ignatius*, Waterhouse comments:

> It is a work of extravagant, and rather enchanting, absurdity. From most points of view—and especially from the sides of the church—the effect is wholly unnerving. Columns fall inward or sideways and the spectator feels as Samson must have felt after he had started work on the Temple at Gaza. But there is one point in the center of the nave (marked by an indicator on the floor) from which all this nonsense appears in correct perspective—and the effect is extremely impressive. It is not a point at which the worshiper in the church would naturally place himself, and one may be permitted to wonder if the Jesuits conceived this bizarre scheme of decoration as a lesson to those who were not altogether on the correct spot in their religious beliefs.[23]

Attempts at such effects were also being made in the 1660s in England, as in Robert Streater's ceilings for the Sheldonian Theatre and Isaac Fuller's ceiling for the Chapel of All Souls in Oxford, in which the artist "ignored the force of gravity almost entirely."[24] Whether in England or on the Continent, such illusionist ceilings spun gymnastic figures whirling and tossing through the sky, freed from all the normal laws of physical force and movement in a space distorted and swirling with multiple trajectories and oblique axes. The visual effects are dizzying.

146 Let us now return to *The Apotheosis of James I* in the Whitehall ceiling, the painting which Milton can be presumed to have known best. The aging monarch rises from the "lower" end of the oval, with one foot placed on an eagle and another on an imperial globe, assisted by a rapidly turning figure of Justice, as he ascends toward Heaven to receive the reward for his earthly achievements. Cherubs blow a fanfare in honor of the royal entry into Heaven, and the King is accompanied by the royal panoply of crown and orb, and welcomed with the palms of peace and the laurel wreath of victory. The composition is filled with boiling movements, whirling, spinning, spiraling figures, and with tossing garments, garlands, and assorted paraphernalia. Rubens' achievement is immensely impressive, both as a work of art and as a glorification of divine right monarchy. He has gone beyond the decoration of a ceiling to persuade the viewer that the ceiling simply does not exist.

Milton refused to be persuaded by the illusionistic and apotheosis paintings, just as he refused to be persuaded by royal absolutism and papal infallibility. Rejecting the ideational content of these paintings, he refused to accept the *sotto in sù* perspective, and so converted the whole visual scheme into the anarchic confusions

---

[22] Held, "Rubens' Glynde Sketch," 278.
[23] Waterhouse, *Italian Baroque Painting*, pp. 69 and 75.
[24] Kerry Downes, "Fuller's 'Last Judgment,'" *Burlington Magazine* 102 (1960), 451-52.

of his Limbo of Vanity. Milton satirizes the pretentious souls by reducing their movements in space to an undignified and ridiculous jumble, which contrasts with the graceful, orderly, and harmonious movements of the faithful angels in their joyful song and dance about the celestial throne and in their purposeful and majestic journeys through space. Visually considered, Milton's Limbo represents the *reductio ad absurdum* of creaturely sin and presumption: elsewhere throughout *Paradise Lost*, the heavens declare the glory of God, as the beauty of their majesty reflects the mind of their Creator; in the Limbo of Vanity, on the contrary, there is no majesty, no dignity. Man's false claims to dignity and to majesty "in this or the other life" have vitiated his native nobility, the gift of God, and have interjected this grotesquerie into the magnificence of the created universe. As Milton's descriptions of Hell provide a perfect visual equivalent to the evil minds of the fallen angels, so does his Paradise of Fools give visual expression to the sin of man. Imagistically, dramatically, and intellectually, the episode is integral to the epic.

XIII

Landscape Art and Milton's Garden of Eden

LANDSCAPE AS MOOD AND MIMESIS IN RENAISSANCE AESTHETICS

LANDSCAPE descriptions abound in Milton's epics, but they are almost never independent units existing by and for themselves. Our first impression is that they serve the narrative by providing scenes for the action, but this is only the beginning of their function: they also express something about the character of the actors and prepare us for the response which Milton wishes us to feel to the action. This critical understanding may be epitomized in Cope's observation that in *Paradise Lost* "scene continually acts as mimesis of argument," and in Spencer's definition for both epics of the function of Milton's ideal landscapes: "they symbolically represent or objectify the poems' thematic content; the poet's argument is obliquely set forth in the iconography of his landscapes."[1]

Our first introduction to the Garden of Eden comes after we have followed Satan's flight through what seems infinity, as Milton has carefully set the terms of his effective and significant contrast. The pastoral intimacy of the Garden impresses us even more fully when we see it set against the background of the cosmos.[2] As with his other epic locales, so with Eden: Milton wishes us to see its landscape not as an end in itself, but so that we may enter into its mood, its consciousness, and understand its significance.[3] In this sense, visual description is an important means to an even more important end.

Very much the same function and priority which we find in Milton's descriptions may also be discovered in the landscape paintings of the Renaissance. In his fascinating study entitled *The Vision of Landscape in Renaissance Italy*, A. Richard Turner finds principles and methods at work in landscape painting which Miltonists will see as almost equally relevant to *Paradise Lost*. Through the diverse operations of various artists Turner finds a common principle: "that landscape is not seen for itself, but as a commentary upon the human condition, as a speculation upon the tension between order and disorder in the world," and he concludes that "the Renaissance artist like Dante before him (*Purg.* x, 31) knew that Nature had been put to shame by Art, and that the business of landscape painting was to evoke a moment of contemplation, wherein a man might discover his just relationship to an

---

[1] Cope, *Metaphoric Structure*, p. 76, and Spencer, *Heroic Nature*, p. 104.

[2] Spencer, *Heroic Nature*, pp. 107-8. Spencer proceeds to note Milton's conjunction in his descriptions of Eden of a classical stasis reminiscent of Titian with a Baroque opulence which recalls Rubens.

[3] Knott, *Milton's Pastoral Vision*, pp. 36-37.

often tumultuous world."[4] The Renaissance artists and their successors who perfected landscape painting produced believable spaces and places on their canvasses in order to create moods. To speak of this process "in terms of the imitation of nature is to miss the point, but to consider it as more of the emotions than of the intellect, and hence like in quality to man's reaction to natural beauty, is to begin aright. Only then will we perceive how the artists' intellect has operated in order to achieve his evocative results." Furthermore, what Turner observes of Leonardo da Vinci defines the terms within which Milton's natural descriptions operate: ". . . for Leonardo and for many after him, the poetic aspect of a landscape was far more important than its topographical verisimilitude. His essential modernity as a landscapist is the discovery of mood as the content of landscape."[5] Similarly apposite are Turner's observations on Giovanni Bellini: "His beautiful landscapes are but backgrounds for Madonnas, Christs, and saints. As backgrounds, however, their function is more than decorative, for the landscape is humanized. By this I mean that its forms and light are not arbitrary, but directed specifically to an enlargement of the spiritual meaning of the figures."[6] Tracing the same conception through Giorgione and Titian, he concludes that "in sixteenth-century Venice this attitude is pervasive, and the great painted landscapes have meaning insofar as they echo and magnify the actions and thoughts of their inhabitants."[7]

In the north, Dutch landscape painting was less concerned than Italian with identifiable people and well-known stories, but nonetheless we almost always find people represented in those landscapes. What this means, as Wolfgang Stechow concludes in his *Dutch Landscape Painting of the Seventeenth Century*, is "that man does not lose himself in nature, that there is no attempt at a glorification or deification of nature beyond man's scope or control . . . . It is an animation which rarely involves a story; if the story is important the figures are apt to predominate over the landscape . . . . But it is an animation which provides a human scale; it prevents the widest panorama, tallest trees and wildest seas from going beyond man's compass and comprehension." By contrast, according to Stechow, "in a Cezanne landscape man, if at all present, means little or nothing."[8]

None of this is intended to deny the presence in the sixteenth and seventeenth centuries of paintings intended to convey mimesis of nature, recorded with greater or lesser verisimilitude, but such intent was not predominant either in the visual arts[9] or in Milton. There were some efforts in painting to provide "unvarnished reports of actual peasant life," which might perhaps best be compared in English literature to Touchstone's famous comments upon shepherds in *As You Like It*, and "the

---

[4] A. Richard Turner, *The Vision of Landscape in Renaissance Italy*, Princeton, 1966, p. 212.

[5] *Ibid.*, pp. 32-33.

[6] *Ibid.*, p. 79.

[7] *Ibid.*, p. 112.

[8] Wolfgang Stechow, *Dutch Landscape Painting of the Seventeenth Century*, London, 1966, p. 8.

[9] Turner, *The Vision of Landscape*, p. 132. Altdorfer's *Landscape with a Footbridge* in the National Gallery of London is perhaps the earliest instance of pure landscape in art.

realities of peasant existence" were made the subject of many of Jacopo Bassano's paintings, for example.[10]

The landscape Milton describes in the Garden is designed to remove us as far as possible from the everyday working world of the Veneto peasant, as painted by Bassano, and from the practical realism and the tar of shepherd's life in Arden, as described by Touchstone. Milton's landscape is of "another heaven/ From Heaven gate not far, founded in view . . ." (VII, 617-18). Scholars of Milton have generally recognized the close relationship, amounting almost to identity, between the Garden in Eden and Heaven.[11] Here, as in so many other ways in *Paradise Lost*, Milton followed the same strategy which had long been used by artists in treating the same subject, for as we have seen in an earlier chapter, "l'art ne distingue pas le Paradis céleste du Paradis terrestre."[12]

In this operation there was undeniably an interaction between Christianity and classical culture, an interaction so pervasive that it is sometimes difficult to sort out with precision. A powerful ingredient of this mixture or amalgam was, as we know, literary Arcadianism, which overlapped with the Christian understanding of the unfallen world. Erwin Panofsky reminds us of the birth of Arcady in the imagination of Virgil,[13] while Italian writers such as Bembo and Sannazzaro naturalized it in the consciousness of Renaissance Europeans, establishing a literary vogue which achieved its finest English expression in Sir Philip Sidney. These literary developments, especially on the continent, fed directly into landscape painting. "There is no doubt," Turner writes, "that this taste for the pastoral developed in literature before the visual arts, and a work such as *L'Arcadia* is strongly pictorial in effect," but the blending was so strong under Renaissance influences that "both literature and painting offer evocative images, suggestive notations rather than finished statements."[14] Milton relied upon the developments in this tradition, as well as upon Genesis, the Song of Songs, the Apocalypse, the hexameral literature, and theological exegesis, so as to produce without loss of fidelity a Christianized Arcadia.[15] Edward W. Tayler compares the natural effusion of Milton's Garden with the earlier tradition, and aptly summarizes the process: "Arcadia, early linked to the Golden Age in Virgil, coalesced with Eden to form a new whole—the Christian landscape of Renaissance pastoral."[16]

Aesthetic practice and aesthetic theory alike had combined to prepare Milton's audience for the very contrasts in landscape description which he provides in *Paradise Lost*. Much of this relevant background in Italian Renaissance art is summarized by Berenson: ". . . for nature is a chaos, indiscriminately clamoring for attention. . . . For art is a garden cut off from chaos wherein there is provided, not only an accord like that of the beasts between our physical needs and our

[10] Turner, *The Vision of Landscape*, pp. 119-20 and 127-28; *As You Like It*, 3.2.11-90.
[11] For example, Knott, *Milton's Pastoral Vision*, p. 53, quoted above, pp. 193-94.
[12] Réau, *Iconographie*, II, ii, p. 750.
[13] Panofsky, *Meaning in the Visual Arts*, pp. 299-300.
[14] Turner, *The Vision of Landscape*, pp. 97-98.
[15] Knott, *Milton's Pastoral Vision*, pp. xi-xii, and 47.
[16] Edward W. Tayler, *Nature and Art in Renaissance Literature*, New York, 1964, pp. 99-100, and also 16, 162.

environment, but a perfect attuning of the universe to our entire state of conscious-ness."[17] In addition to the chaos and the garden to which Berenson refers, Milton's landscape descriptions show the vast reaches of space, the pretentious human distor-tions of the Limbo of Vanity, and the demonic destructiveness of Hell. Each of these "places," as Milton describes them, provides apposite visual metaphors for particular spiritual conditions.

In the Garden before the Fall and in Heaven, the conditions are most similar, and in both Milton employs many of the conventions of post-Renaissance landscape art to provide what Berenson has described as "the consciousness of an unusually intense degree of well-being."[18] Most supportive of Milton's poetic efforts here are three forms of art: Italian landscape gardening, landscape painting in its most popular manifestations, and Biblical paintings devoted to Eden. These are so interpenetrated by influences and attitudes that they cannot be entirely separated, but the first two can now be taken up in turn, after which a separate chapter will consider analogues from explicitly Biblical art. Overlapping cannot, however, be avoided.

ITALIAN GARDENS

The beauties of the Italian landscape in general, and of Italian gardens in particular, made a profound impression upon many English travelers. Among them, Coryate, Stone, Evelyn, Reresby, and Raymond specifically compared what they saw with Paradise.[19] Comparisons of particular gardens to Eden, or Heaven, or Elysium were frequent, and should not be surprising to us: the gardens were designed to suggest just such analogies, and the extent to which they succeeded in creating a paradisial sense of well-being makes them directly pertinent to our interests here. This does not mean that we can find a single paradigm for Milton's Garden, be-cause Milton's purpose was "not to force on us the personal paradisial vision of one man, but rather to distill to an essence all the variegated conceptions that men have ever held of Paradise."[20]

Furthermore, the Italian garden was laid out according to formal and geo-metric design, and although that formality was modified in important ways which we shall note, we nonetheless find here a basic dissimilarity to Milton's Garden. "All Italian gardens are therefore geometric," Jellicoe writes, "and their beauty lies largely in the reconciliation of the upsurging, logical, scientific, and ordered mind of man searching for its objective, with the waywardness of nature."[21] The new gardens became "an expression of Renaissance man's attitude to nature: man

---

[17] Berenson, *Italian Painters of the Renaissance*, pp. 171-72.

[18] *Ibid.*, pp. 101-2.

[19] Amy Lee Turner, *The Visual Arts in Milton's Poetry*, pp. 282 and 334n.; Sells, *The Paradise of Travellers*, pp. 156, 166, and 221; and Evelyn, *Diary*, II, pp. 187, 251, 484, and 487. John W. Stoye, *English Travellers*, p. 203, notes that large numbers of engraved views of Italian gardens were brought back to England, but unfortunately identification of subject and artist are usually unknown to us.

[20] Broadbent, "Milton's Paradise," 176, following C. S. Lewis, *A Preface to "Paradise Lost,"* London, 1949, p. 47.

[21] G. A. Jellicoe, *Studies in Landscape Design*, 3 vols., London, 1960-70, I, p. 2.

was the center of the universe and need no longer fear nature."[22] Seventeenth-century engravings demonstrate how that attitude was expressed in the geometrical landscaping of such famous gardens as the Borghese, the Farnese, the Ludovisi, the Medici on the Pincio, the Quirinal, and the Vatican.[23] Milton could scarcely have escaped seeing some of these, and in addition there was the similar arrangement of the gardens at the Palazzo Barberini.[24]

At least equally famous, and perhaps more so, were the Boboli Gardens laid out around the Pitti Palace of the Medici in Florence, initially by Tribolo in 1550, and completed by Buontalenti during the remainder of the sixteenth century.[25] A plat of the Boboli will show its basically geometrical design, but a walk through these gardens will demonstrate conclusively that they convey a sense of the natural when explored on the ground, a sense which contrasts markedly with the impression we get by merely consulting a landscape chart.[26] The design is artful, even artificial, but as we "feel" the gardens *in situ* we are at least as conscious of nature as we are of art. Though Milton struck a different balance between nature and art in his Eden from that we find in Italian gardens, that difference is less obvious in reality than in theory.[27]

When we walk through these formal gardens, we are made most conscious of their geometrical design when one or both of two conditions are met: when the ground is relatively flat, and when the plantings are so low that our eyes may take in the regularity and symmetry of the whole. In many parts of the Boboli Gardens these conditions are not met: the tall plantings of the shaded alleys along with the rising and falling contours of hills and valleys interfere with our consciousness of the geometrical design so that we can readily forget the overall plat of the landscaping and become primarily conscious of nature rather than of art. Under these circumstances, even when we are aware of the relations between nature and art, we feel these relations as a paradox heightened by contrast: we find that Elisabeth MacDougall calls "formal gardens created from the materials of nature and natural settings created by the skill of the designer."[28] But it is not only a matter of perceiving natural exuberance even in areas of precisely ordered design, for MacDougall has demonstrated "the existence of groves and irregular or naturalistic areas in Renaissance gardens" which have too often been ignored but which were nonetheless of "importance to the garden design." Her examination of many Italian gardens "shows that *boschetti* [i.e., wild woods] and informal planting occurred everywhere," and that by the 1580s "the naturalistic plantings often were equal in

[22] Susan and Geoffrey Jellicoe, *Water: The Use of Water in Landscape Architecture*, New York, 1971, p. 66.

[23] Cesare D'Onofrio, *Roma nel Seicento*, Florence, 1969, pp. 309, 314-15, 322, 250, and 337.

[24] Amato Pietro Frutaz, *Le Piante di Roma*, Rome, 1962, III, pl. 325.

[25] John C. Shepherd and G. A. Jellicoe, *Italian Gardens of the Renaissance*, New York, 1966, pp. 12-13.

[26] Francesco Gurrieri and Judith Chatfield, *Boboli Gardens*, Florence, 1972, figs. 1-12.

[27] Nicolson, *John Milton: A Reader's Guide*, p. 238, comments that debaters in the art-versus-nature controversies could get something for each position from *Paradise Lost*.

[28] Elisabeth MacDougall, "*Ars Hortulorum*: Sixteenth-Century Garden Iconography and Literary Theory in Italy," in *The Italian Garden* (ed. David R. Coffin), p. 52.

area and importance to the formal."²⁹ Rucellai referred to his informal walks as *viottole*, meaning field paths, and to his formal paths as *viali*.³⁰

A large part of the pleasure of Renaissance Italian gardens was in such walks and paths which threaded the whole landscape, providing not only variety of views, but also of scents (blended by the careful planting of herbs and flowers), and of sounds, from birds and running water. In Milton's Garden we find a combination of just "those delicacies . . . of taste, sight, smell, herbs, fruits, and flowers,/ Walks, and the melody of birds" (VIII, 526-28). Walks are repeatedly mentioned in *Paradise Lost*, and we cannot escape the fact that Milton's Garden, like those of Italy, was threaded throughout by walks. Gabriel refers to "the circuit of these walks," and Adam to his "walks, and bowers" (IV, 586-87, and VIII, 304-6). Just as in the Boboli, some of the walks in Eden form arbors and alleys "with branches overgrown," while others are covered only by tall trees "of stateliest covert, cedar, pine, or palm" (IV, 625-27 and 434-38). After the Fall, when she still hopes that they may be allowed to endure their punishment in the Garden, Eve asks, "what can be toilsome in these pleasant walks," and when she learns of their banishment, her lament begins by reference to leaving "these happy walks and shades,/ Fit haunt of Gods" (XI, 179, and 269-71).³¹

Another standard feature of the Renaissance garden was the fountain, which could be designed to emphasize architectural and sculptural achievement, or which could be so skillfully introduced as to seem the product of nature itself. In 1543 the humanist scholar Claudio Tolomei describes fountains "where art was so blended with nature that one could not discover whether the fountains were the product of the former or the latter. Thus some appeared to be a naturalistic artifice while others seemed an artifice of nature. In these times they endeavor to make a fountain appear made by nature itself, not by accident, but with a masterful artistry."³² With that description in mind, let us turn now to the principal fountain we find in the Garden in *Paradise Lost*. A river passed southward through Eden, and

> through the shaggy hill
> Passed underneath engulfed, for God had thrown
> That mountain as his Garden mould high raised
> Upon the rapid current, which through veins
> Of porous earth with kindly thirst updrawn,
> Rose a fresh fountain, and with many a rill
> Watered the garden.
>
> (IV, 224-30)

---

²⁹ *Ibid.*, pp. 41-43.

³⁰ *Ibid.*, p. 44.

³¹ Milton provides another fine garden image in the Indian fig tree which forms "a pillared shade,/ High overarched, and echoing walks between" (IX, 1106-7), and it would be interesting to know whether the famous Medici collection of botanical specimens from throughout the world included such a fig tree.

³² MacDougall, "*Ars Hortulorum*," p. 52.

Here God is the landscaper, and he uses rivers and hills as the materials with which he shapes a "natural" fountain by his divine art. Milton's description corresponds to the taste for fountains designed to appear natural which he would have encountered in Italy,[33] and in the next chapter we shall see how these fountains became normative in sixteenth- and seventeenth-century paintings of the Garden of Eden.

The blending of nature and art in the fountain was typical of the whole thrust of Renaissance gardens, which were understood as reminders of "the role of man in the world of nature, and the creation of order from chaos."[34] Milton's Garden had to be more perfect than even the most successful Renaissance counterpart, for its landscape architect was God, but human landscape gardeners had attempted to suggest that original perfection and also to presage its ultimate fulfilment in the joys of the celestial Paradise. Thus the great gardens of Italy were designed, in Mac-Dougall's words, to reveal "to the world a shadow of Heaven's repose."[35] What Milton provided in his description of the Garden of Eden was a further variation or mutation upon this fundamental conception, a mutation so profound that it may indeed have influenced the future development of landscape architecture in the direction of the greater "naturalness" which Capability Brown achieved in his English garden. Helen Gardner finds in *Paradise Lost* "a conception that comes to perfection in eighteenth-century garden parks and that spread all over Europe as *le jardin anglais*."[36]

The naturalness or informality of the Garden in *Paradise Lost* is one of Milton's great achievements, but it was not so far removed from the Italian gardens he knew as might at first appear. The Italian landscapers achieved an extension into nature of the intimacy and joy of the house, even of the home, and "the psychological purpose of the garden was to give pure contentment to the owner," as Shepherd and Jellicoe have said. "The term 'formality' as applied to the garden is often misread as being cold and stiff. The informality of nature can be a beautiful serene thing in itself. So, too, can the formality of a home; but when the two are brought into immediate contrast without compromise, the charm of both may be lost in abrupt contrast. Italian gardens preserve harmony and repose," because "the most general conscious principle suggested that the lines of the garden should grow less defined as they left the house, like water ripples spreading from a center, to die away gradually in their surroundings—lines always formal but less and less emphasized."[37]

Though the influence of the home upon the garden was not lost upon Milton, the villa itself could of course find no place in the Garden of Eden. Other structures of the Renaissance garden could provide him with models for what he needed, and

[33] Broadbent, "Milton's Paradise," 162, suggests North African gardens as a likely influence.

[34] MacDougall, "*Ars Hortulorum*," p. 53.

[35] *Ibid.*, p. 55.

[36] Gardner, *A Reading of "Paradise Lost*," p. 79, and also Spencer, *Heroic Nature*, p. 120. Milton's impact upon these developments could be made the subject of a fascinating study, but our concern here is not for Milton's influence on the visual arts but for his use of them as resources.

[37] Shepherd and Jellicoe, *Water*, pp. 31, 26, and 28; see also Spencer, *Heroic Nature*, p. 15.

these were the rustic bowers that were carefully placed throughout Italian gardens.[38] These bowers were influenced by the interest in the primeval life of man which found its literary expression in Arcadianism,[39] and they conveyed a simplicity that would for every reason be appropriate to the abode of Adam and Eve. In a typical example, "branches tied together, probably according to a system which Lomazzo attributes to Leonardo, created a mysterious kind of ceiling," perhaps symbolizing "a kind of mystical dissolution into a green atmosphere." Just as Milton describes Eve's bower, these were interlaced and "formed entirely from branches of trees and other living plants."[40] So popular were these structures, that they were often simulated by painted walls and ceilings within villas and palaces, which provide well-preserved representations of actual garden bowers. Thus the Villa Papa Giulia, built between 1550 and 1555, contains a fine cortile with a semicircular barrel vault, decorated in fresco as though it were a trellis of vines.[41] In the loggia of the Palazzo Rospigliosi, there is a beautifully designed bower ceiling, with vines and leaves and birds, and a similar room in the Palazzo Barberini shows ceiling decorations of fir branches crossing each other at intervals to form a kind of trellis work, but not so regular as to preclude the touch of nature.[42]

Curiously, this fascination with primitive bowers rarely if ever found expression in artistic renditions of the Garden of Eden, and Adam and Eve seem generally not to have been shown with a dwelling place until after their expulsion from the Garden.[43] It is in the gardens, then, that we find the closest analogues to Adam's "sylvan lodge" with "shady arborous roof" (v, 377 and 137). As in *Paradise Lost*, "the roof/ Of thickest covert" (IV, 692-93) would provide protection both from sun and rain, and the whole was framed not only with colorful flowers but also with "fragrant leaf" and "odorous bushy shrub," a blending of delightful sensations such as Milton loved to describe and the Italian landscape gardeners loved to achieve.

Though Milton went beyond any single source to create the quintessential Paradise, parallels abound with *topoi* often found in individual gardens. Thus the "mossy seats" of the dining terrace in Eden correspond with those seats "covered with grass" which Battisti tells us were often seen in France as well as Italy (v, 392).[44] The immense popularity of grottoes, artificially constructed for Italian gardens, also lies behind the natural scenery of Milton's Eden:

[38] Battisti, "*Natura Artificiosa* to *Natura Artificialis*," p. 13.

[39] Lionello Puppi, "The Villa Garden of the Veneto from the Fifteenth to the Eighteenth Century," in *The Italian Garden* (ed. David Coffin), p. 91.

[40] Battisti, *op. cit.*, p. 22.

[41] E. March Phillipps, *The Gardens of Italy*, London, 1919, pp. 47-50 and fig. 53.

[42] Vincenzo Golzio, *Palazzi romani dalla rinascita al neoclassico*, Bologna, 1971, figs. 50, 52, and 213-15.

[43] Postlapsarian bowers are sometimes provided for Adam and Eve, as in the tenth-century Grandval Bible in the British Museum, reproduced in Sigrid Esche, *Adam und Eva*, Dusseldorf, 1957, fig. 6, and in Theodor de Bry's engraving in *Admiranda narratio fida tamen, de commodis et incolarum ritibus Virginiae*, Frankfurt am Main, 1590, sig. D6.

[44] Battisti, "*Natura Artificiosa* to *Natura Artificialis*," p. 13.

> umbrageous grots and caves
> Of cool recess, o'er which the mantling vine
> Lays forth her purple grape, and gently creeps
> Luxuriant.
>
> (IV, 257-60)

Outside of *Paradise Lost*, that scene is probably most familiar to us today from the Boboli Gardens, but it was not unique there, nor was the pattern of running water falling into a still lake:

> murmuring waters fall
> Down the slope hills, dispersed, or in a lake,
> That to the fringed bank with myrtle crowned,
> Her crystal mirror holds. . . .
>
> (IV, 260-63)

The theater was also often an important part of the Italian garden, and Milton appositely refers in his Eden to "a woody theater/ Of Stateliest view" (IV, 141-42). Merritt Y. Hughes interprets this phrase as an allusion to "the terraced seats of a Greek theater,"[45] and though there is no reason to overlook that analogy, the allusion fits more comfortably with a garden setting such as that for the "woody theater" in the Boboli, surrounded at the top by a wall-like stand of trees.

The whole ambience of Eden extends out of, even as it goes far beyond, the Renaissance gardens which so caught the imagination of English travelers, and we can apply to the epic poet the words which Jellicoe uses to describe the typical Italian landscapist as "a master of the delights which play upon the senses: dapple shadows, the patterning of box parterre, the inviting glimpse of distant views, the sound of water, . . ."[46] Adam's description of his first delight in the Garden records exactly what the Italian landscape architect wished to achieve:

> about me round I saw
> Hill, dale, and shady woods, and sunny plains,
> And liquid lapse of murmuring streams; by these
> Creatures that lived, and moved, and walked, or flew,
> Birds on the branches warbling; all things smiled,
> With fragrance and with joy my heart o'er flowed.
>
> (VIII, 261-66)

Here we see the merging of what Lionello Puppi has aptly called "the poetics of the garden" with what we might call "the gardening of poetry."[47]

The historical associations between poetry and art in the Renaissance were close and their relations complex. MacDougall has shown how "the revival of epic poetry with its extended landscape descriptions and its new emphasis on the relationship between action and setting" influenced landscape art. Many of these

---

[45] Hughes, ed., *PL* IV, 141n. The world, of course, was also frequently referred to as a theater.

[46] Jellicoe, *Studies in Landscape Design*, I, p. 2.

[47] Puppi, "The Villa Garden of the Veneto," p. 86.

developments stemmed from the court of Ferrara, where Boiardo, Bernardo Tasso, and Ariosto were officials, and Torquato Tasso was court poet. "Thus the practice of using groves and other natural landscape forms developed in the center where a revival of ancient epic and pastoral poetry and drama was taking place. Themes or *topoi* from literary sources provided the general mood evoking either the pastoral, such as the Villa Mattei's grove with its shepherd and sheep, or thoughts of the Golden Age or Garden of the Hesperides in the wandering paths of the Villa Giulia, or the park of the Ferrarese Belvedere."[48] As we find evidence of literary Arcadianism in the landscaped gardens, so, too, those gardens supplied visible *topoi* which figure prominently in Milton's Eden. Within the cultural nexus of the Renaissance, each form of art inevitably influenced and reinforced the others.

LANDSCAPE AND VIEW PAINTINGS

In the later Middle Ages, views painted into illuminated manuscripts begin to show new appreciations of depth and perspective, and similar developments may be traced in larger paintings. In 1444, Konrad Witz incorporated into his *Christ Walking on the Water* one of the earliest recognizable views in modern art, painted so as to present a particular area of Lake Geneva. At about the same time similar work came into prominence in Italy, and Berenson writes that Fra Angelico "was not only the first Italian to paint a landscape that can be identified (a view of Lake Trasimene from Cortona), but the first to communicate a sense of the pleasantness of nature. How readily we feel the freshness and springtime gaiety of his gardens in the frescoes of the *Annunciation* and the *Noli Me Tangere* at San Marco!"[49]

Gombrich shows that the first technical term for the genre of landscape was introduced in Venice, as early as 1521, in the phrase "molte tavolette de paesi," and he traces a significant interest in landscape painting among Italian collectors in the sixteenth century.[50] In their study of the developing taste for landscape in England, Henry and Margaret Ogden find that Englishmen showed "little indication of interest in landscape in the sixteenth century until the later decades, and not very much then," though there was some "forestry work" and landscape backgrounds in tapestry and in portraits.[51] For educated Englishmen, landscape was accepted as an independent genre during or shortly after the first decade of the seventeenth century.[52] Milton was aware of the term and its artistic significance as early as "L'Allegro," where he writes that

> Straight mine eye hath caught new pleasures
> Whilst the landscape round it measures,
> Russet lawns, and fallows grey,
> Where the nibbling flocks do stray,

[48] MacDougall, "*Ars Hortulorum*," p. 51.
[49] Berenson, *Italian Painters of the Renaissance*, pp. 78-79.
[50] E. H. Gombrich, "Renaissance Artistic Theory and the Development of Landscape Painting," *Gazette des Beaux-Arts* 41 (1953), 339.
[51] Henry V. S. and Margaret S. Ogden, *English Taste in Landscape in the Seventeenth Century*, Ann Arbor, 1955, p. 1a, and 2b-3a.
[52] *Ibid.*, pp. 5b-6a.

> Mountains on whose barren breast
> The laboring clouds do often rest:
> Meadows trim and daisies pied,
> Shallow brooks, and rivers wide.
> Towers, and battlements it sees
> Bosomed high in tufted trees. . . .
>
> ("L'Allegro," 69-78)

It is a temptation to continue the quotation, for Milton here provides a splendid visualization, a perfect literary counterpart to the painter's landscape, but our concern is with the epic poetry. There again the word recurs, as "darkened landscape," "so lovely seemed that landscape," and "discovering in wide landscape" (II, 491; IV, 152-53; V, 142).

In each of these epic references we find examples of what has already been called the landscape of mood, a typically post-Renaissance use of natural scenery to evoke and channel human emotions. In the first place we find an extended simile explaining the change of mood among the demonic chieftains who began in "doubtful consultations dark" and yet "ended rejoicing":

> As when from mountain tops the dusky clouds
> Ascending, while the North Wind sleeps, o'erspread
> Heaven's cheerful face, the lowering element
> Scowls o'er the darkened landscape snow, or shower;
> If chance the radiant sun with farewell sweet
> Extend his evening beam, the fields revive,
> The birds their notes renew, and bleating herds
> Attest their joy, that hill and valley rings.
>
> (II, 488-95)

Moving from the "lowering element" through to the "radiant sun," Milton here epitomizes the characteristic psychological uses of landscape in art.[53] Also oriented toward the establishment of personal emotion and response is Milton's second explicit use of landscape, when Satan views the Garden after his hazardous flight through Chaos as though the sun had suddenly reappeared after a shower:

> so lovely seemed
> That landscape: and of pure now purer air
> Meets his approach, and to the heart inspires
> Vernal delight and joy, able to drive
> All sadness but despair: now gentle gales
> Fanning their odoriferous wings dispense
> Native perfumes, and whisper whence they stole
> Those balmy spoils.
>
> (IV, 152-59)

The last of the specific uses of the technical term landscape also involves the

[53] See the comments of A. Richard Turner, quoted above, pp. 218-19.

emergence of the sun after darkness, when Adam and Eve arise in the morning and see that

> the sun, who scarce uprisen
> With wheels yet hovering o'er the ocean brim,
> Shot parallel to the earth his dewy ray,
> Discovering in wide landscape all the east
> Of Paradise and Eden's happy plains,
> Lowly they bowed, adoring, and began
> Their orisons, each morning duly paid.
>
> (v, 139-45)

In each of these descriptions, Milton had chosen the very elements of visualization which his cultivated contemporaries found most delightful in landscape painting. The Ogdens have painstakingly identified what it was that made landscape painting so popular with seventeenth-century Englishmen, and associated the achievement with what they call "essentially Christian optimism." Their definition of the visual process is directly pertinent to Milton: "Man and nature are accomplishing their appointed tasks. The emotion is one of sympathy with such activity, of satisfaction in it, and of approval that the activity of the world is prospering. There is a diffused euphoria, a sense of well-being, in most of the landscapes of the period, which evokes a corresponding feeling in the spectator and which constitutes their essential mood."[54] Milton's topographical descriptions do not and should not always achieve such results (as in Hell, and the Limbo of Vanity, for example), but they always do so in those instances where he specifically labels his descriptions as landscapes. Milton both uses and illustrates the term in precise conformity with the terminology of seventeenth-century aesthetics.

Milton appears also to have been aware, whether consciously or unconsciously, of another salient factor in the development of landscape art. As Turner has showed, "the rise of landscape painting accompanied the flowering of city life, for only with the development of a complex money economy did the great landscapists appear. Their art brought an illusion of the country into the city. . . ."[55] In the light of that history, Milton's choice of a simile to express Satan's admiration of the Garden and of Eve takes on greater force:

> Much he the place admired, the person more.
> As one who long in populous city pent,
> Where houses thick and sewers annoy the air,
> Forth issuing on a summer's morn to breathe
> Among the pleasant villages and farms
> Adjoined, from each thing met conceives delight,
> The smell of grain, or tedded grass, or kine,
> Or dairy, each rural sight, each rural sound.
>
> (IX, 444-51)

[54] Ogden and Ogden, *English Taste in Landscape*, p. 50a-b.
[55] Turner, *The Vision of Landscape*, p. 193.

The image not only conveys the delights of natural scenery, but does so while incorporating a reference to the cultural factors which lay behind the development of such pleasures. Typical of his practice elsewhere, Milton goes beyond the purely visual here to provide a fully sensuous response by references also to the sounds and scents of the countryside.

The increasing popularity of pastoral visions in art provided a cultural context in which Milton's own poetic evocation could operate effectively with his audience. As Knott has recognized, Milton's problem in creating Paradise was to make nature perfect without making it unbelievable, and that problem would have been far more formidable, had it not been for a common visual culture to which Milton could refer, in addition to a common literary culture. A case in point is Milton's exclusion of seasonal change from Paradise, for "Spring and Autumn here/ Danced hand in hand," and here we have only "the eternal Spring" (v, 394-95, and iv, 268). Had it not been for the Fall of man, "the Spring/ Perpetual" would have "smiled on Earth with vernant flowers" (x, 678-79). Now it is important to recognize, as Leland Ryken has helped us to do, that "the entire contradictory fusion of spring and harvest is best understood as an attempt to portray apocalyptic reality through a technique of mystic oxymoron," but it is also important to recognize that Milton could muster strong visual reinforcement for this attempt.[56] This is neither to overlook nor to deny the presence in Milton's background of that brief, but highly influential, Ovidian assertion, "Ver erat aeternum," but such literary Arcadianism had long since moved over into pictorial art, where it was repeatedly given the most charming visual persuasiveness.[57]

What is perhaps Milton's most effective visualization of this theme has often been compared with one of the most famous of quattrocento paintings:

147

> The birds their choir apply; airs, vernal airs,
> Breathing the smell of field and grove, attune
> The trembling leaves, while universal Pan
> Knit with the Graces and the Hours in dance
> Led on the eternal Spring.
>
> (iv, 264-68)

In his edition of *Paradise Lost*, Hughes noted of these lines that "comparison with Botticelli's *Spring* is inevitable," while Jeffry Spencer carries the suggestion somewhat further: "One is struck by the resemblance between the lines above and Botticelli's *Primavera* which presents a similar tableau of frozen movement in a timeless spring landscape. Like Botticelli, Milton used such a moment of stasis to heighten and universalize his mythic material, until the dance itself represents something ritual and holy, an iconographic embodiment of an eternal present, like the figures on Keats' urn."[58] What Botticelli painted was virtually an allegorizing of

---

[56] Knott, *Milton's Pastoral Vision*, p. 47, and Ryken, *The Apocalyptic Vision*, p. 93.

[57] Ovid, *Metamorphoses*, i, 107. Knott, *Milton's Pastoral Vision*, p. 37n. notes later literary developments of the theme.

[58] Spencer, *Heroic Nature*, p. 112. So far as I have been able to discover, Hughes was the first to cite this parallel in his edition of *Paradise Lost* (iv, 266n.), but Charles G. Osgood, *The Classical Mythology of Milton's English Poems*, p. lxvi, noted the relationship between

the theme of eternal spring, of which Milton's poetic description provides a brief but crisply visual vignette.[59]

What Botticelli allegorized, other painters merely accepted. The pastoral idea in Italian, and especially in Venetian, painting continued as a major influence in which a seasonless paradise was often assumed. According to Turner, "it involves either the pagan or the Christian, at home in bountiful land, blessed by the sun yet endowed with cool shade, a place that knows neither season nor weather."[60] We find the same visual conception evident in the Eden paintings of Jan "Flower" Bruegel the Elder, for whom "Paradise was the place where all the flowers of the year bloomed simultaneously," as Gertraude Winkelmann-Rhein has observed.[61] Milton's seasonless Garden would have raised no problems, either visual or conceptual, for cultivated readers whose imagination had been schooled by such art.

The variety and contrast of views Milton provides in his scenic descriptions also accorded well with the aesthetic tastes and principles of his culture. Thomas Kranidas has properly observed that "for all its magnificent unity, *Paradise Lost* is not monolithic. Variety coexists with decorum. Indeed these two important Renaissance concepts enrich and control one another in critical ways."[62] Not only does variety coexist with decorum, but in landscape art especially decorum required variety. As the Ogdens have conclusively shown, "scenery was praised and landscapes admired" for the two principles of variety and contrast, above all others, among seventeenth-century Englishmen. How these principles affected Milton's poetry has been demonstrated by Ogden in greater detail than is possible to recount here, so a few examples must suffice.[63]

Milton early places an emphasis upon variety in the Garden, which was "a happy rural seat of various view," where there were not only rich groves of trees, but

> Betwixt them lawns, or level downs, and flocks
> Grazing the tender herb, were interposed,
> Or palmy hillock, or the flowery lap
> Of some irriguous valley spread her store,
> Flowers of all hue, and without thorn the rose.
>
> (IV, 247, 252-56)

"the flowery-kirtled Naiades" of *Comus*, 254, with "the figure of Primavera in Botticelli's *Spring*. Her robe, loose and flowing, is richly embroidered all over with a pattern consisting of little bunches of flowers."

[59] For close analyses of Botticelli's *Primavera*, see Gombrich, *Symbolic Images*, pp. 31-35, 37-64, and Erwin Panofsky, *Renaissance and Renascences*, New York, 1972, pp. 193-200.

[60] Turner, *The Vision of Landscape*, p. 125, and also p. 212.

[61] Gertraude Winkelmann-Rhein, *Paintings and Drawings of Jan "Flower" Bruegel*, New York, 1969, p. 22.

[62] Kranidas, *The Fierce Equation*, p. 143.

[63] Ogden and Ogden, *English Taste in Landscape*, p. 37a, and Henry V. S. Ogden, "The Principles of Variety and Contrast in Seventeenth Century Aesthetics, and Milton's Poetry," 159-82. Hannah D. Demaray uses the phrase "controlled irregularity" in discussing the landscape variety and contrast in Eden, in her "Milton's 'Perfect' Paradise and the Landscapes of Eden," *Milton Quarterly* 8 (1974), 37-38.

The sweep of Milton's description is representative of landscape painting in general, after the time when perspective was firmly and skilfully employed by artists. Again and again in his visualization of Eden (and indeed of earthly geography elsewhere), Milton insisted upon a variety of contour and topography, contrasting rock and water, hill and plain, forest and open field. To achieve such sweeping effects, he often established his point of vision high above the terrain he set out to describe.

Point of view is important in all painting, and in landscape painting a high point of view is often essential. The advantage of painting from raised ground is obvious, was early established by Antonio Pollaiuolo and Alesso Baldovinetti, and not even the innovative Leonardo da Vinci chose to depart from this convention.[64] There were of course circumstances in which a long view could be achieved from relatively low ground, but these did not so often occur. In those instances when artists virtually "mapped" the possessions of their patron in a landscape view, the paintings remind us somewhat of photographs taken from an aircraft or balloon. In the Palazzo Vecchio in Florence, the frescoes about the central courtyard are devoted to suggesting the major possessions of the royal house of Austria, and these "might better be described as aerial maps than as landscapes."[65]

The same observation might be made of some of Milton's vast panoramas, which are designed to suggest the majesty of God's Creation and of Adam's domain. Though prospect paintings could be executed for the aggrandizement of some particular family or regime, as in the Palazzo Vecchio murals and *mutatis mutandis* in Milton's panoramas, they need not have any such propagandistic purpose. Prospect paintings were in great demand in the seventeenth century, and in no country was this vogue more pronounced than in England. Indeed, as the Ogdens have concluded, "the liking for an extensive and variegated view was the dominant characteristic of English taste in landscape at this period," and Milton's epic descriptions both represent and appeal to that established taste.[66] A representative expression of the English preferences along this line may be found in an anonymous manuscript entitled "A Short Treatise of Perspective," assigned on the basis of handwriting to the late sixteenth century, where the author praises as the chief form of landscape that "which expresseth places of larger prospecte, as whole countries where the eye seemeth not to be hindred by any objectes . . . ether of nature or arte, but to passe as farre as the force thereofe can pierce."[67] Typical of his time and country, Milton delighted in such wide vistas as exposed whole countries to the view, and they are encountered frequently in both his epics. Outdoing the prospect of a single country alone, Satan at the foot of the golden stairs "looks down with wonder at the sudden view/ Of all this world at once," (III, 542-43) while his view of the created universe is compared to that of a scout who

> at last by break of cheerful dawn
> Obtains the brow of some high-climbing hill,

[64] Turner, *The Vision of Landscape*, p. 18.
[65] *Ibid.*, p. 200.
[66] Ogden and Ogden, *English Taste in Landscape*, p. 48a-b.
[67] *Ibid.*, pp. 1b-2a.

Which to his eye discovers unaware
The goodly prospect of some foreign land
First seen, or some renowned metropolis
With glistering spires and pinnacles adorned,
Which now the rising sun gilds with his beams.

(III, 544-51)

The Mount of Vision provides Adam with a somewhat similar prospect, and Milton with another opportunity for a poetic description of sweeping landscape:

He looked and saw wide territory spread
Before him, towns, and rural works between
Cities of men with lofty gates and towers,
Concourse in arms, fierce faces threatening war. . . .

(XI, 638-41)

In *Paradise Lost*, it is only in the last books that Milton's panoramic descriptions can include cities and activities of men, but in *Paradise Regained* his opportunities are unfettered. When Satan takes Christ "up to a mountain high" to view the kingdoms of this world, Milton indulges to the full his delight in landscape poetry, with vast fields and mountains and with "huge cities and high towered, that well might seem/ The seats of mightiest monarchs" (*PR*, III, 261-62). Those descriptions will be treated in more detail in the chapter on *Paradise Regained*, but they should be recalled here as indicative both of Milton's interests and of his skill in presenting what the Ogdens have called "the long view with its multiplicity of objects."[68]

The taste for huge vistas was not purely English, of course, and may be found in many seventeenth-century painters, perhaps most notably in Poussin and Claude. It was also evident in French landscape architecture, especially in the works of André Le Nôtre, who at the château of Vaux-le-Vicomte between 1656 and 1661 "created the first of those huge vistas of his, with their wide surfaces of water and green framed by groves of trees, which gave the inhabitant of the château a seemingly limitless view, an imposing avenue that continues the architecture into the midst of nature." The gardens at Versailles again demonstrate "the manner by which Le Nôtre draws the eye of the observer to the distant horizon in a leisurely progress in which the natural and artificial elements of trees, grass, and water are skillfully composed."[69]

Though Milton seems to have delighted most in sweeping panoramic views, he also on occasion briefly describes closed-in perspectives, as in his shaded bowers and alleys. Bowers would obviously be enclosed, so that the view would be restricted, and also so that the sense of color and light would be affected. Milton thus wrote that "the unpierced shade/ Embrowned the noontide bowers" (IV, 245-46), and John Peter has found awkward connotations in those lines and the "inadvertent suggestion that 'the noontide bowers' are dry and sunburned."[70] The Italian *imbrunire*, from which it is universally agreed that Milton's word was

[68] *Ibid.*, p. 59a.
[69] Bazin, *Baroque and Rococo*, pp. 118 and 123, and see also 125.
[70] Peter, *A Critique of "Paradise Lost,"* p. 87.

derived, does not suggest parching at all, but rather making dark and overcast, surely the most appropriate conception for the interior of a bower. In *Paradise Regained* (II, 293), Milton does indeed refer directly to "alleys brown," just as *Paradise Lost* (IV, 626) has "alleys green." That distinction is valid, and depends upon the kind of planting used to create the alleys. In the development of Italian gardens, Shepherd and Jellicoe tell us, "the necessity of getting from one place to another in shade suggested pleached alleys, such as those of the Villa Gori at Siena, which form practically the entire garden, and those in Valzanzibio, which enable one to make almost a complete circuit in shade."[71] Often and perhaps usually, such pleached alleys, formed as they were by interweaving the branches of plants, exposed to the view of one walking within them the brownish impression of branches and bark, to give a predominant color sensation of brownness, whereas other alleys, especially those without a pleached covering of bare limbs and vine stalks, would expose primarily the greenery of the leaves. Depending upon the setting, we may have embrowned bowers, or alleys brown, or alleys green: each phrase conveys an accurate perception of what Milton wishes us to see.

Color perceptions ranging between brown and embrowned (in the Italian sense) may also be found in a certain type of landscape painting, devoted to the forest interior, which was largely developed by late sixteenth- and seventeenth-century Flemish artists. Taking the works of Paolo Fiammingo and of Gillis van Coninxloo as typical, the Ogdens note that in these pictures "the spectator is placed within the forest, immediately in front of large-limbed, heavy-foliaged trees. His viewpoint is relatively low; he does not look down upon the scene, but straight ahead at the tree trunk and up at the leaves."[72] In such views, the reflection of light will obviously be largely from the trunks and branches of trees, and from the soil, so as to give a decidedly brownish visual impression. Milton's descriptions of landscapes with shallow perspectives thus accurately represent both the visual experience of Renaissance gardens and of paintings of forest interiors—and, indeed, of nature itself. Whether the predominant impression, for Milton or for us, be of green or of brown, primarily depends upon the surfaces from which the light reflects.

As we have seen thus far, Milton's landscape descriptions accord well both with the general aesthetic principles and the practical preferences of his culture, whether in landscape architecture or in landscape painting. Having established Milton's relationship to that general background, we can now turn to the details, both greater and lesser, of his description of the Garden in Eden, and correlate those with similar details in pictorial representations of the same subject.

[71] Shepherd and Jellicoe, *Italian Gardens of the Renaissance*, p. 43.
[72] Ogden and Ogden, *English Taste in Landscape*, p. 41a.

XIV

The Garden of Eden in Milton and in Pictorial Art

LARGER FEATURES OF THE LANDSCAPE

AESTHETIC theory, landscape architecture, and landscape painting all lie behind the perfection of the Garden in *Paradise Lost* and help us to understand Milton's achievement. In addition, many art works were expressly devoted to representing the Garden, and it is with these works that Milton's descriptions must now be compared. We will see that Milton conformed rather closely with the traditions of representing Eden which prevailed in art between the Renaissance and the seventeenth century, but also that he was quite willing to introduce very ancient visual motifs which were no longer fashionable, though still accessible, in his own time.

A case in point is the Mount of Paradise, which in the earliest Christian art was shown as a typical mesa formation, with steep sides and a flat top. It is this visual conception which Milton evokes in his description of "A woody mountain, whose high top was plain,/ A circuit wide" (VIII, 303-4). In Paleo-Christian art, Christ may be shown as standing on such a mountain with precipitate sides and a top almost as flat as a table, or the Heavenly City may be built on it, or sheep may be shown grazing there. Whether with Christ or the city or the lamb, this mesa recurs again and again in early Christian, Romano-Byzantine, and Byzantine art.[1] Milton could have encountered this view in mosaics of ancient churches in Rome, as in SS. Cosmo e Damiano, or he might have seen it in the newly rediscovered catacombs. On all the ancient Christian sarcophagi illustrated in Bosio's *Roma Sotterranea* of 1632 on which the mount appears, it is presented in just this form.

III

This conception of the Mount of Paradise with the top "plain" of a mesa occurs only once in *Paradise Lost*, and is contradicted by Milton's more consistent emphasis upon the mountains, valleys, and hills of Paradise (IV, 254-55, 260-61; IX, 116). The discrepancy is irreconcilable, though it is usually overlooked and I recall no critic who has questioned it. Milton's predominant view accords with the variety and contrast usually found in the Garden of Eden paintings of the sixteenth and seventeenth centuries. The introduction of these two discrepant geological formations is another instance of Milton's attempt to vivify his epic descriptions by recalling elements of the visual tradition to the maximum feasible extent.

The four rivers which issue from Paradise may be traced to Genesis 2:10.

---

[1] Réau, *Iconographie*, II, i, p. 80, and Giuseppe Bovini, *Ravenna: An Art City*, Ravenna, n.d., p. 64.

"A favorite subject in early Christian mosaics in Rome and Ravenna," as Helen Gardner has written, these waters run under the surface of the ground, as in Milton's account, and they are shown as issuing from the sides of the mesa (IV, 223-35).[2] Renaissance gardens often tried to imitate the Garden of Eden or to recapture a sense of it, as we have seen, and such attempts were carried even to the point of providing four streams or rivulets, a landscaping tradition traceable to thirteenth- and fourteenth-century France.[3] After the Renaissance, artists showed as little concern as Milton does for a precise tracing of the four rivers, but streams and fountains could still be found in representations of the Garden.

149, 156, 59

The wall surrounding Eden was a visual feature upon which most medieval artists insisted, and various types of walls are encountered in art over a period of several hundred years. Constructed of stone or brick, though sometimes of plaited wickerwork, their designs usually expressed the architectural and building skills of the period in which they were painted. Such a masonry wall appears as late as a *Biblia Historiale* published in Paris in 1517 and presumably may be found even later, but it was no longer a common element of Biblical paintings and illustrations. Milton's continuation of this largely outdated structure may be due to the popularity of the *hortus conclusus* tradition in poetry from the Song of Songs down to his own day, and it may also represent another instance of his consistent attempt to introduce into his epic descriptions the most salient features of the pictorial renderings of the same subject.

156, 160

At all events, the wall is there as a striking feature of Milton's Garden landscape, though he perfectly adapts it to his own conception by making it no longer a masonry wall but rather a "verduous wall," composed of thickets of tall trees (IV, 142-49). By this expedient, he was able to preserve the *hortus conclusus*, and yet to maintain consistency with the more realistic visions of Eden inculcated by the arts of the preceding two centuries. Verduous walls were frequently one of the more striking features in Renaissance gardens. Trees and shrubs were trained and intertwined so as to provide "hairy sides/ With thicket overgrown," which denied access, and which "overhead upgrew/ Insuperable heighth of loftiest shade" (IV, 135-38). Venturini's engravings of the Tivoli Gardens in the seventeenth century show a number of such walls, which extend upward to four times the height of a man.[4] It was a "natural" wall of this kind which Milton provided for the Garden and which Satan overleaped.

The motifs of the mesa, the four rivers, and the garden wall of Eden were all traceable to Paleo-Christian or medieval art. In other regards, Milton's vision ac-

[2] Gardner, *A Reading of "Paradise Lost,"* p. 78.

[3] Battisti, "*Natura Artificiosa* to *Natura Artificialis*," p. 10. The prototype is clearly Near Eastern, and the tradition was still vital enough in seventeenth-century India to be represented in the Taj Mahal.

[4] Coffin, *The Villa d'Este*, figs. 14-15 and 29. Milton's descriptions repeatedly invite comparison with later developments of English landscape gardening, and his verduous wall had a number of the advantages of the "ha-ha," which Bridgeman designed for Vanbrugh so as to provide a man-made fence for an estate, but excavated so that its harsh lines could not clash with the gentleness of the landscape views.

cords fully with artistic developments of the Renaissance and after—most pervasively perhaps in his insistence upon sweeping panoramas of the Garden. Medieval views, by and large, were severely restricted in scope, and featured only a few *161* details. Experiments in perspective, such as were carried out in the fifteenth century, were necessary before artists could begin to envision anything approaching the "circuit wide" of Milton's Eden (VIII, 304). With expanded scope and improved perspective, it became possible to present in paintings the variety and contrast which became such favorite elements of seventeenth-century taste. As early as the year 1500 or thereabout, even a manuscript illumination such as the Eden scene in the Grimani Breviary showed not only the first parents and the *162* Tempter, but a grove of trees, a natural fountain, and an open glade within the surrounding woods. Cranach's *Paradise* of a few years later provides even greater *163* variety as between clearings and forest, and contrasts both with rocky hills in the upper left of the canvas, but the land contours are more monotonous than would soon be found in such paintings. The Eden paintings by Rubens at The Hague, and *VII* by Jan Bruegel in London and in Rome, are more typical of the later develop- *158, 159* ments, with a lavish variation between woods, forest glade, and flowing water. Closest of all to Milton is the Edenic landscape found in the backgrounds of those tapestries devoted to the story of Adam and Eve which were executed by unknown Flemish masters for the Medici and delivered to them in Florence in the fifteen fifties. There we can find virtually every aspect of Milton's varied scenic concep- *148-54* tion of Eden, as we shall see.

The most conspicuous feature of the skyline of Milton's Paradise is the huge rock mountain at the eastern gate, which is described with vivid poetic detail:

> it was a rock
> Of alablaster, piled up to the clouds,
> Conspicuous far, winding with one ascent
> Accessible from earth, one entrance high;
> The rest was craggy cliff, that overhung
> Still as it rose, impossible to climb.
>
> (IV, 543-48)

Visually, Milton's description continues a tradition that goes back as far as those craggy hills of cold, white rock which the artists of International Gothic loved to paint.[5] Though the Gothic style went out of fashion, craggy rock formations continued to provide interest in landscape backgrounds for such paintings as Filippo Lippi's *Madonna and Child* at the Uffizi and his *Virgin and Child with Saints* at the National Gallery in London, where it is also seen in the *Adoration of the Kings* by Bramantino, as well as in the *Adoration of the Child* painted in the mid-sixteenth century by Gerolamo da Carpi, now in the Uffizi. In each of these Renaissance and Mannerist paintings, the material of the mountain continues to show the hue and

---

[5] Bottrall, "The Baroque Element in Milton," 38, takes Milton's rock of alabaster to be Baroque, but therein we see one of the dangers of a Baroque preoccupation. As a description, Milton's eastern mountain could as well be taken to evoke International Gothic as Baroque.

texture of alabaster or alablaster, which was defined in Cockeram's English dictionary of 1623 as "a very cold marble, white and clear."[6]

Seventeenth-century Englishmen were particularly taken with great masses of bare rocks rising in the landscape paintings they most admired, as the Ogdens have shown: "The liking for great rock masses in the foreground and the frequent use of mountains and hills at the horizon, not to mention the Alpine landscapes, make it clear that painters and picture collectors admired mountainous scenery as much as any other kind."[7] Basing their conclusions not only on the art works collected, but also on the opinions of representative Englishmen, the Ogdens demonstrate a widespread seventeenth-century fascination with great rocks, precipices, and stone mountains.[8] Citing the popularity of Brill's pictures of "bare rock masses rising at steep angles," and sketches by Inigo Jones representing irregular Alpine scenery and dolomitic peaks, they associate the popularity of such views with the universal emphasis upon variety and contrast. On the masquing stage in London, such rock scenery was so overworked as to provoke Chapman to comment: "Rocks? Nothing but rocks in these masquing devices? Is invention so poor she must needs ever dwell among rocks?"[9]

Milton's description of those cliffs at the eastern gate of Paradise provide as fine an example as one might wish of this pervasive English taste. The taste was not merely general in landscape, however, and not merely English—rocky masses were standard features in pictorial renditions of the Garden of Eden. In the sixty-volume, profusely illustrated Kitto Bible at the Huntington Library, a steep stone mountain is so frequently found in the background of pictures illustrating the Creation and the Garden that it would be impracticable to list every instance prior to Milton's time. These illustrations are for the most part engravings, but the alabaster mountain also appears with great regularity in famous oil paintings such as the Paradise panel of Bosch's *Hay Wain*, where the mountain is unmistakably of alabasterlike stone. Mabuse's *Fall of Man* is enacted at the foot of a huge and

157 precipitous mountain of whitish stone which towers over the landscape of Eden. Cranach's *Paradise* shows a more level terrain, but is still dominated by two "rocky pillars" of precipitate angle and alabaster appearance, such as those between which

163 Milton had seated Gabriel. Finally, there are the Medici tapestries of the Eden saga, which accord with Milton's descriptions in this as in other ways. When God conveys Adam into the Garden, the tapestry sets the scene before a craggy peak of

149 alabaster; similarly, the tapestry illustrating the Fall shows Adam and Eve clothing themselves in fig leaves beneath the towering silhouette of that alabaster mountain

152 on the far horizon; finally, the tapestry of the Expulsion represents those same

154 peaks on the horizon behind the couple as they leave the Garden. It would be possible to cite many other pictorial representations of analogues to Milton's moun-

[6] In the note on this passage in his edition of *The Complete Poems*, Hughes identifies Milton's "alablaster" with the modern alabaster, quotes the definition in Cockeram, and cites various literary and geographical parallels.

[7] Ogden and Ogden, *English Taste in Landscape*, p. 36b.

[8] *Ibid.*, pp. 37ff.

[9] *Ibid.*, pp. 45a-b, and 22a.

tains of Paradise, but enough has been said to establish the tradition to which he adheres in his poetic descriptions.[10] Though Milton gave that "craggy cliff" its immortal expression in verse, it already existed in pictorial art, ready at hand as a vision for the poet to evoke and for the reader to recognize with pleasure.

FAUNA AND FLORA

Readers have been repeatedly struck by the sheer luxuriance of the Garden in *Paradise Lost*.[11] The scenes to which we are introduced are flowery, sweetly perfumed by natural scents, varied in light and shade and contour of forest, glade, and water, and in sum totally delicious. But there are occasional signs of excess in such delights, even if it be what Arnold Stein has called an "authorized excess."[12] Adam speaks of "branches overgrown," or "wanton growth," and of blossoms and dropping gums which "ask riddance" as they "lie bestrown unsightly and unsmooth" (IV, 627-32). What Adam and Eve can prune or "lop" away, they find that "one night or two with wanton growth derides/ Tending to wild" (IX, 210-12). We are shown where "fruit trees overwoody reached too far/ Their pampered boughs," and are told that "Nature here/ Wantoned as in her prime, . . . pouring forth more sweet,/ Wild above rule or art" (V, 213-14 and 294-97).

Such excess demands the best efforts of Adam and Eve to prune and remove the unwanted growth. This work of "tending" the Garden had been allegorized from the time of Philo through that of Raleigh, More, and Milton: according to this moral interpretation of the Garden, "Reason was to control the Passions, protect the Virtues, and generally keep the Soul in good order."[13] Barbara Lewalski in a cogent analysis connects the situation here with Milton's views expressed in *Areopagitica* and elsewhere and observes that "for Adam and Eve the external paradise can be secure only so long as they cultivate and enhance the paradise within."[14] In Italy, gardening as such had long been taken as symbolic of the conquest of virtue over vice, whereas the development of the *jardin anglais* at a later date was postulated upon a distinctive English assumption: "the aristocrat's acceptance of nature as an equal (provided she were properly groomed)," as Jellicoe puts it in a phrase which captures many elements of the attitude Milton displays in *Paradise Lost*.[15]

Milton has been credited with notable innovations here, as when Evans tells

[10] See Lars-Ivar Ringbom, *Paradisus Terrestris, Myt, Bild Och Verklighet*, Helsingfors, 1958, pp. 39-45, 57, 60, 66, and 69.

[11] See MacCaffrey, *"Paradise Lost" as Myth*, pp. 148-56; Stein, *Answerable Style*, pp. 58-72; A. Bartlett Giamatti, *The Earthly Paradise and the Renaissance Epic*, Princeton, 1966, pp. 299-313.

[12] Stein, *Answerable Style*, p. 63.

[13] Evans, *"Paradise Lost" and the Genesis Tradition*, p. 250. See also Jean Daniélou, *Primitive Christian Symbols*, Baltimore, 1964, pp. 25-35, and Stewart, *The Enclosed Garden*, p. 51.

[14] Barbara Lewalski, "Innocence and Experience in Milton's Eden," in *New Essays on "Paradise Lost"* (ed. Kranidas), p. 96.

[15] Battisti, *"Natura Artificiosa to Natura Artificialis,"* p. 23, and Jellicoe, *Studies in Landscape Design*, I, p. 33.

us that this "Eden, in all its order and beauty, does not have the stability attributed to it by earlier poets. It does not share the timeless perfection of medieval paintings of it, because the difference between art and nature is that nature grows."[16] I had expected that Edenic perfection to be a consistent feature in the visual arts, but found to my surprise that this was not so, and that artists often implied a situation very similar to what Milton describes in *Paradise Lost*. We find a manuscript illumination of the Fall as early as the thirteenth century which shows a small branch broken off the right side of the Tree of Knowledge. In a print of 1530 by Lucas van Leyden, many branches have been broken off, leaving jagged splinters on the parent trees—but there are no branches lying on the ground. They cannot simply have disappeared, and there was not time enough for them to have rotted into humus. In the woodcut of the Fall (attributed to Dürer) for the 1544 Lyons edition of Luther's Bible, the tree to Eve's right has several stubs of branches, of which at least the lower two appear to have been cut off rather than broken; again the absence of branches beneath the tree implies that someone has been policing the grounds. In the oil by Frans Floris, the two limbs under Adam's left hand have been chopped off or severed in some way. The drawing by Mabuse, on the other hand, shows a broken branch, with the irregular splintering effect which comes from breaking rather than cutting, and the same applies to the painting by Cornelisz van Haarlem. The tree in the foreground of the elder Jan Bruegel's *Garden of Eden* in London has lost a branch on its right side, but whether by breaking or clipping I cannot be sure.

How are we to interpret these hewn and splintered branches, which show that growth has been removed from the trees and also from the area around the trees, leaving no trace of debris? A cultivated seventeenth-century European, accustomed to "reading" the meaning of pictures, may very well have concluded from this visual evidence that Adam and Eve had been busy dressing and keeping the Garden, as Genesis 2:15 indicates they were required to do even before the Fall. Where "branches overgrown" required attention, they would "lop their wanton growth," or remove the detritus which lay "bestrown unsightly and unsmooth" so that the Garden might be "tread with ease," as in *Paradise Lost* (IV, 629-32). Such an hypothesis has much to commend it, but it must remain tentative because the evidence to support it is entirely deductive and inferential, and I have found no pictorial representations of prelapsarian Adam and Eve actually pruning and clearing the Garden. In the most active representation I have found of Adam and Eve as gardeners, the frontispiece to John Parkinson's *Paradisi in Sole* of 1629, Adam is shown apparently plucking fruit and Eve stooping to pick a flower, but neither is pruning. In the absence of what lawyers call dispositive evidence, it is still possible to interpret the missing branches as purely a symbolic foreshadowing in visual allusion to the words of Christ in John 15:4-6: "As the branch cannot bear fruit itself, except it abide in the vine, no more can ye, except ye abide in me . . . . He that abideth in me, and I in him, the same bringeth forth much fruit . . . . If a man abide not in me, he is cast forth as a branch, and is withered; and men gather them and cast them into the fire, and they are burned."

[16] Evans, *"Paradise Lost" and the Genesis Tradition*, p. 249.

Michelangelo also comes to mind here, for in his Sistine painting of the Fall there is, to the left of the Tree of Knowledge, the barren stump of another tree— lifeless, dry, and dead. This evidence of pruning or clearing (again there is no fallen *169* trunk by the stump) is as close an approach to Milton as can be found in Michelangelo. Otherwise, the two men are polar opposites in their visions of Eden. Where Milton gives us luxuriance, Michelangelo provides little more than a sandy desert. As Wölfflin describes his painting, "there is no landscape, not even a blade of grass if it is not essential; here and there, tucked away in a corner, there is an indication of fern-like vegetation—this expresses the appearance of vegetation on the earth, and one tree signifies the Garden of Eden."[17] Michelangelo's landscape of Paradise is so pervasively unattractive, so desolate, that we may well wonder whether his Adam and Eve were driven to hopelessness, so as to sin out of despair rather than presumption.

The utter desolation of Michelangelo's Paradise sets him apart not only from Milton but from most other artists. Eden was traditionally represented in art as an abundantly fertile paradise of fauna and flora. We find this tradition as early as the fifth century in an ivory diptych now in Florence, and insofar as was possible within the limits imposed by what Kenneth Clark has called "the symbolic landscape," medieval artists often suggested a richness of life.[18] After the fifteenth century, luxuriance abounds in virtually every view of Eden, even on occasions *156, 160* suggesting "a vast wild park" as in the Window of Chariots created for St. Vincent in Rouen about 1525.[19] It is in the seventeenth century, however, that we find the closest pictorial analogues to the fertile luxuriance of Milton's Garden. In England, the stained glass window executed in 1641 by Abraham van Linge for University *VI* College, Oxford, shows Eden with the lush overgrowth of a rain forest. On the continent, it was Rubens, as we would expect, who comes closest to the opulence *VII* of Milton's conception of Eden, in his *Fall of Adam and Eve at the Hague.* Jan "Velvet" Bruegel's several paintings of Paradise visualize a similar opulence and *158, 159* even exuberance in nature.[20] What David Daiches has written of Milton's Eden could apply equally well to such paintings as those I have illustrated: "Nature, both animal and vegetable, is described with an almost Baroque luxuriance, but a heraldic formality controls the profusion and prevents any suggestion of the florid."[21] Milton's paradise of all the senses (VIII, 526-28) is suggested in many art works, but it is given full symbolic statement in a lovely unsigned engraving of the late sixteenth or early seventeenth century.[22] Here we see Eve presented to Adam, *170*

[17] Wölfflin, *Classic Art,* p. 53.

[18] Lowrie, *Monuments,* fig. 113, and p. 285.

[19] Mâle, *Religious Art,* pp. 138-39, and reproduced as fig. 90 in von Witzleben, *Stained Glass in French Cathedrals.*

[20] See also Bruegel's painting at Hampton Court Palace, and the Adam and Eve paintings by Jordaens in the museums at Varsovie and Budapest, reproduced as plates 84 and 85 in Leo van Puylvelde, *Jordaens,* Paris, 1953. Hannah D. Demaray, Milton's 'Perfect' Paradise and the Landscape of Italy," 37-38, considers Jacopo Bassano's *Earthly Paradise,* as well as *The Garden of Eden* by Rubens and Bruegel and other works, as related to Milton's Garden.

[21] David Daiches, *Milton,* London, 1957, p. 188.

[22] The engraving is mounted in the *Kitto Bible,* I, p. 171. I am indebted to R. R. Wark of the Huntington Art Gallery for consultation on the date of this anonymous work.

each arousing an immediate and electric response in the other, within a scene of Paradise which is surrounded by figures personifying the five senses—in all, such "a wilderness of sweets" as we find in Milton (v, 294). This does not mean that Milton need have seen any of these particular pictures. Such pictorial renderings of the Garden were traditional, and Milton's descriptive greatness consists neither in having copied their visual programs nor in having originated the concept but rather in having given to the form its ultimate expression in verse.

Usually Milton conforms rather closely to one or another of the established visual traditions, but at other times he introduces scenes rarely encountered in art, as in his description of the lion who "in his paw/ Dandled the kid" (iv, 343-44). This seems to be a development of the Biblical image of the lion lying down with the lamb, and one would expect to find that scene frequently in art, but I have not *VII* been able to do so. In one Rubens' painting, we see two leopards "fighting" play-fully, and two lions do the same in the Bruegel painting in the Galleria Doria, while *158, 159* in Bruegel's Victoria and Albert painting two spaniels bark innocuously at swans, who hiss back in reply, as though it were all an idyllic pastime. Dürer's famous *164* print of 1504 shows a singularly unpredacious cat sleeping quietly, while flanked by a relaxed mouse and a lethargic rabbit. Such representations of the peaceable kingdom were standard in art, but Milton's lion dandling the kid strangely seems not to have been so popular.

Adam's naming of the animals does not appear to have achieved the same popularity in art as did the procession of animals into Noah's Ark, though the two stories offered very much the same visual opportunities. Milton's account of the naming shows "each bird and beast . . ./ Approaching two by two" (viii, 348-50), and Fowler has annotated the line as "a grim reminder of the next mythic gathering of the beasts, 'two and two unto Noah into the Ark' (Gen. 7:9)." This suggestion is attractive, and is in keeping with Milton's frequent ironic foreshadowings. It should also be noted that the two by two procession of animals before Adam in visual art antedated *Paradise Lost* by at least one century: we find it already in one *150* of the Medici tapestries, where the animals proceed in a delightfully childlike vision, divided into three columns according to their kind, while above, "the total kind/ Of birds in orderly array on wing/ Came summoned over Eden to receive/ Their names" (vi, 73-76). And in the background, above Adam's head, is the familiar silhouette of those alabaster peaks.

As "the unwieldy elephant" marches past, we note that he has "wreathed/ His lithe proboscis." A similar wreathing may be observed in Queen Mary's Psalter, in the Creation ceiling of the Chapel of the Trinity in the Gesù in Rome, *159* and also in Bruegel, but in none of these instances is the gesture designed "to make them mirth," as it is in *Paradise Lost* (iv, 345-47). One must strain in order to interpret many elephants in pictorial representations of Eden as analogous to Mil-ton's comic conception, because the elephant had for centuries been taken as the symbol for chastity. In the bestiary legends, elephants were unable to conceive unless the female could get fruit from a tree in a sacred garden, beguile the male into eating it, and then follow the course of nature. This story was repeatedly alluded to in the Middle Ages as exemplifying the virginity of Adam and Eve in the Garden until they ate the fruit of the Tree.[23] Roman Catholic tradition continued to use the elephant as a symbol of virtually absolute chastity even well into the seventeenth century. To return to the Medici tapestry, we note that the elephant there is single, which clearly indicates that the artist wishes to suggest, by long-standing association, the story of the sexlessness of the life of Adam and Eve in Eden. In this respect, these tapestries, in so many ways very close to Milton's descriptions, are farthest from *Paradise Lost*, so that the wreathed proboscis is probably only coincidental. In Milton, as Heckscher has noted, that gesture reduces the elephant to "little more than a clown entertaining Adam and Eve," and it strikes me as more than a little likely that Milton was purposely converting the elephant, and his traditional significance, into a *jeu d'esprit* for the entertainment of Adam and Eve, and of the reader.[24]

As with the animals, many different kinds of trees are found in Milton's Eden: these include laurel, myrtle, acanthus, cedar, palm, fir, pine, banyan, gourd, elm, plantan, and citron.[25] In his edition of *Paradise Lost*, Fowler notes (IV, 138-43) that "the only unconventional tree in Milton's list is the palm, which is possibly to be accounted for by Psalm 92:12: 'the righteous shall flourish like the palm tree; he shall grow like a cedar in Lebanon,' " and he cites Du Bartas who takes the palm as an emblem of chastity or marital loyalty. Fowler's literary analogues are illuminating, but it should be noted that the palm was not "unconventional" in artistic representations of Eden: it appears in Raphael's *Creation of the Animals*, and repeatedly in the Medici tapestry series. The Kitto Bible volumes devoted to Genesis contain so many instances of palm trees in woodcuts and engravings that it would be tedious to list them. Milton mentions no variety of tree in Eden more often than the palm, and in giving it this prominence he is in close accord with the visual tradition.[26]

113
148, 149,
153

The most important tree in the Garden is unquestionably the Tree of the Knowledge of Good and Evil, and Milton describes it in a number of visual contexts. He places it next to a fountain, and in so doing follows a convention which can be found in works of art over many centuries. Paul A. Underwood informs us that "the fountain, whether or not it has any connotation of baptism, has a setting in Paradise or Eden always described in texts or depicted in art as a park," and he adds that the flowing water of Eden was taken from early Christian times as a symbol or image of Christ flowing from his Father.[27] In addition to the fountain, Milton specifies that the Tree grows on level ground—"Beyond a row of myrtles, on a flat,/ Fast by a fountain" (IX, 627-28). On the row of myrtles I can contribute

---

[23] G. C. Druce, *The Elephant in Medieval Legend and Art*, London, 1919, pp. 6-8.

[24] William S. Heckscher, "Bernini's Elephant and Obelisk," *The Art Bulletin* 29 (1947), 177n. For other symbolic uses of the elephant, see Klingender, *Animals in Art*, fig. 329b., and pp. 396-97. Baldwin, "Some Extra-Biblical Semitic Influences upon Milton's Story of the Fall of Man," 368, proposes rabbinical lore as the source of Milton's conception.

[25] IV, 139, 478, 693-94; V, 22, 216, 327; IX, 219, 431, 627, and 1101-18.

[26] IV, 139, 254; VI, 885; VIII, 212; and X, 435.

[27] Underwood, "The Fountain of Life in Manuscripts of the Gospels," 46-48.

nothing, but the rest of the description was standard in the visual arts at least from the fourteenth to the sixteenth century. We find the Tree on a level plot next to a fountain in the early fourteenth-century bas relief carvings by Lorenzo Maitani at Orvieto Cathedral, in the Eden fresco executed somewhat later in the same century for the Camposanto at Pisa, and in two early fifteenth-century manuscripts, *Les Très Riches Heures du Duc de Berry* and in the Bedford Book of Hours. In the first two, the fountain is little more than a simple baptismal font of the kind found in most parish churches, whereas in the latter two it is surrounded and surmounted by an elaborate Gothic tabernacle, a form which frequently appears late in the fifteenth and early in the sixteenth centuries, and is represented in England by the window in King's College Chapel, Cambridge.[28] However the fountain was designed, it typically appeared on a level place beside the Tree. Early printed books made use of this arrangement, as may be seen in the illustration for Hartmann Schedel's *Liber Chronicarum* printed at Nuremberg in 1493, and in the Bible published by Barthelmy Verard in Paris in about 1517. Among later illuminated manuscripts, the Grimani Breviary of about 1500 maintains the traditional flat ground by the Tree but it represents the fountain as a natural spring emerging from the ground in a little pool: here we see a change in one of the traditional motifs in the iconography of Eden.

The placing of baptismal fonts, whether plain or elaborate, as fountains in Eden had achieved widespread popularity in medieval art, but by Milton's time this motif no longer exerted its former appeal. The seventeenth-century attitude may be evidenced by John Evelyn who cites as a ridiculous anachronism "that *piece* of *Malvogius* in His *Majesties Gallery* at *Whitehall*" which shows "an *Artificial* stone Fountain carv'd with *imagerys* in the midst of his *Paradise*."[29] Medieval conceptions of landscape in art as a set of signs and signals allowed the presence of artificial fountains in Eden, but Renaissance artists explored a new concept, according to which landscape is treated with an apparent realism but with underlying sacramental significance.[30] According to this approach landscape becomes an external and visible sign of inner and spiritual significance, so that the external objects embody and suggest religious and other meanings even as they maintain a realistic appearance.[31] This development in painting and sculpture parallels what we have already observed in landscape gardening:[32] as Tolomei wrote in the early sixteenth century, landscapists "endeavor to make a fountain appear made by nature itself," and after about 1500 we find most artists painting fountains in Eden along natural lines.[33]

---

[28] Hilary Wayment, *The Windows of King's College Chapel, Cambridge*, Oxford, 1972, p. 52, and reproduction of window 3.1.

[29] Evelyn's "To the Reader" in Fréart's *An Idea of the Perfection of Painting*, 1668, sigs. b5-b5v.

[30] See "The Landscape of Symbols" in Kenneth Clark, *Landscape into Art*, Harmondsworth, 1966, pp. 17-30, and Hagstrum, *The Sister Arts*, pp. 44-47.

[31] See Spencer, *Heroic Nature*, pp. 29-30 and 38-39.

[32] See above, pp. 223-24.

[33] Pictorial representations of the fountain in various forms may be found in Ringbom, *Paradisus Terrestris*, pp. 63-66, 88-95.

In Cranach's *Paradise* at Vienna, there appears in the upper left a craggy rock formation, not unlike Milton's "shaggy hill" (IV, 224), from which a spring of water pours outward and downward into a pool. A similar "shaggy hill" appears to the right of the Tree of Knowledge in the *Adam and Eve* panel of the Mabuse triptych at Palermo, though the water issues from a lower part of the rock mass and falls into a stream. The relevance to Milton is that both of these are natural fountains, such as the one he describes, as artists solved the problem of presenting a fountain in Eden without objectionable anachronism. In two Eden paintings by the elder Jan Bruegel, there is no longer a fountain as such, but a small pool, and the tree adjacent to it is not the Tree of Knowledge, which is placed far behind the pool in the background of both canvasses. Other artists abandoned the fountain altogether, as we may see in the paintings by Tintoretto and Cornelisz van Haarlem. In short, the combination of the Tree on a flat by a fountain, which had once been so common, tends to dissolve in the sixteenth century. Executed near the watershed of this evolution, the Grimani Breviary preserves the medieval association while introducing the natural fountain, and so comes closer to Milton's description than any other single picture I know. Later, after the fountain was far removed from the Tree or had disappeared altogether, the Tree was still represented on flat ground, as in virtually all the paintings and prints of Eden reproduced in this book.[34]

163

157

158, 159

173

167

162

Of the Tree itself, only Satan identifies its species, when he reports to his demonic confreres that he has seduced man "with an apple" (X, 487). We have only the word of the master liar to rely upon here, yet I see no compelling reason to doubt Satan at this point.[35] Though early Christians did not generally assume the apple to be the fruit of the Fall, the apple is most frequently found in illustrations of various kinds in British churches. The apple was popular in continental art as well, but the fig also figured prominently, as in the Creation cupola of the atrium of S. Marco in Venice, in Della Robbia ware, and in Raphael's *Fall* in the Vatican, but it rarely if ever appeared in British art.[36] Late in the Middle Ages, and continuing into the sixteenth century, we find some representations with a death's head displayed in the Tree, or even with a skeleton replacing trunk and branches, but this view was clearly out of keeping with Milton's epic form.[37] Mil-

[34] The Frans Floris *Fall* (fig. 165) appears to place Adam and Eve at the Tree on the edge of a precipice, thus achieving a fine metaphorical effect by visual means. The painting is so much in need of cleaning that it cannot be interpreted with great confidence, but we may have in it an interesting foreshadowing of a later treatment in art: Kester Svendsen, "John Martin and the Expulsion Scene in *PL*," 67, notes of Martin's *PL* illustrations that "in nearly every landscape a deep center of recession makes Adam and Eve seem perilously near the edge of a pit or of slopes falling away from them."

[35] Brief exchanges on the identity of the forbidden fruit may be found in the notes contributed by W. W. S., Hibernicus, Percival-Kaye, and Sayar, in *N&Q* 183 (1942), 226-27, 323, and 383. Patrides correctly insists that the *raison d'être* of prohibiting the fruit is far more important than its genus ("The Tree of Knowledge in the Christian Tradition," *SN* 34 [1962], 239-42).

[36] Anderson, *Imagery of British Churches*, p. 89.

[37] Réau, *Iconographie*, II, i, p. 85, and Hollstein, *German Engravings*, II, p. 173, and III, pp. 5 and 172.

ton leaves us free to accept the conventional identification with the apple, as Satan reports, but he does not insist on any species.[38]

When Satan describes the Tree to Eve, his word picture accords with one of the most popular and influential versions of the scene, which may be illustrated by Cranach's arrangement of animals crowding near the Tree about which the serpent
174   is wound:

> About the mossy trunk I wound me soon,
> For high from ground the branches would require
> Thy utmost reach or Adam's: round the Tree
> All other beasts that saw, with like desire
> Longing and envying stood, but could not reach.
>
> (IX, 589-93)

Within the very familiarity of that scene there is one jarring note—all the animals longing for the forbidden fruit. However many animals there may be in traditional pictorial representations, and however closely they may be gathered about the Tree, they never show the slightest interest in the forbidden fruit—with a single exception: the only animal who eats the fruit of the Tree, to my knowledge, is the ape, whose apparent imitation of humanity made him a fit and almost universal symbol for presumptuous sin, and a parallel to Satan who was the ape of God.[39]
The trees of interest to all other animals are legitimately edible: the stag in the
152   Medici tapestry of the *Fall* is browsing the leaves of a different tree, quite naturally, as does a doe in one of the Bruegel scenes, while in another a goat leaps up on the
158, 159 trunk of a tree, seeking its fruit, and an engraving by Jean Mignon shows a horse nibbling the grass. That was the kind of animal activity which the pictorial tradition had accustomed people to expect in the Garden of Eden, and Satan's description distorts without entirely destroying the expected picture: it is another example of Satan's use of a half truth so as to be convincing and deceptive at the same time.
VII   The situation of the fruit so "high from ground" as to require Eve's "utmost reach or Adam's" corresponds to the scene usually found in pictorial art (IX, 589-91): the fruit is almost always over the heads of Adam and Eve, yet not quite out of their reach, a visual metaphor which would have been clear even to the least learned viewer. Sometimes the serpent passes the fruit down, as in Cornelisz van
167   Haarlem, and sometimes Eve reaches gracefully over her head to pluck it as in the
IV   Medici tapestry, while Michelangelo gives us an avaricious grasping gesture on

[38] For various pictorial representations, see Cabrol *et al.*, *Dictionnaire d'archéologie chrétienne*, I, pp. 2699-2706. Dalton, *Byzantine Art*, p. 699, writes that "as the original sacred trees were never real trees of any known species, but artificial compounds of lotus elements, so its descendents in later centuries are always composite," but I have often found the Tree not to be a composite. Trapp, "Iconography," p. 179, cites rare examples of pictorial representations of the forbidden fruit as a grape or a peach, and traces the *malum* pun on evil-apple to the fifth century. He also notes Cranach's use of a dead tree in association with sin in an allegorical altarpiece (p. 181).

[39] See H. W. Janson, *Apes and Ape Lore in the Middle Ages and the Renaissance*, London, 1952, pp. 13-27, 107-44. For the general crowding of the animals about Adam and Eve in art, see Fowler IV, 340-52n. Also see Isa. 11:6-9.

Adam's part. Only rarely is the fruit within easy reach as in the painting by *169*
Francesco Floris, and the drawing by Mabuse. *165, 166*

One of the more memorable images in *Paradise Lost* is that of the vine winding around the elm, implicitly suggesting the proper relationship between Eve and Adam. In their gardening, Milton tells us,

> they led the vine
> To wed her elm; she spoused about him twines
> Her marriageable arms, and with her brings
> Her dower the adopted clusters, to adorn
> His barren leaves.
>
> (v, 215-19)

Milton reintroduces the vine image just before the Fall, when Eve goes to tend her roses alone, and leaves Adam "to wind/ The woodbine round this arbor, or direct/ The clasping ivy where to climb" (ix, 215-17). The symbolism was firmly established in literature: we find it in Horace, Ovid, Virgil, among the classics, and in the Renaissance in Tasso, Spenser, and Shakespeare, to mention but a few.[40] Displaying the proper relationship between wife and husband in marriage, the vine and elm were also taken in the emblem books to suggest *Amicitia*, and the "friendship which lasts after death."[41]

These rather general associations of the feminine vine with the masculine tree had been directly connected, in the visual arts, with the story of the first parents long before Milton wrote *Paradise Lost*. Dalton has pointed out that Byzantine ivory carvings placed borders of vine-scrolls about the story of Adam and Eve, and notes that this presentation was picked up by Italian carvers in the twelfth century and carried on thereafter in the Italian tradition.[42] In the relief of the Creation of Eve executed by Andrea Pisano for the Campanile in Florence, Eve is *176* drawn by the hand from the side of Adam, and directly above her head we see a tree, wound about by a vine. This visual scheme is rich in suggestiveness. The entwined vine may suggest the mercies of Christ (and it is Christ here who creates Eve). In a more sinister sense it foreshadows the familiar shape of the serpent coiled about the Tree of Knowledge, while another visual premonition is provided by the presence, in the left-hand side of the panel, of a fig tree, all reminders of tragedy to come which are quite comparable to the premonitions Milton scatters through his epic account. Pisano's relief may also be taken as a commentary on the marriage relationship, here being created by the emergence of Eve from Adam's rib, and defined by the vine encircling the tree.

[40] See the footnotes in the editions by Hughes, and by Carey and Fowler; and Peter de Metz, "The Elm and the Vine: Notes toward the History of a Marriage *Topos*," *PMLA* 73 (1958), 521-32.

[41] Gombrich, *Symbolic Images*, pp. 139-41 and figs. 150-51, and Mario Praz, *Studies in Seventeenth-Century Imagery*, pp. 96-97.

[42] Dalton, *Byzantine Art*, pp. 218-20. Daniélou, *Primitive Christian Symbols*, pp. 35-40, traces the association of the vine with the Tree of Life in Judaic and primitive Christian art, but that is a somewhat different story, for the vine and its grapes became symbolic of sacrifice and redemption through Christ.

Similarly, the relief of the Fall on the first pilaster in the cathedral of Orvieto frames the episode by placing a tree limb across the top of the carving, and coiling a vine about the limb. In the Medici tapestries, vines coiling about tree trunks are consistently used to fine symbolic and thematic effect. In the tapestry representing the Presentation of Eve to Adam, the two trees which frame the scene, to the left and the right, are both entwined with vines, providing a double emphasis for the symbolism. In the *Fall* tapestry, we see Adam clothing Eve with fig leaves near the right margin, and directly along that margin there is a tree entwined with a vine, visually suggesting the relationship which has now become distorted. A similar irony is achieved in the Judgment tapestry, in which Adam points an accusing finger at Eve, as he kneels at the foot of a vine-covered tree, and Eve sits beneath and to the right of another. Finally, in the Expulsion tapestry, we see in the left margin a tree heavily encased with vines, by which a subdued Adam and Eve pass as they leave the Garden. In each of these pictorial representations, the image of the encircling vine is visually self-explanatory, and could be introduced to similar effect in the visual arts and in poetry, without need for explicit commentary.

151

152

153, 154

Another Miltonic comparison relates Eve to an unsupported flower, but here verbal explanation is necessary. When Satan finds Eve, she is alone among her flowers, which

> she upstays
> Gently with myrtle band, mindless the while,
> Her self, though fairest unsupported flower,
> From her best prop so far, and storm so nigh.
>
> (IX, 430-33)

Jeffry Spencer's analysis of this passage along with that treating the tree and vine is so perceptive of relations between the arts as to require full quotation:

> Through the images of tree, vine, and flower, then, Milton has employed visually striking, concrete equivalents to help express an intangible and abstract moral thesis. However, whereas in the vine imagery the moral point has been completely and fully stated in a pictorial emblem that is understandable by itself, the "fairest unsupported flower" metaphor is still dependent upon a verbal explanation of its moral point. Here, unlike the emblematic vine-elm passage, the flower image cannot stand alone. Eve as the fairest flower in a field of fragrant, colorful blooms is effectively poetic, but Milton has to point the explicit moral, telling us she is "From her best prop so far." Metaphoric tenor and vehicle merge completely as they do in a painting only in the tree and vine image, not in the flower image, though both make the same thematic point.[43]

Milton's use of flowers in other contexts is also interesting. Among those he cites are the acanthus, iris, jessamine, violet, crocus, hyacinth, and of course the rose (IV, 696-701; IX, 218, 426). As one would expect, flowers were also common

[43] Spencer, *Heroic Nature*, pp. 116-17.

in paintings of the Garden of Eden, but they do not appear so extensively as in Milton's poetic descriptions. I know of no "spring" or grove of roses, such as that which Eve tends, where the flowers bush around her so as to conceal half her figure (IX, 218-19, and 425-27). Similarly of the lower-growing flowers, I know of no instance in paintings where they are shown so thick as to form a "wrought/ Mosaic, . . . with rich inlay" bordering the ground (IV, 699-703). In art, the flowers of Eden are far more scattered, appearing as occasional ornaments to the earth, and not as the thick groundcover Milton describes. Here, Milton's descriptions are visually innovative to a significant degree.

Milton also appears unusual when we consider the reaction to living flowers on the part of most visitors to actual gardens. John Shearman points out that it was "rare for an early visitor to a sixteenth-century garden to mention the flowers."[44] If Shearman is correct about visitors' comments, then Milton's emphasis upon flowers is exceptional enough to be worthy of critical note. As for the importance of flowers in the Italy Milton knew, Georgina Masson has conclusively demonstrated that Italian gardens displayed a richness of colored flowers in the seventeenth century far beyond anything we see there today.[45] In Milton's time, the *cassette* or compartments of the garden parterre were so thickly set with blossoming plants as to give the effect of what Masson calls a "carpet of flowers"—essentially the same effect that Milton ascribes to his groundcovering flowers.[46] Such garden arrangements are less carefully cared for in Italy today than they were during Milton's tour, and so give a less concentrated and luxurious impression, but we can still see them in full glory in the well-tended gardens of England. Parterres like those Milton would have known both in England and in Italy display flowers in ornamental beds, each with its own variety, laid out contiguously in plots of different shapes and sizes. The visual effect of such gardens is persuasively rendered by Milton's metaphoric description of "wrought mosaic" and "rich inlay," in which the color of the different flowers suggests the color of stones set close together in artistic designs.

Milton's introduction of mosaic patterns as a metaphor for garden parterres is not only visually appropriate in the ways just noted but it sets the poet off on an exploration of "wrought mosaic" which is full of artistic references, all adapted to his visual intent: "underfoot the violet,/ Crocus, and hyacinth with rich inlay/ Broidered the ground, more colored than with stone/ Of costliest emblem" (IV, 698-703). Though there may be a secondary and derivative reference here to the symbolic pictures or emblems popular in the seventeenth century, the primary reference is to the arrangements of colored stones in inlaid designs technically known as *emblemata*, usually enclosed by a framing pattern (corresponding here to the sides of Eve's bower).[47] Milton may be thinking of the use of earth and

---

[44] Shearman, *Mannerism*, p. 133.

[45] Masson, "Italian Flower Collector's Gardens in Seventeenth-Century Italy," pp. 63-80.

[46] *Ibid.*, p. 71.

[47] Rossi, *Mosaics*, p. 12, defines the technical term, while Freeman, *English Emblem Books*, p. 37, cites Geoffrey Whitney's acknowledgement of its derivation from mosaic art and Milton's use of it in that sense in *PL* IV, 700-3.

vegetable colors in floor mosaics, as in Saint John Lateran where the patterns resemble formal gardens and the colors include tans, pinks, reds, greens, and whites. Similar arrangements may be seen in many other churches, as for example in Santa Maria in Aracoeli in Rome, in the Cosmatesque pavements of Westminster Abbey in London, and somewhat differently in the fourteenth-century *opus sectile* of Prior Crauden's Chapel at Ely where the true earth and vegetable colors are combined in what Pevsner calls "one of the most important tile mosaics pavements of England."[48]

Furthermore, the phrases "rich inlay" and "stone/ Of costliest emblem" would seem to suggest the *commesso* or *pietre dure* mosaics which were probably the most famous art works being produced in Florence during Milton's stay there, when he could have observed the actual operations of the Medici workshop on the ground floor of the Uffizi.[49] *Commesso* was surely the richest of all mosaics. Using rare and semiprecious stones, the artisans inlaid "patterns and shapes which bear an odd resemblance to the corollae of flowers, the tendrils of the vine, or the leaves of trees—a resemblance so close that it would be difficult to imitate it with a brush and paints." The eminent seventeenth-century art historian Baldinucci declared that from the opening of the Medici workshops, mosaics were produced which not only "compare with the finest painting of an object, but seem to be the very thing itself."[50] The achievement of such effects was something of a tour de force, for the artist had to find stones which when cut, laid together, and polished would produce almost exactly the effect of the plants or flowers represented. As Baldinucci put it, "He has no opportunity to mix one color with another to produce a third; rather he must discover precisely what he needs already formed in nature."[51] In this sense, *commesso* faithfully reproduces the original creation of God. If Milton's mind turned to such masterpieces of "rich inlay" mosaic when he described the flowers in the Garden, he was thinking of works which achieved a remarkably high degree of verisimilitude while achieving a permanence rarely available in art. Like the "immortal amarant" of prelapsarian Eden and like the flora of Heaven, these brilliantly colored mosaic flowers "never fade" (III, 353-360) and so are an appropriate image for Milton's Garden.

The comparison of flowers in Eden with mosaics is closely related to the enameled imagery used to describe Heaven, which we have already considered.[52] In both instances we are concerned with a going beyond ordinary experience in order to suggest the transcendent. But Milton's going beyond is also a going through, a use of materials and a reference to techniques which were well known in art so as to evoke in us visions of more than ordinary beauty and richness. Probably the most famous of such oxymorons is *Paradise Lost*, and surely the most controversial, is "vegetable gold," to which we will now turn.

[48] Nikolaus Pevsner, *Cambridgeshire: The Buildings of England*, Harmondsworth, 1970, p. 374.

[49] Rossi, *Mosaics*, p. 133.

[50] *Ibid.*, p. 117.

[51] *Ibid.*, p. 118.

[52] See above, pp. 36, 200-5, 249-55.

VEGETABLE GOLD

None of Milton's imagery has caused more consternation than his insistence upon mixing vegetable and mineral in his descriptions of fruit in the Garden. Such descriptions are provided not once only, but a full five times: we are shown "blossoms and fruits at once of golden hue," "fruit/ Of vegetable gold," "fruit burnished with golden rind," while flowers are "specked with gold," and the forbidden fruit is "ruddy and gold" (IV, 148, 219-20, 249; IX, 429 and 578). Mythical precedents abound in classical literature, but these have not protected Milton from the assault of critics who regard his description at least as visually obtuse, and perhaps even as visually impossible.

In 1753 Joseph Warton forcefully stated his objections, and these were echoed as much as two centuries later.[53] T. S. Eliot takes "vegetable gold" as evidence that Milton may never be said to have seen anything properly, while F. R. Leavis treats the phrase as "incompatible with sharp, concrete realization."[54] Milton has not been without his advocates here, and the defenders have followed several major lines of argument. In a closely reasoned reply to Leavis, Douglas Bush argues that Milton uses the phrase so as to gather us "into the artifice of eternity":

> While the critic seems to think the Tree of Life should have been presented in terms acceptable to the horticulturist, Milton wishes, with an oblique glance at the apples of the Hesperides, to suggest a mysterious growth hardly to be approached in words. In the paradoxical phrase "vegetable gold," which Mr. Leavis especially scorns, each word is altered and quickened by the other; the richness of "gold" glorifies the simple product of nature, and the rich natural life applied in "vegetable" gives pliant form and vitality to metallic hardness and removes the idea of unhealthy artifice and evil which in *Paradise Lost* is associated with gold.[55]

Knott takes a somewhat similar line, placing the fruit with golden rind among those things which Milton asks us to take on faith, as features "of an idealized scene that can stand for a heightened version of the nature we know."[56] A different emphasis is supplied by Giamatti, who finds "something sinister in the idea of 'vegetable gold,' something unnatural and unhealthy," which makes us recall "sinister fruits in evil gardens."[57] For Giamatti, that sinister element serves as a premonitory warning about the Garden as a whole. For so perceptive a critic, he oddly misses an important point when he declares that "the poet never describes the fruit when he mentions the Tree of Knowledge," which is true enough for the first description of fruit generally but which misses the later characterization of

---

[53] Warton, in *Adventurer* 101, reprinted in *Eighteenth-Century Critical Essays* (ed. Scott Elledge), Ithaca, N.Y., 1961, II, p. 713.

[54] Leavis, *Revaluation*, p. 50, and for Eliot see above pp. 13-14. Demaray, "Milton's 'Perfect' Paradise and the Landscapes of Italy," 36, praises Milton's enameled imagery.

[55] Douglas Bush, *"Paradise Lost" in Our Time*, New York, 1948, pp. 96-97, and 95.

[56] Knott, *Milton's Pastoral Vision*, p. 34.

[57] Giamatti, *The Earthly Paradise*, pp. 308 and 309-10.

that particular fruit as "ruddy and gold" (IX, 578).[58] Koehler takes this latter description very seriously, contrasts it with the more simple "vegetable gold" and as a result of his analysis finds a "suspicious complexity of color" in the forbidden fruit.[59] Ryken takes a different tack: denying that gold is always associated with evil in *Paradise Lost* (and in this he seems to me to be entirely convincing), he declares that "we will have no difficulty in accepting gold and mineral images as good when they appear in apocalyptic situations if we allow the principle of contextual qualification its proper due."[60] He would therefore place the images of vegetable gold among those mystic oxymorons "whose contradiction is real and cannot be resolved in terms of ordinary experience," where we see Milton "portray the transcendental realm by combining two terms which in empirical reality contradict each other."[61]

These defenses of Milton are impressive examples of close argument, but they suffer from the same fault that undercuts the original attacks on Milton's descriptions: in each case, the visual evidence has been entirely ignored. If an examination of that evidence shows that "vegetable gold" is an accurate or even widely accepted description of what is seen in nature, and if it is repeatedly associated with pictorial renderings of the fruit in Eden—then not only the original objections to Milton's description but also the replies in his defense become irrelevant. And that, I suggest, is the case.

As for the fruits present in nature, perception varies to some extent between individuals as does the choice of color words, but to many eyes the adjective "gold" applies accurately to a considerable number of fruits and flowers, an hypothesis which can readily be tested by visiting orchards and gardens. The Italians demonstrably see certain vegetables in this way, and incorporate the word for gold into the names of at least two varieties: the tomato is called *pomidoro*, or apple of gold, while Venetians have long taken delight in those particularly succulent plums which they call *góccie d'oro*, or drops of gold. That evidence rebuts the contention that Milton never saw anything, unless it be presumed that the Italians also saw nothing, and it raises a legitimate question as to how much Eliot and Leavis and Warton actually observed in nature.

In pictorial art there is overwhelming evidence to support Milton's visual description. Indeed, art frequently endows vegetable forms with golden colors not associated with them in nature itself. The earliest Christian art in Rome abounds with such representations: the lovely fourth-century vault of the Mausoleum of S. Costanza is adorned with vines bearing golden fruit, while in the Chapel of SS. Cyprian and Justina in the Lateran Baptistry the mosaics show both golden and greeen branches against a blue background, bearing golden fruit and flowers, and displaying some leaves of gold, and some of green. Several centuries later in France, King Dagobert donated to the Basilica of Saint-Denis hangings

[58] *Ibid.*, p. 307.
[59] Koehler, "Milton's Use of Color and Light," 60.
[60] Ryken, *The Apocalyptic Vision*, pp. 86-87.
[61] *Ibid.*, pp. 88-89.

decorated with flowers of gold and pearls, which Mâle says were not uncommon.[62] Birch and Jenner, in their study of the illuminated manuscripts in the British Library, report that French and Flemish miniaturists were especially given to ornamenting pages with "golden leaves and sprigs."[63] Golden flowers, leaves, and vines are characteristic of work in champlevé enamel, as in the twelfth-century Alton Towers Triptych in the Victoria and Albert Museum and in the *Noli Me Tangere*, a sixteenth-century Limoges enamel plaque in the Fitzwilliam Museum in Cambridge, to cite only two examples.

An examination of any extensive collection of fifteenth-century paintings reveals the same: in the Uffizi, for example, the fruit in Botticelli's *Primavera* is of a light golden color, while the *Birth of Venus* by the same artist shows golden leaves of grass in the lower right and outlines the leaves of trees elsewhere in gold. The conventional coloring applied in sacred subjects as well as in mythological ones, as may be seen in the same gallery in Filippino Lippi's *Adoration of the Child*, where the flowers are given a light golden color, while the Northern artist Hans Memling, in his *Madonna Enthroned between Two Angels*, depicts garlands made up of golden fruit. The ornamental triangles of the ceiling about Raphael's *Disputa* in the Vatican show trees entirely of gold. In tapestry work, golden thread is abundantly used to represent verdure: in the late fifteenth-century *Episodes of the Passion*, there is a heavy emphasis on vegetable gold in the leaves, even when green thread is also available, and in the 1549 *Death of Julius Caesar* tapestry we find very little green in the floral border, which is mostly decorated with compositions of gold, blue, and red thread—both of these works being in the Vatican gallery. Vegetable gold is equally frequent in the tapestries of the Victoria and Albert collection, including work made in the Low Countries, France, and England in the sixteenth and seventeenth centuries. The products of the famous English Mortlake tapestry works display a frequent and conspicuous use of gold thread in leaves, flowers, and branches, whether executed early or late in the seventeenth century, and the same may be said for most of the English needlework in that museum. In Milton's own Cambridge, vegetable gold was abundantly visible, as in what Pevsner has aptly called the "gorgeous display of heraldic carving" at St. John's College. In Christ's, Milton's Cambridge college, there is an elaborate heraldic carving over the doorway to the Master's Lodge, which contains, just below the oriel, horizontal bands of foliage. Assuming the accuracy of the restoration (for which Pevsner vouches), we see there an example of what Milton could have seen in the heraldic displays of Cambridge during his college years—leaves veined and fruit painted in heraldic gold.[64]

The color of the gold varies, depending upon the artistic medium, and even within a single medium it varies depending upon whether and how the colors are

---

[62] Mâle, *Religious Art*, p. 46.

[63] Birch and Jenner, *Early Drawings and Illuminations*, p. 64.

[64] Pevsner, *Cambridgeshire*, p. 144. What we see today can be accepted as visual evidence if we accept the accuracy of the restoration, as Pevsner does, for such displays were widespread in the Cambridge of Milton's time, but the Master's Lodge at Christ's is not shown as carved in Loggan's *Cantabrigia Illustrata* of 1690.

mixed. Mosaic tesserae range from light to dark gold, whereas in the tapestries with which I am familiar the golden threads usually seem to be of a light color, perhaps due to fading. Illuminated manuscripts often show pure gold color, and heraldic carvings are decorated in bright gilt. Paints, and especially oil, may be so mixed as to provide a wide range of hues, embracing greenish gold, red gold, and yellow gold. Again, the application of paint with a brush allows the artist to mix colors variously. If we recall here Milton's references, we also see a considerable range of effect: flowers and fruit appear "of golden hue . . . with gay enamelled colors mixed," along with fruit described merely as "vegetable gold," or fruit qualified as "burnished with golden rind," or mixed as "ruddy and gold," while flowers are "specked with gold" (iv, 148-49, 219-20, 249; ix, 578, and 429). While it is possible that these expressions are varied merely for rhetorical effect, it may be that Milton had in mind some rather specific differences in hue. Further study of the vocabularies of artists and art critics of Milton's time might perhaps enable us to identify the individual colors he wished to evoke, within the golden range, but such specificity (apart from the fairly obvious speckling with gold and mixture of ruddy with gold) is not necessary for our purposes here.

Having seen that art of all kinds and of various media abounds in vegetable gold, we would expect to find the same color renditions in representations of the Garden of Eden, as indeed we do. In the *Creation* mosaic of the S. Marco atrium in Venice, the Garden of Eden bears golden fruit, and in the miniature by the Limbourg brothers for the *Trés Riches Heures* the forbidden fruit is painted in pure gold. In the Grimani Breviary, the fruit is ruddy and gold, and in the *Fall* by Tintoretto in the Accademia in Venice we see a pure, light-golden fruit. Golden fruit appears in all the major paintings of the subject of the Fall at the Prado, by Dürer, Titian, and Rubens, as also in Rubens' great canvas at The Hague. The Cranach *Eve* holds a fruit which is "ruddy and gold," while the *Paradise* by Bruegel in the Victoria and Albert shows various shadings of gold. The Fall of Man was not only a frequent subject for major art, but was also represented on glazed dishes made for household use, and in all the examples of these with which I am familiar the fruit is golden, as in the 1623 dish made in Rome, the 1635 dish made in London, and in the tin-glazed earthenware plates of English manufacture dating from about 1720 and from 1741, all in the Victoria and Albert Museum. A study of English stained glass yields the same results: though the forbidden fruit itself is bright red in the Fall window of King's College Chapel, Cambridge, other fruit in the Garden in the same window is gold. In the east window of 1631 in Lincoln College Chapel, Oxford, the forbidden fruit is vegetable gold, as also in the stunningly beautiful Fall window executed in 1641 by Abraham van Linge for University College Chapel. And of course there are the Medici tapestries.

The validity of describing certain fruits as gold in color is so readily established that one wonders why Warton, Eliot, and Leavis ever raised the issue at all. As we have noted, the Italian language incorporates gold into the names of at least two fruits, and vegetable gold abounded in many forms of art for many different subjects for twelve centuries up to Milton's time. Finally, representations of the

Garden of Eden, ranging in quality from the greatest paintings to the most utilitarian household utensils, again and again visualize fruit in the Garden as of golden hues. It is only because certain critics systematically ignored this mass of evidence that they have been able to sustain for over two hundred years a controversy centered on Milton's descriptions of vegetable gold. Here as elsewhere, there is abundant evidence that critics themselves should look long and hard before they take the leap of assuming that Milton's imagery is lacking in visual perception.

Part Five
The Human World

XV

Adam and Eve

THE CREATION OF ADAM AND EVE

PICTORIAL representations of the creation of Adam in most cases show Adam lying upon a slightly elevated bank of earth and he is usually in much the same position in pictures of the creation of Eve. During the emergence of Eve from his rib, Adam is described in Genesis as asleep, though nothing is said of his sleeping upon a bank. Similarly, nothing is said in Genesis about his appearing to be asleep at any point during his own creation, but the artists usually represented him as sleeping prior to the call of God. The bank upon which he rests and the sleep (*sommus Adae*) from which he is awakened at the time of his own "enlivement" are thus extra-Biblical elements, which came to figure in the Western imagination through the influence of the pictorial arts, and Milton incorporates these details into his own descriptions.[1]

151, 163, 179, 180

156

Adam's first recollection of himself is of one "new waked from soundest sleep/ Soft as on the flowery herb," from which he arises in wonder at himself and his surroundings (VIII, 253-54). Shortly he falls asleep again "on a green shady bank profuse of flowers" and dreams until the Son comes and raises him by the hand (VIII, 286, 300). That familiar bank upon which Adam sleeps prior to recognizing his own creation may be illustrated in the bas reliefs designed by Giotto and carved by Pisano for the Campanile in Florence, where, too, the creation of Eve finds Adam in much the same posture he assumed at the time of his own "enlivement."

175, 176

Sometimes God extracts Eve fully formed from Adam's side by taking her hand, as in the bronze doors at S. Zeno in Verona, sometimes he holds her by the shoulders and gently draws her forth as in the carved pilaster in the cathedral at Orvieto and in the frescoes at the Camposanto in Pisa, or by grasping her beneath her armpits, as in Cranach's *Paradise*, or he may merely bring her forth by a majesterial gesture of his right hand, as in the cupola mosaics in the Florentine Baptistry. In each of these instances, the *sommus Adae*[2] is pictured upon a bank, as in Milton. This immensely popular visual convention continued well into the sixteenth and even the seventeenth centuries.[3] One particularly charming vision of the creation of Eve[4] is that which shows God drawing a rib from Adam's side,

179

172

163

---

[1] Another tradition, much less popular, showed Adam emerging from the earth itself, as in the Medici tapestries (fig. 159), where God has drawn him forth to his shins.

[2] Evans, *"Paradise Lost" and the Genesis Tradition*, pp. 291-92, points out that Christian commentators on Genesis almost invariably provided Adam with a vision of the future during this sleep.

[3] Ehrenstein, *Das Alte Testament in der Graphik*, figs. 1, 4, 6, 13, 15, 17-18, 20-21, and 27.

[4] In medieval art, Eve's creation was a more popular subject than Adam's, for reasons made clear by Anderson, *The Imagery of British Churches*, p. 88.

while Eve emerges in her feminine beauty from the rib, as may be seen in the Grabow Altarpiece of Master Bertram, a delightfully naive rendering of Genesis 2:22, but this visual motif seems to have died out with the rise of the printed book.[5] In the ordinary medieval form of the story, according to Rosalie Green, "Eve is shown rising or being drawn by God fully formed from the side of Adam" as in the plates already cited.[6] God's drawing Eve forth by hand or by the word of his command is not the picture Milton chooses to give us.

Milton's description of the creation of Eve corresponds to that artistic conception of the Creator as "le souverain Plasmateur," to which Réau refers:[7] "The rib he formed and fashioned with his hands;/ Under his forming hands a creature grew,/ Manlike, but different sex, so lovely fair . . ." (VIII, 469-71).[8] Where God uses both hands to draw Eve forth, as in the Camposanto fresco and in Cranach's *Paradise*, the divine "shaping" of Eve is perhaps suggested, though it does not become so explicit as in Milton's description, perhaps because it might in explicit visual form have given rise to some ribald responses.[9] Lucas van Leyden's copper engraving of the scene carries the shaping process as far as is visually tactful.

172
163

182

As for the rib itself, Milton three times specifies that it was taken from the left side of Adam (IV, 484; VIII, 465-66; and X, 884-88). Genesis does not supply that detail, and although there had been some speculation about the question among theologians, such speculation was often ridiculous and often ridiculed. The left side allowed a certain didactic symbolism, by placing the origin of the wife closest to the heart of the husband. Milton gives this traditional meaning[10] when he has Adam address Eve for the first time:

> to give thee being I lent
> Out of my side to thee, nearest my heart
> Substantial life, to have thee by my side
> Henceforth an individual solace dear;
> Part of my soul I seek thee, and thee claim
> My other half.
>
> (IV, 483-88)

Adam's later remarks give the rib a radically different meaning, during his savage

---

[5] Gibbs, "Creation of Eve," p. 4.

[6] Rosalie B. Green, "The Adam and Eve Cycle in the *Hortus Deliciarum*," in *Late Classical and Mediaeval Studies in Honor of Albert Mathias Friend, Jr.* (ed Kurt Weitzmann), Princeton, 1955, p. 344.

[7] Réau, *Iconographie*, II, i, p. 71.

[8] For the "shaping" and "enlivenment" of the first parents at Creation, see Kurt Weitzmann, *Illustrations in Roll and Codex: A Study of the Origin and Method of Text Illustration*, Princeton, 1970, pp. 176-77.

[9] God does appear to be shaping Eve in the eleventh-century Aelfric Manuscript, British Library *MS* Cotton Claudius B IV, fol. 6v., reproduced in Kirschbaum, *Lexikon*, I, p. 58, fig. 6, and in Veronese's *Creation of Eve* at the Art Institute in Chicago. Leclercq discusses and illustrates the "shaping" of Eve by God on an early (but undated) sarcophagus in *Manuel d'archéologie chrétienne*, II, pp. 299-300.

[10] The left rib was less often taken to suggest a sinister influence; that interpretation would have been suspect, as implying an evil design on the part of God at the Creation.

verbal assault upon Eve: she was "but a rib/ Crooked by nature, bent, as now appears,/ More to the part sinister," a sarcastic comment which shows how far Adam's reason has been corrupted by the Fall from his earlier understanding, and which at the same time serves as a vicious insult not only upon Eve but by implication even upon the Creator (x, 884-86).[11]

Pictorial representations of Eve's creation varied as to the side from which she emerged, and there seems to have been no standard form. For some time I kept records of the different presentations, and found them to be almost equally divided. It appears likely that for many, and perhaps most, artists the decision as to the side from which Eve emerged was based not on intellectual or theological considerations, but on whether Adam's head was placed toward the left or the right side of the picture, and depending on that decision it would then be necessary for Eve to emerge on the right or left side, as the case might be.

For convenience, I have analyzed the creations of Adam and Eve together, though in *Paradise Lost* they are separated not only by some time but also by distance: Eve was created within the Garden, but Adam's creation took place outside it, and it was necessary to take him into the Garden, just as Genesis 2:8 and 15 specify. Réau indicates that the act of flying Adam into the Garden was a major part of the visual tradition.[12] In the Bedford Book of Hours, the Christ-Logos, supported by winged cherubs, carries the rigid body of Adam over the wall into the Garden. The illuminator here is obviously attempting to suggest levitation, but despite the charm of his design he conveys no sense of movement. At this point as in a number of other scenes, Milton's vision comes closest to that in the Medici tapestries. There we see the Almighty with his left arm holding Adam, and his right pointing to the manifold beauty and diversity of the Garden as the two move gently through the air. Milton's description could scarcely find a closer correspondence than in this tapestry:

> So saying, by the hand he took me raised,
> And over fields and water, as in air
> Smooth sliding without step, last led me up
> A woody mountain; whose high top was plain,
> A circuit wide, enclosed, with goodliest trees
> Planted, with walks, and bowers, that what I saw
> Of earth before scarce pleasant seemed.
>
> (VIII, 300-6)

[11] See the notes in the Carey and Fowler edition, and also John Halkett, *Milton and the Idea of Matrimony*, New Haven, 1970, pp. 87-88 and 132-33. For a general treatment of the significance symbolically of the left and right hands, see Howard Patch, *The Goddess Fortuna in Medieval Literature*, Cambridge, Mass., 1927, pp. 44-45.

[12] Réau, *Iconographie*, II, i, p. 79, and Peter Brieger, *English Art: 1216-1307*, p. 181, and pl. 67a, where Brieger illustrates and discusses a picture from the Oscott Psalter in which "God the Father carries the sleeping Adam like a babe in his arms" as "a strange scene." Perhaps Brieger is correct if applied only to English usage up to the early years of the fourteenth century, while Réau's statement may be allowed to stand unqualified for the broader usage.

Both poet and artist have conveyed a sense of easy, even effortless, flight ("smooth sliding without step"), and have also taken the opportunity to provide a lovely and varied view of the circuit of Paradise.

NUDE BEAUTY

The nudity of Adam and Eve is a given of the account in Genesis, and although nothing is said there about their beauty of form and face, it is possible to infer from God's assertion of the goodness of all creation that the first parents were ideally beautiful creatures before the Fall. This assumption dominates the earliest Christian art, and it is dominant again after the Renaissance, but in the intervening centuries the vision of Adam and Eve is not so easy to summarize.[13] As Trapp has written, Adam and Eve are "invariably in early Christian art an ideally handsome pair, Adam stalwart and beardless (there are some exceptions to this, which may represent the Eastern tradition), and Eve beautiful and longhaired."[14] On the sarcophagus of Junius Bassus at the Vatican, we see the first parents represented as beautiful *54* in their nakedness, an example of *lo stile bello* operating in Paleo-Christian art. An ivory diptych of the fifth century, now in Florence, continues this clear attempt to represent the naked Adam as the figure of human perfection.[15] We have here the artistic counterparts to the poetic descriptions by Dracontius, the early Christian poet, who envisioned Eve "with her snowy body naked like a nymph of the sea. . . . And everything about her was beautiful, eyes, mouth, neck and hands. . . ."[16] In the verse and in the carvings, we see represented that "honesta voluptas" in which Adam and Eve are commanded to live by Dracontius' Creator.

Medieval representations evoke quite different responses, ranging from representations which appear moderately attractive to others which seem ungainly in the extreme. The Adam and Eve cast in bronze panels for the doors of S. Zeno in *179* Verona by the Secondo Maestro in the mid-twelfth century scarcely impress us as physically attractive, but neither are the Creator and the angel in the same series. The Adam and Eve carved for the ivory diptych of the *Passion of Christ*, a French work of the late thirteenth century now in the Wallace Collection in London, are unusually handsome and graceful, whereas the *Descent into Hell* relief of ivory from fourteenth-century France in the same collection shows Adam and Eve in quite homely form. Similarly crude are the Adam and Eve figures which we find at Ely, from the early fourteenth century, as roof bosses in the Lady Chapel and in the mosaic tile floor of Prior Crauden's Chapel. Of the Adam and Eve illustrations in the Saint Albans Psalter of the earlier twelfth century, Boase comments

[13] A general survey of the first parents in pictorial art may be found in Sigrid Esche, *Adam und Eva*, while the concentration is upon the folk art traditions in Lutz Röhrich, *Adam und Eva*, Stuttgart, 1958. Infrequently seen reproductions of Adam and Eve in early Christian art may be found in Leclerq, *Manuel d'archéologie chrétienne*, II, pp. 330, and 491.

[14] Trapp, "The Iconography of the Fall," p. 233.

[15] Reproduced in Lowrie, *Monuments of the Early Church*, fig. 113, and p. 285.

[16] Evans, *"Paradise Lost" and the Genesis Tradition*, p. 130.

that "these gaunt, overanatomized nudes have an archaic, retrograde appearance."[17] It is difficult to interpret some of these medieval representations of Adam and Eve without reference to medieval asceticism, for they seem to imply a depreciation of the values of the human body. Sometimes the female breasts are so undeveloped that it can be difficult to tell Adam from Eve, apart from hair length and distinctive actions. The question of the significance of these gaunt figures must be recognized, but fortunately it is not our responsibility to solve that problem. As Trapp has written, "It is next to impossible to conclude anything on the score of whether these figures are an exact reflection of current ideals of beauty or to draw conclusions from any real or suspected expressions of face, pose or gesture."[18] If we find these figures strangely unattractive, our reactions may well be due to our own cultural provincialism, and we should bear in mind that Michael Levey has dismissed as erroneous those "ideas that the Gothic nude was meager because shamed, and quite unsensuous. Concepts of beauty change much more rapidly than concepts of morals."[19] In the fifteenth century, surely, it is possible to document fashions in individual beauty that are no longer quite to our taste, as with the round-faced and slit-eyed Eve of Van Eyck's *Ghent Altarpiece*, which has been shown to represent ideals of beauty shared by Van Eyck, François Villon, and others of the time.[20] Similarly, Jean Longnon shows that in the *Très Riches Heures* Eve was painted "after the type of female fashionable at the time, with a high bosom, thin waist, and slightly protruding stomach."[21]

160

The Renaissance introduced conceptions of nude beauty closer to our own. According to Trapp, "by the beginning of the sixteenth century we have figures of Adam and Eve which are explicitly intended as expressions of an ideal beauty and proportion—at least of body. Among them are the most celebrated northern representations, namely Albrecht Dürer's."[22] The repudiation of asceticism was influential here, as may be illustrated in the widespread idealization of the human nude in sculpture and in painting, and there were other important philosophical and symbolic influences at work. The nude figure of Veritas was one of the most popular of Renaissance and Baroque personifications, and Panofsky observes that "nudity as such, especially when contrasted with its opposite, came to be understood as a symbol of truth in a general philosophical sense."[23] In the Renaissance, the nudity of Adam and Eve thus takes on a new explicitness, an affirmative joy akin to that of the Greek deities in art and legend.[24] The appropriation of classical

---

[17] T. S. R. Boase, *English Art: 1100-1216*, Oxford, 1953, p. 105.

[18] Trapp, "The Iconography of the Fall," p. 250.

[19] Michael Levey, *Themes and Painters in the National Gallery: The Nude*, London, 1972, pp. 8-9.

[20] Panofsky, *Early Netherlandish Painting*, I, pp. 223 and 449n.

[21] Jean Longnon, ed., *Très Riches Heures*, note to pl. 20.

[22] Trapp, "The Iconography of the Fall," p. 250.

[23] Panofsky, *Studies in Iconology*, p. 159, and for the traditional Hebrew and Roman conception of nudity as objectionable, "because it indicated either poverty, or shamelessness," see also *op. cit.*, p. 155. Mario Praz, *Studies in Seventeenth-Century Imagery*, p. 46, relates the symbolic use of nudity in emblem books to "the Spartan custom of making maidens go naked and matrons clothed," and cites also Titian's *Sacred and Profane Love*.

[24] Spencer, *Heroic Nature*, p. 110.

perfection of form was even given a theological basis, as Panofsky observes in connection with Dürer:

> While medieval art had appropriated classical motifs without much reflection, the Renaissance tried to justify this practice on theoretical grounds: 'the pagan people attributed the utmost beauty to their heathen god Apollo,' Dürer says, 'thus we shall use him for Christ the Lord who is the most beautiful man, and just as they represented Venus as the most beautiful woman we shall chastely display the same features in the image of the Holy Virgin, mother of God.'[25]

Dürer's Adam was just as Apollonian as his Christ, as Wölfflin points out:

> Reality alone was not enough for him. He wanted to advance from naturalism, which does not go beyond the depiction of a given reality, to an art which represented the typical, the conclusive. He wanted to show man as he should be according to the design of God. He was confused and alarmed by the infinity of individual appearances and searched for the ultimate image of beauty which must be contained in definite proportions. How else was it possible to say that one man was more beautiful than another? He found a formula with which he was content for the time being. It was applied to the engraving of Adam and Eve, dated 1504. . . .[26]

164, 184   Dürer's conception of ideal beauty obviously changed, as a comparison especially of the faces of Eve between the 1504 engraving and his later oils will show, but the effort remained constant.

Problems arise for an artist not only from the attempt to arrive at ideal proportions, but also from the very practical necessity of incorporating these within a single art work. Panofsky makes the crucial distinction:

> There is a great difference between the question: 'What is the normal relationship between the length of the upper arm and the length of the entire body in a person standing quietly before me?' and the question: 'How shall I scale the length of what corresponds to the upper arm, in relation to the length of what corresponds to the entire body, on my canvas or block of marble?' The first is a question of 'objective' proportions—a question whose answer precedes the artistic activity. The second is a question of 'technical' proportions—a question whose answer lies in the process itself.[27]

Milton's problem was simpler than that of the artist, in that he did not need to arrive at an "objective" mathematical proportion between upper arm and body,

---

[25] Panofsky, *Studies in Iconology*, p. 70.

[26] Wölfflin, *The Art of Albrecht Dürer*, p. 27. For a discussion of the preliminary work in drawings which led Dürer to this particular idealization, see the notes by Gaillard F. Ravenel and Jay A. Levenson in *Dürer in America* (ed. Charles W. Talbot), Washington, 1971, pp. 50-52.

[27] Panofsky, *Meaning in the Visual Arts*, p. 56.

and so forth, nor was he required, as the artist was, to give a "technical" proportion in his representation. With no possibility of rivaling the graphic particularity of the visual artist, Milton could concentrate upon eliciting the appropriate response to beauty as such. Once the conception of ideal beauty had been firmly associated with Adam and Eve in the minds of his readers, he could allow each to conclude how, and even whether, to apply precise physical proportions to that ideal.

In conveying a picture of Adam and Eve to us, Milton relies upon what Ryken has aptly called "a poetic texture of conceptual images," to which we may supply objective components. We see this operation in the first extended description of Adam and Eve in *Paradise Lost*:

> Two of far nobler shape erect and tall,
> Godlike erect, with native honor clad
> In naked majesty seemed lords of all,
> And worthy seemed, for in their looks divine
> The image of their glorious Maker shone,
> Truth, wisdom, sanctitude severe and pure,
> Severe, but in true filial freedom plac't;
> Whence true authority in men. . . .
>
> (IV, 288-95)

Ryken observes of this passage that "no fewer than fourteen conceptual terms comprise the poetic texture of the description: nobleness, Godlikeness, honor, majesty, lordship, worthiness, glory, truth, wisdom, sanctitude, severity, purity, freedom, and authority. Each of the terms names a quality which is no less real and distinct than a tangible object perceived through the senses. . . ."[28] The reliance on conceptual images here is indisputable, but Ryken seems on less safe ground when he assumes that these images are no less real and distinct than tangible objects. It would be more accurate to observe that each brings to individual minds tangible objects appropriate to associate with the first parents, allowing thus for distinctions of taste between individuals and even between cultural periods. When Milton summarizes his description of the first parents, it is as "Adam the goodliest man of men since born/ His sons, the fairest of her daughters Eve," which provides a conceptual breadth adaptable to almost any taste (IV, 323-24).

But there is more to Milton's description than a mere reliance upon conceptual terminology, as Ryken recognizes when he comments upon how "the patterns of conceptual images [are] consistently complementing the sensory descriptions of the human pair."[29] There are details in Milton's sensory descriptions which can easily be missed, amid the wealth of conceptual imagery, and these details may furnish insight into Milton's own understanding of ideal beauty. To these we shall turn in considering the individual descriptions of Adam and Eve, but first something must be said about Milton's insistence upon the unmitigated nudity of the first parents.

[28] Ryken, *The Apocalyptic Vision*, pp. 199, 193-94.
[29] *Ibid.*

While pictorial art had for centuries represented Adam and Eve as completely nude, artists repeatedly found means for concealing "those mysterious parts" of their bodies which Milton so insisted upon as visible:

> Nor those mysterious parts were then concealed,
> Then was not guilty shame, dishonest shame
> Of nature's works: honor dishonorable,
> Sin-bred, how have ye troubled all mankind
> With shows instead, mere shows of seeming pure,
> And banished from man's life his happiest life,
> Simplicity and spotless innocence.
> So passed they naked on, nor shunned the sight
> Of God or angel, for they thought no ill.
>
> (IV, 312-20)

The prudery or "dishonest shame" against which Milton so eloquently protests in these lines was not just a psychological condition but a visual reality in representations of Adam and Eve even in his own time. In Abraham van Linge's stained *VI* glass window of 1641 in University College, Oxford, a branch conveniently extends its leaves from the trunk of the Tree to conceal Adam's pudendum, while Eve's is concealed by her long hair, and we find precisely the same strategies of concealment in the carved marble font executed shortly after Milton's death by Grinling Gibbons for St. James's Church in Piccadilly. This convenient placing of leaves began early in the visual tradition, and is frequently encountered in every century.[30] Even before the Fall has taken place, the private parts of Adam and Eve were usually concealed by one subterfuge or another, as a glance through the pictures reproduced in this book will indicate. Milton's repudiation of this conception could not have been more complete, or more explicit. Indeed, it may be one reason for his having Eve's hair fall only to her waist, for Eve's hair had frequently been used as a means for concealing her nakedness, as in the two seventeenth-century English works just cited, and we shall return to this subject in connection with the specific description of Eve.

ADAM

Of the first visual impression *Paradise Lost* provides of Adam and Eve (IV, 288-324), Wayne Shumaker writes that "if Milton had been asked what he had accomplished in these . . . lines, he might very well have answered that he had given an introductory description of Adam and Eve and, indeed, in a loose sense of the phrase, this is what he has accomplished. More strictly, he has hardly described *objects* at all."[31] That critical judgment has some merit, but its conclusion will not stand up under close analysis. It is true that we have few explicit details of Adam's

---

[30] Trapp, "The Iconography of the Fall," p. 236.
[31] Shumaker does go on to observe that "Adam's hair is more tightly curled than Eve's" (*Unpremeditated Verse*, pp. 52-53).

appearance beyond Milton's reiterated insistence upon his perfection, yet those details should not be overlooked, for they are sufficient to identify one of the traditional conceptions of Adam. The large forehead which is ascribed to him through the phrases "fair large front" and "front serene" (IV, 300, and VII, 509) at once sets him apart from such medieval representations as may be seen in the twelfth-century doors of S. Zeno in Verona, the Genesis mosaics in the S. Marco atrium, and the frescoes in the Pisan Camposanto, and mark him as a distinctively Renaissance Adam, of the kind represented by Masolino, Dürer, and Michelangelo. The emphasis upon his "shoulders broad" (IV, 303) likewise sets him apart not only from such medieval examples as those on the doors of S. Zeno and the cupola mosaics of the Florentine Baptistry, but also from such *retardataire* Adams as are to be seen in the Grimani Breviary of about 1500, in Cranach's *Paradise*, and in the painting at Bologna attributed to Met de Bles. Again, that phrase assures us of an ideal Renaissance Adam, such as we see in the bronze figure by Rizzo ornamenting the courtyard of the Ducal Palace in Venice, or the Creation paintings by Michelangelo in the Sistine Chapel, and many others, perhaps most notably Dürer's 1504 engraving.

179, 177

185, 164, 181
172
179

162, 163
186

187
181
164

Adam is described by Eve as tall when she first perceives him under the platan tree, "fair indeed and tall" (IV, 477), which presumably indicates that she perceives him as taller than she is, but Milton makes no explicit comparison of their heights, contrasting them not to each other but to the animals in the Garden: "Two of far nobler shape erect and tall,/ Godlike erect, with native honor clad" (IV, 288-89). The explicit differences between them—"For contemplation he and valor formed,/ For softness she and sweet attractive grace" (IV, 297-98)—do not distinguish between them as to their relative stature, though we might have expected Milton to use relative height symbolically here. It may be relevant, and it is interesting, to note that in art they are usually represented as almost the same in stature, as for instance in the paintings of Masolino, Masaccio, Cranach, the pseudo Met de Bles, in the Grimani Breviary, in the Florentine Baptistry, in the sculpture by Rizzo, and in engravings by Baldung and Holbein. Mabuse does make Adam almost a head taller than Eve, but it is rare to see Adam given any more advantage than about half a head, as we find in Dürer, Cornelius van Haarlem, Naccherino and the Medici tapestries. In general the artists minimized, and Milton left unspecific, differences in their height.

185, 189, 163,
186
162, 187, 188
191, 192, 190
157
164, 167, 193
151-54,
IV, V

What Milton and the artists alike do emphasize is the erect stature of the first parents standing upright, and towering not over each other but over other creatures. In almost every representation of prelapsarian man in Renaissance art with which I am familiar, Adam and Eve are accorded an unmistakable authority in stature and in posture; it is only with the Fall that they begin to slump, cringe, or assume other awkward positions, as may be seen by contrasting Masolino's yet unfallen couple with the fallen counterpart in Masaccio's painting, both in S. Maria del Carmine in Florence. It is in these terms that Milton has insisted upon the tallness of Adam and Eve, not so much as a distinction between the sexes as between the creatures. As God the Father says in *Paradise Lost*, man is

185, 189

> a creature who, not prone
> And brute as other creatures, but endued
> With sanctity of reason, might erect
> His stature, and upright with front serene
> Govern the rest, self-knowing, and from thence
> Magnanimous to correspond with Heaven.
>
> (VII, 506-11)

As for Adam's hair, we are twice informed that he is "fair," once by the epic voice and again by Eve (IV, 300 and 477), and the word is sufficient to place Adam's hair somewhere within the usual artistic range from light yellow to brownish. As "fair" establishes the range of color for Adam's hair, so the reference to "hyacinthine locks" establishes the shape (IV, 301).[32] What Denys Haynes has found in the sculptured Pergamon fragment from the famous seventeenth-century collection of the Earl of Arundel is typical of the classical representations of heroes, athletes, and divinities in general: "The hair was treated in short, chunky curls with deep-grooved contours."[33] Although I have been unable to discover a classical painting or sculpture which was definitely thought to be Hyacinth in Milton's time,[34] there can be no doubt that Renaissance and Baroque artists were agreed as to how Hyacinth should be represented, for they consistently give him the close, tightly curling locks of the Greek hero. The hyacinthine hair to which Milton referred may be illustrated by two famous examples: the engraving of *Apollo and Hyacinth* by Marcantonio Raimondi, and the marble group of *Apollo and Hyacinth* by Benvenuto Cellini. In both we see the hair curling close to the skull, like the blossoms of the bluebell, or as close set as grapes, an impression which Milton evokes by the word "clustering (IV, 303).[35] The same general pattern is observable in the

195
196

[32] Attempts to read "hyacinthine" as a color reference can lead only to confusion. The phrase is ultimately derived from a description of Odysseus (*Odyssey* VI, 231, and XXIII, 158), but Liddell and Scott identify the Greek hyacinth flower and stone as blue, whereas Odysseus is given auburn or dark yellow hair (*Odyssey* XXIII, 399). After analyzing the possibilities, W. B. Stanford concludes that the comparison is "between Odysseus's short curls (as in later Greek athletic statues) and the curling petals of the bluebell" (*The Odyssey of Homer*, 2 vols., London, 1950, I, pp. 316-17). In seventeenth-century England, the hyacinth was a well-known flower of many different colors, but with a preponderant consistency of shape, with close-curling bells or ringlets (John Parkinson, *Paradisi in Sole: Paradisus Terrestris*, London, 1629, pp. 111-13 and 115-16, and Sir Thomas Hanmer, *Garden Book* [a manuscript of 1659, ed. Elenour S. Rohde], London, 1933, pp. 35-36 and 66). Fowler's note (*PL* IV, 301-8) concludes that the reference is to shape.

As for Homer's references to "blue-hair" heroes and deities, it may be worth noting that excavations on the Greek island of Thera, exposing a civilization from the Bronze Age of about 1500 B.C., shows at least one girl in a fresco with a blue scalp and a lock of dark hair—see Cokie Roberts and Steven V. Roberts, "Atlantis Recaptured," *New York Times Magazine* (Sept. 6, 1976), p. 36.

[33] Denys Haynes, "The Worksop Relief," *Jahrbuch der Berliner Museen* V (1963), p. 6.

[34] Greek vases frequently show Hyacinth, but vases were unknown or unregarded in Milton's time. Adolf Michaelis, *Ancient Marbles in Great Britain*, pp. 281-82, scientifically discusses a "Hyacinth" marble which was brought to England in the famous Hope Collection, but this was much later.

[35] Rubens did a famous painting of the same subject, but the painting has been destroyed,

prints illustrating Ovid's account of the Hyacinth story in *Metamorphoses* x, 162–219, though of course with less detail.[36]

The convergence of visual evidence allows us to eliminate certain traditional hair styles for Adam, and to focus upon the one Milton intended.[37] In the first place, we eliminate the straight and close cropped, almost crew cut, vision of Adam to be found on the sarcophagus of Junius Bassus, in the paintings for S. Maria del Carmine in Florence by Masaccio and Masolino, in Michelangelo's *Fall*, and in Tintoretto's *Fall*. Milton's Adam was no roundhead. Neither did he show the long, stringy or only slightly wavy locks ascribed to him in many medieval works, as on the doors at S. Zeno by Secondo Maestro, in Paolo Uccello's fresco for the Chiostro Verde, in the Camposanto frescoes in Pisa, in the illumination for the Grimani Breviary, or in the great window by Abraham van Linge for University College, Oxford. After the Renaissance, the hyacinthine pattern predominates in artistic representations of Adam. Of the works reproduced here, it may be seen in Raphael's *Fall* in the Stanza della Segnatura in the Vatican, in the statues by Michelangelo Naccherino and Cristoforo Solario, in paintings by Cranach, by Mabuse, and by Salviati, and in the Medici tapestries.

The locus classicus of this conception may be found in Dürer's famous 1504

54

185, 189
169, 173

179
197, 172
162
VI
198
193, 199
163, 174
157, 166
155, 148

---

and only a sketch remains, in which the hair is similar to that in Cellini and Raimondi, but lacking in detail. See Max Rooses, *L'Oeuvre de P. P. Rubens*, Antwerp, 1890, III, p. 22, entry 533, and Svetlana Alpers, *Decoration of the Torre de la Parada*, Brussels, 1971, fig. 123.

[36] Mrs. Arthur Vershbow has kindly reported upon the illustration in the 1599 Lyons edition of Ovid in the Vershbow Collection, and also on the 1557 Lyons edition, the 1582 Leipzig edition, and the undated Tempesta illustrations of Ovid which are in the Lamont Library at Harvard, and she finds in these essentially the same pattern of nape-length fluffy or wavy hair, with no parting. For the kind help of Charlotte and Arthur Vershbow, I am indeed grateful. The illustration for George Sandys' *Ovid's Metamorphoses*, London, 1640, as a frontispiece to Book x, in the Firestone Library in Princeton, is sketchy, but to the same effect. The illustrated Bartsch index in the Institute of Fine Arts in New York contains a Galestruzzi print after the antique showing Hyacinth with curly bangs in front, curly shoulder length hair behind (B XXI.69.74), a Tempesta engraving with short curly ringlets (B XVII.151.638-787), and a Cesio after Carracci of curly shoulder-length hair as a back view (B XXI.111.41). The Carracci fresco (sometimes attributed to Domenichino) in the Palazzo Farnese, Rome, shows a back view of Hyacinth's head, with curling locks down the nape of his neck, and what appear to be curling bangs about his averted face.

[37] It is curious that in a single artistic cycle, an artist may give several different shapes to Adam's hair. *Genesis B* often shows it as close cropped, curling about the skull, but sometimes (even on the same page as on p. 31) allows it to wave down below Adam's shoulders (fig. 37). Michelangelo treats Adam's hair in a variety of ways: in the *Creation of Man* it is mostly straight, though with a few slight waves; in the *Creation of Eve*, it curls in the hyacinth pattern, where it also has a forelock over the forehead (but unparted); in the *Fall*, Adam in reaching for the fruit seems to have curly hair, though the damage to the paint makes it impossible to be sure, whereas his hair is clearly not curly as he is being expelled from Eden (fig. 169). In the Baptistry Font attributed to Antonio Federighi in the Chapel of San Ansano in the Cathedral in Siena, we have the most curious variations of all: the panel devoted to the Creation of Adam shows him with close-cropped hair, whereas his hair clusters to his shoulders at the Creation of Eve and at her Fall; by the time of his own Fall he has had a haircut, and is again closely cropped; at the Judgment and Expulsion, his hair is clustering again and amply covers the skull in rich curls.

164 engraving, where we have the perfect Renaissance Adam, with "shoulders broad" and "fair large front" as well as hyacinthine locks:

> His fair large front and eyes sublime declared
> Absolute rule; and hyacinthine locks
> Round from his parted forelock manly hung
> Clustering, but not beneath his shoulders broad.
>
> (IV, 300-3)

The inclusion of Renaissance ideals in Dürer's engraved Adam gives almost complete visual expression to Milton's descriptions, both in physical details and in conceptual qualities. It is considerably more difficult for an artist to achieve a conceptual impression through the use of lines and volumes than it is for a poet to achieve it through words, but Dürer has conveyed through his pictorial statement the essential impression of Milton's Adam, as he goes forth to meet the Archangel Raphael:

> Meanwhile our primitive great sire, to meet
> His god-like guest, walks forth, without more train
> Accompanied than with his own complete
> Perfections; in himself was all his state,
> More solemn than the tedious pomp that waits
> On princes, when their rich retinue long
> Of horses led, and grooms besmeared with gold
> Dazzles the crowd, and sets them all agape.
>
> (V, 350-57)

164, 169 Surely, Dürer comes closer than Michelangelo to conveying a Miltonic sense of the majesty and dignity of unfallen man, as may be seen by comparing their renditions of the Fall. I do not argue for the Dürer engraving as the source of Milton's conception, though I regard it as the closest single artistic counterpart to that conception. What is important to recognize, I suggest, is that Milton combines physical detail and conceptual generalization in such a way that any thoughtful reader of his descriptions of Adam can, by drawing upon the various elements of the traditional pictorial representations, arrive at a basic visual image of the figure Milton describes.[38]

A curious exception to the general likeness of Milton's Adam to the Adams of Renaissance and later art is what Milton refers to as "his parted forelock" (IV, 302). This phrase is clear and explicit: we are to envision a lock of hair growing from the forepart of the head, brought forward over the forehead, and parted into two strands. The forelock is unmistakably singular, though parted, and so cannot be confused with several separate strands of hair brushed over the forehead, nor with bangs falling in a solid front over the forehead. It obviously has no connection with

---

[38] In choosing to leave Adam unbearded, Milton was again in accord with the predominant post-Renaissance pictorial tradition, from which, however, there were notable departures, such as, for example, those by Masolino, Cranach, Mabuse, the Medici tapestries, Titian and Rubens (figs. 185, 163, 157, 166, 148-54, 171).

that long strand of hair called the "lovelock" which cavaliers separated from the rest of their hair and wore hanging down over the right shoulder, nor can it be associated with the short fringe of hair (*corta frangetta* or *frangetta sulla fronte*) which was also sometimes encountered in the seventeenth century.[39] It was not usually associated with hyacinthine locks, for as Calderini observes "the tightly waved hair is not parted" in this typical classical style.[40] Roman portrait sculpture frequently shows the hair brushed forward upon the forehead, either as bangs, or as a series of forelocks, but not as a parted forelock.[41] The forelock ascribed in emblems to Time or Occasion was far too scraggly to have furnished a visual model for the handsome Adam; furthermore, it was not parted, but was a long and fairly heavy lock of hair hanging down before the face.[42] In the pictorial representations of Adam, I have seen numerous examples of bangs, fringes, and perhaps even multiple forelocks, but never that single parted forelock which Milton so carefully specifies. In Michelangelo's *Risen Christ* in S. Maria sopra Minerva, the Second Adam is given what might be mistaken for a parted forelock, but which is in reality more nearly a parted fringe or a part in the bangs falling over the forehead. That, at all events, is the closest I have come to finding a counterpart in sacred art to Milton's phrase, and possible analogues in representations of Adam are far less convincing.

162, 154 157, 190 166, 155, 201

If we turn from art to the fashions of male hair styling in the sixteenth and seventeenth centuries, we will at first be disappointed, but we will at least be moving in a direction which can, as I will suggest, show what Milton had in mind. In sixteenth-century England, men almost without exception wore their hair shorter than in the seventeenth, and forelocks are comparatively rarer. Nicholas Hilliard portrayed himself with a decided forelock, and also showed one in his portrait of Sir Francis Drake, and William Camden is sometimes portrayed with a short forelock in the center of his high domed forehead, while Sir Nicholas Hyde was shown with three.[43] Single and undivided forelocks also appear in portraits of Algernon Sidney and Bulstrode Whitelock, while William Prynne, John Lilburne, and the Earl of Strafford all wore decided bangs over their foreheads.[44] Bangs and/or multiple forelocks appear frequently elsewhere, but where a single forelock appears, it is not parted.[45] Whatever else may be said about it, the "parted forelock"

[39] Emma Calderini, *Acconciature antiche e moderne*, Milan, 1963, figs. 449, 462, 541, and 551.

[40] Calderini, *Acconciature*, fig. 16.

[41] See L. Goldscheider, *Roman Portraits*, New York, 1940, and Antal Hekler, *Greek and Roman Portraits*, New York, 1912, *passim*.

[42] Milton refers to "Occasion's forelock" in *PR* III, 173. The following studies treat the literary and visual iconography of the motif: John E. Matzke, "On the Source of the Italian and English Idioms Meaning 'to take Time by the Forelock'," *PMLA* 8 (1893), 303-34; G. L. Kittredge, "To Take Time by the Forelock," *MLN* 8 (1893), cols. 459-69; Rudolph Wittkower, "Chance, Time and Virtue," *JWCI* 1 (1937-38), 313-21; and Erwin Panofsky, *Studies in Iconology*, pp. 71-72.

[43] Roy Strong, *Tudor and Jacobean Portraits*, 2 vols., London, 1969, II, figs. 67, 70, 125, 340; see also figs. 116-17, 378, and 611.

[44] Wolfe, *Milton and his England*, figs. 93a and b, 44c, 45, and 49a.

[45] David Piper, *Catalogue of Seventeenth-Century Portraits in the National Portrait*

Milton ascribes to Adam set him apart from the overwhelming majority of historical and legendary characters whose portraits have been preserved for us.

The Adam of *Paradise Lost* is in this regard almost unique, but not quite. We know two men who wore their hair with a parted forelock just like that of Milton's Adam: they were Oliver Cromwell and John Milton. The famous portrait of Cromwell executed by Peter Lely, showing warts and all, also shows a forelock neatly parted so as to fall toward the left and the right eye respectively, while the two miniatures of Cromwell by Samuel Cooper again show him wearing a forelock which was literally parted and falling to the left and right over his forehead.[46]

202

As for Milton himself, the engraved portrait of 1670 by William Faithorne shows a clearly parted forelock, falling symmetrically on his forehead over the left and right eyes, which John Martin describes as "two strands [lying] to right and left on the forehead."[47] The pastel portrait of Milton in the Firestone Library at Princeton shows the same unmistakable detail. Martin holds (rightly, I think) that this pastel was the original on which the Faithorne engraving was based, and though some critics disagree as to the priority, there is no doubt that the pastel was accepted by Milton's daughter, Deborah Clarke, as a living likeness of the poet.[48] The evidence seems incontrovertible: the kind of parted forelock Adam wears in *Paradise Lost* was rare indeed, but it was a characteristic shared also by Oliver Cromwell and John Milton.

203

EVE

As for Adam, the description of Eve is relatively brief, but it, too, contains significant physical details:

> She as a veil down to her slender waist
> Her unadorned golden tresses wore
> Dishevelled, but in wanton ringlets waved
> As the vine curls her tendrils. . . .

(IV, 304-7)

In this description there is nothing so puzzling as the parted forelock of Adam but the passage is nonetheless interesting for the insights it affords into Milton's choice of visual images.

Let us begin with Eve's "slender waist." The phrase immediately excludes the

---

Gallery: 1625-1714, Cambridge, 1963, pls. 2e, 3e and h, 4g, 5b and 7a. For Sir John Suckling, who usually arranged his hair with a single forelock, see Thomas Clayton, "An Historical Study of the Portraits of Sir John Suckling," *JWCI* 23 (1960), 105-26.

[46] See the illustrations facing pp. 245, 289 and 304 in Maurice Ashley, *The Greatness of Oliver Cromwell*, New York, 1958, and Wolfe, *Milton and His England*, fig. 93c.

[47] John R. Martin, *The Portrait of John Milton at Princeton*, Princeton, 1961, p. 6.

[48] The Hollis bust at Christ's College, Cambridge, which is accepted as a likeness of Milton and which Vertue ascribed to Pierce, also shows the parted forelock separated from the major portion of the hairline, falling toward either eye. See David Piper, "The Portraits of John Milton," *Christ's College Magazine* 60 (1970), 156-61.

possibility of associating Eve with the typical Rubens' nude, whose waist is hardly *VII*
slender. Nor could we accept the waist of Michelangelo's Eve of the Expulsion,
where the muscles seem already to have sagged as from the strains of childbirth
which has not yet occurred. The illustration of the 1544 Lyons Bible, ascribed to *169*
Holbein, shows Eve with a waistline which might almost indicate the early stages *190*
of pregnancy, though presumably it was not intended to do so. Again, the Eve of
the University College stained glass window is too full-bodied to qualify. The Eve *VI*
in Dürer's celebrated engraving shows a waist considerably narrower than her hips, *164*
but not appreciably narrower than her shoulders, and the same may be said for the
marble figure outside the cathedral in Milan carved by Cristoforo Solario. A survey *200*
of the Eves reproduced in the plates of this book will indicate that after about
1500 there was a marked division among artists as to whether Eve should appear
with a slim or full-bodied waist. Cranach consistently preferred slender waists. *163, 174,*
Dürer also painted a slim-waisted Eve, as may be seen in the Uffizi oil and in its *178*
prototype at the Prado, while Masolino's long-limbed Eve would qualify, and so *184*
would the more curvaceous Eve of the Medici tapestries. A comparison between *185*
these lists of slim and buxom Eves indicates the absence of any single convention *IV, V*
or standard, and here we would seem to gain at least some slight insight into
Milton's personal tastes in feminine beauty.

Milton's Eve wears her hair "as a veil" only to her waist, as do the Eves of *163, 174,*
Cranach. An individual artist could vary his handling here, as a comparison of *178*
Dürer's oil and his print shows. It may be that Milton cut short Eve's hair at the *164, 184*
waist in order to reinforce his assertion that "those mysterious parts" were not
then concealed (IV, 312), as I have already suggested, or again he may have been
merely following his own personal taste, and I can see no way to judge between
these two possibilities. At all events, Milton's description excludes any visual image
of the long hair that falls to, or even below, Eve's buttocks, as it is shown in the
Grimani Breviary, Dürer's oils, the Lyons Bible, the University College windows, *162, 184, 190*
and the Medici tapestries. *VI, IV, V*

When it came to describing the color of Eve's hair as golden, Milton had very
little, if any, choice, given the pervasive iconographical traditions.[49] It is interesting
to know, as Giamatti has informed us, of parallels in the description of Aphrodite
by Homer and Marino, and of Horace's "yellow-haired Pyrrha."[50] Ancient literary
attitudes toward feminine beauty must surely have had considerable influence upon
the complexion generally ascribed to Eve, but Milton did not need to think of
"golden Aphrodite" in order to imagine his Eve. At least from the Renaissance on,
Eve's hair was always blonde, and I know of no example in art which could not be
described, *mutatis mutandis*, by Milton's phrases "golden tresses" or "flowing gold"
(IV, 305 and 496), as we find in paintings by Masolino, Michelangelo, Tintoretto,
and virtually all others. The color reproductions shown here of the Medici tapestry, *IV, V*
the van Linge window, and the Rubens painting are representative.[51] *VI, VII*

[49] Réau, *Iconographie*, II, i, p. 78.
[50] Giamatti, *The Earthly Paradise*, pp. 319-20 and 323.
[51] There were a few dark-haired Eves prior to the Renaissance, as may be seen most
conspicuously in the Creation cupola of San Marco in Venice.

Milton also describes Eve's hair as "dishevelled," and in so doing he excludes a frequent, though not predominant, feature in representations of her. In Tintoretto's painting of the Fall, Eve's hair is rather neatly set about her head, and it is bound up in tiny encircling braids in the painting by Salviati. Michelangelo's Eve at the Fall has her hair similarly bound up, but it is flowing in a disheveled fashion at the Expulsion, which might seem to suggest a rather obvious difference between her prelapsarian and postlapsarian appearance. If so, however, the iconographic distinction was not generally accepted, for there are many examples of free-flowing hair on Eve prior to the Fall. I have seen at least two instances in which Eve is shown binding up her hair after the Fall, as she does in the Medici tapestries, but there Eve's hair again flows loosely as she is expelled from the Garden; in *The Judgment of Adam and Eve* by Paolo Farinati, in SS. Nazaro e Celso in Verona, dated 1557, Eve is again shown binding up her hair in a pose which suggests the influence of the Medici tapestries. In Bassano's *Paradise* in the Galleria Doria in Rome, where the chronology is somewhat ambiguous, Eve's hair is bound up, as it is in the *Expulsion* by Andrea del Minga and in Cristoforo Solario's marble figure of the postlapsarian Eve. In these representative examples, I can find no consistent prelapsarian or postlapsarian significance for disheveled hair.

When Milton described how Eve's hair "in wanton ringlets waved/ As the vine curls her tendrils, which implied/ Subjection," he was evoking the familiar vine symbolism which we have already treated, but he was doing so in a way which had long been established in the artistic tradition. To be sure, there had been some straight-haired Eves prior to 1600, as in the paintings by Masolino and Massaccio and in the Bedford Book of Hours; the *formella* executed by Andrea Pisano for the Florentine Campanile shows only the slightest waves. Barely waving hair may also be found on Eve in the Chiostro Verde and the Camposanto frescoes, in the S. Marco mosaics, in the 1544 Lyons Bible, and in the Altdorfer painting; of these, only the latter two date from as late as the sixteenth century. After about 1500, Eve's hair is typically curly, as in the Medici tapestries. Frequently, artists painted precisely the vinelike curls Milton described, as we may see in Dürer's engraving, Rizzo's statue, Mabuse's drawing, and almost invariably in Cranach.

Milton's visualization of Eve is an instructive example of his descriptive techniques, and as such should now be summarized. Above all, he wishes to create an image of Perfect Woman, and in so doing he will not allow a too particularized description to stand between his readers and their own conceptions of ideal beauty. But he does not rely upon a purely conceptual set of images, and he does select and exclude from the possibilities available to him. Only the golden tresses were an absolute given of the visual formula, so widespread that it is doubtful whether Milton or anyone else in his age could have imagined Eve with hair of any other color. At other points, Milton directed our imaginations to particular features of the visual tradition, such as describing Eve's hair as disheveled rather than neatly bound about her head or even carefully combed—another example of his insistence upon the native freedom and luxuriance of the Garden, where "not nice art" prevailed. As we have noted, the length of Eve's hair, extending only to the waist,

173
155
169
153, 154
204
205
200
185
189, 156
176
197
172, 177
190, 206
151-54
164, 166,
188
163, 174,
178

may be a reflection of Milton's personal taste, or may be a means of avoiding any intrusion of postlapsarian prudery. It is possible that the tendrillike ringlets of Eve's hair also reflect Milton's personal preference, but we cannot be sure, for the choice might on any grounds have been dictated by the same iconographic considerations that led so many other artists to make use of the motif. Only the slender waist, which is totally dissociated from any symbolic significance, can be interpreted with reasonable certainty as an indication of Milton's personal preference in ideal beauty. Even so, the whole figure is so carefully universalized, so discreetly made up of details chosen from the most beautiful representations of Eve, that the Eve of *Paradise Lost* evokes ideal feminine beauty in the mind of virtually every reader.

The five particulars which we have just considered represent either the standard view or accepted variations within the visual tradition. At other points, Milton's descriptions take him so far beyond the usual bounds of pictorial representations that I have been unable to find analogues. As already noted, I have found no example of Eve half concealed in a thick garden of roses, nor have I found any paintings of her as a flower-gardener and only one engraving, in an English gardening book of 1629. Again, though there are many instances of Eve's weeping as she leaves the *168* Garden, I know of none in which she sheds "a gentle tear" before the Fall, as Milton has her do after her devil-inspired dream (v, 129-35). Milton's graphic description of a Narcissus-like Eve lying on a green bank to look at her own image in "the clear smooth lake" is also unsupported by visual analogues (IV, 453-62). None of this should be surprising, for these incidents could not be self-explanatory as they would have to be in pictorial art, but demand the explanatory context that literature can provide. On the other hand, I had expected to find many examples of the flushed face which Milton ascribes to Eve after her Fall—"in her cheek distemper flushing glowed" (IX, 887). Such heightened color does appear in Eve's face as represented by Salviati, but whether it is part of the original paint, *155* I cannot say. The abrasion of skin tones is commonplace in older paintings, and perhaps inevitable after the passage of several centuries. I suspect that in Milton's time many Eves were painted at the Fall with flushed countenances but have since lost much of their heightened color.

Eve is repeatedly compared in *Paradise Lost* to other women in history and legend, and something should now be said about these.[52] Most important, perhaps, is the association of her with "blest Mary, second Eve" which occurs twice (v, 387, and x, 183). As those allusions are without visual content, there is no need to go beyond the written traditions in search of analogues, but it should be mentioned that there are also many such associations in the visual arts. The earliest linking of Eve with Mary in art occurred about 1015, and the two were repeatedly connected in art works until long after Milton's death.[53] So far as I can determine, nothing in

[52] See D. C. Allen, *Mysteriously Meant*, Baltimore, 1970, pp. 292-93.

[53] Ernst Guldan, *Eva und Maria*, Graz-Cologne, 1966, gives the fullest analysis of these, and appends approximately 175 reproductions of art works, of dates continuing through the life of Milton, in which the association of Eve and Mary is represented. See also Esche, *Adam und Eva*, especially figs. 30-40, and Trapp, "The Iconography of the Fall of Man," p. 258.

these art works would lead us to alter the conclusion reached by Sister Mary Christopher Pecheux in discussing Milton's use of the theme:

> It will be seen that the study of the concept of the Second Eve in *Paradise Lost* reveals nothing basically new (and this is a tribute to the skill with which Milton has integrated the idea with other parts of his theme), but it does show the richness of certain aspects of the poem. . . . Finally, it helps to substantiate the view of the poem as one of profound Christian optimism; for it does not permit us to forget the eventual happy ending. From the very beginning we know that the Fall is to come; but the hints and suggestions embodied in Eve's double role give the needed counter-point, which swells into a triumphant though muted climax at the end of Book XII.[54]

Long antedating Milton was the practice of associating figures of classical mythology with Eve, either directly in her own person or indirectly through that Second Eve, Mary. The earliest such association was with Pomona, and Bourguet suggests that early Christian artists, seeking some visual model for representing the Virgin and finding Venus and other well-known goddesses unsuitable, turned to Pomona.[55] Applying this analogy to Eve, Milton writes that she seemed most like "Pomona thus adorned," and declares that her bower "like Pomona's smiled" (IX, 393, and V, 378). Joannes Saenredam had made the same comparison in engravings executed in 1597 and 1605, in which analogy virtually becomes identity: Pomona and Eve (as also Vertumnus and Adam) are so alike in physical appearance that we must rely on their surroundings and attributes in order to distinguish them from each other.

207

The comparison with Venus came considerably later in Christian iconography and was not necessarily a direct influence even so. Kenneth Clark reminds us of a "diffused memory of that particular physical type developed in Greece between the years 480 and 440 B.C., which in varying degrees of intensity and consciousness furnished the mind of Western man with a pattern of perfection from the Renaissance until the present century."[56] In terms of that strong visual tradition, it was probably inevitable that Milton should have exalted Eve's beauty above that of Venus: "Eve/ Undecked, save with herself more lovely fair/ Than wood-nymph, or the fairest goddess feigned/ Of three that in Mount Ida naked strove" (V, 379-82). Just as Adam was visually compared to Apollo, so was Eve with Aphrodite. Indeed, the same print representing a nude woman, fig-leafed, with an apple extended in her right hand, was used to illustrate both Eve and Venus in the 1506 Venice edition of Boccaccio's *De Mulieribus Claris*. This conflation of images was not uncommon, but is epitomized in the paintings of Cranach, where the figures of Venus and of Eve often seem virtually indistinguishable. In Cranach's *Venus and Cupid* in the National Gallery, London, Venus is shown in Eve's typical posture

208

---

[54] Pecheux, "The Concept of the Second Eve in *Paradise Lost*," *PMLA* 75 (1960), 366; see also A. B. Chambers, "Three Notes on Eve's Dream in *Paradise Lost*," 191-93.

[55] Bourguet, p. 17.

[56] Clark, *The Nude*, Garden City, New York, 1959, p. 35.

by a fruit-laden tree which is visually reminiscent of the Tree of Knowledge, with the customary stag in the background, the principal differentiation being in the necklace and the hat Venus wears and in the fact that she is accompanied by Cupid.[57]

Milton's comparison of Eve with Proserpina ("while Proserpin gathering flowers/ Herself a fairer flower by gloomy Dis/ Was gathered, which cost Ceres all that pain" [IV, 269-71]) was an easy extension of an ancient iconographic motif. As Bernheimer has noted, "Berchorius gave an entire allegorical interpretation of the rape of Proserpina, claiming that Pluto was the devil, Proserpina the Christian soul, her mother Ceres the Church, and the flowers the vain temporal attractions of the world."[58] So understood, it was appropriate that the "enlèvement de Proserpine" should appear on the sarcophagus of Charlemagne.[59] Rosemond Tuve has long since commented that, although Milton usually found Christian allegorizings of pagan mythology to be silly, "his Ceres and Proserpina figure seems to have its poignant stab of loving compassion from unmentioned suggestions of the love of a truer redeeming Divinity that seeks us through the world."[60]

More extensive is the comparison Milton makes between Eve and Pandora:

> Espoused Eve deckt first her nuptial bed,
> And heavenly choirs the hymenaean sung,
> What day the genial angel to our sire
> Brought her in naked beauty more adorned,
> More lovely than Pandora, whom the gods
> Endowed with all their gifts, and O too like
> In sad event, when to the unwiser son
> Of Japhet brought by Hermes, she ensnared
> Mankind with her fair looks, to be avenged
> On him who had stole Jove's authentic fire.
>
> (IV, 710-19)

Milton had already observed in the *Doctrine and Discipline of Divorce* "what a consummate and most adorned Pandora was bestowed upon Adam to be the nurse and guide of his arbitrary happiness and perseverance, I mean his native innocence and perfection, which might have kept him from being our true Epimetheus."[61] The box Pandora opened, thus loosing all manner of afflictions upon mankind, had been compared to the forbidden fruit eaten by Eve as early as Gregory Nazianzus and Origen.[62] This patristic conception was revived at the time of the Renaissance, and was given its most famous artistic expression in the *Eva Prima Pandora* painted

---

[57] See the comment by Michael Levey, *The Nude*, p. 25.

[58] Richard Bernheimer, *Wild Men in the Middle Ages*, Cambridge, Mass., 1952, p. 133; see also pp. 133-35 and figs. 25 and 28.

[59] Cabrol, *Dictionnaire*, III, 795.

[60] Tuve, *Allegorical Imagery*, p. 228.

[61] *CE*, III, p. 441.

[62] Dora and Erwin Panofsky, *Pandora's Box: The Changing Aspects of a Mythical Symbol*, New York, 1962, pp. 12-13. This fascinating study is the definitive treatment of the subject.

209 by Jean Cousin in the 1540s.[63] As his title indicates, Cousin has cast Eve in the guise of Pandora.[64] Other artists reversed the process, and cast Pandora in the role and stance of Eve, holding the pyxis where Eve holds her fig leaf, as may be seen in drawings by Abraham van Diepenbeeck and, derivatively, an engraving by Abraham Bloemaert.[65] In addition, there are two rather attractive Spanish statuettes, dating between 1600 and 1610 and made of wood painted in flesh color, which have been attributed to El Greco, though without absolute certainty.[66] These figures so closely resemble those in traditional representations of the Fall, and even certain features of Dürer's famous 1504 engraving, that they have been taken as Adam and Eve. As the Panofskys note, however, "the very fact that the head of the male figure is covered with a kind of Phrygian cap and that its right hand gingerly holds a sealed vase—both motifs incompatible with the Garden of Eden —suffices to prove that the so-called Adam is really Epimetheus . . . and that the so-called Eve is in reality Pandora."[67] It is not necessary to assume that Milton was inspired by these pictorial, rather than literary, associations between Pandora and Eve: wherever the comparison may first have been suggested to him, the point is that his usage was reinforced both by the pictorial and the written traditions.

The comparison of Adam's awakening of Eve to "when Zephyrus on Flora breathes" is a typically Miltonic adaptation of a mythological theme, and one which has an interesting parallel in representational art (v, 16). The complexity of the visual and personal characteristics of Flora in art made her particularly apt for comparison to Eve. As we have already noted, Eve was not particularly distinguished in paintings by her association with flowers, but in a fascinating study entitled "Flora, Goddess and Courtesan," Julius Held has analyzed the artistic representations of Flora in a way which can be highly suggestive for Miltonists. He says that "after the middle of the sixteenth century we find Flora surrounded by . . . an ever increasing profusion of all kinds of flowering plants," which no doubt represent the increasing popularity of gardening, and which make Milton's allusion to Flora in connection with Eve especially rewarding.[68] Furthermore, the goddess acquired an unmistakably erotic character both in literature and in painting. "The simple fact that she had gained her position because of her amorous union with Zephyrus was enough to lend her a voluptuous character," as Held points out. "Thus it was inevitable that in pictorial representations of the nymph of spring, the bride of Zephyrus and the goddess of flowers, the erotic appeal of the figure would

---

[63] Trapp, "The Iconography of the Fall," pl. 26, reproduces this painting, but regards it as the only pictorial statement of the identification (p. 261), whereas the Panofskys reproduce several other examples.

[64] Hatzfeld, *Literature through Art*, pp. 58-59, discusses Cousin's painting in connection with the writings of Marot and others in France at the same period.

[65] Reproduced as figs. 35 and 36 in Dora and Erwin Panofsky, *Pandora's Box*, pp. 75-76.

[66] Harold Wethey, *El Greco*, I, figs. 353-54, and II, figs. 160-61.

[67] Dora and Erwin Panofsky, *op. cit.*, p. 155.

[68] Julius S. Held, "Flora, Goddess and Courtesan," in *Essays in Honor of Erwin Panofsky* (ed. Millard Meiss), New York, 1961, I, 206.

be emphasized in various ways."[69] This erotic character was often quite legitimate, but there was also a frequent tendency to treat Flora as a harlot, with "all the hallmarks of a portrait of a *cortigiana*."[70] Of such interpretations, Titian's *Flora* is probably the most famous. Suggestions of the courtesan Flora might have lent visual support to Milton's sometimes ironical treatments of Eve, but these would have formed no more than a possible undertone to Milton's comparison in the lines in question.

Milton's obvious intent in this passage was to associate Eve with the erotically attractive floral goddess, all within the authorized freedom of pure married love. His introduction of Flora is thus less like Titian's treatment and more like Rembrandt's. Postulating that Rembrandt had seen Titian's painting while it was in Amsterdam, Professor Held suggests that Rembrandt in a sense reversed Titian's conception so as to render Flora a perfect embodiment of honest married love by painting her in the person of his beloved wife Saskia. Rembrandt's rendition of the Flora theme is so like Milton's as to deserve comment, not because Milton saw the painting (which seems impossible, and I have found no evidence of etched or engraved copies) but because we have here two deeply religious and sectarian Protestants using the same subject to the same end, as both the painter and the poet exalt the pure physical love between husband and wife. As Held points out, when Rembrandt

> painted the portrait of Saskia in 1641 he completely changed the pattern, moved no doubt by the impression of Titian's painting. Like Titian's *Flora*, Saskia offers a flower with her right hand while the position of her left hand and her discreetly but unmistakably loosened dress and shirt give to the offer precisely the same meaning it had in Titian's work. Yet, with the artist's wife serving as the model, the picture has primarily a personal, private significance. . . . [Rather than] an image of a siren turning coyly chaste, Rembrandt painted Flora as a chaste woman giving herself trustingly to her wedded love. As a typical artist of the Renaissance, Titian dignified Flora's profession by making of her a figure of perfect beauty and grace. Rembrandt, the artist of the northern baroque, derived from the sensual image of the Renaissance a formal pattern with which to express a private and intimate sphere of experience. In borrowing Flora's language of signs Saskia hallows them. It is perhaps not too much to say that in this picture of Saskia as Flora, the courtesan of the early Fathers and of Boccaccio was finally redeemed.[71]

The inescapable implication of the contrast between Rembrandt's wedded *Flora* and Titian's courtesan *Flora* is precisely parallel to the contrast Milton draws between wedded love as the "Perpetual fountain of domestic sweets,/ Whose bed is undefiled and chaste pronounced,/ Present, or past, as saints and patriarchs used,"

[69] *Ibid.*, pp. 203 and 204. Classical writers made similar connections.
[70] *Ibid.*, p. 217, and pp. 208ff.
[71] *Ibid.*, p. 218.

on the one hand and on the other "the bought smile/ Of harlots, loveless, joyless, unendeared,/ Casual fruition" (IV, 760-67).

THE LOVE OF ADAM AND EVE

Milton's descriptions of the relations between Adam and Eve contain some of the finest love poetry ever written. "The loveliest pair/ That ever since in love's embraces met" are again and again described in attitudes of love, before the Fall, in *Paradise Lost* (IV, 321-23). Even at luncheon, they are shown as romantic lovers: "Under a tuft of shade . . . by a fresh fountain side,"

> side-long as they sat recline
> On the soft downy bank damaskt with flowers:
> The savory pulp they chew, and in the rind
> Still as they thirsted scoop the brimming stream;
> Nor gentle purpose, nor endearing smiles
> Wanted, nor youthful dalliance as beseems
> Fair couple, linkt in happy nuptial league,
> Alone as they.
>
> (IV, 333-39)

Again, Eve

> with eyes
> Of conjugal attraction unreproved,
> And meek surrender, half embracing leaned
> On our first father, half her swelling breast
> Naked met his under the flowing gold
> Of her loose tresses hid.
>
> (IV, 492-97)

At night,

> These lulled by nightingales embracing slept,
> And on their naked limbs the flowery roof
> Showered roses, which the morn repaired. Sleep on,
> Blest pair; and O yet happiest if ye seek
> No happier state, and know to know no more.
>
> (IV, 771-75)

Corcoran finds relatively little precedence for Milton's descriptions of the sexual life of Adam and Eve before the Fall, and Knott finds little emphasis even on the mere repose of Adam and Eve in the earlier literary traditions.[72]

[72] Mary Irma Corcoran, *Milton's Paradise with Reference to the Hexameral Background*, Washington, 1945, pp. 76ff., and Knott, *Milton's Pastoral Vision*, p. 48. Knott's view seems well substantiated, but I am less convinced of Corcoran's: sexual intercourse before the Fall seems to be implied in the *Adamus Exul* of Grotius, as translated in Kirkconnell, *The Celestial Cycle*, pp. 107, 139, and 203.

I have been unable to find many art works which correspond to Milton's descriptions of the prelapsarian lovemaking of Adam and Eve. Adam and Eve are shown with arms about one another as they walk through the Garden in Joannes Sadeler's engraving after a Marten de Vos painting (where the fig leaves were *180* added in ink to the print by some prudish owner), and their loving pose there is copied in an illustration for Joseph Fletcher's *Historie of the Perfect-Cursed-Blessed Man*, published in London in 1628. Similarly, Adam is shown with his arm *210* around Eve as they stroll through a glade in the background of a painting by Cornelius van Haarlem, but it is not absolutely certain that this is a prelapsarian *167* scene, though it probably is. Other such representations may be found, but they would surely be rare and would provide very little visual reinforcement from pictorial art for what we find in *Paradise Lost*. Essentially innovative, Milton's conception represents a poetic affirmation of those Puritan doctrines of the purity of married love which I and others have traced elsewhere.[73] Milton was at one with his coreligionists in repudiating ascetic doctrines such as those promulgated by the fourteenth-century Augustinian preacher Fra Simone Fidati, who declared that "married couples should not touch one another, neither seductively nor playfully, because this puts the fire of desire in their flesh,"[74] and by the *Ethiopic Book of Adam and Eve* which maintained that "the righteous regard marriage with reluctance. Adam has intercourse with Eve only three times in nine hundred and thirty years."[75] Denying this largely medieval asceticism, Milton and the Puritans could find support not only in the Bible but in the Rabbinic and patristic writers.[76] I have found no conclusive evidence of widespread support from pictorial art.

From our first view of Adam and Eve in *Paradise Lost* to our last, we see them holding hands. In his initial description of the pair, Milton writes that "hand in hand they pass" before Satan's eyes, and Eve recalls to Adam how at their first meeting "thy gentle hand/ Seized mine" (IV, 321, and 488-89). They never seem to walk without holding hands: "Thus taking hand in hand alone they passed" and again "into their inmost bower/ Handed they went" (IV, 689 and 738-39). On the morning of the Fall, Eve sets herself on a disaster course when "from her husband's hand her hand/ Soft she withdrew," as she goes to garden alone (IX, 385-86). Their hands are rejoined after the Fall only when Adam "seized" hers as a prelude to their debauched and newly exploitative orgy (IX, 1037). Their union is fully restored only in the last two lines of the epic when "they hand in hand with wandering steps and slow,/ Through Eden took their solitary way" (XII, 648-49). As has been widely recognized, the joining of hands is a very ancient symbol for the plighting and keeping of faith in marriage, as also in friendship and even in various kinds of social bonds. Milton can and does use the hieroglyph with the assurance that it will be understood.

Granting all this, it is surprising that Adam and Eve are so very rarely shown

[73] Frye, "The Teachings of Classical Puritanism on Physical Love in Marriage," *Studies in the Renaissance* 2 (1955), 148-59, and Halkett, *Milton and the Idea of Matrimony*.

[74] Quoted by Meiss, *Painting in Florence and Siena*, p. 26.

[75] Kirkconnell, *The Celestial Cycle*, p. 509.

[76] Adams, *Ikon: Milton and the Modern Critics*, p. 142.

by artists as holding hands. Having now examined many hundreds of art works representing the first parents, I have found only three examples in which they are visualized prior to the Fall in much the same way as Milton describes them. Here a distinction is basic: though Milton's insistence upon joined hands brings to mind the familiar joining of hands in the marriage ceremony, the *dextrarum iunctio*, or *fides manualis*, a moment's reflection will reveal how extraordinarily awkward it would be for a couple to walk through a garden holding each other by the *right* hands in the marriage gesture.[77] That gesture is appropriate to *stasis*, as when a bride and groom stand before a priest in the marriage ceremony: representations of "the marriage of Adam and Eve" sometimes picture them in this statuesque pose, as in Duvet's engraving. By holding hands, Adam and Eve evoke the meaning of that formal and hieratic gesture, but they do not physically conform to it, and indeed they scarcely can. They move gracefully, walk, "pass" before us repeatedly, holding hands in the only way possible for such sustained movements—namely, a joining of right and left hands. And it is precisely this joining of hands which is so extraordinarily rare in art.[78]

211

The only examples I know of prelapsarian Adam and Eve holding hands are to be found in three works: in Cranach's *Paradise* of 1530, Adam's left hand envelops Eve's wrist and right hand as the couple stand in the foreground before the Creator; in the frontispiece of the English Matthew Bible of 1537, Adam's left hand holds Eve's right as they sit upon the ground, surrounded by animals; and in an engraving by Saenredam after Bloemart, the couple is holding hands as they walk in the Garden. Of these, the Saenredam seems closest to Milton, not only for the closely interlocked fingers of the hands as Adam and Eve stroll but also for the pervasive sense of "youthful dalliance as beseems/ Fair couple, linkt in happy nuptial league,/ Alone as they" (IV, 337-40). As for the Expulsion, I have been able to find only three examples, and these are restricted to the twelfth and thirteenth centuries: the Index of Christian Art at Princeton identifies a twelfth-century sculpture at the cathedral in Skara in which Adam is said to be holding Eve's hand as the angel drives them out of Paradise, and there is a twelfth century stone carving in Malmesbury Abbey in which they do indeed hold hands.[79] In addition, there

163

212

213

[77] For the iconography of the *dextrarum iunctio*, the following may be consulted: Guy de Tervarent, *Attributs et symboles dans l'art profane*, pp. 258-60; Kirschbaum, *Lexikon der Christlichen Ikonographie*, I, 318ff. s.v. "Bräutigam und Braut"; Raimond van Marle, *Iconographie de l'art profane*, I, pp. 121-25; Erwin Panofsky, "Jan van Eyck's Arnolfini Portrait," *Burlington Magazine* 64 (1934), 117-27, esp. 123. In an especially interesting article, Phyllis L. Williams, "Two Roman Reliefs in Renaissance Disguise," *JWCI* 4 (1941), 47-66, traces Renaissance uses of the joined hands of marriage in Roman marriage portraits and emblems with inscriptions of *Fidei*, *Amor*, and *Virtus*, to which Milton has Adam specifically refer in his expostulations to Eve (IX, 335). I am indebted to William S. Heckscher for calling my attention to an association of the clasped hands with *amicitia* in O. Scarlatini, *Homo symbolicus*, Augsburg-Dillingen, 1695, pt. I, pp. 193 and 212. Though Scarlatini does not sufficiently define the clasped-hand gesture, I judge him to be concerned with the *dextrarum iunctio*.

[78] Emile Mâle notes of the redeemed at the general resurrection that "at Notre-Dame in Paris a husband and wife meet once more and walk hand in hand, united to all eternity" (*Gothic Image*, p. 384).

[79] See Fritz Saxl, *English Sculptures of the Twelfth Century*, London, 1954, pl. LXXI, but Saxl provides no iconographic comment.

is an illumination of the Expulsion executed by the thirteenth-century English miniaturist, William de Brailes, which shows the first parents leaving the Garden with Adam holding Eve's right hand in his right hand, though not so stiffly as in the conventional marriage gesture.[80] The pictorial examples I have cited here are unlikely to be the only ones produced, and others will undoubtedly be added to this list by other scholars, but illustrations of Adam and Eve holding hands can only be regarded as highly exceptional, a minuscule proportion of all the pictorial works devoted to them.[81] Rare examples occur in the hexameral writings, as when Vondel describes Eve "as her spouse led her across the meadows by the hand," but there is surely nothing here which can explain Milton's consistent use of this motif.[82]

Despite the paucity of examples for Adam and Eve, we would naturally expect that holding hands would have been as popular a custom in and before Milton's time as it is in our own. And, as art works have been proved invaluable sources for establishing such social customs and conventions in previous centuries, we would expect to find numerous examples of handholding in those art works which illustrate popular and courtly life. But again the visual evidence is strangely disappointing. Raimond van Marle's *Iconographie de l'art profane* provides a treasure of visual evidence on the daily life of all classes of society from the thirteenth to the sixteenth centuries, and it is surprising how rarely we see a man and woman walking hand in hand. The natural joining of hands may be found in representations of the dance, where it was indisputably common, but it almost never appears under other circumstances. In the 160 illustrations of the two chapters entitled "Les Rapports entre les deux sexes" and "L'Amour," van Marle shows none of a couple walking as Adam and Eve habitually do in *Paradise Lost*. Even his illustrations of *promenades d'amoureux* show only one couple holding hands and they are seated.[83] Aldegrave's *Dansers des noces* series shows a man holding a woman's hand as he kisses her, and there is some hand play in other scenes, while a man in a bathhouse takes a nude woman's hand to draw her into bed, but that is just about the extent of what we find.[84] Van Marle surely does not exhaust all of the visual evidence of customs and behavior, but he provides a strong cross-section of that evidence, in which hand-holding is startlingly rare. A perusal of Arthur M. Hind's *Engraving in England in the Sixteenth and Seventeenth Centuries* yields much the same results. Two examples may suffice as illustrations. Family trees for the House of Stuart engraved

[80] Eric Millar, "Additional Miniatures by W. de Brailes," *Journal of the Walters Art Gallery* 2 (1939), 106-9, reproduced as fig. 3 on p. 107. The miniature is one of seven from the Georges Wildenstein Collection, and unfortunately I have been unable to secure a reproduction.

[81] I am indebted to Mrs. Martha Lively for a survey of illuminations in the Western manuscripts of the Bodleian Library, on the basis of which she reports that she "found nothing of them holding hands."

[82] Vondel's *Lucifer* in Kirkconnell, *The Celestial Cycle*, p. 365.

[83] Raimond van Marle, *Iconographie de l'art profane*, I, fig. 460 on p. 464, reproducing a sixteenth-century French tapestry. There may be one additional instance in the late fifteenth-century Italian *Fountain of Youth* engraving, II, fig. 466 on p. 437, but the poor detail makes it impossible to be certain.

[84] *Ibid.*, I, fig. 479 on p. 479, fig. 460 on p. 464, fig. 465 on p. 467, and fig. 517 on p. 515.

by William Kip and by Benjamin Wright show portraits of the royal couples among the vines of the family tree, and the clasped hands of the standard *fides manualis* are used emblematically. A somewhat later engraving by Francis Delaram showing the betrothal of Charles I and Henrietta Maria blessed by an angel, combines features of the popular portrait with the emblem,[85] but the pose is static and unsuited to the kind of walking which is characteristic of Milton's descriptions of Adam and Eve.[86]

Representations in art have preserved much of what we know of the daily life, customs, and behavior of earlier cultures, yet apart from the dance and from the patently symbolic *dextrarum iunctio*, the rarity of hand-holding in the pictorial records must be regarded as curious. Perhaps the actual practice was uncommon.[87]

[85] Hind, *Engraving in England in the Sixteenth and Seventeenth Centuries*, II, pls. 4 and 34.

[86] Though it does not conform to Milton's description of holding hands, there is a portrait of Charles I and Henrietta Maria at Hampton Court, by Daniel Mytens, in which the Queen has placed her right hand extended and flat, with the fingers together, palm down, directly over the extended hand of the King, with palm upward. A couple might stand in a formal arrangement for a portrait in this pose, but could scarcely walk very far this way through Eden. A reproduction may be seen in Oliver Millar, *Tudor, Stuart and Early Georgian Pictures in the Collection of Her Majesty the Queen*, London, 1963, II, pl. 59. The painting of the Salusbury Family, about 1640, which is reproduced as 149 in Oliver Millar's *The Age of Charles I*, does show Sir Thomas Salusbury holding his wife's hand, as he apparently prepares to mount his horse. The hand-holding here would allow the couple to walk "handed" together, but in context it appears to be a farewell gesture. In a still different context, mortuary representations of husbands and wives with hands joined in the marriage gesture were popular in England, as may be seen in Herbert Haines, *A Manual of Monumental Brasses*, Bath, 1970, LXI-LXII; Arthur Gardner, *English Medieval Sculpture*, figs. 462 and 473; Thomas S. R. Boase, *Death in the Middle Ages*, pp. 86-87; and Fred H. Crossley, *English Church Monuments*, pp. 18, 34, 243, 251, and 254. Marriage portraits in England in the Tudor and Stuart periods sometimes represented husband and wife with the *dextrarum iunctio*, as may be seen in the painting executed in 1602 of Sir Thomas and Lady Helen Fane, now hanging at Fulbeck Hall in Lincolnshire, reproduced in *Country Life* (Feb. 17, 1972), p. 398. John Dixon Hunt and Peter Willis in *The Genius of Place*, London, 1975, p. 68, reproduce Cornelius Holsteyn's *Reynier Pouw with His Wife*, ca. 1650, which shows this couple "handed" in their garden like Adam and Eve, while Joris Hoefnagel's *A Marriage Feast in Bermondsey*, ca. 1570, shows two couples holding hands in the left foreground (collection of the Marquess of Salisbury, Hatfield House). Finally, there is a portrait of husband and wife, showing Walter Devereux, Lord Ferrers of Chartley, Viscount Hereford, with his wife Lettice, daughter of Sir Francis Knollys, which is or was in the possession of the Viscount Hereford at Hampton Court, Leominster, showing the couple holding hands in the Miltonic gesture (left hand and right hand), which is reproduced in E. M. Tenison, *Elizabethan England*, 1933, bk. I, vol. III, opposite p. 18.

[87] Meetings between human beings and God or an angel often involve a contact of hands, but this usage rarely corresponds to Milton's descriptions of Adam and Eve walking hand in hand. In *PL* VIII, 300, and XI, 421, Milton has first God and then Michael raise Adam "by the hand," whereas in the visual arts this gesture is far rarer than that in which Adam is grasped by the wrist, as in Ghiberti's Creation panel for the Florentine Baptistry doors, and in the fresco by Paolo Uccello for S. Maria Novella in Florence. Representations of Christ in Limbo are similar, as in the nave mosaic in S. Marco, Venice, where Christ grasps the wrist of the patriarch, though we do encounter a handshaking gesture in the Limbo window of King's College Chapel in Cambridge. In early Christian representations of the Ascension of Christ, a hand from Heaven reaches down to take Christ's hand, but in the

However that may be, there can be no doubt that Milton's repeated descriptions of Adam and Eve walking hand in hand represented a striking innovation, for which there was only the slightest pictorial precedence and reinforcement. The appropriateness of the gesture as expressing the innocent and loving intimacy of prelapsarian life cannot be denied, and has often been remarked upon. The evidence developed here not only shows the extent of Milton's originality but may also indicate something very individual and even personal about Milton himself. When *Paradise Lost* was published in 1667, Milton had been totally blind for fifteen years, "In power of others, never in my own," as his Samson said, and as he moved about in darkness he must himself often have made Samson's request: "A little onward lend thy guiding hand" (*SA*, 78, and 1). As a blind man, the experience of walking hand in hand must have seemed to him almost the ultimate expression of human affection and mutuality. As such, he used it as a descriptive detail which, both actually and symbolically, characterized the ideal relationship between Adam and Eve.

---

late tenth century the gesture of the heavenly hand changes, and Christ tends thereafter to be grasped about the wrist, and not by his hand (Schiller, *Ikonographie*, III, figs. 451, 457, 477, 480, 484, and 500, and Réau, *Iconographie*, II, i, p. 7). The Byzantine Painters' Manual directs that the Lord in Heaven should be represented as taking by the hand the soul who has mounted to the top step of the Ladder of Salvation (Didron, *Christian Iconography*, II, p. 380). The characteristic gesture of a Divinity leading a human being by the wrist, rather than by the hand, may be traced as far back as about 2150 B.C., in the Stele of Gudea, now in the Vorderasiatisches Museen in Berlin. Representations of Tobias and the Angel usually do show Raphael leading the boy by the hand, and the rescuing angel leads Peter by the hand out of prison in Raphael's *The Freeing of Peter*, in the Vatican.

XVI

The Fall and its Effects

174
169
88
152, IV
VI, VII

THE FALL

MILTON systematically described each of the principal pictorial types for the Tempter in the Garden, as we have seen: the purely herpetological snake wound around the Tree appears in the serpent-devil's account to Eve of his own eating of the Fruit; the hybrid serpent-woman appears as Sin at the Gates of Hell; finally, Milton adopts for the operative Fall in his epic the erect serpent such as we see on the frontispiece of Luther's first Bible and in the Medici tapestries. As for the forbidden fruit itself, Milton's description of it as ruddy and gold conformed to the most widely accepted representation in art, as we have also seen. Finally, the placing of the Fruit on a bough so high as to require Eve to reach for it was also a standard feature of the visual representations. In each of these ways, Milton's descriptions would have been reinforced by the familiar representations in the visual arts.

Milton's most important divergence from the typical pictorial representations of the Fall is predictable, given the inherent differences between visual and verbal opportunities. In the overwhelming majority of visual representations, Adam and Eve are shown at the Tree together, and it is at least strongly implied that Adam's Fall follows immediately upon Eve's. This conflation of time may well have been forced upon most artists by the limits of space available, but such restriction did not apply to Milton. He was able to expand the action for narrative and dramatic effect. Adam and Eve are separated at the time of her Fall, and his Fall does not take place at the Tree but at some little distance away where "he her met,/ Scarce from the Tree returning" (IX, 849-50).

Immediately after Eve's Fall, Milton introduces a visual episode which is far removed from the mainstream of pictorial representation. Intoxicated as she is with the effects of the Fruit, Eve promises to give song and due praise to the Tree each morning, just as she has previously given these honors to God (IX, 800). Then, just before she sets out to meet Adam, she actually performs this blasphemous rite before the Tree:

> from the Tree her step she turned,
> But first low reverence done, as to the power
> That dwelt within, whose presence had infused
> Into the plant sciental sap, derived
> From nectar, drink of Gods.

(IX, 834-38)

For this dramatic episode, I know of only one possible parallel in art: in the lower register of an illumination in *Genesis B*, the postlapsarian Adam is shown kneeling in prayer to God, while Eve bows all the way to the ground in "low reverence," virtually prostrating herself before the Tree.¹ This drawing is but one of several striking examples of coincidences between *Paradise Lost* and the illustrations in this eleventh-century English manuscript, but we have no contemporary evidence that Milton ever saw the manuscript. However the idea of Eve's idolatry may first have been suggested to Milton, his description here would have struck his readers as one of his most brilliant innovations, for which nothing in the commonly known visual tradition would have prepared them.

When Eve leaves the Tree and goes to meet Adam, she breaks off a bough with fruit to take to him. In the meanwhile, he has prepared a garland of flowers for her, which he brings to their meeting. One could scarcely find a stronger antithesis than between the two gifts each has plucked for the other, with profound symbolic implications in each case. Milton's development of this garland episode is, as far as I have been able to learn, unique in literary treatments of the Fall.² In the absence of Eve,

> Adam the while
> Waiting desirous her return, had wove
> Of choicest flowers a garland to adorn
> Her tresses, and her rural labors crown,
> As reapers oft are wont their harvest queen.
>
> (IX, 838-42)

When the couple meet again and Adam learns of her trespass, he drops the garland, from which the roses fall apart disjointed and begin to fade: "From his slack hand the garland wreathed for Eve/ Down dropped, and all the faded roses shed" (IX, 892-93). Milton's poetic innovation here could scarcely be more apposite, for as Professor Knott has written, "Adam's fading roses suggest not only Eve's alienation from nature but the inability of nature to withstand the presence of sin."³ That idea is conveyed in lines which are equally successful as verbal picture and as expressive symbol.

A striking parallel to Milton's garland may be found in a painting by Salviati

---

¹ The illustrator has here departed from the Anglo-Saxon text which he is supposedly illustrating, for it contains nothing that would account for Eve's worship of the Tree.

² Milton's uniqueness, of course, consists only in having introduced the garland into this episode of the Genesis story. In other contexts the garland had a long history in poetry: it was not uncommon in the classical period but disappeared for centuries, only to reappear in Sannazaro and to be continued by later poets including Marot, Spenser, Shakespeare, and Milton. See C. Ruutz-Rees, "Flower Garlands of the Poets, Milton, Shakespeare, Marot, Sannazaro," in *Mélanges offerts à M. Abel Lefranc.*

³ Knott, *Milton's Pastoral Vision*, p. 122. Evans, *"Paradise Lost" and the Genesis Tradition*, pp. 58 and 284, notes a Jewish tradition that all the trees shed their leaves when Eve ate the fruit, and notes also that Martin Luther had used a garland to teach that man's original purity was like "a wreath on a pretty girl. The wreath is not part of the virgin's nature; it is something apart from her nature," and suggests that Milton "fused these two ideas together."

in the Palazzo Colonna in Rome. Executed in the middle years of the sixteenth century, this is the only painting I know which incorporates this detail, just as Milton's is the only literary treatment to do so. In Salviati's painting, we see Adam receiving the Fruit from Eve, as he sits upon the ground. At his feet in the lower part of the canvas we see a number of roses which have been plucked and are now fallen in confusion. One or two are upside down, and some of the blossoms are already withering where they lie. The implication is obvious and even inescapable: Salviati's Adam, like Milton's, had picked these flowers for Eve, and had dropped them in the same circumstances.[4]

What are we to make of this striking coincidence in which a visual motif, otherwise apparently unique both in literature and in art, is used to precisely the same visual and symbolic effect by a sixteenth-century painter and a seventeenth-century poet? In the present state of our knowledge, each of us must apply his own scale of probability, and no definitively conclusive answer seems possible. Milton could certainly have seen this painting while he was in Italy, and it could have planted in his mind an association which later bore fruit in his account of the Fall in *Paradise Lost*, and I suspect that this is what happened. Or the two men may have been influenced by a common source. On the other hand, Milton's imagination was certainly creative enough to have arrived at the conception without Salviati's prompting. What is surely more important than any possible source relationship, is the powerful effectiveness with which each of these artists has employed the same device.

Eve's gift of the bough of fruit is as common in art as Adam's picked flowers are rare. Like the artists, Milton does not picture Eve's breaking of the bough from the Tree, but he does describe it—"in her hand/ A bough of fairest fruit that downy smiled,/ New gathered, and ambrosial smell diffused," and in a slightly later scene he notes that "the bough/ She gave him of that fair enticing fruit" (IX, 851-52 and 995-96). There was no need, of course, for Eve to offer Adam more than the Fruit itself, and sometimes the incident is so illustrated, as in the Medici tapestry devoted to the Fall. More typically, however, a bough or branch with leaves and fruit is shown, and may be passed from the Serpent to Eve, from Eve to Adam, or simply be held by one of the three principals in the scene. In addition to bearing the Fruit, which was the essential property of the story, the bough was useful because of its leaves, and these were often deployed to cover the private parts of Adam and Eve. In Dürer's influential 1504 engraving we see Eve holding the Fruit in her left hand with a branch attached which performs this function for her, whereas Adam is covered by a leafy branch from a nearby tree. Cranach sometimes allowed neighboring foliage to provide this concealment, as in the Courtauld painting, but more often he used the leaves of a bough broken from the Tree, as

[4] An almost identical painting by Salviati may be seen in the Chigi Chapel of S. Maria del' Popolo in Rome, though without the fallen roses. It is interesting to note, and it may possibly have some slight relevance, that "Francesco Salviati is the one contemporary painter whom the young Tasso mentions," according to E. K. Waterhouse, "Tasso and the Visual Arts," p. 151.

in the Uffizi paintings and in the *Paradise* from Vienna.[5] The bough operates to the same purpose in the Prado paintings by Dürer, and in their replicas at the Uffizi, and also in the woodcut (ascribed to Holbein) in the 1544 Luther Bible. Hans Brosamer incorporated the motif into his print, as did Cornelius van Haarlem in his painting. It was represented also in Limoges enamels, and was one of the standard features found in engravings of the subject.[6] Once established as a part of the visual tradition, the leaves of the bough do not always serve for covering. The popular engraving by Marcantonio Raimondi, based upon Raphael, shows a completely exposed Adam and Eve, and in Adam's upraised left hand a small twiglike bough with two pieces of fruit and two leaves. In Abraham van Linge's 1641 stained glass rendition, the serpent holds a bough with leaves and fruit above Eve's head, but within her reach while she holds another piece of fruit in her hand.

178, 163
183, 184
190
214
167

VI

Milton explicitly disavowed any such concealment prior to the Fall, for reasons we have already examined, and so the bough could not perform for him its original and persistent function in pictorial art.[7] Why then did he choose to provide two descriptions of the bough Eve brought to Adam, when the simple Fruit would have been enough? Here the answer would appear to be quite simple: the branch with fruit and leaves had been so firmly established in scenes of the Fall that it appeared natural, and perhaps even inevitable. In Milton's time, one almost always *saw* the Fall in this way. Granted this almost universal visual tradition to which Milton's imagery conforms, we can be far more confident in assuming that Milton was influenced by the visual arts than even in the case of so striking and unique a correspondence as that between Milton's and Salviati's introduction of the gift of roses, fallen and scattered by Eve's Fall.

Milton provides extensive insight into the psychological reactions of the first parents to the Fruit and to the Fall. His achievement here cannot be traced to any source in art, but from the Renaissance on artists had helped people to think of the Fall in psychological terms. Prior to the fifteenth century, artists had done little more than provide visual reminders of the story. In the Quattrocento, Italian artists hesitantly began to suggest the feelings of the tempted couple at the Tree. In the first half of that century, Michele di Matteo painted Adam holding a branch

---

[5] For other examples of Cranach's typical usage, see his paintings in the collections of Norton Simon, Inc., and in the museums at Breslau, Dresden, Braunschweig, Strasbourg, and Berlin, most of which are reproduced by Heinrich Lilienfein, *Lukas Cranach und Seine Zeit*, Leipzig, 1942.

[6] See the Small Passion series of plaques from the sixteenth century in the Wallace Collection in London, and the enamel of about 1570, signed Pierre Reymond, in the Victoria and Albert; also the prints by H. S. Beham in Hollstein, *German Engravings*, III, p. 172; by Jacob Matham in Hollstein, *Dutch and Flemish Engravings*, XI, p. 215; the frontispiece to the 1633 Edinburgh edition of the Authorized Version; and the prints dated 1562 in the Kitto Bible, I, 8v. and 9v.

[7] A very different use of a bough may be seen in an engraving by Robert van Voerst of Charles I and Henrietta Maria: the Queen is shown with a small bough in her left hand, and passing a larger one with her right hand to the King. The use of boughs here is interesting, but is patently unrelated to the Fall. See Hind, *Engraving in England*, III, pl. 99.

in his left hand, and smelling the Fruit, which he holds in his right hand.[8] The
suggestion here is not altogether successful or convincing, for the visual artist lacks
that sensual range of possibilities which enabled Milton to introduce not only the
attractive appearance but also the "ambrosial smell" of the Fruit. Painting is better
able to show a close visual inspection of the Fruit, and thereby to suggest a mental
appraisal of the Temptation, and Mantegna in his *Vierge de la Victoire* at the
Louvre shows Eve much as Milton envisioned her when "fixed on the Fruit she
gazed" (IX, 735). Again, Milton's description of how "greedily she engorged without restraint" and of how Adam, once he has made his fatal decision, "took no
thought,/ Eating his fill" can more readily be given full and unambiguous expression in painting, as we find when Mantegna shows Adam greedily eating the Fruit
from one hand while reaching with the other for another piece from the Tree
(IX, 791 and 1004-5).

In the High Renaissance and later, psychological reactions were increasingly
emphasized in representations of the Fall, and in the later renderings, as Trapp has
observed, Adam was shown to run "the gamut from doubt and hesitation to fear
and recoil."[9] No single pictorial representation can incorporate the entire gamut,
of course, but virtually every conceivable reaction may be found. Lucas van
Leyden shows Adam with a blank and almost stupefied stare in his eyes, as he
215 reaches eagerly for the bough of fruit presented by a coy and calculating Eve,
while the painting by Jordaens shows Adam eagerly reaching out to take the apple
from Eve even as she is about to bite into it.[10] In the Medici tapestries, Adam
IV appears less eager, but still open and susceptible: Eve extends her right hand and
arm almost to their full length in passing him the Fruit, and while his receiving arm
is only half extended, he does lean forward, and gaze intently upon her face, as
152 though listening attentively to her persuasive words. Cranach shows a nonplused
174 Adam, who scratches his head in perplexity even as he takes the Fruit from Eve.
162 In the Grimani Breviary, Eve stares away from Adam with eyes which seem
almost to imply that she has been drugged, and Adam raises both hands as though
in protest against the Fruit which she is passing to him. Altdorfer paints an authori-
206 tative Adam, whose alert and serious face and magisterially raised hand and forefin-
ger seem to rebuke Eve, who holds the already bitten apple in the stance of a somewhat shamefaced school girl who is enduring reproof. It is Burgkmair who perhaps
216 most effectively suggests that a Miltonic discussion or even debate is taking place, as
Eve invitingly extends the Fruit in her right hand and gestures with her left as
though to depreciate Adam's objections, while Adam stands with his lips parted
171 as in speech and his left hand raised in admonition. Titian and Rubens show Adam
seated with his back toward the viewer, his right arm extended with his hand
touching Eve's shoulder in a gesture implying remonstrance and restraint. Tinto-
173 retto's Adam is drawing back in consternation, away from Eve's proffered hand,
with one hand raised to his chin in shocked recognition of what she has done and

---

[8] Reproduced in Esche, *Adam und Eva*, fig. 37.
[9] Trapp, "The Iconography of the Fall," p. 264.
[10] Van Puyvelde, *Jordaens*, pl. 84.

would lead him to do. In Rembrandt's 1638 etching, the first parents confound us with their homeliness, as though their native beauty has been lost even as they consider the Fruit. Adam is caught in a tension between attraction and revulsion, at once desirous of the Fruit and horrified by it, raising his right hand in a gesture of rejection even as his left hand reaches out to grasp the forbidden Fruit.

In these paintings and prints we find occasional counterparts to Milton's eagerly persuasive Eve and amazed Adam who "astonied stood and blank, while horror chill/ Ran through his veins" (IX, 890-91), but we cannot find the full range of the emotions presented by Milton in any one of these examples. Here, differences between the visual and verbal forms of art control differences of effect. Because the story of the Fall was universally known, the artists were able (once they became seriously interested in doing so) to postulate psychological reactions for the characters involved, and to do so by purely visual means. The range of their interpretations and the extent of their successes are impressive and demonstrate beyond doubt the possibilities for characterization inherent in line, color, and volume. There is no way that Milton or any other poet could have duplicated these achievements by purely verbal descriptions of facial expression and bodily posture, for words can only very incompletely suggest the direction of lines, the contour of shapes, and the tones of color through which the artist achieves his effects. Milton's description of the Fall is carried out preponderantly through the use of psychological, spiritual, and conceptual terms, for these offered him as a poet the most direct access to his chosen effects. His primarily pictorial words and phrases are thus restricted in effect, but are nonetheless carefully chosen and combined. So understood, Milton's account of the Fall may not be maximally visual, but it is optimally so, and as a poet he can of course explain psychological reactions more extensively than can a painter.

THE EFFECTS OF THE FALL

Having presented the Fall, Milton's next task is to show its effects upon Adam and Eve. The initial effect upon both of them is the lustful orgy, "of their mutual guilt the seal," in which they indulge for the first time in sexual predation and exploitation of each other (IX, 1043). With "carnal desire inflaming, . . . in lust they burn," as Adam "on Eve/ Began to cast lascivious eyes, she him/ As wantonly repaid," as her "eye darted contagious fire" (IX, 1013-15 and 1036). Eve had already embraced Adam as he prepared to eat the Fruit (IX, 990), and now he "seized" her hand and "led her nothing loth" to their couch (IX, 1037-39). Their orgiastic union at this point is in every way a debasement of the unalloyed happiness of the intercourse they had enjoyed in their state of innocence.

Sex had also been associated with the Fall in many famous art works, but these allow ambiguities which Milton has carefully avoided. An artist can show physical contact between Adam and Eve at the time of the Fall, and imply that a sexual union will follow it immediately, but no picture alone can tell whether the Fall was caused by the first recognition of sexual desire, or sexual desire by the Fall, and so forth. All that the artist can do is to provide hints and innuendoes by a graphic association of the two, without defining their causative and sequential relationships.[11] Milton's narrative form with event following event, and his epic sweep which provided for ample commentary on each event, allowed him to communicate his meanings with a specificity and to an extent which would be impossible in any nonverbal form of art. In *Paradise Lost* as in Genesis, man brings on his fall not by sexual activity but the presumptuous attempt to "be as God." For Milton, the postlapsarian orgy is a parody of what has existed before, a parody because Adam and Eve no longer enjoy each other as creatures under God, but rather exploit each other as presumptuous and even rival deities. An artist who provides a visual association of the Fall with sex may agree with Milton's understanding, or he may believe that sex began as a result of the Fall, or he may hold that the Fall was the result of sex—but he cannot make a single picture tell us explicitly which views he holds.

That generic distinction between the possibilities of visual and verbal art is absolutely basic, and once it has been recognized, we can go on to note that pictorial art, particularly that of in the sixteenth century, provided strong visual reinforcement for Milton's descriptions. The sexual intentions of the first parents are clear enough in the 1511 engraving by Baldung Grien, where Adam's hand is cupped around Eve's breast, and matters seem to have progressed even a stage

191, 192 further in Baldung's 1519 engraving where they regard each other as in Milton
165 with "lascivious eyes." In a painting by Frans Floris, Eve sits in Adam's lap as she
157, 218 offers him the Fruit and in an oil by Mabuse, as in a Dürer print, the standing
166 couple embrace as they prepare to eat. Most explicit of all is a drawing by Mabuse, where the sexual reverberations are as unmistakable as an artist could possibly make them within the limits of tact and good taste; to have gone further would have been to enter the realm of pornography. Other examples could be cited, but these are sufficient to establish the range of artistic analogies to Milton's treatment.[12]

Pictorial representations of Adam and Eve directly after the Fall are less numerous than those which show them before and during the Fall. Consequently, there are not many visual analogies to Milton's descriptions of how Adam and Eve recognize and eventually come to terms with their guilt. After their postlapsarian orgy, Milton describes that they "rose/ As from unrest," and found themselves "destitute and bare/ Of all their virtue: silent, and in face/ Confounded long they sat, as strucken mute" (IX, 1051-52, 1062-64). We find much the same scene in the

[11] Trapp, "Iconography," p. 167, mentions a twelfth-century manuscript illumination which shows the serpent kissing Eve's lips, but I have found no other examples of this treatment.

[12] For example, the engraving of 1536 by H. S. Beham (Hollstein, *German Engravings*, III, p. 4), the Grisaille enamel signed by Pierre Courtois in the Victoria and Albert, Dürer's later print (fig. 218), a drawing by Spranger, paintings of the Fontainebleau School, and of the school of Bronzino, several of which are reproduced by Trapp, who comments that "certainly as the sixteenth century progresses there is what looks like strong emphasis on sexuality" in representations of the Fall ("The Iconography of the Fall," pp. 251-52 and 264, and pls. 16, 17, 22, and 27). Trapp seems to read more sexual significance into Tintoretto's painting of the Fall (fig. 173) than is explicitly there.

lower register of one of the illustrations in *Genesis B*, where both remorse and *40*
silence are powerfully conveyed through a few strokes of the artist's pen. Effective
as this Anglo-Saxon illumination is, it can scarcely compare in profundity to
Rembrandt's drawing of the scene. Rotermund aptly characterizes Rembrandt's *219*
nervously sketched lines as "almost stenographic reports of psychic processes," and
here we find an almost perfect counterpart of Milton's poetic rendering of despair
and psychic devastation.[13]

Milton's next visual reference comes when Adam wonders aloud how he can
again behold the dazzling light of God or angel, "erst with joy/ And rapture so oft
beheld" (IX, 1081-82). This visual motif is most often seen in paintings of the
Expulsion, where Adam and Eve frequently shield their eyes from the brilliant
sight of the angel. As Milton wishes to conclude his epic on another note, he places
this reference to a brightness now grown insufferable immediately after the Fall.
The same strategy is evident in his treatment of their weeping. In Milton's Expulsion, they soon wipe the tears from their eyes, whereas in some of the most famous
representations of the Expulsion they are shown to be dissolved in tears, as we
shall see. Milton antedates this motif when he declares, soon after the Fall, that
"tears/ Rained at their eyes" (IX, 1121-22), but he does not go beyond this
torrential weeping to give further visual expression to their anguish. We even miss
the standard physical gesture of pictorial representations where the "emotional
note of remorse is added by the bowing of their heads upon their hands."[14] That
gesture may be seen in Rembrandt's drawing, and repeatedly in the illuminations of *219*
Genesis B, but Milton does not need it and does not use it. Aside from the visual *38-40*
details already cited, the overwhelming remorse of Adam and Eve is conveyed in
their own words, which are predominately conceptual and psychological.

In Genesis, when the fallen Adam and Eve stand under the judgment of God,
Adam seeks to shift his responsibility to Eve, and Eve attempts to shift hers to the
serpent. Artists frequently translated this story into visual terms by showing Adam
pointing accusingly toward Eve, and Eve pointing to the serpent, in gestures
which are known in art history as the transference of blame.[15] This naive but
effective representation of the Biblical story may be found in the bronze doors of
Saint Bernward, erected in Hildesheim early in the eleventh century, in the relief
carvings on the baptismal font in the Chapel of St. John in the Siena cathedral, and
in the Medici tapestry. So far as I know, no artist has succeeded in communicating *153*
by visual means alone a sense of the bitter accusations Adam and Eve level against
each other in *Paradise Lost*. There are examples of their turning away from each
other, beginning with the Junius Bassus sarcophagus of 359, but though the sug- *54*
gestion in such visual accounts is clear, it necessarily remains rudimentary. Milton
develops verbal exchanges between them which extend the transference of blame

[13] Hans-Martin Rotermund, *Rembrandt's Drawings and Etchings for the Bible*, Philadelphia, 1969, p. 10. For purposes of compositional balance, Rembrandt has shown Eve as standing, whereas she is seated in Milton (as in *Genesis B*), but the import of the figures remains
the same.

[14] Green, "The Adam and Eve Cycle," p. 345.

[15] *Ibid.*

to each other, and these exchanges are profoundly revelatory of human nature.[16] In these episodes, Milton's method is almost purely conceptual, with the minimum of visual projection: he allows us to hear and follow their diatribes, and then he comments in summary upon them that "thus they in mutual accusation spent/ The fruitless hours, but neither self-condemning,/ And of their vain contest appeared no end" (IX, 1187-89). All mutuality has been lost, and Milton portrays each as sunk within himself or herself, isolated from the other. The *Genesis B* artist gives fine visual expression to this understanding when he shows each of the first parents alone, absorbed in individual guilt, and separated by the trees of the forest. It is this artist who has also come closest to conveying in pictorial form what at least appears to be an argument between them after the Fall, and I know of nothing quite so Miltonic until after the publication of *Paradise Lost*.

38, 40

The recovery of Adam and Eve comes only when they begin to feel the possibility of divine forgiveness, consequently show concern for each other, and finally kneel in a prayer of confession and petition to God. Visually, Milton's picture of both Adam and Eve kneeling in prayer has relatively few counterparts in art. Farinati shows Adam at prayer while Eve adjusts her hair, a trivializing of Eve very far from Milton's conception in which she plays a decisive role in the couple's repentance and reconciliation. Representations of Adam and Eve kneeling together in prayer occur in the atrium mosaics of S. Marco in Venice, in the stained glass Fall window in the Toledo cathedral, and in *Genesis B*.

204

37, 41

As for artistic representations in which either of the first parents shows compassion toward the other, I know of only two possible examples. Cristoforo Solari carved pendant statues of Adam and Eve outside the cathedral in Milan which show Adam in a pose redolent of physical exhaustion and spiritual anguish, while Eve gazes upon him with a loving concern no less deep for the serenity of its expression. This conception prefigures Milton's in that the woman first shows signs of love and mutual concern while the man is still lost in his own anguish. The correspondence, however, is at best only partial, because the presence of the hoe upon which Adam wearily leans, and the introduction of the infants Cain and Abel indicate that the incident took place after the Expulsion, rather than before it.[17]

199, 200

Perhaps the fullest artistic prefiguration of Milton at this point is to be found in the marble carving by Michelangelo Naccherino which confronted seventeenth-century visitors entering the public gates to the Boboli Gardens. As should be recalled, it is also in this work that we find the only visual counterpart to Milton's devil shedding tears over the first parents. The psychological meaning of the grouped figures is unmistakable: the grief-stricken Adam and Eve here stand together, physically comforting and supporting each other in their anguish and guilt.

193

[16] Evans, *"Paradise Lost" and the Genesis Tradition*, pp. 204-6 and 289, shows that Milton was here echoing "earlier treatments of the same extra-biblical episode" in the hexameral literature.

[17] Eve leans against a stump about which is entwined the serpent with a female face; this may suggest a multiscenic conception, but is more likely to have been inserted as an attribute which makes inescapable the identification of Eve.

Naccherino does not show their alienation, nor does he reveal an Eve who has fallen humbly at the feet of Adam to embrace them and beseech reconciliation, as Milton does, and Milton never describes the two as standing together in Naccherino's pose of mutual support. The marble does represent Eve's "tears that ceased not flowing,/ And tresses all disordered," but it is the psychological implications which bring Naccherino's couple so close to the Adam and Eve in *Paradise Lost* who agree to "strive/ In offices of love, how we may lighten/ Each other's burden in our share of woe" (x, 910-11, and 959-61). Neither Naccherino nor Cristoforo Solari is a famous artist, and in their statues the features most relevant to Milton do not represent a popular and widely known visual tradition. These figures are interesting because of their attempt to do in visual terms what Milton later accomplished in verbal, but they remain so isolated that we cannot cite them as providing visual reinforcement which Milton could have expected his readers to call upon as they read his poetic descriptions.

Between the Fall and the Expulsion, the story of Adam and Eve was rarely told in the visual arts, so that there was very little in the way of visual precedent upon which Milton and his readers could rely. This fact may help to account for the overwhelming preponderance of conceptual and psychological terms to be found in his descriptions after the Fall. When he chooses to introduce physical descriptions in these passages, they are effective and apposite, but they remain limited. We find very much the same patterns operative when we analyze his descriptions of the effects of the Fall on nature, and here he has approximately the same measure of precedent and support in pictorial art. Poetically he makes the most of broadly sensual descriptions, in which purely visual elements are rarely primary. When Eve ate the Fruit, "Earth felt the wound," and when Adam also ate "Earth trembled from her entrails," for the Fall brought in its wake "changes in the Heavens" and introduced "pinching cold and scorching heat" (ix, 782 and 1000, and x, 692-93). Within the total sensual ambience, vision is also evoked, as we see that the "sky lowered, and muttering thunder some sad drops/ Wept at completing of the mortal sin," while even more awesome changes are observed in the animal world, where "Beast now with beast gan war, and fowl with fowl,/ And fish with fish; to graze the herb all leaving, Devoured each other" (ix, 1002-3 and x, 710-12). From having been an external paradise of the senses fitting for the abode of pure beings, the Garden loses its sensuous harmony when Adam and Eve lose their inner righteousness, and the disruption of their essential nature is made sensible by the outward disruptions of nature in Eden. The visual components are present in the tempestuous winds "shattering the graceful locks/ Of these fair spreading trees" (x, 1066-67). We have also the "lateral noise" of high winds and the sounds of thunder rolling "with terror through the dark aerial hall" (x, 705, 666-67), and we are even introduced to smells at once "corrupt and pestilent" (x, 695).

Visual precedent for Milton's description of Nature turning against man are both rare and limited in relevance. Stanley Stewart has identified an engraving in Joseph Fletcher's *Perfect-Cursed-Blessed Man* as making Milton's essential point.

"After the Fall," Stewart writes, "the animals once named by Adam rise up against him. Barren of growth, his land is swept by storms. In every way natural man is exposed to the brunt of nature's hostile forces; not only does the fruitless tree now fail to cover his head but in general nature assaults him from all sides."[18] The sorely beset figure in this engraving is even directly attacked by animals, as a panther charges him from the left and a lion chews on his leg from the right, whereas in *Paradise Lost* the animals do no more than glare on man (x, 712-14). However impressive the parallel may be, it remains incomplete, and the pathetic figure so assaulted by nature is not Adam but a fully clothed man of later date, while in the background we see a tall building out of keeping with the dawn of human history as we find it treated in seventeenth-century art. Other visual similarities to Milton's treatment may be found in Abraham van Linge's Oxford windows in which the mountains behind Adam and Eve before the Fall are without snow but in the postlapsarian window are covered with it. These analogies are unmistakable, but we do not find many such prior to Milton's *Paradise Lost*. After Milton's time, we find engravings which illustrate the postlapsarian animosity among the animals, with a snarling hippopotamus, a predacious eagle, and the like, but these developments were presumably influenced by *Paradise Lost*.[19]

The most famous pictorial representation of animal predation in the Garden is found in the *Eden* panel of Bosch's *Garden of Earthly Delights*, where we have the notorious instance of the cat eating the mouse even in the presence of Adam, Eve, and God in the Garden. If we assume that this predation occurs before the Fall, then Bosch's vision differs in every way from Milton's, as from all other Christian interpreters of the subject with whom I am familiar. On the other hand, it is possible that Bosch is painting here in the tradition of the medieval telescoping of time sequences into a single panel, where the viewer is intended to sort out the order of events, and to recognize that the cat eating the mouse is intended as postlapsarian. If so, Bosch provided a visual counterpart to Milton's descriptions, but the matter is too perplexing for easy assurance. In general, Bosch's postlapsarian landscapes are far more distorted and extreme than any Milton leads us to envision. Of the antagonistic nature painted by Bosch, Max J. Friedlander has written:

> The country landscape never offers friendly homesteads, it is much more
> the enemy of man, whether it is just a wasteland or a desert, or bears a
> parched vegetation whose thorns recall instruments of torture. Each
> individual form appears sharply delineated but the infinite variety of form
> motifs in the broken and diversified matter gives uncanny life to the
> picture. It is not only the animal world and its monstrous, hybrid creatures
> that threaten with tooth and claw; even the vegetation seems to scratch

---

[18] Stanley Stewart, *The Enclosed Garden*, p. 64.

[19] See the Kitto Bible, III, pp. 401 and 405; the engravings are anonymous, or to be more accurate they are so closely cropped that it is impossible to determine their authorship. On the basis of the style of the printing in the legend and of the engraving itself it is possible to be sure that these engravings are too late to have influenced Milton, whether their provenance is eventually established as late seventeenth century or early eighteenth century.

and wound with its twisted branches and twigs. The earth itself threatens with snares and pitfalls.[20]

Though Milton's earth did feel the wound, it is never so devastated, so disgraced, so deformed as in Bosch. It is still possible for a repentant Adam to reassure Eve that "we need not fear/ To pass commodiously this life, sustained/ By Him with many comforts" (x, 1082-84).

THE EDUCATION OF ADAM: BOOKS XI-XII

The last two books of *Paradise Lost* give Milton's epic a "comforting" and affirmative ending. Dealing primarily with Adam's education by Michael, these books provide a sweeping perspective on human history[21] in which Adam and Eve serve as what F. T. Prince has called "registers" of consciousness, and the reader is instructed by experiencing the effects of the vision on them.[22] For Adam himself, as an epic character, the books also provide time in which "he becomes a conscious tragic hero (both actor and spectator) accepting, with all passion spent, fully man's condition, and he himself now a fully experienced man; and becomes a mythic hero reborn; and finally becomes man, with all his history behind and before him."[23]

This vision of humanity's history could have been so brilliantly projected only by Milton, as F. T. Prince has suggested, and Milton's originality is in no way diminished when we recognize that there were literary precedents for it.[24] After the Expulsion, as Dick Taylor has shown, "writers customarily presented accounts of the ills of the new world, the dislocations in Nature and the numerous troubles of Adam and Eve and their descendents from death, disease, pain, a host of psychological and emotional disturbances, and from the general problem of wresting a living from an unfriendly earth. Later in Medieval and Renaissance drama these various ills were represented by allegorical figures, Death, Care, Sin, Guile, Hunger and the like, who came and menaced or persecuted Adam." Accepting the usefulness of such a vision of postlapsarian life, Milton went beyond his predecessors when he "integrated these evils into a pattern of growing hope."[25] Previous Jewish and Christian writers on the Fall had variously located Adam's vision of the future, but it was a common feature of the hexameral tradition. Jewish commentators sometimes placed the vision before Adam's soul entered his body, or when he ate

---

[20] Max J. Friedlander, "The Art of Hieronymous Bosch" in *Hieronymous Bosch: The Garden of Delights* (ed. Wolfgang Hirsch), London, 1954, p. 7.

[21] Barbara Lewalski has called the final books "a highly complex aesthetic structure, organized so as to project the great themes of the poem on the epic screen of all human history" ("Structure and the Symbolism of Vision in Michael's Prophecy, *PL* XI-XII," *PQ* 42 [1963], 25).

[22] F. T. Prince, "On the Last Two Books of *PL*," in *Milton's Epic Poetry: Essays on "Paradise Lost" and "Paradise Regained"* (ed. C. A. Patrides), Harmondsworth, 1967, p. 237; see also Lawrence A. Sasek, "The Drama of *Paradise Lost*, Books XI and XII," in *Milton: Modern Essays in Criticism* (ed. Arthur E. Barker), pp. 349 and 355.

[23] Arnold Stein, *Answerable Style*, p. 161.

[24] Prince, "On the Last Two Books of *PL*," p. 238.

[25] Taylor, "Milton's Treatment of Judgment and the Expulsion in *Paradise Lost*," 61 and 74.

the fruit, or after the Expulsion. Among Christian commentators, the vision was usually conveyed to Adam in a dream while Eve was being formed from his rib. Once again we see Milton's adaptive imagination at work, reshaping traditions to which he gives the highest literary and religious expression.[26]

If pictorial parallels exist to Milton's overall treatment of the vision, I have not found them.[27] Artists do provide Adam with some instruction after the Fall, but it is instruction at a fairly rudimentary level. An early tradition provides angelic tutelage for Adam in digging, a practical though primitive and fore-shortened equivalent of Michael's instruction of Adam. A fresco executed about 1200 for the Chapter House of the Monastery at Sigena shows a nimbed angel digging with a spade, while Adam holds a hoe and looks on, as though learning his trade. The same tradition is found in ecclesiastical art in England, and on the font at East Meon we see an angel teaching Adam how to dig,[28] while a thirteenth- or fourteenth-century fresco at All Saints Church in East Hanningfield shows the angel giving tools to Adam. The only pictorial parallels to Adam on the Mount of Vision with which I am familiar are of very different subjects—either Moses being shown the Promised Land, which is based in Old Testament accounts, or the legendary appearance of the Christ Child on a mountaintop to show the coming events of his life to John the Baptist, so that John can prophesy correctly in his ministry.[29]

Postlapsarian representations of Adam and Eve are not uncommon, but these do not provide very rewarding analogues to Milton's accounts. Most frequently in the Middle Ages, Adam is shown delving and Eve spinning, as in the formella relief on Giotto's Campanile in Florence. In the Renaissance, we find other treatments of Adam, emphasizing not so much the effort of his labors as his fatigue after them, and perhaps an air of resignation. Thus we see a seated Adam, with Eve and the young twins, in the painting by Fra Bartolomeo in the Johnson Collection in Philadelphia, and an Adam seated in weary thoughtfulness in the postlapsarian window by Abraham van Linge in University College, Oxford. Otherwise, Adam may be shown standing, leaning on a spade or hoe or other gardening tool, as in the drawing by Pollaiuolo in the Uffizi, or in the marble figure on the Milan cathedral executed *199, 200* by Cristoforo Solari. There, Adam looks up under furrowed brows, with weariness marking every aspect of his pose, though the body remains strong and muscular, the total effect being one of ineffable sadness and regret. Such works give us evidence as to how the postlapsarian Adam and Eve were visually conceived, but are not highly pertinent to Milton's descriptions.

Allegorical paintings of the Fall and its results may correspond somewhat more closely with Milton's thematic conception. Thus the Fall of Man triptych *206* by Albrecht Altdorfer shows the Fall of Adam and Eve in the center, while we

---

[26] Evans, *"Paradise Lost" and the Genesis Tradition*, pp. 291-92.

[27] I have made only a partial examination of the hexameral literature in search of pictorial illustrations, but found little of relevance.

[28] Anderson, *Imagery of British Churches*, p. 89.

[29] See Adelheid Heimann, "Moses shown the Promised Land," *JWCI* 34 (1971), 321-24, and Marilyn Aronberg Lavin, "Giovannino Battista: A Study in Renaissance Religious Symbolism," *Art Bulletin* 37 (1955), 85-101, and supplement in *Art Bulletin* 43 (1961), 319-26.

see to the left the reign of Bacchus and to the right the reign of Mars. Representing concupiscent and irascible sins in these side panels, Altdorfer is effectively leading his viewers to understand how the originating sin in the center proliferates through human experience, and the impression gained from the painting may be epitomized in Adam's words after the fifth vision of Book XI: "for now I see/ Peace to corrupt no less than war to waste" (XI, 783-84). A similar, but more detailed, analysis is provided in a late sixteenth- or early seventeenth-century engraving by Philip Galle, in which an illustration of the Fall is surrounded by roundels illustrating each of the seven deadly sins in turn, with a scriptural reference to the fifth chapter of Romans.[30] The Window of Chariots executed about 1525 for St. Vincent in Rouen, shows Evil triumphant as a result of the Fall: the demonic serpent-woman rides in a chariot, with a flag bearing the image of Death, while Adam and Eve are led captive with their hands tied and their heads bowed, accompanied by Toil and Grief and a long procession of Vices.[31] Bosch's *Haywain* illustrates the Fall to the left, Hell to the right, and in the center the hayride of humanity through a course of sin and death.

Whereas such works visualize the consequences of the Fall in allegorical terms, others do so typologically. In this category we have many works, usually put together into series, which illustrate representative examples chosen from the Scriptures so as to convey an understanding of human life and history. C. A. Patrides accords these artistic treatments a prominent place in his study of the Christian understanding of history:

> Visual expositions of the Christian view of history were even more memorably undertaken by several great artists. Here we encounter yet another imposing tradition, for the artists of the Renaissance had been preceded by the artists of the Middle Ages. Mediaeval representations were commonly sequential arrangements of the principal events from the creation to the Last Judgement; they were most often executed in stained glass or painted panels, and not infrequently in sculpture. Examples in stained glass are legion; some are major works of art in their own right, like the Great East Window (1405-8) of the York Minster—the work of John Thornton of Coventry—whose central panels depict twenty-seven episodes from the Old Testament starting with the creation, followed by eighty-one illustrations of the Johannine Apocalypse. The continuity of tradition is even more interestingly displayed at Exeter Cathedral. The elaborately-carved pulpitum or quire screen erected in the early fourteenth century is crowned by a series of thirteen panels painted in the seventeenth century and so arranged as to advance from the Creation and the Expulsion, through several episodes drawn from the Old Testament, to the ascent of the Christ into Heaven and the descent of the Holy Spirit into history.[32]

[30] Kitto Bible, II, p. 313.
[31] Mâle, *Religious Art*, pp. 138-39.
[32] Patrides, *The Grand Design of God*, pp. 53-54.

In England, these pictorial narratives were frequently used to adorn medieval castles and palaces, as well as churches.[33] They were popular in the illuminations for manuscript Bibles, and continued popular after the introduction of printing.[34] Such panoramic histories were just as popular in Italy, one of the best known being the mosaic series from Old Testament history in the cupola of the Florentine Baptistry. The most famous example is Michelangelo's Sistine Ceiling, but that ceiling is only one aspect of the universal history portrayed in the Sistine Chapel: while the ceiling carries human history from Creation through the Flood, the left wall (when facing the altar) represents the Law, and the deliverance of the Jews from Egypt, while the right wall is devoted to Grace, with representations of Christ and Redemption, and the climactic altar wall shows Michelangelo's *Last Judgment*. In equally instructive epitomes of human history and human destiny, Europe was for centuries familiar with painted or sculptured representations of incidents from the Old and New Testaments, similar to those Milton has chosen for the instruction of Adam. Many incidents appear again and again in such series, but there was no invariable pattern, and I have found no pictorial version which corresponds throughout and in precise detail with Milton's account in the last two books of *Paradise Lost*. For our interest, then, the importance of such pictorial cycles is that they establish, not Milton's own selection of incidents, but a familiarity on the part of his audience with the use of a sequence of "views" to convey a Christian understanding of the nature and destiny of man.[35]

In connection with a particular incident chosen for representation, there would inevitably be a certain carryover of iconographic significance from the visual arts to the epic narrative. The first Biblical incident Michael chose to show Adam is the story of Cain and Abel, which frequently appeared in the pictorial cycles. Cain came to represent the first of the damned, and in certain late fifteenth- and early sixteenth-century book illustrations Cain was shown as the leader of the company of the damned, standing at their head at the Last Judgment, and holding a staff in his hand from which flowed a banner with his name lettered upon it.[36] The story of the first fratricide "prefigured the killing of Christ by his fellow Jews," as M. D. Anderson writes. "The scholarly observer would have been reminded of the contrast between the blood of Abel, which is described in Genesis as crying from the ground for vengeance, and the blood of Christ which calls for God's mercy upon sinful men."[37] With that significance in mind, we see that even the first murder can take on ironic overtones of the eventual redemption of man: perhaps the better-informed among Milton's early readers would have caught these overtones and would have seen a possibility of hope where Adam sees only terror.

[33] Tristram, *English Medieval Wall Painting: The Thirteenth Century*, I, p. 59.

[34] Brieger, *English Art: 1216-1307*, *passim*; Stewart, *The Enclosed Garden*, p. 38; and Koch and Bryan, eds., *Five Themes from Genesis*, p. 1.

[35] I have found no comprehensive history of the development of pictorial cycles such as those described above. Such a study would be a notable contribution to learning.

[36] Prince d'Essling, *Les Livres à figures vénitiens*, Florence and Venice, 1914, II, p. 122, reproduces such an illustration from Voragine, *Legendario de Sancti*, Modena, 1492, and it also appeared in the 1519 Milan edition.

[37] Anderson, *History and Imagery of British Churches*, pp. 91-92.

Visual representations of such an incident as this of Cain and Abel may also be related to Milton's verse in terms of focus and composition. In Early Christian art, Cain and Abel appear primarily in connection with their sacrifices, not in connection with the murder.[38] Later, the murder itself became a very popular theme and was frequently represented with great violence.[39] In the Middle Ages, artists developed conventions for presenting several such foci within a single scene —a synoptic combination of successive actions within a single painting or piece of sculpture. Spencer notes that an "especially memorable example, one which Milton may have seen in Italy, is the great bronze relief of Cain and Abel by Ghiberti, done for the doors of the Baptistry in Florence in about 1436. Ghiberti's subject, one of a series on Biblical scenes, is, like Milton's poetic passage, treated in six sequential episodes."[40] Whereas Milton and Ghiberti do not correspond precisely with each other in their composition, Milton does construct his picture according to the established principles of multiscenic design in pictorial art. Adam's first vision is of

> a field
> Part arable and tilth, whereon were sheaves
> New reapt, the other part sheep-walks and folds;
> I'th' midst an altar as the landmark stood
> Rustic, of grassy sward; thither anon
> A sweaty reaper from his tillage brought
> First fruits, the green ear, and the yellow sheaf,
> Unculled, as came to hand; a shepherd next
> More meek came with the firstlings of his flock
> Choicest and best; then sacrificing, laid
> The inwards and their fat, with incense strewed,
> On the cleft wood, and all due rites performed.
> His offering soon propitious Fire from Heaven
> Consum'd with nimble glance, and grateful steam;
> The other's not, for his was not sincere;
> Whereat he inly raged, and as they talked,
> Smote him into the midriff with a stone
> That beat out life; he fell, and deadly pale
> Groaned out his soul with gushing blood effused.
>
> (XI, 429-47)

Milton first gives us an overall view of the field, both as pasture and as farmland (where Ghiberti had shown Abel watching his flock and Cain plowing). Milton then adds the altar as his second detail, Cain bringing to it fruit and grain as the third detail, and as the fourth, the coming of Abel with a sacrificial lamb. Fifthly, the fire comes down from Heaven as a mark of acceptance and consumes Abel's

---

[38] André Grabar, *Christian Iconography: A Study of its Origins*, Princeton, 1968, pp. 137 and 144-45.

[39] Ehrenstein, *Das Alte Testament*, pt. III, figs. 1-19.

[40] Spencer, *Heroic Nature*, p. 114.

offering. These scenes are telescoped by Ghiberti into a single view of the two brothers kneeling by their sacrifices, while the fire descends to consume Abel's. Finally, in Milton's account, there is the murder itself, which is also represented in Ghiberti's bronze door panel. Whatever may be the incidental differences in details included, it is clear that Milton is composing his vision in patterns very similar to those used by artists in rendering a multiscenic representation.

Two details should be singled out for particular attention here. That flame which comes down from Heaven to light Abel's offering has no counterpart in the Biblical source; Genesis 4:4-5 merely informs us that the Lord had respect unto Abel and his offering, but not unto Cain. In pictorial art, the flame was universally employed to objectify God's approval of Abel, and even to distinguish him from his evil brother. Visually, artists could not have told the story without using that flame, but Milton could readily have reverted to the purely literary explanation provided in the Scripture. Here his description follows an artistic motif so widespread that most of his readers, both in his own time and since, have probably been unaware that the detail is not to be found in Genesis.[41]

That detail is standard enough, but the other is extraordinary in the extreme: Cain kills his brother by smiting him "into the midriff with a stone/ That beat out life" (XI, 445-46). It would be hard to find a less efficient method for killing a man, and no critical explanation with which I am familiar adequately explains Milton's choice. Two literary sources have been suggested. Cowley in his *Davideis* of 1656 has Cain knock Abel on the head with a great stone, and then ingeniously converts the stone into his monument. Citing this passage, Shumaker quite properly observes that "from such frigid ingenuity as this Milton's description is happily free," which none can regret, and yet it must be granted Cowley that a man could more readily be slain by beating him over the head with a large stone than by throwing it into his midriff.[42]

There is also a rabbinical account which shows certain similarities to Milton's: "The manner of Abel's death was the most cruel conceivable. Not knowing what injury was fatal, Cain pelted all parts of his body with stones, until one struck him on the neck and inflicted death."[43] Milton's account differs in that he does not provide a general pelting of the whole body, nor is the fatal blow struck in the neck. This account of the stoning occurs in a fantastic romantic legend of a kind which surely would not have appealed to Milton in any way: it is embellished with Cain's jealousy of Abel's lovely fiancée, well before the fatal quarrel, and includes Cain's justification of himself by saying that he did not know that thrown stones could be fatal, and concludes with God's lamenting that it was not Abel who had killed Cain.[44] I cannot believe that Milton would have taken this legend seriously enough to have adopted its methodology in his account of the murder, any

---

[41] Shumaker, *Unpremeditated Verse*, pp. 204-5, recognizes the influence of pictorial art here.

[42] *Ibid.*, pp. 205-6; see also the note in the Carey and Fowler edition.

[43] Louis Ginzberg, *The Legends of the Jews*, I, p. 109.

[44] *Ibid.*, pp. 108-10.

more than it seems to me likely that he would have been influenced at this point by Cowley.

In pictorial art, Cain is very often represented as clubbing Abel to death with a wooden stave or limb from a tree, as in Ghiberti's bronze relief. The visual tradition which showed the murder weapon to be the jawbone of an animal originated in the British Isles, and spread thence to achieve great popularity on the continent as well.[45] The club and the jawbone are the most frequently encountered murder weapons, but one may much more rarely find some farm implement such as a scythe employed. In the bronze doors executed by Primo Maestro for S. Zeno in Verona, Cain apparently kills Abel by a jiujitsu toss, which is an unusual method for homicide but entirely believable. Secondo Maestro for the same church chose to have death delivered by a club.

Milton's choice of murder by stoning is supported by the visual tradition, but by an extraordinarily narrow stream of that tradition: bas relief carvings on Byzantine ivory boxes.[46] The examples in the Index of Christian Art at Princeton all date between the tenth and twelfth centuries, and the discovery of all these items outside the bounds of the Byzantine Empire indicates that they were probably especially carved for export trade. In the version at the Ducal Palace in Pesaro, Cain is throwing ball-like stones at Abel's midriff, and Abel is bent over stiffly from the waist under the impact of the blows. The version at the Palais des Arts in Lyons shows Abel falling down under the blows of many stones, as does also the casket at the Hermitage in Leningrad. The version I illustrate here, from the Cleveland   220
Museum, shows Cain throwing stones, one hitting Abel high on his thigh and another squarely in the solar plexus. I have found no examples of this motif in Western art before Milton's time, and when it eventually appears, it is under the influence of *Paradise Lost*.[47]

Of the possible sources and analogues we have been considering, only the Byzantine ivories correspond precisely to Milton's detail of the stones to the midriff. Milton may well have seen one of these ivory caskets, of which more examples would have been extant in his time than in our own, but even had Milton seen such a representation, it is impossible that many of his intended readers would have been familiar with it. Apposite though it may be, this visual tradition is so narrow and so restricted that it could have provided only the scantest visual reinforcement for Milton's description. That death should have come by stoning does suggest an iconographical association between Abel, as the first human martyr, and Stephen, as the first Christian martyr, but the account of Stephen's martyrdom in Acts 7:58-59 makes no reference to the midriff, and the familiar artistic representa-

[45] Shapiro, "Cain's Jaw-Bone."

[46] The fullest treatment is given by Kurt Weitzmann, "Zur Frage des Einfluss jüdischer Bilderquellen auf die Illustration des Alten Testamentes," *Festscrift Theodor Klauser*, Munster, 1964, pp. 405-6; see also Shapiro, "Cain's Jaw-Bone," 209; Anderson, *Imagery of British Churches*, p. 90; and Réau, *Iconographie*, ii, i, p. 96.

[47] The Kitto Bible, iv, pp. 555 and 565, presents two engravings after a design by G. Hoet (1648-1733), the first executed by J. Baptist, who died in London in 1691, and the second by L. M. S., whom I have been unable to identify.

tions of Stephen show him with stones embedded in his skull.[48] I cannot explain why Milton chose to describe the murder in terms that are at once so bizarre and so inherently improbable, but he did not haphazardly introduce such details and there must be a richness of meaning here which I have been unable to discover.

In the education of Adam, the vision of Cain and Abel is followed by a vision of the Lazar-house, between them summarizing the sins of violence and of intemperance which Altdorfer epitomized in somewhat different fashion in the triptych *206* we have already considered. For the invocation of death which Milton describes in the Lazar-house (for which analogues exist in literature) we find an immensely *221, 222* moving parallel in work attributed to Andrea di Cione and Nardo Orcagna. There we see miserable wretches, wracked with much the same kinds of affliction that Milton describes in his Lazar-house, extending their hands toward the flying figure of Death to beseech an instant end to their miseries, but Death ignores them, as in Milton:

> And over them triumphant Death his dart
> Shook, but delayed to strike, though oft invoked
> With vows as their chief good, and final hope.
>
> (XI, 491-93)

A fragment of a similar scene, also attributed to Andrea Orcagna, is preserved in *223* Florence. It is hard to imagine that anyone could look at these paintings without being profoundly moved. Milton precisely conveys their effect as well as the effect he intends for his poetic counterpart: "Sight so deform what heart of rock could long/ Dry-eyed behold? Adam could not, but wept . . ." (XI, 494-95). Adam responds to those beseeching gestures as would almost any sensitive person standing before a *Triumph of Death* painting.

The only non-Biblical and allegorical vision in Book XI is this of the Lazar-house, and after it Milton returns to his basic literary source in Genesis. The third vision presents the fathers of the trades, based upon the account in the fourth chapter of Genesis. First we have the prototype of the herding, then of music, and finally of metal work—Jabal, Jubal, and Tubalcain respectively. These three worthies, along with personifications of the liberal arts, were popular figures in medieval and later art, and many examples may be found in the Index of Christian Art. The most familiar medieval examples known in the twentieth century are probably in the *formelle* on Giotto's Campanile, which represent rather simple figural reliefs. In the late sixteenth and early seventeenth centuries, pictorial representations became more complex, as may be seen in the series of engravings on subjects from Genesis executed by Joannes Sadeler after designs by Marten de Vos. *224* The print devoted to Jabal in this series is far more detailed than Milton's brief treatment: "he looked and saw a spacious plain, whereon/ Were tents of various hue; by some were herds/ Of cattle grazing" (XI, 556-58). Immediately thereafter,

[48] Huge, boulderlike stones were used as weapons by the giants and other primitive peoples in Greek art, as may be seen in Maximilian Mayer, *Die Giganten und Titanen in der Antik in Sage und Kunst*, Berlin, 1887, pp. 11f. Still, this offers no parallel for the midriff as a target.

Milton shifts to the father of music, where the development is somewhat fuller. Adam sees other tents

> whence the sound
> Of instruments that made melodious chime
> Was heard, of harp and organ; and who moved
> Their stops and chords was seen: his volant touch
> Instinct through all proportions high and low
> Fled and pursued transverse the resonant fugue.
>
> (XI, 558-63)

The Sadeler-de Vos print reveals a different emphasis from Milton's, concentrating *225* rather upon the manufacture of musical instruments than upon their playing, though dancers are a prominent feature. Next comes the inventor of metal work, Tubalcain:

> In other part stood one who at the forge
> Laboring, two massy clods of iron and brass
> Had melted (whether found where casual fire
> Had wasted woods on mountain or in vale,
> Down to the veins of earth, thence gliding hot
> To some cave's mouth, or whether washt by stream
> From underground); the liquid ore he drained
> Into fit moulds prepared; from which he formed
> First his own tools; then, what might else be wrought
> Fusile or graven in metal.
>
> (XI, 564-73)

In the background of the engraving we see caves like Milton's with miners work- *226* ing, and in the right margin a mill separating the metal "washed by stream/ From underground," while in the foreground Tubalcain himself is working the metal on his forge. This plate is closer in conception to Milton than are the other two, but in no instance are the similarities close enough to demonstrate a source relationship. What Milton and the artists unquestionably share is the popular seventeenth-century interest in the early history of human technology.[49]

Milton next introduces the just men who come down from the hills to the plains and enter into marriages based on mere appetite rather than on rational choice (XI, 573-97). In Genesis (6:1-8), this story comes two chapters after the treatment of the invention of trades, but the chronology based upon the Genesis genealogies is not entirely clear, and was subject to different interpretations. Our series of engravings follows Genesis more faithfully than Milton does at this point, and places the episode immediately before Noah is chosen to build the ark, but the series also pictures a growth of frivolity and lasciviousness in the time of Jubal and of Lamech, as does Milton. The Jubal engraving shows dancers who suggest, *225*

[49] Panofsky, *Iconology*, pp. 33-49 discusses the treatment of Greek myths of such developments in the paintings of Piero di Cosimo.

as in Milton, women "Bred only and completed to the tastes/ Of lustful appetance, to sing, to dance,/ To dress, and troll the tongue, and roll the eye" (XI, 618-20).

227 The other relevant engraving contains a Latin motto of Lamech's lamentation for the manner in which Cupid is plaguing the people, and shows feasting, dancing, and lovemaking in the background, intended to suggest the debasement of relations between the sexes, similar to what we find in Milton. The presence in the center foreground of a he-goat mounting a she-goat, driven on by Cupid, serves as a visual commentary and identification of the meaning of the dancing and love-making figures. In place of such a visual key, Milton provides a verbal commentary, but the result is similar:

> All now was turned to jollity and game,
> To luxury and riot, feast and dance,
> Marrying or prostituting, as befell,
> Rape or adultery, where passing fair
> Allured them.
>
> (XI, 714-18)

228 The Latin verses appended to the Sadeler-de Vos engraving on the sons of God and the daughters of men convey much the same irony and ambiguity we find in Milton's lines paralleling "marrying or prostituting, as befell,/ Rape or adultery," as "all in heat" rush into marriage "with feast and music," and the incident is visualized with the same emphases we find in *Paradise Lost*.[50]

Between the third and fifth visions, both concerned with cupidity, comes a vision which returns to irascible sins, represented for the first time by war when "infinite/ Manslaughter shall be held the highest pitch/ Of human glory" (XI, 693-94). Here Enoch is introduced, protesting the evils of violence, the first in that series of outspoken prophets who prefigures the ultimate redemption in Christ. Genesis 5:24 recounts that "Enoch walked with God; and he was not, for God took him," without giving any details of the manner of his ascent into Heaven. Milton, too, might have left it at that, but instead he follows the pictorial tradition and declares that "a cloud descending snatched him thence" (XI, 670), which is exactly the mode of ascension delineated in the

229 Sadeler-de Vos engraving.[51]

The fifth and sixth visions recount the destruction wrought by the Flood, and the salvation of the chosen men and animals aboard Noah's Ark. The story of Noah was immensely popular in art, giving rise to innumerable representations. Iconographically, of course, the Ark represented the Church in which the faithful were redeemed from the general destruction of mankind, and Noah was taken as an early prefiguration of the Redeemer himself. These interpretations were so firmly estab-

[50] A somewhat similar print was executed by Crispin de Pas, also in the Kitto Bible for Genesis 6, showing the union of the sons of God and the daughters of men.

[51] At *PL* XI, 706, Milton extends and modifies the description to show him "rapt in a balmy cloud with winged steeds," perhaps recalling the method of Elijah's translation in 2 Kings 2:11. In his note to XI, 655-71, Fowler recognizes a "possible" influence from pictorial sources.

lished that Milton could confidently expect them to be applied by his readers to the accounts in *Paradise Lost*. Shumaker has rightly pointed out the powerful effect of the "chiefly motor" imagery in these passages,[52] but equally impressive is the visual recreation of the effects of wind on water in Milton's description of "a keen north wind that blowing dry/ Wrinkled the face of Deluge," which provides a fine and lively verbal picture (XI, 842-43). And we have also another of Milton's notable underwater scenes, not so precisely detailed as in the earlier description (VII, 399-410) which we have treated elsewhere, but still vivid and impressive: "sea covered sea,/ Sea without shore; and in their palaces/ Where luxury late reigned, sea-monsters whelped/ And stabled" (XI, 749-52). The picture has its own power, but as usual with Milton the picture is not an end in itself: it deepens our understanding by showing palaces which were once filled with the specious luxury of a bestialized humanity and which are now, with even greater propriety, luxuriating with sea-monsters.

As for the appearance of the Ark itself, there were two standard versions. Early Christian art represented it as a kind of box, literally an *arca* or shrine, which floated on the waters. It continued to be more a symbol than a ship well into the Middle Ages, but then some efforts were made to suggest "a ship of sorts, albeit of most doubtful seaworthiness," and these efforts were extended in later art until it became at least a passably navigable vessel.[53] Milton chooses to evoke this later form of visualization, as evidenced by his references to the vessel's "beaked prow" and "hull" (XI, 746, 840).

Far more significant is the overall composition and focus of Milton's description, which corresponds to the predominant emphases of pre-sixteenth-century art. Prior to Michelangelo, artists centered the attention of their viewers upon the Ark itself, thus magnifying the theme of redemption. Even when drowning figures and other instances of destruction were included, these were given a subordinate place in the design. It is this vision which Milton chooses to bring before the eyes of his readers, and in the course of some 175 lines of description, only about a dozen or so are devoted to pictures of devastation and destruction. In thus concentrating our attention upon visions of redemption, Milton by-passed and ignored the predominant visual emphases of his own and the preceding century. The decisive artistic influence here was Michelangelo, and F.J.P. Broun summarizes his achievement and influence:

> Now in the fresco on the Sistine ceiling, we are confronted by a spectacle which is almost entirely new. The Ark, always the focus of attention in any Deluge scene, has been pushed so far into the background that it virtually disappears, and the viewer is faced not by the dove with its comforting message of peace and hope, but by the agonized contortions of condemned mankind. . . . Never had help been so far from hand, never had those who did survive the Flood been so forgotten. By minimizing the idea of divine preservation, Michelangelo deliberately shifts our

[52] Shumaker, *Unpremeditated Verse*, pp. 211-13.
[53] Anderson, *Imagery of British Churches*, pp. 91-92.

thoughts from the blessed to the damned, and from now on the artists who follow his lead will concentrate more and more on the cataclysmic aspects of the event, often to such an extent that the Ark is omitted altogether.[54]

In D. J. Vellart's 1544 engraving *The Deluge* the dramatic visual concentration is upon incidents of people who have found some temporary position of safety, and are blocking others from their fragile security by beating them off with clubs, jawbones, or whatever may come to hand. Such conceptions continued to dominate art through Milton's time and beyond. Milton must, and does of course, indicate the scope of the loss, as when he describes Adam mourning like a father "his children, all in view destroyed at once" (XI, 761), but in the context of his overall treatment, the emphases of the previous century and a half are reversed, and he concentrates our vision upon the Ark, its passengers, and its whole symbology of redemption. Here, as in so many other instances, we see the critical differences which separate Milton's Christian optimism from the Christian pessimism of Michelangelo.[55]

After the six visions of Book XI, Book XII shifts from visual to narrative instruction. Michael tells Adam that "I perceive/ Thy mortal sight to fail," and adds "henceforth what is to come I will relate" (XII, 8-9, 11). Thereafter Michael's approach remains generally consistent throughout Book XII. Occasionally the lines evoke physical images, but only rarely so, and the effect remains primarily non-visual. The reason is not hard to find. Milton is attempting to summarize, or more precisely to evoke and epitomize, the understanding of human history as it extends from the tenth chapter of Genesis through to the Last Judgment and beyond, and he is doing so in only 605 lines. The achievement is impressive in itself, and is possible only because Milton observes the most rigorous poetic economy. A startling range of historical events is included, but none are sharply visualized in details. In the accounts of Noah and the Ark, Milton had provided sufficient particulars, both large and small, to guide his readers in choosing between the different visualizations which were familiar to them; but the remaining instructions which Michael imparts to Adam on the mountain are pervasively conceptual.

THE EXPULSION

The affirmative and consolatory tone of the Expulsion in *Paradise Lost* sets Milton's conception apart from the general literary traditions which preceded him. Whether narrative, dramatic, or exegetical, earlier writings on this subject had yielded strikingly less in the way of compassion and hope. A point-by-point com-

---

[54] F.J.P. Broun, "The Flood," in *Five Themes from Genesis* (ed. Koch and Bryan), p. 8.

[55] In even more pronounced ways, Milton differs from Bosch. E. H. Gombrich maintains that Bosch's *Garden of Earthly Delights* should be retitled "The Lesson of the Flood," because it deals with the sins of man in that context. Milton can never be said to have allowed the "human face divine" to have been so degraded and deformed as is typically the case with Bosch. See Gombrich, "Bosch's 'Garden of Earthly Delights': A Progress Report," *JWCI* 32 (1969), 162-70.

parison between *Paradise Lost* and its predecessors in prose and verse led Dick Taylor to identify the distinctively Miltonic contributions to the story: "It had been conventional that Adam and Eve leave the Garden bemoaning their fate in terror and despondency; and in previous works the emphasis had been upon their fright at the ills and evils which lay before them, at the terror and uncertainty of the horrible new existence in a sadder home, a sorrier land." Without minimizing the evil consequences of the Fall, Milton emphasized "moral and spiritual strength, . . . a strong sense of personal confirmation."[56] The calm resignation and muted optimism of the Expulsion in *Paradise Lost* is one of Milton's greatest achievements, for which critical praise has never been lacking. It was possible only by virtue of Milton's careful modulation of literary means and effects.

Milton defines our attitudes toward the Expulsion both through conceptual statement and through visual descriptions.[57] The conceptual statements appeal directly to our psychological and spiritual understanding. The Almighty sends Michael not only to expel the couple, but to prepare them with infinite kindness for their new life. Michael is specifically directed to hide all terror, and to "dismiss them not disconsolate . . . , though sorrowing yet in peace" (XI, 111, 113-17). Even before Michael's arrival, Adam begins to feel the results of interaction between penitence and divine forgiveness, and understands God to be "placable and mild" (XI, 151). When Michael appears, Adam sees him as "not terrible,/ That I should fear, nor sociably mild,/ As Raphael, that I should much confide,/ But solemn and sublime" (XI, 233-36). Michael's behavior confirms that balanced appraisal, and Adam comments appreciatively upon how "gently hast thou told/ Thy message" (XI, 298-99). Michael's tuition is through progressive revelation, and Adam is gradually led by stages of increasing understanding until he is "replete with joy and wonder" at the "goodness infinite, goodness immense,/ That all this good of evil shall produce,/ And evil turn to good" (XII, 468-71). Our own education continues with Adam's, until the archangel promises "a paradise within thee happier far," and in his final words to Adam and to us sublimates sadness within an ultimate vision "much more cheered/ With meditation on the happy end" (XII, 587, 604-5). Like Adam, Eve responds to her own dream vision with "words not sad" and "consolation yet secure" (XII, 609, 620).

The physical departure from Eden is described in words which pictorially reinforce these conceptual statements. Taking them by the hand, Michael leads Adam and Eve to the gate of Paradise, the blazing sword going before them. When they have been led out of the Garden and to the plain beneath, they look back with some nostalgia, and some natural tears which they soon wipe away. Then, taking each other by the hand, they move into their new world and new life (XII, 632-49). The epic's conclusion is so poetically majestic and moving and its pictorial details so simple and unobtrusive that we can all too easily overlook the sophistica-

---

[56] Taylor, "Milton's Treatment of Judgment and the Expulsion in *Paradise Lost*," 76 and 74.

[57] The music of the verse also contributes, but that is another and equally complex matter.

tion of Milton's visual iconography here. Milton has included almost every detail of the traditional pictorial representations of the Expulsion, but has rearranged them in such a way as to create an entirely original vision. The traditional sword is there and the angel "handing" them out, the gate and the backward glance, all of which his readers would have expected, but each of which he subtly turns away from its traditional presentation so as to create from standard materials a vision which is fresh and wondrous.

Long before Milton, artists had begun to introduce into the story two details that differ from the account in the last verses of the third chapter of Genesis. According to Genesis, it was not an angel, but the Lord God himself who expelled Adam and Eve from the Garden. For the first twelve centuries of Christian art, the Expulsion was personally executed by God, as in the Biblical account, but thereafter it was an angel who executed the sentence and pushed the delinquents *179* from the gate of Paradise.[58] On the critical point of identifying the agent of the Expulsion, Milton departs from Biblical authority to follow the visual tradition that had dominated the European imagination for four and a half centuries before him. Similarly, Milton follows the artists in introducing the sword into the Expulsion scene even before Adam and Eve leave the Garden, whereas in Genesis it appears over the gate only after they have left.

Alternative modes of angelic action in the Expulsion were to be found in the pictorial tradition, and Milton had to choose between these. In many versions, the angel appeared with his sword in the sky, behind and above the departing couple. *189* The angel so appears in the famous painting by Masaccio, but there the angel discharges a merely supervisory role, without threatening the already severely distraught couple. In later renditions, the flying angel takes on a tremendously menacing aspect, perhaps under the influence of Michelangelo's angel who swings his sword with great vigor immediately behind Adam's neck, so that Adam appears *169* to wince from the threatened blow. In the print from the 1529 *History of Adam and Eve* series by Lucas van Leyden, the angel appears to be dive-bombing Adam and Eve as he flails with his sword, and Hans Brosamer treats the subject in much *214* the same way. The seventeenth-century oil painting of the Expulsion by Gazzola and Strozzi is equally vigorous, as the angel slashes away at the fleeing Adam and *230* Eve, and a similar impression is given in the canvas by Cavaliere d'Arpino in Christ Church, Oxford. Such immensely punitive representations of the airborne angel continued throughout the seventeenth century, as may be seen in the painting attributed to Gisbert Hondecouter in the Galleria Corsini. The image of the flying angel of the Expulsion was so firmly associated with terror that Milton could not

---

[58] Réau, *Iconographie*, II, i, p. 89; the earlier tradition may be seen in the Creation cupola of the atrium of S. Marco, and in illuminated manuscripts such as the English St. Albans Psalter and Cotton Genesis (Trapp, "The Iconography of the Fall," p. 241); for the later motif of expulsion by an angel, see Rosalie Green, "The Adam and Eve Cycle," pp. 346-47, and Anderson, *Imagery of British Churches*, p. 89. In "Two Milton Notes," *MLR* 44 (1949), 91, William B. Hunter, Jr., suggests that it was Milton who popularized the view of the Expulsion which most people take for granted today, but in point of fact Milton was merely transmitting the long-established pictorial representation.

have used it and still achieved his purpose of dismissing Adam and Eve "not disconsolate . . . though sorrowing, yet in peace."

Walking angels could also be immensely terrifying in Expulsion scenes, but were less consistently so. In the crude but powerful bas relief panels for the doors of S. Zeno in Verona, the angel holds the sword erect, but the gesture is hieratically authoritative rather than physically menacing. In Uccello's fresco, the sword is held below the waist, with the point slightly raised, but the angel's arm is relaxed, and not preparing to strike; Fra Angelico could convert the same posture into an even more gentle suggestion. Somewhat more menacing is the holding of the sword about shoulder level and pointed at one of the first parents, a stance which is seen both in the fresco by Pietro di Puccio at the Camposanto in Pisa, and in the illumination for the Bedford Book of Hours.

179
197

172
156

These examples illustrate the irenic possibilities of the motif of the walking angel, as distinguished from the flying angel, but they represent renditions before the sixteenth century. In the sixteenth and seventeenth centuries, even footborne angels used their swords so as to inspire Adam and Eve at least with fear, and often with terror. In Cranach's *Paradise*, a running angel raises his sword above his head, and the fleeing Adam and Eve clearly expect him to bring it down upon them, as they raise their arms to protect themselves, and essentially the same action is represented by Mabuse and by Tintoretto. In the representation by Andrea del Minga, Adam dances and twists as though the raised sword in the vigorous arm of the angel was being used to flay him, and the bronze relief after Peter Flötmer in the Victoria and Albert shows the same flaying swing of the angelic sword.

163

157, 173
205

Enough has been said about the angelic sword to indicate the problems it raised for Milton's conception of the Expulsion. He might have followed the Genesis account and avoided the problem altogether by merely showing the sword over the gate to the Garden after Adam and Eve had departed, but centuries of artistic usage had so firmly established the traditional visualization that it may never have occurred to Milton to abandon it. Instead, he adapted and altered the tradition to suit his own ends. We are explicitly told that Michael wears a sword, "Satan's dire dread," when he comes into the Garden, but that sword remains in its "glistering zodiac" by his side, and is never drawn (XI, 246-48): all the terror of that weapon was for Satan, not for Adam and Eve. But this alone would not be enough to meet the universal expectation of an active use of a sword during the process of the Expulsion. In citing "the brandisht sword of God" which blazed "fierce as a comet," Milton did something like what was expected of him, but with a pronounced and unmistakable difference. In pictorial art, that "brandisht" sword always *followed* Adam and Eve, driving them before it with greater or lesser implications of immediate physical harm, whereas Milton reverses its position, and explicitly places it "before them," where it was "high in front advanced" (XII, 632-34). At this point and for this visual motif, that shift of position makes all the difference. Milton's description shows Adam and Eve led out of Paradise, rather than forcibly driven from it. So used, the sword becomes processional, leading them forth in dignity and grace rather than driving them in terror.

What the angel is doing with his hands contributes importantly to the tone and mood of the representation. As two-handed long-swords were rare in these scenes, the angel of the Expulsion usually had one hand free. This free hand was rarely allowed to fall limply by the side, or to remain unused.[59] As early as the tenth century, the angel placed one hand on Adam's shoulder, as may be seen in the illuminations for the Grandval Bible in London and the Karls des Kahlen Bible in Paris, and in the Alcuin Bible in Bamburg, and still later in the St. Albans Psalter.[60] In the San Marco atrium in Venice, where the Expulsion is still carried out by the Son, a hand is also lightly placed upon Adam's shoulder. In these early uses, the gesture impresses us as gentle, and perhaps even compassionate, as it is at S. Zeno in Verona.[61] In the quattrocento bas relief carved by Jacopo della Quercia for the entrance to San Petronio in Bologna, the angel is pushing so forcefully with that hand that Adam's shoulder blade seems almost forced out of joint, and his arm is raised in a very awkward position.[62] Jacopo's typical straining after muscular effect places a disproportionate emphasis upon physical force, as may also be seen in his carvings of the Expulsion in the Piccolomini Library and in the Museo Civico in Siena. The gesture has been technically identified in German scholarship as the "Handauflegung auf die Schulter," a fine phrase whose harsh and grating sound seems highly appropriate to the visual sense of the motif.[63] With threatening sword and pushing hand, Adam and Eve are physically driven and shoved out of the Garden.[64]

In the strict course of justice, they deserve no better, and such artistic representations generally throw a heavy emphasis upon retribution. Some artists represent the Expulsion as less oppressive than others, but the visual message always emphasizes the infliction of punishment, and either minimizes or ignores the promises of grace. Milton's description, on the contrary, throws the emphasis upon grace, forgiveness, reconciliation, and hope. As with the sword, so with the *Handauflegung*, Milton alters the overall meaning of the traditional visualization by changes in the treatment of details. Not only is the familiar pushing gesture not mentioned by Milton, but it is excluded and explicitly replaced: "In either hand the hastening angel caught/ Our lingering parents" (XII, 637-38). I know of nothing like that in pictorial art: when Michael takes the hands of Adam and Eve in his

179

---

[59] It so appears in Lucas van Leyden's *Adam and Eve*, fig. 215.

[60] Esche, *Adam und Eva*, figs. 6, 7, and 9; and Otto Pacht, C. R. Dodwell, and Francis Wormald, *The St. Albans Psalter*, London, 1960, pl. 15a.

[61] The gesture becomes increasingly popular in and after the thirteenth century in England, and may be found in numerous stone carvings and illuminated manuscripts. See Gardner, *English Medieval Sculpture*, figs. 106, 141, and 150; Eric G. Millar, *English Illuminated Manuscripts of the XIVth and XVth Century*, Paris, 1928, pls. 21 and 33. In subsequent centuries, the gentleness tended to be lost, and the hand on Adam's shoulder became a fitting counterpart to the upraised and threatening sword. For renderings by Dürer and Baldung, see Hollstein, *German Engravings*, II, p. 77, and VII, p. 115.

[62] Reproduced in Louis Gielly, *Jacopo della Quercia*, Paris, 1930, pl. 32.

[63] Kirschbaum, *Lexikon*, I, p. 65. See also Réau, *Iconographie*, II, i, p. 89.

[64] Examples of the Expulsion in Jewish art may be found in Cecil Roth, ed., *Jewish Art: An Illustrated History*, New York, 1961, illustrations opposite col. 399 and on p. 490.

hands and leads them through the gate, we have a radically new version of an old and familiar scene. The picture of the expelling angel hand in hand with the first parents gives a perfect visual expression to the union of justice with mercy, and of the reconciliation between the human and the divine.[65]

The movement of the angelic hosts set to guard Eden is rendered with equally impressive decorum. We do not find here the martial airs and epic parade of the plains of Heaven, nor even the idyllic garrison life of Gabriel and his young sentinels which we earlier saw in the Garden. By a bold and masterly stratagem, Milton shifts from the heroic to the genre. He describes how from the surrounding hills the cherubim in bright array descend,

> on the ground
> Gliding meteorous, as evening mist
> Risen from a river o'er the marish glides,
> And gathers ground fast at the laboror's heel
> Homeward returning.
>
> (XII, 628-32)

The grand style of *Paradise Lost* is not generally suitable to such homely imagery, but at this particular point where Adam and Eve are being conducted from the perfect garden into an everyday world of toil and woe, no description could have been more appropriate than these lines which so brilliantly and poignantly introduce the whole atmosphere of genre. What Milton achieves with this visual simile is the essence of the genre painting which had achieved such popularity at this very time in Protestant Holland: the ordinary workaday life of mankind is dignified and ennobled, but without the slightest trace of romanticizing or sentimentalizing.

One final detail requires attention. In most artistic representations of the Expulsion from the Renaissance on, one or both of the first parents is shown as looking back toward the angel and the lost Garden. In the most devastating of all renderings of the Expulsion, that by Masaccio, there is and can be no looking back—only a *189* bleak and desolate facing ahead, a wailing entry into the future. Michelangelo's fresco is somewhat less oppressive (though it is terrifying enough): in it, Adam *169* attempts almost half-heartedly to ward off a blow from the angel, but his tear-swollen eyes look directly ahead out of a face contorted with weeping, while it is Eve who casts a furtive and futile glance behind them.[66] In the oil by Cranach and *163* the print by Brosamer the backward glances are cast in frightened apprehension *214* at the pursuing angel. In the version by del Minga, the first parents look in conster- *205* nation and fear directly at the angel, as they also do in the more powerful and moving canvas by Gazzola and Strozzi. Variations upon this visual motif, within *230* the same range of implication, may be found in the painting by Cavaliere d'Arpino in Christ Church, Oxford, and in the van Linge windows at University College, Oxford. Again, Milton incorporates the conventional motif in his description:

[65] See Baldwin, "Some Extra-Biblical Semitic Influences," 395, for a somewhat similar description of the Expulsion in a rabbinical source.

[66] Trapp observes that in such scenes, Eve "is usually shown as the more sorrowful and regretful" ("Iconography," p. 173).

Adam and Eve look back, and they see the flaming sword at the gate, but the sadness they show contains neither terror nor despair: "some natural tears they dropped, but wiped them soon" (XII, 645). No one could expect, or even hope, in the paintings of Masaccio and Michelangelo that the tears of Adam and Eve could be wiped away soon, or that their despair could give place to the muted optimism of Milton's closing lines.

When we consider what Adam and Eve have lost, and what now lies before them, Milton's achievement seems little short of the miraculous. It is theologically justified by the grace of God, and is made psychologically credible by the instructed faith which was imparted through Michael, but the aesthetic achievement is Milton's alone. Neither in the visual nor in the verbal arts had anything comparable been created before him. The mood upon which he chose to end his epic was effected almost equally by conceptual and visual descriptions in his verse. Conceptual phrases such as "not disconsolate" and "sorrowing yet in peace" define what he wishes us to feel, but such definitions alone are not sufficient to explain his success, which derives also and perhaps equally from the objective visual descriptions he provides as the external expression of the conceptual understanding.

To that end, Milton's adaptation and manipulation of visual details evidences the greatest care. I cannot suggest the degree to which he consciously recalled the visual traditions in framing his own account, but it must surely be clear that he was at the very least subconsciously aware of the established iconographies. With a meticulous attention to familiar pictorial details, he chose, changed, and manipulated his visual expressions until they precisely evoked the desired effects.

Finally, he added a particular which might almost be his own distinctive colophon: when Michael releases their hands from his, Adam and Eve, now alone, join hands once more in that symbol of mutuality and confidence Milton has so carefully developed and enriched throughout his epic. The only comparable picture I know is in the Medici tapestries where the first parents walk slowly out of Eden with Adam's hand resting in an affectionate and comforting gesture on Eve's shoulder, while their physical and facial expressions show them to be chastened but not overwhelmed. But the mutual linking of their hands does not appear in any artistic representation of the Expulsion with which Milton and his contemporary audience could have been familiar.[67] The addition of that detail returns Adam and Eve to each other and completes Milton's exacting visual description of the Expul-

154

[67] Adam and Eve are sometimes represented at the Expulsion with their arms linked, as in the early fourteenth-century French Bible Historiale (Bodley MS Douce 211, fol. 6v.), and in the fourteenth-century English Queen Mary's Psalter (reproduced in George F. Warner, *Queen Mary's Psalter*, London, 1912, pl. 6). In these instances, the gesture is rather awkward, and conveys little emotional significance. In a thirteenth-century illumination in the Wildenstein Miniatures (reproduced in *Journal of the Walters Art Gallery* 2 [1939], fig. 3 on p. 107), Adam takes Eve by the right hand with his right hand, but this grasp is more for leading or even pulling her than for holding hands. Eve's left hand appears to touch Adam's arm above the right elbow as they leave the Garden in *Genesis B* (reproduced in Sir Israel Gollancz, *The Caedmon Manuscript*, Oxford, 1927, p. 45). For a slightly different linking of arms, see the rather crude design from a church wall in Mauchenheim, reproduced in *Archives alsaciennes d'histoire et de l'art* 11 (1932), fig. 3 on p. 57.

sion, as he concludes *Paradise Lost* with some of the most hauntingly moving lines in literature:

> The world was all before them, where to choose
> Their place of rest, and providence their guide:
> They hand in hand with wandering steps and slow,
> Through Eden took their solitary way.
>
> (XII, 646-49)

Part Six

The World Redeemed

XVII

Paradise Regained

THE WILDERNESS TEMPTATIONS IN PICTORIAL ART AND THE PROBLEMS OF "PARADISE REGAINED"

Paradise Regained was published in 1671, four years after *Paradise Lost*. A short epic, it adheres to different formulas and moves to a slower music in a lower key, patterned to some extent after the Book of Job. Milton's young Quaker friend Thomas Ellwood claims to have suggested to Milton the idea of writing the latter epic immediately after the completion of the earlier one. Whatever its genesis, the poem strongly complements *Paradise Lost* in a briefer and more muted way. Elizabeth Pope and Barbara Lewalski, to mention only the most prominent commentators, have recreated for us the intellectual and literary backgrounds for the poem, and have amply shown its brilliant and psychologically perceptive forensics, as well as its theological subtlety.[1]

Paradise Regained consists of a number of debates between Christ and Satan, set against the backdrop of a wilderness landscape. The subject matter was provided for Milton by the first thirteen verses of the fourth chapter of Luke, which treat Satan's temptation of Christ in a slightly different order from that found in the parallel account in Matthew. These episodes were a frequent subject of commentary in the early centuries of the Church, but were not represented in Christian art until the ninth century, when a number of examples appear.[2] Thereafter the visualization of the devil followed historically the developments we have already observed, evolving from an initially beautiful figure[3] to quite degraded forms[4] during the Middle Ages. With the Renaissance, we begin to see the same kind of rehabilitation of Satan we have found elsewhere, though representative details differ in ways which we shall observe at a later point in connection with Milton's descriptions.

In the sixteenth century, artists began to move beyond what Wölfflin has described as the "visual pleasure in gaily colored miscellanies" which had delighted the Quattrocento, and to exploit artistically the world of human emotions, to show "a strong interest in the psychology of events" and exploit "significant and emotionally expressive action." For these reasons, Wölfflin notes that "the Temptation

---

[1] Elizabeth Pope, *"Paradise Regained," The Tradition and the Poem*, Baltimore, 1947, and Barbara K. Lewalski, *Milton's Brief Epic*, Providence, R.I., 1966.

[2] Schiller, *Iconography*, I, pp. 143-44, and Réau, *Iconographie*, II, ii, pp. 307-8.

[3] Schiller, *Iconography*, I, figs. 389-92.

[4] *Ibid.*, figs. 393-400, for example.

of Christ was a theme admirably adapted to the spirit of the new age,"[5] as indeed it was, and there were notable pictorial renderings of it during this period which correspond to Milton's visualized conception.[6]

The original story in the Gospels naturally lent itself to dramatization as a debate. Whether due to the New Testament narrative or to medieval stagings of it, the Holkham Picture Bible represented the scene as an argument in progress, with numbered scrolls provided for each of the antagonists so as to trace the course of the dramatic dialogue.[7] Verbal scrolls were not necessary in order to indicate that a debate was taking place: oratorical gestures and facial expressions would serve almost as well, and more subtly. In the early thirteenth-century stained glass from the cathedral of Troyes, we clearly understand that the devil is speaking and that Christ is about to reply, whereas in Ghiberti's bronze relief Satan's posture indicates that he has just been rebuked by Christ. In post-Renaissance examples, Dirk Vellert shows the devil speaking to a listening Christ, whereas Bloemaert shows Christ speaking patiently to an alertly observant devil. By Milton's time, the convention of treating the Temptations as a debate was firmly established.

231

232

233

234

235

But despite successes such as these in the visual representations of the story, Milton as a poet risked being unable to elevate his brief epic above the level of masterfully versified forensics. His subject is heavily abstract, and his two antagonists argue like skillful theologians. Indeed, some of Milton's most brilliant theology is found in this poem, though not, I think, his finest poetry, and if properly taught *Paradise Regained* might be received with at least equal enthusiasm in a course on Christology as in one on literature. It remains a major poem by one of our greatest poets, however, and it is as such that it interests us here.

Jeffry Spencer pointed to a difficulty which lies close to our concern for the relations between Milton's verse and the visual arts when he observed that "*Paradise Regained* reveals itself to the reader conceptually rather than pictorially. Its method is dialectical, not metaphorical, for the most part," and he goes on to add that "Milton himself seems to have realized that the impact of his epic argument would be increased if, at strategic intervals, he interrupted his dialogue to introduce passages of descriptive power."[8] It is to those descriptive passages that we will now turn.

[5] Wölfflin, *Classic Art*, pp. 217-18.

[6] Schiller, *Iconography*, i, p. 145, observes that it was never a "particularly prominent" theme in art, but Pigler's list of Mannerist and Baroque examples runs for almost two pages.

[7] Holkham Picture Bible (ed. Hassall), fol. 11v., and pp. 83-84. In the scrolls, the Holkham devil orders Christ to depart, claiming authority to rule humanity until the impossible event of a virgin conceiving, and Christ replies that the new order is now being instituted. Hassall reports without citing his source (p. 84) that M. R. James regarded this treatment of the encounter as probably original, and it does appear separately from the illustrations of the Temptations in the Wilderness on fols. 19-19v.

[8] Spencer, *Heroic Nature*, pp. 125 and 126. Equally apposite is Spencer's comment, p. 136, that "for an epic containing little more action than a series of dramatized debates between Christ and Satan, the Baroque theatricality of the landscapes contributes a good deal to the pictorialization of themes that would be otherwise almost wholly abstract, ethical, and intellectual."

INCIDENTAL IMAGES AND PANORAMIC VIEWS

The physical conditions of *Paradise Regained* are far closer to ordinary human experience than those of *Paradise Lost*. Put differently, the reader is only finitely separated from the place and action of the brief epic, whereas he lives at an infinite remove from the same aspects of the earlier work. Though Christ in the Wilderness is the Son of God, he is fully incarnate, and though his antagonist is the Prince of Darkness, he appears for most of the epic in forms readily conformable to our own observation of historical persons. This basic fact underlies virtually all Milton's descriptions in *Paradise Regained*, whether they be large and pervasive or brief and incidental. Turning first to the latter, let us examine three small verbal pictures. The first is pure genre, the second partially so, and the third a seascape vignette.

In the seventeenth century, genre painting gained a strong hold upon the popular imagination, especially in northern Europe, depicting everyday scenes and surroundings of ordinary and unidealized life. Milton's earlier form and subject matter allowed scant opportunity for genre descriptions, but toward the end of *Paradise Lost* we do find that evocative image of the laborer homeward returning which we discussed in Chapter XVI. We might expect more frequent examples of such homely imagery to appear in *Paradise Regained*, but though the short epic lacks the grandeur of the longer one, the awesome and stark isolation of its subject precludes very much in the way of ordinary and everyday scenes. There is a brief moment in connection with those "plain fishermen" Andrew and Peter when a genre description is both possible and appropriate, and with a simplicity reminiscent of the black and white lines of a Rembrandt etching, Milton shows their "cottage low" "on the bank of Jordan, by a creek/ Where winds with reeds and osiers whispering play" (*PR* II, 25-28). A longer description would be distracting, but just enough is said here to provide a graphic and indelible impression of the simple men and the everyday, unheroic landscape in the midst of which the Gospel of Redemption was revealed. The mystery of God's grace was that the Son of Glory should live and minister in a genre world. The theological idea has been given a perfect visual expression.

Another brief and genrelike image conveys the nagging persistence of Satan when Milton describes how "a swarm of flies in vintage-time,/ About the wine-press where sweet must is poured,/ Beat off, returns as oft with humming sound" (*PR* IV, 15-18). The picture is not only sharply drawn, but combines tactile and aural senses with the sense of sight, and we feel ourselves surrounded by the total sensuous experience of swarming insects. Reinforcing this sensation, with which everyone is familiar, is our knowledge of the artistic representations of swarming insect-devils. That image is immediately followed by another in which Milton describes how the "surging waves against a solid rock,/ Though all to shivers dashed, the assault renew,/ Vain battery, and in froth or bubbles end" (*PR* IV, 18-20). There is an almost instinctive human identification of bubbles with evanescence, and there is a widespread Biblical association between faith, God's assurances, and the solid immobility of rock, but the visual details which Milton joins together do not rely upon any major iconographical tradition in art. We do not need here that understanding of pictorial art which so enriches the insect simile, but this image is nonetheless visual: its effect upon us comes directly from an immediate sharing in a strongly visual experience. These three images exemplify what we may call snapshots in the visual portfolio of *Paradise Regained* and we must look elsewhere for the meticulous composition and coordinated sweep of the great landscapes.

The Temptations of the Kingdoms provided Milton with opportunities for describing the same kind of sweeping panoramic views with which he delights his readers in *Paradise Lost*. Satan first directs the Savior's attention to Assyria and the East:

> It was a mountain at whose verdant feet
> A spacious plain outstretched in circuit wide
> Lay pleasant; from his side two rivers flowed,
> Th' one winding, the other straight, and left between
> Fair champaign with less rivers interveined,
> Then meeting joined their tribute to the sea:
> Fertile of corn the glebe, of oil and wine,
> With herds the pastures thronged, with flocks the hills,
> Huge cities and high towered, that well might seem
> The seats of mightiest monarchs, and so large
> The prospect was, that here and there was room
> For barren desert fountainless and dry.
>
> (*PR* III, 253-64)

The visual details here are differently assembled from anything we have seen in Milton's earlier panoramas, but the methods and effects are essentially the same, with the same emphases on variety, contrast, and scope of vision, so that much of what was said in our earlier discussion of landscape views in *Paradise Lost* would apply here. So too, though to a lesser extent, with the brief placing of Rome in its geographical setting:

> He brought our Savior to the western side
> Of that high mountain, whence he might behold
> Another plain, long but in breadth not wide;
> Washed by the southern sea, and on the north
> To equal length backed with a ridge of hills
> That screened the fruits of the earth and seats of men
> From cold Septentrion blasts, thence in the midst
> Divided by a river, of whose banks
> On each side an imperial city stood.
>
> (*PR* IV, 25-33)

In this description, Milton quite naturally does not indulge in an "ideal" view, as he could in his broader sweep over Assyria, but seeks to reproduce a particular geographical site (and one he knew well) with marked fidelity; nonetheless, the scene still accords with the landscape art we have already discussed.

Milton could have presented all the kingdoms of the world in a similar way, and perhaps to good effect, at least theoretically, for the very conception of a kingdom suggests a vast and varied domain. But he chose not to do so. He does list many realms which were tributary to Rome (*PR* IV, 70-85), but the effect is a musical evocation of exotic places and peoples, underscoring the universality of Roman power, and we do not see the landscapes. In the midst of this resonant geographical fugue, Milton has inserted one sharply visual line: "Dusk faces with white silken turbans wreathed." Though it is almost engulfed by the surrounding music, that brief picture is startlingly beautiful. Otherwise the geopolitical catalog is utterly unpictorial. Nowhere else do we see anything approaching the hills, valleys, plains, rivers, lakes, and seas which would make up any large empire. Instead, Milton typified the kingdoms of this world through their capital cities.[9] Most often he merely mentions the cities by name (Nineveh, Babylon, Persepolis, Ctesiphon), but Athens, Jerusalem, and Rome are each given their own descriptions. On any count this may seem to limit visual possibilities in an odd way, and especially so for the poet who in *Paradise Lost* had created such magnificently successful landscapes sweeping over widely diversified and contrasting terrain. But the reasons for Milton's apparently curious choice here are not hard to discern. In the first place, too many versified panoramas during the same relatively brief episode would have become monotonous. Furthermore, Milton's epitomizing of entire kingdoms by reference to cities conformed to a major tradition in pictorial renderings of the temptation on the mountain. From the Middle Ages on, the visual arts had accustomed people to imagining the kingdoms offered to Christ as figuratively represented by fortified cities.[10]

This concentration upon the topography of cities sets the landscape views of *Paradise Regained* apart from those in the earlier epic. There are three such views: that of Athens is brief and sketchy, while that of Jerusalem provides only enough detail to serve as a setting for the Temptation on the pinnacle of the Temple, but the description of Rome is extensive and fully developed. Jeffry Spencer finds sufficient visual quality in Milton's Rome to suggest a "counterpart in many of the heroic landscapes of Nicholas Poussin," but he holds nonetheless that Milton "has carefully kept the impression nonparticularized enough to remain general."[11]

That comment could be applied more accurately to Milton's treatment of Athens and of Jerusalem than to his description of Rome. Milton refers to Athens as "the eye of Greece, mother of arts/ And eloquence, native to famous wits/ Or

---

[9] As a variant upon this basic scheme, Milton epitomizes Parthia by a vivid description of the Parthian army issuing from Ctesiphon in active campaign against the Scythians (*PR* III, 310-15, 322-44). The picture is full of life, movement, and action, conveyed through lively kinematic verbs and kinesthetic adjectives and nouns. There is no comparable description of Roman armies, though we are shown the busy comings and goings of government officials and soldiers at the gates (*PR* IV, 61-69).

[10] Réau, *Iconographie*, II, ii, p. 308.

[11] Spencer, *Heroic Nature*, p. 134.

hospitable, in her sweet recess,/ City or suburban, studious walks and shades," and points particularly to "the olive grove of Academe" (*PR* IV, 240-44). Even with the reference to walks, shades, and the olive grove, the description is unparticularized, and provides no details which distinguish Athens from almost any other "city or suburban" scene. Milton's concentration is upon the city as "mother of arts and eloquence," and there is only one brief and minimally visualized reference to "the low-roofed house/ Of Socrates" (*PR* IV, 273-74). One cannot fault Milton for this emphasis, for Athens was introduced into the debate only because of its intellectual achievements. Even had Milton wished to provide more in the way of physical particularity, he would have found little in the way either of information or support from pictorial representations. The *Nuremberg Chronicle* of 1493 had illustrated Athens as though it were a medieval German city, and no topographical account appeared again until the *Athenae Atticae* of 1624 by Johannes Meursius, which was seriously handicapped by the fact that Meursius had never seen the city he described.[12] And neither, of course, had Milton.

Though city views of Athens were rare, many existed of Jerusalem. The illustrations of Jerusalem in George Sandys' *Relations of a Journey* of 1632 show towers, domes, pinnacles, and columned porticoes, and Thomas Fuller's *A Pisgah-Sight of Palestine* of 1650 is amply supplied with maps and sketches which show many towers, crenellated walls, domes, pinnacles, and flags flying from flagstaffs; some of the roofs are peaked, while others are flat; Solomon's Temple is a classical building, with courts, balustraded walkways, cloisters, and a total effect which would not have displeased Inigo Jones. Similar features are found in the engraving of Jerusalem executed by Jacques Callot in 1618-19, indicating a general consensus of understanding.[13] Milton makes relatively little use of this substantial body of topographical views of Jerusalem, and his description is only somewhat less generalized than that of Athens:

> fair Jerusalem,
> The Holy City lifted high her towers,
> And higher yet the glorious Temple reared
> Her pile, far off appearing like a mount
> Of alabaster, topped with golden spires.
> There on the highest pinnacle he set
> The Son of God. . . .
>
> (*PR* IV, 544-50)

Milton does include the high towers which were insisted upon in the topographical prints, but otherwise we have only the sketchiest of outlines, sufficient to arouse our memories of impressions of Jerusalem gained from the Bible, and to set our imaginations at work, but not to channel them in particular directions and toward particular details—with one exception: upon the roof of the Temple are the

---

[12] Weiss, *Renaissance Discovery of Classical Antiquity*, p. 131.

[13] Walter Vitzthum and Maurizio Calvesi, *Jacques Callot: Incisione*, Florence, 1971, pl. xxxvi.

pointed shapes of spire and pinnacle, as is required by Milton's interpretation of the final Temptation. Otherwise, visual explicitness remains minimal. Ruskin's comment that Milton's lines here describe "exactly what St. Mark's [in Venice] is" seems to me extraordinarily lax: true, S. Marco is large and topped with many spires, but so were hundreds of other buildings, and Ruskin must surely have been in a singularly uncritical mood when he reached this identification.[14] Milton's lines on Jerusalem are so generalized that they cannot be productively related either to particular topographical art or to particular architecture.

Milton's description of Rome (*PR* IV, 25-68) is not only far longer, but is more carefully designed to adduce the image of one particular city and no other, perhaps because this was the only one of the three cities which Milton knew both from inspection and study and perhaps also because of the easy access to visual reconstructions which were accepted as trustworthy in his own time. Not only are we shown the geographical environs of the city without and the seven hills within, but we are called upon to notice distinctively Roman buildings such as baths, aqueducts, and triumphal arches,[15] in addition to the more generalized porches, theaters, gardens, and groves. The Tarpeian Rock and Mount Palatine are also specified, and we are told of "carved work, the hand of famed artificers." Though the lines here are not sharply drawn, and though we are not provided with a close-up view of any of the constituent buildings and other features, Milton's description is sufficiently comprehensive and detailed to evoke in each reader's mind distinctive features of Rome—of Rome in particular, and not of a generalized cityscape. We have already noted Spencer's comparison of Milton's effect with the effects of paintings by Poussin, but a comment by Mario Praz on Poussin's typical cities will enable us to set them apart from Milton's Rome: "Whether Poussin is depicting the plague of Athens or the blind men of Jericho, the triumph of David or the rape of the Sabines, the background is the same classical city of majestic temples, of massive buildings, of harmonious spaces. . . ."[16] Milton has surely achieved a more individual effect than that for Rome, though not for Athens and Jerusalem.

It is usually assumed that Milton's imaginary reconstruction of ancient Rome was the product of his long study of Latin literature and history, and it cannot be denied that a lifetime of classical learning is reflected here as elsewhere in Milton's verse.[17] Many of the visual features of Rome can be accounted for on the basis of literary sources alone,[18] but it is impossible to leave the matter simply at that, for

[14] Ruskin, letter of 10 Jan., 1852, in *Works* x, p. 112.

[15] Turner, *The Visual Arts in Milton's Poetry*, pp. 289-90, holds that "triumphal arcs" (*PR* IV, 37), were not present in Rome at the time of Christ. It is true that the first arch decorated with bas-relief sculpture was erected by Titus in A.D. 81, but simpler arches long antedated this one. The first were erected in 196 B.C. in the Forum Boarium and Circus Maximus by L. Stertinius, while Q. Fabius Maximus Allobrogicus erected another in 108 B.C. There was also a plain travertine arch of 10 A.D. inscribed with the names of Publius Dolabella and of *flamen martialis* C. Junius Silanus. There may have been others, but these instances demonstrate Milton's accuracy at this point.

[16] Praz, *Neoclassicism*, p. 33.

[17] Smith, "The Source of Milton's Pandaemonium," 187.

[18] Kliger, "The 'Urbs Aeterna' in *Paradise Regained*," PMLA 61 (1946), 491.

Milton has introduced a very specific descriptive phrase which cannot be derived from either the classical literary texts or the actual classical architecture: "glittering spires" are conspicuously placed along the rooflines of the imperial palace on Mount Palatine (*PR* IV, 54). There is simply no way to reconcile that Gothic detail with the literary and historical accounts of Rome from which Milton is assumed to have created his description.

This word "spire" developed from the Old English *spīr*, meaning a shoot or blade of grass. It could also refer to other vegetable forms, but always of the same shape, as in the pointed top of a tree or other tapering plant. In addition, it could apply to a tongue of fire or flame, as when Milton writes of the "pointing spires" of flames on the burning lake (*PL* I, 223), but the *pointed* shape was essential. The association becomes clearer when we recognize that "spire" in popular usage succeeded upon the now obsolete "spear," according to the Oxford English Dictionary, and both forms were applied to the architectural steeple. We cannot doubt that Milton understood this etymology when we note his puns on the various verbal forms of spire/spear in *The Reason of Church Government*: there he declares of Episcopacy that "her pyramid aspires and sharpens to ambition, not to perfection" and that polemicists who claim prelacy to be the peak of the church, "gore one another with their sharp spires for upper place and precedence."[19] The "glistering spires and pinnacles" of the Gothic city referred to in *Paradise Lost*, III, 550, virtually duplicate the "glittering spires" ascribed to Rome in *Paradise Regained*, and, again, as with the spires and pinnacles of the Temple in Jerusalem, we are to envision the pointed shape.[20]

No such spire was ever seen in classical Rome, where flat-roofed towers with crenelations were the architectural standard until long after the time of Christ.[21] Aside from the cupola tower which did not antedate the third century, one can find squat pyramidal roofs atop towers in Roman architecture. No one could possibly confuse any of these with the spires and pinnacles which, a thousand years later, developed from them.[22]

Milton's interpretation of the pinnacle on the Temple in Jerusalem as an elongated spire was necessary to the way in which he chose to tell the story. He surely knew that the New Testament Greek word translated as "pinnacle" in English did not define a sharp point on which no mere human could remain standing, and many theologians and exegetes maintained that the position in which Satan placed Christ on the Temple posed no immediate physical threat or danger in itself.[23] Elizabeth Pope has long since suggested that Milton's description here

---

[19] *CE* III, p. 218.

[20] The only contrary use of "spire" in Milton with which I am familiar comes at *PL* IX, 502, where the erect serpent stands "amidst his circling spires"—but the word here, though a homophone, is semantically and etymologically distinct, derivative from the Latin word for "loop" or "coil" which is primarily represented in modern English by "spiral."

[21] Smith, *Architectural Symbolism of Imperial Rome and the Middle Ages*, pp. 41 and 66.

[22] Arthur K. Porter, *Medieval Architecture: Its Origins and Developments*, New York, 1969, II, pp. 93-94.

[23] Pope, "Paradise Regained," pp. 84-87.

may be indebted to the popular representations of pictorial art,[24] and there can be little doubt that her hypothesis is valid. Spires and pinnacles of various heights and numbers appear in representations of the Temptation of Christ by Georg Pencz, Hans Sebald Lautensack, Martino Rota, J. Cornelicz, P. Cornelisz, and L. van Valkenborg,[25] and may be seen in the background of engravings by Vellert and Hondius, reproduced here.

234, 236

For spires and pinnacles in Jerusalem there is justification aplenty, in terms both of Milton's narrative design and of the relevant visual tradition, but he was under no necessity whatsoever to put spires in imperial Rome. Why did he do it? It is of course possible that he merely nodded and let an obvious faux pas slip by him, but this was not his usual way: he was no Shakespeare who introduced anachronisms with a fine creative abandon. From all that we know of Milton's scholarship and of his writing, it appears more likely on the face of it that he was here relying upon some source or sources which he regarded as authoritative when he placed those spires across the skyline of imperial Rome.

It was not until well over a century after Milton's death that archeological advances made it possible to produce accurate reconstructions of classical Rome, but this is not to say that attempts were not made before that time. With the renascence of classical learning in the fifteenth century, and the fascination with all aspects of classical life and culture, scholars and artists naturally turned to the task of showing Rome as it appeared during its centuries of greatness. A splendid example of such endeavors may be found in the work of Giovanni Marcanova, who combined the skills of physician, philosopher, and antiquarian in the manner so distinctive of the quattrocento. A manuscript at Princeton of Marcanova's *Antiquitates*, executed with the date 1465, contains anonymous sepia drawings which illustrate Marcanova's conception.[26] These views present a lively recreation of ancient Rome, and combine a surprising accuracy at points with equally striking anachronisms, including just such steepled towers as Milton describes. In the reconstruction reproduced here, we encounter Roman legionnaires entering a fortification in which two towers are topped by medieval conical spires, while even more sharply elongated pinnacles are illustrated on the hills in the right background.

237

Advances over Marcanova were made in the course of the sixteenth century, but Gothic details continued to intrude upon the classical city. Even the great Raphael became involved in the effort to represent the ancient appearance of Rome, and it is indicative of the state of archeology at the time that the primary responsibility for recapturing a vision of the city was placed upon an artist rather than an historian. Raphael embarked upon the project in the last years of his life and pursued it with enthusiasm, but he had apparently achieved very little toward its completion before his death in 1520. Thereafter Marco Fabio Calvo, a serious

[24] *Ibid.*, p. 99.

[25] The first three are in the file of Bartsch photographs at Princeton (Bartsch VI.361.1, VIII.331.39, and XVI.249.4 respectively), and the latter three in the Digital Index of the Art of the Low Countries at Princeton and elsewhere (under DIAL 73C2 and 73C22.1).

[26] For a brief account of the Marcanova codices, see Erna Mandowsky and Charles Mitchell, *Pirro Ligorio's Roman Antiquities*, London, 1963, p. 9.

scholar who had close associations with Raphael, brought forth some printed views of ancient Rome, as also did Andrea Fulvio. In 1544, Giovanni Battista Palatino, working under the guidance of Bartolomeo Marliani, produced a printed plan of Rome which was the most satisfactory reconstruction up to that time.[27]

Pirro Ligorio entered the field in 1553 with his engraved view of the ancient city. Ligorio continued to address himself to the subject, and his work became the best known and probably the most widely accepted among the versions Milton is likely to have seen. In 1561 he issued the most elaborate and detailed of all topographical visions of the ancient city, printed in fifteen separate sheets, which could be assembled into a single engraved view measuring four feet by five feet. Ligorio had taken advantage both of ancient texts and of recent studies, but "the 1561 plan was a 'synthetic' creation, rising on the wings of Ligorio's learned imagination above the particular world of specific archeological remains into an ideal exemplary sphere where all is made perfect. It was Ligorio's vision of *Roma Triumphans*."[28] Ligorio's huge topographical plan was at once popular and influential, and it brings us fairly close to Milton's conceptions. We see here the same terraces we find on the Palatine Hill in *Paradise Regained* (which were also described in Latin literature), but we notice, too, an elongation of some pyramidal roofs on the towers, a stretching of the squat Roman shapes up toward the pinnacle form.[29] This tendency to draw out and extend pyramidal shapes of ancient Rome into pointed roofs was continued in the map by Mario Cartaro of 1579 and in views executed in the early seventeenth century by Giacomo Lauro, which also show close approaches to the pinnacle shape.[30]

Ligorio was influential not only because of his massively detailed topographical engravings, but also for a famous three-dimensional reconstruction of the ancient city. As archeologist to Cardinal d'Este, Ligorio was charged with responsibility for constructing in the Tivoli Gardens a model of Rome, known as the Rometta. Work was commenced in 1567 or 1568, and the Eternal City was reconstructed along the lines of a theatrical set on a raised stagelike plateau where small buildings were "scale modeled" to reconstruct the most familiar sights of Rome. Below this model was a fountain. The whole endured into the middle of the nineteenth century, when the collapse of a sustaining wall destroyed most of the small buildings. The original effect has fortunately been preserved in a seventeenth-century engraving by Venturini which provides an accurate impression of the Rometta as it appeared in Milton's time.[31] One of the first three-dimensional models to be used for archeological reconstruction, Ligorio's creation was immensely popular. Early seventeenth-century accounts indicate that visitors came daily in great

238

---

[27] Weiss, *Renaissance Discovery of Classical Antiquity*, pp. 93-97; Ferdinando Castagnoli, "Raphael and Ancient Rome," in *The Complete Work of Raphael*, New York, 1969, pp. 569-84; and Turner, *The Vision of Landscape*, p. 168; Mandowsky and Mitchell, *op. cit.*, p. 20.

[28] *Ibid.*, pp. 40-41 and 43.

[29] Amato Pietro Frutaz, *Le piante di Roma*, II, pls. 26-32.

[30] *Ibid.*, pls. 53, 59-61; in pl. 62, the tendency is less observable in Goffredo van Schayck's representation.

[31] Coffin, *The Villa d'Este at Tivoli*, pp. 23-27.

numbers to see Tivoli and its wonders, as John Evelyn certainly did, and many were particularly fascinated by the Rometta.[32] Like Evelyn, Milton could readily have visited the Rometta, and his classical interests would presumably have attracted him to it. On the right side of the model, the battlemented city wall shows two towers capped by elongated pyramidal roofs.[33] The tall needlelike spire or flèche on the dome in the center background is especially unclassical, but quite Miltonic. Toward the right margin and again in the background, there is an architectural form which may have been intended to represent an obelisk, but which is so slender in shape and raised so high against the skyline that it gives exactly the effect of an architectural spire, even after the fashion of Chartres. That Gothic skyline which *Paradise Regained* pictures for Rome in the time of Christ is, I suggest, most likely due to Milton's accepting the authority of what he had seen in the Rometta by Ligorio, or in one or more of the numerous "archeological" engravings of the time.[34] Spires and pinnacles in first-century Rome and Jerusalem remain an error, but an error which Milton and his contemporaries were led to accept on the basis of famous pictorial representations.[35]

"PAYSAGE MORALISÉ": THE WILDERNESS AND THE GROVE

The views shown by Satan from the mountain all take us outside the desert, but the stage setting for the action, or the arena for the contest, remains the Wilderness itself. The physical environs in which Christ and Satan meet are of extraordinary importance in setting the tone for their extended debate, and contribute to its meaning. In this sense, Milton brilliantly adapts to his own ends the broad tradition of the *paysage moralisé* in art. Everything in the desert is described in terms of that tradition: physical landscape is used to create moral, spiritual, and psychological moods and conditions, almost always representing a choice between styles of life and action.

[32] *Ibid.*, pp. 127-30, and John Evelyn, *Diary*, II, p. 396, for the account of Evelyn's visit on May 7, 1645.

[33] These pyramidal roofs are topped by balls. Such topping elements sometimes appeared on tombs outside the walls of Rome, but though they were not a feature of Roman architecture in the city, they appear again and again in the Rometta.

[34] It may also be that Milton's conception of Gothic elements on the classical Roman skyline was indebted to Italian theatrical scenery. Irving Lavin has kindly allowed me to examine his extensive collection of photographic reproductions of stage designs from this period, and in these one frequently finds the mixture of spires and pinnacles with a purely classical architecture, but a full evaluation of this evidence would involve the identification of plays, the dating of sets, the determination of when and where they were employed, the nature and period of the subject dramatized, and a series of other problems in Italian stage history which I am unable to investigate. The subject does, however, deserve inquiry.

[35] For generous consultations on ancient Rome and Milton's description of it, I am particularly indebted to David R. Coffin of Princeton University's Department of Art and Archaeology, to my colleague Robert E. A. Palmer of the University of Pennsylvania's Department of Classical Studies, and to the following colleagues at the Institute for Advanced Study in Princeton: J. F. Gilliam, Emilio Gabba, G. Nicolaus Knauer, and Peter Kussmaul in Classical Studies and to Irving Lavin in Art History. The solutions I have proposed in the foregoing text are, however, entirely my own, and should not be held against these worthy gentlemen.

Various landscapes conveyed differing meanings, but by Milton's time the kind of landscape appropriate to spiritual conflict and spiritual heroism had been firmly established, as A. Richard Turner tells us: "In the hands of a major artist the forms of the landscape became virtually an extension of the saint's quality of soul."[36] The visual conventions may be epitomized in the works of Titian, where "the world of the hermit ceases to be a pleasant place within a stone's throw of civilization. Rather one enters the unkempt forest, a place of rushing waters and gnarled trees evoked by a detail from the painter's *John the Baptist*, done at mid-century. For a brief moment the Italian artist set aside that domesticated landscape which had been groomed over the centuries, and ascended the forbidding hills above the plain," as we may see in Titian's representations of St. John and St. Jerome.[37] Grünewald's *St. Anthony and St. Paul the Hermit* shows that Northern artists understood this iconographic landscape as well as the Italians, and used it to equally dramatic effects of spiritual discipline and worldly renunciation. There were differences of visual dialect in these representations, but all within a well-understood lingua franca. Writing of English taste in the seventeenth century, Ogden and Ogden declare that "the kind of landscape regarded as conducive to religious ecstasy was mountain scenery with rocky crags and ravines, twisted trees and broken limbs. The wilder the scene, the more fitting it was thought for religious contemplation and exaltation, because the farther removed from worldly associations."[38]

This firmly established scenic convention provided Milton with a means for objectifying and visualizing themes which would otherwise remain forbiddingly conceptual and abstract. The text of *Paradise Regained* shows that he made the most of this visual tradition to vitalize his epic narrative by reference and reinforcement. "Hard are the ways of truth, and rough to walk," as Satan says, and in so saying he epitomizes the rationale for the *paysage moralisé*. When he later describes the Son "seated as on the top of Virtue's hill," he introduces another familiar iconographic detail (*PR* I, 478, and II, 216-17).[39] What Satan briefly recognizes in these lines constitutes the basic symbolic import of the wilderness landscape in *Paradise Regained*.

Milton at the same time introduces us to the traditional setting, and defines its traditional rationale when he describes how the Son of God

> Musing and much revolving in his breast,
> How best the mighty work he might begin
> Of Savior to mankind, and which way first
> Publish his Godlike office now mature,
> One day forth walked alone, the Spirit leading,
> And his deep thoughts, the better to converse

[36] Turner, *The Vision of Landscape*, p. 113.
[37] *Ibid.*, pp. 115-16 and fig. 67.
[38] Ogden and Ogden, *English Taste in Landscape*, p. 52b.
[39] Associated with the same conception is Milton's reference in Sonnet IX to those few who are "eminently seen,/ That labor up the Hill of Heavenly Truth."

With solitude, till far from track of men,
Thought following thought, and step by step led on,
He entered now the bordering desert wild,
And with dark shades and rocks environed round,
His holy meditations thus pursued.

(*PR* I, 185-95)

There we have the dark shades, the wilderness, and rocky terrain considered appropriate to spiritual resolution. Subsequent descriptions throughout the four books of the short epic add cumulatively to the visual and spiritual effect. The thoughts of the Savior were such "as well might recommend/ Such solitude before choicest society," and the "pathless desert, dusk with horrid shades . . . by human steps untrod" were just what Milton's contemporaries would see in many paintings and etchings of a saint's spiritual struggle and victory (*PR* I, 296-302). Whether "on hill" or "in shady vale," some covert might be provided by an "ancient oak/ Or cedar," or by a cave, but in "this barren waste" water was far removed, even the sticks on the ground were "withered," and for food there was only "tough roots and stubs" (*PR* I, 303-7, 316, 325, 339-40, and 352-54). The protective "covert" in Book I seems to be an occasional single tree, whereas in Book II we have moved into a dark forest "Of trees thick interwoven," and in Book IV we are still in a wilderness of "branching arms thick intertwined" (*PR* II, 263, and IV, 405). It is also in the last book that we have the fierce demonic storm in which "tallest pines,/ Though rooted deep as high, and sturdiest oaks/ Bowed their stiff necks, loaden with stormy blasts,/ Or torn up sheer" (*PR* IV, 416-19). On the final day of the Temptations we observe Christ "walking on a sunny hill . . ./ Backed on the north and west by a thick wood" (*PR* IV, 447-48).

The vegetation cited in these passages does not represent the deserts of the Holy Land, but the range both of geology and vegetation which Milton describes may be precisely paralleled in pictorial renderings of the Temptation in the Wilderness: in the sixteenth-century prints by Antonio Tempesta, and the anonymous illustrator of the 1563 Greek New Testament, we see the rocky barrenness of Milton's earliest descriptions, punctuated with only a few trees, whereas Schaufelein and the monogrammatist D. P. show such a barren foreground merging into a wooded background, and Bloemaert, Hondius, and Cock represent the Temptation as occurring within leafy northern forests. Galle's engraving includes elements of all these features.[40] Milton's settings also correspond, though in different order, to Botticelli's fresco in the Sistine Chapel which shows the first Temptation as taking place within a forest, and the last as occurring on a barren rocky plateau. What Arnold Stein has written of *Paradise Regained* can as well be applied to the pictorial representations of the same story: "The images are those of profound, labyrinthine self-search."[41] Whether in pictorial art or in poetry, the picture of

240
241
242, 243
235, 236,
244
248

246

[40] Pope, "*Paradise Regained*," reproduces as her plate IV the engraving by Galle.
[41] Arnold Stein, *Heroic Knowledge: An Interpretation of "Paradise Regained" and "Samson Agonistes*," Hamden, Conn., 1965, pp. 53-54, 128-30.

Christ "wandering this woody maze," "by human steps untrod," is supported by a consistent imagery (*PR* ii, 246, and i, 298).[42]

Into such desolate landscapes it was not unusual to introduce contrasting scenery, so as to provide a clear expression of the moral struggles and choices involved. Thus the Ogdens point out how "often a small area of such pictures represents a peaceful valley or a group of buildings, suggesting the contrast between worldly and otherworldly values."[43] In *Paradise Regained*, Milton establishes this exact antithesis in his descriptions of the "barren waste" in which Christ explores the implications of his own mission and the "pleasant grove" and luxurious banquet which Satan introduces to deceive and betray him. Panofsky observes that the *paysage moralisé* "is frequent in religious pictures where the '*Aera sub lege*' is contrasted with the '*Aera sub gratia*,' and, more particularly, in the representation of subjects like 'Hercules at the Crossroads' where the antithesis between Virtue and Pleasure is symbolized by the contrast between an easy road winding through beautiful country and a steep, stony path leading to a forbidding rock."[44] As Christ had taught, the road to Hell is broad and easy, whereas the road to Heaven is narrow and hard, and similar contrasts were perennially employed in the moral and religious allegorization of classical mythology. "In representations of Hercules at the Crossroads," Panofsky continues, "the barren and desolate scenery stands for praiseworthy virtues, while the rich and beautiful one stands for reprehensible pleasures."[45] As a prime example, he cites Annibale Carracci's painting of this scene, where the barren and rocky wilderness contains the figure of Athena who personifies Virtue, while the lush and deceptive garden landscape contains the figure of Venus, personifying Vice or Voluptuousness, and the canvas is appropriately divided between the two.[46] Whether in allegorized myth or in Christian story, scenic backgrounds are not merely decorative, but are constructs of meaning. "The landscape is humanized," as Turner puts it, while "forms and light are not arbitrary, but directed specifically to an enlargement of the spiritual meaning of the figures."[47]

This second phase[48] of *paysage moralisé* in *Paradise Regained* comes in the "pleasant grove" of the Satanic Temptation in Book ii. Hungry now for the first time; the Savior awakes, and climbs a hill in search of a cottage, but sees instead

> a pleasant grove,
> With chant of tuneful birds resounding loud.
> Thither he bent his way, determined there

[42] The theme is also treated in Mary's reflections upon the time when the boy Jesus was lost, and then found in the Temple: "when twelve years he scarce had seen,/ I lost him, but so found, as well I saw/ He could not lose himself" (*PR* ii, 96-98).

[43] Ogden and Ogden, *English Taste in Landscape*, p. 52b

[44] Panofsky, *Studies in Iconology*, p. 64.

[45] *Ibid.*, p. 65.

[46] Panofsky, *Hercules am Scheidewege*, Leipzig, 1930, pl. xliv.

[47] Turner, *The Vision of Landscape*, p. 79.

[48] It would be possible, of course, to interpret the Kingdoms in a similar way, but for convenience I have associated them with the panoramic views and cityscapes to which they are visually related.

> To rest at noon, and entered soon the shade
> High rooft, and walks beneath, and alleys brown
> That opened in the midst a woody scene;
> Nature's own work it seemed (Nature taught Art)
> And to a superstitious eye the haunt
> Of wood gods and wood nymphs.
>
> (*PR* ii, 289-97)

This passage is carefully designed to elicit the second of the antithetical and allegorical landscapes which Panofsky identified in art, the rich and gardenlike scene representing the easy temptations of thoughtless vice, which may divert the hero or saint from fulfilling his high calling.[49] We shall return to this scene at a later point in connection with the temptation of the false banquet.

One further aspect of Milton's *paysage moralisé* concerns the peacefulness of the wild animals in the presence of Christ: "they at his sight grew mild,/ Nor sleeping him nor waking harmed, his walk/ The fiery serpent fled, and noxious worm,/ The lion and fierce tiger glared aloof" (*PR* i, 310-13). Old Testament prophets had predicted that the Messiah would apocalyptically establish such a "peaceable kingdom" although nothing in the Gospel accounts explicitly connects this situation with Christ's Temptation in the Wilderness.[50] Some later Christian commentators added that the wild animals were as harmless in the presence of Christ as they had been in the presence of Adam, because they recognized here the same perfect unfallen innocence. Giles Fletcher, in a fictionalized treatment of the Temptation in the Wilderness which preceded Milton's, went so far as to declare that the wild animals had accompanied and even comforted Christ during his forty-day stay in the desert, but this charming suggestion undercuts the necessary solitariness of the wilderness experience. Milton stops well short of that extreme, but he does show the animals as mild and harmless.[51]

Milton's description of the wild animals grown peaceful in the presence of Christ accords with popular visual representations not only of Christ in the Wilderness[52] but of Christian saints[53] as well. At Merton College, Oxford, there is a fine

[49] For a comparison of this grove with the gardens of Armida and Alcina, and of Spenser's Bower of Bliss, see Spencer, *Heroic Nature*, p. 129. The literary history of such places is traced in Giamatti, *The Earthly Paradise*.

[50] Isa. 11:6-9 and 65:25, and Ezek. 34:25.

[51] Pope, "*Paradise Regained*," p. 110, understands that the serpent, lion and tiger are classed with the other animals, though Jackson I. Cope denies this in his "Satan's Disguises: *Paradise Lost* and *Paradise Regained*," *MLN* 73 (1958), 9-11. I prefer Pope's interpretation.

[52] The earliest British example is the late seventh-century carving on the Ruthwell Cross in Dumfriesshire, which goes far beyond Milton in showing "a full length figure of Christ being worshipped by the beasts in the desert." See Laurence Stone, *Sculpture in Britain: The Middle Ages*, Harmondsworth, 1972, p. 11 and fig. 3, and also Burgess, *English Churchyard Memorials*, p. 160, which refers to similar reliefs at Easby Bewcastle, also of the Anglo-Saxon period.

[53] Engelbert of Nassau's *Book of Hours*, fol. 36v.-37, in the Bodleian Library, shows St. Anthony Abbot in the Wilderness surrounded by wild animals who harm neither him nor each other; in another illuminated manuscript, St. Mary of Egypt is shown feeding a lion (fig. 623 in Lilian M. C. Randall, *Images in the Margins of Gothic Manuscripts*, Berkeley,

fifteenth-century stone carving of the Agnus Dei in the Wilderness surrounded by animals peaceful and unafraid. In the stained glass window at King's College Chapel, Cambridge, the animals with Christ include a bear playing with a log in the presence of unconcerned deer and rabbits, while a cat sits quietly and peaceably, watching a rabbit frolic safely within easy reach.[54] Prints by Gatti and Tassari show predatory animals friendly and harmless in the presence of each other and of Christ in the Wilderness,[55] and we see predator and prey in the same irenic disposition in a Slavic woodcut of about 1573.[56] Among our reproductions here we may note how "the fiery serpent fled" from Christ in the engraving by Hondius, while Bloemaert shows the lion and the lamb coexisting without threat or fear. Milton's descriptions accord with the predominant artistic treatment in showing the animals as mild in the presence of Christ, but not as crowding about to reassure and comfort him during the Wilderness Temptation. In this as in other ways, Milton's verbal pictures exploit to their optimal effect the traditional features of the *paysage moralisé* in pictorial art.

236
235

EXTRA-BIBLICAL TEMPTATIONS

Milton introduces into *Paradise Regained* two temptations which are nowhere found in the New Testament accounts. The first of these is Satan's "pleasant grove" with its luxurious al fresco banquet, which as we have seen completes a traditional contrast within the *paysage moralisé*. The second is the frightful storm and hideous demonic assault which is visited upon the Savior in the "night of terror" (*PR* IV, 401-31). These two incidents represent major innovations by Milton, and although they do not appear elsewhere in literary renditions of the story, we can find instructive examples of their use in the pictorial tradition.[57] Let us begin with the banquet.

As Christ descends into the grove, he is met by Satan once again, but now "not rustic as before, but seemlier clad,/ As one in city, or court, or palace bred," an appearance more suitable to the temptations which will now be offered (*PR* II, 299-300). After a brief exchange, Satan points to

> A table richly spread, in regal mode,
> With dishes piled, and meats of noblest sort

1966). John the Baptist is shown in the Wilderness with a wide variety of animals who evidence neither antagonism nor alarm in a French stained glass window made in the middle of the sixteenth century at Rouen and now at the Victoria and Albert Museum. For other such representations, see Lavin, "Giovanino Battista."

[54] Wayment, *The Windows of King's College Chapel*, p. 66, and reproduction of window, 7.4.

[55] Bartsch XIX.8.14, and XVII.30.14, included in the illustrated Bartsch file under New Testament 13a, at the Institute of Fine Arts in New York.

[56] Reproduced as pl. XXXIX.12 in Zoltánné Soltész, *A Magyarországi Könyvdíszítés A XVI. Századbdan*, Budapest, 1961.

[57] Lewalski, *Milton's Brief Epic*, p. 119, finds "little foundation in the Christiads for Milton's banquet sequence," but cites some possible parallels.

And savor, beasts of chase, or fowl of game,
In pastry built, or from the spit, or boiled,
Grisamber steamed; all fish from sea or shore,
Freshet, or purling brook, of shell or fin,
And exquisitest name, for which was drained
Pontus and Lucrine Bay, and Afric Coast.
Alas how simple, to these cates compared,
Was that crude apple that diverted Eve!
And at a stately sideboard by the wine
That fragrant smell diffused, in order stood
Tall stripling youths rich clad, of fairer hue
Than Ganymede or Hylas; distant more
Under the trees now tripped, now solemn stood
Nymphs of Diana's train, and Naiades
With fruits and flowers from Amalthea's horn,
And ladies of th' Hesperides, that seemed
Fairer than feigned of old, or fabled since
Of fairy damsels met in forest wide
By knights of Logres, or of Lyones,
Lancelot or Pelleas, or Pellenore;
And all the while harmonious airs were heard
Of chiming strings or charming pipes, and winds
Of gentlest gale Arabian odors fanned
From their soft wings, and Flora's earliest smells.
Such was the splendor, and the tempter now
His invitation earnestly renewed.

(*PR* II, 340-67)[58]

The basic temptation, of course, is to misuse the bounties of nature. Milton's references to incidents in the Arthurian romances links this episode in *Paradise Regained* with those questing knights who were seduced by the temptation of women in the wilderness and diverted from their missions; the passage also clearly alludes to other famous and equally sumptuous groves and banquets which divert the soul from its divine quest, and we find conspicuous parallels both in Tasso and in Spenser.[59] These literary parallels have long been known, and they provide at least part of the cultural context for Milton's introduction of the banquet temptation.

But some critics are unsatisfied. Charles Lamb found the banquet, with its "mighty artillery of sauces," to be altogether a profanation of the story, and Landor held similar reservations, while Van Doren judged it so overdone and

---

[58] Satan assures the Son that "these are not fruits forbidden," but shellfish were explicitly prohibited by the Mosaic dietary laws, and very few of the delicacies specified here would not come under the same prohibition, as Michael Fixler has shown in "The Unclean Meats of the Mosaic Law and the Banquet Scene in *Paradise Regained*," *MLN* 70 (1955), 573-77.

[59] Lewalski, *Milton's Brief Epic*, pp. 224-25; Spencer, *Heroic Nature*, p. 130, and Frye, *The Return of Eden*, p. 127.

"Baroque" as to show an "obtuseness scarcely to be matched in all poetry."[60] An analysis of similar banquets in art will establish the context for Milton's description and show it to be less shocking and inappropriate than it has seemed to such critics as these.

Rich vessels as a display of regal opulence and luxury were introduced into the earliest known illustration of the Temptation in the Wilderness, the Stuttgart Psalter of the early ninth century, where Satan directs Christ's attention to rich vessels suitable for serving a royal banquet of food and wine.[61] In the illuminated

249   eleventh-century Gospel Book belonging to Matilda of Tuscany, we see a horned devil tempting Christ and pointing to a draped entablature on a column, below which are goblet, bowl, and candlesticks. This motif was popular in illuminated manuscripts over several centuries, and included several types of dishes and cups, sometimes filled, sometimes not.[62] The motif was not restricted to illuminated manuscripts, as may be seen in the carvings on a late twelfth-century stone capital, probably from the Ile-de-France and now in the Metropolitan Museum. Four sides show the three Biblical Temptations of Christ and one other: after the Temptation of the stones, a scene is inserted where Jesus "is tempted by the devil who points to food and drink."[63]

After the end of the thirteenth century, I have been able to find no such explicit scenes of Satan tempting Christ by food, but pictorial works continue to show devils tempting men (whether saints or ordinary mortals) with food, variously presented. Bartolomeo di Giovanni painted a bishop eating dinner with a beautiful woman who was later exposed as a demon, and Nicholas Manuel Deutsch drew a picture of St. Anthony being offered food on a platter by a handsome female demon.[64] The diabolical feast was a standard part of witch lore, and F. M. Guazzo's *Compendium Maleficarum* illustrates these feasts with pictures of three

250   al fresco banquet tables, richly spread and served by demons.[65]

Reports of the menus varied from country to country, and Owen finds several examples in medieval French literature of infernal banquets served for the demons and a human guest which afford such prime delicacies as "roast heretics, the

[60] Wittreich, *Romantics on Milton*, pp. 300-301, and 324; and Van Doren, *The Noble Voice*, p. 139.

[61] Reproduced as fig. 389 in Schiller, *Iconography*, I.

[62] The following examples are taken from the Index of Christian Art in Princeton, where reproductions may be consulted: the Gospel Book of Henry III, fol. 26, in the Escorial; the Prayer Book of St. Hildegardis, fol. 21v., in the Staatsbibliothek, Munich; a Psalter of ca. 1200, fol. 10v., in Emmanuel College, Cambridge; two lectionaries, Bibl. Roy. 9428, fol. 32v., and Bibl. Roy. 9222, fol. 39, in Brussels; a Pericope, Stadtbibliothek, b. 21, fol. 25v., in Bremen; and in the Psalter, Bibliothèque de la Ville 539, fol. 235, in Lyons. These manuscripts date from the eleventh through the thirteenth centuries.

[63] B[rech], J[oseph], "A King of Judah and Other Medieval Sculptures," *Bulletin of the Metropolitan Museum of Art* 16 (1921), 48-52, where the scene is reproduced as fig. 2, and described on p. 51.

[64] Reproduced in Kaftal, *Iconography of the Saints in Tuscan Painting*, fig. 41, and in André Chastel, "La Tentation de Saint Antoine; ou Le Songe du Mélancholique," *Gazette des Beaux-Arts* 15 (1936), fig. 4.

[65] Alan C. Kors, and Edward Peters, eds., *Witchcraft in Europe 1100-1700: A Documentary History*, Philadelphia, 1972, p. 230.

tongues of false advocates choicely grilled," or "roast monk with usurer or lecher sauce," or "heretic with renegade Beguine sauce."[66] Such dishes are a far cry from those which Milton stipulates in *Paradise Regained*, but would perhaps accord with the satiric tone of Bosch's *Temptation of St. Anthony* in Lisbon and the related panels on the same subject in the Prado. Of the former, Walter S. Gibson notes that "the open-air table, the cloth slung tent-like over the tree stump beside the temptress, and the servants pouring wine seem like a grotesque parody of the traditional Garden of Love." In the central panel of the same triptych, we see another table offering food and drink: "On a platform before the tomb, an elegantly dressed pair have set up a table from which they dispense drink to their companions."[67] In one form or another, there are numerous instances in art from the eleventh into the seventeenth century of the demonic use of food in temptation scenes.

In pictorial works devoted to saints in the desert, there are many instances of devils appearing to tempt in attractive as well as ugly guises.[68] Milton's Satan is perceptive enough to reject Belial's proposal that he tempt Christ to lust after beautiful women (*PR* II, 153), but when he presents the banquet as a temptation to abandon a mission of salvation for all mankind in favor of a personal enjoyment of the bounties of nature, the service staff are the fairest of youths and maidens, obviously that "chosen band/ Of spirits likest to himself in guile" which he brings with him from the demonic council (*PR* II, 236-37). Milton's description at this point of "stripling youths . . . of fairer hue/ Than Ganymede or Hylas" closely corresponds with famous paintings of the Temptation in the Wilderness by Titian and by Tintoretto, in which Satan appears as a kind of Ganymede or Hylas. Raymond Henniker-Heaton comments upon "the golden tone of the boy's head" in Titian's *Temptation* and also upon "the luminosity of the flesh."[69] Tintoretto's painting in the Scuola di San Rocco, Venice, shows the Tempter as a bit older, *251, 252* literally a stripling youth, and so carries Titian's conception to the point where it is very close indeed to Milton's suggestion of the demonic youths in the grove, as we can see. Tintoretto's achievement here is so like Milton's that the comments of art historians upon the painting may almost equally well be applied to the poem. Seeing Tintoretto's tempter as "the prototype of material splendor and opulent beauty," Osmaston declares that "here we have the ideal of the human form itself in its sensuous or material manifestation. He [the Tempter] is the glory of nature disjoint from her ideal significance. His appeal to Christ is that of the materialist to have that which is entirely material absorbed within the ideal totality of life for purely selfish ends. It is the direct negation of the dictum of the idealist, 'My kingdom is not of this world.' "[70] That is, of course, essentially the appeal which Satan

---

[66] Owen, *The Vision of Hell*, pp. 159, 207, and 210.

[67] Gibson, *Bosch*, pp. 143-44.

[68] Levron, *Le Diable dans l'art*, p. 18.

[69] Harold Wethey, *The Paintings of Titian*, London, 1969-71, I, p. 162, and Raymond Henniker-Heaton, *Panel Picture Representing The Temptation of Christ by . . . Titian*, New York, 1925, p. 13.

[70] Osmaston, *The Art and Genius of Tintoret*, I, p. 168.

makes with his banquet "scene" in *Paradise Regained*. Tietze emphasizes another aspect relevant both to paintings and poem when he notes that Tintoretto has "adorned the Prince of Evil with all the seductive glitter of outward appearance" and has shown him as rising in ideal beauty "to joyful pride in order to render the divine victory more striking."[71] A final example of the Tempter as a handsome youth may be found in an engraving by Cornelius Galle based upon a sixteenth-century painting by Marten de Vos, where the beauty is not so sustained, but still obvious. Close as Milton's "stripling youths" are to these handsome young devils, his introduction of the nymphs and naiades is without any counterpart, as far as I have been able to determine, in pictorial representations of the story, though lovely female demons do appear frequently in paintings of human saints in the wilderness.

Not only are the handsome servers important, but so is the banquet itself. In his lavish description of the proffered meal, Milton has created a poetic counterpart of the still-life paintings which became increasingly popular in Europe after the Renaissance. Representing a heaped abundance of edible delicacies, these still-lifes often achieved great refinement, with their subtle combinations of color, light, and form.[72] So complete is the mimetic triumph of these representations, especially those executed in oil, that it would be easy to regard them as merely secular examples of a voluptuous tour de force, and where this may be a proper interpretation, any comparison between such still-life paintings and Milton's exquisite banquet would be no more than the recognition of a coincidence.

But much more is implied by many of these paintings than meets the uninstructed eye, as a number of art historians have shown. What Erwin Panofsky has called concealed or disguised symbolism is operative here,[73] and by Milton's time still-life paintings of such a larder as he describes had long since been established as *vanitas* symbols. Raimond van Marle finds this understanding as early as the year 1500, and his comment is almost as apposite to Milton as to the artistic examples: "Les excès de table fournissent le sujet d'une allégorie, intitulée, 'Le Banquet' ou encore 'La Condamnation de Banquet et de Souper,' mais qui est en réalité une glorification de la Tempérance, par la démonstration de ce qui est le contraire, et surtout des maladies qu' entraînent les excès de tout genre."[74] These tendencies which van Marle finds before the Reformation were considerably strengthened by Protestant emphases in the sixteenth century, and Dutch still-life paintings have even been referred to as "tal modo dei 'luterani'" which transmuted a genre or still-life scene into an allegory.[75]

For our purposes this still-life tradition may be epitomized by a Dutch larder painting of the late sixteenth or early seventeenth century, now at the Van Abbe Museum in Eindhoven and sometimes attributed to Pieter Pieterse. The artist has provided a lifelike spread of various kinds of food and drink, laid out in profusion

[71] Tietze, *Tintoretto: The Paintings and Drawings*, p. 49.
[72] Bazin, *Baroque and Rococo*, pp. 73, and 98-99.
[73] Panofsky, *Early Netherlandish Painting*, I, p. 141.
[74] Van Marle, *Iconographie*, II, p. 101.
[75] *La Natura Morta Italiana: Catalogo della Mostra: Napoli-Zurigo-Rotterdam*, Milan, 1964, p. 15.

upon a table covered with a white linen cloth. He has made his meaning unmistakably clear by inscribing upon the wall behind the table and directly above the right-hand tankard a reference from Milton's primary Biblical source for the Temptation in the Wilderness: Luke 4:7 ("if thou therefore wilt worship me, all shall be thine"). The artist has thus presented an attractive picture of the good things of created nature, but has placed them under the explicit Biblical reminder that they can be used by the devil for our destruction, just as he attempted to destroy Christ in the Wilderness.[76] The banquet described by Milton thus conveys the same meaning that may be found in still-life larders of the artists, especially among Milton's co-religionists of the Low Countries.[77] In the earliest pictorial representation in the Stuttgart Psalter and in this Dutch painting of about 1600, a richly displayed larder was directly and explicitly associated with Satan's temptation of Christ, just as it is in *Paradise Regained*.

That the temptations of prosperity were epitomized by the *vanitas* banquet scene makes this an appropriate and effective addition to Milton's story, even though it had no direct Biblical warrant. Milton's other major non-Biblical addition represents the trial by adversity—a fitting pendant to the trial by prosperity.[78] This second trial is found in the tempest and the night of terror with which Christ is afflicted prior to his final meeting with Satan.[79] The two types of temptation are represented in a single fresco of St. Anthony by Michelangelo Aliprandi, in which the female devil with the bare breast behind the saint represents the trial of prosperity, while the adversity trial is inflicted as a beating by two satyrlike devils. 254

During the night of terror, the Savior is plagued both by a horrendous tempest

[76] See Ingvar Bergström, *Dutch Still-Life Painting in the Seventeenth Century*, New York, 1956, p. 26, for comments on this work, and for a more general account, pp. 10, 14, 22, and 291. Bergström interprets the pictures or scenes through windows in the background of this anonymous painting as directly connected with the Temptation of Christ by Satan. One would expect him to be correct in this identification, but I am not convinced, though my difficulty may be with the quality of the reproduction I have been able to study. If the background view is in fact of the Wilderness Temptation, as Bergström maintains, the relevance of the painting to Milton's iconography would be even more interesting, but the Biblical inscription alone makes the relationship undeniable.

[77] A tantalizing possibility is raised by a Rembrandt drawing illustrating Luke 4:7, or Matt. 4:8, the verse in question. A double circle surrounds Christ and Satan, and appears again on the edge of the sheet, which has suggested to some that we may have here Rembrandt's "sketch for a plate or bowl, perhaps a piece of Delft faience or a piece of gold work like that of Jan Lutma" (Hans-Martin Rotermund, *Rembrandt's Drawings and Etchings for the Bible*, fig. 166 and p. 179). Rembrandt did not generally do this kind of decorative work but he may have occasionally. At all events, the *vanitas* traditions in still-life would have made it appropriate to depict a *Temptation in the Wilderness* on a plate or bowl for fruit or other foods.

[78] For comparable renditions of St. Anthony in the Wilderness, Réau, *Iconographie*, III, i, p. 107, points out that the attack of the devil should most properly be called the truth or tribulation of St. Anthony, reserving the word temptation for the carnal temptations, or the trial by prosperity, but his terminology has not been generally accepted.

[79] For a learned analysis of the two trials, especially the later one, and a correlation with the emblematic title page of John Downame's *The Christian Warfare* of 1634, see John M. Steadman, "Like Turbulences: The Tempest of *Paradise Regain'd* as Adversity Symbol," *MP* 59 (1961), 81-88, and *Milton's Epic Characters*, pp. 90-101.

which blends "water with fire/ In ruin reconcile" and winds which tear up the tallest pines and sturdiest oaks and also by a pack of hideous demonic visitors:

> Infernal ghosts, and hellish furies, round
> Environed thee, some howled, some yelled, some shrieked,
> Some bent at thee their fiery darts, while thou
> Satest unappalled in calm and sinless peace.
> Thus passed the night so foul till morning fair
> Came forth with pilgrim steps in amice gray.
>
> (*PR* IV, 422-27)

Milton identifies these as "grisly spectres which the Fiend had raised/ To tempt the Son of God with terrors dire," and Satan himself uses "this ominous night that closed thee round,/ So many terrors, voices, prodigies" as a warning and threat to Christ (*PR* IV, 430-31 and 481-82). In all these lines, Milton descriptively evokes for Christ, "this glorious eremite" in the desert, the demonic terrors which artists had painted in their representations of later desert saints and hermits (*PR* I, 8). When Romney came to illustrate Milton's description of the demonic visitation, he imitated the patterns established for sixteenth-century Temptations of St. Anthony, and quite properly so, for that association was what Milton obviously wished to evoke.[80]

Seznec has traced the history of this subject in pictorial art in ways which are highly instructive for our purposes. The iconography of Wilderness Temptation for St. Anthony and others had been fairly restrained until about 1470, when Martin Schongauer converted the whole episode into a visual teratology which 255 was spread throughout Europe by his engravings. For the first time here we have what Seznec refers to as "a real feeling of terror," with the "ruthless violence of the tormentors," and "the unwonted shapes" of real monsters, "ghastly combinations of all animal species, squamous and shaggy, with trunks and suckers."[81] 256 Grünewald adopted the new iconography in his Isenheim Altarpiece which is filled with almost every variety of horrid fiend—the scraggly medieval demons of vaguely human proportions, insect devils, and devils showing features of pig, fish, fowl, and serpent, in what Seznec calls "a sickening confusion of wings and shells and antlers." Bosch provided his own distinctive nightmares, in "the most elaborately grotesque combinations," a private nightmare world which caught the popular imagination and through the engravings of Bruegel and others soon became a 257 public and widely employed visual idiom.[82] In the seventeenth century, Callot

[80] Pointon, *Milton and English Art*, p. 127, strangely misses the point that Romney was drawing upon sources which had influenced the Milton passage he illustrated.

[81] Seznec, "Temptation of St. Anthony in Art," 89. It may be that Schongauer assembled horrors from some of the written sources which Barbara Lewalski suggests may have contributed to Milton's vision, but my point is that the various furies and terrors had been assembled in pictorial art long before Milton brought them to bear upon the Savior in *Paradise Regained*; see Lewalski, *Milton's Brief Epic*, pp. 305-14.

[82] Those interested in this pictorial tradition should see, in addition to Seznec, André Chastel, "La Tentation de Saint Antoine; ou Le Songe du Mélancholique," and Sydney

carried on the tradition in a strongly Gallic but nonetheless frightening vein. *13*
After Milton's time, these horrors and terrors lost their fascination and were rarely
exploited in the eighteenth century, but when Milton described the trial by terror
he knew that he could rely upon strong visual reinforcement from a widespread
and immensely popular pictorial convention. Milton's conception was obviously
not derived from any single work in this tradition, but rather sought to exploit the
whole visual nexus by the introduction of infernal ghosts and hellish furies, some
howling, some shrieking, and some actively threatening, as may be seen in our
reproductions. In general, this iconography served not only to dramatize the trial
of the saint, but also served as a wild and violent foil to set off and display his
spiritual peace, as may be seen in all our reproductions, and perhaps especially in
that of the Carracci painting. Milton brings home the same contrast when he   *258*
describes how the Savior, during all this howling and shrieking assault, "satest
unappalled in calm and sinless peace" (IV, 425).

THE BIBLICAL NARRATIVE ENVISIONED

The Son of God is never given a physical description in *Paradise Regained*.
Whether he is tall or short, massive or lean, blond or brunet, bearded or clean
shaven, we simply do not learn from Milton. This omission cannot be attributed
to Protestant doctrine, for the decalogue's prohibition against "graven images"
of the Deity was not interpreted as precluding representations of the incarnate
Son, which may be found in pictures by Calvinist and Lutheran artists alike. But
the artist who told a Biblical story in line and color of necessity had to represent
Christ in physical terms, and Milton was under no such constraint. Perhaps his
reticence was due to his knowledge that he had no firm historical evidence as to
the actual appearance of Jesus. As for the Christ of pictorial art, there was a recog-
nizably standard conception, but with marked variations, and Milton's readers are
not given the slightest hint as to whether they should imagine Christ in the Wilderness after the fashion of, say, Botticelli or Tintoretto, Ghiberti or Mattia Preti,   *246, 251, 233*
Cock or Rubens.   *261, 245, 259*

In one brief passage Milton did indicate a preference for one of the conceptions of the child Jesus. For centuries artists had shown not a boy but an hieratic
little icon, as in Byzantine art and comparable early works of Western Europe.
Then there was a shift toward a greater personalism, and in the thirteenth century
it was possible to represent the Lord as an agile lad sliding down a sunbeam with
charming joie de vivre. Along with more serious representations, that conception   *125*
of the playful child continued throughout the fifteenth century, during which the
Christ Child was again and again pictured as merry and even mischievous, digging
a seed out of a pomegranate and offering it to his mother, reacting pleasantly to
an amusing incident, or enjoying childish play with his slightly older cousin John.

Cockerell, "Two Pictorial Lives of St. Anthony the Great," *Burlington Magazine* 62 (1933),
59-66; for the barbaric oriental pantheon which Cartari and others introduced to the West,
see Seznec, *The Survival of the Pagan Gods*, p. 252.

But in the sixteenth century a change occurred, in the course of which the buoyant little fellow was replaced by a very grave child indeed: he no longer plays with John, but soberly accepts his adoration. As Wölfflin has observed, the young Jesus usually appears as "serious, very serious, as Raphael's Roman pictures testify. Michelangelo, however, was the first to represent the Child in this way, without imposing unchildlike attitudes—such as blessing—upon him. He gives us a truly natural boy, whether sleeping or waking, but He is a joyless Child."[83] When the Savior in *Paradise Lost* describes himself as a boy, the image is decidedly in the tradition of Raphael and Michelangelo:

> When I was yet a child, no childish play
> To me was pleasing, all my mind was set
> Serious to learn and know, and thence to do
> What might be public good.
>
> (*PR* I, 201-4)

Professor Hanford and others have interpreted those lines as autobiographical, as John Milton reading his own childhood back into the childhood of the Savior.[84] Perhaps so, and there is no way to prove or disprove the theory, but it is surely relevant to observe that whether or not these verses represent Milton's boyhood, they do indeed accord with the image of the young Jesus which major artists had been inculcating since shortly after 1500. Nowhere else in *Paradise Regained* is it possible to discover a closer correlation between Milton's divine protagonist and historical developments in pictorial art.

For the demonic antagonist, art parallels abound. When we see Satan set out to find and challenge Christ in the Wilderness, we are told that he is "girded with snaky wiles" (*PR* I, 120). The phrase is obviously metaphoric, and not literal, but it is a metaphor which had been given visual expression for hundreds of years before Milton incorporated it into his poem.[85] The visual convention goes back to what may very well be the first pictorial representation of the devil in human form —the carved ivory book cover for the manuscript Gospel of Charles the Bald, where a serpent is coiled about the demonic body.[86] Serpentine girdings are shown on devils in the celebrated fourth pillar at Orvieto and in Signorelli's *Separation of the Blessed and the Damned* in the same cathedral, on the demonic papal chancellor in Michelangelo's *Last Judgment* (lower right), in the *Madonna of Succor* by Jacopo Chimenti da Empoli in the Palazzo Pitti, in Lanfranco's *Chaining of Satan* and *Salvation of a Soul*, and in Luca Giordano's *Michael Overcoming Satan* in Berlin. Milton's younger contemporary Mattia Preti painted Satan girt in just this

61

23

80

---

[83] Wölfflin, *Classic Art*, p. 220. Wölfflin does not identify any particular work by Michelangelo, but his pertinent reproductions include the relief of the Madonna and Child in the Bargello, the painting of the Holy Family in the Uffizi, and the Medici Madonna in S. Lorenzo. Not all artists followed Michelangelo's lead, of course, as may be exemplified by the laughing Child of Murillo's *Holy Family with the Little Bird* in the Prado.

[84] Hanford, *John Milton Englishman*, p. 17.

[85] Similar phrases to describe tricky characters are used by Virgil (*Aen.* II, 152) and Homer (*Il.* IV, 339), and there is of course the ironic contrast to the girding of the faithful man's loins with righteousness and truth in Isa. 11:5 and Eph. 6:14.

[86] Wall, *Devils*, p. 69.

way at the moment of his overthrow by Christ in the final temptation. Further-   *261*
more, devils were frequently belted with serpents when they appeared on the
sixteenth- and seventeenth-century Italian stage.[87] This particular visual metaphor
continued to be popular until well after Milton's time.

Between the fifteenth century and the seventeenth, the Tempter in the Wilderness appeared in several standard forms. Most frequently, he was shown as the
falsus frater, as an old Franciscan friar, or as a hermit, often with a rosary, as Botticelli represented him in his Sistine Chapel frescoes.[88] This is the only disguise   *246, 247*
which Milton entirely ignores in *Paradise Regained* and the omission must surely
be significant. Perhaps Milton was unwilling to indulge in an anachronism, but if so
he still could have maintained the traditional association of the Tempter with the
religious orders of Roman Catholicism by employing one of those similes which he
often used to link earlier and later historical events. Had the story been told by a
younger Milton, the Milton of the polemical prose tracts, we would surely expect
him to have dramatized the anticlerical and antipapal possibilities of this established visual motif, but the Milton of the epics consistently maintains and displays
a more ecumenical spirit.

Each of the other Renaissance guises he does incorporate into his treatment.
We have already noted his introduction into the banquet temptation of the handsome young angel-devil created by Titian and by Tintoretto. Other well-known
guises for the Tempter in sixteenth- and seventeenth-century art cast him as an
old peasant or shepherd, as Milton does in the first temptation, or as a richly dressed
man of the world, as he does in the second. In the final temptation, the devil is
usually shown as unmistakably demonic in physical appearance, or in what Milton
calls his "wonted shape" (*PR* IV, 449). Aside from the final temptation, there was
no fixed order of the disguises employed, and each artist was apparently free to
choose at will among the possibilities.[89]

[87] Again I am indebted to Irving Lavin for allowing me to study the large collection of
photographs he has assembled from early Italian drawings, prints, and engravings of the
theater.

[88] For the very common representation of the Tempter in religious habit, see Réau,
Iconographie, II, ii, pp. 307-8. David Novarr, "'Gray Dissimulation': Ford and Milton," *PQ*
41 (1962), 500-4, treats the possible relations between *Paradise Regained* and Ford's *The
Broken Heart* on this subject, and properly recognizes (p. 503) that "Milton's Satan in
Book I is not a Franciscan friar." The similarities between the old swain Tempter of *Paradise
Regained* and Archimago of the *Faerie Queene* are apparent, and have frequently been
remarked upon, as for example by John M. Major, "*Paradise Regained* and Spenser's Legend
of Holiness," *Ren.Quar* 20 (1967), 465-70. Archimago seems to me more closely related
to the pictorial traditions of the *falsus frater*, but the *vetus homo* representations of Satan in
the Wilderness are also a relevant part of his background. There were also presentations of
the Tempter as a scholar, as Wall, *Devils*, p. 74, notes of the School of Giotto, and Rudwin,
The Devil in Legend and Literature, pp. 51-52, in the case of Lucas ven Leyden. It is not
always easy to know where to place these representations in relation to Milton's descriptions:
some show a scholar not far removed from the traditional *falsus frater* and so out of Milton's
range, while other scholar-tempters are "not rustic as before, but seemlier clad,/ As one in
city, or court, or palace bred," and so fit with Satan's second disguise (*PR* II, 299-300).

[89] Pope, "*Paradise Regained*," pp. 42-47, provides a useful analysis of the tradition, and
concludes that it was so flexible that it "left every writer free to do very much what he
pleased."

When Satan first accosts Christ in *Paradise Regained*, he is "an aged man in rural weeds," a "swain," peasant or herdsman (*PR* 1, 314, 337), just as he appears in the engravings by Bloemaert and Schaufelein. Cock supplies him with a rosary, but dresses him as a peasant rather than a friar, so that his usage essentially parallels Milton's, as does that of the monogrammatist D. P., except that his peasant Tempter is in the vigorous prime of life. Milton agrees with most of these engravers when he makes the Tempter both old and a peasant, but differs from them in his omission of any telltale physical sign which would identify the stranger as the devil. Such a sign was quite unnecessary in *Paradise Regained*, where the narrative has already prepared us for Satan's advent so that we know just who he is when he arrives on the scene. The artists' problem was different, and most felt it advisable to provide some visual signal which would aid viewers to identify the action and the actors. The figure of Christ was unmistakable, but the figure approaching him might be confusing, so D. P. makes sure that we will penetrate the disguise by providing the Tempter with small horns and satyr ears, while Schaufelein introduces webbed feet and Bloemaert harpy feet.

In Cock the signals are exceptionally interesting, for the feet trail off into dry, twiglike toes, just as the curious cap terminates in dead branches. I have found only one plausible explanation for these details, and suggest that they are visual allusions to the statement by Christ in John 15:6 that "if a man abide not in me he is cast forth as a branch, and is withered," fit only to be cast into the fire and burned. A seventeenth-century public intimately familiar with the Gospels would have recognized Cock's engraving as a brilliant visual pun incorporating into Satan's physical appearance the telltale withered branches of damnation. Milton alludes to the same New Testament passage when he suggests that the peasant Tempter may be looking for withered sticks to burn, as John Carey explains in his note on this passage (*PR* 1, 315-16): "Satan's apparent occupations relate to his usual occupation," looking for lost souls, symbolized as strayed sheep and dead branches. If these interpretations are correct, Milton and Cock correspond not only in introducing the Tempter as an old swain but also in associating him symbolically with the same Biblical verse on the damned.

Rubens' painting of the Temptation incorporates no such sophisticated allusion, nor does it provide any identifying deformity for the Tempter, as may be seen in Jegher's engraving which popularized Rubens' conception of a handsome Christ interrupted in his meditations by a gnarled old peasant devil. By eliminating any deformity and by choosing the peasant disguise, both Rubens and Milton were returning to the practice of the earliest stage of such representations in Christian art, though surely neither of them did so knowingly: an illuminated initial in the Sacramentary of Bishop Drogo, executed by the School of Metz about 830-850, presents Christ with a Tempter who appears to be no more than a poor peasant or shepherd.[90]

[90] Reproduced in Schiller, 1, fig. 390. Henry J. Todd cited *vetus homo* representations of the Tempter in a 1518 woodcut and in an engraving by Vischer, but I have been unable to find either of these (see Shawcross, *Milton 1732-1801*, p. 406). Todd also mentions a Salvator Rosa painting, but it is much too late to be of relevance to our inquiry here.

When Satan next appears to the Savior in *Paradise Regained*, he is "not rustic as before, but seemlier clad,/ As one in city, or court, or palace bred,/ And with fair speech" (*PR* II, 299-301). Here he is a very sophisticated character indeed, or as Lewalski has identified him, "the Prince of this World."[91] Numerous visual examples correspond to Milton's description. A fifteenth-century Arras tapestry from the Abbaye de la Chaise-Dieu in Haute Loire shows the Tempter as a self-assured and authoritative figure dressed in a magnificent robe with ermine hood and lining.[92] A fresco by Fra Angelico in San Marco, Florence, shows Christ on the mountain top dismissing the Tempter, who is dressed in the cap and robes similar to those worn by Renaissance princes and courtiers.[93] The frontispiece in Jacques de Théramo's *Belial*, published at Lyon in 1481, shows the Tempter in a somewhat less elaborate but nonetheless courtly costume of the time.[94] In a print of 1523 by T. van Star the Savior is confronted by a handsome Tempter beautifully dressed right down to his fashionable shoes.[95] The Tudor stained glass window of the Wilderness Temptation in King's College Chapel, Cambridge, shows Satan with white hair and beard, distinguished facial features and frighteningly piercing eyes; he wears a dazzling white robe, with a blue over-robe and a ruby colored hood—all very brilliant, rich, and handsome.[96] This tradition may be epitomized in the engraving by Dirk Vellert which shows an immensely impressive figure, a sharply intelligent Renaissance man dressed in the most fashionable attire of the early sixteenth century, and fit to be an ornament to any court in Europe. For almost half of the total lines in the epic, Satan is in this disguise, far more than in the other two appearances combined.

234

When Satan fails in presenting the Temptation of the Kingdoms of this World, he disappears from the sight of Christ, only to stage-manage the night of terror which we have already discussed. On the final day he erupts upon us once again: "out of the wood he starts in wonted shape," an undisguised devil at this point, "the fiend now swollen with rage" (*PR* IV, 449, 499). As Lewalski puts it, his accustomed demonic shape is "appropriate to him now that he has no more guiles and gifts to offer but can only display the violence and brutality which comprise his essential self."[97] In Milton's brief and fast-moving account of the final temptation, two descriptive features are emphasized, both of which had become

[91] Lewalski, *Milton's Brief Epic*, p. 221.

[92] Didron, *Christian Iconography*, II, p. 127, sees the Tempter here as "a doctor clad in the ample robes of his profession," but I would add that the richness of his attire and his princely bearing clearly mark him "as one in city, or court, or palace bred." As is frequently the case in art, this scene is directly linked in the same tapestry with the Temptation and Fall of Adam and Eve. I am indebted to K. Lea of St. Catherine's College, Oxford, for reminding me of this work.

[93] Reproduced in Frida Schottmüller, *Fra Angelico da Fiesole*, Stuttgart and Leipzig [c. 1911], p. 126.

[94] There were many editions of the Belial in this period, and the illustrations do not always show the demon confronting Christ in disguise.

[95] Bartsch VIII.28.5 in the Institute of Fine Arts (New York City) Bartsch Catalogue, under New Testament 13a.

[96] Wayment, *The Windows of King's College Chapel*, p. 66, records that he has cloven feet and horns, but when I examined the window *in situ* it took a fieldglass to disclose those details. See the reproduction of window 7.4 in Wayment.

[97] Lewalski, *Milton's Brief Epic*, pp. 303-4.

traditional in the pictorial representations of the subject: in the first place, Satan appears in demonic form, and in the second place, he falls precipitously from the height of his arrogant presumption. On that second point, *Paradise Regained* was apparently unique among literary treatments of the subject: Elizabeth Pope writes that "it is noteworthy that no other writer that I know of states that Satan *fell* after his final defeat: they simply say that he 'departed' or that he 'fled away,' " and she suggests the influence of pictorial representations.[98]

Not only for the literarily unique fall of Satan (whether from Luke's Temple pinnacle or from Matthew's mountain peak), but also for his final appearance in demonic form, there were strong precedents in pictorial art. In the thirteenth-

260 century mosaic at S. Marco in Venice, Satan's physique remains clothed until after the last temptation, when he is stripped of his robes and headgear, symbols of his

247 disguise and pretension, and plunges toward Hell in his nude essence. Botticelli's

246 *Temptation* in the Sistine shows Satan as a Franciscan friar until the final scene, when his robes are thrown back to reveal the obscene and hairy body of a fiend, and he is driven over the precipice. The intarsia pictures executed in the 1540s by Fra Damiano da Bergamo for the choir of San Domenico in Bologna show the Satan of the first two temptations as a properly dressed elderly gentleman, perhaps a clergyman, whereas he returns to fully demonic form in the third temptation,

242 and falls from the mountain. One of Schaufelein's engravings transforms the benign old peasant of the first temptation of stones into an unmistakably demonic

240 figure on the peak. In the Tempesta engraving of about 1590, the religious figure of the first temptation is unmasked as a satyr-devil in the last, and as such he plunges out into empty space after his final defeat.

261 The painting by Mattia Preti,[99] executed in the latter half of the seventeenth century, epitomizes at once the visual tradition and Milton's poetic descriptions. Here we see the nude figure of Satan, stripped of all covering except that familiar girding with serpent wiles. His feet have slipped from "whence he stood to see his victor fall," his eyes stare widely as though "smitten with amazement," and his taloned hands flail the air "for grief and spite," as he tumbles backward over the precipice in the triumphant presence of the Son of God whose power he now fully understands: "So struck with dread and anguish fell the Fiend" (*PR* iv, 562-76). Preti and Milton worked in the same period, and they treated the same episode with essentially the same visual and psychological effect—so much so that the painting could be mistaken for an illustration of the poem or the verse as a description of the painting. But of course there was no such direct relationship: painter and poet worked in ignorance of each other, yet in reliance upon a central pictorial tradition of which Milton was obviously just as aware as was Preti. Here in the climactic episode of *Paradise Regained*, Milton relied once again upon the traditional vision of the artists. From the beginning to the end of his brief epic, he used familiar pictorial representations to enliven, dramatize, and objectify a debate which otherwise might have seemed impossibly abstract.

[98] Pope, "*Paradise Regained*," pp. 10-11 and 99; see also Spencer, *Heroic Nature*, p. 135.
[99] For Mattia Preti, see the article by Georgiana Goddard King, "Mattia Preti," *The Art Bulletin* 18 (1936), 371-86.

Conclusion

MILTON'S principal subjects in *Paradise Lost*, and therefore his primary descriptions of them, do indeed "surmount the reach of human sense," as the Archangel Raphael said of his own tale, but they rarely surmount the reach of sacred art. For centuries before Milton's time, artists had represented in painting, sculpture, tapestry, and mosaic, those very conditions and characters and episodes which were in the central focus of Milton's epic concern—Heaven and Hell, angels and devils, Adam and Eve, the Garden of Eden, and all the rest. Such subjects were to be encountered in the visual arts throughout the Europe Milton knew: hundreds of examples were to be seen even in the relative isolation of England, and thousands in Italy. When Adam asks that Raphael "relate/ To human sense th' invisible exploits/ Of warring spirits" and "the secrets of another world," Raphael replies that what is "perhaps not lawful to reveal" has been dispensed for Adam's good, and informs his human pupil that "I shall delineate so,/ By likening spiritual to corporal forms,/ As may express them best" (v, 563-74). Those words spoken to Adam are, in effect, Milton's words to us.

Readers who have followed my argument throughout this book will, I trust, be prepared to agree that the "corporal forms" which Milton chose to "delineate" in *Paradise Lost* and *Paradise Regained* were largely derived from the traditions of sacred art. It should be equally clear that Milton's epic employment of those traditions was never slavish or mechanical. He never merely copied what he had seen in art, anymore than he reproduced what he had read in literature. No man has ever been more his own master, under God, than John Milton. His wide learning not only becomes more impressive when we recognize his awareness of the arts, but so, too, does the synthetic imagination by which he transmuted knowledge into poetry. The same may be said of his literary tact: he did not demand that his readers accept and envision things which would have seemed ridiculous or outlandish, but rather that they draw upon readily available sets of images with which the visual arts had stocked the mind of Western man. When we recapture and recall that stock of images, we find that many of the most damaging objections to Milton's epic poetry lose their force, and his writing strikes us with a greater brilliance than ever before.

Those critics who have agreed with Johnson, Coleridge, and Eliot in denying or depreciating Milton's visual powers have not thereby missed all his achievements, many of which are definitely nonvisual; but they have missed enough to make Milton's epic poetry appear considerably less great than in fact it is. Other critics have acknowledged Milton's visual powers, but have not fully recognized them. In any case, we will understand *Paradise Lost* and *Paradise Regained* only partially if we cannot accept the poet's invitation to *see* persons, events, and things. For Milton, imagery was rarely if ever merely decorative, but was developed to express or suggest or support an idea. Time and again, his challenge to us as readers is both visual and intellectual, and we cannot meet such a challenge without some familiarity with traditional systems of visual iconography. It was by carefully wrought and carefully selected poetic references to such iconography, still familiar when he wrote his great epic, that he sought to guide the vision of his audience and to vitalize subjects which might otherwise have seemed forbiddingly remote and abstract.

A basic acquaintance with the visual lexicon available to Milton is needed, but what he chose to use from that lexicon is no more important than what he chose to ignore, and indeed the one can scarcely be understood apart from the other. Milton's visual selectivity was governed by his own epic and religious intentions, rather than by allegiance to any artist, or studio, or even school, and his descriptions correspond with motifs drawn from every period, sect, and artistic medium, while some were entirely original with him. We find here the same eclecticism which characterized his thought in every field. For his angels, he created movements and actions which correspond with sixteenth- and seventeenth-century art, but he also invented the scene of all the demons fallen prostrate in reverence before Satan, and as a happy contrast to that gesture of infernal tyranny he described serene and dignified angels seated upon their thrones in the court of Heaven, a representation which had been popular in the fifteenth century but which rarely appeared thereafter. Similarly, he dressed his "stripling cherub" with the girded robe and staff of those guardian angels who were so often represented in his own period, but he chose also to show Raphael clad in the feathered mail which was characteristic of angels in medieval England, and to adorn the hair of his heavenly hosts with the chaplets of flowers which had been standard in the fourteenth and fifteenth centuries, though infrequent thereafter. In his descriptions of the Creation, he evoked the infinite space of Baroque ceilings, as also of the telescope, but along with these up-to-date features he introduced the timeless symbol of the golden compasses turned by the hand of God. It was usual in sixteenth- and seventeenth-century art to show God the Father as the divine agent of creation, but Milton rejected this conception because it did not allow the epic aggrandizement of the Son which he wished to achieve, and his descriptions evoked earlier and once popular visions of the Son not only as Creator, but also as sole victor of the War in Heaven and as judge of fallen man.

In describing the fallen angels he was no less eclectic. He chose to introduce a distinctively medieval vision, rarely used in later art but still widely accessible, in making his Satan tower above all his cohorts, but at the same time he either excluded or carefully distanced from his own demons those horrible deformities which characterized medieval fiends. Here he preferred to describe handsome and princely devils such as those painted by High Renaissance and later artists, and he gave to his princes of Hell the kind of differentiated and even individualized appearance which was found in the art of his time. His War in Heaven evoked the visual arts in similar ways, the antagonists being accoutred in fine armor and mounted on fiery steeds, fighting with weapons and feeling pain or even bleeding when wounded. For the Expulsion of the Rebel Angels, he provided both traditional views—the uninhibited fall into Hell, and the harrying pursuit—but he had to choose between the instant transformation and the gradual degeneration of his demons, and he chose the latter. In these and other choices, he was motivated by differing considerations, related sometimes to his epic design, sometimes to characterization, and sometimes to theology, but in each also he wrote so as to evoke the aid of visual traditions in generating understanding of the thought he wished to convey.

Of all the scenes in his epic, those in the Garden of Eden probably conform most closely to the artistic tastes of the sixteenth and seventeenth centuries. Milton's conception of the ideal garden owes much to landscape gardening and painting, and even more to paintings of Paradise. The "vegetable gold" was perennial, but otherwise his evocations conform almost exclusively to conceptions popularized in the High Renaissance and thereafter. So, too, with Adam and Eve: both represent post-Renaissance ideals, individuated by such distinctively Miltonic touches as holding hands and Adam's parted forelock. Except of course for these, most of Milton's visualized details may be found in those superb tapestries of the Eden saga to which we have often referred.

A few works conform to Milton's descriptions in such striking and apparently unique details that they may be postulated as sources: so Raphael's animals erupting from the ground at Creation, Naccherino's maudlinly tearful tempter serpent, and perhaps Beccafumi's fallen angels rising from the lake of Hell and the somewhat similar scene carved on the oak screen in King's College Chapel. Milton could have seen these works, and I suspect that he probably did, but I am unwilling to press the point: striking and even unique analogues are not necessarily sources, and within the particular scope of our concerns here we can be more confident of direct influence from widespread traditions than from single instances. Thus, Milton's account of Eve as bringing Adam a bough broken from the Tree of Knowledge, rather than just the Fruit alone, almost certainly evidences the influence of pictorial representations in which that detail repeatedly appeared, whereas Adam bringing Eve a flower garland for her hair is seen only in Salviati and in *Paradise Lost*. Again, I suspect that Milton saw Salviati's painting and that its moving symbol of love and loss influenced his own account, but the case for the importance of the visual arts for a full understanding of *Paradise Lost* does not rest upon such singular instances. We are on safer ground when we find Milton's descriptions evoking popular iconography which he could have expected his audience to recognize and to recall in their reading.

Certain correspondences between Milton and particular artists have been noted in the course of our study, as for example the general affinity with the angels and devils of Signorelli, but Signorelli's influence in these particular matters was great, and we cannot be sure whether Milton was primarily impressed by him or by those who followed him. With Michelangelo, Milton shares much: the grandeur of the two men's careers and achievements, as well as the majesty and *terribilità* which pervade their works, set them apart from others and in a class by themselves. Beyond that, they could scarcely be more different, either essentially or in detail. It is true that in one brief passage on the Last Judgment, Milton endows the Son with a slinging away of evil which is most comparable to Michelangelo's rendition in the Sistine, but Milton pervasively epitomized a Christian optimism poles apart from the great Italian's Christian pessimism. We may see that contrast by comparing the bleak and barren Eden of the painter with the opulent descriptions of the poet, and in many other ways as well. Comparisons of this kind can only be suggested here, for to work them out in detail would require almost another book. This applies, too, to another important subject repeatedly touched upon, namely, the difference between the ways a particular subject can be treated by the visual and verbal arts.

My purpose in this book has been to reestablish the principal visual frames of references upon which Milton could rely when he invited his readers to envision his epic actions and actors. It has not been my intent to defend Milton from aspersions (he is, in every sense, beyond the need for such defense as I might offer), but rather to defend us as readers from misunderstanding and misjudging his poetry. To that end, I have sought to recover as far as I was able the visual lexicon upon which he drew, so that we may today see more clearly and more fully what he has so masterfully evoked in his descriptions. In this sense, I have merely written an introduction to reading Milton with a more adequate visual recognition. Other scholars will surely amplify what I have done here, and correct my oversights, omissions, and errors, but at least a beginning has been made: I hope that it will lead to the fuller appreciation of a great poet whose inherent stature and whose value for us increase the more we understand him.

Bibliography

Adams, Robert M. "Contra Hartman: Possible and Impossible Structures of Miltonic Imagery," in *Seventeenth-Century Imagery* (ed. Earl Miner), pp. 117-32.

———. *Ikon: Milton and the Modern Critics*. Ithaca, N.Y., 1955.

Adamson, J. H. "The War in Heaven: Milton's Version of the *Merkabah*." *JEGP* 57 (1958), 690-703.

Alciati, Andrea. *Omnia Emblemata*. Paris, 1618.

Allen, Don Cameron. *The Harmonious Vision: Studies in Milton's Poetry*. Baltimore, 1970.

———. *Image and Meaning: Metaphoric Traditions in Renaissance Poetry*. Baltimore, 1960.

———. "Milton and the Name of Eve." *MLN* 74 (1959), 681-83.

———. "Milton's Amarant." *MLN* 72 (1957), 256-58.

———. "Milton's Winged Serpents." *MLN* 59 (1944), 537-38.

———. *Mysteriously Meant: The Rediscovery of Pagan Symbolism and Allegorical Interpretation in the Renaissance*. Baltimore, 1970.

———. "The Scala Religionis in *Paradise Lost*." *MLN* 71 (1956), 404-5.

———. "Two Notes on *Paradise Lost*." *MLN* 68 (1953), 360-61.

Alpers, Svetlana. *The Decoration of the Torre de La Parada*. New York, 1971.

Anderson, Jeffery. "Jacob's Ladder," in *Five Themes from Genesis* (ed. Koch and Bryan), pp. 16-20.

Anderson, M. D. *History and Imagery in British Churches*. Edinburgh, 1971.

———. *The Imagery of British Churches*. London, 1955.

Armstrong, John H. *The Paradise Myth*. London, 1969.

Arthos, John. *Dante, Michelangelo, and Milton*. London, 1963.

———. *Milton and the Italian Cities*. London, 1968.

Ashley, Maurice. *The English Civil War*. London, 1974.

———. *The Greatness of Oliver Cromwell*. New York, 1958.

Aubin, Robert Arnold. *Topographical Poetry in XVIII-Century England*. New York, 1936.

Auerbach, Erna. *Tudor Artists*. London, 1954.

———, and C. Kingsley Adams. *Paintings and Sculpture at Hatfield House*. London, 1971.

Augustine. *Earlier Writings* (trans. and ed. John H. S. Burleigh). Philadelphia, 1953.

Aurenhammer, Hans. *Lexikon der Christlichen Ikonographie*. Vienna, 1959-67.

B., C. W. "Milton and Mabuse." *TLS* (10 Feb. and 3 Mar., 1927), 92 and 144.

Bach, Eugène. "Le Tombeau de François Ier de la Sarra-Montferrand à La Sarraz." *Congrès Archéologique de France* cx (1952), 369-74.

Baker, Charles H. Collins. *British Painting*. London, 1933.

———. "Some Illustrators of Milton's *Paradise Lost* (1688-1850)," *The Library* 5th ser. vol. 3 (1948), 1-21 and 101-19.

Baker, Charles H. Collins, and William G. Constable. *English Painting of the Sixteenth and Seventeenth Centuries*. Florence and Paris, 1930.

Baker, Donald C. "On Satan's Hair." *N&Q*, 202 (1957), 69-70.

Baldwin, Edward C. "Some Extra-Biblical Semitic Influences upon Milton's Story of the Fall of Man." *JEGP* 28 (1929), 366-401.

Baltrušaitis, Jurgis. *Le Moyen Age fantastique: Antiquités et exotismes dans l'art gothique*. Paris, 1955.

————. *Réveils et prodiges: Le gothique fantastique*. Paris, 1960.

Banks, Theodore H. *Milton's Imagery*. New York, 1969.

Barb, A. A. "Antaura. The Mermaid and the Devil's Grandmother." *JWCI* 29 (1966), 1-23.

Barfucci, Enrico. *Giornate Fiorentine*. Florence, 1961.

Bargellini, Piero. *Florence: An Appreciation of her Beauty; Historical and Artistic Guide*. Florence, 1969.

Barker, Arthur E. ". . . And on his Crest Sat Horror: Eighteenth Century Interpretations of Milton's Sublimity and His Satan." *UTQ* 11 (1942), 421-36.

————, ed. *Milton: Modern Essays in Criticism*. New York, 1965.

Barron, John. *Greek Sculpture*. New York, 1970.

Bates, Ernest S. *Touring in 1600*. New York, 1911.

Bateman, Stephen. *A Christall Glasse of Christian Reformation*. London, 1569.

————. *The Doom Warning All Men to Judgemente*. London, 1581.

Battisti, Eugenio. "*Natura Artificiosa* to *Natura Artificialis*," in *The Italian Garden* (ed. David R. Coffin), pp. 1-36.

Bazin, Germain. *Baroque and Rococo*. London, 1964.

Beckmann, Josef Hermann and Ingeborg Schroth. *Deutsche Bilderbibel aus dem späten Mittelalter*. Stuttgart, 1960.

Beckwith, John. "Byzantium: Gold and Light," in *Light* (ed. Thomas Hess and John Ashbery), pp. 67-81.

Bender, John B. *Spenser and Literary Pictorialism*. Princeton, 1972.

Benesch, Otto. *The Drawings of Rembrandt*, 6 vols. London, 1954-57.

Berefelt, Gunnar. *A Study on the Winged Angel: The Origin of a Motif*. Stockholm, 1966.

Berenson, Bernard. *The Italian Painters of the Renaissance*. New York, 1964.

————. *Lorenzo Lotto*. London, 1956.

Bergström, Ingvar. *Dutch Still-Life Painting in the Seventeenth Century* (trans. Christina Hedström and Gerald Taylor). New York, 1956.

Bernheimer, Richard. *Wild Men in the Middle Ages: A Study in Art, Sentiment, and Demonology*. Cambridge, Mass., 1952.

Bibliothèque Nationale. *Byzance et la France médiévale: Manuscrits à peintures du IIe au XVIe siècle*. Paris, 1958.

————. *Les Manuscrits à peintures en France du VIIe au XIIe siècle*. Paris, 1954.

Billioud, Joseph. *Manuscrits à enluminures*. Marseille, 1924.

Binyon, Laurence. "A Note on Milton's Imagery and Rhythm," in *Seventeenth-Century Studies Presented to Sir Herbert Grierson*. Oxford, 1938, pp. 184-91.

Birch, Walter de Gray, and Henry Jenner. *Early Drawings and Illuminations: An Introduction to the Study of Illustrated Manuscripts with a Dictionary of Subjects in the British Museum*. London, 1879.

Blacker, Irwin R. "Did Milton Visit Hell?" *SCN* 9 (1951), 54.

Bland, David. *A History of Book Illustration; the Illuminated Manuscript and the Printed Book*. London, 1958.

———. *The Illustration of Books*. London, 1951.

Bloomfield, Morton W. *The Seven Deadly Sins*. East Lansing, Mich., 1952.

Blunt, Anthony. "El Greco's 'Dream of Philip II': An Allegory of the Holy League." *JWCI* 3 (1939-40), 58-69.

———. "The Heroic and the Ideal Landscape in the Work of Nicolas Poussin." *JWCI* 7 (1944), 154-68.

———. "The Palazzo Barberini." *JWCI* 21 (1958), 256-87.

Boase, Thomas S. R. *Death in the Middle Ages: Morality, Judgment, and Remembrance*. London, 1972.

———. *English Art, 1100-1216*. Oxford, 1953.

Bodkin, Maud. *Archetypal Patterns in Poetry; Psychological Studies of Imagination*. London, 1958.

Bodleian Library. See *Italian Illuminated Manuscripts from 1400 to 1550*.

Bohigas, Balaguer Pedro. *La Illustración y la decoración del libro manuscrito en Cataluña; Contribución al estudio de la historia de la miniatura Catalana*, 3 vols. Barcelona, 1960-67.

Bonnefoy, Yves. *Rome 1630: L'horizon du premier baroque*. Paris, 1970.

Bonnell, John K. "The Serpent with a Human Head in Art and in Mystery Play." *American Journal of Archaeology*, 2nd ser. 21 (1917), 255-91.

Borenius, Tancred and E. W. Tristram. *English Medieval Painting*. Florence and Paris, 1927.

Borsook, Eve. *The Companion Guide to Florence*. London, 1966.

Bosio, Antonio. *Roma Sotterranea*. Rome, 1632.

Bottrall, Margaret. "The Baroque Element in Milton." *English Miscellany: A Symposium of History, Literature and the Arts* 1 (1950), 31-42.

Bouquet, A. C. *European Brasses*. New York, 1967.

Bourguet, Pierre du. *Early Christian Painting*. New York, 1965.

Bovini, Giuseppe. *Ravenna: An Art City*. Ravenna, n.d.

Bowie, Theodore, ed. *East-West in Art, Patterns of Cultural and Aesthetic Relationships*. Bloomington, Ind., 1966.

Bowra, Cecil M. *From Virgil to Milton*. London, 1945.

Braham, Allan. "Two Notes on El Greco and Michelangelo." *Burlington Magazine* 108 (1966), 307-308.

Brassinne, Joseph. *Livre d'Heures de Gysbrecht de Brederode*. Brussels, 1924.

———. *Psautier Liégeois du XIIIe siècle*. Brussels, 1923.

Braunfels, Wolfgang. *Die Heilige Dreifaltigkeit*. Dusseldorf, 1954.

B[rech], J[oseph]. "A King of Judah and Other Medieval Sculptures." *Bulletin of the Metropolitan Museum of Art* 16 (1921), 48-52.

Bridaham, Luther Burbank. *Gargoyles, Chimeres, and the Grotesque in French Gothic Sculpture*. New York, 1969.

Brieger, Peter. *English Art 1216-1307*. Oxford, 1957.

———, Millard Meiss, and Charles S. Singleton. *Illuminated Manuscripts of the Divine Comedy*, 2 vols. Princeton, 1969.

Brion, Marcel. *Animals in Art* (trans. Frances Hogarth-Gaute). London, 1959.

———. *Art fantastique*. Paris, 1961.

British Museum. *Catalogue of Early Italian Engravings . . . in the British Museum* (ed. A. M. Hind and S. Colvin) 2 vols. London, 1909-10.

Broadbent, John B. (ed.). *John Milton: Introductions*. Cambridge, 1973.

———. "Milton's Hell." *ELH* 21 (1954), 161-92.

———. "Milton's Paradise." *MP* 51 (1954), 160-76.

———. *Some Graver Subject*. London, 1960.

Brooke-Rose, Christine. "Metaphor in *Paradise Lost*: A Grammatical Analysis," in *Language and Style in Milton* (ed. Emma and Shawcross), pp. 252-303.

Broun, F.J.P. "The Flood," in *Five Themes from Genesis* (ed. Koch and Bryan), pp. 6-10.

Brown, Eleanor G. *Milton's Blindness*. New York, 1934.

Brown, Frank P. *London Buildings, Paintings, and Sculpture*, 3 vols. London, 1933-34.

Bruck, Robert. *Die Malereien in dem Handschriften des Königreichs Sachsen*. Dresden, 1906.

Bry, Theodor de. *Admiranda narratio fida tamen, de commodis et incolarum ritibus Virginiae*. Frankfurt am Main, 1590.

Buchthal, Hugo. *Historia Troiana: Studies in the History of Mediaeval Secular Illustration*. London, 1971.

———. *Miniature Painting in the Latin Kingdom of Jerusalem*. Oxford, 1957.

Bühler, Curt. *The Fifteenth Century Book, the Scribes, the Printers, the Decorators*. Philadelphia, 1960.

Bunim, Miriam Schild. *Space in Medieval Painting and the Forerunners of Perspective*. New York, 1940.

Burden, Dennis H. *The Logical Epic: A Study of the Argument of "Paradise Lost."* Cambridge, Mass., 1967.

Burgess, Frederick. *English Churchyard Memorials*. London, 1963.

Burke, Edmund. *The Sublime*. London, 1757.

Bush, Douglas. "Ironic and Ambiguous Allusion in *Paradise Lost*." *JEGP* 60 (1961), 631-40.

———. *"Paradise Lost" in Our Time*. New York, 1948.

Byvanck, A. W. *De middeleeuwsche Boekillustratie in de noordelijke Nederlanden*. Antwerp, 1943.

Cabrol, Fernand, et al. *Dictionnaire d'archéologie chrétienne et de liturgie*, 15 vols. Paris, 1907-53.

The Caedmon Manuscript (ed. Sir Israel Gollancz). Oxford, 1927.

Calderini, Emma. *Acconciature antiche e moderne*. Milan, 1963.

Campbell, Malcolm. *Pietro da Cortona at the Pitti Palace*. Princeton, 1977.

[Carmelite Fathers]. *Satan*. New York, 1952.

Carver, P. L. "The Angels in *Paradise Lost*." *RES* 16 (1940), 415-31.

Castagnoli, Ferdinando. "Raphael and Ancient Rome," in *The Complete Work of Raphael*, New York, 1969, pp. 569-84.

Cavalli, Gian Carlo, and Gnudi, Cesare. *Guido Reni*. Florence, 1955.

Centro Internazionale di Studi Umanistici. *L'Umanesimo e il Demonaica nell'Arte*. Rome, 1952.

Chambers, A. B. "Three Notes on Eve's Dream in *Paradise Lost*." *PQ* 46 (1967), 186-93.

Chambers, Douglas. "'A Speaking Picture': Some Ways of Proceeding in Literature and the Fine Arts in the Late-Sixteenth and Early Seventeenth Centuries," in *Encounters, Essays on Literature and the Visual Arts* (ed. J. D. Hunt), pp. 28-57.

Charcot, J.-M., and Richer, P. *Les Démoniaques dans l'art.* Paris, 1887.

Charlton, John. *The Banqueting House Whitehall.* London, 1964.

Chastel, André. "La Tentation de Saint Antoine; ou Le songe du mélancholique." *Gazette des Beaux-Arts* 15 (1936), 218-29.

———. *Studios and Styles of the Italian Renaissance.* New York, 1966.

Chew, Samuel C. *The Pilgrimage of Life.* New Haven, 1962.

Ciardi, John. "A Poem Talks to Itself: One Thing Calls another into Being." *Saturday Review* (Jan. 24, 1959), 12-13.

Cipriani, R., et al. *La Capella Portinari in Sant' Eustorgio a Milano.* Milan, 1963.

Cirillo, Albert R. "Tasso's *Il Mondo Creato*: Providence and the Created Universe." *Milton Studies* 3 (1971), 83-102.

Clark, Evert M. "Milton's Abyssinian Paradise." *UTSE* 29 (1950), 129-50.

Clark, Kenneth. *Landscape into Art.* Harmondsworth, 1966.

———. *The Nude: A Study in Ideal Form.* Garden City, N.Y., 1959.

Clavering, Rose, and John T. Shawcross. "Anne Milton and the Milton Residences." *JEGP* 59 (1960), 680-90.

Clayton, Thomas. "An Historical Study of the Portraits of Sir John Suckling." *JWCI* 23 (1960), 105-26.

Clement, Clara Erskine. *Angels in Art.* Boston, 1898.

Clements, Rex. "The Angels in *Paradise Lost*." *QR* 264 (1935), 384-93.

Cockerell, Sydney C. *Old Testament Miniatures: A Medieval Picture Book.* New York, 1969.

———. "Two Pictorial Lives of St. Anthony the Great." *Burlington Magazine* 62 (1933), 59-66.

Coffin, David R., ed. *The Italian Garden.* Washington, 1972.

———. *The Villa d'Este at Tivoli.* Princeton, 1960.

Cohen, Gustave. *Histoire de la mise en scène dans le théatre religieux français du Moyen Age.* Paris, 1906.

Coleridge, Samuel Taylor. *Shakespearean Criticism*, 2 vols. (ed. Thomas Middleton Raysor). London, n.d. [1962?].

———. *Specimens of the Table Talk*, 2 vols. London, 1885.

Colie, Rosalie. *Paradoxia Epidemica: The Renaissance Tradition of Paradox.* Princeton, 1966.

Collin de Plancy, J.A.S. *Dictionnaire infernal.* Brussels, 1845.

Congresso Internazionale di Studi Umanistici, Rome, 1952. *Christianesimo e ragion di stato; l'umanesimo e il demoniaco nell' arte*, Rome, 1953.

Conway, Moncure D. *Demonology and Devil-Lore.* New York, 1881.

Cook, Walter W. S. "The Earliest Painted Panels of Catalonia." *Art Bulletin* 6 (1923), 31-60.

Cope, Gilbert. *Symbolism in the Bible and the Church.* New York, 1959.

Cope, Jackson I. *The Metaphoric Structure of "Paradise Lost."* Baltimore, 1962.

———. "Satan's Disguises: *Paradise Lost* and *Paradise Regained*." *MLN* 73 (1958), 9-11.

Corcoran, Sister Mary Irma. *Milton's Paradise with Reference to the Hexameral Background.* Washington, 1945.

Coulange, Fr. Louis [pseud. of Joseph Turmel]. *The Life of the Devil* (trans. Stephen H. Guest). New York, 1930.

Croft-Murray, Edward. *Decorative Painting in England, 1537-1837*, vol. I. London, 1962.

Crossley, Fred H. *English Church Craftsmanship*. London, 1941.

———. *English Church Monuments A.D. 1150-1550*. London, [1921?].

Curry, Walter C. "Milton's Chaos and Old Night." *JEGP* 46 (1947), 38-52.

———. *Milton's Ontology, Cosmogony and Physics*. Lexington, Ky., 1957.

Curtius, Ernst Robert. *European Literature and the Latin Middle Ages* (trans. W. R. Trask). New York, 1953.

Dacos, Nicole. *La Découverte de la "Domus Aurea" et la formation des grotesques à la Renaissance*. London, 1969.

Daiches, David. *Milton*. London, 1957.

Dalton, Ormonde M. *Byzantine Art and Archaeology*. New York, 1961.

d'Alano, Redento. *Fra Semplice da Verone*. Padua, 1970.

Daniel, Howard. *Devils, Monsters and Nightmares: An Introduction to the Grotesque and Fantastic in Art*. New York, 1964.

Daniells, Roy. *Milton, Mannerism and Baroque*. Toronto, 1963.

———. "Milton and Renaissance Art," in *John Milton: Introductions* (ed. John Broadbent), pp. 186-207.

Daniélou, Jean, S. J. *Primitive Christian Symbols* (trans. Donald Attwater). Baltimore, 1964.

Daniels, Edgar F. "Thomas Adams and Darkness Visible (*Paradise Lost*, 1, 62-63)." *N&Q*, 204 (1959), 369-70.

Darbishire, Helen. *The Early Lives of Milton*. London, 1932.

———. *The Manuscript of Milton's "Paradise Lost," Book I*. Oxford, 1931.

Davidson, Gustav. *A Dictionary of Angels Including the Fallen Angels*. New York, 1967.

Davies, Randall. "An Inventory of the Duke of Buckingham's Pictures, etc., at York House in 1635." *Burlington Magazine* 10 (1906-07), 376-82.

Day, Lewis. *Windows: A Book about Stained and Painted Glass*. London, 1897.

De Jesus-Marie, Bruno: *see* Carmelite Fathers.

Demaray, Hannah Disinger. "Milton's 'Perfect' Paradise and the Landscapes of Italy." *Milton Quarterly* 8 (1974), 35-41.

Demaray, John G. *Milton and the Masque Tradition: The Early Poems, "Arcades," and Comus*. Cambridge, Mass., 1968.

———. "The Thrones of Satan and God: Backgrounds to Divine Opposition in *Paradise Lost*." *HLQ* 31 (1967), 21-33.

De Metz, Peter. "The Elm and the Vine: Notes toward the History of a Marriage *Topos*." *PMLA* 73 (1958), 521-32.

Demus, Otto. *Byzantine Art and the West*. New York, 1970.

———. *The Church of San Marco in Venice; History, Architecture, Sculpture*. Washington, 1960.

der Nersessian, *see* Nersessian.

de Solms, E., and Louis Bouyer. *Anges et Demons*, n.p., 1972.

Deuchler, Florens. "Gothic Glass" in *Light* (eds. Thomas Hess and John Ashbery), pp. 55-66.

De Wald, Ernest T. *The Illustrations of the Utrecht Psalter*. Princeton, n.d.

de Witt, Antonio. *Marcantonio Raimondi Incisioni*. Florence, 1968.

Didron, Alphonse N., and Margaret Stokes. *Christian Iconography: The History of Christian Art in the Middle Ages*, 2 vols. (trans. E. J. Millington). New York, 1968.

Diekhoff, John. *Milton on Himself: Milton's Utterances upon Himself and His Works*. New York, 1939.

Dodgson, Campbell. *Catalogue of Early German and Flemish Woodcuts . . . in the British Museum*, 2 vols. London, 1903.

Dodwell, C. R. *The Great Lambeth Bible*. London, 1959.

D'Onofrio, Cesare. *Roma nel Seicento*. Florence, 1969.

Douce, F. *Holbein's Dance of Death*. London, 1858.

Douglas, R. Langton. "*The Fall of Man* by Piero di Cosimo." *Burlington Magazine* 86 (1945), 134-39.

Downes, Kerry. "Fuller's Last Judgment." *Burlington Magazine* 102 (1960), 451-52.

Druce, G. C. *The Elephant in Medieval Legend and Art*. London, 1919.

Drummond, Andrew L. *The Church Architecture of Protestantism: An Historical and Constructive Study*. Edinburgh, 1934.

Duncan, Joseph E. *Milton's Earthly Paradise: A Historical Study of Eden*. Minneapolis, 1972.

————. "Milton's Four-in-One Hell." *HLQ* 20 (1957), 127-36.

Dussler, Luitpold. *Raphael: A Critical Catalogue of his Pictures, Wall-Paintings and Tapestries*. London, 1971.

Dustdoor, P. E. "Legends of Lucifer in Early English and in Milton." *Anglia* 54 (1930), 213-68.

Duthuit, Georges. "Représentations de la mort." *Cahiers d'art* 14 (1939), 25-39.

Dvorak, Max. *Die Gemälde Peter Bruegels des Alteren*. Vienna, 1941.

Ehl, Heinrich. *Die Ottonische Kölner Buchmalerei*. Bonn, 1922.

Ehrenstein, Theodor. *Das Alte Testament in der Graphik*. Vienna, 1936.

Eisler, Colin. "The Athlete of Virtue. The Iconography of Asceticism," in *Essays in Honor of Erwin Panofsky* (ed. Millard Meiss), I, 82-97.

Eliot, T. S. "A Note on the Verse of John Milton." *E&S* 21 (1936), 32-40.

————. "Milton." *Proceedings of the British Academy* 33 (1947), 61-79.

————. *On Poetry and Poets*. New York, 1957.

Emma, Ronald D., and John T. Shawcross, eds. *Language and Style in Milton: A Symposium in Honor of the Tercentenary of "Paradise Lost."* New York, 1967.

Empson, William. *Milton's God*. London, 1965.

————. *Some Versions of Pastoral*. London, 1935.

Esche, Sigrid. *Adam und Eva*. Dusseldorf, 1957.

Esdaile, Katharine A. *English Church Monuments 1510-1840*. New York, n.d. [1946?]

Essling, Victor Massena, Prince d'. *Les Livres à figures vénitiens*, 6 vols. Florence and Paris, 1907-14.

Ettlinger, L. D. "Virtutuum et Viciorum Adumbracio." *JWCI* 19 (1956), 155-56.

Evans, Joan. *English Art, 1307-1461*. Oxford, 1949.

————. *Monastic Iconography in France from the Renaissance to the Revolution*. Cambridge, 1970.

————. *Pattern: A Study of Ornament in Western Europe from 1180 to 1900*, 2 vols. Oxford, 1931.

Evans, J. M. *"Paradise Lost" and the Genesis Tradition*. Oxford, 1968.

Evelyn, John. *Diary*, 6 vols. (ed. E. S. De Beer). Oxford, 1955.

———, trans. of Roland Fréart de Cambray. *An Idea of the Perfection of Painting*. 1668.

Ferrari, Oreste, and Giueseppe Scavizzi. *Luca Giordano*, 3 vols. n.p. [Naples?], 1966.

Ferry, Ann D. *Milton's Epic Voice, the Narrator in "Paradise Lost."* Cambridge, 1963.

Fiore, Amadeus P., O.F.M. "Satan is a Problem. The Problem of Milton's 'Satanic Fallacy' in Contemporary Criticism." *Franciscan Studies* 17 (1957), 173-87.

———, ed. *Th' Upright Heart and Pure*. Pittsburgh, 1967.

Firth, Sir Charles H. *Oliver Cromwell and the Rule of the Puritans in England*. London, 1947.

Fish, Stanley Eugene. *Surprised by Sin: the Reader in "Paradise Lost."* New York, 1967.

Fischel, Oskar. *Raphael* (trans. Bernard Rackham), 2 vols. London, 1948.

Fixler, Michael. "The Apocalypse within *Paradise Lost*," in *New Essays on Paradise Lost* (ed. Thomas Kranidas), pp. 131-78.

———. "The Unclean Meats of the Mosaic Law and the Banquet Scene in *Paradise Regained*." *MLN* 70 (1955), 573-77.

Flannagan, Roy C. "Editor's Note." *Milton Newsletter* 2 (1968), 73.

———. "Vallombrosa and Valdarno." *Milton Newsletter* 2 (1968), 47-48.

Fletcher, Harris. *Milton's Rabbinical Readings*. Urbana, Ill., 1930.

Fletcher, Joseph. *The Historie of the Perfect-Cursed-Blessed Man*. London, 1628.

Fox, Robert C. "Milton's Sin: Addenda." *PQ* 42 (1963), 120-21.

———. "The Allegory of Sin and Death in *Paradise Lost*." *MLQ* 24 (1963), 354-64.

Frank, Joseph. "The Unharmonious Vision: Milton as a Baroque Artist." *CLS* 3 (1966), 95-108.

Freeman, Rosemary. *English Emblem Books*. London, 1970.

French, Joseph Milton. *Life Records of John Milton*, 5 vols. New Brunswick, 1949-58.

———. "Milton's Homes and Investments." *PQ* 28 (1949), 77-97.

Friedlaender, Walter. *Mannerism and Anti-Mannerism in Italian Painting*. New York, 1970.

———. *Nicolas Poussin: A New Approach*. New York, n.d.

Frisch, Ernst. *Mittelalterliche Buchmalerei Kleinodien aus Salzburg*. Vienna, 1949.

Frutaz, Amato Pietro. *Le piante di Roma*, 3 vols. Rome, 1962.

———. *Piante e vedute di Roma e del Vaticano dal 1300 al 1676*. Vatican City, 1956.

Frye, Northrop. *The Return of Eden: Five Essays on Milton's Epics*. Toronto, 1965.

Frye, Roland Mushat. *God, Man, and Satan: Patterns of Christian Thought and Life in "Paradise Lost," "Pilgrim's Progress," and the Great Theologians*. Princeton, 1960.

———. "Milton's Florentine Friend, Bishop Frescobaldi: A Biographical Note and Portrait." *Milton Quarterly* 7 (1973), 74-75.

———. "Milton's Paradise Lost and the Visual Arts," *Proceedings of the American Philosophical Society* 120 (1976), 233-44.

———. "The Teachings of Classical Puritanism on Conjugal Love." *Studies in the Renaissance* 2 (1955), 148-59.

Fuller, Thomas. *A Pisgah-Sight of Palestine*. London, 1650.

Fulvio, Andrea. *L'antichità di Roma*. Venice, 1588.

Funck, M. *Le Livre belge à gravures . . . imprimés en Belgique avant le XVIIIe siècle*. Paris and Brussels, 1925.

Furbank, P. N. *Reflections on the Word "Image."* London, 1970.

Galavaris, George. *The Illustrations of the Liturgical Homilies of Gregory Nazianzenus.* Princeton, 1969.

Garber, Marjorie B. "Fallen Landscape: The Art of Milton and Poussin." *ELR* 5 (1975), 96-124.

Gardner, Arthur. *A Handbook of English Medieval Sculpture.* Cambridge, 1935.

Gardner, Helen. *A Reading of "Paradise Lost."* Oxford, 1965.

Gardner, Stephen. "The Tower of Babel" in *Five Themes from Genesis* (ed. Koch and Bryan), pp. 11-15.

Garvin, Katharine. "Snakes in the Grass (with particular attention to Satan, Lamia, Christabel)." *REL* 2 (April 1961), 11-27.

Gazzola, Piero. *La porta bronzea di S. Zeno a Verona,* Milan, n.d.

Geiger, Benno. *Magnasco.* Bergamo, 1949.

Geisberg, Max. *Die Deutsche Buchillustration in der ersten Hälfte des XVI Jahrhunderts,* 9 vols. Munich, 1930-32.

George, Wilma. *Animals and Maps.* Berkeley and Los Angeles, 1969.

Giamatti, A. Bartlett. *The Earthly Paradise and the Renaissance Epic.* Princeton, 1966.

Gibbs, Mary Laura. "The Creation of Eve" in *Five Themes from Genesis* (ed. Koch and Bryan), pp. 3-5.

Gibson, Walter S. *Hieronymus Bosch.* London, 1973.

Gielly, Louis. *Jacopo della Quercia.* Paris, 1930.

Gilbert, Allan H. *A Geographical Dictionary of Milton.* New Haven, 1919.

———. "Milton's China." *MLN* 26 (1911), 199-200.

———. *On the Composition of "Paradise Lost," A Study of the Ordering and Insertion of Material.* Chapel Hill, 1947.

Gilbert, Creighton, ed. *Renaissance Art.* New York, 1970.

Gilliam, J. F. "Scylla and Sin." *PQ* 29 (1950), 345-47.

Ginzberg, Louis. *The Legends of the Jews,* 7 vols. (trans. Henrietta Szold). Philadelphia, 1909-38.

Goldscheider, L. *Roman Portraits.* New York, 1940.

Goldschmidt, Adolph. "English Influence on Medieval Art on the Continent," in *Medieval Studies in Memory of A. Kingsley Porter* (ed. Wilhelm R. W. Koehler), Cambridge, Mass., 1939, II, pp. 709-28.

Gollancz, Sir Israel. *The Caedmon Manuscript.* Oxford, 1927.

Golzio, Vincenzo. *Palazzi romani dalla rinascità al neoclassico.* Bologna, 1971.

Gombrich, E. H. *Aby Warburg: An Intellectual Biography.* London, 1970.

———. "Bosch's 'Garden of Earthly Delights': A Progress Report." *JWCI* 32 (1969), 162-70.

———. "Hypnerotomachiana." *JWCI* 14 (1951), 119-25.

———. "Personification," in *Classical Influences on European Culture A.D. 500-1500* (ed. R. R. Bolger), Cambridge, 1971, pp. 247-57.

———. "Renaissance Artistic Theory and the Development of Landscape Painting." *Gazette des Beaux-Arts* 41 (1953), 335-60.

———. *Symbolic Images: Studies in the Art of the Renaissance.* London, 1972.

Goodspeed, Edgar J., Donald W. Riddle, and Harold R. Willoughby. *The Rockefeller McCormick New Testament,* 3 vols. Chicago, 1932.

Gossman, Ann. "Milton, Prudentius, and the Brood of Sin." *N&Q* 202 (1957), 439-40.

Gossman, Ann. "Two Milton Notes; 1: Milton, Plutarch, and Darkness Visible; 2: The Iron Rod and Golden Sceptre in *Paradise Lost*." *N&Q* 206 (1961), 182-83.

Gould, Cecil. *The School of Love and Correggio's Mythologies*. London, n.d. [1970].

Grabar, André. *Christian Iconography: A Study of Its Origins*. Princeton, 1968.

Graham, Rose. "A Picture-Book of the Life of St. Anthony the Abbot." *Archaeologia* 83 (1933), 1-26.

Green, Rosalie B. "The Adam and Eve Cycle in the *Hortus Deliciarum*," in *Late Classical and Mediaeval Studies in Honor of Albert Mathias Friend, Jr.* (ed. Kurt Weitzmann). Princeton, 1955, pp. 340-47.

Greene, Thomas. *The Descent from Heaven; A Study in Epic Continuity*. New Haven, 1963.

Grose, Christopher. "Some Uses of Sensuous Immediacy in *PL*." *HLQ* 31 (1968), 211-22.

Guazzo, F. M. *Compendium Maleficarum*. Milan, 1608.

Guccerelli, Demetrio. *Stradario storico biografico della città di Firenze*. Rome, 1969.

Guldan, Ernst. *Eva und Maria: Eine Antithese als Bildmotiv*. Graz-Cologne, 1966.

Gurrieri, Francesco, and Judith Chatfield. *Boboli Gardens*, Florence, 1972.

Gurteen, S. Humphreys. *The Epic of the Fall of Man: A Comparative Study of Caedmon, Dante, and Milton*. New York, 1896.

Haberly, Lloyd. *Mediaeval English Pavingtiles*. Oxford, 1937.

Hadermann-Misguich, Lydie. "Deux nouvelles sources d'inspiration du polyptyque de Modène." *Gazette des Beaux-Arts* 63 (1964), 355-58.

Hadfield, Miles and John. *Gardens of Delight*. Boston, 1964.

Hagstrum, Jean H. *The Sister Arts. The Tradition of Literary Pictorialism and English Poetry from Dryden to Gray*. Chicago, 1958.

Halkett, John. *Milton and the Idea of Matrimony; A Study of the Divorce Tracts and "Paradise Lost."* New Haven, 1970.

Haines, Herbert. *A Manual of Monumental Brasses*. Bath, 1970.

Hammond, Mason. "Concilia Deorum from Homer through Milton." *SP* 30 (1933), 1-16.

Hanford, James Holly. *John Milton, Englishman*. New York, 1949.

———. "Milton in Italy." *Annuale Médiaévale* 5 (1964), 49-63.

Hankins, John E. "Milton and Olaus Magnus," in *Studies in Honor of T. W. Baldwin* (ed. by Don C. Allen). Urbana, 1958, pp. 205-10.

———. "The Pains of the Afterworld: Fire, Wind, and Ice in Milton and Shakespeare." *PMLA* 71 (1956), 482-95.

Hanmer, Sir Thomas. *The Garden Book* (ed. Eleanour S. Rohde). London, 1933.

[Harbison, Craig, ed.]. *Symbols in Transformation. Iconographic Themes at the Time of the Reformation; An Exhibition of Prints in Memory of Erwin Panofsky*. Princeton, 1969.

Hard, Frederick. "E. K.'s References to Painting: Some Seventeenth Century Adaptations." *ELH* 7 (1940), 121-29.

Harding, Davis P. *The Club of Hercules: Studies in the Classical Background of "Paradise Lost."* Urbana, 1962.

———. "Milton's Bee-Simile." *JEGP* 60 (1961), 664-69.

Hartt, Frederick. *History of Italian Renaissance Art*. New York [c. 1969].

Haskell, Francis. *Patrons and Painters: A Study in the Relations Between Italian Art and Society in the Age of the Baroque*. New York, 1963.

Hassall, W. O. See *Holkham Bible*.

Hatzfeld, Helmut A. *Literature through Art: A New Approach to French Literature.* New York, 1952.

Haynes, Denys. "The Worksop Relief." *Jahrbuch der Berliner Museen* 5 (1963), 1-13.

Hazlitt, William. *Works*, 21 vols. (ed. P. P. Howe). London, 1930-34.

Heckscher, William S. "Bernini's Elephant and Obelisk." *The Art Bulletin* 29 (1947), 155-82.

Heimann, Adelheid. "Moses Shown the Promised Land." *JWCI* 34 (1971), 321-24.

———. "Three Illustrations from the Bury St. Edmunds Psalter and Their Prototypes: Notes on the Iconography of Some Anglo-Saxon Drawings." *JWCI* 29 (1966), 39-59.

———. "Trinitas Creator Mundi." *JWCI* 2 (1938-39), 42-52.

Hekler, Antal. *Greek and Roman Portraits*. New York, 1912.

Held, Julius S. "Flora, Goddess and Courtesan" in *Essays in Honor of Erwin Panofsky* (ed. Millard Meiss), I, pp. 201-18.

———. "Rubens Glynde Sketch and the Installation of the Whitehall Ceiling." *Burlington Magazine* 112 (1970), 274-81.

Henderson, G. "Late-Antique Influences in Some English Medieval Illustrations of Genesis." *JWCI* 25 (1962), pp. 172-98.

Henkel, Arthur, and Albrecht Schöne. *Emblemata; Handbuch zur Sinnbildkunst des XVI and XVII Jahrhunderts*. Stuttgart, 1967. With bibliographical supplement by William S. Heckscher and Cameron F. Bunker in *Renaissance Quarterly* 23 (1970), 59-80.

Henniker-Heaton, Raymond. *Panel Picture Representing the Temptation of Christ by Tiziano Vecelli called "Titian."* New York, 1925.

Henry, Françoise. *Early Christian Irish Art*. Dublin, 1954.

———. *Irish Art in the Romanesque Period 1020-1170 A.D.* Ithaca, N.Y., 1970.

Herbert, Carolyn. "Comic Elements in the Scenes of Hell of *Paradise Lost*," in *Renaissance Papers*, Columbia, S.C., 1956, pp. 92-101.

Hess, Thomas B., and John Ashbery, eds. *Light in Art*. New York, 1971.

Heywood, Thomas. *The Hierarchie of the Blessed Angells*. London, 1635.

Hibernicus. "The Forbidden Fruit." *N&Q* 183 (1942), 323.

Hildburgh, W. L. "An English Alabaster Carving of *St. Michael Weighing a Soul*." *Burlington Magazine* 89 (1947), 129-31.

———. "English Alabaster Carvings as Records of the Medieval Religious Drama." *Archaeologia* 93 (1949), 51-101.

Hill, Christopher. *God's Englishman: Oliver Cromwell and the English Revolution.* Harmondsworth, 1970.

Hill, D. M. "Satan on the Burning Lake." *N&Q* 201 (1956), 157-59.

Hind, Arthur M. *Early Italian Engraving*. (7 vols. in 4). London, 1970.

———, Marjorie Corbett, and Michael Norton. *Engraving in England in the Sixteenth and Seventeenth Centuries; A Descriptive Catalogue with Introductions*, 3 vols. Cambridge, 1952-64.

———. *Marcantonio and Italian Engravers and Etchers of the Sixteenth Century.* New York [1912].

Hirsch, Wolfgang, ed. *Hieronymus Bosch: The Garden of Delights*. London, 1954.

Hobsbaum, Philip. "The Criticism of Milton's Epic Similes." *SN* 36 (1964), 220-31.

Hogarth, William. *The Analysis of Beauty, with the Rejected Passages from the Manuscript Drafts and Autobiographical Notes* (ed. Joseph Burke). Oxford, 1955.

Holbein, *see* F. Douce.

Holkham Bible Picture Book (ed. W. O. Hassall). London, 1954.

Holkham Bible Picture Book: The Anglo-Norman Text (ed. F. P. Pickering). Oxford, 1971.

Hollstein, F.W.H. *Dutch and Flemish Etchings, Engravings, and Woodcuts c. 1450-1700*, 19 vols. Amsterdam, 1949-1969.

———. *German Engravings, Etchings, and Woodcuts c. 1400-1700*. Amsterdam, 1954-.

Howard, Clare. *English Travellers of the Renaissance*. New York, 1914.

Howard, F. E., and F. H. Crossley. *English Church Woodwork: A Study in Craftsmanship during the Mediaeval Period A.D. 1250-1550*. London, n.d.

Huckabay, Calvin. "The Satanist Controversy of the Nineteenth Century" in *Studies in English Renaissance Literature* (ed. Waldo F. McNeir), Baton Rouge, 1962, pp. 197-210.

Hughes, Merritt Y. "Milton and the Symbol of Light." *SEL* 4 (1964), 1-33.

———. "Milton's Limbo of Vanity" in *Th' Upright Heart and Pure* (ed. Amadeus P. Fiore, O.F.M.), pp. 7-24.

———. "Satan Now Dragon Grown (*Paradise Lost*, x, 529)." *EA* 20 (1967), 356-69.

———. "Some Illustrators of Milton: The Expulsion from Paradise." *JEGP* 60 (1961), 670-79.

Hughes, Robert. *Heaven and Hell in Western Art*. New York, 1968.

Hunt, John Dixon. "Milton's Illustrators" in *John Milton: Introductions* (ed. John Broadbent), pp. 208-25.

———, ed. *Encounters, Essays on Literature and the Visual Arts*. London, 1971.

Hunt, John Dixon, and Peter Willis. *The Genius of Place: The English Landscape Gardens 1620-1820*. London, 1975.

Hunt, Winifred. "On Even Ground: A Note on the Extramundane Location of Hell in *Paradise Lost*." *MLQ* 23 (1962), 17-19.

Hunter, William B., Jr. "Eve's Demonic Dream." *ELH* 13 (1946), 255-65.

———. "Satan as Comet: *Paradise Lost*, II, 708-11." *ELN* 5 (1967), 17-21.

———. "Two Milton Notes." *MLR* 44 (1949), 89-91.

———, C. A. Patrides, and J. H. Adamson. *Bright Essence: Studies in Milton's Theology*. Salt Lake City, 1971.

Huntley, Frank L. "A Justification of Milton's 'Paradise of Fools.'" *ELH* 21 (1954), 107-13.

———. "Milton, Mendoza, and the Chinese Landship." *MLN* 69 (1954), 404-7.

Huntley, John F. "The Ecology and Anatomy of Criticism: Milton's Sonnet 19 and the Bee Simile in *Paradise Lost*, I, 768-76." *JAAC* 24 (1966), 383-91.

Hütt, Wolfgang. *Albrecht Dürer 1471 bis 1528: Das gesamte graphische Werk*, 2 vols. n.p. [Munich], n.d. [1970].

Huxley, Aldous. "Death and the Baroque." *Horizon* 19 (1949), 281-91.

Huyghe, René, ed. *Larousse Encyclopedia of Renaissance and Baroque Art*. New York, 1967.

Illo, John. "Animal Sources for Milton's Sin and Death." *N&Q* 205 (1960), 425-26.

Italian Illuminated Manuscripts from 1400 to 1550: Catalogue of an Exhibition held in the Bodleian Library. Oxford, 1948.

Jacob, Henriette s'. *Idealism and Realism: A Study of Sepulchral Symbolism.* Leiden, 1954.

James, Montague R. *Abbeys.* London, 1926.

———. *The Apocalypse in Art.* London, 1931.

———. *The Apocryphal New Testament.* Oxford, 1924.

Jameson, Anna and Lady Eastlake. *The History of Our Lord as Exemplified in Works of Art: with that of His Types; St. John the Baptist; and Other Persons of the Old and New Testament,* 2 vols. London, 1864.

———. *Sacred and Legendary Art,* 2 vols. New York, 1970.

Janson, H. W. *Apes and Ape Lore in the Middle Ages and the Renaissance.* London, 1952 (*Studies of the Warburg Institute,* vol. 20).

———. 'The Image of Man in Renaissance Art: From Donatello to Michelangelo,' in *The Renaissance Image of Man and the World* (ed. Bernard O'Kelly). Columbus, Ohio, 1966, pp. 77-103.

———. *The Sculpture of Donatello,* 2 vols. Princeton, 1957.

Jellicoe, G. A. *Studies in Landscape Design,* 3 vols. London, 1960-70.

Jellicoe, Susan and Geoffrey. *Water: The Use of Water in Landscape Architecture.* New York, 1971.

Johnson, James Rosser. *The Radiance of Chartres: Studies in the Early Stained Glass of the Cathedral.* New York, 1965.

———. "Stained Glass and Imitation Gems." *Art Bulletin* 39 (1957), 221-24.

Johnson, Samuel. *Lives of the English Poets* (ed. George Birkbeck Hill), 3 vols. New York, 1967.

Jónsdóttir, Selma. *An 11th Century Byzantine Last Judgment in Iceland.* Reykjavík, 1959.

Jonson, Ben. *Works,* 11 vols. (ed. C. H. Herford and Percy Simpson). Oxford, 1925-52.

Kaftal, George. *Iconography of the Saints in Central and South Italian Schools of Painting.* Florence, 1965.

———. *Iconography of the Saints in Tuscan Painting.* Florence, 1952.

Katzenellenbogen, Adolph. *Allegories of the Virtues and Vices in Mediaeval Art from Early Christian Times to the Thirteenth Century.* New York, 1964.

Kauffmann, Georg. *Florence: Art Treasures and Buildings* (*A Phaidon Guide*). London, 1971.

Kelemen, Pál. *El Greco Revisited: Candia, Venice, Toledo.* New York, 1961.

Kellogg, Alfred L. "Some Patristic Sources for Milton's Gehenna." *N&Q* 195 (1950), 10-13.

Kendon, Frank. *Mural Paintings in English Churches during the Middle Ages; An Introductory Essay on the Folk Influence in Religious Art.* London, 1923.

Kendrick, T. D. *Late Saxon and Viking Art.* London, 1949.

Kennedy, Charles W. *Early English Christian Poetry.* London, 1952.

Kessler, Herbert Leon. "The Solitary Bird in Van der Goes' 'Garden of Eden.'" *JWCI* 28 (1965), 327-29.

Keutner, Herbert. *Sculpture: Renaissance to Rococo.* Greenwich, Conn., 1969.

King, Georgiana Goddard. "Mattia Preti." *Art Bulletin* 18 (1936), 371-86.

Kirkconnell, Watson. *The Celestial Cycle; The Theme of "Paradise Lost" in World Literature with Translations of the Major Analogues.* Toronto, 1952.

Kirschbaum, E. "L'Angelo rosso e l'angelo turchino." *Rivista di archeologia cristiana* 17 (1940), 209-48.

Kirschbaum, Engelbert (S.J.). *Lexikon der Christlichen Ikonographie*, 7 vols. Freiburg im Breisgau, 1968-74.

Kitto Bible. Extra-illustrated collection of Biblical illustrations at the Huntington Library.

Kittredge, G. L. "To take Time by the Forelock." *MLN* 8 (1893), cols. 459-69.

Klauser. *Festschrift Theodor Klauser*. Münster, Westfalen, 1964.

Klein, H. Arthur. *Graphic Worlds of Peter Bruegel the Elder*. New York, 1963.

Kliger, Samuel. "The 'Urbs Aeterna' in *Paradise Regained*." *PMLA* 61 (1946), 474-91.

Klingender, Francis. *Animals in Art and Thought to the End of the Middle Ages* (eds. Evelyn Antal and John Harthan). Cambridge, Mass., 1971.

Knight, G. Wilson. *The Burning Oracle; Studies in the Poetry of Action*. London, 1939.

Knott, John R., Jr. *Milton's Pastoral Vision, An Approach to "Paradise Lost."* Chicago, 1971.

———. "Symbolic Landscape in *Paradise Lost*." *Milton Studies* 2 (1970), 37-58.

———. "The Visit of Raphael: *Paradise Lost*, Book v." *PQ* 47 (1968), 36-42.

Koch, Robert A. "The Salamander in van der Goes' 'Garden of Eden.'" *JWCI* 28 (1965), 322-26.

———, and Mina R. Bryan, eds. *Five Themes from Genesis*. Princeton, 1972.

Koehler, G. Stanley. "Milton's Use of Color and Light." *Milton Studies* 3 (1971), 55-81.

Kors, Alan C., and Edward Peters, eds. *Witchcraft in Europe 1100-1700: A Documentary History*. Philadelphia, 1972.

Kranidas, Thomas. *The Fierce Equation: A Study of Milton's Decorum*. The Hague, 1965.

———. "Satan's First Disguise." *ELN* 2 (1964), 13-15.

———, ed. *New Essays on "Paradise Lost."* Berkeley, 1969.

Kristeller, Paul. *Biblia Pauperum. Unicum der Heidelberger Universitäts-Bibliothek*. Berlin, 1906.

———. *Kupferstich und Holzschnitt in vier Jahrhunderten*. Berlin, 1922.

Krouse, Patricia. "The Story of Joseph" in *Five Themes from Genesis* (ed. Koch and Bryan), 21-28.

Künstle, Karl. *Ikonographie der Heiligen*. Freiburg, Breisgau, 1926.

Kurth, Burton O. *Milton and Christian Heroism: Biblical Epic Themes and Forms in Seventeenth Century England*. Berkeley, 1959.

Laborde, Alexandre de. *La Bible Moralisée illustrée . . . du manuscrit du XIIIe siècle*, 5 vols. Paris, 1911-27.

Ladner, Gerhart B. *Ad imaginem Dei; The Image of Man in Medieval Art*. Latrobe, Pa., 1965.

———. "Vegetation Symbolism and the Concept of Renaissance," in *Essays in Honor of Erwin Panofsky* (ed. Millard Meiss), 1, 303-22.

Laking, Sir Guy Francis. *A Record of European Armour and Arms through Seven Centuries*, 5 vols. London, 1920-22.

Lamberton, Clark D. *Themes from St. John's Gospel in Early Roman Catacomb Painting*. Princeton, n.d.

Lanciani, Rodolfo. *The Golden Days of the Renaissance in Rome from the Pontificate of Julius II to that of Paul III*. Boston, 1906.

———. *Pagan and Christian Rome*. Boston, 1893.

———. *The Ruins and Excavations of Ancient Rome: A Companion Book for Students and Travellers*. Boston, 1897.

———. *Storia degli Scavi di Roma e Notizie Intorno le Collezioni Romane di Antichità*, 2 vols. Rome, 1902-03.

Langdon, Ida. *Milton's Theory of Poetry and Fine Art: An Essay with a Collection of Illustrative Passages from His Works*. New Haven, 1924.

Langton, Edward. *Good and Evil Spirits: A Study of the Jewish and Christian Doctrine, Its Origin and Development*. London [1942].

———. *Satan: A Portrait*. London, n.d.

Lassels, Richard. *An Italian Voyage, Or A Complete Journey Through Italy*. Paris, 1670.

Lavin, Marilyn Aronberg. "Giovannino Battista: A Study in Renaissance Religious Symbolism." *Art Bulletin* 37 (1955), 85-101 with supplement in *Art Bulletin* 43 (1961), 319-26.

Law, Ernest. "Milton and Mabuse." *TLS* (27 Feb., 1927), 126.

Leavis, F. R. "Mr. Eliot and Milton," in *The Common Pursuit*. New York, 1952, pp. 9-32.

———. *Revaluation: Tradition and Development in English Poetry*. London, 1936.

Leclerq, H. *Manuel d'archéologie chrétienne depuis les origines jusqu'au VIIIᵉ siècle*, 2 vols. Paris, 1907.

Le Comte, Edward S. "Milton's Infernal Council and Mantuan." *PMLA* 69 (1954), 979-83.

Leeming, Bernard. "The Adversary," in *Satan* [Carmelite Fathers], pp. 19-39.

Lees-Milne, James. *Saint Peter's*. Boston, 1967.

Lehmann, Karl. "The Dome of Heaven." *Art Bulletin* 27 (1945), 1-27.

Lehner, Ernst and Johanna. *Devils, Demons, Death and Damnation*. New York, 1971.

Leitch, Vincent B. "The Landscape of Hell in *Paradise Lost*, Book I." *Xavier University Studies* 9 (1970), 26-30.

Leroquias, Victor. *Supplément aux Livres d'heures manuscrits de la Bibliothèque Nationale (Acquisitions récentes et donation Smith-Lesouëf)*. Mâcon, 1943.

Lever, J. W. "*Paradise Lost* and Anglo-Saxon Tradition." *RES* 23 (1947), 97-106.

Levey, Michael. *Themes and Painters in the National Gallery: The Nude*. London, 1972.

Levin, Harry. *The Myth of the Golden Age in the Renaissance*. Bloomington, Ind., 1969.

Levron, Jacques. *Le Diable dans l'art*. Paris, 1935.

Lewalski, Barbara Kiefer. "Innocence and Experience in Milton's Eden," in *New Essays on Paradise Lost* (ed. Thomas Kranidas), pp. 86-117.

———. *Milton's Brief Epic: The Genre, Meaning, and Art of "Paradise Regained."* Providence, R.I., 1966.

———. "Structure and the Symbolism of Vision in Michael's Prophecy, *Paradise Lost*, Books XI-XII." *PQ* 42 (1963), 25-35.

Lewis, Clive Staples. *The Discarded Image; An Introduction to Medieval and Renaissance Literature*. Cambridge, 1964.

———. *A Preface to "Paradise Lost."* London, 1949.

Lieb, Michael. *The Dialectics of Creation: Patterns of Birth and Regeneration in "Paradise Lost."* Amherst, Mass., 1970.

Lightbown, R. W. "Time and Death: A New Relief by Zumbo." *Victoria and Albert Museum Bulletin* 3 (1967), 39-44.

Lilienfein, Heinrich. *Lukas Cranach und seine Zeit.* Leipzig, 1942.

Limbourg Brothers. *The "Très Riches Heures" of Jean, Duke of Berry.* New York, 1969. (Also under Longnon, Jean.)

Lloyd, Joan Barclay. *African Animals in Renaissance Literature and Art.* Oxford, 1971.

Löffler, Karl. *Schwäbische Buchmalerei in Romanischer Zeit.* Augsburg, 1928.

Longnon, Jean, Raymond Cazelles, and Millard Meiss. *The "Très Riches Heures" of Jean, Duke of Berry.* New York, 1969.

Lowrie, Walter. *Art in the Early Church.* New York, 1969.

———. *Monuments of the Early Church.* New York, 1901.

Ludovici, *see* Samek Ludovici.

Lum, Peter. *Fabulous Beasts.* New York, 1951.

Luther, Martin, and Lucas Cranach the Elder. *Passional Christi und Antichristi.* Leipzig, n.d.

MacCaffrey, Isabel G. *"Paradise Lost" as "Myth."* Cambridge, Mass., 1959.

———. "The Theme of *Paradise Lost,* Book III" in *New Essays on Paradise Lost* (ed. Thomas Kranidas), pp. 58-85.

McCarthy, B. Eugene. "Defoe, Milton, and Heresy." *Milton Newsletter* 3 (1969), 71-73.

Macaulay, Thomas B. "Milton," in *The Works of Lord Macaulay,* v, New York, 1900, pp. 1-46.

MacClaren, Neil, and Allan Braham. *The National Gallery Catalogue: The Spanish School.* London, 1970.

McColley, Grant. "Milton's Golden Compasses." *N&Q* 176 (1939), 97-98.

———. *"Paradise Lost": An Account of Its Growth and Major Origins, with a Discussion of Milton's Use of Sources and Literary Patterns.* Chicago, 1940.

MacDougall, Elisabeth. *"Ars Hortulorum*: Sixteenth-Century Garden Iconography and Literary Theory in Italy" in *The Italian Garden* (ed. David R. Coffin), pp. 37-60.

Mace, Dean Tolle. "Ut Pictura Poesis: Dryden, Poussin and the Parallel of Poetry and Painting in the Seventeenth Century," in *Encounters, Essays on Literature and the Visual Arts* (ed. J. D. Hunt), pp. 58-81.

Mackenzie, Phyllis. "Milton's Visual Imagination: An Answer to T. S. Eliot." *UTQ* 16 (1946), 17-29.

McNamee, M. B. "Beowulf—An Allegory of Salvation?" in *An Anthology of Beowulf Criticism* (ed. Lewis E. Nicholson), Notre Dame, Indiana, 1963, pp. 331-52.

Madsen, William G. *From Shadowy Types to Truth: Studies in Milton's Symbolism.* New Haven, 1968.

Major, John M. *"Paradise Regained* and Spenser's *Legend of Holiness." Ren. Quar.* 20 (1967), 465-70.

Mâle, Emile. *L'Art religieux de la fin du XVIe siècle, du XVIIe siècle et du XVIIIe siècle.* Paris, 1951.

———. *The Gothic Image; Religious Art in France of the Thirteenth Century* (trans. Dora Hussey). New York, 1958.

———. *Religious Art from the Twelfth to the Eighteenth Century.* New York, 1949.

Malins, Edward. *English Landscaping and Literature 1660-1840*. London, 1966.

Mandowsky, Erna, and Charles Mitchell. *Pirro Ligorio's Roman Antiquities*. London, 1963.

Marcanova, Giovanni. *Antiquitates*, manuscript dated 1465 in Princeton University Library.

Marilla, Esmond L. "Milton's Paradise of Fools." *ES* 42 (1961), 159-64.

Marle, Raimond van. *Iconographie de l'art profane au moyen-âge et à la Renaissance*, 2 vols. The Hague, 1931-32.

Martin, André. *Le Livre illustré en France au XVᵉ siècle*. Paris, 1931.

Martin, Gregory. *Roma Sancta 1581* (trans. George B. Parks). Rome, 1969.

Martin, John Rupert. *The Illustration of the Heavenly Ladder of John Climacus*. Princeton, 1954.

———. *The Portrait of John Milton at Princeton; and its Place in Milton Iconography*. Princeton, 1961.

Martinelli, Fioravante: *See under* D'Onofrio, Cesare.

Martinelli, Giuseppe, ed. *The World of Renaissance Florence* (trans. Walter Darwell). New York, 1968.

Martz, Louis L. *The Paradise Within; Studies in Vaughan, Traherne, and Milton*. New Haven, 1964.

Masson, Georgina. "Italian Flower Collectors' Gardens in Seventeenth Century Italy," in *The Italian Garden* (ed. David R. Coffin), pp. 63-80.

Masson, David. *The Life of John Milton*, 6 vols. New York, 1946.

Master of Mary of Burgundy. *A Book of Hours for Engelbert of Nassau* (ed. J.J.G. Alexander). New York, 1970.

Matzke, John E. "On the Source of the Italian and English Idioms meaning 'To take Time by the Forelock.'" *PMLA* 8 (1893), 303-34.

Maunde-Thompson, Sir E. "The Grotesque and the Humorous in Illuminations of the Middle Ages." *Bibliographica* 2 (1896), 309-32.

Mayer, Maximilian. *Die Giganten und Titanen in der Antik in Sage und Kunst*. Berlin, 1887.

Meiss, Millard. *French Painting in the Time of Jean de Berry*, 3 vols. London, 1967-68.

———. "Light as Form and Symbol in Some Fifteenth-Century Paintings," in *Renaissance Art* (ed. Creighton Gilbert), pp. 43-68.

———. *Painting in Florence and Siena After the Black Death; the Arts, Religion and Society in the Mid-Fourteenth Century*. Princeton (1951) 1976.

———, ed. *Essays in Honor of Erwin Panofsky*, 2 vols. New York, 1961.

Mercer, Eric. *English Art, 1553-1625*. Oxford, 1962.

Meulen, *see* Van der Meulen.

Michaelis, Adolf. *Ancient Marbles in Great Britain*. Cambridge, 1882.

Michigan, University, Museum of Art. *Italy through Dutch Eyes: Dutch Seventeenth-Century Landscape Artists in Italy*. Ann Arbor [1964].

Middleton, J. Henry. *Illuminated Manuscripts in Classical and Mediaeval Times: Their Art and Their Technique*. Cambridge, 1892.

Milburn, R.L.P. *Saints and Their Emblems in English Churches*. London, 1949.

Miles, Josephine. "From 'Good' to 'Bright': A Note in Poetic History." *PMLA* 60 (1945), 766-74.

Millar, Eric. "Additional Miniatures by W. deBrailes." *Journal of the Walters Art Gallery* 2 (1939), 106-9.

————. *English Illuminated Manuscripts from the Xth to the XIIIth Century*. Paris and Brussels, 1926.

————. *English Illuminated Manuscripts of the XIVth and XVth Centuries*. Paris, 1928.

Millar, Oliver. *The Age of Charles I: Painting in England 1620-1649*. London, 1972.

————. *The Tudor, Stuart and Early Georgian Pictures in the Collection of Her Majesty the Queen*, 2 vols. London, 1963.

Miller, Ella, ed. *Forest Hill with Shotover . . . The Village Book*. Oxford [1933].

Milton, John. *The Poems* (ed. John Carey and Alastair Fowler). New York, 1972.

————. *Complete Poems and Major Prose* (ed. Merritt Y. Hughes). New York, 1957.

————. *Paradise Lost* (ed. Merritt Y. Hughes). New York, 1935.

————. *The Works*, 18 vols. in 21 (ed. Frank A. Patterson et al.). New York, 1931-38.

[Miner, Dorothy Eugenia] The Walters Art Gallery. *Illuminated Books of the Middle Ages and Renaissance: An Exhibition Held at the Baltimore Museum of Art*. Baltimore, 1949.

Miner, Earl, ed. *Seventeenth-Century Imagery; Essays on Uses of Figurative Language from Donne to Farquhar*. Berkeley, 1971.

Molajoli, Bruno. *Naples: Museo e Gallerie Nazionale di Capodimonte*. Naples, 1964.

Mollenkott, Virginia R. "A Note on Milton's 'Materialistic' Angelology." *SCN* 22 no. 1 (1964), item 9.

Molsdorf, Wilhelm. *Christliche Symbolik der Mittelalterlichen Kunst*. Leipzig, 1926.

Montagu, Jennifer. "Antonio and Giuseppe Giorgetti: Sculptors to Cardinal Francesco Barberini." *Art Bulletin* 52 (1970), 278-98.

Morris, Edward. "John Gibson's Satan." *JWCI* 34 (1971), 397-99.

Morris, Harry. "Some Uses of Angel Iconography in English Literature." *CL* 10 (1958), 36-44.

Mortoft, Francis. *Francis Mortoft His Book. Being His Travels Through France and Italy 1658-59* (ed. Malcolm Letts). London, 1925.

Muir, Kenneth. *John Milton*. London, 1960.

Muir, Lynette R. "A Detail in Milton's Description of Sin." *N&Q* 201 (1956), 100-1.

Müntz, Eugène. *Raphael, His Life, Works and Times*. London, 1888.

Murray, Patrick. *Milton: The Modern Phase, A Study of Twentieth-Century Criticism*. London, 1967.

Murray, Peter. *Piranesi and the Grandeur of Ancient Rome*. London, 1971.

Narkiss, Bezalel. *Hebrew Illuminated Manuscripts*. New York, 1969.

Nash, Ernest. *Pictorial Dictionary of Ancient Rome*, 2 vols. New York, 1961-62.

La natura morta italiana. Catalogo della mostra. Napoli, Zurigo, Rotterdam. Milan, 1964.

Nelson, James G. *The Sublime Puritan: Milton and the Victorians*. Madison, 1963.

Nelson, Lowry, Jr. *Baroque Lyric Poetry*. New Haven, 1961.

Nersessian, Sirapie der. *Armenian Manuscripts in the Freer Gallery of Art*. Washington, 1963.

Neuss, Wilhelm. *Die Apokalypse des Hl. Johannes in der Altspanischen und Altchristlichen Bibel-Illustration (Das Problem der Beatus-Handscriften)*, 2 vols. Münster in Westfalen, 1931.

Nicoll, Allardyce. *Stuart Masques and the Renaissance Stage*. London, 1937.

Nicolson, Marjorie Hope. "The Discovery of Space." *Medieval and Renaissance Studies: Proceedings of the Southeastern Institute of Medieval and Renaissance Studies, 1965* (ed. O. B. Hardison, Jr.). Chapel Hill, 1966, pp. 40-59.

———. *John Milton: A Reader's Guide to his Poetry*. New York, 1966.

———. "Milton's Hell and the Phlegraean Fields." *UTQ* 7 (1938), 500-13.

———. "The Telescope and Imagination." *MP* 32 (1935), 233-60.

Nogara, Bertolomeo. *Art Treasures of the Vatican*. New York, 1950.

Novarr, David. " 'Gray Dissimulation': Ford and Milton." *PQ* 41 (1962), 500-4.

Nuttall, W.L.F. "King Charles I's Pictures and the Commonwealth Sale." *Apollo* 82 (October, 1965), pp. 302-9.

Nuttgens, Patrick. *The Landscape of Ideas*. London, 1972.

Oakeshott, Walter. *The Sequence of English Medieval Art, Illustrated Chiefly from Illuminated Manuscripts, 650-1450*. London, 1950.

Ogden, Henry V. S. "The Principles of Variety and Contrast in Seventeenth Century Aesthetics, and Milton's Poetry." *JHI* 10 (1949), 159-82.

———, and Margaret S. Ogden. *English Taste in Landscape in the Seventeenth Century*. Ann Arbor, 1955.

O'Keeffe, Timothy J. "An Analogue to Milton's Sin and More on the Tradition." *MQ* 5 (1971), 74-77.

O'Kelly, Bernard, ed. *The Renaissance Image of Man and the World*. Columbus, Ohio, 1966.

Onofrio, *see* D'Onofrio.

Oras, Ants. "Darkness Visible: Notes on Milton's Descriptive Procedures in *Paradise Lost*" in *All These to Teach: Essays in Honor of C. A. Robertson* (ed. Robert A. Bryan and others), Gainesville, Fla., 1965, pp. 130-43.

Ortelius, Abraham. *The Theatre of the Whole World—London, 1606* (intro. R. A. Skelton). Amsterdam, 1968.

Osgood, Charles G. *The Classical Mythology of Milton's English Poems*. New York, 1964.

Osmaston, Francis P. B. *The Art and Genius of Tintoret*, 2 vols. London, 1915.

Otten, Charlotte F. " 'My Native Element': Milton's Paradise and English Gardens," *MS* 5 (1973), 249-67.

Ovid. *Metamorphoses Englished, Mythologized, and Represented in Figures* (trans. George Sandys, ed. Karl K. Hulley and Stanley T. Vandersall). Lincoln, Neb., 1970.

Owen, Douglas D. R. *The Vision of Hell: Infernal Journeys in Medieval French Literature*. Edinburgh, 1970.

Pächt, Otto, and J. J. G. Alexander. *Illuminated Manuscripts in the Bodleian Library, Oxford*. Oxford, 1966.

———, C. R. Dodwell, and Francis Wormald. *The St. Albans Psalter*. London, 1960.

Palme, Per. *Triumph of Peace, A Study of the Whitehall Banqueting House*. Stockholm, 1956.

Panofsky, Dora and Erwin. *Pandora's Box: The Changing Aspects of a Mythical Symbol*. New York, 1962.

Panofsky, Erwin. *The Life and Art of Albrecht Dürer*, Princeton, 1971.

Panofsky, Erwin. "Comments on Art and Reformation," in *Symbols in Transformation: Iconographic Themes at the Time of the Reformation; An Exhibition of Prints in Memory of Erwin Panofsky* (ed. Craig Harbison), pp. 9-14.

———. *Early Netherlandish Painting*, 2 vols. Cambridge, Mass., 1966.

———. *Galileo as a Critic of the Arts*. The Hague, 1954.

———. *Hercules am Scheidewege*. Leipzig, 1930.

———. "Jan van Eyck's *Arnolfini* Portrait." *Burlington Magazine* 64 (1934), 117-27.

———. *Meaning in the Visual Arts*. New York, 1955.

———. *Renaissance and Renascences in Western Art*. New York, 1972.

———. *Studies in Iconology*. New York, 1939.

———. *Tomb Sculpture: Four Lectures on its Changing Aspects from Ancient Egypt to Bernini* (ed. H. W. Janson). New York, 1964.

Pantini, Romualdo. *San Gimignano e Certaldo*. Bergamo, 1904.

Papini, Giovanni. *Il Diavolo*. Florence, 1954.

Parish, John E. "Standing Prostrate: The Paradox in *Paradise Lost*, x, 1099, and xi, 1." *EM* 15 (1964), 89-101.

Parker, William Riley. *Milton: A Biography*, 2 vols. London, 1968.

Parkinson, John. *Paradisi in Sole: Paradisus Terrestris*. London, 1629.

Parks, George B. *The English Traveler to Italy*. Stanford, Cal. [1954].

Patch, Howard R. *The Goddess Fortuna in Medieval Literature*. Cambridge, Mass., 1927.

———. *The Other World, According to Descriptions in Medieval Literature*. Cambridge, Mass., 1950.

Patrick, John M. "Milton, Phineas Fletcher, Spenser, and Ovid—Sin at Hell's Gates." *N&Q* 201 (1956), 384-86.

Patrides, C. A., ed. *Approaches to "Paradise Lost": The York Tercentenary Lectures*, London, 1968.

———. *The Grand Design of God*. London, 1972.

———. "John Milton: The Poet Who Gave us Paradise." *The Observer* (Color Supplement) Aug. 13, 1967, pp. 3-9.

———. *Milton and the Christian Tradition*. Oxford, 1966.

———. "Milton and His Contemporaries on the Chains of Satan." *MLN* 73 (1958), 257-60.

———. "Renaissance Interpretations of Jacob's Ladder." *Theologische Zeitschrift* 18 (1962), 411-18.

———. "Renaissance Thought on the Celestial Hierarchy: The Decline of a Tradition." *JHI* 20 (1959), 155-66.

———. "Renaissance and Modern Views on Hell." *HTR* 57 (1964), 217-36.

———. "Renaissance Views on the Unconfused Orders Angellick." *JHI* 23 (1962), 265-67.

———. "The Tree of Knowledge in the Christian Tradition." *SN* 34 (1962), 239-42.

———, ed. *Milton's Epic Poetry: Essays on "Paradise Lost" and "Paradise Regained."* Harmondsworth, 1967.

Pearce, Donald R. "The Style of Milton's Epic" in *Milton: Modern Essays* (ed. Arthur E. Barker), pp. 368-85.

Pecheux, Mother Mary Christopher, O.S.U. "The Concept of the Second Eve in *Paradise Lost*." *PMLA* 75 (1960), 359-66.

———. "The Conclusion of Book vi of *Paradise Lost*." *SEL* 3 (1963), 109-17.

Penrose, Boies. *Urbane Travelers 1591-1635*. Philadelphia, 1942.

Percival-Kaye, George. "The Forbidden Fruit." *N&Q* 183 (1942), 323.

Perry, Mary P. "On the Psychostasis in Christian Art." *Burlington Magazine* 22 (1912-13), 94-105, 208-18.

Peter, John. *A Critique of "Paradise Lost."* New York, 1960.

Petrucci, Alfredo. *Panorama della incisione italiana; il cinquecento*. Rome, n.d.

Puyvelde, *see* Van Puyvelde.

Pevsner, Nikolaus. *Cambridgeshire: The Buildings of England*. Harmondsworth, 1970.

———. *The Englishness of English Art*. Harmondsworth, 1964.

Philip, Lotte Brand. *The Ghent Altarpiece and the Art of Jan van Eyck*. Princeton, 1971.

Phillipps, E. March. *The Gardens of Italy* (ed. Arthur T. Bolton). London, 1919.

Phillips, John. *The Reformation of Images: Destruction of Art in England, 1535-1665*. Berkeley, Cal., 1975.

Phillips, Norma. "Milton's Limbo of Vanity and Dante's Vestibule." *ELN* 3 (1966), 177-82.

Philostratus. *Imagines* (ed. Arthur Fairbanks). New York, 1931.

Pigler, A. *Barockthemen*, 2 vols. Budapest and Berlin, 1956.

Piper, David. *Catalogue of Seventeenth-Century Portraits in the National Portrait Gallery 1625-1714*. Cambridge, 1963.

———. *The English Face*. n.p. [London?], 1957.

———. "The Portraits of John Milton." *Christ's College Magazine* 60 (1970), 156-61.

Plancy, *see* Collin de Plancy.

Pointon, Marcia R. *Milton and English Art*. Toronto, 1970.

Pollard, A. W. "The Transference of Woodcuts in the Fifteenth and Sixteenth Centuries." *Bibliographica* 2 (1896), 343-68.

Pope, Elizabeth M. *"Paradise Regained": The Tradition and the Poem*. Baltimore, 1947.

Pope-Hennessey, Sir John. *Catalogue of Italian Sculpture in the Victoria and Albert Museum*, 3 vols. London, 1964.

Porter, Arthur K. *Medieval Architecture: Its Origins and Development*, 2 vols. New York, 1969.

Portoghesi, Paolo. *Roma Barocca; The History of an Architectonic Culture* (trans. Barbara Luigia La Penta). Cambridge, Mass., 1970.

———. *Rome of the Renaissance* (trans. Pearl Sanders). London, 1972.

Prampolini, Giacomo. *L'annunciazione nei pittori primitivi Italiani*. Milan, n.d.

Praz, Mario. "Baroque in England." *MP* 61 (1964), 169-79.

———. "The Metamorphoses of Satan" in *The Romantic Agony* (trans. Angus Davidson). London, 1933, pp. 51-92.

———. "Milton and Poussin" in *Seventeenth-Century Studies Presented to Sir Herbert Grierson*, Oxford, 1938, pp. 192-210.

———. *On Neoclassicism* (trans. Angus Davidson). Evanston, 1969.

———. *Studies in Seventeenth-Century Imagery*, Rome, 1964.

Prince, F. T. "On the Last Two Books of *PL*," in *Milton's Epic Poetry* (ed. C. A. Patrides), pp. 233-48.

Prior, E. S. "The Sculpture of Alabaster Tables," in *Illustrated Catalogue of the Exhibition of English Medieval Alabaster Work*. London, 1913.

———, and A. Gardner. *An Account of Medieval Figure-Sculpture in England*. Cambridge, 1912.

Puppi, Lionello. "The Villa Garden of the Veneto from the Fifteenth to the Eighteenth Century," in *The Italian Garden* (ed. David R. Coffin), pp. 83-114.

Quistorp, Heinrich. *Calvin's Doctrine of the Last Things*. Richmond, Va., 1955.

Qwarnström, Gunnar. *The Enchanted Palace: Some Structural Aspects of "Paradise Lost."* Stockholm, 1967.

Raftery, Joseph. *Christian Art in Ancient Ireland*. Dublin, 1941.

Ragusa, Isa, and Rosalie B. Green. *Meditations on the Life of Christ: An Illustrated Manuscript of the Fourteenth Century*. Princeton, 1961.

Rajan, Balachandra. *The Lofty Rhyme: A Study of Milton's Major Poetry*. Coral Gables, Fla., 1970.

Randall, Lilian M. C. *Images in the Margins of Gothic Manuscripts*. Berkeley, 1966.

Raphael. *The Complete Work of Raphael*. New York, 1969.

Raw, Barbara. *The Story of the Fall of Man and of the Angels in Junius XI and the Relationship of the Manuscript Illustrations to the Text*, unpublished University of London thesis, 1953.

Raymond, John. *Il Mercurio Italico*. London, 1648.

Read, Sir Edward. *Icon and Idea*. New York, 1972.

Réau, Louis. *Iconographie de l'art chrétien*, 3 vols. in 6. Paris, 1955-59.

Redig De Campos, D. *Il Giudizio Universale di Michelangelo*. Milan, 1964.

Reinach, Salomon. *Répertoire de la statuaire grecque et romaine*, 6 vols. in 7. Paris, 1904-30.

Relazione del Solenne Funerale e Catafalco fatto dalli Pedri della Compagnia di Giesu. Rome, 1639.

Reutersward, Patrik. "What Color is Divine Light" in *Light* (eds. Hess and Ashbery), pp. 101-24.

Reville, Albert. *The Devil, His Original Greatness and Decadence*. London, 1871.

Ricci, Corrado, and Guido Zucchini. *Guida di Bologna*. Bologna, 1968.

Rice, D. Talbot. *English Art 871-1100*. Oxford, 1952.

Rickert, Margaret. *Painting in Britain: The Middle Ages*. London [c. 1954].

Ricks, Christopher. *Milton's Grand Style*. Oxford, 1963.

Riggs, William G. *The Christian Poet in "Paradise Lost."* Berkeley, 1972.

Ringbom, Lars-Ivar. *Paradisus Terrestris, Myt, Bild och Verklighet*. Helsingfors, 1958.

Ringling Museum of Art. *Salvator Rosa: His Etchings and Engravings After His Work*. Sarasota, Fla., 1971.

Ripa, Cesare. *Iconologia*. Padua, 1618.

Robb, David N. "The Iconography of the Annunciation in the Fourteenth and Fifteenth Centuries." *Art Bulletin* 18 (1936), 480-526.

Robertson, Alexander. *The Bible of St. Mark: St. Mark's Church*. London, 1898.

Robins, Harry F. *If This Be Heresy; A Study of Milton and Origin*. Urbana, Ill., 1963.

———. "Milton's Golden Chain." *MLN* 69 (1954), 76.

———. "Satan's Journey: Direction in *Paradise Lost*." *JEGP* 60 (1961), 699-711.

Röhrich, Lutz. *Adam und Eva: Das erste Menschenpaar in Volkskunst und Volksdichtung*. Stuttgart, 1968.

Rooses, Max. *L'Oeuvre de P. P. Rubens*. Anvers, 1890.

Rosenau, Helen. *The Ideal City in Its Architectural Evolution*. London, 1959.

Rosenberg, Alfons. *Michael und der Drache: Urgestalten von Licht und Finsternis*. Freiburg im Breisgau, 1956.

Rosenblatt, Jason P. "Celestial Entertainment in Eden: Book v of *Paradise Lost.*" *HTR* 62 (1969), pp. 411-27.

———. "Structural Unity and Temporal Concordance: The War in Heaven in *Paradise Lost,*" *PMLA* 87 (1972), 31-41.

Rossi, Ferdinando. *Mosaics: A Study of Their History and Techniques.* New York, 1970.

Rostvig, Maren-Sofie. "Images of Perfection" in *Seventeenth-Century Imagery* (ed. Earl Miner), pp. 1-24.

Roth, Cecil, ed. *Jewish Art: An Illustrated History.* New York, 1961.

Roth, Leon. "Hebraists and Non-Hebraists of the Seventeenth Century." *Journal of Semitic Studies* 6 (1961), 204-21.

Rothenstein, Sir John. *An Introduction to English Painting.* London, 1933.

Rotermund, Hans-Martin. *Rembrandt's Drawings and Etchings for the Bible.* Philadelphia, 1969.

Rougemont, Denis de. *The Devil's Share.* New York, 1952.

Rowse, Alfred L. "The Milton Country" in *The English Past, Evocations of Persons and Places.* New York, 1952, pp. 85-112.

Royal Commission on the Ancient and Historical Monuments and Constructions of England. *An Inventory of the Historical Monuments in the City of Cambridge.* London, 1959.

———. *An Inventory of the Historical Monuments in the City of Oxford.* London, 1939.

Rudrum, Alan, ed. *Milton: (Modern Judgments).* London, 1968.

Rudwin, Maximilian. *The Devil in Legend and Literature.* Chicago, 1931.

Ruskin, John. *Works,* vols. 4, 10, and 11 (ed. E. T. Cook and Alexander Wedderburn). London, 1903-4.

Ruutz-Rees, C. "Flower Garlands of the Poets, Milton, Shakespeare, Spenser, Marot, Sannazaro," in *Mélanges offerts à M. Abel Lefranc.* Paris, 1936, pp. 75-90.

Ryken, Leland. *The Apocalyptic Vision in "Paradise Lost."* Ithaca, N.Y., 1970.

Rykwert, Joseph. *On Adam's House in Paradise: The Idea of the Primitive Hut in Architectural History.* New York, 1972.

John Rylands Library. *The Beginnings of Printed Book Illustration.* Manchester, 1933.

———. *Descriptive Catalogues of Printed Book Illustrations of the Fifteenth Century.* Manchester, 1933.

S., W. W. "The Forbidden Fruit." *N&Q* 183 (1942), 226-7.

Saint Albans Psalter, *see* Pächt.

Salerno, Luigi. "Seventeenth-Century English Literature on Painting." *JWCI* 14 (1951), 234-58.

Samek Ludovici, Sergio. *Illustrazione del libro e incisione in Lombardia nel '400 e '500.* Modena, 1960.

Samuel, Irene. *Dante and Milton: The 'Commedia' and 'Paradise Lost.'* Ithaca, N.Y., 1966.

Sander, Max. *Le Livre à figures italien depuis 1467 jusqu'à 1530,* 6 vols. plus supplement. Milan, 1942-69.

Sandys, George. *Ovid's Metamorphoses.* London, 1640.

———. *A Relation of a Journey.* London, 1632.

Sandys, John E. *A History of Classical Scholarship,* 3 vols. New York, 1967.

Santoro, Caterina. *I Tesori della Trivulziana: La storia del libro dal secolo VIII al secolo XVIII.* Milan, 1962.

Sasek, Lawrence A. "The Drama of *Paradise Lost,* Books XI and XII," in *Milton: Modern Essays in Criticism* (ed. Arthur E. Barker), pp. 342-55.

Saunders, O. Elfrida. *English Illumination,* 2 vols. Florence and New York, 1928.

———. *A History of English Art in the Middle Ages.* Oxford, 1932.

Saxl, Fritz. *English Sculptures of the Twelfth Century.* London, 1954.

———. *A Heritage of Images: A Selection of Lectures* (eds. Hugh Honour and John Fleming). Harmondsworth, 1970.

———. "A Spiritual Encyclopedia of the Later Middle Ages." *JWCI* 5 (1942), 82-134.

———, and Rudolf Wittkower. *British Art and the Mediterranean.* Oxford, 1948.

Sayar. "The Forbidden Fruit." *N&Q* 183 (1942), 383.

Schaar, Claes. "Vida, Ramsay, and Milton's Bees." *ES* 46 (1965), 417-18.

Schade, Herbert. *Dämonen und Monstren; Gestaltungen des Bösen in der Kunst des frühen Mittelalters.* Regensburg, 1962.

Schaefer, Lucie. "Die Illustrationen zu den Handschriften der Christine de Pizan." *Marburger Jahrbuch für Kunstwissenschaft* 10 (1959), 119-208.

Schanzer, Ernest. "Milton's Hell Revisited." *UTQ* 24 (1955), 136-45.

Schiller, Gertrud. *Ikonographie der Christlichen Kunst,* 3 vols. Gütersloh, 1966-71.

———. *Iconography of Christian Art (Ikonographie der Christlichen Kunst,* vols. I and II, trans. Janet Seligman). Greenwich, Conn., 1971-72.

Schmidt, Ph. *Die Illustration der Lutherbibel 1522-1700.* Basel, 1962.

Schottmüller, Frida. *Fra Angelico da Fiesole.* Stuttgart and Leipzig [c. 1911].

Schultz, Howard. "A Fairer Paradise?" *ELH* 32 (1965), 275-302.

———. "Satan's Serenade." *PQ* 27 (1948), 17-26.

Scott-Giles, C. W. *Sidney Sussex College. A Short History.* Cambridge, 1951.

Scudder, Harold H. "Satan's Artillery." *N&Q* 195 (1950), 334-37.

Scuricini Greco, Maria Luisa. *Miniature Riccardiane.* Florence, 1958.

Sells, A. Lytton. *The Paradise of Travellers: The Italian Influence on Englishmen in the Seventeenth Century.* London, 1964.

Seznec, Jean. *The Survival of the Pagan Gods; The Mythological Tradition and its Place in Renaissance Humanism and Art.* New York, 1953.

———. "Temptation of St. Anthony in Art." *Magazine of Art* 40 (1947), 87-93.

Shapiro, Meyer. "Cain's Jaw-Bone That Did the First Murder." *Art Bulletin* 24 (1942), 205-12.

———. "'Muscipula Diaboli,' The Symbolism of the Mérode Altarpiece," in *Renaissance Art* (ed. Creighton Gilbert), pp. 21-42.

Shawcross, John T. "The First Illustrators of *PL.*" *MQ* 9 (1975), 43-46.

———. "The Metaphor of Inspiration in *Paradise Lost,*" in *Th' Upright Heart and Pure* (ed. Amadeus Fiore), pp. 75-85.

———. "Paradise Lost and the Theme of Exodus." *Milton Studies* 2 (1970), 3-26.

———, ed. *Milton: The Critical Heritage.* London, 1970.

———, ed. *Milton 1732-1801: The Critical Heritage.* London, 1972.

Shearman, John. *Mannerism.* Harmondsworth, 1969.

Shepherd, John C., and Jellicoe, G. A. *Italian Gardens of the Renaissance.* New York, 1966.

Shumaker, Wayne. *Unpremeditated Verse: Feeling and Perception in "Paradise Lost."* Princeton, 1967.

Simon, Ulrich. *Heaven in the Christian Tradition*. New York, 1958.

Sims, James H. *The Bible in Milton's Epics*. Gainesville, Fla., 1962.

Slater, Eliot. "The Colour Imagery of Poets." *Schweizer Archiv für Neurologie, Neurochirurgie und Psychiatrie* (Zurich) 91 (1963), 303-8.

Sloane, William. "Milton's Rooms at Christ's College." *N&Q* N.S. 6 (1959), 357-8.

Sluys, Felix. *Didier Barra et François de Nome, dits Monsu Desiderio*. Paris, 1961.

Smith, Earl Baldwin. *Architectural Symbolism of Imperial Rome and the Middle Ages*. Princeton, 1956.

Smith, Rebecca W. "The Source of Milton's Pandaemonium." *MP* 29 (1931), 187-98.

The Society of Antiquaries. *Illustrated Catalogue of the Exhibition of English Medieval Alabaster Work*. London, 1913.

Solier, René de. *L'Art Fantastique*. Paris, 1961.

Soltész, Zoltánné. *A Magyarországi Könyvdíszítés A XVI Században*. Budapest, 1961.

Spencer, Jeffry B. *Heroic Nature: Ideal Landscape in English Poetry from Marvell to Thompson*. Evanston, Ill., 1973.

Squires, V. P. "Milton's Treatment of Nature." *MLN* 9 (1894), 454-74.

Stanford, W. B., ed. *The Odyssey of Homer*, 2 vols. London, 1950.

Starnes, D. T. "Gehenna and Tophet." *N&Q* 192 (1947), 369-70.

——. "Tityos and Satan." *N&Q* 197 (1952), 379-80.

Steadman, John M. "The Bee-Simile in Homer and Milton." *N&Q* 201 (1956), 101-2.

——. "The Devil and Pharaoh's Chivalry." *MLN* 75 (1960), 197-201.

——. "*Ethos* and *Dianoia*: Character and Rhetoric in *Paradise Lost*," in *Language and Style in Milton* (ed. Emma and Shawcross), pp. 193-232.

——. "Eve's Dream and the Conventions of Witchcraft." *JHI* 26 (1965), 567-74.

——. "Grosseteste on the Genealogy of Sin and Death." *N&Q* 204 (1959), 367-8.

——. "Iconography and Renaissance Drama." *RORD* 13-14 (1970-71), 73-122.

——. "John Collop and the Flames without Light (*Paradise Lost*, I, 62-3)." *N&Q* 200 (1955), 382-3.

——. "Leviathan and Renaissance Etymology." *JHI* 28 (1967), 575-6.

——. "Like Turbulences: The Tempest of *Paradise Regain'd* as Adversity Symbol." *MP* 59 (1961), 81-8.

——. "Meaning and Name: Some Renaissance Interpretations of Urania." *NM* 64 (1963), 209-32.

——. *Milton and the Renaissance Hero*. Oxford, 1967.

——. *Milton's Epic Characters; Image and Idol*. Chapel Hill, N.C., 1968.

——. "Milton's Giant Angels: An Additional Parallel." *MLN* 75 (1960), 551-53.

——. "Milton's Rhetoric: Satan and the 'Unjust Discourse.'" *Milton Studies* 1 (1969), pp. 67-92.

——. "Milton and Patristic Tradition: The Quality of Hell-Fire." *Anglia* 76 (1958), 116-28.

——. "Milton and St. Basil: The Genesis of Sin and Death." *MLN* 73 (1958), 83-84.

——. "Milton's Walls of Glass (Psalm 136)." *Archiv* 198 (1961), 34-37.

——. "Satan's Metamorphoses and the Heroic Convention of the Ignoble Disguise." *MLR* 52 (1957), 81-85.

——. "Sin, Echidna and the Viper's Blood." *MLR* 56 (1961), 62-66.

——. "'Sin' and the Serpent of Genesis 3: *Paradise Lost*, II, 650-53." *MP* 54 (1957), 217-20.

——. "The Suffering Servant and Milton's Heroic Norm." *HTR* 54 (1961), 29-43.

Steadman, John M. "Tantalus and the Dead Sea Apples (*Paradise Lost*, x, 547-73)." *JEGP* 64 (1965), 35-40.

―――. "Tradition and Innovation in Milton's 'Sin': The Problem of Literary Indebtedness." *PQ* 39 (1960), 93-103.

Stechow, Wolfgang. *Dutch Landscape Painting of the Seventeenth Century*. London, 1966.

―――. *See* Michigan, University of, Museum of Art.

Stein, Arnold. *Answerable Style: Essays on "Paradise Lost."* Seattle, 1967.

―――. *Heroic Knowledge: An Interpretation of "Paradise Regained" and "Samson Agonistes."* Hamden, Conn., 1965.

―――. "Milton and Metaphysical Art: An Exploration." *ELH* 16 (1949), 120-34.

Sterling, Charles. *La Nature Morte de l'antiquité à nos jours*. Paris, 1952.

―――. *Metropolitan Museum of Art: A Catalogue of French Paintings, XV-XVIII Centuries*. Cambridge, Mass., 1955.

Stewart, Stanley. *The Enclosed Garden; The Tradition and Image in Seventeenth-Century Poetry*. Madison, Wisc., 1966.

Stone, George Cameron. *A Glossary of the Construction, Decoration and Use of Arms and Armor*. Portland, Me., 1934.

Stone, Lawrence. *Sculpture in Britain: The Middle Ages*. Harmondsworth, 1972.

Stoye, John W. *English Travellers Abroad 1604-67: Their Influence in English Society and Politics*. London, 1952.

Strachan, James. *Pictures from a Mediaeval Bible*. Boston, 1961.

Strong, D. E. *Roman Imperial Sculpture*. London, 1961.

Strong, Roy. *The English Icon: Elizabethan and Jacobean Portraiture*. London, 1969.

―――. *Tudor and Jacobean Portraits*, 2 vols. London, 1969.

Summers, Joseph H. *The Muse's Method: An Introduction to "Paradise Lost."* New York, 1968.

Summerson, John. *The Classical Language of Architecture*. Cambridge, Mass., 1971.

Svendsen, Kester. "John Martin and the Expulsion Scene of *Paradise Lost*." *SEL* 1 (1961), 63-73.

―――. "Milton's Chariot of Paternal Deity," *N&Q* 193 (1948), 339.

―――. *Milton and Science*. Cambridge, Mass., 1956.

Swidler, Arlene A. "Milton's *Paradise Lost*, ii, 866-70." *Expl.* 17 (1959), item 41.

Symonds, John Addington. *Sketches in Italy*. Leipzig, 1883.

Sypher, Wylie. *Four Stages of Renaissance Style: Transformations in Art and Literature 1400-1700*. Garden City, N.Y., 1955.

Talbot, Charles W., ed. *Dürer in America: His Graphic Work*. Washington, 1971.

Tayler, Edward W. "Milton's *Samson*: The Form of Christian Tragedy." *ELR* 3 (1973), 306-21.

―――. *Nature and Art in Renaissance Literature*. New York, 1964.

Taylor, Dick, Jr. "Milton's Treatment of the Judgment and the Expulsion in *Paradise Lost*." *TSE* 10 (1960), 51-82.

―――. "The Storm Scene in *Paradise Regained*: A Reinterpretation." *UTQ* 24 (1955), 359-76.

Taylor, Francis Henry. "The Triumph of Decomposition." *Parnassus* 4 (April, 1932), 4-9, 39.

Tempesta, Antonio, des. *Sanctum Dei Evangelium Arab. Lat.* (ed. Alfred Aspland for Holbein Society). London, 1873.

Tervarent, de, Guy. *Attributs et symboles dans l'art profane, 1450-1600; dictionnaire d'un langage perdu.* Geneva, 1958.

Thomas, P. W. "Two Cultures? Court and Country under Charles I," in *The Origins of the English Civil War* (ed. Conrad Russell). London, 1973, pp. 168-93.

Thompson, Richard Lowe. *The History of the Devil: The Horned God of the West.* London, 1929.

Tietze, Hans. *Tintoretto: The Paintings and Drawings.* London, 1948.

Tillyard, E.M.W. "Causeway from Hell to the World." *SP* 38 (1941), 266-70.

———. *The Miltonic Setting, Past and Present.* New York, 1949.

———. *Milton.* London, 1956.

Titi, Filippo. *Descrizione delle pitture, sculture, e architetture esposte al pubblico in Roma,* 2 vols. Rome, 1763, facsimile ed., Florence, 1966.

Trapp, J. B. "Iconography," in *John Milton: Introductions* (ed. John Broadbent), pp. 162-85.

———. "The Iconography of the Fall of Man," in *Approaches to "Paradise Lost"* (ed. C. A. Patrides), pp. 223-65.

Trefman, Simon. "A Note on the Bridge of Chaos in *Paradise Lost* and Matthew XVI." *SCN* 20 (1963), item 204, pp. 18-19.

Trevor-Roper, Hugh. *The Plunder of the Arts in the Seventeenth Century.* London, 1970.

Trevor-Roper, Patrick. *The World Through Blunted Sight: An Inquiry into the Influence of Defective Vision on Art and Character.* London, 1970.

Tristram, Ernest W. *English Medieval Wall Painting: The Twelfth Century.* Oxford, 1944.

———. *English Medieval Wall Painting: The Thirteenth Century,* 2 vols. Oxford, 1950.

———. *English Wall Painting of the Fourteenth Century.* London, 1955.

Turner, Amy Lee. "Milton and Jansson's Sea Atlas." *Milton Quarterly* 4 (1970), 36-39.

———. "Milton and Jodocus Hondius the Elder." *Milton Newsletter* 3 (1969), 26-30.

———. *The Visual Arts in Milton's Poetry,* unpublished Rice University doctoral dissertation, 1955.

Turner, A. Richard. *The Vision of Landscape in Renaissance Italy.* Princeton, 1966.

Tuve, Rosamond. *Allegorical Imagery: Some Medieval Books and Their Posterity.* Princeton, 1966.

———. "Baroque and Mannerist Milton?" in *Essays by Rosamond Tuve: Spenser, Herbert, Milton* (ed. Thomas P. Roche, Jr.). Princeton, 1970, pp. 262-80.

Ugloff, L. "Drawings by Jacques Callot for the Temptation of Saint Anthony." *Burlington Magazine* 67 (1935), 220-24.

Underwood, Paul A. "The Fountain of Life in Manuscripts of the Gospels." *Dumbarton Oaks Papers* no. 5 (1950), 43-138.

Utrecht Psalter. *See* DeWald.

Van der Meulen, Jan. "A *Logos Creator* at Chartres and its Copy." *JWCI* 29 (1966), 82-100.

Van Doren, Mark. *The Noble Voice: A Study of Ten Great Poems.* New York, 1946, pp. 122-47.

Van Puyvelde, Leo. *Jordaens.* Paris, 1953.

Varty, Kenneth. *Reynard the Fox. A Study of the Fox in Medieval English Art.* Leicester, 1967.

Vetter, Ewald. "Necessarium Adae Peccatum." *Ruperto-Carola* 18 (1966), 144-81.

Villeneuve, Roland. *Le Diable dans l'art*. Paris, 1957.

Viswanathan, S. "Milton and Purchas' Linschoten: An Additional Source for Milton's Indian Fig-tree." *MN* [now *MQ*] 2 (1968), 43-5.

Vitzthum, Walter, and Calvesi, Maurizio. *Jacques Callot: Incisioni*. Florence, 1971.

Volkmann, Ludwig. *Iconografia Dantesca*. Leipzig, 1897.

Vondel, Joost van den. *Werken*, 11 vols. Amsterdam, 1927-40.

Von der Osten, G. "Job and Christ: The Development of a Devotional Image." *JWCI* 16 (1953), 153-58.

Waddington, Raymond B. "Appearance and Reality in Satan's Disguises." *TSLL* 4 (1962), 390-98.

Waldock, A.J.A. *"Paradise Lost" and its Critics*. Cambridge, 1964.

Walker, Daniel P. *The Decline of Hell: Seventeenth Century Discussions of Eternal Torment*. London, 1964.

Wall, J. Charles. *Devils*. London, 1904.

Warner, George F. *Queen Mary's Psalter. Miniatures and Drawings by an English Artist of the Fourteenth Century*. London, 1912.

————. *Miniatures and Borders from the Book of Hours of Bona Sforza*, London, 1894.

Warton, Joseph. *Adventurer* 101, reprinted in *Eighteenth-Century Critical Essays* (ed. Scott Elledge), Ithaca, N.Y., 1961, II, 713-17.

Waterhouse, Ellis K. *Italian Baroque Painting*. London, 1962.

————. "Tasso and the Visual Arts." *Italian Studies* 3 (1946-48), 146-62.

Wayment, Hilary. *The Windows of King's College Chapel, Cambridge*. Oxford, 1972.

Weber, F. P. *Aspects of Death and Correlated Aspects of Life in Art, Epigrams and Poetry*. New York, 1920.

Webster, T.B.L. "Personification as a Mode of Greek Thought." *JWCI* 17 (1954), 10-21.

Weiss, Roberto. *The Renaissance Discovery of Classical Antiquity*. Oxford, 1969.

Weitzmann, Kurt. *Ancient Book Illumination*. Cambridge, Mass., 1959.

————. *Aus den Bibliotheken des Athos*. Hamburg, 1963.

————. *Illustrations in Roll and Codex: A Study of the Origin and Method of Text Illustration*. Princeton, 1970.

————. "Zur Frage des Einfluss jüdischer Bilderquellen auf die Illustration des Alten Testamentes," in *Festschrift Theodor Klauser*. Münster, 1964, pp. 401-15.

Wellek, René. "The Parallelism between Literature and the Arts." *English Institute Annual (1941)*, New York, 1942, pp. 29-63.

Welsford, Enid. *The Court Masque: A Study in the Relationship between Poetry and the Revels*. Cambridge, 1927.

Wessel, Klaus, ed. *Reallexikon zur Byzantinischen Kunst*. Stuttgart, 1966–.

West, Robert H. "Elizabethan Belief in Spirits and Witchcraft," in *Studies in Shakespeare*, Miami, Fla., 1953, pp. 65-73.

————. *Milton and the Angels*. Athens, Ga., 1955.

Westwood, J. O. *Palaeographia Sacra Pictoria*. London, 1845.

Wethey, Harold E. *El Greco and His School*, 2 vols. Princeton, 1962.

————. *The Paintings of Titian*, 2 vols. London, 1969-71.

Whaler, James. "Animal Simile in Paradise Lost." *PMLA* 47 (1932), 534-53.

————. "The Compounding and Distribution of Similes in *Paradise Lost.*" *MP* 28 (1931), 313-27.

————. "Grammatical Nexus of the Miltonic Simile." *JEGP* 30 (1931), 327-34.

————. "The Miltonic Simile." *PMLA* 46 (1931), 1034-74.

Wheatley, Dennis. *The Devil and All His Works.* New York, 1971.

Whinney, Margaret. *Sculpture in Britain: 1530-1830.* London, 1964.

————, and Oliver Millar. *English Art, 1625-1714.* Oxford, 1957.

White, Christopher. *Dürer, The Artist and His Drawings.* London, 1971.

Whiting, George W. "The Golden Compasses in *Paradise Lost.*" *N&Q* 172 (1937), 294-95.

————. *Milton and This Pendant World.* Austin, Tex., 1958.

————. "Tormenting Tophet." *N&Q* 192 (1947), 225-30.

Whitney, Geoffrey. *Choice of Emblemes* (ed. Henry Green). n.p., 1866.

Whittick, Arnold. *Symbols, Signs and Their Meaning.* Newton, Mass., 1960.

Widmer, Kingsley. "The Iconography of Renunciation: The Miltonic Simile." *ELH* 25 (1958), 258-69.

Wiesel, J. M., and B. Cichy. *Rom, Veduten des 14-19 Jahrhunderts.* Stuttgart, 1959.

Wildridge, Thomas T. *The Grotesque in Church Art.* Detroit, Michigan, 1969.

Williams, Arnold. *The Common Expositor: An Account of the Commentaries on Genesis, 1527-1633.* Chapel Hill, N.C., 1948.

Williams, Ethel Carleton. "The Dance of Death in Painting and Sculpture in the Middle Ages." *Journal of the British Archaeological Association*, 3rd ser., 1 (1937), 229-57.

————. "Mural Paintings of the Three Living and the Three Dead in England." *Journal of the British Archaeological Association*, 3rd ser., 7 (1942), 31-40.

Williams, Phyllis L. "Two Roman Reliefs in Renaissance Disguise." *JWCI* 4 (1941), 47-66.

Wind, Edgar. *Pagan Mysteries in the Renaissance.* New York, 1968.

Winkelmann-Rhein, Gertraude. *Paintings and Drawings of Jan "Flower" Bruegel.* New York, 1969.

Wittkower, Rudolf. "Chance, Time, and Virtue." *JWCI* 1 (1937-38), 313-21.

————. "Inigo Jones—Puritanissimo Fiero." *Burlington Magazine* 90 (1948), 50-51.

————. "Marvels of the East: A Study in the History of Monsters." *JWCI* 5 (1942), 159-97.

Wittreich, Joseph Anthony, Jr., ed. *The Romantics on Milton: Formal Essays and Critical Asides.* Cleveland, Ohio, 1970.

Witzleben, Elisabeth von. *Stained Glass in French Cathedrals.* New York, 1968.

Wolf, Edwin, II. *A Descriptive Catalogue of the John Frederick Lewis Collection of European Manuscripts in the Free Library of Philadelphia.* Philadelphia, 1937.

Wolfe, Don M. *Milton and His England.* Princeton, 1971.

Wölfflin, Heinrich. *The Art of Albrecht Dürer* (trans. Alastair and Heide Grieve). London, 1971.

————. *Classic Art: An Introduction to the Italian Renaissance* (trans. Peter and Linda Murray). New York, 1968.

Worringer, Wilhelm. *Die Altdeutsche Buchillustration.* Munich, 1912.

Wrangel, C. de (Preface). *Choix d'incunables illustrés de la Bibliothèque Bodmer.* Zurich, 1954.

Wundram, Manfred. *Donatello und Nanni di Banco*. Berlin, 1969.

Yates, Frances A. "Paolo Sarpi's 'History of the Council of Trent.'" *JWCI* 7 (1944), 123-43.

Zarnecki, George. *English Romanesque Sculpture, 1066-1140*. London, 1951.

———. *Later English Romanesque Sculpture, 1140-1210*. London, 1953.

Zerner, Henri. *The School of Fontainebleau: Etchings and Engravings*. London, 1969.

Index

GENERAL

Individuals quoted or cited within the text are listed by page reference to the text, without reference to pertinent footnote, but where such citations are restricted to a footnote, the index indicates page and footnote. Anthologists and editors are not indexed unless directly quoted in their editorial capacity.

Abdiel, 74
Abel, 294, 300-4, fig. 220
Abraham, 149, 169, 170, 173, 182, 193
acanthus, 243, 248
accommodation, 10, 36, 43, 125, 189, 190, 201, 347
Achilles, 187
Acts, Book of, 303
Adam: appearance of, 266-72; creation of, 150n, 259-61; fall of, 286-91; and garland for Eve, 287-88; hair of, 268-72; instructed by Michael, 297-308; instructed by Raphael, 153, 179-80; nakedness of, 262-66, 288, 289; postlapsarian, 267, 291-97; taken into Garden, 261; weeping, 293, 309, 313, 314; *see also* Adam and Eve
Adam and Eve: creation of, 259-61; expulsion of, 163, 293, 308-15; fall of, 286-91; holding hands, 281-85, 291, 309, 312, 314; judgment of, 163; love of, 243, 260, 278-85, 291-92; postlapsarian, 298-99; reconciliation between, 294, 295; repentance of, 294; tending the Garden, 239-41; transference of blame, 293
Adams, Robert M., 5, 281n
Adams, Thomas, 130n
Adamson, J. H., 157n
Addison, Joseph, 9, 75, 174, 211
adversity, trial by, 339-41
Aelfric Manuscript, 57, 61, 67, 75, 140, 156, 260n, fig. 42
Aelst, Coecke van, 131n
Aera sub gratia, 332
Aera sub lege, 332
agate, *see* stones, precious
Age of Reason, 10, 12, 174
agitation, 189

alabaster, 237, 242, 324; *see also* Garden of Eden: mountains
Albani, Francesco, 181n
Alberti, 87
Albumaser, 55n
Alciati, 187
Alcina, 333n
Alcuin Bible, 312
Aldegrave, 283
Algardi, Alessandro, 50
Aliprandi, *Temptation of St. Anthony*, 339, fig. 254
Allen, Don Cameron, 6, 14, 73n, 101n, 130n, 171n, 174n, 180n, 186, 190n, 198, 203, 275n
alleys, 222, 232-34
"alleys brown," 234
"alleys green," 234
Allori, Alessandro, 70
All Souls, Oxford, 216
Alpers, Svetlana, 268n
Alpine landscapes, 238
Alsloot, D. Van, 178
Altdorfer, Albrecht, *Fall of Man*, 219n, 274, 290, 298, 304, fig. 206
Altdorfer, Erhard, 45n
Alton Towers Triptych, 253
Alunno, *see* Nicolò di Liberatore
amarant, 185-86, 205
ambition, 189
Ambra, 16
Amicitia, 247
Amor, 282n
amorini, 177
Anderson, M. D., 68, 93n, 103, 114n, 127n, 140n, 143, 149n, 158n, 159n, 160n, 161n, 170, 175n, 180n, 182n, 187n, 190n, 191n, 194n, 245n, 259n, 298n, 300n, 303n, 307n

Andrea da Firenze, *Christ in Limbo*, 68, 75, 139, 141, 236, fig. 59
Andrea del Minga, *The Expulsion of Adam and Eve*, 104, 274, 311, 313, fig. 205
Andrea Del Sarto, 24, 50
Andreani, Andrea, 76, 156
Andrew, apostle, 321
Andromeda, 93n 4
Angelico, Fra: *Last Judgment*, 127, 139, 193, 197, fig. 100; detail of Heaven, 193, 194, 199, fig. 137; other references, 86, 185, 227, 311, 345
angel roofs, English, 170
angels: ages of, 176-77; apathetic, 53-54; blue, 66; as cavalry, 47-49; carrying deity, 184; clothing of, 45, 177; colors of, 66, 171, 179; diet of, 181-83; at expulsion from Garden, 308-14; "feathered mail" of, 180; games of, 179; globes of, 183-84, 193, 212; guardian, 87, 175-79, 348; guarding Garden, 179, 313; hair arrangement of, 177, 185-87, 348; hierarchy of, 183; at Last Judgment, 164; movements of, 171-75; music and dance of, 187-88; seated, 185, 348; sex life of, 181-83; weeping, 105, 181; wings of, 169-71; *see also* armor, ordnance, War in Heaven
anger, 54
animals: creation of, 12, 161-62; postlapsarian, 296-97; with Savior, 333-34
Anne of Denmark, 192
Annunciation, 100, 169, 171, 175
Anonymous engraving, Kitto Bible: *Christ and Satan* (1563), 331, fig. 241; *Paradise of the Senses*, 241, fig. 170
Anonymous ivory carving, *Cain and Abel*, 303, fig. 220
Anonymous painted utensil, *Truth the Daughter of Time*, 121, fig. 94
Anonymous painting, *The Fall*, 104, fig. 87
Anonymous stained glass, *Christ and Satan*, 112, 320, fig. 232
Anonymous tapestries, *see* Medici Tapestries
Anonymous wax models, *The Blessed* and *the Damned*, 71, fig. 72
Antaura, 121n
Anthony Abbot, St., 48, 70, 77, 91, 97, 98, 120n, 330, 333n, 336, 339n, 340-41
Antichrist, 77
Apakas, 71, 137
Apennines, 16
Apocalypse, 47, 61n, 196
Apollo, 276
apotheosis, 65, 111, 212-17
apple, 245, 251
aqueducts, 325
Arcadianism, 220, 225, 227, 230

arch, triumphal, 325
archeology, 31-33, 327
Archimago, 343n
architecture: 133-37, 153n, 157n, 194; ancient, 323-29; Baroque, 196; Gothic, 37, 324-29; of Heaven, 133, 194-98; of Hell, 128, 133-38, 140-41, 196; Renaissance, 196; *see also* Pandaemonium, Rome: St. Peter's Church
Argenton-Château, 67
Ariosto, 49, 211, 215n, 227
Ark, 306-8
Armida, 333n
armor, 11, 43-49, 63, 179-81, 349
Armstrong, John, 103n
Arpino, Cavaliere di, 310, 313
arrow, 116
art and literature: 33, 44, 51, 54-56, 65, 71, 79, 83-91, 98, 109, 115, 116, 124, 125, 142, 164, 187, 211n, 226, 248, 264, 275, 286, 290-95, 344; *see also* Milton compared with artists
Arthos, John, 19, 24n, 26n, 29n
Arthurian romances, 335
artillery, demonic, 48-49, 55
Arundel, Earl of, 26, 268
asceticism, 263, 281; *see also* prudery
Ashley, Maurice, 46n, 272n
Ashmole, Elias, 58n
Asmodeus, 179
Aspland, A., 120n
asses' ears, 62
Assyria, 322
astronomy, 55
As You Like It, 219
Athena, 322
Athenae Atticae, 324
Athens, 323-25
Atlantis, 268n
Augsburg Cathedral, 107
Augustine, St., 65, 194-95, fig. 140
Aulnay, 67
avarice, 122, 126

Babel, 135, 153, 214
Babylon, 323
Bacchus, 299
Bach, Eugene, 100n
Baciccia, 186, 199, 209, 215
Baglione, Giovanni, 28n
Baker, C. H. Collins, 5n, 119
Baker, Donald C., 75n
Baldinucci, 250
Baldovinetti, Alesso, 232
Baldung Grien: 118n, 312n; *Adam and Eve* (1511), 267, 292, fig. 191; *Adam and Eve* (1519), 267, 292, fig. 192

Baldwin, Edward C., 106, 243n, 313n

Baltrusaitis, Jurgis, 69n, 138n

Banks, Theodore, 14, 94n, 98

banquet, false, 333-39

Banqueting House, Whitehall, 22, 213, 216

banyan tree, 243

Baouit, Egypt, 66

baptismal font, 243-44

Baptist, J., engraver, 303n

Baptistry mosaics, *see* Florence, Baptistry

Barb, A. A., 121n

Barberini, Antonio, 29n

Barberini, Francesco, 28, 96, 202, 212, 215

Barberini, Palazzo, 96, 97, 212, 225

Barberini Garden, 222

Barfucci, Enrico, 24n

Bargellini, Piero, 25n, 30n

Barker, Arthur E., 9n, 75n

Barlow, Francis, 119

Baroque, 6, 17-18, 134-35, 172, 174, 182, 200, 205, 209-10, 215, 218n, 237n, 241, 279, 320n, 336, 348

Barri, Giacomo, 28n

Barron, John, 44n

Bartoli, Taddeo di, 86, 112, 118n

Bartolomeo, Fra, 298

Bartolomeo di Giovanni, 336

bas relief in Cambridge, 84

Bassano, Jacopo, 220, 241n, 274

Bassano, Leandro, 74, 165

Bassus, Junius, Sarcophagus of, 66, 102, 262, 269, 293, fig. 54

Bateman, Stephen, 152n, 158n

Bates, Ernest S., 27n

baths, Roman, 325

Batoni, Pompeo, 186n

Battisti, Eugenio, 38, 225, 236n, 239n

Battle of Angels, *see* War in Heaven

bat wings, 62

Bayerische Staatsbibliothek MS 8201, *see* Frau Welt

Bazin, Germain, 209, 213n, 233n, 338n

beatitude, 189

beauty, conceptions of: 33, 262-65, 270, 276, 291; Milton's conception of, 273-75

Beccafumi, Domenico: 85-86, 132; *Michael and the Fallen Angels*, 54, 80, 83, 84, 85, 90, 129, 131, 132, 179, figs. 29, 30; and Milton, 83-86

Beckwith, John, 157n, 201

Bede, Venerable, 103

Bedford Book of Hours, *Story of Adam and Eve*, 236, 241, 244, 259, 261, 274, 311, fig. 156

Beelzebub, 56, 80, 86, 88

bees, *see* devils, analogies to insects

Beethoven, 15n

Beham, H. S., 289n, 292n

Belial, 52, 56, 86, 88

Bellini, Giovanni, 219

Bembo, Pietro, 220

Benevento Cathedral, 77

Benlowes, Edward, illus. *The Soul Fights Temptation*, 119, fig. 91

Benozzo Gozzoli, 152

Berchorius, 277

Berefelt, Gunnar, 169n, 182-83

Berenson, Bernard, 7, 39, 62n, 142n, 143n, 150, 199, 210-11, 220-21, 227

Bergström, Ingvar, 339n

Bernard, Saint, 69

Bernheimer, Richard, 277

Bernini, Gianlorenzo: 134, 177n, 189, 200; *St. Theresa*, 177, 200, fig. 128

Bertram, Master, 260

bestiaries, 63, 93, 242, fig. 85

Bettini, Antonio, illus. *Ladder of Salvation*, 192, fig. 136

Beza, Theodore, 105n

Biardeau, Pierre, 81

Bible, Protestant, 46, 48, 97, 107, 117, 152, 158n, 159, 175, 195n, 240, 267, 271-74, 282, 286, 289, 310, 313, figs. 6, 88, 190, 214

Bible Historiale, 57, 48n

Biblioteca di S. Marco, Venice, *see* Grimani Breviary

Bibliothèque Nationale MS lat. 873, *see* Missal of Poitiers

Bibliothèque Royale Albert Ier MS 9001, *see* Desmoulins

Binyon, Laurence, 14

Birch, Walter, 45n, 68n, 158n, 253

birds, black, 98

Biverus, 103n

Black Death, 166

Blacker, Irwin R., 132

Blake, William, 9

Bles, Herri met de, *The Inferno*, 97, 128, 131, 132, 137, 139, 140, 142, 144, fig. 101

Bles, Pseudo Met de, *The Fall*, 267, fig. 186

blessed, at Last Judgment, 165

Bloemaert, Abraham: 178, 278; *Christ and Satan*, 320, 331, 334, 344, fig. 235; *Adam and Eve, see* Saenredam, Joannes

Bloomfield, Morton, 68n, 191n

Blunt, Anthony, 29n, 143n

Boase, T.S.R., 113n, 183n, 191n, 193n, 263n, 284n

Boboli Gardens, 30, 105, 222-23, 226

Boccaccio, 276

Bodkin, Maud, 16

Bodleian Library: MS Ashmole 1511, *see* Bestiary; MS Douce 93, *see* Utrecht Book of Hours; MS Douce 134, *see* Treatise on Antichrist; MS Douce 374, *see* Tavernier; MS Junius 11, *see* Genesis B; MS Selden supra 38, *see* Enfancie de Nostre Seigneur, MS Tanner 184 Apocalypse, *see Satan Leading his Troops Out of Hell*

Boiardo, 227

Bol, Hans, 178

Bologna, Giovanni, *Siren* in *Neptune Fountain*, 121, fig. 93

Bologna, San Petronio, 312

Bonnell, John K., 100-4, 103, 119

Bonifacio di Pitati, 52n, 137, 179

Bononi, Carlo, *The Guardian Angel*, 87, 88, 178, fig. 83

Boorsch, Suzanne, 5n

Borden, Kent, 49n

Borenius, Tancred, 45n, 158n

Borghese Gardens, 30, 186, 222

Borsook, Eve, 105

Bosch, H., 46, 48, 58, 69n, 74, 97, 98, 116, 132, 136n, 238, 296, 299, 308n, 337, 340; *Hell*, 70, 74, 86, 90, 118, 128, 131, 132, 136, 138, 144, fig. 68; and Milton, 297, 308n

boschetti, 222

Bosio, Antonio, 27, 155n, 157n, 182, 235

Botticelli: 112, 182, 186, 230, 253; *Primavera*, 87, 230, fig. 147; *Christ and Satan*, 331, 341, 343, 346, figs. 246, 247; and Milton, 230

Botticini, 185

Bottrall, Margaret, 177n, 210, 237n

bough of fruit, 288

Bourguet, Pierre du, 155n, 157n, 170n, 190n, 276

Bouts, Dirk, 97

Bovini, Giuseppe, 235n

bowers, 225, 233

Bowra, Cecil N., 94n

Braham, Allan, 143n

Brailes, W. de, 130, 141, 283

Bramantino, 237

Brantzius, Johannes illus., *The Devil and the Invention of Gunpowder*, 49, fig. 14

Braunfels, Wolfgang, 159n, 182n

Bray, Salomon de, 196n

B[rech], J[oseph], 336n

Brentwood, John, 183

Breviary of St. Louis, 58

Bridaham, Luther B., 69n, 99n, 121n

bridge, from Hell to earth, 143-45

Bridgeman, 236n

Bridge of Dread, 143

Brieger, Peter, 180n, 261n, 300n

Brill, 238

Brion, Marcel, 69n

British art, 68, 140

British Library: add. MS 11639 Bible and Prayer Book, *see The Fall*; add. MS 18850, *see* Bedford Book of Hours; add. MS 27695, *see* Treatise on the Seven Vices; add. MS 34294 Book of Hours, *see Michael and the Expulsion of the Rebel Angels*; add. MS 47682, *see* Holkham Bible; MS 2 B VII, *see* Queen Mary's Psalter; MS Cotton Claudius B IV, *see* Aelfric MS

Broadbent, J. B., 36, 85n, 94n, 98n, 104, 115, 126, 135, 136n, 174n, 180n, 221n, 224n

Bronzino, Agnolo: 70, 103n, 292n; *Allegory*, 121, figs. 95, 96

Brooke-Rose, Christine, 14n

Brosamer, Hans, *Adam and Eve*, 289, 310, 313, fig. 214

Broun, F.J.P., 307

Brown, Capability, 224

Brown, Eleanor G., 15

Bruegel, Jan the Elder, 231, 240

Bruegel, Peter the Elder: 53n, 56, 97, 116, 340; *Fall of the Rebel Angels*, 46, 50, 57, 58, 68, 70, 97, 115, 142, 179, fig. 5; *Garden of Eden* (London), 237, 240, 241, 242, 245, 246, 254, fig. 158; *Garden of Eden* (Rome), 237, 241, 242, 245, 246, fig. 159; *Temptation of St. Anthony*, 340, fig. 257

Bruegel, Peter the Younger, *Orpheus in Hades*, 97, fig. 86

Brutus, 112

Bry, Theodor de, 101n, 225n

Bryan, Nina R., 300n

bubbles, 321

bubonic plague, 113

Buckingham, Duke of, 26, 213

Bunim, Miriam S., 210n

Buontalenti, 222

Burden, Dennis, 182n

Burgess, Frederick, 117n, 333n

Burke, Edmund, 75

Burkmair, Hans: 47n, 95; *The Fall*, 290, fig. 216

Burney, E. F., 108n

Burton, Robert, 35

Bush, Douglas, 4, 251

Byzantine Painter's Manual, 59, 191, 284n

Cabrol, Fernand, 246n, 277n

Cain, 294, 300-4, fig. 220

Calderini, Emma, 271n

Callot, Jacques, *The Temptation of St. Anthony*, 47n, 48-49, 70-71, 90-91, 137, 340-41, fig. 13

Calvaert, Dionisio, *The Virgin with Child and Michael*, 57, 87-88, 179, figs. 25, 26
Calvin, John, 70
Calvo, Marco Fabio, 195, 327
Camassei, Andrea, 184
Cambridge: Christ's College, 253, 272n; Holy Sepulchre Church, 170-71, 187, fig. 118; King's College Chapel, 71, 158, 170-71, 186, 244, 254, 284n, 344-45; *Angel in Feathered Mail*, 171, 180, fig. 119; *Expulsion of the Rebel Angels*, 57, 61, 83, 128, 137, 185, fig. 44; St. John's College, 253; Sidney Sussex College, 97
Camden, William, 271
camel, 102, 106
cannon, *see* artillery, demonic
Cano, Alonzo, *Vision of St. John*, 194, 195, fig. 141
Canterbury Cathedral, 114
"capitall"/ "capitoll," 137
Care, 297
Carey, John, 344
Carleton, Ambassador, 26
Caron, Antoine: 55; *see also* Leu, Thomas de
caro vilis, 114, 116
Carracci, Annibale: 269n, 332; *Temptation of St. Anthony*, 98, 341, fig. 258
Carracci, Ludovico, *The Praise of Angels*, 188, fig. 135
Cartari, 70
Cartaro, Mario, 328
Carver, P. L., 181n
cassette, 249
Cassius, Caius, 112
Castagnoli, Ferdinando, 328n
catacombs, 27, 107, 190
Cathedra Petri, 200
Catholicism, *see* Roman Catholicism
Cavalli, Gian Carlo, 55n
Cavallini, 181, 185
cavalry, angelic, 43, 47-49
Cecil, Sir Robert, 26n
Cecill, L., *The Ladder of Angels and the Fall of the Devils*, 61, 190, 192, fig. 50
cedar, 223, 243, 331
ceiling painting, *see* illusionist ceilings
Cellini, Benvenuto: *Apollo and Hyacinth*, 268, fig. 196
Cenni di Francesco, 54
centaurs, 47
Centro Internazionale di Studi Umanistice, 69n, 126n, 137n, 158n
Cerberus, 120
Ceres, 277
Cesio, 269n
Cézanne, 219

chain, golden, 190
Chaldon church, 191
Chambers, A. B., 100, 276n
Chancellor of Hell, 80, 88
Chaos, 56-57, 142, 173
Chapel of the Princes in S. Lorenzo, 204
Chapman, George, 238
Chapron, Nicholas, 161n
Charcot, J.-M., 66n
chariot: 47, 122; of Egypt, 94-95; of Son, 156-57, 190; wheels, 43
Charlemagne, 277
Charles I, King, 22, 26n, 34, 213, 284, 289n
Charlton, John, 214n
Charon, 128, 165
Chartres, 329
Chastel, André, 340n
chastity, 242
Chatfield, Judith, 222n
cherub, 98, 176-79
Chichele, Henry, 114
Chinese land-ship, 35
Christ: child, 175, 298, 341-42; in Limbo, 67; Logos, 57, 60, 66, 149, 155, 159-60; Victor, 44, 55, 57, 60, 156, and *see also* God the Son, and War in Heaven; for *PR*, *see also* Savior
Christina, Queen, 28
Christus, Petrus, 118n
2 Chronicles, 68n
Chrysostom, Saint John, 70, 120
Church, 306,
Ciardi, John, 108
Cione, Andrea di, 304
Cione, Nardo di: 75; *The Inferno* (Florence), 126, 127, 128, fig. 99
Cione, Nardo di and Orcagna, Andrea, *The Inferno* (Pisa), 74, 76, 86, 89, 112, 118, 127, 138, fig. 73; *Last Judgment*, 165, 193, fig. 115; *The Triumph of Death*, 139, 304, figs. 221, 222
Cipriani, 183n
Circe, 120
circle, 195-96
Circus Maximus, 325n
Cirillo, Albert R., 171n, 198n
cities, views of, 323-29
citron, 243
City of God, 194-98
cityscapes, *see* cities, views of
Civetta, *see* Bles, Herri met de
Civil Wars, English, 20
Clark, Evert M., 35n
Clark, Kenneth, 241, 244n, 276
Clarke, Deborah, 272
Clarke, John, 11

classics, the, 4, 6, 55
Claude, 132, 233
claws, 62, 63, 67
Clayton, Thomas, 271n
Clement, Clara Erskine, 53n, 178n, 183n
Clement of Alexandria, 186
Clements, Rex, 177n, 183n, 215n
Climacus, John, 190, 191n
cloud, 152
Cock, H., *Christ and Satan*, 331, 334, figs. 244, 245
Cockeram, 238
Cockerell, 340n
Coecke, van Aelst, 144
Coffin, David R., 30n, 236n, 328n, 329n
Cohen, Gustave, 49, 137n
Coleridge, S. T., 12, 14, 116, 161, 347
Collop, John, 130n
color, 36, 66, 171, 179, 198-205, 232-34, 273-74; *see also* vegetable gold
Comestor, Peter, 103
comet, 75
commesso, 204-5, 250; *see also* mosaics
Commonwealth and Protectorate, 20, 22
compasses, 160, 201, 348
Comus, 230n
Concilia Deorum, 6n
Coninxloo, Gillis van, 234
Conques, 126
Constantine, 157n
continental tour, 23
Cook, Walter W. S., 158n
Cooper, Samuel, 272
Cope, Jackson I., 130n, 210n, 218, 333n
Corbett, Marjorie, 58n
Corcoran, Mary Irma, 280n
cormorant, 98
Cornelisz, P., 327
Cornelius van Haarlem, 55-56
coronets, 60
corta frangetta, 271
Cortona, Pietro da: 53, 209; *The Triumph of Glory*, 97, 213, fig. 144
Coryate, 221
Cosimo I, 212, 215
cottage, 321
Council in Hell, *see* devils, council of
Counter Reformation, 114
Courtois, Pierre, 292n
Cousin, Jean, *Eva Prima Pandora*, 278, fig. 209
Cowley, 302, 303
Cozza, 215
Cranach, Lucas: *Eve*, 254, 273, 274, 289, fig. 178; *The Fall*, 104, 106, 246, 269, 273, 274, 286, 288, 290, fig. 174; *The Garden in Eden* print (1534), 107, 286, fig. 88; *Paradise*

(Vienna), 237, 238, 245, 259, 260, 267, 269, 270n, 273, 274, 282, 289, 311, 313, fig. 163; *Venus and Cupid*, 276, fig. 208; *War in Heaven*, 46, 48, 117, 269, fig. 6
Creation: 150n, 155, 159, 348; of Adam and Eve, 149, 259-61; of animals, 161; of universe, 159-62; theological understanding of, 65
Creator: 149; *see also* God the Son
Crivelli, Carlo: 52n; *Annunciation*, 100, 175, 177, fig. 124; *Pietà*, 181, fig. 131
crocus, 248-49
Croft-Murray, Edward, 213n, 214n
Cromwell, Oliver, 20-22, 272
Cross, Thomas, 116
Crossley, Fred H., 45n, 72, 121n, 171n, 187n, 284n
crown, 60, 64, 117, 177, 201
Crucifixion, 104, 113n
crystal, *see* stones, precious
Ctesiphon, 323
Cupid, 277, 306
cupidity, 306
Curry, Walter Clyde, 6n, 139, 142n, 195

Dagobert, King, 252
Daiches, David, 241
Dalton, Ormonde M., 52n, 149n, 157n, 169n, 172n, 246n, 247
Damiano da Bergamo, Fra, 96, 346
dance, 283
Dance of Death, 113-15
dancers, 305
Daniel, Book of, 52n
Daniel, Howard, 47n
Daniells, Roy, 210
Daniélou, Jean, 239n, 247n
Daniels, Edgar F., 130n
Dante, 89n, 112, 126, 127, 141, 184n, 215n, 218
Darbishire, Helen, 31n, 137
darkness, 116
dart, 116
Dati, Carlo, 24-25
Davies, Randall, 213n
Day, Lewis, 37
Death: 35, 111-19, 122, 166, 297, 299; appeal for, 304; Dance of, 113-15; Satan and, 117; weapons of, 115-17, 304
debates, between Christ and Satan, 319-20
Deceit, 119, 121-22
Defoe, Daniel, 10
Delaram, Francis, 284
Della Bella, 94
della Robbia, *see* Robbia, della
Demaray, Hannah D. 211n, 231, 251n
Demary, John G., 135n, 157n

de Metz, Peter, 247n
Demogorgon, 142
demons, *see* devils
Demus, Otto, 201n
Dennis, John, 11
descriptio rei, 17
desert, *see* wilderness
Desmoulins, Guyart, 57, 140, fig. 48
despair, 54
de Terverant, *see* Terverant, de
Deuchler Florens, 203n
Deutsch, N. M., 336
Devereux, Walter, 284n
devils: activities, 46-49, 88, 90, 96, 111, 164;
   analogies to, 92-98; deterioration of, 54, 57-
   58, 61-63, 73-77, 80-82, 85, 89, 109, 124-25,
   246; differences between, 80, 86-90; fall into
   Hell, 39, 55-64, 81-82, 214, 345-49; hateful-
   ness, 65, 67, 75-76, 79, 111-12, 118, 125-27;
   in *PR*, 337-48; *see also*: artillery, demonic;
   armor; Death; Hell; Hell Hounds; Pandemonium; Satan; Sin; War in Heaven
———, physical appearance: absurdity, 72,
   246
———, animalistic: dragons, 45-46, 52-53, 63;
   goats, 58; insects, 89, 94-98, 321, 340; serpents, 57, 66, 89, 100-10, 112, 286, 342, 346;
   toads, 98-100, 115; whale, 92
———, bodily parts: blood, 54; eyes, 73;
   feet, 71, 75; gastrocephalic, 74, 123; hair,
   60-61, 67, 75, 79, 85; polymorphic, 50, 69,
   123, 340; triprosope, 112
———, clothing: 46, 59-61, 67, 78, 85, 342
———, darkness of: 58-59, 67, 78, 89, 127
———, disguises: 96-102, 342-45
———, humanoid: 46, 50-52, 60-67, 70-72,
   77-91, 337-38, 342-46, 348
———, identifying attributes, 78, 81, 342,
   345-46
———, problems of visualizing: 65-67
———, ugly: 50, 57, 60-77, 87, 111, 124, 340-
   41, 345-46, 348
———, pretensions to deity, 64-65, 72, 109-15,
   191, 214, 246
———, psychology: character differences,
   80, 86-90; distortions, 73-77, 111; emotions,
   54, 79, 105, 111
———, social ranks, 79-80, 87-90, 96, 185, 348
———, theological understanding of, 51, 58,
   65-67, 70, 73, 86, 111
De Wald, Ernest T., 136n
dextrarum iunctio, 282, 284
Diabolus, 113
diamond, *see* stones, precious
Didron, A. N., 58, 103n, 116n, 121n, 191n,
   345n

Diekhoff, John, 15n
Diepenbeeck, Abraham van, 278
Dijk, Abraham van, 178
dishes, 254
Disney, Walt, 43
Dives, 91
divine right, paintings of, 213-17
Dodgson, Campbell, 123n
Domenechino, 87, 175, 178, 209, 269n
Donatello, 187, fig. 134
Donducci, Andrea, 95
D'Onofrio, Cesare, 28n, 222n
Douce, F., 117n
dove, 100, 153, 175
Downame, John, 339n
Downes, Kerry, 216n
Dowsing, William, 20
D. P., Christ and Satan, 331, 344, fig. 243
Dracontius, 262
dragon, 48, 67, 72, 84, 87, 89-90
Drake, Sir Francis, 271
drama, 49, 72, 100, 103, 151, 180, 320, 329n,
   343, *see also* masque
Drayton, Michael, 36n
Droeshout, John, *Michael and the Demons*,
   58, 89, 97, fig. 49
Druce, G. C., 243n
Du Bartas, Salluste, 243
Duccio, 139, 141, 178, fig. 103
Duncan, Joseph E., 128n
Dürer, Albrecht: 47, 71, 254, 263-64, 278,
   312n; *Adam*, 289, fig. 183; *Eve*, 264, 273,
   289, fig. 184; *The Fall* (from *Small Pas-
   sion*), 292, fig. 218; *The Fall* (1504), 104,
   240, 242, 264, 267, 270, 273, 274, 288, fig. 164
Dustdoor, P. E., 57n, 60n, 112n, 156, 183n
Dutch art, 35
Duthuit, G., 113n
Duvet, Jean, 46, 71, 282, fig. 211
Dvorak, Max, 64n

Easby Bewcastle, 333n
East Hanningfield, All Saints Church, 298
Eastlake, Lady, 163n
East Meon, 298
Eden, *see* Garden of Eden
Edward VI, 21
Egypt, 135
Egyptians, 93-95
Ehrenstein, Theodor, 103n, 107n
   259n, 301n
elephant, 242
El Greco, *see* Greco, El
Elijah, 157
Eliot, T. S., 13-14, 92, 130, 251, 252, 254, 347
Ellwood, Thomas, 319

elm, 243, 247

Ely, 250, 262

Elysium, 193n, 221

emblems, 18, 93, 142, 249

Empedocles, 214

Empoli, Jacopo Chimenti da, 342

Empson, William, 43, 111n

"enameled imagery," 36, 200, 249-55; *see also* "vegetable gold"

Enfancie de Nostre Seigneur, *Christ Child on Sunbeam*, 175, 341, fig. 125

Engelbert of Nassau, 333n

English College in Rome, 29

Enoch, 157, 306

envy, 54, 123

Ephesians, Epistle to, 44n, 342n

Epimetheus, 277-78

Equicola, Marius, 187

Esche, Sigrid, 225n, 262n, 275n, 290n, 312n

Esdaile, Katharine A., 49n

Essling, V. M., 300n

Este, Cardinal d', 328

Ettlinger, L. D., 143n

Euripides, 116n

Eusebius, 157n

Evans, Joan, 34n, 177n, 200

Evans, J. M., 6n, 60n, 82n, 89n, 100n, 103n, 105n, 162n, 239n, 240n, 259n, 262n, 287n, 294n, 298n

Eve: appearance of, 246, 267, 272-79; creation of, 150n, 259-61; fall of, 246, 286-91; as gardener, 239-41, 248, 275; hair of, 266, 272-75, 294; and Mary, 100, 122, 275; and mythical women, 276-80; nakedness of, 262-66, 273, 288-89; postlapsarian, 267, 286, 291-97; temptation of, 98-110, 120, 246; weeping, 275, 293, 295, 309, 314; *see also* Adam and Eve

Evelyn, John, 24, 27, 29, 134, 161, 204, 221, 244, 329

Ewelme, Oxfordshire, 114

Exeter Cathedral, 299

Exodus, 94-96

Expulsion, of Adam and Eve, 163, 293, 308-15

Expulsion, of the Rebel Angels, 56-64, 349

Eyck, Jan van, 70, 118n, 127, 142, 170, 199, 263, 282n

eye, of God, 151

Ezekiel, 150, 156, 157, 169n, 195n

Fabritius, B., 178

faculty psychology, 74

Fairford Church, 131, 158

Faithorne, William, *John Milton*, 272, fig. 203

The Fall, MS. illumination, 237, 240, fig. 161

Fall of Man: 100-10, 115, 120, 214, 286-97; effects of, 267, 287, 295-98; psychological visualizations, 289-91; and sex, 100, 104, 291-92; *see also* Adam, Eve, Fruit, Tree

falsehood, 121-22

falsus frater, 343, 346

Fane, Sir Thomas, 284n

Farinati, Paolo: *The Judgment of Adam and Eve*, 274, 294, fig. 204; *Michael and Lucifer*, 53, 87, 88, fig. 24

Farnese Garden, 222

Father, *see* God the Father

faun, 68

"feathered mail," 180

Federighi, Antonio, 269n

Ferrarese Belvedere, 227

Ferrari, Oreste, 63n, 176n

Ferry, Ann D., 215n

Feti, Domenico, 186

Fiammingo, Paolo, 234

Fidati, Fra Simone, 281

fides manualis, 282, 284

Fielding, Basil, 26

fig, 36, 223n, 245, 247

Fiore, Jacobello del, *Michael and the Dragon*, 53, 62, 72, 179, 185, fig. 22

fir, 243

Fischel, Oskar, 53, 156, 172

Fish, Stanley E., 89n

fish-siren, 120

Fixler, Michael, 92n, 335n

flames, 60

Flaxman, J., 108n

Fletcher, Giles, 333

Fletcher, Harris F., 160

Fletcher, Joseph, 281, 295, fig. 210

Fletcher, Phineas, 109n, 119n

flies, diabolic, 321

Flood, 306-8

Flora, 278-79

Florence: 183, 232, 259, 267, 300, and *see also* Milton in Italy; Accademia, anonymous tapestries, *see* Medici Tapestries; Baptistry mosaics, *Christ in Judgment*, 158, fig. 112; *Satan in Hell*, 68, 76, 89, 99, 112, 118, 128, 138, fig. 55

Floris, Frans, *The Fall*, 240, 245n, 247, 292, fig. 165

Flötmer, Peter, 122, 311

font, baptismal, 243-44

Fontainebleau School, 62n, 292n

Fontana, G. B., *Last Judgment*, 144, fig. 105

Fools, Paradise of, *see* Paradise of Fools

Ford, John, 343n

forelock, parted, 270-72

Fortitude, 192

Forum Boarium, 325n

Fowler, Alastair, 58, 105, 154n, 168n, 243, 247n, 261n, 268n, 306n
Fox, Robert C., 112n, 119n
Francesco di Giorgio, 152
Francini, Antonio, 24n
Franciscan friar, 343, 346
Francken, Frans, 70
Franco, Iacomo, 121
frangetta sulla fronte, 271
Fraud, 121
Frau Welt, 97, 119, 122-24, figs. 97, 98
Freeman, Rosemary, 93n
French, J. Milton, 23n, 31n
Frescobaldi, Bishop Piero, 24-25
Frey, Michael, 53
Friedlaender, Walter, 18, 183n, 213
Friedlander, Max J., 296
Frisch, Ernst, 77n
Fruit, forbidden, 246, 251-55, 288-90, 335n; *see also* Tree, "vegetable gold"
Frutaz, Amato Pietro, 28n, 222n
Frye, Northrop, 6n, 18n, 126n, 132, 335n
Frye, R. M., 25n, 281n
Fuller, Isaac, 71, 216
Fuller, Thomas, 324
Fulvio, Andrea, 28n, 328
Furbank, P. N., 84n, 89n
Fuseli, Henry, 9

Gabba, Emilio, 329n
Gabriel, 43, 62, 152, 171, 173, 179
Gaddi, Jacopo, 24, 25
Galavaris, George, 56n
Galileo, 209
Galle, Cornelius, *Christ and Satan*, 331, 338, fig. 248
Galle, Philip, 299
games, 90, 179n
Ganymede, 337
garden, 30, 38, 220
Garden of Eden: 6, 36, 349; artists' version of, 235-55 *passim*; bowers in, 225, 233; decay and disruption in, 239-41, 295; and English gardens, 6, 224; fauna of, 98, 106, 242-43, 246, 295; flora of, 223, 236, 239-55; and Heaven, 193, 201, 220-21, 224; informality of, 6, 224; and Italian gardens, 221-27; and landscape painting, 227-34; mountains in, 237-39, 242, 245; panoramic views of, 231-39; scents in, 38, 223, 225, 239; and seasons, 230-31; and symbolic landscape, 218-21; walks and alleys in, 222-23, 225, 232-34; wall of, 226, 236; water and fountains, 16, 222-24, 226, 235, 243-45
gardens, English, 6, 38n, 224, 239, 249
gardens, formal, 6, 221-24

gardens, Italian, 186, 221-27, 236, 249
Gardner, Arthur, 45n, 171n, 180n, 182n, 284n, 312n
Gardner, Helen, 5n, 6, 17, 38, 49n, 68n, 84, 127, 160n, 224, 236
gargoyles, 69
garland, for Eve, 287-88
Garvin, Katharine, 109n
gastrocephalic, 74, 123
Gatti, 334
Gaulli, Giovanni Battista, 209
Gazzola, Dono, and Strozzi, Bernardo, *The Expulsion*, 310, 313, fig. 230
Geiger, Benno, 120n
Geisberg, Max, 45n, 47n, 48n
gems, 198-205
Genesis, Book of: I: 154, 159, 162; II: 235, 240, 260, 261, III: 310; IV: 302, 304; V: 306; VI: 305, 306n; XXVIII: 190
Genesis B: 60, 74, 140, 269n, 293, 314n; compared with Milton, 60, 100, 287, 294; *Creation of Man and the Ladder to Heaven*, 190, fig. 35; *The Fall and Postlapsarian Prayers*, 67, 100, 269n, 287, 294, fig. 37; *The Fall of the Rebel Angels into Hell*, 67, 75, 126, 128, 136, fig. 34; *Judgment of Adam, Eve, and the Serpent*, 107, 294, fig. 41; *Lucifer's Presumption and Expulsion*, 57, 59, 64, 67, 74, 75, 139, 156, fig. 33; *Recrimination and Alienation of Adam and Eve*, 293, 294, fig. 40; *The Remorse of Adam and Eve*, 293; 294, fig. 38; *Temptation of Eve*, 100, fig. 36; *The Tempter Demon Returns to Hell*, 67, 293, fig. 39
Geneva Bible, *Adam and Eve*, 152, fig. 109
Geneva, Lake, 227
genre painting, 313, 321
Gentileschi, Artemisia, 175
Gentileschi, Orazio, 186
Gentleman's Magazine, 10, 11, 49
George III, 13
Gerolamo da Carpi, 237
Gherardi, Filippo, 215
Ghiberti, Lorenzo: 284n, 301, 302, 303; *Christ and Satan*, 78, 320, 341, fig. 233
Ghirlandaio, Domenico, 179, 185
Giamatti, A. B., 239n, 251, 273, 333n
Gianbologna, *see* Bologna, Giovanni
giants, 55
Gibbons, Grinling, 266
Gibbs, Mary Laura, 159n, 260n
Gibson, Walter S., 91n, 136, 337
Gielly, Louis, 312n
Gilbert, Allan H., 35, 56n, 59n, 128, 129
Gilliam, J. F., 120, 329n

Giltlinger, Andreas, *Nativity with Annunciation to Shepherds*
Ginzberg, Louis, 106n, 302n
Giordano, Luca: 62, 95, 176, 342; *Michael and Lucifer* (Madrid), 46, 50, 52, fig. 11; *St. Michael Archangel* (Vienna), 50, 57, 63, fig. 47, pl. VIII
Giorgione, 219
Giotto, 112, 118n, 127, 177, 181, 185, 298
Giovanni di Balduccio, 183
Giovanni di Paolo, *Paradise*, 185n, 194, fig. 138
gisant, 113
Giulio Romano, 55
glass, stained, *see* stained glass
Glover, G., *Fall of the Rebel Angels*, 46, 61, 71n, fig. 10
Gluttony, 98
Gnudi, Cesare, 55n
goats, 66, 68, 306
góccie d' oro, 252
God: and angels, 184; and Heavenly Ladder, 191; and light, 152, 198-205
God the Father: 149-55, 160, 310; as Creator, 159-62, 260; and War in Heaven, 57, 155-59
God the Holy Spirit, 100, 153-55, 175, 330
God the Son: 44, 73, 150, 153-68; as Creator, 149, 155-56, 159-62, 259-61, 348; as Judge of Adam and Eve, 156, 160, 163, 312; at Last Judgment, 163-68, 193; and War in Heaven, 53, 57, 60, 155-59, 163; *see also* Savior
gods, Aztec, 71
Goes, Hugo van der, 177n
gold, color, 273-74, 251-55
gold, metal, *see* metals, precious
gold, vegetable, 251-55
Golden Age, 220
Goldscheider, L., 271n
Goldschmidt, Adolph, 68n
Gollancz, Sir Israel, 60n
Goltzius, Hendrik, *The Disgracers: The Fall of Icarus*, 56, fig. 32
Golzio, Vincenzo, 225n
Gombrich, E. H., 84n, 87, 112n, 123n, 178n, 227, 231n, 247n, 308n
Good Shepherd, 155
Gossaert, Jan, *see* Mabuse
Gossman, Ann, 119n, 120, 130n
Gothic, 202
gourd, 243
Grabar, André, 301n
Graham, Rose, 78n, 120n
Grandval Bible, 107, 225n, 312
"Great Turk," 32
Greco, El, 129, 140, 144, 156, 278, fig. 102
Greece; 32-33; art of, 44, 268n, 271, 304n

Greed, 122
Greek New Testament (1563), illus. *Christ and Satan*, 331, fig. 241
Green, Rosalie, 260, 293n, 310n
Greene, Thomas, 170
Gregory, Saint, 139
Gregory Nazianzus, 95n, 277
Grief, 299
griffin, 47
Griffith, Matthew, 192
Grimani Breviary, *The Fall*, 102, 131, 237, 244, 245, 254, 267, 269, 271, 273, 290, fig. 162
Grose, Christopher, 14n, 72n
Grosseteste, 130n
grotesquerie, 69, 128, 217
Grotius, 280n
grottoes, 226
grove, of temptation, 332, 334-39
Grünewald: 58, 112; *St. Anthony and St. Paul the Hermit*, 330, fig. 239; *Temptation of St. Anthony*, 340, fig. 256
grylli, 69
Guazzo, illus. *Diabolical Feast*, 336, fig. 250
Guccarelli, Demetrio, 24n
guidebooks, 27-28
guides, 29
Guile, 297
guilt, 294
Guldan, Ernst, 101n, 107n(two), 275n
gunpowder, 49
Gurrieri, Francesco, 222n
Gurteen, S. Humphreys, 60n
Guthlac, St., 68

Haarlem, Cornelis van, *Adam and Eve in Paradise*, 240, 245, 246, 267, 281, 289, fig. 167; *The Disgracers: The Fall of Icarus, see* Goltzius, Hendrik
Hadermann-Misguich, Lydie, 156n
Hagstrum, Jean, 6, 14, 19, 37, 46n, 135, 202, 244n
"ha-ha," 236n
Haines, Herbert, 284n
hair: of Adam, 268-72; of angels, 177, 185-87, 348; of devils, 60, 61, 67, 75, 79, 85; of Eve, 265, 272-75, 294; "parted forelock," 270-72; styles in Milton's England, 271-72
Halkett, John, 261n, 281n
halo: 59, 61, 78, 85, 112, 149, 163, 185; black, 66
Hamlet, 86
Hammond, Mason, 6n
Hamner, Sir Thomas, 268n
Hampton Court, 22
hand, of God, 150
Handauflegung, 312

hands, holding, *see* holding hands

hands, right and left, 261n

Hanford, James Holly, 17, 24n, 29n, 342

Hankins, John E., 130, 132n

Harding, Davis P., 4, 96n

harpies, 71, 75

Harrowing of Hell, 105, 138, 141; *see also* Limbo

Hartt, Frederick, 55n, 83

Haskell, Francis, 29n

hate, 111

Hatzfeld, 6n, 278n

Haynes, Denys, 268

Hazlitt, William, 13, 77n

Heaven: 125, 187-98; city of, 56, 133, 190, 193-205, 235; color and light in, 129, 193, 198-205; and garden landscapes, 152, 193, 201, 220-21, 224; and Hell, 189, 196-98; shape of, 195-96; sill of, 58, 61, 156, 190; stairs of, 190-92, 201, 214, 232, 284n; *see also* War in Heaven

Heckscher, William S., 243, 282n

Heemskerck, Maerten van: *Death and Judgment*, 140, 144, fig. 104; *Raphael and Tobias*, 178, fig. 130

Heimann, Adelheid, 57n, 152n, 159n, 161n, 175, 298n

Hekler, Antal, 271n

Held, Julius S., 214n, 215, 278, 279

Hell: 10, 15, 75, 90, 221; bridge to, 143-45; buildings in, 49, 59, 128, 133-38, 140-41; darkness of, 127-32; gate of, 10, 120, 139-41, 143, 197; geography of, 60-61, 63, 82-83, 85, 92-93, 127-33, 141-42; Harrowing of, 49, 53, 67; and Heaven, 189, 193, 196-98, 221; at Last Judgment, 164-68; psychological, 74, 125; symbols of, 58-61, 68, 118n, 128, 139-40, 144, 156, 167, 197; theological understanding of, 125-28; tortures of, 90, 125-27, 145, 167; *see also* Pandemonium

Hell Hounds, 68, 119, 123, fig. 57

Hellenistic art, 27, 32; *see also* Greece, art of

Henniker-Heaton, Raymond, 337

Henrietta Maria, 284n, 289n

heraldic carving, 253

Hercules, 332

Hesiod, 54n

Heywood, Thomas: 46, 50n, 71n, 89; illus.: *Fall of the Rebel Angels*, *see* Glover, G.; *The Ladder of Angels and the Fall of the Devils*, *see* Cecill, L.; *Michael and the Demons*, *see* Droeshout, John

Hibernicus, 245n

hierarchy of angels, 183

Hildburgh, W. L., 151n, 180n

Hildesheim, Saint Michael's Church, 163, 293

Hill, Christopher, 21

Hill, D. M., 93

Hilliard, Nicholas, 271

Hind, Arthur M., 58n, 71n, 192n, 283, 289n

Hoefnagel, Joris, 284n

Hoet, G., 303n

Hogarth, William, 9

Holbein: 115, 117n; *The Fall* (1544), 107, 267, 271, 273, 274, 289, fig. 190

holding hands, 281-85, 291, 309, 312, 314

Holkham Bible: 101n, 160n, 186, 320n; *Debate between Christ and Satan*, 320, fig. 231; *Last Judgment*, 197, fig. 142; *Lucifer Enthroned, Christ Creating, and the Jaws of Hell*, 64, 142, 161, fig. 53

Hollstein, F.W.H., 137n, 245n

Holstenius, Lucas, 25, 29

Holsteyn, Cornelius, 284n

Holy Land, 331

Holy Sepulchre Church carving, *see* Cambridge, Holy Sepulchre Church

Holy Spirit, *see* God the Holy Spirit

Homer, 9, 11, 12, 44, 96, 152n, 211, 268n, 273, 342n

Hondecouter, Gisbert, 310

Hondius, Hendrik I, *Christ and Satan*, 327, 331, 334, fig. 236

Hondius, J., *Christian Knight Map*, 35, 112, 122, fig. 2

Horace, 247, 273

hornets, *see* devils, as insects

horns, 62

horses, 156

hortus conclusus, 236

Howard, Clare, 27n, 29n

Howard, F. E., 171n

Hughes, Merritt Y., 5n, 109n, 135n, 160, 171n, 195n, 198n, 215n, 226, 230, 238n, 247n

Hughes, Robert, 185n

humanoid devil, *see* devils, humanoid

Hume, David, 11

Humility, 189, 192

Hunger, 297

Hunt, John Dixon, 5n, 284n

Hunt, Leigh, 19

Hunt, Winifred, 141

Hunter, William B., Jr., 75n, 99n, 310n

Huntley, F. L., 35, 215n

Huntley, John F., 97

Huyghe, René, 18, 202n

Huys, 137, 140

Hyacinth, 267-70

hyacinth, 248

"hyacinthine locks," 268-70

Hyde, Sir Nicholas, 271

Hylas, 337

Icarus, 56, fig. 32
iconoclasm, 20
Illo, John, 119n
illusionist ceilings, 209-17
illustrators, of Milton, 5, 9, 108n
imagery, enameled, *see* "enameled imagery"
imago dei, 196
imago diaboli, 111
inaccessible, the, 3
Incarnation, 100, 321
indebtedness, *see* influences, sources
indescribable, the, 3
influences: 4-5, 347, 349; *see also* sources
Innocent VIII, 27
insects, 89, 94-98, 321, 340
iris, 248
Isaiah, Book of: VI: 169; XI: 342n; XIII: 68n;
    XIV: 56n; XXX: 101n; XXXIV: 94n; XL: 152n,
    160n
Islamic art, 69
Italy, *see* Milton in Italy
Ixion, 56

Jabal, 304
Jacob, 190
Jacob, Henriette s', 114n, 116n, 150n
Jacopino da Bologna, 52n
Jacques de Théramo, 345
James, M. R., 64n, 97n, 320n
James I, 213-16
Jameson, Anna B., 59n, 163n, 172n, 176, 177n,
    178n
Janson, H. W., 187, 246n
Jansson's Sea Atlas, 35
jasper, *see* stones, precious
Jean de Jandun, 204
Jegher, C., *Christ and Satan*, 341, 344, fig. 259
Jellicoe, Geoffrey, 221, 222n, 224, 226, 234,
    239
Jellicoe, Susan and Geoffrey, 222n
Jenner, Henry, 45n, 68n, 158n, 253
Jerusalem, 323-27
jessamine, 248
Jesuits, 29, 114, 115
Jesus in *PR*, *see* Savior
jewels, *see* stones, precious
Jimenez, Juan, *Michael and the Dragon*, 50,
    51, 53, 54, 62, 179, figs. 20, 21
Job, 78, 130, 187, 139
John, Gospel of, 240, 344
John the Baptist, 298
Johnson, James Rosser, 202-3
Johnson, Samuel, 3n, 11-12, 14, 43, 44, 144,
    174, 347
Jones, Inigo, 28n, 137n, 324
Jónsdóttir, Selma, 126n

Jonson, Ben, 73n
Jordaens, Jacob, 20n, 178, 241n, 290
Jordan, river, 321
Joshua, 169
Juanes, Juan de, 52n
Jubal, 304-5
Judas, 77, 112, 126
Judgment, Last, *see* Last Judgment
Julio Romano, 55
Julius II, 27
Junius, Francis, 60
Jupiter, 55, 149-50
Justice, 152n, 192

Kaftal, George, 64n, 120n
Karls des Kahlen Bible, 312
Katzenellenbogen, Adolph, 45n, 52n, 67n,
    99n, 126n, 152n, 191n
Kauffmann, Georg, 25n
Kavertzàs, 71
Keats, 38, 230
Kellogg, Alfred L., 132n
Kendon, Frank, 117n, 189n
Kennedy, Charles W., 60n, 84n
Keutner, Herbert, 50n
Keyser, Henrik de, 196n
kinaesthetics, 14, 37, 39, 143, 223, 225, 230,
    241, 321
King Lear, 86, 155
kings, divine right of, 213-17
Kip, William, 284
Kirkconnell, Watson, 49, 60n, 76n, 119n, 130n,
    137n, 280n, 281n
Kirschbaum, E., 66n, 195, 260n, 282n, 312n
Kitto Bible, 62n, 161n, 238, 241n, 289n, 296,
    303n
Kittredge, G. L., 271n
Kliger, Samuel, 325n
Klingender, Francis, 93n, 98n, 99n, 243n
Klotzas, 47, 71, 107, 137
Knauer, G. Nicolaus, 329n
Knight, G. Wilson, 38
knights, questing, 335
Knott, John R., 6n, 36n, 76, 111, 140n, 181n,
    187, 193n, 194, 195n, 218n, 220n(two),
    230, 251, 280n, 287
Koch, Robert A., 102n, 300n
Koehler, G. Stanley, 16, 171, 180n, 200n, 201
Konecny, Ludomir, 18n
Kors, Alan C., 336n
Kranidas, Thomas, 8n, 101n, 181, 231
Krapp, George P., 60n
Kussmaul, Peter, 329n

Laborde, Alexandre de, 94n, 95n, 101n, 163n

Ladder: of Heaven, 190-92, 201, 214, 220-21, 224, 232, 284n; of Salvation, 284n; of Virtues, 191-92

Ladner, Gerhart B., 159n

Lake of Fire, *see* Hell, geography of

Laking, Sir Guy Francis, 180n

Lamb, Charles, 335

Lamech, 305-6

Landor, Walter Savage, 12

landscape, symbolic uses of, 125, 127-32, 138-41, 189, 193, 197, 217, 218-21, 228-29, 329-34

Lanen, Jasper van der, 178

Lanfranco, Giovanni: 161n, 209, 215; *Michael Chaining Satan*, 53, 342, fig. 23; *The Virgin Delivers a Child from Satan*, or *The Salvation of a Soul*, 87, 88, 342, fig. 80

Langdon, Ida, 17n

Langton, Edward, 101n

Lankrink, P. H., 178

lapis lazuli, *see* stones, precious

Lassels, Richard, 26, 161

Last Judgment: 158, 163-68, 350; *see also* God the Son

Lateran Baptistry, 252

Laud, Archbishop, 20, 183, 214

laughter, 153

laurel, 243

Lauro, Giacomo, 328

Lautensack, Hans Sebald, 327

Lavin, Irving, 329n(two), 343n

Lavin, Marilyn Aronberg, 298n, 333n

Lazar-house, 304

LD, *see* Master LD

Lea, K., 345n

leaves, 93, 266, 288

Leavis, F. R., 13, 128, 129, 251, 252, 254

le Blanc, Abbé, 9

Lebrun, Charles, 62

Leclercq, H., 17n, 260n, 262n

Leeming, Bernard, 70n

Lees-Milne, James, 115n

Lehmann, Karl, 194n

Leitch, Vincent B., 130n, 132n

Leithgow, 27

Lely, Peter, *Oliver Cromwell*, 272, fig. 202

Le Nôtre, André, 233

Leo X, 27, 212

Leonardo da Vinci, 24, 62, 219, 225, 232

Lerouquais, V., 78n

Leslie, Reverend Charles, 11

Leu, Thomas de, *A Giant Destroyed by Jupiter*, 55, fig. 31

Levenson, Jay A., 264n

Lever, J. W., 60n

Levey, Michael, 263, 277n

Leviathan, 74, 89, 92-93, 118n, 123, 128, 139, 144, 197; *see also* whale

Leviathan and the Seamen, 93, fig. 85

Levin, Harry, 55, 189

Leviticus, Book of, 68n

Levron, J., 48, 66n, 68, 81n

Lewalski, Barbara, 239, 297n, 319, 334n, 335n, 340n, 345

Lewis, C. S., 93n, 221n

lexicon, visual, 4, 7, 348, 350

Leyden, *see* Lucas van Leyden

Lieb, Michael, 118n, 140n

Lier, I. van, *Christ and Satan*, *see* Hondius, Hendrik I

light, 152, 171, 179, 185, 193, 198-205, 293

Lightbown, R. W., 100n

Ligorio, Pirro, *Rometta*, 327-29, fig. 238

Lilburne, John, 271

Lilienfein, Heinrich, 289n

Limbo, 49, 53, 67, 78, 105, 137, 138, 141, 284n

Limbo of Vanity, *see* Paradise of Fools

Limbourg Brothers: *Expulsion of the Rebel Angels*, 57, 61, 78, 117, 131, 185, fig. 45; *Satan and Hell*, 68, 75, 78, 117, 131, fig. 46; *Story of Adam and Eve*, 236, 241, 244, 254, 263, fig. 160

Limoges, 253, 289

Linge, *see* van Linge

lion, 44, 98

Lippi, Filippino, 182, 185, 253

Lippi, Fra Filippo: 175, 185, 237; *Annunciation*, 171, 186, fig. 120

Lively, Martha, 283n

L. M. S., 303n

Lochner, Stephen, 136, 194

locusts, *see* devils, as insects

Lodge, William, *see* W. L.

Loggan, 253n

Lomazzo, 225

Longnon, Jean, 61n, 78n, 263

Lorenzetti, Ambrogio, 185

Lorenzetti, Pietro, 177

Lorenzo the Magnificent, 16

Lotto, Lorenzo: 96, 142, 211; *The Fall of Lucifer*, 53, 62, fig. 27

lovelock, 271

Lowrie, Walter, 149n, 150, 155n, 166n, 241n, 262n

Lubeck Bible, 45n

Lucas van Leyden: 99n, 240, 310, 343n; *Adam and Eve*, 290, 312n, fig. 215; *Creation of Eve*, 260, fig. 182

Lucretius, 162

Ludovisi Garden, 222

Luke, Gospel of, 56n, 319, 339

lust, 99, 111, 122, 126, 291, 306

Luther, Martin: 46, 48, 287n; illustrations for 1534 and 1522 Bibles, *see* Cranach, *The Garden in Eden*, and *War in Heaven*; Bible 1544, *see* Holbein; Bible 1565, *see* Brosamer

Mabuse: *Adam and Eve*, 240, 247, 269, 270n, 271, 274, 292, fig. 166; *The Fall*, 238, 245, 267, 269, 270n, 271, 292, 311, fig. 157
MacCaffrey, Isabel, 72, 149n, 196, 210n, 239n
McCarthy, B. Eugene, 10n
Macaulay, Thomas, 89n
McColley, Grant, 160
MacDougall, Elisabeth, 222-24, 226
MacKenzie, Phyllis, 14n
Maclaren, Neil, 143n
McNamee, M. B., 132n
Madsen, William G., 23n, 191n
Maitani, Lorenzo, 244
Major, John M., 343n
Mâle, Emile, 45n, 69n, 74n, 89n, 99n, 113n, 114, 122n, 126n, 139n, 140, 164, 177, 178n, 184n, 191, 193n, 241n, 253, 282n, 299n
Malins, Edward, 6n
Malmesbury Abbey, 282
Malory, 119n
Malvogius, 244
Mammon, 88
Mandowsky, Erna, 327n, 328n
Mannerism, 6, 18, 205, 210
Manso, Giovanni Battista, 25
Mantegna, 290
maps, 34-35, 112, 122, figs. 1, 2
Marcanova, Giovanni, illus. *Ancient Rome*, 327, fig. 237
Marco Benefial, 185n
Marco d'Oggiono, *The Angelic Triumph over Satan*, 62, 75, 139, fig. 51
Marilla, Esmond L., 212n
Marino, 273
Mark, Gospel of, 58n
Marle, Raimond van, *see* van Marle
Marliani, Bartolomeo, 328
Marot, 186n, 278n, 287n
marriage, 261n, 279, 281
Mars, 299
Martin, John Rupert, 191n(two), 245n, 272
Martinelli, Fioravante, 28n
Martinelli, Giuseppe, 28n, 30n
Martini, Simone, *Annunciation*, 171, 186, 235, pl. II
Martz, Louis L., 14
Marvell, 36n
Mary, the Virgin, 87, 100, 122, 275, 332n
Masaccio, *The Expulsion*, 267, 269, 274, 310, 313-14, fig. 189

Masolino, *The Fall*, 185n, 267, 269, 270n, 273, 274, fig. 185
masque, 73, 135, 137n, 139, 157, 238; *see also* drama
Masson, David, 35n, 60n
Masson, Georgina, 186n, 249
Mastelletta, Il, 95
Master LD, *Pride*, 62, 75, fig. 52
Master of Saint Giles, 199
Matham, Jacob, 289n
Matilda of Tuscany's Gospel Book, *Christ and Satan*, 336, fig. 249
Matteo di Giovanni, 185
Matthew, Gospel of, 58, 139, 143, 164, 339n
Matthew Bible, *Adam and Eve*, 282, fig. 212
Matzke, John E., 271n
Maunde-Thompson, E., 69n, 72
Mayer, Maximilian, 304n
Mazzaroli, I. O., 55
medal, 187
Medici Tapestries: 314; *Adam Names the Animals*, 108, 237, 242, fig. 150; *Adam Taken into the Garden*, 108, 236, 237, 238, 243, 261, fig. 149; *Creation of Adam*, 108, 237, 243, 269, fig. 148; *Eve Presented to Adam*, 108, 237, 248, 259, 267, 274, fig. 151; *Expulsion of Adam and Eve*, 108, 237, 238, 248, 267, 270-71, 274, 314, fig. 154; *The Fall*, 106, 108, 109, 237, 238, 246, 248, 254, 267, 273-74, 286, 288, 290, fig. 152, pl. IV; *Judgment of Adam and Eve*, 108, 115, 237, 243, 248, 267, 273-74, 293, fig. 153, pl. V
Medina, J. B., 68n, 108n
Medusa, 70, 75n, 121, 122, 123n
Meiss, Millard, 7, 52n, 113n, 127, 152n, 159n, 165, 211n, 281n
memento mori, 100, 116
Memling, Hans, 253
memory, 14-15
Mercator, 35n
Merkabah, 157
mermaid, 120
mesa, 235
Messiah in *PL*, *see* God the Son
metals, precious: 171, 179, 198-205; *see also* "vegetable gold"
metal work, 304
Meursius, Johannes, 324
Michael: and Adam and Eve, 164, 179, 192, 297-314; appearance of, 45, 171, 179; on horseback, 47-48; as judge, 45, 152, 180n; and Satan, 50-53, 87, 172; as warrior, 45, 50, 64n, 179; *see also* armor, ordnance, War in Heaven
Michaelis, A., 22n, 268n

Michelangelo: 50, 74, 79-80, 104, 150n, 159, 166n, 170, 196, 269n, 300, 307, 314, 342, 369n; compared with Milton, 80, 166, 241, 308, 314, 342, 349; *Creation of Adam*, 159, 267, fig. 181; *The Fall and Expulsion*, 104, 120, 121, 241, 247, 269, 270, 273, 274, 286, 310, 313, fig. 169; *God the Father Separating Land and Water*, 150, 151, 159, fig. 106; *Last Judgment*, fig. 60; det. Charon Delivers the Damned, 76, 79, 128, 165, 342, fig. 61; det. Charon, 74, 165, fig. 62; det. Christ in Judgment, 166, fig. 67; det. Hades or Screaming Demon, 70, 74, fig. 63; det. Head of Devil, 79, fig. 65; det. Papal Chancellor, 79, 80, 88, fig. 64; det. One of the Damned, 74, fig. 66; *The Risen Christ*, 271, fig. 201

Michele di Matteo, 289

Mignon, Jean, 246

Milburn, R.L.P., 180n

Miles, Josephine, 171n, 198

Millar, Eric, 158n, 184n, 283n, 312n

Millar, Oliver, 213n, 284n

Milton, John: attitudes to visual arts, 23, 31-37; cultural awareness of, 6, 350; eclecticism of, 5-6, 113, 347-50; eyesight of, 14-15, 16n, 23, 60, 285; illustrators of, 5, 9, 108; and Italy, 16, 17n, 19, 23-39, 132, 202, 218-27, 328; memory of, 7; musical effects, 13, 39, 108, 309n, 319, 323; office of, 23, 213, 216; parted forelock of, 272; and Roman Catholicism, 135, 343; *see also* Index to Milton's Poetry

Milton compared with artists: Beccafumi, 83-86; Bosch, 297, 308n; Botticelli, 230; *Genesis B*, 60, 100, 287, 294; Lotto, 211; Masaccio, 314; Medici tapestries, *see* Medici tapestries; Michelangelo, 80, 166, 241, 308, 314, 342, 350; Naccherino, 105, 294, 349; Raphael, 161-62, 342, 349; Rembrandt, 270; Rubens, 63; Salviati, 287-89, 349; Signorelli, 79-80, 85, 167, 188, 349; Tintoretto, 51, 337

Milton's prose works: *Apology Against a Pamphlet*, 33-34; *Areopagitica*, 239; *Church Government*, 35n; *Doctrine and Discipline of Divorce*, 18, 277; *Eikonoclastes*, 34-35; *The First Defense*, 33n, 35n; *Logic*, 34; *Of Education*, 24, 34, 38n; "Of Statues and Antiquities," 31-32; *Pro Se Defenso*, 35; *The Reason of Church Government*, 23-25, 326; *see also* Index to Milton's Poetry

mimesis, 218-21

mirror, art as, 3

Missal of Poitiers, *Devils, Hell-hounds and Hell*, 68, 123, fig. 57

mist, 98-99

Mitchell, Charles, 327n

Molinos, Miguel de, 202

Mollenkott, Virginia R., 181n

Moloch, 43, 56, 63, 86, 88

monkey, 112

Montagu, Jennifer, 25n

Montaigne, 121

More, Thomas, 239

Morland, Sir Samuel, 11-12

Morone, 186n

Morris, Edward, 5n

Mors, 113, 122

Mortlake, 253

Mortoft, Francis, 27-30

Moryson, Fynes, 27, 55

mosaics, 30, 35-36, 44, 150, 169-70, 201-5, 249-50

Moses, 298

Mostaert, Jan, 152

mountains, 54-55, 91, 152, 235, 237

Mount of Vision, 192, 233, 297-308

mounts, *see* cavalry

Muchelney Abbey, 182

Muir, Kenneth, 76, 128

Muir, Lynette R., 119n

Mulciber, 133

multiscenic design, 296, 301

Murillo, 342n

Murray, Patrick, 13n

museums, 27-28

music: at Cambridge, 61; in Heaven, 187-88; in Hell, 90; and Jabal, 304-5; in Milton's verse, 13, 39, 108, 309n, 319, 323

Mylius, 23

myrtle, 243

Mytens, Daniel, 284n

Naccherino, *Adam, Eve and Satan*, 105, 120, 267, 269, 294, 349, figs. 193, 194

Nadobocchi, 161n

Nanni di Banco, 187

Naples, *see* Milton in Italy

Narcissus, 275

Nativity, 169, 174

nature, 7, 10, 12, 15n, 16, 94, 96, 98-99, 102, 133, 192n, 232-34, 249, 307, 323

Nazarene, 155

Nazianzus, Gregory, 95n, 277

needle, 94

Neer, E. van der, 178

Nelson, James G., 77n

Nero, 69

Neuss, Wilhelm, 61n

New Jerusalem, 194

Newton, Thomas, 9, 77n

Niccoli, Niccolò, 187

Nicolas of Verdun, 103

Nicoll, A., 137n, 139n

Nicolo di Liberatore, *The Virgin Delivers a Child from Satan*, 76, 87, 185, fig. 79

Nicolson, Marjorie, 15, 128n, 132, 135n, 209, 222n

night of terror, 339-41

Nike, 169-70, 182

Nimrod, 153

Ninevah, 323

Niphates, 73

Noah, 242, 305-8

Noailles Bible, 163

nobilitas, 203

Nogara, Bartolomeo, 120n

Norton, Michael, 58n

Novarr, 343n

nudity, 32, 262-66, 273, 288-89

Nuremberg Chronicle, 324

Nuttall, W.L.F., 20

Nuttgens, Patrick, 203n

Nys, Daniel, 26n

oak, 331, 340

Oakeshott, Walter, 184n

"objects," 31

observation, 24

Occasion, 271

Octateuchs, Byzantine, 102

Odysseus, 268n

Ogden, Henry V. S. and Margaret S., 18-19, 22, 35n, 227, 229-32, 234, 238

O'Keefe, Timothy J., 119n

Ophiucus, 75n

opus sectile, 250

orantes, 113

Oras, Ants, 131

Orcagna, Andrea: 74, 127; *The Triumph of Death*, 304, fig. 223; *see also* Cione, Nardo di

Orcagna, Nardo, 304

ordnance, 11, 43-52, 55, 63, 115-17, 156, 179-81, 309-11, 349

Origen, 277

original sin: *see* apotheosis; devils, pretension to godhead; fall of man; sin, theological understanding of; sin, as pretension to godhead

Ortelius, 35, fig. 1

Ortolano, 177

Orvieto, cathedral of, 248-49

Oscott Psalter, 261n

Osgood, Charles G., 6n, 7n, 116n, 142n, 230n

Osmaston, F.P.B., 152n, 173, 337

Otten, Charlotte F., 38n

overreachers, 55

Ovid, 54, 119n, 120, 230, 247, 269

Owen, D.D.R., 49n(two), 67n, 98n, 130n, 137n, 143n, 336-37

Oxford: Lincoln College, 254; Magdalen College, 97, 158; Queen's College, 71, 74, 158; St. John's College, 183; St. Mary's Church, 20; Sheldonian Theatre, 216; University College, 158, VI; *see also* van Linge

Oxymoron, 116, 120, 252

Pacher, 139

Pacht, Otto, 312n

painted glass, *see* glass, stained

Palatine, Mount, 325-26, 328

Palatino, Giovanni Battista, 328

Palazzo Barberini, 225

Palazzo Rospigliosi, 225

Palazzo Vecchio in Florence, 232

Palladio, 28n

palm, 223, 243

Palma Giovanni, 165, 193

Palme, Per, 22, 214n

Palmer, Robert E. A., 329n

Pandemonium, 11, 33, 64, 88, 96, 128, 133-38, 140-41, 196

Pandora, 277-78

Panofsky, Dora and Erwin, 277n, 278n

———, Erwin, 18n, 20n, 59n, 70, 100n, 113n, 116n, 117n, 118n, 121, 127, 133n, 135n, 149n, 152n, 170, 187n, 220, 231n, 263, 264, 271n, 305n, 332-33

panoramas, 231-33, 237, 322-25

Pantokrator, 158

Paolo Uccello, *The Expulsion*, 269, 274, 311, fig. 197

Papal Chancellor, 80, 88

Paradise of Fools, 126, 209-17, 221

Paris, churches: Ste. Chapelle, 204; St.-Denis, 252

Parker, W. R., 15n, 23n, 29n

Parkinson, John, illus. *Terrestrial Paradise*, 240, 268n, 275, fig. 168

parrot, 112

"parted forelock," 270-72

Parthia, 323n

Passe, Crispin van de, *Christ Triumphing over Sin, Death and Hell*, 306n, 113, fig. 89

pastoralism: *see* Arcadianism, gardens, landscape

Patch, Howard R., 143n, 261n

Patinir, Joachim, 128, 131

Patrick, John M., 119n

Patrides, C. A., 17, 46n, 128n, 183n, 191, 245n, 299

paysage moralisée, *see* landscape, symbolic use of

Peacham, Henry, 28n, 121
peacock, 60, 122
Pearce, Donald R., 33n, 38
pearl, *see* stones, precious
Peccatum, 113, 122
Pecheux, Mary C., 58n, 276
Pencz, Georg, 327
Percival-Kaye, 245n
Perry, Mary P., 45n, 152n, 180n
Persepolis, 323
Perugino: 210; *Virgin in Glory with Saints and Angels*, 177, fig. 127
1 Peter, 98n, 186
Peter, apostle, 321
Peter, John, 15, 43, 94n, 133, 189, 233
Peters, Edward, 336n
Petrucci, A., 121n
Pevsner, N., 250, 253
Phaeton, 55-56
Pharaoh, 94-95
Philadelphia Museum of Art, Philip S. Collins MS, *see* Augustine, St.
Philip, Lotta Brand, 210
Phillipps, E. March, 30n, 225n
Phillipps, Sir Thomas, 31
Phillips, John, 21n, 31
Phillips, Norma, 211
Philo, 239
Phlegraean Fields, 15, 132
Piccolomini Library, 312
Pierce, Edward, 272n
Piero della Francesco: 46n, 170, 185; *Michael and the Dragon*, 50, 54, fig. 18
Piero di Cosimo, 133n, 305n
Pierpont Morgan Library MS 492 Gospel Book, *Christ and Satan*, 339, fig. 249
Pieterse, Pieter, *Banquet Larder*, 338, fig. 253
pietre dure, 204-5, 250; *see also* mosaics
Pigler, A., 50n, 178n, 182n, 192, 320n
pine, 223, 243, 331, 340
pinnacle, *see* spires
Pintorricchio, 186
Piper, David, 271n, 272n
Pisano, Andrea: *The Creation of Adam*, 259, fig. 175; *Creation of Eve*, 247, 259, 274, fig. 176
Pisano, Nicolò, 118n, 163
plantan, 243
Plot, Dr., 49n
Pluto, 277
Pointon, M., 5, 77n, 340n
Poitou, 107
Poliziano, 16
Pollaiuolo, Antonio, 232, 298; *Michael and the Dragon*, 50, 52, 54, 72, 87, fig. 19

Pollaiuolo, Piero, 185
pomidoro, 252
Pomona, 276
Pope, Elizabeth, 7, 19, 319, 326, 331n, 333n, 343n, 346
Pope-Hennessey, Sir John, 25n
porphyry, *see* stones, precious
Porter, Arthur K., 326n
Portoghesi, Paolo, 28n, 30n
Poussin, 18, 132, 181n, 183n, 233, 323, 325
Pouw, Reynier, 284n
Pozzo, Andrea, 209, 213n, 215, 216
Prampolini, Giacomo, 175n, 186n
Praz, Mario, 13, 18, 94, 247n, 263n, 325
Preti, Mattia, *Christ and Satan*, 341, 343, 346, fig. 261
pride, 54, 122
Primo Maestro, 303
Prince, F. T., 297
Prior, E. S., 180n
promenades d'amoreux, 283
Proserpina, 277
prosperity, trial by, 334-39
Protectorate, *see* Commonwealth and Protectorate
Protestantism, 10, 20-23, 150-53, 281
Prudence, 192
Prudentius, 67
prudery, 266, 275
Prynne, William, 271
Psalms, 93n, 150, 187, 193, 243
psychomachia, 45, 52n, 67, 87
Psychostasis, 45n
pulvis, 114, 116
Puppi, Lionello, 225n, 226
Puritanism, 20-23, 150, 281
putti, 177

Queen Mary's Psalter: 242, 314n 67; *Christ Creating and the Fall of the Rebel Angels*, 68, 72-75, 142, fig. 56
Quercia, Jacopo della, 312
Quirinal Garden, Rome, 222
Quistorp, Heinrich, 70n

rabbinical lore, 106
Radi, Bernardo, 25
Raimondi, Marcantonio, *Apollo and Hyacinth*, 268-69, fig. 195
Rajan, B., 143, 159
Raleigh, 239
Randall, Lilian M. C., 333n
Raphael, Archangel: 56, 62, 171, 173; and Adam and Eve, 153, 179-80; "feathered mail" of, 180; and Tobias, 178-79

Raphael, Sanzio, 22, 74, 87, 159, 161, 172, 184, 188, 191, 210, 243, 245, 253, 284n, 289, 327, 342; and Milton, 161-62, 342, 349; *The Fall*, 104, 120, 269, fig. 198; *Michael and the Dragon*, 51, 53, 70, 131, 136, fig. 69; *Michael Vanquishing the Devil*, 51, 70, 172, fig. 70; *The Vision of Ezekiel*, 150, fig. 107

Raphael Sanzio and school, *God Creating the Animals*, 161, 243, fig. 113

"rarities," 25n

Rashi, 93n

rats, 115

Ravenna mosaic: 101n, 170; *Abraham Entertains the Angels*, 170, 182, fig. 116; *Christ Separating Sheep from Goats*, 66, 155, pl. I; *Christus Victor*, 53, 155, 199, fig. 3; *The Heavenly City*, 154, 194, pl. III

Raw, Barbara, 6n

Raymond, John, 28n, 30n, 221

reason, 74, 239, 268

Réau, Louis, 20n, 47, 72n, 73, 74n, 78, 98n, 103n, 107n, 120n, 127n, 149n, 150n, 152n, 157n, 159n, 166n, 170n, 182, 190n, 193, 195n, 196, 220, 235n, 245n, 260, 261, 284n, 303n, 310n, 319n, 323n, 339n, 343n

reconciliation, 294-95

Red Sea, 92-96

Reformation, 23

Reichle, Hans, 50

Rembrandt: 132, 170, 173, 178, 279, 321n, 339n; *The Fall*, 291, fig. 217; *Postlapsarian Adam and Eve*, 293, fig. 219

Reni, Guido: 55, 184, 188; *Michael and Satan*, 53, 81, 87, 88, 109, 131, 132, 179, fig. 28

repentance, 294

repetition, incremental, 53, 56

Reresby, 221

Restoration, 22

"restorers," 21

Resurrection, 173

Reutersward, Patrik, 199, 203n, 204n

Revelation, Book of, 54, 56n, 96-97, 99n, 158, 177n, 185n, 187, 195n, 220, 289n

Rheims, miniaturists of, 67

rib, 260-61

Richardson, Jonathan, 9, 77n

Richer, P., 66n

Ricks, Christopher, 6n, 39n, 98n(two), 183n

"Riesenbibel von Saint Peter," 77

Riggs, William G., 135n

Ring, Hermann Tom, 158

Ringbom, Lars, 239, 244n

Ripa, Cesare, 119, 121, 123n

river gods, statues of, 83n

Rizzo, Antonio: *Adam*, 267, fig. 187; *Eve*, 267, 274, fig. 188

Robb, David N., 175n

Robbia, della: 187, 245; *Michael*, 177, fig. 126

Roberts, Cokie, 268n

Roberts, Steven V., 268n

Robins, Harry F., 6n, 139, 190n, 195n

rock, 321

rocks in art, 238

Röhrich, Lutz, 262n

Roman Catholicism, 27, 135, 215n

Romans, Epistle to, 299

Rome, ancient: 322-29; art of, 27, 69, 271, 282n; maps of, 195, 327-28; model of, 327-29, fig. 238; *see* Milton and Italy

Rome, Churches of: S. Clemente, 150, fig. 108; SS. Cosma e Damiano, 235; St. John Lateran, 250; S. Maria in Aracoeli, 250; S. Maria Maggiore, 169; St. Peter's, 134-35, 196; *see also* San Costanza

Rometta, the, 327-29, fig. 238

Romney, 340

Rooses, Max, 268n

Rosa, Salvator, 55, 344n

rosary, 214, 344

rose, 248, 287

Rosenau, Helen, 195n, 196n

Rosenberg, Alfons, 50n

Rosenblatt, Jason P., 93n, 150n, 157n, 182n

Rossi, Bartolommeo, 28n

Rossi, Ferdinando, 202n(two), 204n(two), 249n, 250n

Rossi, Filippo de, 28n

Rostvig, Maren, 157n, 191n

Rota, Martino, 327

Rotermund, Hans, 293, 339n

Roth, Cecil, 312n

Rouen: 122, 333n; St. Vincent, 241, 299

Rougemont, Denis de, 70n

rout, 63

Rubens: 53n, 54, 56, 63, 140, 213-16, 218n, 242, 268n, 273; *Adam and Eve in Paradise*, 237, 241, 242, 246, 254, 273, 286, pl. VII; *Apotheosis of Buckingham*, 213, fig. 145; *Apotheosis of James I*, 214, 216, fig. 146; *Christ and Satan*, 341, 344, fig. 259; *The Fall*, 103, 106, 270n, 290, fig. 171; *The Fall of the Damned into Hell*, 63, 164, fig. 114; *Michael and the Expulsion of the Rebel Angels* (Munich), 50, 54, 57, 63, 81, 87, 90, 179, fig. 17

Rucellai, 223

Rudwin, M., 103n

Ruskin, John, 66, 72, 74n, 150n, 325

Ruthwell Cross, 333n

Ruutz-Rees, C., 186n, 287n

Ryken, Leland, 15, 150, 153n, 171n, 181n, 184n, 194, 198, 200, 201n, 210n, 230, 252, 265

Saenredam, Joannes: *Adam and Eve*, 282, fig. 213; *Vertumnus and Pomona* and *Adam and Eve*, 276, fig. 207
Saint Albans Psalter, 101n, 262, 310n, 312
Saint-Denis, Basilica of, 252
Ste. Chapelle, 204
saints, temptation of, 330-33, 340-41
salamander, 102
Salusbury, Sir Thomas, 284n
Salviati, *Adam and Eve*, 103, 269, 271, 274, 275, 287-89, 349, fig. 155
Samson, 169, 216
Samuel, Irene, 134n
San Costanza, Mausoleum of, 252
Sandys, George: 120, 269n, 324
Sannazzaro, 186n, 220
Sansovino, Jacopo, 25
Santi di Tito, 95
sapphire, *see* stones, precious
Sarah, 170, 182
Sarpi, Paolo, 26n
Sasek, L. A., 297n
Satan: as debater, 319-20; degeneration of, 81, 85, 109, 124; disguises of, 78, 98-101, 176-79, 342-46; fall of, 214; flight through Chaos, 173, 210; and Hell within, 74, 125; as hero, 71, 76; as parody of God, 112, 191, 246; as prince, 46-48, 50, 51, 78, 117, 185; prostrate, 51-53; as serpent-tempter, 100-10; stature of, 89-90, 348; transfiguration of, 73, 109; at Tree, 120, 246; triprosope, 112, 118; weeping, 104-5; as wilderness tempter, 342-46; *see also* Death, devils (all headings), Hell, Michael and Satan, Pandemonium, Sin, Throne, War in Heaven
Saturn, 55
satyrs, 58, 63, 68, 71, 121
Saunders, O. Elfrida, 170n
Savior: appearance of, 341; as child, 175, 332n, 341-42; debates Satan, 319-20; visual types of, 155; wilderness trials of, 334-41; *see also* Satan; Son of God
Savry, Salomon, 47n
Saxl, Fritz, 55n, 121n, 123n, 169, 282n
Sayar, 245n
scala coeli, 190-92, 201
scales, 45, 152, 180n, 201
Scarlatini, O., 282n
Scavizzi, Giuseppe, 63n, 176n
scents, 223
Schaar, Claes, 96
Schaefer, Lucie, 93n

Schanzer, Ernest, 126n
Schaufelein, Hans, *Christ and Satan*, 331, 344, 346, fig. 242
Schayck, Goffredo van, 328n
Schedel, Hartmann, 244
Schiller, Gertrud, 113n, 122, 141, 156n, 158n, 175n, 284n, 219n(two), 320n, 336n, 344n
Schmidt, Ph., 159n
Scholes, P., 21
Schongauer, Martin, *Temptation of St. Anthony*, 340, fig. 255
Schott, François, 28n
Schottmüller, Frida, 345n
Schultz, Howard, 99n
scientists, 153
Scott, Thomas, illus. *Christ Triumphing over Sin, Death and Hell*, *see* Passe, Crispin van de
Scott-Giles, C. W., 97n
Scudder, Harold H., 48n
sculpture, 32
Scylla, 119-20
Scythians, 323n
seamen, and Leviathan, 92-93
seasons, 230
Secondo Maestro, *Story of Adam and Eve*, 259, 262, 267, 269, 310, 311, 312, fig. 179
Sells, A. Lytton, 26n, 30n, 55n
seraphim: 169n; *see also* angels
serene, the, 189
serpent: 44; in Garden, 101-9; in Hell, 109-10; *see also* devils: serpents; Sin
serpent woman: 103-5, 117-23; *see also* devils: serpents; Sin
sex relations: and Adam and Eve, 100, 182, 242, 278-85, 291-92; and angels, 181-83; and devils, 111; and Fall of Man, 100, 104, 291-92; sinful uses of, 305
Seznec, Jean, 55n, 69, 70, 142n, 340
Sforza Book of Hours, *Michael and The Expulsion of the Rebel Angels*, 50, 51, 87, fig. 16
Shakespeare, 49n, 69, 86, 155, 186n, 219, 247, 287n, 327
Shapiro, Meyer, 139, 175, 303n(two)
Shawcross, John T., 5n, 94n
Shearman, John, 37n, 73n, 249
Sheldonian Theatre, 216
Shepherd, John C., 221, 222n, 224, 226, 234, 239
Shumaker, Wayne, 14, 44, 47n, 55, 153n, 266, 302, 307
Sidney, Algernon, 271
Sidney, Sir Philip, 220
Siena cathedral, 293
Sigena, Monastery, 298

"Sightsman," 29

Signorelli: 78, 80, 86, 172; *Angels Conducting the Elect*, 167, 188, fig. 77; *The Calling of the Elect*, 167, 188, fig. 78; *The Damned in Hell*, 62, 76, 78, 79, 85, 91, figs. 74, 75; *The Reception of the Damned into Hell*, 62, 76, 78, 79, 85, fig. 76

Silentiarius, Paulus, 202

silver, *see* metals, precious

Sims, James H., 7n, 56n, 101n, 160, 182n

Sin: 35, 56, 101-9, 111-15, 117-24, 166, 286, 297; *see also* devils: serpents; original sin; sin

sin: 64-65, 212-17, 292; *see also* original sin

sins, deadly, 67-68

siren, 120

Sistine Chapel: 300, 331, 341, 343, 346; *see also* Michelangelo

Sixtus IV, 27

Skara, cathedral, 282

skirts, 151

slander, 121

sloth, 122

smiles of God, 153

Smith, Earl Baldwin, 157n, 326n

Smith, Rebecca W., 96, 134, 325n

Socrates, 324

Solario, Cristoforo: *Adam*, 269, 294, 298, fig. 199; *Eve*, 273, 274, 294, 298, fig. 200

Solier, René de, 69n

Solimena, Francesco, 50

somnus Adae, 259

Son of God, *see* God the Son; Savior

Song of Songs, 193, 220, 236

sotto in sù, *see* illusionist ceilings

soul, contest over, 87

sources, 4-5, 288, 289, 305, 341, 347, 349

space, 55, 209-17

spear, 116

specificity, 9-10, 12

Spencer, Jeffry B., 8n, 9n, 14, 36n, 49, 119n, 172, 186n, 210n, 211, 218, 224n(two), 230, 244n, 247, 248, 263n, 287n, 301, 320, 323, 333n(two), 335, 343n, 346n

sphinx, 102

Spinello Aretino, *Expulsion of the Rebel Angels*, 46, 50, 54, 57, 58, fig. 4

spires and pinnacles, 324-29

Spirit of God, *see* God the Holy Spirit

sports, 179n

Springer, Anton, 87

Spranger, 292n

square, 195-96

Squires, V. P., 15n

stag, 246

stained glass, 37, 71, 112, 122, 131, 158, 199, 202-4, 254, 320

Stanford, W. B., 268n

Star, T. van, 345

Starnes, D. T., 89n, 132n

Steadman, John M., 5n, 62n, 81n, 82, 89n, 93n, 94n, 96n, 98n, 99n, 101n, 104n(two), 112n, 119, 130n, 139n

Stechow, Wolfgang, 131n, 219

steeds, *see* cavalry

Stein, Arnold, 16, 82n, 125, 145n, 149n, 239, 297n, 331

Steinhard, Francis and Dominic, 161n

Stele of Gudea, 284n

Stephen, St., 303

Stewart, Stanley, 7n, 239n, 295, 300n

stile bello, 262

still-life, 337-39

sting, 122

Stokes, Margaret, 59n

Stone brothers, 29, 221

Stone, George Cameron, 180n

Stone, Laurence, 333n

stones, precious, 37, 198-205

Stoye, John W., 23n, 26n, 29n, 161n, 221n

Strafford, Earl of, 271

stream: 16; *see also* Garden of Eden: water

Streater, Robert, 216

"stripling cherub," *see* angels: ages of

Strong, Roy, 217n

Strozzi, Bernardo, *see* Gazzola, Dono

Stuart dynasty, 213-17

Stuttgart Psalter, 336

Suckling, Sir John, 271n

Suger, Abbot, 199, 203

Sultan, 32, 46

Summers, Joseph H., 117n

Sunbeam, Christ Child on, *see* Enfancie de Nostre Seigneur

Svendsen, Kester, 5n, 93n, 157n, 245n

Swanenburgh, Jacob van, 137, 144

Swidler, Arlene A., 124n

sword, of expulsion, 309-11

Symonds, John Addington, 79n, 188

synecdoche, 150-52

Sypher, Wylie, 135n

Tacca, Ferdinando, 71

Tacca, Pietro, *Devil Running a Footrace*, 90, fig. 84

tactile values, 39, 143

tails, 63

Taj Mahal, 236n

talons, 60, 63, 75

Tantalus, 56

tapestries: 22-23, 35, 107-8, 253; *see also* Medici tapestries
Tarpeian Rock, 325
Tassari, 334
Tasso, Bernardo, 227
Tasso, Torquato, 96, 171n, 198n, 227, 247, 288n, 335
taste, 21
Tate, Allen, 189
Tavernier, Jean, *The Devil asks for a more Flattering Portrait*, 78, fig. 81
Tayler, Edward W., 150n, 220
Taylor, Dick, Jr., 112n, 162, 297, 309
tears, 105
telescope, 209, 348
temperance, 192, 338
tempest, in wilderness, 339-41
Tempesti, Antonio: 96, 120n, 269n; *Christ and Satan*, 331, 346, fig. 240
Temple, Solomon's, 324, 326
Temptation in the Wilderness: 19, 78, 319-20; *see also* Savior; trial
Teniers, David II, *Dives in Hell*, 70, 91, 139, fig. 71
Tenison, E. M., 284n
teratology, 340
Tervarent, Guy de, 157n, 186, 282n
Thanatos, 116n
theater, in gardens, 226
Thera, Isle of, 268n
Théramo, *see* Jacques de
Thetis, 187
Thévenot, Doctor, 15
Thomas, P. W., 22
Thomassin, Philippe, 101n
Thornton, John, 299
Throne: of angels, 185, 348; of the Father, 151; of Satan, 58, 63-64, 109, 117, 137-38; of the Son, 157-59
Tiarini, Allesandro, 186n
Tibaldi, Pellegrino, 62
Tietze, Hans, 174n, 338
tiger, 98, 99
Tillyard, E.M.W., 143n
Time, 121, 271
Tinner, B. J., 60n
Tintoretto: 50n, 152, 159, 173, 174, 184, 191, 254, 292n; *Christ and Satan*, 337, 341, figs. 251, 252; *The Fall*, 245, 269, 273, 290, 311, fig. 173; *Michael and the Dragon*, 46, 51, 80, figs. 8, 9; *Paradise*, 184, 199, 201, fig. 132; *The Ressurection*, 173, fig. 122; *St. George and the Dragon*, 152, fig. 110
Titian, 103, 121n, 171, 175, 178, 218n, 219, 254, 263n, 279, 290, 330, 337
Titus, 325n

Tivoli Gardens, 30, 236, 327-29
toad, 98-100, 115
Tobias, 178, 284n
Todd, Henry J., 9, 344n
Toil, 299
Toledo cathedral, 294
Tolomei, Claudio, 223, 244
tombs, 100, 113-15
topographical views, 34, 324, 327-29
Torcello, 77
tortures, *see* Hell, tortures of
Totti, P., 28n
Touchstone, 219
Toulouse Cathedral, 126
tournament, 43
towers, 194
trades, fathers of, 304-5
tranquility, 189
transis, 100, 114
Trapp, J. B., 59n, 89n, 99n, 100n, 101n, 102-3, 107, 182n, 246n, 262, 263, 266n, 275n, 278n, 290, 292n(two), 313n
Trasimene, Lake, 227
travelers, 23-31, 36
Treatise on Antichrist, *Christ the Judge, and Devils*, 68, 72, 74, fig. 58
Treatise on the Seven Vices, *Fall of the Rebel Angels*, 57, 61, 140, 156, fig. 43
Trechsel, 107
Tree of Knowledge, 66, 101n, 103, 106, 120, 237, 243-47, 251-55, 277, 286, 288; *see also* Fall of Man, Fruit, "vegetable gold"
trees, 102, 239-48, 330-33, 340
Très Riches Heures du Duc de Berry, see Limbourg Brothers
Trevor-Roper, Patrick, 202n
trial: by adversity, 339-41; by prosperity, 334-39
Tribolo, 222
Trinity: holy, 159, 175, 182, 193; infernal, 111-15
triprosope, 112
Tristram, Ernest W., 37n, 45n(two), 69, 75n, 158n(two), 172n, 191n, 194n, 300n
trompe l'oeil, see illusionist ceilings
trumpets, 164
Truth, 121, 330
Truth the Daughter of Time, anonymous painted utensil, 121, fig. 94
Tubalcain, 304-5
Tudor dynasty, 23
Tundalus, 68
turbulent, the, 189
Turk, 32, 46
Turner, A. Richard, 218, 228n, 330

Turner, Amy Lee, 17n, 27n, 28n, 29n, 35, 93n, 112, 123n(two), 134n, 161n, 221n, 325n
Turner, J.M.W., 9
Turner, Richard, 219, 220, 229, 231, 232, 328, 332
Tuve, Rosemond, 18, 67, 93n, 277
Tyndale's Bible, *War in Heaven*, 46, 48, 97, 117, fig. 7
Typus Praedestinationis, 103n

Uccello, Paolo, 46n, 284n
ugliness: 67, 87 *see also* devils: ugly
Ugloff, L., 48n
Underwood, Paul A., 153n, 243
Urban, VIII, 28, 202, 212, 213
Uriel, 73, 174-75
Ussher, Archbishop James, 60
utensils, household, 71, 121, 161n, 254
Utrecht Book of Hours, *Last Judgment*, 194, 197, fig. 139
Utrecht Psalter, 48n, 136, 139, 156

Valkenborg, L. van, 327
Valla, *see* Manso, 25
Vallombrosa, 50, 92-96
Valturius, Robertus, 49
Valvasone, 49, 76n
Valzanzibio, 234
Vanbrugh, 236n
van der Meulen, Jan, 159n
Van Doren, Mark, 3n, 43, 157, 335
Vanitas paintings, 337-39
Vanity, Limbo of, *see* Paradise of Fools
van Linge, Abraham: 131, 165, 182, 296, 298, 313; *The Fall*, 14n, 103, 241, 254, 266, 269, 273, 286, 289, 296, pl. VI
van Marle, Raimond, 113n, 118n, 122n, 152n, 282-83, 338
van Puylvelde, 241n, 290n
Vasari, Giorgio: 83n, 101n, 103, 112, 118n, 165; *Triumph of Cosimo I*, 212, fig. 143
Vatican collection, 25
Vatican Garden, 222
Vaughan, 58
Vaux-le-Vicomte, chateau of, 233
Vecchietta, 191
"vegetable gold," 251-55
Vegetius, Flavius Renatus illus., "Dragon," 49, fig. 15
Vellart, D. J., 308
Vellert, Dirk, *Christ and Satan*, 320, 327, 345, fig. 234
Venice: San Marco mosaics, 78, 245, 284n, 294, 310n, 312, 325; *Christ and Satan*, 346, fig. 260; *Christ-Logos as Creator*, 155, 160,

254, fig. 111; *The Judgment of Adam and Eve*, 163, 267, 274, fig. 177
Venturini, G. F., *see* Ligorio, Pirro
Venus, 276
Verard, Barthelmy, 244
"verduous walls," 222
Veritas, 263
vermis, 114, 116, 123
Verona, 163, 303
Veronese: 159, 175, 260n; *Consecration of St. Nicholas*, 172, fig. 121
Verrocchio School, *Raphael and Tobias*, 178, fig. 129
Versailles, gardens, 233
Vershbow, Charlotte and Arthur, 269n
Vertue, 272n
Vertumnus, 276
vetus homo, 343n
viali, 223
via negativa, 152
Vice: 299, 332-33; *see also* psychomachia
Victoria and Albert Museum, *see* entries under anonymous, for painted utensil, stained glass, wax models
Victory, 169, 170, 182
Villa d'Este, 30
Villa Giulia, 227
Villa Gori, 234
Villa Mattei, 227
Villa Papa Giulia, 225
Villa Poggio, 16
Villon, François, 263
vine, 247-48, 274
violet, 248-49
viottole, 223
Virgil, 9, 35n, 96, 101n, 152n, 211, 220, 247, 342n
Virtues: 191-92, 282n, 330; *see also* ladder of virtues; psychomachia; Vices
Virtus, 282n
Vischer, 344n
The Vision of St. Paul, 127
visual lexicon, *see* lexicon, visual
Vita, 122
Vitzhum, Walter, 324n
vocabulary, of visual imagery, *see* lexicon, visual
Voerst, Robert van, 289n
Volkmann, Ludwig, 184n
Voltaire, 11, 49, 111, 115, 135
Voluptuousness, 332
Vondel, 47n, 76n, 283
von Pflaumen, J. H., 28n
Voragine, 300n

Vos, Marten de: *Adam and Eve, see* Sadeler,
  Joannes I; *Christ and Satan, see* Galle,
  Cornelius
Vulcan, 133n

Waddington, Raymond B., 98-99
Waldock, 43, 44, 81n, 105n, 126n
Walker, Daniel P., 126n
Wall, J. C., 101n, 103n(two), 120n, 342n,
  343n
wall: 226, 236; *see also* Heaven, city of
Waller, 36n
Walpole, Horace, 5
War in Heaven, 11-12, 43-64, 155-59, 163,
  348
Wark, R. R., 241n
Warner, George F., 314n
War of the Angels, *see* War in Heaven
Warton, Joseph, 205, 251, 252, 254
Warwick, Saint Mary's Church, 183
wasps, *see* devils; insects
water: 16, 222-24, 321; *see also* Garden of
  Eden: water
Waterhouse, E. K., 204n, 215n, 216, 288n
Wayment, Hilary, 244n, 334n, 345n
weapons, 43-52, 55, 63, 115-17, 156, 309-11,
  349
Webster, T.B.L., 112n
Weiss, Roberto, 27n, 195n, 324n, 328n
Weitzmann, Kurt, 94n, 260n, 303n
Wellek, René, 18
Welsford, Enid, 135n, 157
Welt, *see* Frau Welt
Wessel, Klaus, 126n
West, Nicholas, 21
West, Robert, 11n, 12, 44, 130n, 176, 178n,
  181n(two)
Westminster Abbey: 170, 250; *Censing
  Angel*, 171, fig. 117
Wethey, Harold, 156n, 278n, 337n
whale: 58, 60, 93, 113, 139; *see also*
  Leviathan
Whaler, James, 93n, 96n
Whitehall Banqueting House, 22, 213-17
Whitelock, Bulstrode, 271
Whiting, George W., 35, 127, 130n, 132n,

160, 191n
Whitney, Geoffrey, 18, 142, 249n
Whittick, Arnold, 186n
Widmer, Kingsley, 96
Wierix, Hieronymus, 107
Wildenstein Miniatures, 314n
wilderness, of temptation, 329-34
Williams, E. Carleton, 113n
Williams, Phyllis L., 282n
Willis, Peter, 284n
Wilton Diptych, 186, fig. 133
Wind, Edgar, 49n, 151n
Winkelmann-Rhein, Gertrud, 231
Wisdom, 192
Witart, 101n
witches, 91, 336, fig. 250
Wittkower, Rudolph, 69n, 121n, 271n
Wittreich, Joseph A., Jr., 5n
Witz, Konrad, 227
Witzleben, Elisabeth Von, 122n, 241n
W. L. [William Lodge], 28n
wolf, 98
Wolf, Edwin, II, 78n
Wolfe, Don M., 77n, 94n, 161, 272n
Wölfflin, Heinrich, 34n, 47n, 95, 172, 177n,
  182, 183, 241, 264, 319, 342
"Worksop Relief," 268n
World, *see* Frau Welt
worms, 114-15
Worringer, Wilhelm, 107n
Wotton, Sir Henry, 26, 32, 134n
Wrath, 123
Wren, Christopher, 196
Wright, Benjamin, 284

Yates, Frances A., 26n
York Minster, 299

Zanfurmaris, 71
Zephyrus, 278
Zerner, Henri, 62n
Zeus, 150
Zuccari, Federico, 81, 112, 118n, 121, 140,
  165, 184
Zumbo, Gaetano: 100; *The Corruption of
  Corpses*, 115, fig. 90

Paradise Lost

I, 6: p. 154
I, 19-24: p. 154
I, 44-49: pp. 39, 56
I, 45: p. 63
I, 46: p. 63
I, 51-53: pp. 82, 132
I, 56: p. 74
I, 59-67: p. 129
I, 77: p. 132
I, 84: pp. 57, 86
I, 91-92: p. 139
I, 152: p. 129
I, 169: p. 56
I, 169-77: p. 56
I, 173: p. 190n
I, 180-83: p. 129
I, 193-96: p. 82
I, 195-210: p. 92
I, 221-24: p. 83
I, 222: p. 85
I, 223: p. 326
I, 226: p. 129
I, 228-29: p. 132
I, 236-37: p. 132
I, 244: p. 129
I, 249: p. 194
I, 249-52: p. 84
I, 254-55: p. 125
I, 263: p. 117
I, 301-313: p. 94
I, 325-30: p. 56
I, 326: p. 56
I, 327-28: p. 53
I, 330: p. 84
I, 340-43: p. 96
I, 348: p. 46
I, 358-59: pp. 80, 85
I, 364-521: p. 70n
I, 381: p. 139
I, 423-24: p. 182
I, 547: p. 46n
I, 570: p. 80
I, 589-91: p. 89
I, 591-94: pp. 73, 86
I, 596: p. 85
I, 599-600: p. 89
I, 606: p. 84
I, 616-18: p. 184
I, 619-21: p. 105
I, 620: p. 105n
I, 657: p. 139
I, 670-71: p. 132
I, 679-84: p. 36

I, 682: p. 200
I, 692-99: p. 33
I, 710-12: p. 135n
I, 710-23: p. 134
I, 726: p. 134
I, 732: p. 151n
I, 747: p. 63
I, 756: p. 137
I, 762: p. 134
I, 764: p. 46
I, 767-76: p. 96
I, 768-76: p. 98n
I, 789-93: p. 89

II, 1-10: p. 138
II, 44-45: p. 88
II, 67: p. 130
II, 77-81: p. 56
II, 78-79: pp. 56, 63
II, 106: p. 74
II, 106-8: p. 88
II, 110-17: p. 88
II, 165: p. 57
II, 165-68: p. 56
II, 174: p. 151n
II, 176: p. 132
II, 183: p. 132
II, 195: p. 52
II, 300-7: p. 80
II, 343: p. 194
II, 353: p. 195
II, 374: pp. 56-57, 63
II, 375-77: p. 152
II, 377-78: p. 131
II, 383-84: p. 79
II, 436: p. 10
II, 477-79: p. 185
II, 488-95: p. 228
II, 491: pp. 34n, 228
II, 511-13: p. 184
II, 521-628: p. 90
II, 529-30: p. 90
II, 531: p. 47
II, 532-8: p. 179n
II, 539-41: p. 91
II, 552-55: p. 91
II, 596: p. 75
II, 616: pp. 73, 79
II, 621: p. 133
II, 622-27: p. 126
II, 624-28: p. 75
II, 644-48: p. 197
II, 645-48: p. 141

II, 650-61: p. 119
II, 651-53: p. 122
II, 654: p. 124
II, 656: p. 124
II, 660: p. 120
II, 662: p. 124
II, 666-69: p. 115
II, 670: p. 116
II, 672: p. 116
II, 673: p. 117
II, 681-82: p. 124
II, 688: p. 124
II, 698-99: p. 117
II, 704: p. 124
II, 708-11: p. 75
II, 710: p. 85
II, 713: p. 74
II, 719: p. 74
II, 724: p. 124
II, 727: p. 151n
II, 731: p. 153
II, 735: p. 124
II, 743: p. 124
II, 744-45: p. 124
II, 764: p. 111
II, 767-77: p. 56
II, 770: p. 63
II, 772: pp. 57, 63, 190n
II, 795-802: pp. 123-24
II, 811: p. 116
II, 812: p. 43
II, 817-18: p. 124
II, 843-44: p. 118
II, 850: p. 139
II, 862: p. 124
II, 866-70: p. 112n
II, 880-83: p. 197
II, 888-89: p. 197
II, 890-94: p. 142
II, 929: p. 173
II, 940-42: p. 173
II, 947-50: p. 143
II, 948-50: p. 173
II, 993-98: p. 56
II, 995-96: p. 63
II, 997-98: p. 57
II, 1005-6: p. 190n
II, 1013-14: p. 173
II, 1026-28: p. 144
II, 1034-40: p. 198
II, 1047-48: p. 195
II, 1047-52: p. 194
II, 1049-50: p. 200

II, 1051-53: p. 190n

III, 56-59: p. 151
III, 60-63: p. 184
III, 63: p. 154
III, 138-42: p. 155
III, 206: p. 214
III, 257: p. 153
III, 279: p. 151n
III, 323-33: p. 164
III, 333: p. 167
III, 333-41: p. 166
III, 352: pp. 177, 185
III, 353-360: p. 250
III, 355-56: p. 186
III, 358-59: p. 16
III, 361: p. 185
III, 362: p. 185
III, 363: p. 200
III, 363-64: p. 200
III, 365-71: p. 188
III, 377-80: p. 151
III, 385-87: p. 154
III, 390-99: p. 56
III, 416-17: p. 188
III, 418-19: p. 142
III, 438-39: p. 35n
III, 440-97: p. 211
III, 441: p. 76
III, 448-53: p. 212
III, 455-56: p. 212
III, 466-71: p. 214
III, 476-80: p. 214
III, 487-89: p. 212
III, 487-94: p. 215
III, 501-25: p. 190
III, 505-8: pp. 197, 200, 205
III, 508-9: p. 190
III, 510-12: p. 190
III, 510-18: p. 198
III, 516: p. 192
III, 518-19: p. 200
III, 520-21: p. 185n
III, 540-43: pp. 191, 214
III, 541: p. 200
III, 542-43: p. 232
III, 544-51: p. 233
III, 550: p. 326
III, 560-67: p. 210
III, 563-64: p. 173
III, 625: pp. 177, 185
III, 636-44: p. 176
III, 640: p. 177
III, 691: p. 176
III, 694: p. 176

IV, 3: p. 63
IV, 3-4: p. 101n
IV, 21-22: p. 125
IV, 75: pp. 74, 125
IV, 91-92: p. 79
IV, 98f.: p. 79
IV, 108-13: p. 79
IV, 110: p. 125
IV, 114-17: p. 54
IV, 116: p. 73
IV, 127-28: p. 73
IV, 128-29: p. 73
IV, 135-38: p. 236
IV, 138-43: p. 243
IV, 139: p. 243n
IV, 141: p. 226n
IV, 141-42: p. 226
IV, 142-49: p. 236
IV, 148: p. 251
IV, 148-49: pp. 36, 254
IV, 152-53: p. 228
IV, 152-59: p. 228
IV, 153: p. 34n
IV, 166-71: p. 179
IV, 219-20: pp. 251, 254
IV, 223-35: p. 236
IV, 224: p. 245
IV, 224-30: p. 224
IV, 245-46: p. 233
IV, 247-56: p. 231
IV, 249: pp. 251, 254
IV, 254: p. 243n
IV, 254-55: p. 235
IV, 257-60: p. 226
IV, 260-61: p. 235
IV, 260-63: p. 226
IV, 264-68: p. 230
IV, 266: p. 230n
IV, 268: p. 230
IV, 269-71: p. 277
IV, 288-89: p. 267
IV, 288-95: p. 265
IV, 288-324: p. 266
IV, 297-98: p. 267
IV, 300: pp. 267, 268
IV, 300-3: p. 270
IV, 301: p. 268
IV, 301-8: p. 268n
IV, 302: p. 270
IV, 303: pp. 267, 268
IV, 304-7: p. 272
IV, 305: p. 273
IV, 312: p. 273
IV, 312-20: p. 266
IV, 321: p. 281
IV, 321-23: p. 280

IV, 323-24: p. 265
IV, 333-39: p. 280
IV, 337-40: p. 282
IV, 343-44: p. 242
IV, 345-47: p. 242
IV, 388-89: p. 104
IV, 403-8: p. 99
IV, 434-38: p. 223
IV, 453-62: p. 275
IV, 477: pp. 267, 268
IV, 478: p. 243n
IV, 483-88: p. 260
IV, 484: p. 260
IV, 488-89: p. 281
IV, 492-97: p. 280
IV, 496: p. 273
IV, 503: p. 74
IV, 543-49: p. 237
IV, 550-54: p. 179
IV, 555-56: pp. 173, 174, 176
IV, 570-71: pp. 73, 79
IV, 576: p. 179
IV, 586-87: p. 223
IV, 590: p. 174
IV, 625-27: p. 223
IV, 626: p. 234
IV, 627-32: p. 239
IV, 629-32: p. 240
IV, 677-88: p. 188
IV, 689: p. 281
IV, 692-93: p. 225
IV, 693-94: p. 243n
IV, 696-701: p. 248
IV, 698-703: p. 249
IV, 699-701: p. 36
IV, 699-703: p. 249
IV, 700-3: p. 249n
IV, 701-3: p. 36
IV, 710-19: p. 277
IV, 738-39: p. 281
IV, 760-67: p. 279
IV, 771-75: p. 280
IV, 780: p. 179
IV, 782-85: p. 173
IV, 797-98: p. 171
IV, 800: p. 99
IV, 821: p. 73
IV, 835-40: p. 89
IV, 840: p. 86
IV, 846: p. 89
IV, 850: pp. 79, 85, 89
IV, 869-70: pp. 85, 89
IV, 870: p. 79
IV, 873: p. 79
IV, 924: p. 74
IV, 965: p. 139

IV, 965-66: p. 43
IV, 973-74: p. 184
IV, 996-97: p. 152

V, 16: p. 278
V, 22: p. 243n
V, 129-35: p. 275
V, 137: p. 225
V, 139-45: p. 229
V, 142: pp. 34n, 228
V, 156-58: p. 149
V, 178: p. 188
V, 213-14: p. 239
V, 215-19: p. 247
V, 216: p. 243n
V, 261-62: p. 209
V, 266-71: p. 173
V, 280-85: p. 171
V, 284: p. 180
V, 285-87: p. 173
V, 294: p. 242
V, 294-97: p. 239
V, 306: p. 16
V, 310: p. 171
V, 327: p. 243n
V, 333-36: p. 38
V, 350-57: p. 270
V, 377: p. 225
V, 378: p. 276
V, 379-82: p. 276
V, 387: p. 275
V, 392: p. 225
V, 394-95: p. 230
V, 509-12: p. 192n
V, 546-48: p. 188
V, 563-74: p. 347
V, 594-95: p. 184
V, 594-96: p. 184
V, 598-99: p. 152
V, 600: p. 198
V, 606: p. 151n
V, 619-27: p. 188
V, 622-24: p. 188
V, 631: p. 184
V, 635-36: p. 194
V, 636: p. 185
V, 718: p. 153
V, 725-26: p. 64
V, 737: p. 153
V, 864: p. 151n

VI, 16-17: p. 47
VI, 28: p. 152n
VI, 41-43: p. 74
VI, 51-52: p. 190n

VI, 71-75: p. 43
VI, 73-76: p. 242
VI, 93-96: p. 188
VI, 103: p. 64
VI, 110: p. 43
VI, 114-16: p. 80
VI, 139: p. 151n
VI, 149: p. 74
VI, 154: p. 151n
VI, 167-68: p. 188
VI, 181: p. 74
VI, 194: p. 51
VI, 209: p. 43
VI, 260-61: p. 54
VI, 300-7: p. 52
VI, 327-40: p. 51
VI, 328: p. 53
VI, 331-33: p. 54
VI, 334: p. 43
VI, 340: p. 53
VI, 355-62: p. 43
VI, 362: p. 63
VI, 368: p. 43
VI, 372: p. 57
VI, 387: p. 57
VI, 387-88: p. 63
VI, 388-91: p. 43
VI, 389-91: p. 47
VI, 399-400: p. 43
VI, 482-627: p. 48
VI, 504: p. 49
VI, 541-43: p. 43
VI, 598: p. 63
VI, 644-45: p. 55
VI, 660: p. 198
VI, 660-61: p. 79
VI, 661: p. 85
VI, 665: p. 54
VI, 680-84: p. 154
VI, 683: p. 156
VI, 713: p. 156
VI, 720-21: p. 155
VI, 747: p. 151n
VI, 749-66: p. 156
VI, 757-59: p. 200
VI, 759: p. 158
VI, 762: p. 151n
VI, 772: p. 200
VI, 784: p. 194
VI, 807: p. 151n
VI, 824-77: p. 56
VI, 835: p. 151n
VI, 835-55: p. 156
VI, 836: p. 156
VI, 840: p. 43
VI, 845: p. 156

VI, 854: p. 156
VI, 855-58: p. 58
VI, 856-57: p. 58n
VI, 859: p. 156
VI, 865: p. 156
VI, 866: p. 139
VI, 873: p. 63
VI, 885: p. 243n
VI, 890: p. 194
VI, 892: p. 151n

VII, 148: p. 194
VII, 197: p. 170
VII, 205-7: p. 197
VII, 211-12: p. 209
VII, 225-33: p. 160
VII, 233-37: p. 154
VII, 256-60: p. 188
VII, 275: p. 188
VII, 309-28: p. 14n
VII, 399-410: p. 307
VII, 453-70: p. 162
VII, 463-73: p. 14n
VII, 480-81: p. 102
VII, 484: p. 101
VII, 497: p. 101
VII, 500: p. 151n
VII, 506-11: p. 268
VII, 509: p. 267
VII, 547: p. 116
VII, 557-64: p. 188
VII, 575: p. 197
VII, 586: p. 184
VII, 587: p. 159
VII, 594-634: p. 188
VII, 599: p. 152n
VII, 617-18: p. 220
VII, 619: pp. 200, 202n

VIII, 78: p. 153
VIII, 212: p. 243n
VIII, 253-54: p. 259
VIII, 261-66: p. 226
VIII, 263: p. 16
VIII, 286: p. 259
VIII, 300: pp. 259, 284n
VIII, 300-6: p. 261
VIII, 303-4: p. 235
VIII, 304: p. 237
VIII, 304-6: p. 223
VIII, 348-50: p. 242
VIII, 465-66: p. 260
VIII, 469-71: p. 260
VIII, 526-27: p. 38
VIII, 526-28: pp. 223, 241
VIII, 589-92: p. 192n

VIII, 612-630: p. 182
VIII, 626: p. 182

IX, 116: p. 235
IX, 120-21: p. 125
IX, 121-22: p. 74
IX, 122f.: p. 79
IX, 123: p. 125
IX, 126-30: p. 79
IX, 128-29: p. 74
IX, 129: p. 129
IX, 158-60: p. 99
IX, 180: p. 99
IX, 210-12: p. 239
IX, 215-17: p. 247
IX, 218: p. 248
IX, 218-19: p. 249
IX, 219: p. 243n
IX, 335: p. 282n
IX, 344: p. 151n
IX, 385-86: p. 281
IX, 393: p. 276
IX, 425-27: p. 249
IX, 426: p. 248
IX, 429: pp. 251, 254
IX, 430-33: p. 248
IX, 431: p. 243n
IX, 444-451: p. 229
IX, 457-58: p. 183
IX, 467-68: pp. 74, 125
IX, 496-500: p. 108
IX, 500-501: p. 109
IX, 501: p. 101
IX, 502: p. 326n
IX, 516-17: p. 108
IX, 525: p. 101
IX, 578: pp. 251, 254
IX, 589-91: pp. 106, 246
IX, 589-93: p. 246
IX, 627: p. 243n
IX, 627-28: p. 243
IX, 631-33: p. 108
IX, 668-69: p. 109
IX, 670-72: p. 106
IX, 670-78: p. 109
IX, 708-14: p. 214
IX, 735: p. 290
IX, 782: p. 295
IX, 791: p. 290
IX, 800: p. 286
IX, 834-38: p. 286
IX, 838-42: p. 287
IX, 849-50: p. 286
IX, 851-52: p. 288
IX, 887: p. 275
IX, 890-91: p. 291

IX, 892-93: p. 287
IX, 934: p. 214
IX, 937: p. 214
IX, 990: p. 291
IX, 995-96: p. 288
IX, 1000: p. 295
IX, 1002-3: p. 295
IX, 1004-5: p. 290
IX, 1013-15: p. 291
IX, 1036: p. 291
IX, 1037: p. 281
IX, 1037-39: p. 291
IX, 1043: p. 291
IX, 1051-52: p. 292
IX, 1062-64: p. 292
IX, 1081-82: p. 293
IX, 1082-84: p. 171
IX, 1101-18: p. 243n
IX, 1106-7: pp. 38, 223n
IX, 1121-22: p. 293
IX, 1187-89: p. 294

X, 22-25: p. 181
X, 64: p. 151n
X, 65-67: p. 154
X, 73: p. 163
X, 183: p. 275
X, 190: p. 53
X, 267-69: p. 118
X, 304-5: p. 114
X, 312-14: p. 144
X, 381: p. 195
X, 392-93: p. 79
X, 424-25: p. 137
X, 435: p. 243n
X, 439: p. 137
X, 464: p. 139
X, 487: p. 245
X, 511-15: p. 110
X, 525: p. 109n
X, 528-32: p. 89
X, 534: p. 63
X, 597-607: p. 118
X, 605-6: p. 116
X, 625-27: p. 73
X, 630-33: p. 118
X, 633-37: p. 165
X, 637: p. 167
X, 641-43: p. 188
X, 666-67: p. 295
X, 678-79: p. 230
X, 692-93: p. 295
X, 695: p. 295
X, 695-707: p. 35
X, 705: p. 295

X, 710-12: p. 295
X, 712-14: p. 296
X, 772: p. 151n
X, 884-86: p. 261
X, 884-88: p. 260
X, 890-93: p. 183
X, 910-11: p. 295
X, 959-61: p. 295
X, 1046-48: p. 163
X, 1058: p. 151n
X, 1059: p. 163
X, 1066-67: p. 295
X, 1082-84: p. 297
X, 1094-96: p. 163

XI, 77-80: p. 193
XI, 80: p. 198
XI, 80-84: p. 185
XI, 111: p. 309
XI, 113-17: p. 309
XI, 127: p. 171
XI, 151: p. 309
XI, 179: p. 223
XI, 206: p. 171
XI, 232-36: p. 180
XI, 233-36: p. 309
XI, 240-49: p. 179
XI, 245-46: p. 176
XI, 246-48: p. 311
XI, 269-71: p. 223
XI, 298: p. 180
XI, 298-99: p. 309
XI, 372: p. 151n
XI, 421: p. 284n
XI, 429-447: p. 301
XI, 445-46: p. 302
XI, 468-70: p. 139
XI, 491: p. 116
XI, 491-93: p. 304
XI, 494-95: p. 304
XI, 556-58: p. 304
XI, 558-63: p. 305
XI, 564-73: p. 305
XI, 573-97: p. 305
XI, 618-20: p. 306
XI, 638-41: p. 233
XI, 655-71: p. 306n
XI, 670: p. 306
XI, 693-94: p. 306
XI, 706: p. 306n
XI, 714-18: p. 306
XI, 746: p. 307
XI, 749-52: p. 307
XI, 761: p. 308
XI, 783-84: p. 299

XI, 840: p. 307
XI, 842-43: p. 307

XII, 8-9: p. 308
XII, 11: p. 308
XII, 59: p. 153
XII, 367-68: p. 43
XII, 432: p. 117
XII, 457: p. 151n

XII, 458-465: p. 167
XII, 468-71: p. 309
XII, 545-51: p. 167
XII, 546-47: p. 168
XII, 581-84: p. 192
XII, 587: p. 309
XII, 604-5: p. 309
XII, 609: p. 309

XII, 620: p. 309
XII, 628-32: p. 313
XII, 632-34: p. 311
XII, 632-49: p. 309
XII, 637-38: p. 312
XII, 645: p. 314
XII, 646-49: p. 315
XII, 648-49: p. 281

Paradise Regained

I, 8: pp. 153, 340
I, 14-15: p. 153
I, 120: p. 342
I, 128-29: p. 170
I, 129: p. 153
I, 168-72: p. 188
I, 171: p. 184
I, 185-95: p. 331
I, 201-4: p. 342
I, 296-302: p. 331
I, 298: p. 332
I, 303-7: p. 331
I, 310-13: p. 333
I, 314-16: p. 344
I, 316: p. 331
I, 325: p. 331
I, 337: p. 344
I, 339-40: p. 331
I, 352-54: p. 331
I, 478: p. 330

II, 25-28: p. 321

II, 96-98: p. 332n
II, 130: p. 170
II, 153: p. 337
II, 216-17: p. 330
II, 236-37: p. 337
II, 246: p. 332
II, 263: p. 331
II, 289-97: p. 333
II, 293: p. 234
II, 299-301: pp. 334, 343n, 345
II, 340-67: p. 335

III, 173: p. 271n
III, 187: p. 151n
III, 253-64: p. 322
III, 261-62: p. 233
III, 288-89: p. 16
III, 310-15: p. 323n
III, 322-44: p. 323n

IV, 15-18: pp. 96, 321
IV, 18-20: p. 321

IV, 25-33: p. 322
IV, 25-68: p. 325
IV, 37: p. 325n
IV, 54: p. 326
IV, 61-69: p. 323n
IV, 70-85: p. 323
IV, 240-44: p. 324
IV, 273-74: p. 324
IV, 401-31: p. 334
IV, 405: p. 331
IV, 416-19: p. 331
IV, 422-27: p. 340
IV, 425: p. 341
IV, 430-31: p. 340
IV, 447-48: p. 331
IV, 449: pp. 343, 345
IV, 481-82: p. 340
IV, 499: p. 345
IV, 544-50: p. 324
IV, 562: p. 172
IV, 562-76: p. 346
IV, 581-85: pp. 172, 184

To Other Poems
(Alphabetically)

Comus, pp. 13, 230n
"Hymn on the Morning of Christ's Nativity," p. 72n
"Il Penseroso," pp. 37-38, 190, 199-204
"In Quintum Novembris," p. 72n
"L'Allegro," pp. 34n, 228
Samson Agonistes, pp. 16, 98n, 285
Sonnet IX, p. 330n

Illustrations

I. *Christ Separating the Sheep from the Goats*, sixth-century mosaic, S. Apollinare Nuovo, Ravenna

II. Simone Martini (1284-1344), *Annunciation* (detail), Gallerie degli Uffizi, Florence

III. *The Heavenly City*, sixth-century mosaic, S. Apollinare in Classe, Ravenna

IV. Medici Tapestries, Flemish, ca. 1550, *The Fall* (detail), Accademia, Florence

V. Medici Tapestries, Flemish, ca. 1550, *God Clothing Adam & Eve* (detail), Accademia, Florence

VI. Abraham van Linge, *The Fall*, 1641, University College Chapel, Oxford

VII. Peter Paul Rubens (1577-1640), *Adam and Eve in Paradise*, Mauritshuis, The Hague

VIII. Luca Giordano (1632-1705), *The Archangel Michael*, Kunsthistorisches Museum, Vienna

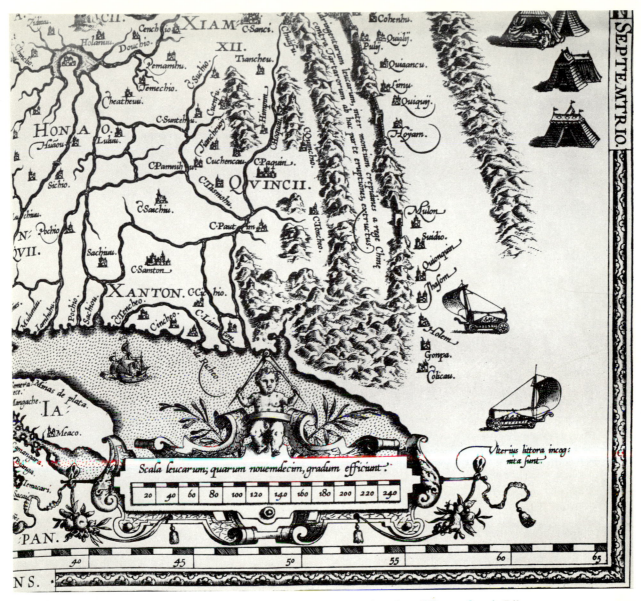

1. Ortelius, "China," from *Theater of the Whole World*, 1606, University of Pennsylvania Library

2. Jodocus Hondius, *Christian Knight Map*, 1597, British Library, London

3. *Christus Victor*, early sixth-century mosaic, Oratory of St. Andrew, Ravenna

4. Spinello Aretino (active 1373-d. 1410/11), *Expulsion of the Rebel Angels*, S. Francesco, Arezzo

5. Peter Bruegel (ca. 1525/30-69), *Fall of the Rebel Angels*, Musées Royaux des Beaux-Arts, Brussels

6. Lucas Cranach (1472-1553), *War in Heaven*, Luther's 1522 Wittenberg New Testament, Princeton University Library: Scheide Collection

7. Anonymous, *War in Heaven*, Tyndale's 1534 Bible, Princeton University Library: Scheide Collection

8. Jacopo Tintoretto (1518-94), *Michael and the Dragon*, S. Giuseppe di Castello, Venice

9. Detail of Figure 8.

10. G. Glover(?), *The Fall of the Rebel Angels*,
in Thomas Heywood, *The Hierarchie of the
Blessed Angells*, 1635, sig. Ee 3v, University of
Pennsylvania Library

11. Luca Giordano (1632-1705), *Michael and
Lucifer*, Palacio Real, Madrid

12. *Satan Leading His Troops Out of Hell*, thirteenth-century
English Apocalypse, Bodleian Library MS Tanner 184, p. 56, Oxford

13. Jacques Callot (1592/3-1635), *The Temptation of Saint Anthony*, National Gallery: Rudolf L. Baumfeld
Collection, Washington

14, 15, 16

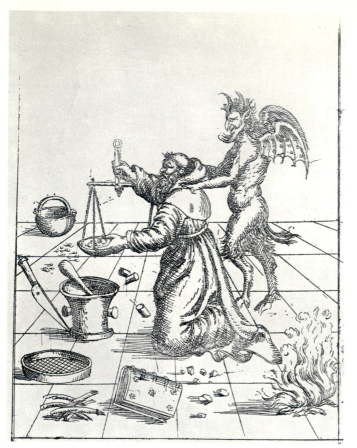

14. *The Devil and the Invention of Gunpowder*, frontispiece in Johannes Brantzius, *Les Artifices de feu*, 1604, Folger Shakespeare Library, Washington

15. Dragon, from Flavius Renatus Vegetius, *De re militari*, Augsburg, 1472, University of Pennsylvania Library

16. *Michael and the Expulsion of the Rebel Angels*, in the Sforza Book of Hours, ca. 1490, British Library add. MS 34298, fol. 186v., London

17. Peter Paul Rubens (1577-1640), *Michael and the Expulsion of the Rebel Angels*, Alte Pinakothek, Munich

19. Antonio Pollaiuolo (ca. 1432–98), *Michael and the Dragon*, Museo Bardini, Florence

18. Piero della Francesca (1410/20–92), *Michael and the Dragon*, National Gallery, London

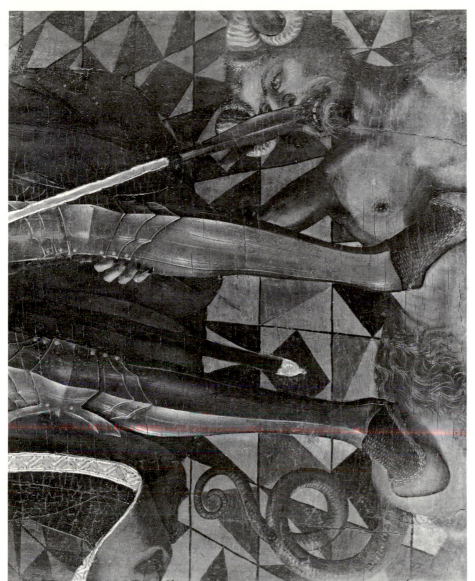

21. Detail of Figure 20

20. Juan Jimenez, *Michael and the Dragon*, ca. 1500, Philadelphia Museum of Art: John G. Johnson Collection

22. Jacobello del Fiore (d. 1439), *Michael and the Dragon*, Accademia, Venice

23. Giovanni Lanfranco (1582-1647), *Michael Chaining Satan*, Museo Capodimonte, Naples

24. Paolo Farinati (1524-1606), *Michael and Lucifer*, S. Maria in Organo, Verona

25. Dionisio Calvaert (ca. 1545-1619), *The Virgin with Child and Michael*, S. Giacomo Maggiore, Bologna

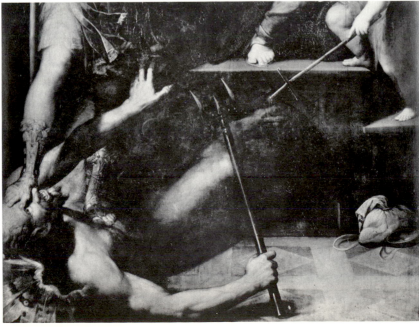

26. Detail of Figure 25

29. Domenico Beccafumi (1484/6-1551), *Michael and the Fallen Angels*, Pinacoteca, Siena

30. Detail of Figure 29

31. Thomas de Leu (1562-ca. 1620) after Antoine Caron, *A Giant Destroyed by Jupiter*, The Art Museum, Princeton University

32. Hendrik Goltzius (1558-1617), after Cornelius van Haarlem, *The Disgracers: The Fall of Icarus*, The Art Museum, Princeton University

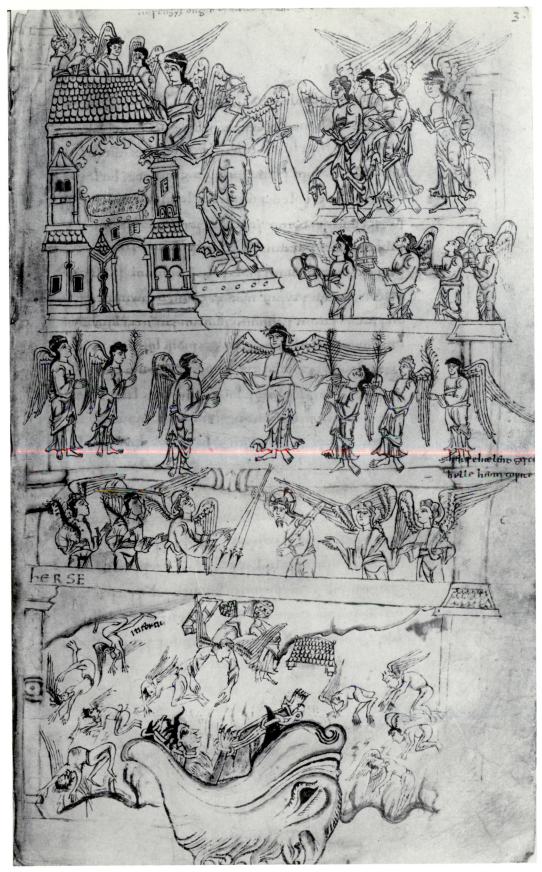

33. *Lucifer's Presumption and Expulsion*, early eleventh-century Anglo-Saxon illumination, *Genesis B*, Bodleian Library MS Junius 11, p. 3, Oxford

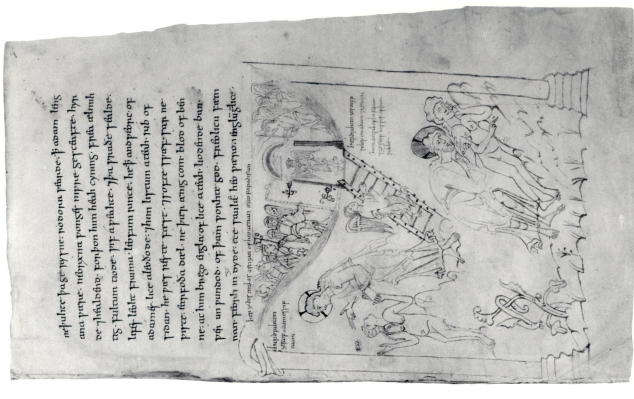

35. *Creation of Man and the Ladder to Heaven, Genesis B, p. 9*

34. *The Fall of the Rebel Angels into Hell, Genesis B, p. 16*

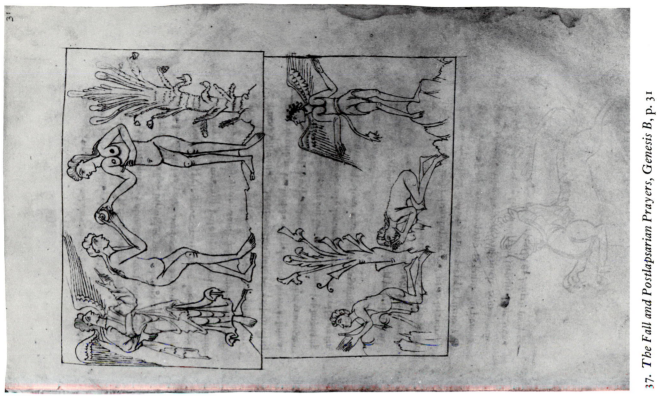

37. *The Fall and Postlapsarian Prayers, Genesis B, p. 31*

36. *Temptation of Eve, Genesis B, p. 24*

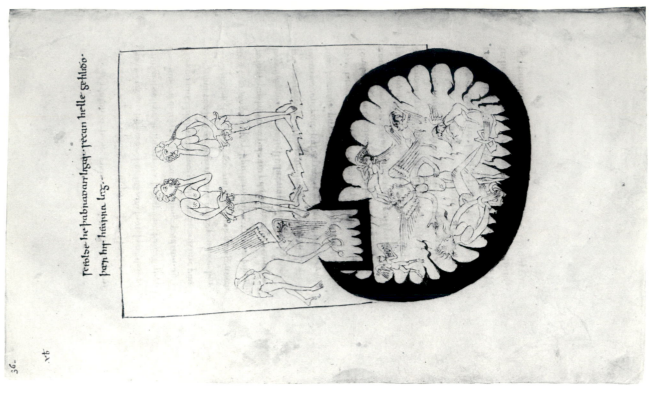

39. *The Tempter-Demon Returns to Hell, Genesis B, p. 36*

38. *The Remorse of Adam and Eve, Genesis B, p. 34*

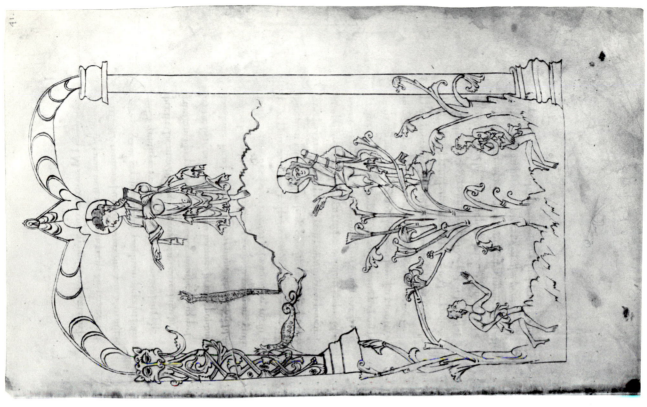

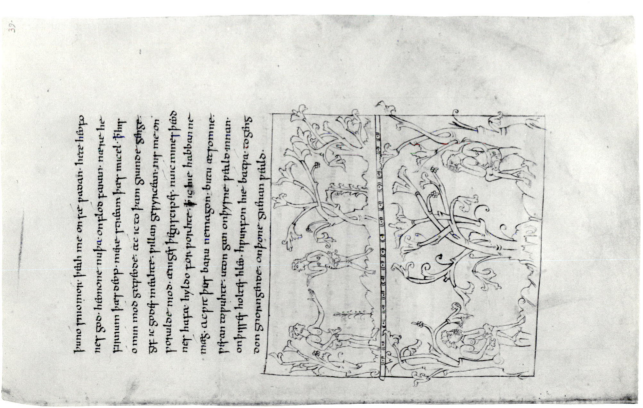

42. *Fall of Rebel Angels*, eleventh-century Anglo-Saxon illumination, Aelfric Manuscript, British Library MS Cotton Claudius B IV, p. 2, London

43. (Opposite) *Fall of the Rebel Angels*, late fourteenth-century Italian illumination in *Treatise on the Seven Vices*, British Library add. MS 27695, fol. 1v., London

44. *Expulsion of the Rebel Angels*, early sixteenth-century oak bas relief, King's College Chapel, Cambridge

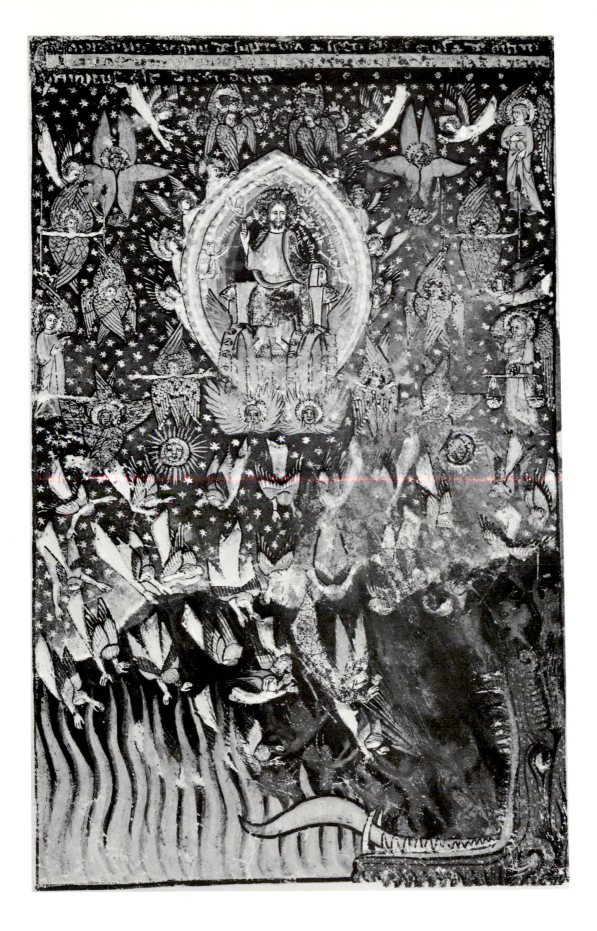

45. Limbourg Brothers, *Expulsion of the Rebel Angels*, early fifteenth-century *Très Riches Heures du Duc de Berry*, fol. 64v., Musée Condé, Chantilly

46. Limbourg Brothers, *Satan and Hell*, early fifteenth-century *Très Riches Heures du Duc de Berry*, fol. 108, Musée Condé, Chantilly

47. Luca Giordano (1632-1705), *S. Michael Archangel*, Kunsthistorisches Museum, Vienna

48. Guyart Desmoulins, Illumination for Bible Historiale, 1390, Bibliothèque Royale Albert Ier, MS 9001, fol. 19, Brussels

49. John Droeshout, *Michael and the Demons*, in Thomas Heywood, *The Hierarchie of the Blessed Angells*, 1635, sig. Tt 1v., University of Pennsylvania Library

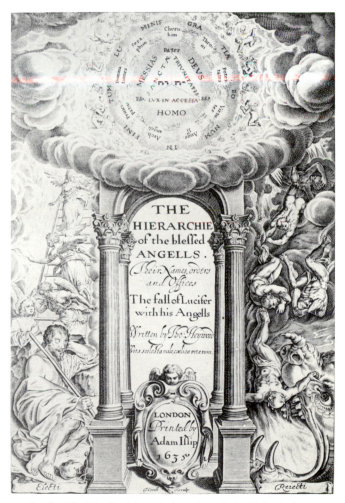

50. L. Cecill, *The Ladder of Angels and the Fall of the Devils*, frontispiece in Heywood, *The Hierarchie of the Blessed Angells*

51. Marco d'Oggiono (ca. 1475-ca. 1530), *The Angelic Triumph over Satan*, Brera, Milan

52. Master LD, *Pride*, mid-sixteenth-century French engraving, University of Pennsylvania Library

53. *Lucifer Enthroned, Christ Creating*, and the *Jaws of Hell*, fourteenth-century English illumination, Holkham Bible, fol. 2, British Library add. MS 47682, London

54. Sarcophagus of Junius Bassus, fourth-century, Vatican Museum

55. Satan in Hell, thirteenth-century mosaics, Baptistry Cupola, Florence

56. *Christ Creating* and the *Fall of the Rebel Angels*, fourteenth-century English illumination, Queen Mary's Psalter, British Library Roy. MS 2B VII, fol. 1v., London

57. *Devils, Hell-Hounds and Hell*, later fifteenth-century illumination, Missal of Poitiers, Bibliothèque Nationale MS lat. 873, fol. 164, Paris

58. *Christ the Judge and Devils*, Treatise on Antichrist, fifteenth-century French illumination, Bodleian Library MS Douce 134, fol. 98, Oxford

59. Andrea da Firenze, *Christ in Limbo* (detail of demons), ca. 1365, Spanish Chapel, S. Maria Novella, Florence

60. Michelangelo Buonarroti (1475-1564), *Last Judgment*, Sistine Chapel, Vatican

61. Detail of Figure 60, *Charon Delivers the Damned*

62. Detail of Figure 69, *Charon*

63. Detail of Figure 60, *Hades* or *Screaming Demon*

64. Detail of Figure 60, *Papal Chancellor as Devil*

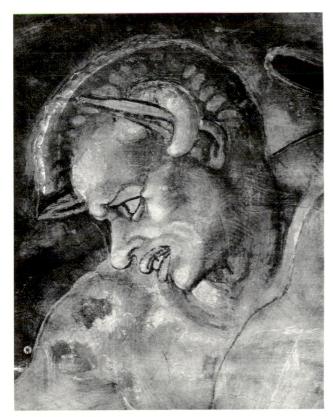

65. Detail of Figure 60, *Head of Devil*

66. Detail of Figure 60, *One of the Damned*

67. Detail of Figure 60, *Christ in Judgment*

68. Hieronymus Bosch (1450-1516), *Hell* from *Garden of Earthly Delights*, Prado, Madrid

69. Raphael (1483-1520), *Michael and the Dragon*,
ca. 1500-4, Louvre, Paris

70. Raphael (1483-1520), *Michael Vanquishing the
Devil*, ca. 1518, Louvre, Paris

71. David Teniers II (1610-90), *Dives in Hell*, National Gallery, London

72. *The Blessed* (left) and *The Damned* (right), seventeenth-century wax models, Victoria and Albert Museum, London

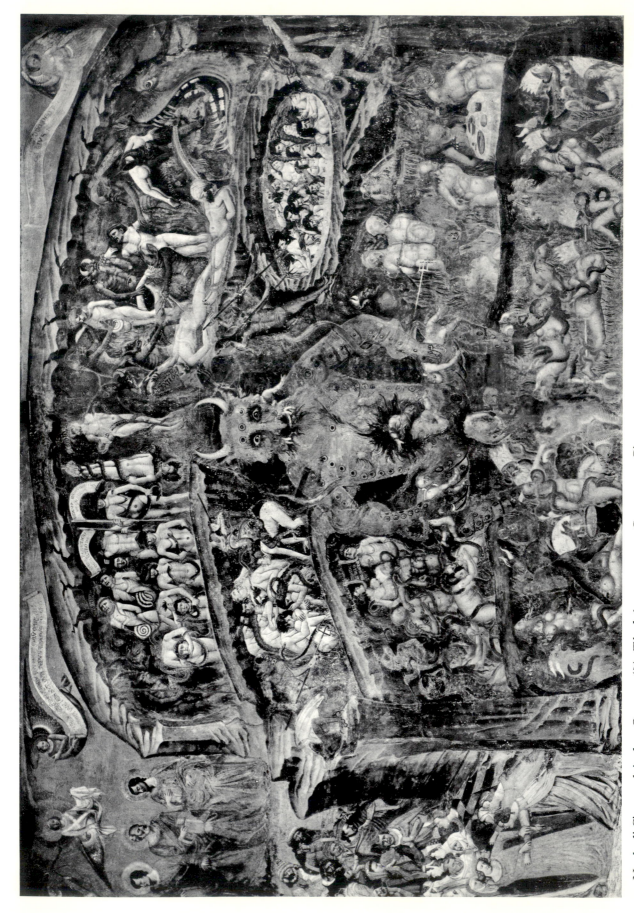

73. Nardo di Cione and Andrea Orcagna (?), *The Inferno*, ca. 1350, Camposanto, Pisa

74. Luca Signorelli (ca. 1441/50-1523), *The Last Judgment: The Damned in Hell*, 1499-1502, Cathedral, Orvieto

79. Nicolò di Liberatore (Alunno) (1425/30-1502),
The Virgin Delivers a Child from Satan, Galleria
Colonna, Rome

80. Giovanni Lanfranco (1582-1647), *The Virgin
Delivers a Child from Satan* or *The Salvation of a Soul*,
Museo Capodimonte, Naples

81. Jean Tavernier, *The Devil Asks for a More Flattering Portrait*, in *Miracles de
Nostre Dame*, ca. 1456, Bodleian Library MS Douce 374, fol. 93, Oxford

82. Domenichino (1581-1641), *The Guardian Angel*, Museo Capodimonte, Naples

83. Carlo Bononi (1569-1632), *The Guardian Angel*, Pinacoteca Civica, Ferrara

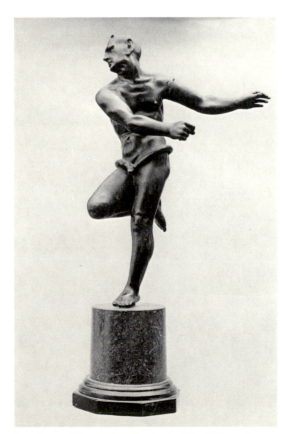

84. Pietro Tacca (1577-1640), *Devil Running a Foot Race*, Museo Capodimonte, Naples

85. *Leviathan and the Seamen*, late twelfth-century illumination, Bestiary, Bodleian Library MS Ashmole 1511, fol. 86v., Oxford

86. Peter Bruegel the Younger (1564-1638), *Orpheus in Hades*, Palazzo Pitti, Florence

87. Anonymous, *The Fall*,
mid-sixteenth-century
Italian oil, author's collection

88. Lucas Cranach (?), *The Garden in Eden*,
illustration for Genesis in Luther's 1534 Bible, Princeton
University Library: Scheide Collection

89. Crispin van de Passe I (1565-1637), *Christ Triumphing
over Sin, Death and Hell*, from Thomas Scott, *Vox Dei*,
London, 1623, Folger Shakespeare Library, Washington

90. Gaetano Zumbo (ca. 1656-1701), *The Corruption of Corpses*, Bargello, Florence

91. *The Soul Fights Temptation*, engraving, frontispiece to Edward Benlowes, *Theophila*, 1652, Folger Shakespeare Library, Washington

92. Engraving, Scylla in frontispiece to Book XIV of Sandys' translation of Ovid's *Metamorphoses*, London, 1632, sig. Hhh4v, University of Pennsylvania Library

93. Giovanni Bologna (1529-1608), Siren in Neptune
Fountain, Bologna

94. *Truth the Daughter of Time*, Italian earthenware dish,
ca. 1540-50, Victoria and Albert Museum, London

95. Agnolo Bronzino (1503-72), *Allegory*, National Gallery, London

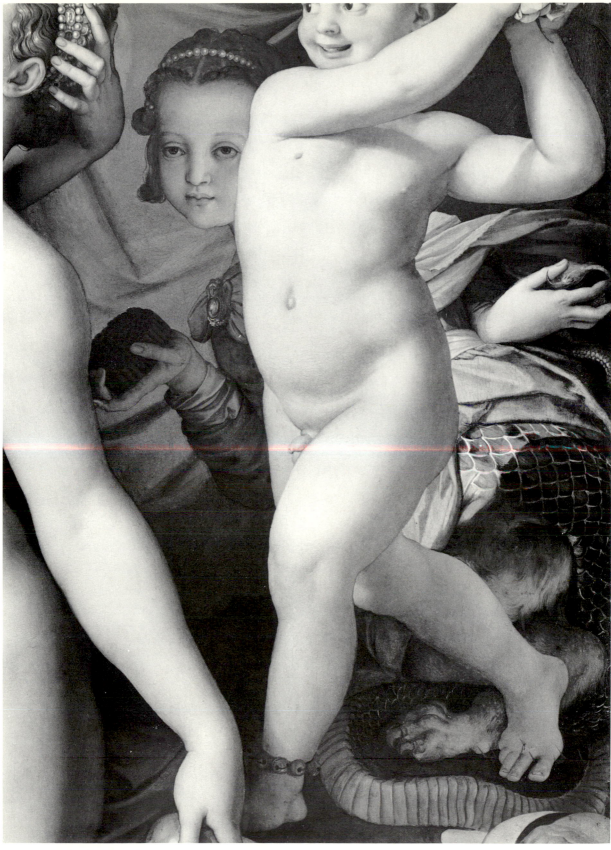

96. Detail of Figure 95, *Deceit*

97. *Frau Welt*, early fifteenth-century illumination,
Codex Latinus monacensis, Bayerische Staatsbibliotek
MS 8201, fol. 95, Munich

98. *Frau Welt*, fifteenth-century woodcut, British
Library, London

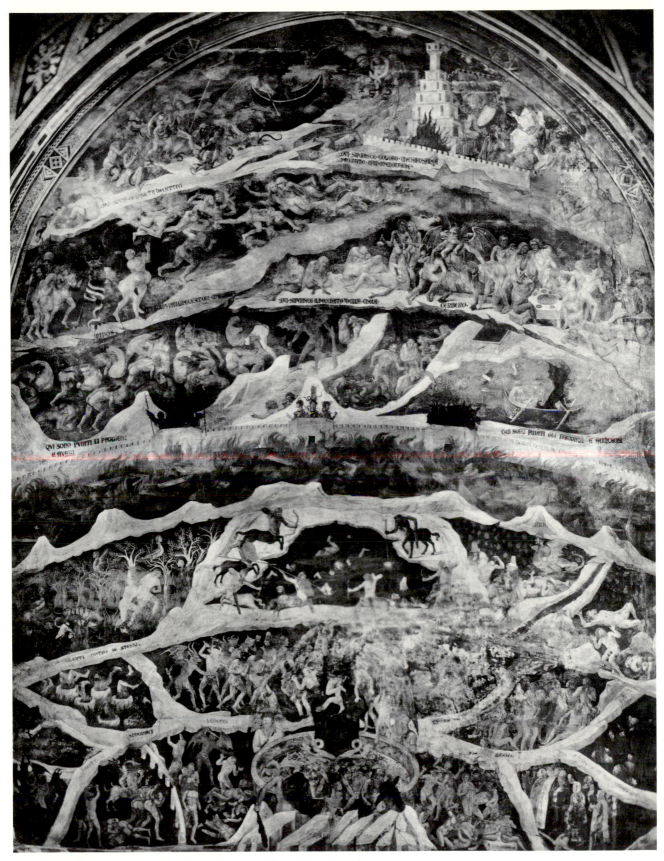

99. Nardo di Cione (d. 1366), *The Inferno*, S. Maria Novella, Florence

100. Fra Angelico (ca. 1400-1455), *Last Judgment*, Museo di S. Marco, Florence

101. Herri met de Bles (Civetta) (d. 1550), *The Inferno*, Doge's Palace, Venice

102. El Greco (1541-1614), *Allegory of the Holy League*, also called *The Dream of Philip II* and *Adoration of the Holy Name of Jesus*, Prado, Madrid

103. Duccio di Buoninsegna (ca. 1255/60-1315/18), *Christ in Limbo*, Cathedral Museum, Siena

104. Maerten van Heemskerck (1498-1574), *Death and Judgment*, Hampton Court Palace

RELIGIONE AC PIETATE INSIGNI
IO THOMAE BRIXINEN
EPISCOPO DESIGNATO·D·
Baptista Fontana Veronensis

105. Giambattista Fontana (1525-87), *Last Judgment*, Institute of Fine Arts, New York

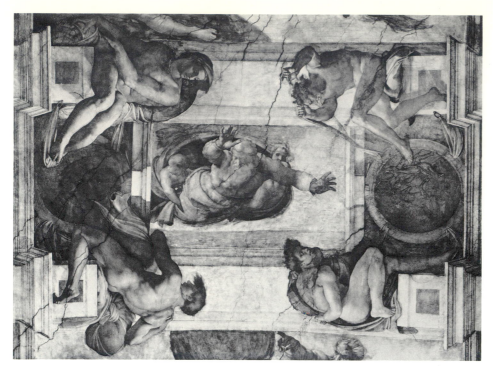

106. Michelangelo Buonarroti (1475-1564),
God the Father Separating Land and Water,
Sistine Chapel, Vatican

107. Raphael (1483-1520), *The Vision of
Ezekiel*, ca. 1516, Palazzo Pitti, Florence

108. *Omnipotent Hand of God*, twelfth-century mosaic, Apse of S. Clemente, Rome

109. *Adam and Eve*, frontispiece to Genesis, Geneva Bible, 1583, University of Pennsylvania Library

110. Jacopo Tintoretto (1518-94), *St. George and the Dragon*, National Gallery, London

111. *Christ-Logos as Creator*, thirteenth-century mosaic, Atrium of S. Marco, Venice

112. *Christ in Judgment*, thirteenth-century mosaic, Baptistry, Florence

113. Raphael (1483–1520) and his school, *God Creating the Animals*, Vatican Loggia

114. Peter Paul Rubens (1577-1640), *The Fall of the Damned into Hell*, Alte Pinakothek, Munich

115. Nardo di Cione and Andrea Orcagna (?), *Last Judgment*, ca. 1350, Camposanto, Pisa

116. *Abraham Entertains the Angels*, sixth-century mosaic, S. Vitale, Ravenna

118. *Angelic Musician*, fifteenth-century carving, Holy Sepulchre Church, Cambridge

117. *Censing Angel*, thirteenth-century sculpture, South Transept, Westminster Abbey, London

119. *Angel in Feathered Mail*, early Tudor sculpture, King's College Chapel, Cambridge

120. Fra Filippo Lippi (1406-69), *Annunciation*, Palazzo Barberini, Rome

121. Paolo Veronese (1528-88), *Consecration of St. Nicholas* (detail),
National Gallery, London

122. Jacopo Tintoretto (1518-94), *The Resurrection* (detail),
Scuola di San Rocco, Venice

123. Andreas Giltlinger (fl. 1563-80), *Nativity with Annunciation to Shepherds*, Rosengarten Museum, Constance

125. *Christ Child on Sunbeam*, early thirteenth-century illumination, from *Enfancie de Nostre Seigneur*, Bodleian Library MS Selden supra 38, fol. 24, Oxford

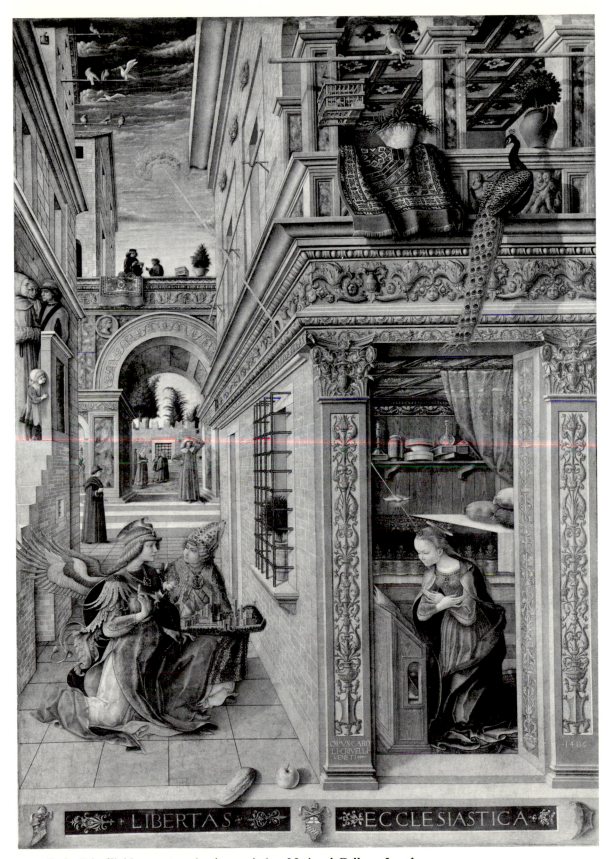

124. Carlo Crivelli (d. 1495/1500), *Annunciation*, National Gallery, London

126. Studio della Robbia, *Michael*, ca. 1475, Metropolitan Museum, New York

127. Perugino (ca. 1445/50-1523), *Virgin in Glory with Saints and Angels*, Pinacoteca Nazionale, Bologna

128. Gianlorenzo Bernini (1598-1680), *Ecstasy of St. Theresa* (detail), S. Maria della Vittoria, Rome

129. School of Verrocchio (1435-88), *Raphael and Tobias*,
National Gallery, London

130. *Raphael and Tobias*, anonymous engraving after Maerten van
Heemskerck (1498-1574), Rijksbureau voor Kunsthistorische
Documentatie, The Hague

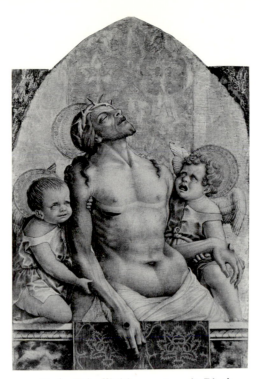

131. Carlo Crivelli (d. 1495/1500), *Pietà*,
Philadelphia Museum of Art: John G.
Johnson Collection

132. Jacopo Tintoretto (1518-94), *Paradise* (detail), Doge's Palace, Venice

134. Donatello (1386-1466), *David*, Bargello, Florence

133. Anonymous late fourteenth-century painter, *Wilton Diptych*, National Gallery, London

136. Antonio Bettini, *Ladder of Salvation*, from *Monte Santo di Dio*,
Florence, 1491, Library of Congress: Rosenwald Collection

135. Ludovico Carracci (1555–1619), *The Praise of Angels*,
S. Paolo, Bologna

137. Fra Angelico (ca. 1400-55), Paradise detail of *Last Judgment*, Museo di S. Marco, Florence

138. Giovanni di Paolo (1403-82/3), *Paradise*, Pinacoteca, Siena

139. *Last Judgment*, late fifteenth-century illumination, Utrecht Book of Hours, Bodleian Library MS Douce 93, fol. 46v., Oxford

140. Augustine's *City of God*, early fifteenth-century illumination, Philadelphia Museum of Art: Philip S. Collins Collection

141. Alonso Cano (1601-67), *The Vision of St. John* (detail), 1635-37,
Wallace Collection, London

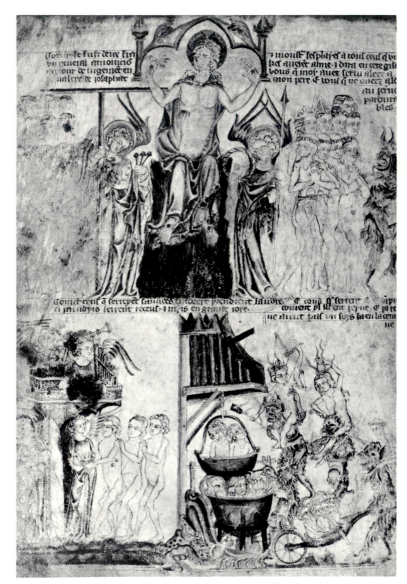

142. *Last Judgment*, early fourteenth-century illumination,
Holkham Bible, fol. 42v., British Library, London

143. Giorgio Vasari (1511-74) and others, *Triumph of Cosimo I*, Palazzo Vecchio, Florence

144. Pietro da Cortona (1596-1669), *The Triumph of Glory*, Palazzo Barberini, Rome

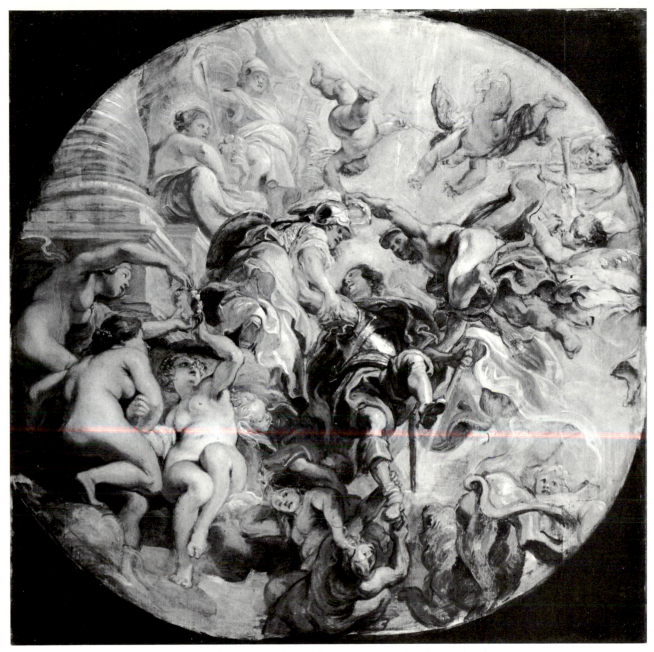

145. Peter Paul Rubens (1577-1640), *Apotheosis of Buckingham*, National Gallery, London

146. Peter Paul Rubens (1577-1640), *Apotheosis of James I*, Whitehall Banqueting House, London

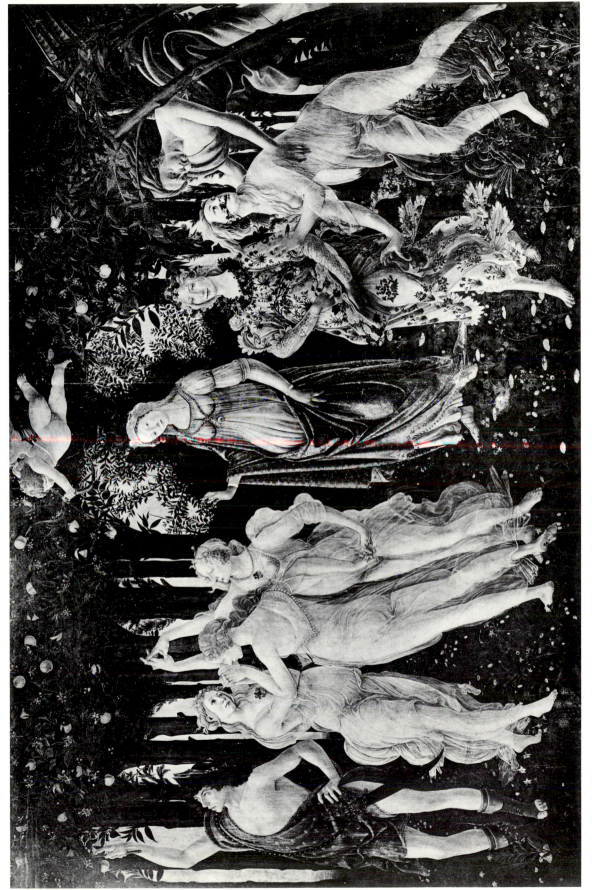

147. Sandro Botticelli (ca. 1445–1510), *Primavera*, Gallerie degli Uffizi, Florence

148. Medici Tapestries, Flemish, ca. 1550, *Creation of Adam*, Accademia, Florence

149. Medici Tapestries, *Adam Taken into the Garden*

150. Medici Tapestries, *Adam Names the Animals*

151. Medici Tapestries, *Eve Presented to Adam*

152. Medici Tapestries, *The Fall*

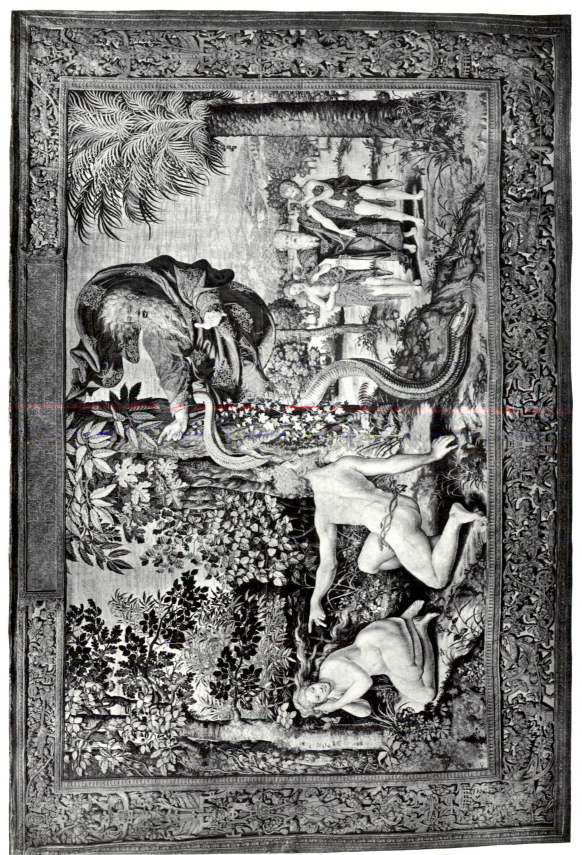

153. Medici Tapestries, *The Judgment of Adam and Eve*

154. Medici Tapestries, *Expulsion of Adam and Eve*

155. Cecchino Salviati (Francesco de' Rossi) (1510-63), *The Fall*, Galleria Colonna, Rome

157. Mabuse (Jan Gossaert) (d. ca. 1533), *The Fall* from the Malvagna Triptych,
Museo, Palermo

156. *Story of Adam and Eve*, early fifteenth-century illumination,
Bedford Book of Hours, British Library add. MS 18850, fol. 14, London

158. Jan Bruegel the Elder (1568-1625), *Garden of Eden*, Victoria and Albert Museum, London

159. Jan Bruegel the Elder (1568-1625), *Garden of Eden*, Galleria Doria, Rome

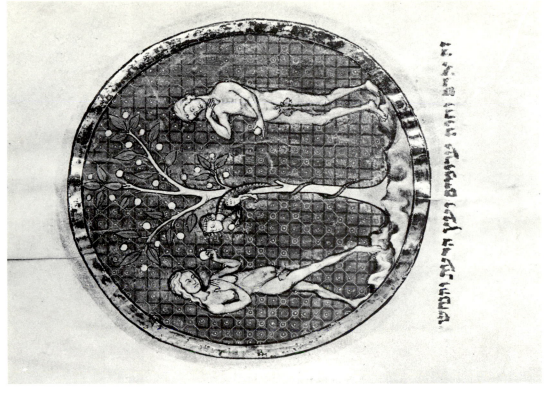

161. *The Fall*, late thirteenth-century illumination, Bible and Prayer Book, British Library add. MS 11639, fol. 520v, London

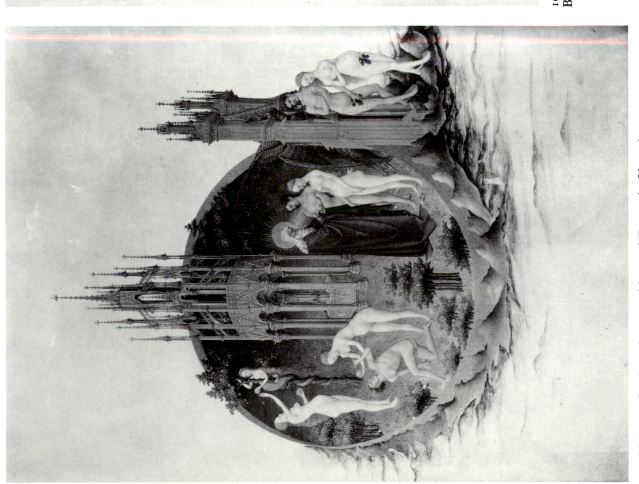

160. Limbourg Brothers, *Story of Adam and Eve*, early fifteenth-century *Très Riches Heures du Duc de Berry*, fol. 25v., Musée Condé, Chantilly

162. *The Fall*, manuscript illumination
ca. 1500, from the Grimani Breviary,
Biblioteca di S. Marco, Venice

163. Lucas Cranach (1472-1553), *Paradise*, Kunsthistorisches Museum, Vienna

164. Albrecht Dürer (1471-1528), *The Fall*, National Gallery: Rosenwald Collection, Washington

166. Mabuse (Jan Gossaert) (d. ca. 1533), *Adam and Eve*, Rhode Island School of Design, Providence

165. Frans Floris (ca. 1517-70), *The Fall*, Palazzo Pitti, Florence

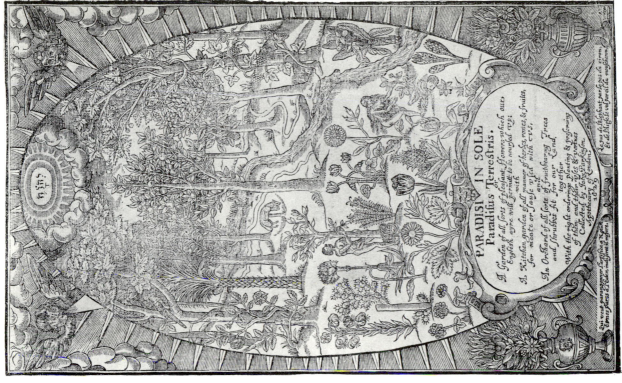

168. *Terrestrial Paradise*, engraved title page to John Parkinson, *Paradisi in Sole*, 1629, Princeton University Library

167. Cornelius van Haarlem (1562-1638), *Adam and Eve in Paradise*, Rijksmuseum, Amsterdam

169. Michelangelo Buonarroti (1475-1564), *The Fall and Expulsion*, Sistine Chapel, Vatican

170. *The Paradise of the Senses in Eden*, unsigned engraving, ca. 1600, Huntington Library, San Marino, California

171. Peter Paul Rubens (1577-1640), *The Fall*, Prado, Madrid

172. Pietro di Puccio, *The Story of Adam and Eve*, ca. 1390, Camposanto, Pisa

173. Jacopo Tintoretto (1518-94), *The Fall*, Accademia, Venice

175. Andrea Pisano (ca. 1290-ca. 1349), *The Creation of Adam*, Campanile, Florence

174. Lucas Cranach (1472-1553), *The Fall*, Courtauld Institute: Lee Collection, London

177. *The Judgment of Adam and Eve*, thirteenth-century mosaic, Atrium of S. Marco, Venice

176. Andrea Pisano (ca. 1290–ca. 1349), *The Creation of Eve*, Campanile, Florence

178. Lucas Cranach (1472-1553), *Eve*, Gallerie degli Uffizi, Florence

179. Secondo Maestro, *Story of Adam and Eve*, twelfth century, S. Zeno, Verona

180. Joannes Sadeler I (1550-1600), after Marten de Vos, *Adam and Eve*, Huntington Library (Kitto Bible), San Marino, California

181. Michelangelo Buonarroti (1475-1564), *Creation of Adam*, Sistine Chapel, Vatican

182. Lucas van Leyden (1494?-1533), *Creation of Eve*, University of Pennsylvania Library

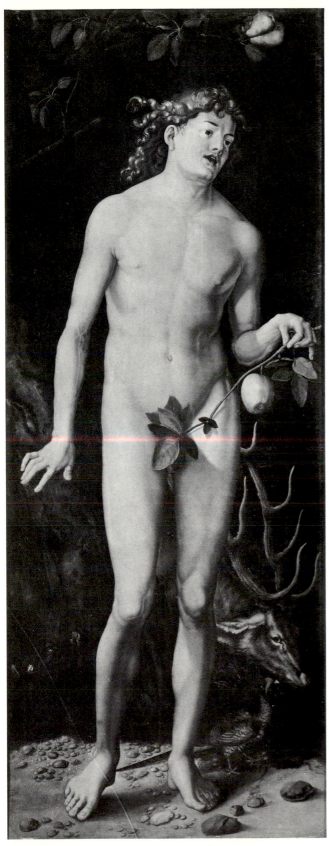

183. Albrecht Dürer (1471-1528), *Adam*, Gallerie degli Uffizi, Florence

184. Albrecht Dürer (1471-1528), *Eve*, Gallerie degli Uffizi, Florence

186. Pseudo Met de Bles, *The Fall*, Pinacoteca, Bologna

185. Masolino (ca. 1383/4–1447?), *The Fall*,
S. Maria del Carmine, Florence

188. Antonio Rizzo (fl. 1465–85), *Eve*, Doge's Palace, Venice

187. Antonio Rizzo (fl. 1465–85), *Adam*, Doge's Palace, Venice

189. Masaccio (1401-28), *The Expulsion*, S. Maria del Carmine, Florence

190. Hans Holbein (1497/8-1543) (attributed to), *The Fall*, Luther Bible, Lyons, 1544, Princeton University Library: Scheide Collection

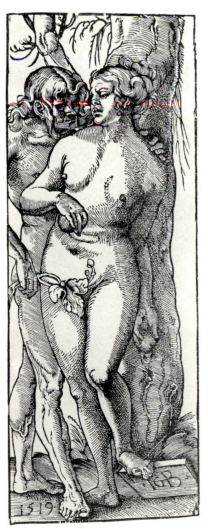

191. Hans Baldung Grien (1484/5-1545), *Adam and Eve*, 1511, National Gallery: Rosenwald Collection, Washington

192. Hans Baldung Grien (1484/5-1545), *Adam and Eve*, 1519, National Gallery: Rosenwald Collection, Washington

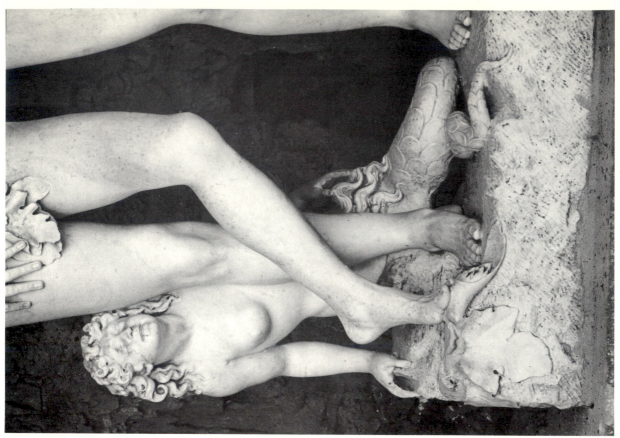

194. Detail of Figure 193

193. Michelangelo Naccherino (1550-1622), *Adam, Eve and Satan*, Boboli Gardens, Florence

196. Benvenuto Cellini (1500–71), *Apollo and Hyacinth*, Bargello, Florence

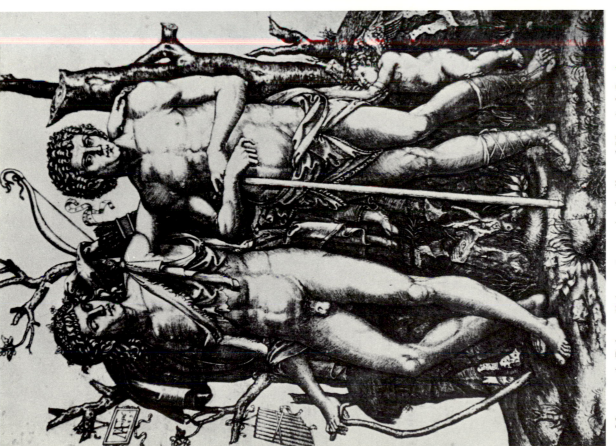

195. Marcantonio Raimondi (ca. 1480–1534), *Apollo and Hyacinth*, Institute of Fine Arts, New York

198. Raphael (1483-1520), *The Fall*, Vatican Apartments

197. Paolo Uccello (1396/7-1475), *The Expulsion*, Chiostro
Verde, S. Maria Novella, Florence

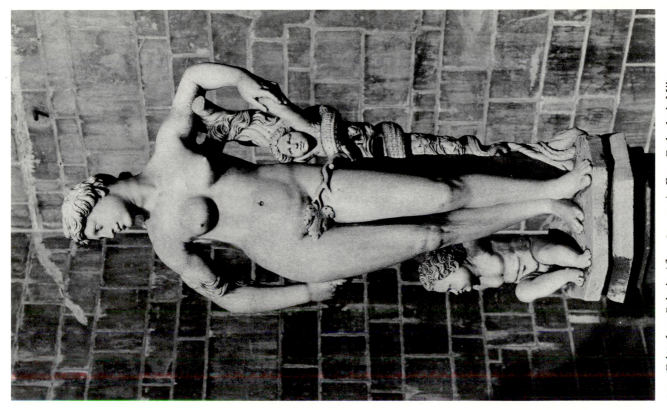

200. Cristoforo Solario (fl. 1489-1520), *Eve*, Cathedral, Milan

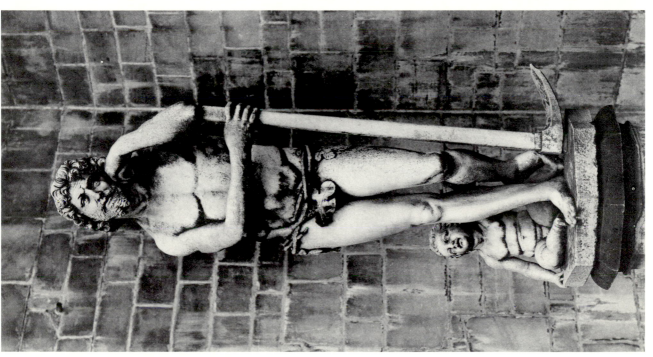

199. Cristoforo Solario (fl. 1489-1520), *Adam*, Cathedral, Milan

201. Michelangelo Buonarroti (1475-1564), *The Risen Christ*, S. Maria sopra Minerva, Rome

203. William Faithorne (1616-91), *John Milton*, Princeton University Library

202. Peter Lely (1618-80), Oliver Cromwell, 1653, Palazzo Pitti, Florence

204. Paolo Farinati (1524-1606), *The Judgment of Adam and Eve*, SS. Nazaro e Celso,
Verona

205. Andrea del Minga (ca. 1540-96), *The Expulsion of Adam and Eve*, Palazzo Pitti,
Florence

206. Albrecht Altdorfer (1480-1538), *Fall of Man*, National Gallery, Washington

207. Joannes Saenredam, *Vertumnus and Pomona* (left), 1605, and *Adam and Eve* (right), 1597, Princeton University Library

208. Lucas Cranach (1472-1553), *Venus and Cupid*, National Gallery, London

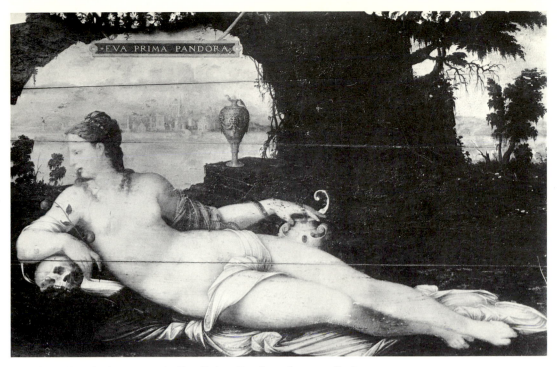

209. Jean Cousin (1490-1560), *Eva Prima Pandora*, Louvre, Paris

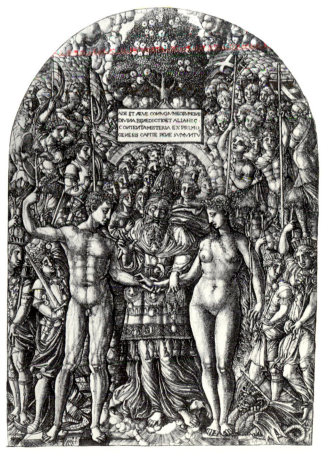

210. *Adam and Eve*, anonymous engraving, in Joseph Fletcher, *Perfect-Cursed-Blessed Man*, 1628, sig. E2v, Huntington Library, San Marino, California

211. Jean Duvet (ca. 1485-1561), *The Marriage of Adam and Eve*, National Gallery: Rosenwald Collection, Washington

213. Joannes Saenredam after A. Bloemart, *Adam and Eve*, ca. 1600, Huntington Library (Kitto Bible), San Marino, California

212. *Adam and Eve*, anonymous engraving, frontispiece to Genesis in the Matthew Bible, London, 1537, University of Pennsylvania Library

215. Lucas van Leyden (1494?-1533), *Adam and Eve*, National Gallery: Rosenwald Collection, Washington

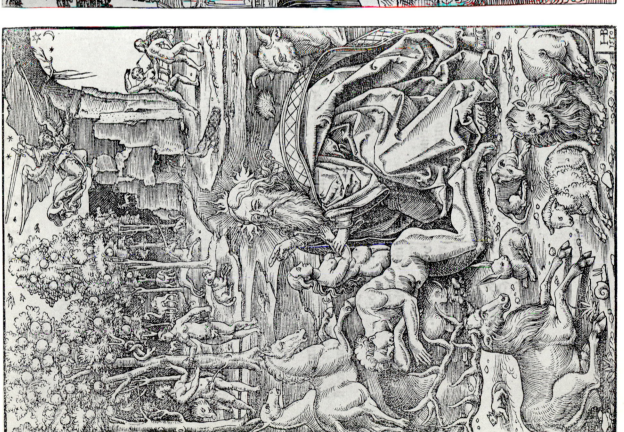

214. Hans Brosamer (1500-54), *Adam and Eve*, frontispiece to Genesis in Luther Bible, 1565, Huntington Library (Kitto Bible), San Marino, California

217. Rembrandt van Ryn (1606-69), *The Fall*, National Gallery: Rosenwald Collection, Washington

216. Hans Burgkmair (1473-1531), *The Fall*, National Gallery: Rosenwald Collection, Washington

219. Rembrandt van Ryn (1606-69), *Postlapsarian Adam and Eve*,
Pierpont Morgan Library, New York

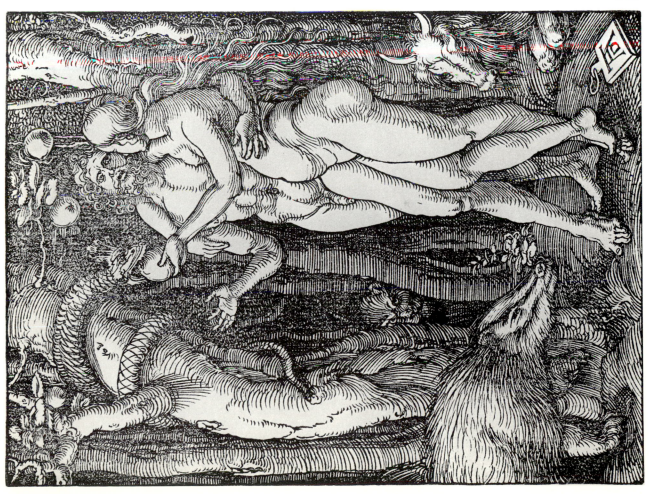

218. Albrecht Dürer (1471-1528), *The Fall*, National Gallery:
Rosenwald Collection, Washington

220. *Stories from Genesis*, eleventh-twelfth-century Byzantine ivory (detail), Cleveland Museum of Art

221. Nardo di Cione and Andrea Orcagna (?), *The Triumph of Death*, ca. 1350, Camposanto, Pisa

222. Detail of Figure 221

223. Andrea Orcagna (1308-68), fragment of *The Triumph of Death*, Museo S. Croce, Florence

224. Joannes Sadeler I (1550-1600) after Marten de Vos, *Jabal*, Huntington Library
(Kitto Bible), San Marino, California

225. Joannes Sadeler I after Marten de Vos, *Jubal* (Kitto Bible)

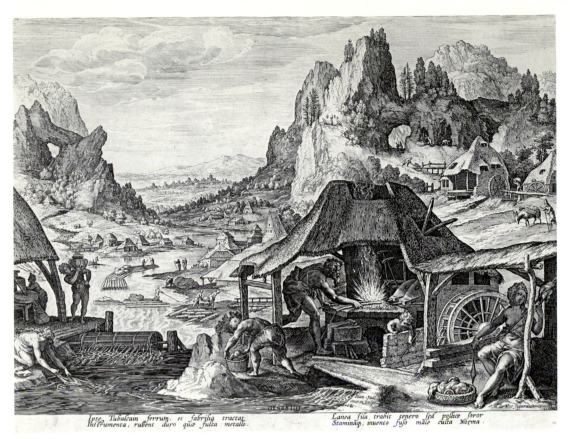

Ipse, Tubalcain ferrum, et fabrilia tractat
Inſtrumenta, rubent duro quæ fulta metallo.

Lanea fila trahit tenero sed pollice ſoror
Staminaq, inuento fuſo male culta Noema.

226. Joannes Sadeler I after Marten de Vos, Tubalcain (Kitto Bible)

Lamech conſilio præstans Noe protulit, illi
Ferret vt auxilium et rebus ſolamen in arctis:

Talia grandæuus depromſit verba palato,
Heu malus exagitat populum dirusq̃ Cupido.

227. Joannes Sadeler I after Marten de Vos, *Lamech's Lament* (Kitto Bible)

Joann. fader auctor
et fculptor excud. Martin de vos figurauit.
Genefis capit: 6

Creuit in immenfum numeru miferabile vulgus,
Illicitos ungens thalamos, vetitofq hymenaeos.

Nullus honor, cultusq Dei pietasq remanfit,
Luftra tamen duodena Deus bis pertulit ifta.

228. Joannes Sadeler I after Marten de Vos, *The Sons of God and the Daughters of Men*
(Kitto Bible)

M. de vos inuen.
feron. W. fecit
Sadleri excud. Antuerpie
C Henoch autem vixit fexaginta quinque annis, et genuit Mathufalam. Et vixit Henoch poftquam genuit
Mathufalam, trecentis annis, et gehuit filios et filias Et facti funt omnes dies Henoch trecenti fexagita
quinque ann. Ambulauitq cum Deo, et non apparuit: quia tulit eum Deus. GENES. V.

229. Joannes Sadeler I after Marten de Vos, *Enoch's Ascent*
(Kitto Bible)

230. Dono Gazzola (?) and Bernardo Strozzi (1581-1644), *The Expulsion*, Castelvecchio, Verona

231. *Debate between Christ and Satan*, fourteenth-century English illumination, Holkham Bible, fol. 11v., British Library, London

232. *Christ and Satan*, thirteenth-
century stained glass, ca. 1225,
Victoria and Albert Museum, London

233. Lorenzo Ghiberti (1378-1455),
Christ and Satan, Baptistry, Florence

234. Dirk Vellert (fl. 1511-44), *Christ and Satan*, National Gallery: Rosenwald Collection, Washington

235. Abraham Bloemaert (1564-1651), *Christ and Satan*, Huntington Library (Kitto Bible), San Marino, California

236. Henric Hondius I (1573-ca. 1649) after I. van Lier, *Christ and Satan*, Huntington Library (Kitto Bible), San Marino, California

237. *Ancient Rome*, illumination, in Giovanni Marcanova,
Antiquitates, 1465, Princeton University Library

238. Giovanni Francesco Venturini (1650-1710+), engraving of Ligorio's *Rometta* in the Tivoli Gardens,
Princeton University Library

239. Grunewald (ca. 1470/80-1528), *St. Anthony and St. Paul the Hermit*, ca. 1510-15, Isenheim Altarpiece, Unterlinden, Colmar

241. *Christ and Satan*, engraving in Greek New Testament, 1563, Huntington Library (Kitto Bible), San Marino, California

240. Antonio Tempesta (1555-1630), *Christ and Satan*, from first Arabic Gospels, 1590-91, Huntington Library (Kitto Bible), San Marino, California

242. Hans Schaufelein (ca. 1483-1539/40), *Christ and Satan*, Institute of Fine Arts, New York

243. D. P., *Christ and Satan*, 1642, Huntington Library (Kitto Bible), San Marino, California

NON IN SOLO PANE VICTVRVS EST HOMO, SED OMNI VERBO QVOD DIGREDITVR PER OS DEI MAR. 4. DEVT. 8

244. Hieronymus Cock (1510-70), *Christ and Satan*, National Gallery: Rosenwald Collection, Washington

245. Detail of Figure 244

246. Sandro Botticelli (ca. 1445-1510), *Christ and Satan*, Sistine Chapel, Vatican

247. Detail of Figure 246

248. Cornelius Galle after Marten de Vos, *Christ and Satan*, Huntington Library (Kitto Bible), San Marino, California

249. *Christ and Satan*, eleventh-century illumination, Matilda of Tuscany's Gospel Book, Pierpont Morgan Library MS 492, fol. 43, New York

250. *Diabolical Feast*, in Guazzo's *Compendium Maleficarum*, 1608, Folger Shakespeare Library, Washington

251. Jacopo Tintoretto (1518-94), *Christ and Satan*, Scuola di San Rocco, Venice

252. Detail of Figure 251

253. Pieter Pieterse (?), *Banquet Larder*, ca. 1600, Van Abbe Museum, Eindhoven, Holland

254. Michelangelo Aliprandi (fl. 1560-82), *Temptation of St. Anthony*, SS. Nazaro e Celso, Verona

255. Martin Schongauer (d. 1491), *Temptation of St. Anthony*, ca. 1470, National Gallery: Rosenwald Collection, Washington

256. Grunewald (ca. 1470/80-1528), *Temptation of St. Anthony*, Isenheim Altarpiece, Unterlinden, Colmar

257. Peter Bruegel the Elder (1525/30-69), *Temptation of St. Anthony*, Ashmolean Museum, Oxford

258. Annibale Carracci (1560-1609), *Temptation of St. Anthony* (detail), National Gallery, London

259. C. Jegher (1596–1652/3) after Rubens, *Christ and Satan*, Huntington Library (Kitto Bible), San Marino, California

260. *Christ and Satan*, thirteenth-century mosaic, S. Marco, Venice

261. Mattia Preti (1613-99), *Christ and Satan*, Museo Capodimonte, Naples

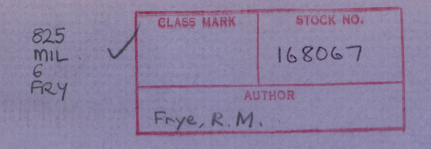